The Collected Courses of the Academy of 1
Series Editors: Professor Philip Alston,
New York University School of Law,
Professor Gráinne de Búrca, and
Professor Bruno de Witte,
European University Institute,
Florence
Assistant Editor: Barbara Ciomei,
European University Institute,
Florence

VOLUME XIII/3

Non-State Actors and Human Rights

The Collected Courses of the Academy of European Law
Edited by Professor Philip Alston, Professor Gráinne de Búrca,
and Professor Bruno de Witte

This series brings together the Collected Courses of the
Academy of European Law in Florence. The Academy's mission is to
produce scholarly analyses which are at the cutting edge of the two
fields in which it works: European Union law and human rights law.
A 'general course' is given each year in each field, by a
distinguished scholar and/or practitioner, who either examines the
field as a whole through a particular thematic, conceptual or
philosophical lens, or who looks at a particular theme in the context
of the overall body of law in the field. The Academy also publishes
each year a volume of collected essays with a specific theme in each
of the two fields.

Non-State Actors and Human Rights

Edited by
PHILIP ALSTON

Academy of European Law

European University Institute
in collaboration with the Center for
Human Rights and Global Justice,
New York University School of Law

OXFORD
UNIVERSITY PRESS

OXFORD
UNIVERSITY PRESS

Great Clarendon Street, Oxford OX2 6DP

Oxford University Press is a department of the University of Oxford.
It furthers the University's objective of excellence in research, scholarship,
and education by publishing worldwide in

Oxford New York

Auckland Cape Town Dar es Salaam Hong Kong Karachi
Kuala Lumpur Madrid Melbourne Mexico City Nairobi
New Delhi Shanghai Taipei Toronto

With offices in

Argentina Austria Brazil Chile Czech Republic France Greece
Guatemala Hungary Italy Japan Poland Portugal Singapore
South Korea Switzerland Thailand Turkey Ukraine Vietnam

Oxford is a registered trade mark of Oxford University Press
in the UK and in certain other countries

Published in the United States
by Oxford University Press Inc., New York

British Library Cataloguing in Publication Data

Data available

Library of Congress Cataloging in Publication Data

Non-state actors and human rights / edited by Philip Alston.
    p. cm.
  "Academy of European Law, European University Institute in collaboration with the
Center for Human Rights and Global Justice, New York University School of Law."
  Includes bibliographical references.
  ISBN 0–19–927281–6 (hardback) — ISBN 0–19–927282–4 (pbk.) 1. Human rights.
2. Juristic persons. 3. International business enterprises—Law and legislation.
I. Alston, Philip. II. Academy of European Law. III. New York University. Center for
Human Rights and Global Justice.
  K3240.N66 2005
  341.4'8—dc22

                                                                2005007553

Typeset by Newgen Imaging Systems (P) Ltd., Chennai, India
Printed in Great Britain
on acid-free paper by the
MPG Books Group, Bodmin and King's Lynn

ISBN 978–0–19–927282–2 (Pbk.)

Contents

Notes on Contributors   vii

Part One: Introduction

1. The 'Not-a-Cat' Syndrome:
   Can the International Human Rights Regime
   Accommodate Non-State Actors?   3
   Philip Alston

2. The Changing International Legal
   Framework for Dealing with Non-State Actors   37
   August Reinisch

Part Two: Non-Governmental Organizations and International Organizations as Non-State Actors

3. The Evolving Status of NGOs under
   International Law: A Threat to the Inter-State System?   93
   Menno T. Kamminga

4. Economic, Social, and Cultural Human Rights and
   the International Monetary Fund   113
   François Gianviti

Part Three: Corporations

5. Catching the Conscience of the King:
   Corporate Players on the International Stage   141
   Celia Wells and Juanita Elias

6. Corporate Responsibility and the International
   Law of Human Rights: The New *Lex Mercatoria*   177
   Ralph G. Steinhardt

7. The Accountability of Multinationals for
   Human Rights Violations in European Law   227
   Olivier De Schutter

8. Human Rights Responsibilities of Businesses
   as Non-State Actors   315
   David Weissbrodt and Muria Kruger

   Bibliography   351
   Mary Rumsey

Index   369

Notes on Contributors

Philip Alston is Professor of Law at New York University Law School and Faculty Director of its Center for Human Rights and Global Justice. He has been Editor-in-Chief of the *European Journal of International Law* since 1997 and is Vice-President of the European Society of International Law. He chaired the UN Committee on Economic, Social, and Cultural Rights from 1991 to 1998 and prior to that was the Committee's Rapporteur from its inception in 1987 until 1990. He is currently Special Advisor to the UN High Commissioner for Human Rights on the Millennium Development Goals, Chairman of the Board of the NY-based Center for Economic and Social Rights and an External Professor at the European University Institute in Florence.

Olivier De Schutter (LL.M., Harvard, 1991; Ph.D., UCL, 1998) is professor of international and European human rights at the University of Louvain (Belgium). He is the director of the CIEDHU Seminar for advanced research in the field of comparative and international human rights at the International Institute of Human Rights (Strasbourg). He is the coordinator of the EU Network of independent experts on fundamental rights, set up in September 2002 by the European Commission upon the request of the European Parliament to monitor the Charter of Fundamental Rights of the EU in the European Union and its Member States. He has acted regularly since 1995 as an expert for the Council of Europe and for the European Union.

Juanita Elias is a Lecturer in International Relations at Manchester University. She has research interests in gender and globalization and multinational corporations. She is author of *Fashioning Inequality: The MNC and Gendered Employment in a Globalising World* (2004).

François Gianviti has been Director of the Legal Department of the International Monetary Fund since 1986 and its General Counsel since 1987. He studied at the Sorbonne, the Paris School of Law, and New York University School of Law. He was awarded a *doctorat d'Etat en droit* in 1967, was *Lauréat de la Faculté de droit de Paris* and *Lauréat du concours général des Facultés de droit*. From 1967 to 1969, he was Lecturer in Law, first at the Nancy School of Law, and subsequently at the Caen School of Law. In 1968, he was admitted to the Paris Bar. In 1969, he obtained the *Agrégation de droit privé et science criminelle* of French universities and was appointed Professor of Law at the University of Besançon. From 1970 to 1974, he was seconded to the IMF Legal Department as Counsellor, and later as Senior Counsellor. In 1974 he became Professor of Law at the University of Paris XII, and was Dean from 1979 to 1985. He is a member of the Monetary Committee of the International Law Association and has been awarded a *Chevalier des Palmes Académiques* (France) and a *Chevalier dans l'Ordre National du Mérite* (France).

Menno T. Kamminga is Professor of International Law at Maastricht University and Co-Director of the Maastricht Centre for Human Rights. He is a former legal adviser of Amnesty International, former member of Amnesty International's International Executive Committee, member of the Editorial Board of the *Netherlands International Law Review*, and Co-Rapporteur of the International Law Association's Committee on International Human Rights Law and Practice. He is the author of *Inter-State Accountability for Violations of Human Rights* (1992) and co-editor with S. Zia-Zarifi of *Liability of Multinational Corporations under International Law* (2000).

Muria Kruger received her J.D. degree from the University of Minnesota Law School in 2001, graduating *magna cum laude*. She is a Legal Associate at Heins, Mills and Olson in Minneapolis and has written on a range of human rights issues especially in relation to business and human rights and the work of the UN Sub-Commission on the Promotion and Protection of Human Rights.

August Reinisch is Professor of International and European Law at the University of Vienna. He also teaches at the Bologna Center/SAIS of Johns Hopkins University and at Bocconi University, Milan. He holds masters degrees in philosophy (1990) and in law (1988) as well as a doctorate in law (1991) from the University of Vienna and an LL.M. (1989) from NYU. He currently serves as arbitrator on the In Rem Restitution Panel established pursuant to the Austrian General Settlement Fund Law 2001, as a member of the International Law Association's Committee on Accountability of International Organisations, and as an expert adviser on international and European law issues in litigation and arbitration. His recent publications include: *International Organizations before National Courts* (2000), 'Developing a Human Rights and Humanitarian Law Accountability of the UN Security Council for the Imposition of Economic Sanctions', 95 *American Journal of International Law* (2001), 851; 'Governance without Accountability', 44 *German Yearbook of International Law* (2001), 270; and 'Selecting the Appropriate Forum for Investment Disputes', in UNCTAD (ed.), *Handbook on Dispute Settlement* (2003).

Mary Rumsey is the Foreign, Comparative and International Law Librarian at the University of Minnesota Law Library. She received her B.A. degree in Philosophy and Political Science from the University of Wisconsin, Phi Beta Kappa, and her law degree from the University of Chicago. In 1998, she received a masters degree in library and information science from Dominican University. With David Weissbrodt and Marci Hoffman, she has published a comprehensive bibliography on international human rights research. Rumsey has also published several other articles and book chapters on legal research, and teaches a seminar on international and foreign legal research at the University of Minnesota Law School.

Ralph G. Steinhardt is Arthur Selwyn Miller Research Professor of Law and International Relations at George Washington University Law School, in Washington, D.C. He is also the co-founder and director of the Programme in International Human Rights Law, at Oxford University. Professor Steinhardt has been active in the domestic litigation of international human rights norms, having represented various human rights organizations, as well as individual human rights victims, before all levels of the federal judiciary, including the U.S. Supreme Court. He is also the founding Chairman of the Board of Directors of the Center for Justice and Accountability, an anti-impunity NGO created by Amnesty International and based in San Francisco. His most recent publications include *International Civil Litigation: Cases and Materials on the Rise of Intermestic Law* (2002), *The Alien Tort Claims Act* (with D'Amato, 1999), and a variety of articles on the relationship between international law and domestic law.

Celia Wells has held the post of Professor of Law at Cardiff University since 1995. Her research has mainly focused on criminal law, in particular the criminal liability of corporations (*Corporations and Criminal Responsibility*, 2nd ed., 2001). With Nicola Lacey and Oliver Quick, she is co-author of *Reconstructing Criminal Law* (3rd ed., 2003), a student text adopting an explicitly feminist perspective. She has also published a number of articles in medical law on topics such as maternal-fetal relations and court-ordered cesareans. In 2001 she held the Pricewaterhouse Coopers Legal Visiting Chair in Women and Law at the University of Sydney. She is joint editor of *Legal Studies*, the Journal of the Society of Legal Scholars, and is a member of the Cardiff University ESRC Centre for Business Relationships, Accountability, Sustainability and Society.

David Weissbrodt has taught at the University of Minnesota Law School since 1975 and is now the Fredrikson & Byron Professor of Law. He teaches International Human Rights Law and other subjects. Weissbrodt has authored a dozen books and more than 120 articles. Weissbrodt helped to establish and continues to work with several organizations including the Center for Victims of Torture, the International Human Rights Internship Program, Minnesota Advocates for Human Rights, and University of Minnesota Human Rights Center. Weissbrodt has served two terms (1996–2004) as a member of the U.N. Sub-Commission on the Promotion and Protection of Human Rights and has also been a member of its Working Group on the Working Methods and Activities of Transnational Corporations. In August 2000 Professor Weissbrodt was named the U.N. Special Rapporteur on the rights of non-citizens. In 2001–02 he served as Chairperson of the Sub-Commission.

Part One

Introduction

1

The 'Not-a-Cat' Syndrome: Can the International Human Rights Regime Accommodate Non-State Actors?

PHILIP ALSTON*

1. THE 'NOT-A-CAT' SYNDROME

When one of my daughters was eighteen months old she deftly transcended her linguistic limitations by describing a rabbit, a mouse, or a kangaroo as a 'not-a-cat'.[1] In the arenas of international law and human rights an almost identical technique is pervasive. Civil society actors are described as *non*-governmental organizations. Terrorist groups or others threatening the state's monopoly of power are delicately referred to as *non*-state actors. But so too are transnational corporations and multinational banks, despite their somewhat more benign influence. International institutions, including those which wield immense influence while disavowing all pretensions to exercise authority *per se*, such as the International Monetary Fund (IMF) and the World Bank, are classified either as *non*-state entities or as *non*-state actors.

Apart from its ability to obfuscate almost any debate, this insistence upon defining all actors in terms of what they are not combines impeccable purism in terms of traditional international legal analysis with an unparalleled capacity to marginalize a significant part of the international human rights regime from the most vital challenges confronting global governance at the dawn of the twenty-first century. In essence, these negative, euphemistic terms do not stem from language inadequacies but instead have been intentionally adopted in order to reinforce the assumption that the state is not only the central actor, but also the indispensable and pivotal one around which all other entities revolve. Accordingly, for the purposes of

* Thanks to Nehal Bhuta for his excellent research assistance in the preparation of this Chapter.

[1] This description of the not-a-cat syndrome draws on Philip Alston, 'The "Not-a-cat" Syndrome: Re-thinking Human Rights Law to Meet the Needs of the Twenty-first Century', in *Progressive Governance for the XXI Century* (Florence, European University Institute and New York University School of Law, 2000) 128.

international legal discourse—the language of human rights—those other entities can only be identified in terms of their relationship to the state. Just like my daughter's rabbit, anything that is not a state, whether it be me, IBM, the IMF, Shell, Sendero Luminoso, or Amnesty International, is conceptualized as a 'not-a-state'.

It is thus neither accidental, nor perhaps surprising, that the United Nations has an editorial rule which requires that the word 'State' should always be capitalized (i.e. that upper-case format be used).[2] Apart from recalling the insistence of religious publications that god must always be acknowledged as God, this usage merely encapsulates the assumptions of 1945. But the problem is that it also sets those assumptions in stone at a time when that particular stone is competing with quite a few others as the embodiment of power and even authority. It is revealing that no matter how subversive of the legitimacy of a given state it might be, every human rights document produced under the auspices of the United Nations requires its author(s) to genuflect in this way before the altar of 'State' sovereignty every time the word is mentioned. None of this is to suggest that the state is not important, let alone to endorse the more extreme versions of the 'state is dead' thesis. It is simply to underline the fact that the world is a much more poly-centric place than it was in 1945 and that she who sees the world essentially through the prism of the 'State' will be seeing a rather distorted image as we enter the twenty-first century.

The thrust of this Chapter is that such a uni-dimensional or monochromatic way of viewing the world is not only misleading, but also makes it much more difficult to adapt the human rights regime in order to take adequate account of the fundamental changes that have occurred in recent years. The challenge that it lays down is one of re-imagining, as the social scientists would put it, the nature of the human rights regime and the relationships among the different actors within it. Lawyers, not being noted for their willingness to depart from precedents, might prefer to see the task in terms of re-interpreting existing concepts and procedures rather than re-imagining. Either way, the nature of the challenges that lie ahead emerge clearly from this volume.

Notwithstanding the questionable utility of the terminology, non-state actors are looming ever larger on the horizons of international and human rights law. They are a recognized category of partners for the European Union in development and humanitarian activities,[3] they are the subject of a specialized law journal in the field

---

[2] Interestingly, the only UN document in which it is not capitalized is the UN Charter itself. That document pays linguistic homage to 'Members' rather than states *per se*.

[3] See Article 4 of the Cotonou Agreement of 2000 between the EU and the African, Caribbean, and Pacific states which recognizes 'the complementary role of and potential for contributions by non-State actors to the development process'. It then provides that 'non-State actors shall, where appropriate:

- be informed and involved in consultation on cooperation policies and strategies...and on the political dialogue;
- be provided with financial resources...to support local development processes;
- be involved in the implementation of cooperation project and programmes...;
- be provided with capacity-building support in critical areas...'

of international law,[4] a separate book series has been dedicated to them,[5] and scholarly articles are emerging at a great rate.[6] Yet the membership of this group is difficult to define and virtually open-ended. The resulting grab-bag of miscellaneous players ranges from transnational corporations and small-time businesses and contractors, through religious and labour groups, organized epistemic communities, civil society more broadly, and international organizations, to terrorist bands and armed resistance groups.[7]

Not much more than a decade ago the category of non-state actors remained all but frozen out of the legal picture by international law doctrines and had received only passing recognition even from scholars. While the case-law of the regional human rights systems had begun to address some violations committed by private actors, the resulting jurisprudence was neither systematic nor especially coherent. At the international level, human rights groups, along with many governments, treated the category with the utmost caution because they were extremely wary of dignifying the nefarious activities of certain such actors by focusing specifically upon them or by seeking to give even a few among them a place at the international table. The result, somewhat ironically, was that groups classified by international law as non-state actors (human rights NGOs) were lobbying strongly against the recognition of other groups classified in the same way.

Today, however, at least a subset of non-state actors has suddenly become a force to be reckoned with and one which demands to be factored into the overall equation

---

http://europa.eu.int/comm/development/body/cotonou/agreement/agr05_en.htm. See also Communication from the Commission to the Council, the European Parliament, and the Economic and Social Committee of 7 November 2002: 'Participation of non-state actors in EC development policy' COM (2002) 598 final, at http://europa.eu.int/scadplus/leg/en/lvb/r12009.htm.

[4] *Non-State Actors and International Law*, published by Brill.

[5] See series entitled: Non-State Actors in International Law, Politics and Governance, published by Ashgate.

[6] See e.g. J. Oloka-Onyango 'Reinforcing Marginalized Rights in an Age of Globalization: International Mechanisms, Non-State Actors, and the Struggle for Peoples' Rights in Africa', 18 *Am. U. Int'l L. Rev.* (2003) 851; William A. Schabas, 'Theorical and International Framework: Punishment of Non-State Actors in Non-International Armed Conflict', 26 *Fordham Int'l L.J.* (2003) 907; Richard A. Rinkema, 'Environmental Agreements, Non-State Actors, and the Kyoto Protocol: A "Third Way" for International Climate Action?', 24 *U. Pa. J. Int'l Econ. L.* (2003) 729; Michael G. Heyman, 'Asylum, Social Group Membership and the Non-State Actor: The Challenge of Domestic Violence', 36 *U. Mich. J.L. Ref.* (2003) 767; Norman G. Printer, Jr., 'The Use of Force against Non-State Actors under International Law: An Analysis of the U.S. Predator Strike in Yemen', 8 *UCLA J. Int'l L. & For. Aff.* (2003) 331; Daniel Wilsher, 'Non-State Actors And The Definition Of A Refugee In The United Kingdom: Protection, Accountability Or Culpability?', 15 *Int'l J. Ref. L.* (2003) 68; Rachel Lord, 'The liability of non-state actors for torture in violation of international Humanitarian Law: an assessment of the jurisprudence of the International Criminal Tribunal for the Former Yugoslavia', *Melbourne J. Int'l L.* (2003) 112.

[7] For three systematic and wide-ranging surveys of the issues see Andrew Clapham, *Human Rights in the Private Sphere* (Oxford, Oxford University Press, 1993); Steven Ratner, 'Corporations and Human Rights: A Theory of Legal Responsibility', 11 *Yale L.J.* (2001) 443; and International Council on Human Rights, *Beyond Voluntarism: Human Rights and the developing international legal obligations of companies* (2002).

in a far more explicit and direct way than has been the case to date. As a result, the international human rights regime's aspiration to ensure the accountability of all major actors will be severely compromised in the years ahead if it does not succeed in devising a considerably more effective framework than currently exists in order to take adequate account of the roles played by some non-state actors. In practice, if not in theory, too many of them currently escape the net cast by international human rights norms and institutional arrangements.

For practical purposes, much of the focus of the international human rights regime in the years ahead will be on transnational corporations and other large-scale business entities, private voluntary groups such as churches, labour unions, and human rights groups, and on international organizations including the United Nations itself, the World Bank, the International Monetary Fund, and the World Trade Organization. The purposes of this Chapter, apart from surveying the issues raised by the various contributors to this volume, include putting the issue very briefly into some historical perspective, examining more closely the issue of definition, and identifying the key contexts in which non-state actors have risen to the fore in the past couple of decades. The Chapter then explores the nature of, and the reasons for, the reluctance of mainstream international law to accord a real place at the table to non-state actors.

2. THE RAPID EVOLUTION OF THE STATUS OF NON-STATE ACTORS

In the early 1980s I was asked by one of the United Nations' specialized agencies to write a consultancy study on legal aspects of the role of non-state actors in the field of human rights. I am ashamed to say that I was as keen to take on the job as I was perplexed about the real meaning or utility of the assignment. Several then recent developments seemed to suggest that my concern should be with armed opposition groups, national liberation movements, and perhaps transnational corporations, although the human rights dimensions of even those issues were, curiously in retrospect, not especially obvious. In relation to the first group, the 1977 Additional Protocol II to the Geneva Conventions had recently given status to certain types of non-state forces involved in an armed conflict within the territory of a state.[8] In relation to the second, the United Nations and other international organizations had been making an effort, under pressure from the non-aligned group of developing states, to take account in its own work of the role played by national liberation movements in a number of key conflict areas, such as in Namibia, South Africa, and Palestine.[9] In relation to the third, the United Nations had been engaged throughout

---

[8] For a critique see Antonio Cassese, *International Law* (Oxford, Oxford University Press, 2001), 346–48.

[9] See Malcolm Shaw, *International Law* (5th ed., Cambridge, Cambridge University Press, 2003) 220–23.

the late 1970s in drafting a code of conduct for transnational corporations.[10] But the bottom line was that the human rights framework remained somewhat distant from these important forays into unknown territory, and the issues were largely absent from the agendas of most international human rights groups. The reasons were not difficult to see: humanitarian and human rights norms were considered separate; national liberation movements were strong on the right to self-determination but not overly concerned with many other rights; and the focus on transnationals had more to do with the New International Economic Order and the sovereignty of host states than with the human rights of workers or anyone else.

But in the space of only a couple of decades, all this has changed. Human rights and humanitarian law have moved much closer together, as the statute of the International Criminal Court attests and the jurisprudence of the International Criminal Tribunals for the former Yugoslavia and for Rwanda illustrate. National liberation movements have either gone into the business of government (as in Namibia, Zimbabwe, South Africa, and East Timor) or been pushed towards outlaw status as terrorist groups. The right to self-determination is now a struggle that is expected to be fought at the ballot box rather than through guerilla warfare in the jungles or urban areas.[11] And consumer movements and human rights groups have reignited international concern about the activities of transnational corporations by successfully focusing public opinion on labour, environmental, and human rights abuses in which those corporations are increasingly seen to be involved.

Perhaps most importantly, in the aftermath of the Cold War and the triumph of liberal economic systems, private actors are being asked to undertake a wide range of functions and responsibilities which it had previously been unimaginable to entrust to them.

3. SOME CASE STUDIES TO ILLUSTRATE THE REAL-WORLD CHALLENGES

Using a term such as non-state actors risks transforming the analysis of very concrete issues into a purely academic exercise, detached from the sometimes harsh realities and often very practical dilemmas that arise. In order to avoid such a sanitizing effect, it will be instructive if we bear in mind some case studies which illustrate the ways in which non-state actor-related issues have arisen in international human

---

[10] For the text of the draft code, work on which was effectively, but not formally, abandoned in 1983 under pressure from the Reagan Administration, see Draft United Nations Code of Conduct on Transnational Corporations, UN doc. E/1983/17/Rev.1 (1983). For a review of this process and its aftermath see Peter Muchlinski, 'Attempts To Extend the Accountability of Transnational Corporations: The Role of UNCTAD', in Menno T. Kamminga and Saman Zia-Zarifi (eds.), *Liability of Multinational Corporations under International Law* (2000) 97.

[11] See generally Philip Alston, 'Peoples' Rights: Their Rise and Fall' in P. Alston (ed.), *Peoples' Rights* (Oxford, Oxford University Press, 2001) 259, at 270–73.

rights law. Four different types of situation are not far below the surface of most of the analyses that are undertaken in the Chapters contained in this volume.

A. Is there Freedom of Speech in a Private Shopping Centre?

The first case study concerns a case brought under the European Convention on Human Rights involving a private shopping centre in which local residents seek to exercise their right to freedom of speech by collecting signatures on a petition.[12] The issue in question is a matter of considerable importance to the residents of the town, but does not directly concern the owners of the Town Centre, as the area is known. A range of public services such as the police station, the public library, and the health and social services centres are all located either in or very close to it. The owners of the shopping centre insist, however, that it is private property and that permitting citizens to gather signatures would violate their 'stance on all political and religious issues [which] is one of strict neutrality'.[13] They are supported by the United Kingdom government which rejects the claim that such gathering places for the citizenry can be considered to be 'quasi-public' land, a designation which might be considered to trigger human rights obligations.[14] The European Court of Human Rights upholds the right of the private owners and dismisses the free speech claim brought by the citizens' group, thus giving strong reign to the notion that human rights do not run in the private sphere.[15]

B. If the United Nations Administers a Territory, is it Bound by Human Rights?

A second, generic, case study involves forces sent under United Nations auspices to take control of a territory after the government has collapsed, fled, or been forced out of office as a result of internationally endorsed measures. The forces take directions from a UN civilian administrator and are subject to exclusive United Nations command. In seeking to establish law and order in a hostile environment they promulgate a range of orders which are not in compliance with international human rights law but which many observers feel are justified under the circumstances. When criticized, UN officials point out that the UN is not a state, and does not have the capacity to become a party to the International Human Rights Covenants, and that it cannot therefore be bound by specific human rights requirements.

A variation on the same theme is illustrated by the position taken in relation to human rights obligations by the International Monetary Fund, and to which various other international organizations would probably be happy to subscribe if they

---

[12] *Appleby and Others v. United Kingdom*, Application no. 44306/98, 6 May 2003.

[13] Ibid., para. 16.   [14] Ibid., para. 38.

[15] For an excellent critique of this case see Oliver Gerstenberg, 'What Constitutions Can Do (but Courts Sometimes Don't): Property, Speech, and the Influence of Constitutional Norms on Private Law', 17 *Canadian Journal of Law and Jurisprudence* (2004) 61.

could. Human rights treaties are addressed to states, international organizations are not permitted to become parties, they were not involved in any way in the drafting, they do not and cannot report to the relevant treaty bodies, and nor can they participate in electing the expert members. Because of the importance of maintaining a workable division of labour within the international system it must be for the human rights bodies to promote and seek to uphold human rights and for the more functionally oriented agencies to do what they, in turn, have been mandated to do. If the governments of the world had wanted all international agencies to have a human rights mandate they would have given them one or would do so now. But they have chosen not to, and the conclusion is that the relevant agencies are, for these purposes at least, non-state actors upon whom human rights obligations do not and cannot fall directly.

C. Are there any Human Rights-Based Constraints on the Actions of Private Security Contractors?

The third case study addresses the role of private contractors in the reconstruction of Iraq following the invasion in 2003. A starting point is to acknowledge that, although Iraq has been the best publicized of the cases in this area, it is not the first and will not be the last, since the 'privatized military industry has been estimated at US$100 billion in annual global revenue'.[16] In Iraq, the number of contractors working as civilian security guards is agreed to be between 15,000 and 20,000. The roles they play range 'from handling military logistics and training the local army, to protecting key installations and escorting convoys'.[17] It has been reported that their conduct 'more and more [gives] the appearance of private, for-profit militias'.[18] According to other reports some of these civilian contractors, who were working as translators and interrogators, were deeply implicated in the torture and humiliation of inmates in the Abu Ghraib prison. A secret report prepared for the U.S. military, but subsequently leaked, recommended disciplinary action for those employees.[19]

But the issues go much further than those well publicized incidents. As a recent report noted: 'Stressed and sometimes ill-trained mercenaries operate in Iraq's mayhem with apparent impunity, erecting checkpoints without authorisation, and claiming powers to detain and confiscate identity cards'.[20] Security contractors who are asked to carry out tasks normally undertaken by public authorities, be they police or military, are in a position to infringe dramatically on the rights of the citizens

[16] Peter Singer, 'Warriors for Hire in Iraq', *Salon.com*, 15 April 2004, at http://www.brook.edu/views/articles/fellows/singer20040415.htm.

[17] Peter Singer, 'Outsourcing the War', *Salon.com*, 16 April 2004, at http://www.brook.edu/views/articles/fellows/singer20040416.htm.

[18] David Barstow, 'Security Companies: Shadow Soldiers in Iraq', *New York Times*, 19 April 2004, p. 1.

[19] Report by Major-General Antonio Tagubas, at http://www.globalpolicy.org/security/issues/iraq/attack/law/2004/0430torture.htm, p. 48.

[20] 'The Baghdad Boom: Mercenaries', *Economist*, U.S. Edition, 27 March 2004, p. 25.

whom they are, in effect, being called upon to police. The situation is thus about as close as one could possibly get to replicating all the elements that underpin the classic doctrine of state responsibility for human rights violations. And yet, the private nature of the forces involved would argue, according to classical international law theory, that there is no human rights accountability. Rather than looking at the individual contractors or the transnational corporations which employ them, the response is that only one or other of the relevant governments can be held to account.

The principal problem is that the legal situation of the contractors, and the means by which they might be held accountable for human rights breaches, remain very unclear. Under an order issued by the Coalition Provisional Authority in 2003, renewed in June 2004, and the content of which the 'sovereign' Iraqi Government was requested to renew or extend for the period following 30 June 2004, all 'Contractors', 'Private Security Companies', and 'International Consultants' are granted immunity from 'Iraqi legal process' with respect to all acts and omissions committed. This would include serious violations of human rights standards. While their home state governments could opt to subject them to their home jurisdiction for crimes committed, there is no obligation to do so. The very first preambular paragraph of the Order signed by Paul Bremer notes that it is being issued in accordance with 'the laws and usages of war, and consistent with relevant U.N. Security Council resolutions . . .'[21]

While the private contractors could be charged with war crimes under international law, this is a relatively high threshold to meet and will not cover a very wide range of human rights violations that might be committed in their daily work. Human Rights Watch has noted that there are various U.S. Federal laws under which contractors could be prosecuted,[22] and indeed the Center for Constitutional Rights filed a lawsuit in June 2004 in a U.S. Federal Court under the Alien Tort Claims Act and the Racketeer Influenced and Corrupt Organizations Act (RICO).[23] Nevertheless, *The Economist* has observed that 'the standards of proof required by a American court are unlikely to be met in Iraq—or in any other war zone, for that matter'.[24] In response to the fear that these contractors have been permitted to operate within a legal vacuum, a group of Democrats in the U.S. Senate has called upon the Pentagon to 'adopt written guidelines, with supporting legal justification, for the rules of engagement security contractors should follow'.[25] But such guidelines were actually being sought by the security companies before that initiative and, according to reports, an initial draft would give the contractors 'the right to detain

---

[21] Coalition Provisional Authority Order Number 17 (Revised): Status of the Coalition Provisional Authority, MNF—Iraq, Certain Missions and Personnel in Iraq, doc. CPA/ORD/27 June 2004/17, at http://www.cpa-iraq.org/regulations/20040627_CPAORD_17_Status_of_Coalition_Rev_with_Annex_A.pdf.

[22] Human Rights Watch, Private Military Contractors and the Law, at http://hrw.org/english/docs/2004/05/05/iraq8547.htm.   [23] See text accompanying note 53 below.

[24] 'Dangerous Work: Private Security Firms in Iraq', *Economist*, 10 April 2004, pp. 26–27.

[25] David Barstow, 'The Struggle for Iraq: The Contractors', *New York Times*, 9 April 2004, p. 1.

civilians and to use deadly force in defence of themselves or their clients'.[26] The bottom line might still be a set of guidelines that lie beyond the reach of either United States or international courts.

D. What Can be Expected of a Transnational Corporation in a Situation in which it is a Dominant Actor?

The fourth and final case study, concerning transnational corporations, is explored in some depth in recognition of the centrality of this issue to a number of the Chapters that follow in this volume. It concerns the Shell Oil Company and its operations in Nigeria. In the early 1990s the Movement for the Survival of the Ogoni People, led by a well known playwright Ken Saro-Wiwa, protested against environmental damage caused by the activities of the oil companies, and in particular Royal Dutch/ Shell, in Ogoniland, an oil-rich state whose people lived in dire poverty. In response, Shell 'acknowledged frequent spills but has said the Ogoni movement exaggerated their impact'. The protesters also demanded that a fairer share of Nigeria's oil wealth should be spent in Ogoniland. The response by the military regime was to mount 'a kind of scorched-earth campaign against the Ogoni, burning villages and committing murders and rapes', and to declare that the death penalty would be carried out against anyone who interfered with efforts to 'revitalize' the oil industry. In November 1995 Saro-Wiwa and eight other protesters were executed.[27]

In March 1996 a complaint was submitted to the African Commission on Human and Peoples' Rights alleging that a consortium consisting of a Nigerian state-owned oil company and Shell had 'exploited oil reserves in Ogoniland with no regard for the health or environment of the local communities, disposing toxic wastes into the environment and local waterways, . . . [caused] numerous avoidable spills in the proximity of villages [resulting in] serious short- and long-term health impacts, including skin infections, gastrointestinal and respiratory ailments, and increased risk of cancers, and neurological and reproductive problems'.[28] The complaint also alleged that the government had 'condoned and facilitated these violations by placing the legal and military powers of the State at the disposal of the oil companies'.[29] Although the Commission did not publish its response to the complaint until 2002, it sent an investigative mission to Ogoniland in March 1997 and kept the matter under active review in the meantime.

Non-state actors were among those bringing pressure to bear on Shell. The Body Shop launched a campaign under the headline 'Someone's Making a Killing in

---

[26] Barstow, note 18 above.

[27] Howard French, 'Nigeria Executes Critic of Regime, Nations Protest', *New York Times*, 11 November 1995, p. 1.

[28] African Commission on Human and Peoples' Rights, Decision Regarding Communication 155/96 (*Social and Economic Rights Action Center/Center for Economic and Social Rights v. Nigeria*), 27 May 2002. Case No. ACHPR/COMM/A044/1. At <http://www.umn.edu/humanrts/africa/comcases/allcases.html>, para. 2. [29] Ibid., para. 3.

Nigeria'. Underneath it was a picture of a petrol pump nozzle looking like a smoking gun. The message about the role of the oil companies was clear but the private enterprise messenger was unusual.

In 1996 Shell produced a 'Plan for Ogoni' in which it commited itself to cleaning up oil spills and underwriting community development. In 1999 Human Rights Watch (HRW) produced a lengthy report which noted allegations that the company had collaborated with the military regime in suppressing protests and violating human rights on a significant scale. 'A document alleged to be a leaked government memorandum from 1994 implicated Shell in planned "wasting operations" by the Rivers State Internal Security Task Force, stating that the oil companies should pay the costs of the operations'. The report also noted that detained protesters had 'alleged that they were detained and beaten by Shell police'.[30]

HRW used the occasion of this report to spell out a long list of demands directed to the various international oil companies operating in Nigeria, but Shell was singled out for a range of specific recommendations which throw into sharp relief the authors' vision of the appropriate limits of human rights-friendly corporate responsibility. Among the recommendations of general applicability were calls to:

develop guidelines on making or maintaining investments in or withdrawing from countries where there is a pattern of ongoing and systematic violation of human rights;
adopt explicit company policies in support of human rights; establish procedures to ensure that company activities do not result in human rights abuses . . .

It was explicitly suggested that Shell should:

. . . call for and cooperate with an independent judicial inquiry into the situation in Ogoni, including the role of Shell staff and contractors, as well as the security forces, in past human rights violations . . .

. . . call on the Nigerian government to allow freedom of assembly, association and expression, in particular with respect to grievances directed against the oil industry . . .

. . . call on the Nigerian government to release unconditionally all those detained for exercising their rights . . . and to ensure fair and prompt trials before independent tribunals for all those charged with criminal offences . . .

review programs of community assistance to ensure that development projects are planned by people who are professionally trained, that all members of communities can participate in devising development plans . . .

develop and publicize policies to provide compensation to victims of human rights abuse committed by the Nigerian security forces or oil company private security . . . . Consider establishing independently and professionally administered funds for this purpose . . .

arrange independently funded verification, by national and international nongovernmental organizations and other appropriate bodies, of compliance by the company with international human rights and environmental standards.

---

[30] Human Rights Watch, *The Price of Oil: Corporate Responsibility and Human Rights Violations in Nigeria's Oil Producing Communities* (New York, 1999).

In 2003, after riots and clashes with security forces around the city of Warri in the Niger Delta in which scores of people were killed, HRW addressed itself to both the Nigerian government and the multinational oil companies in calling for measures to prevent further violence. The companies, including Shell, were urged 'to publicly state that the response of government security forces must not be disproportionate to the threat; that they should only resort to force as absolutely necessary in accordance with international standards; that their operation should be conducted in a manner that ensures respect for due process and fundamental human rights; is focused on arresting and prosecuting the actual perpetrators rather than retaliating against whole communities; and any allegations of human rights violations should be thoroughly and impartially investigated and the perpetrators brought to justice'.[31]

The basis upon which HRW invoked the responsibility of these corporations was their approval of the Voluntary Principles on Security and Human Rights in the Extractive Industries,[32] which had been adopted in 2000 under the auspices of the U.S. and U.K. governments, in conjunction with concerned companies and human rights NGOs. The Principles state, *inter alia*, that '[i]n their consultations with host governments, Companies should take all appropriate measures to promote observance of applicable international law enforcement principles'; urge investigations of violations; and 'actively monitor the status of investigations and press for their proper resolution'. Highlighting the complexity of seeking to hold oil companies account in this way was the fact that even before HRW had sent its letters, the three big foreign oil companies had announced the shutdown of their operations and the evacuation of their staff.[33] In March 2004 Shell indicated that it was planning to cut a significant percentage of its jobs in Nigeria, close various offices, and move more of its drilling activities offshore. These developments meant, as *The Financial Times* put it, 'that the company will need less land-based infrastructures and is likely to experience fewer problems with community protests'.[34]

This final case study, which could readily have been concerned instead with a range of other transnational corporations operating either in the extractive industries or in a wide range of others such as apparel or footwear manufacturing, serves to raise the key issues with which those wanting to apply human rights standards in their fullness to private entities need to grapple. They include the following. Are there any fundamental differences in the nature of the human rights obligations that fall upon governments and those that fall upon corporations? If the only difference is that governments have a comprehensive set of obligations, while those of corporations are limited to their 'spheres on influence', as the Global Compact puts it, how

---

[31] Human Rights Watch, 'Letter to Shell Petroleum Development Company of Nigeria', 7 April 2003, at http://www.hrw.org/press/2003/04/nigeria040703shell.htm.

[32] Available at http://www.state.gov/g/drl/rls/2931.htm.

[33] 'Shell, Chevron and Elf all Quit Nigerian Delta' 24 March 2003, at http://www.srimedia.com/artman/publish/article_466.shtml.

[34] M. Peel, 'Nigerian Moves Come at Time of Turbulence for Shell', *Financial Times*, 22 March 2004, p. 25.

are the latter to be delineated? Does Shell's sphere of influence in the Niger Delta not cover everything ranging from the right to health, through the right to free speech, to the rights to physical integrity and due process? But if the private sphere is distinguished from the public sphere by virtue of its emphasis on autonomy, risk-taking, entrepreneurship, and the rational pursuit of self-interest, what are the consequences of saddling it with all of the constraints, restrictions, and even positive obligations which apply to governments? Are all of the demands articulated by Human Rights Watch reasonable under the circumstances? If many or most of them are, to what extent do similar obligations apply to smaller corporations, and at what point can a corporation plead that although it does not have the resources to fulfil such obligations it is nevertheless in the interests of all concerned that its business enterprise should proceed? And what are the limits of concepts such as complicity to which Human Rights Watch and the International Council on Human Rights Policy[35] have attached such importance?

4. DEFINING NON-STATE ACTORS

Although much discussed in the literature, definitions of the concept of non-state diverge widely.[36] Indeed the concept is often left undefined. As Kamminga notes below, the same is true of the term non-governmental organizations and there are some authors who would define both categories as embracing multinational corporations, national liberation movements, and voluntary agencies.[37] A recent 'Report of the Panel of Eminent Persons on United Nations—Civil Society Relations' bravely begins with a glossary of terms but then goes on to concede that '[t]here is considerable confusion surrounding [the term NGO] in United Nations circles'.[38] NGOs are then described mainly in terms of the roles accorded them within the UN, while civil society is defined very broadly but in a way which excludes the private and public sectors. The problematic nature of such attempts at definition is illustrated by the description of the private sector which notes that although 'the category includes small and medium-sized enterprises, some of these are supported by non-governmental organizations or are cooperatives and may also have characteristics closer to civil society'. It is perhaps noteworthy that, while the report does use the term non-state actors, it does not attempt to define it, although it

---

[35] *Beyond Voluntarism*, note 7 above, 121–42.

[36] Richard A. Higgott *et al.* (eds.) *Non-State Actors and Authority in the Global System* (2000); Bas Arts, Math Noortmann, and Bob Reinalda (eds.), *Non-State Actors in International Relations* (2001); Panel, 'Human Rights and Non-State Actors', 11 *Pace Int'l L. Rev.* (1999) 205; 'Non-State Actors and the Case Law of the Yugoslavia War Crimes Tribunal', 92 *Am. Soc'y Int'l L. Proc.* (1998) 48; Beard, 'International Security: Multiple Actors, Multiple Threats—Countering the Threat Posed by Non-State Actors in the Proliferation of Weapons of Mass Destruction', 92 *Am. Soc'y Int'l L. Proc.* (1998) 173; Farrior, 'State Responsibility in a Multiactor World: State Responsibility for Human Rights Abuses by Non-State Actors', 92 *Am. Soc'y Int'l L. Proc.* (1988) 299.   [37] Kamminga, Chapter 3 below, n. 7.

[38] *We the Peoples: Civil Society, the United Nations and Global Governance*, UN doc. A/55/817 (2004), p. 13.

seems to include, in addition to civil society, at least firms, parliamentarians, and local authorities.[39] The latter two are odd inclusions since they would normally be included in the public sector.

For some groups, the term non-state actors has assumed a specific meaning within their own context. The International Campaign to Ban Landmines, for example, uses the term to refer to 'armed opposition groups who act autonomously from recognised governments'. They thus encompass 'rebel groups, irregular armed groups, insurgents, dissident armed forces, guerrillas, liberation movements, and *de facto* territorial governing bodies'.[40] About 190 such non-state actors have been formally recognized on this basis.[41] While this is an understandable approach in the arms control area, such a definition will not get us very far for general purposes. Similarly the European Commission defines non-state actors as groups which: are created voluntarily by citizens; are independent of the state; can be profit or non-profit-making organizations; have a main aim of promoting an issue or defending an interest, either general or specific; and, depending on their aim, can play a role in implementing policies and defending interests. In trying to be more specific the EU indicates that they can include: 'non-governmental organisations (NGOs), trade unions, employers' associations, universities, associations of churches and other confessional movements, cultural associations, etc.'[42]

Another definition includes 'all those actors that are not (representatives of) states, yet that operate at the international level and are potentially relevant to international relations'.[43] The last of the criteria requires an actor to be sizeable, have a substantial and multinational constituency, to have been granted at least informal access by governments and intergovernmental organizations to political arenas, and to show that it is 'consequential to international politics'.[44] Although Bas Arts seems to adopt a fairly broad interpretation of his criteria, this definition clearly has a potentially quite restrictive set of requirements and one which, albeit not explicitly, seems tailored to fit fairly traditional patterns of international relations scholarship. It is unlikely for example that many of the Landmine Campaign's 190 non-state actors would qualify.

Perhaps the most comprehensive definition put forward in the scholarly literature is that crafted by Josselin and Wallace. It includes all organizations:

- largely or entirely autonomous from central government funding and control: emanating from civil society, or from the market economy, or from political impulses beyond state control and direction;

---

[39] Ibid., p. 25.   [40] http://www.icbl.org/wg/nsa/nsabrochure.html.
[41] This does not include farmers, drug cartels, or many of the smaller loosely organized non-state actors. Margaret Busé, 'Non-State Actors and Their Significance', at http://maic.jmu.edu/journal/5.3/features/maggie_buse_nsa/maggie_buse.htm.
[42] The Commission estimates that 20% of EU development assistance is channeled through non-state actors. 'Participation of non-state actors in EC development policy', note 3 above, p. 1.
[43] Bas Arts, *Non-State Actors in Global Governance: Three Faces of Power*, Max Planck Project Group on Common Goods, Bonn, Working Paper 2003/4, p. 5.   [44] Ibid.

- operating as or participating in networks which extend across the boundaries of two or more states—thus engaging in 'transnational' relations, linking political systems, economies, societies;
- acting in ways which affect political outcomes, either within one or more states or within international institutions—either purposefully or semi-purposefully, either as their primary objective or as one aspect of their activities.

Several characteristics of this definition are worthy of note. First, it is very wide-ranging and has the potential to accommodate a hugely diverse range of actors. Secondly, the focus is on those actors whose activities have a transnational dimension. Actors engaged solely at the national level in one state or another are not part of the definition. Thirdly, there is no necessary commitment to particular values or principles, as has often been suggested should be part of the appropriate definition of a human rights NGO (non-governmental organization). Fourthly, the definition is endlessly debatable, as the very first criterion illustrates: what level of governmental funding, support, or encouragement might disqualify a group as a non-state actor? Fifthly, the category is so open-ended that it will have limited utility as a basis for making specific policy prescriptions in the context of international law or the appropriate approaches to be followed by international organizations.

There have also been some official attempts in the context of the work of international organizations to come up with a definition of the term. Thus in the Cotonou Agreement between the EU and ACP states, in which a variety of specific roles is accorded to non-state actors, the term is defined as encompassing three groups: the private sector; 'economic and social partners, including trade union organisations'; and 'Civil Society in all its forms according to national characteristics'.[45] This wholly benign definition contrasts dramatically with the usage which has evolved in the context of the UN Security Council. This is best illustrated by reference to a 2004 resolution dealing with non-state actors in the context of efforts to contain the spread of nuclear, chemical, and biological weapons. Unusually, the resolution actually contains a definition of the term, albeit said to be for the purpose of this resolution only. It is any 'individual or entity, not acting under the lawful authority of any State in conducting activities which come within the scope of this resolution'.[46] Further elucidation is provided by a later reference to the 'threat of terrorism and the risk that non-State actors such as those identified in the United Nations list established and maintained by the Committee established under Security Council resolution 1267 and those to whom resolution 1373 applies, may acquire, develop, traffic in or use nuclear, chemical and biological weapons and their means of delivery'. The so-called 'Resolution 1267 Committee' oversees the implementation of sanctions imposed on 'individuals and entities belonging or related to the Taliban, Usama Bin Laden and the Al-Qaida organization'.[47]

---

[45] Cotonou Agreement, note 3 above, Article 6(1).

[46] Security Council res. 1540 (2004), first preambular para.

[47] Security Council res. 1267 (1999), para. 6. The Committee's work is described at http://www.un.org/Docs/sc/committees/1267.

Resolution 1373 (2001) was adopted in response to the attacks of 11 September 2001 in the United States and applies to 'entities or persons involved in terrorist acts'.[48] The conclusion then is that the term non-state actors has come to be associated, at least in this central United Nations context, with terrorist groups. This is further evidence of the extent to which the meaning attributed to the phrase has become heavily context-dependent.

For present purposes, therefore, it seems more helpful to identify some of the key factors which are propelling non-state actors to greater prominence within the international human rights regime. They include, but are by no means limited to, the following.

Privatization. At the national level, the tidal wave of privatization that was unleashed in the 1980s has led, in many countries, to private actors being given responsibility for arrangements relating to social welfare services, prisons, asylum processing, schools, adoptions, health care provision for the poor, the supply of water, gas, and electricity, and a great many other functions previously provided or overseen by public actors.

Capital mobilization and private foreign investment flows. Globalization—driven by deregulation, the liberalization of trade, expanded opportunities for foreign investment, and the active promotion by the governments of industrialized countries and international agencies of a free enterprise economic environment—has facilitated an immense expansion since the 1970s in the wealth and power of transnational corporations. In terms of revenues, the 2003 sales of the world's biggest company (Wal-Mart at US$256 billion) made it larger than the economies of all but the world's thirty richest nations.[49] Its sales on a single day alone are greater than the annual Gross Domestic Product (GDP) of thirty-six countries in the world.[50] In Mexico, for example, it has become the largest private employer, accounts for 2 per cent of the country's GDP, and is credited with single-handedly reducing the national inflation rate.[51]

Trade liberalization and its employment consequences. In 1994 the ILO began a process of reinvigorating and adapting its approach to international labour standards. It culminated in the adoption of the International Labour Organization's (ILO) 1998 Declaration on Fundamental Principles and Rights at Work. In launching the process the Director-General of the ILO identified the growing role of non-state actors as one of the principal challenges flowing from globalization. The problem for the ILO, he noted, lies in 'the "state-centred" nature of ILO standards, in other words, the fact that the obligations arising from Conventions apply directly only to States'.[52]

---

[48] Security Council res. 1373 (2001), para. 2(a).

[49] Tim Weiner, 'Wal-Mart Invades, and Mexico Gladly Surrenders', *New York Times*, 5 December 2003, A1 at A9.

[50] Jerry Useem, 'One Nation Under Wal-Mart', *Fortune Magazine*, 3 March 2003, at http://www.ufcw135.org/z_news/n_onenation_under_wmt.htm.   [51] Weiner, note 49 above.

[52] *Defending Values, Promoting Change: Social Justice in a Global Economy: An ILO Agenda*, Report by the Director General for the International Labour Conference 81st Session, 1994, p. 56.

The expanding horizons of multilateral institutions. The United Nations and many other international organizations were recognized as long ago as the early 1950s as enjoying a form of international legal personality. But the implications of this status have changed radically since the end of the Cold War as these organizations and agencies are called upon to exercise a wide range of governmental functions in areas ranging from Kosovo and East Timor, to Afghanistan, and Iraq. Along with this dramatic expansion of functions have come many questions about the relationship between international human rights and humanitarian law and the personnel operating under the relevant international mandates.

The unleashing of civil society. Until the early 1990s the term non-governmental organizations seemed more than adequate to describe the role played by voluntary organizations in relation to the international community. Since then the opening up of all societies in response to global political changes and to the pressures and opportunities of globalization has created vast new opportunities. Civil society organizations today often have multi-million dollar budgets, employ very large staffs, and are engaged in a large number of countries. Their functions are by no means confined to issue advocacy. Many of them are highly operational and exercise great leverage in communities in which they oversee the expenditure of huge amounts of aid, provide a wide range of basic services, or implement major projects in the fields of environment, disarmament, and much else.

The privatization of security provision. While the 1980s saw widespread condemnation of the role of mercenaries in a range of different conflicts, the 2000s are seeing a broad and potentially almost unlimited role being accorded to private contractors in conflict situations. In Iraq for example a class action lawsuit was brought in the US Federal Court in June 2004 against two corporations (Titan International and CACI International) accused of having conspired with U.S. officials to 'humiliate, torture and abuse persons detained' in Iraq. The contractors provided a range of services to the U.S. government, including carrying out prisoner interrogations, a role they had also played in Guantánamo.[53]

The changing nature of conflicts. Although humanitarian law has always sought to reach out to all of the parties to armed conflicts, groups and individuals basing themselves upon the framework of international human rights law were much more wary of following suit. In recent years, however, this has changed significantly. Perhaps the best illustration of this is the work of the Special Representative of the UN Secretary-General for Children and Armed Conflict. Basing himself to a significant extent on the Convention on the Rights of the Child, as well as the Geneva Conventions, the Special Representative has in recent years sought and obtained commitments from groups as diverse as the Sudan People's Liberation Movement, the Revolutionary United Front in Sierra Leone, the Liberation Tigers of Tamil Eelam in Sri Lanka, and the Revolutionary Armed Forces of Colombia.[54]

---

[53] The text of the class action lawsuit is available at http://www.ccr-ny.org/v2/legal/september_11th/docs/Al_Rawi_v_Titan_Complaint.pdf.

[54] http://www.un.org/special-rep/children-armed-conflict/English/Commitments.html.

In all of these contexts the result of recent developments has been to highlight and/or expand the *de facto* roles played by non-state actors in national and international affairs. But the challenge confronting the international human rights regime in particular, and international law in general, is to establish a framework which acknowledges the rights and responsibilities of these diverse actors, while at the same time protecting the principles upon which the regime is based. A refusal to recognize and accommodate the new realities in relation to non-state actors will only serve to marginalize the existing arrangements and underscore the need to bypass it in devising future arrangements. An international human rights regime which is not capable of effectively addressing situations in which powerful corporate actors are involved in major human rights violations, or of ensuring that private actors are held responsible, will not only lose credibility in the years ahead but will render itself unnecessarily irrelevant in relation to important issues.

5. THE RESPONSE OF MAINSTREAM INTERNATIONAL LAW TO THE EMERGENCE OF NON-STATE ACTORS

By the standards of formal international law the question of the status enjoyed by non-state actors is a remarkably straightforward one. Indeed the issue is almost determined before the question can be asked as a result of the very terminology long favoured by international lawyers—the phrase 'non-state actors' makes it abundantly clear that, as far as international law is concerned, the key actors are divided into two categories: states and the rest. And what distinguishes the motley crew that make up the rest is overwhelmingly, if not entirely, the very fact that they are not states and can never aspire to be such. But the concept of international legal personality, and the acknowledgement by the International Court of Justice in its famous comment in 1949 that the 'subjects of law in any legal system are not necessarily identical in their nature or in the extent of their rights, and their nature depends upon the needs of the community',[55] holds open the possibility that the categories might be meaningfully reconsidered in time.

As a result, international lawyers have long debated the circumstances under which entities other than states might also be characterized as 'subjects' of international law. The bottom line for the great majority of commentators is that while various actors have been accorded some form of international legal personality for specified purposes, this does not justify the conclusion that international law should treat them as subjects, and thus place them on a par, for at least some limited purposes, with states. In this sense, the term 'subjects' has been treated as a term of art in international law and one which can meaningfully be contrasted with the 'objects' of international law. Indeed the latter category can be defined not only with flexibility but even with generosity since no particular significance was thought to attach to the concept. Any entity could be deemed an 'object' as long as states chose

---

[55] Reparations for Injuries Case, 1949 *ICJ Rep.* 178.

to treat it as such. The phrase non-state actors, on the other hand, conveniently avoids confronting these terminological debates. From an international legal perspective the term 'actor' is a category seen as quintessentially derived from political science and thus, while carrying useful descriptive power, is (fortunately) unable to capture or convey any significant sense of legal capacity or personality.

International law textbooks continue to be remarkably faithful to this general line of thinking despite its ever-diminishing capacity to describe the evolving reality. This is not the place to enter into a systematic review of the shortcomings of the traditional reasoning but suffice it to say that the exclusionary nature of the conclusions reached almost always reflected the application of somewhat circular tests which were more or less intentionally designed to ensure a highly restrictive outcome. One example is enough. Writing at the beginning of the 1990s in a very lengthy international law textbook which emerged from a major UNESCO-sponsored endeavour, Bin Cheng defined international legal personality as 'the capacity to bear rights and obligations under international law'. It was an eminently reasonable definition but the set of criteria which he then laid out gave a very clear indication of just what types of entity might be able to satisfy the necessary requirements. To ascertain if an actor has international personality all we have to do is to ask if it possesses any duties or rights under international law:

Concrete examples include the right to send and receive diplomatic missions ('rights of legation'), to conclude agreements ('right of treaty'), the right . . . to engage in legitimate armed conflicts; the right to a maritime flag; the right of diplomatic protection of nationals; the right to bring an international claim, to sue and be sued on the international plane; the enjoyment of sovereign immunity within the jurisdiction of other States; and the right to be directly responsible for any breach of one's own legal obligations . . . ; without forgetting above all acknowledged territorial sovereignty over a portion of the surface of the earth.[56]

Any entity can aspire to international personality, but it will need to look an awful lot like a traditional state in order to meet the requirements. Lest it be thought that Bin Cheng's approach reflects a pre-Cold War analysis, it is instructive to compare the response of international lawyers and political scientists in response to developments in international relations over the past fifteen years or so. The great majority of political scientists would endorse the view that since the end of the Cold War, 'state power [has been] in retreat across the globe and [there is] increasing evidence of the influence of transnational private actors in international and domestic politics'.[57] It follows that analytical frameworks, even for the realists, have to be expanded to take account of a wider range of actors than states. But do normative frameworks need to be expanded as a result?

[56] B. Cheng, 'Introduction to Subjects of International Law', in M. Bedjaoui (ed.), *International Law: Achievements and Prospects* (Paris, UNESCO, 1991) 23 at 38.

[57] Josselin and Wallace, 'Non-State Actors in World Politics: A Framework', in Daphné Josselin, and William Wallace, *Non-State Actors in World Politics* (Houndsmills, Palgrave, 2001) 11–12; for a detailed bibliography tracing the relevant international relations and political science literature see Arts, note 43 above, 41–53.

International lawyers have been much less favourably disposed towards such heretical thinking than political scientists or economists. One exception is Michael Reisman who argues that the state-dominated 'international decision process' embodied in the UN Charter has been replaced in recent years by a process in which the lawfulness of international actions is assessed, be it retrospectively or prospectively, by a group consisting not only of governments but also of 'intergovernmental organizations, non-governmental organizations and, in no small measure, the media'. In his view this new 'international legal process is more able than constitutive structures of the past to provide remedies for grave human rights violations'. But Reisman regrets the limitations of the media and the lack of representativeness of some of the NGOs, and ends by calling upon international lawyers 'to improve the world constitutive process so that it can address humanitarian and other issues and thus obviate unilateral action'.[58] While more recent events in relation to the invasion of Iraq by a 'coalition of the willing' do little to encourage a sense that a more improved constitutive process would lead to better decision-making or would eliminate the resort to unilateral action, his analysis is nonetheless amenable to a greatly enhanced role for a wide range of actors. Notably, however, he does not mention transnational corporations as one of the players in the new constellation.

The great majority of international lawyers, however, have been much less sanguine about the possibility of expanding the range of key actors given a place at the top table. Indeed, most of them have shown a marked reluctance to contemplate any fundamental rethinking of the role of the state within the overall system of international law. Various explanations might be suggested: an intrinsic lack of imagination; a natural affinity with the status quo; a deeply rooted professional commitment to internationalism, albeit one premised on the continuity of the system of sovereign equality; a reluctance to bite the hand that feeds; or simply the conviction that respect for that system has taken a great deal of time and human suffering to achieve and that it continues to offer a better prospect than any alternative that has so far been put forward.

It is instructive to consider a cross-section of the responses. A good illustration of affection for the status quo is to be found in the approach of a leading international lawyer in the context of a symposium which sought to explore the implications for the concept of statehood of 'increasing tendencies towards pan-European, international—and, indeed, supranational—institutionalism'.[59] Asked to reflect on the issue, Ian Brownlie wrote dismissively: 'Seeking signs of the "rebirth of statehood" is more than a little premature: there is no evidence that the State has died. It is an intellectual fashion to preach the end of the State and to attack sovereignty. But such iconoclasm has had no impact on the real world.' The fact

---

[58] Michael Reisman, 'Unilateral Action and the Transformations of the World Constitutive Process: The Special Problem of Humanitarian Intervention', 11 *European Journal of International Law* (2000) 3, at 18.

[59] Malcolm Evans, 'Statehood and Institutionalism in Contemporary Europe: An Introduction', in M. Evans (ed.), *Aspects of Statehood and Institutionalism in Contemporary Europe* (Ashgate, 1997) 1.

remains that since 1945 the existence of states has provided the basis of the legal order.[60]

He went on to identify two culprits. The first consists of certain (unnamed) powerful states which encourage talk of the demise of sovereignty in order to use it as a justification for projecting their own power. The second set of culprits are the political scientists who use their 'repertoire of facile abuse' to attack the concept of the state.[61] Insofar as it was useful to ask whether there might be alternative approaches to the traditional state-centrism, Brownlie suggested that those could only be the 'alternative models familiar to international lawyers: the condominium, trusteeship, and federation'. Since they tend to be both 'complex and transitional in purpose' they offer no real solace and so we are back to the state.[62]

Other international lawyers are more willing to comprehend the novelty of the challenges facing the international system but equally convinced that the state system must remain the bedrock of any workable approach. Richard Falk is an example of one who has long challenged the received wisdom in most aspects of the field and who has characterized 'global civil society as a bearer of a hopeful and progressive vision of the future of world order'.[63] Indeed for Falk and his collaborators in the World Order Models Project, transnational civil society holds the key to the future.[64] Firmly committed to the promotion of shared values in terms of peace, ecological awareness, and human rights, and animated by shifting political identities which transcend territorial boundaries, these groups will play an increasingly central role in overall governance structures. Ultimately, to the extent that 'global civil society becomes a reality in the imagination and lives of its adherents, the reality of territorial states will often recede in significance even though it may never entirely disappear'.[65]

But when it comes to the question of whether multinational corporations, the single most relevant category of non-state actors, currently have either moral or legal obligations, Falk answers in the negative. They have no 'established moral obligations beyond their duties to uphold the interests of their shareholders'; the efforts they make to 'improve their public image in relation to human rights are a matter of self-interest that does not reflect the existence or acceptance of a moral obligation'; and even long-term compliance with the standards contained in voluntary codes of conduct would take a long-time to 'ripen into a moral obligation'. He concedes that a 'framework of international legal obligations' for corporations would help protect human rights but applies strong caveats in that respect. Such a framework would

---

[60] Ian Brownlie, 'Rebirth of Statehood', ibid., 5.   [61] Ibid.   [62] Ibid.

[63] Richard Falk, 'Democratizing, Internationalizing, and Globalizing', in Y. Sakamoto (ed.), *Global Transformation: Challenges to the State System* (Tokyo, United Nations University, 1994) 475, 488.

[64] E.g. Richard Falk, 'The World Order Between Inter-State Law and the Law of Humanity: The Role of Civil Society Institutions', in Daniele Archibugi and David Held (eds.), *Cosmopolitan Democracy* 163 (Cambridge, Polity Press, 1995).

[65] Richard Falk, *On Human Governance: Towards a New Global Politics* (Cambridge, Polity Press, 1995) 212.

need to be widely endorsed at both the regional and international levels, by states rather than corporations, and in any event they would be likely in the short-term to 'accentuate human suffering' because international standards would reduce the competitiveness of the poorest countries.[66] Presumably he has in mind the much-contested case of labour rights,[67] rather than the charges of slavery, forced labour, and other fundamental abuses of which various corporations operating in places such as Myanmar have been accused.

Christian Tomuschat, another leading international lawyer with impeccable credentials as a human rights expert, is slightly less categorical than Falk. He emphasizes in a recent book that '[i]n human rights discourse, the State is the key actor', but by the same token he concedes that a 'concept that would visualize human rights exclusively as a burden on the governmental apparatus would be doomed from the very outset'. Lest this be taken as making a case in favour of imposing responsibilities on non-state entities, he adds that it 'does not mean that the individual as a holder of rights should concomitantly be subjected to legal duties either under domestic or international law'. His optimistic prescription is that '[g]overnments have always found ways and means to enforce [their] policies' and all that is really needed is 'that the intellectual frame of society [should condition] its practices in the field of human rights'.[68] In relation to transnational corporations he sums up the received wisdom with remarkable brevity. In response to various claims by human rights lawyers that such corporations should be subject to human rights obligations, he notes that: 'It is true that in particular in developing countries transnational corporations bear a heavy moral responsibility because of their economic power, which may occasionally exceed that of the host State. But on the level of positive law, little, if anything has materialized'.[69] In other words there is a strong moral case to be made but positive international law has not budged in the face of such amorphous pressures.

Finally, mention should be made of the law of state responsibility itself. In 2001 the International Law Commission adopted a set of final Articles on the Responsibility of States for Internationally Wrongful Acts.[70] These were approved by the U.N. General Assembly, which took note of them and commended them 'to the attention of Governments without prejudice to the question of their future adoption or other appropriate action'.[71] One of the questions that arose in the context of the drafting process was whether various developments relating to the role of non-state actors in invoking international the rules of state responsibility at the international level in areas such as human rights, foreign investment, and environmental protection,

[66] Richard Falk, 'Human Rights', *Foreign Policy*, March–April 2004, 18, at 20–22.

[67] For a survey of the literature see Drusilla Brown, *International Trade and Core Labor Standards: A Survey of the Recent Literature*, Department of Economics, Tufts University, Discussion Paper 2000–05 (2000).

[68] Christian Tomuschat, *Human Rights: Between Idealism and Realism* (Oxford, Oxford University Press, 2003) 320.   [69] Ibid., 90–91.

[70] UN doc. A/56/10 (2001).   [71] General Assembly res. 56/83 (2001), para. 3.

should be reflected in the Articles. In the end, the draft goes out of its way to protect any such acquired rights by providing that the part of the Articles dealing with the content of state's responsibility 'is without prejudice to any right, arising from the international responsibility of a State, which may accrue directly to any person or entity other than a State'.[72] This provision was included even though the commentary on the Articles, as approved by the Commission, made clear that they do not 'deal with the possibility of the invocation of responsibility' by non-state actors.[73] That, in other words, is a matter to be determined by the primary rules agreed to by states in whatever context and the Commentary notes that some procedures may well be available which would enable a non-state entity 'to invoke the responsibility on its own account and without the intermediation of any State'.[74]

Thus, from a non-state actor's point of view, the Articles are essentially neutral in that they neither discourage nor seek to promote those trends which favour an enhanced role for non-state actors in terms of invoking state responsibility. By the same token, they very clearly leave the door open for further developments in the future. Nevertheless, the Articles have been criticized by some commentators for not having gone further. Edith Brown Weiss, in arguing that more could have been done, points to two steps that might have been taken. One would have been to confirm that non-state actors are entitled to invoke state responsibility 'if the obligation breached is owed to them or an international agreement or other primary rule of international law so provides'.[75] That step would not seem to add a great deal but it would have made the existing approach more explicit. The other step would have been to recognize that non-state actors 'of one state *may* be entitled in certain circumstances to invoke the responsibility of another state if the obligation is owed to the international community as a whole'.[76] This second step would have been more dramatic and it is not surprising that the Commission, anxious to complete work which had taken too many decades already, did not wish to provoke the fears of states with the inclusion of such an additional element.

In its subsequent work, begun in 2002, the Commission has adopted an equally cautious approach but also one which does not close the door to non-state actors in its examination of the topic of the 'responsibility of international organizations'.[77] Draft Article 2 defines the term 'international organization' as referring to 'an organization established by a treaty or other instrument governed by international law and possessing its own international legal personality. International organizations

---

[72] Draft Articles, UN doc. A/56/10 (2001), Art. 33(2).

[73] The Commentary has been reprinted in James Crawford, *The International Law Commission's Articles on State Responsibility: Introduction, Text and Commentaries* (Cambridge University Press, 2002), Art. 33, para. 4.   [74] Ibid.

[75] Edith Brown Weiss, 'Invoking State Responsibility in the Twenty-First Century', 96 *AJIL* (2002) 798, at 816.   [76] Ibid., emphasis in original.

[77] *Report of the International Law Commission on the Work of its 54th Session*, UN doc. A/57/10 (2002), chap. VIII, para. 458.

may include as members, in addition to States, other entities.'[78] The second sentence makes clear that the draft will not apply to any entity which is not composed, at least in part, by states or state organs or agencies.[79] The Commentary on the draft points out that it is designed to accommodate 'a significant trend in practice' according to which international organizations have a mixed membership including private entities. The report gives the World Tourism Organization as an example in that respect.[80]

6. OUTLINE OF THE BOOK

A. The Framework for Non-State Actors

As noted at the outset, the potential scope of an analysis dealing with non state actors is almost without limit. In certain contexts, and particularly from a political science perspective of trying to map and navigate the new terrain, a wide-ranging approach is both appropriate and necessary. But in the context of a book dealing with the ways in which the international human rights regime has sought to come to grips with the rapidly changing role of non-state actors a significantly narrower approach is called for. In particular, the most important current debate relates to the role of 'transnational corporations and other business enterprises', to use the formula agreed upon by the drafters of the Norms proposed by the UN Sub-Commission for the Promotion and Protection of Human Rights in 2003. For that reason, the majority of the contributions to this volume address the legal and practical difficulties of holding such entities to account for conduct which violates international human rights law but is not adequately dealt with by the domestic law of the state in which the entity is operating. The remaining Chapters address the case of non-governmental organizations and of a particular international organization, the International Monetary Fund.

Before focusing individually on specific actors, August Reinisch in 'The Changing International Legal Framework for Dealing with Non-State Actors' (Chapter 2 below) provides an overview of the current state of the law. He notes that the increased concern with trying to hold corporations accountable for human rights violations represents a shift in the conventional understanding of human rights principles as limitations on state power.[81] Indeed, the focus on corporate behaviour may be regarded as an instance of a broader movement towards concern with the actions of non-state actors in international law. There has been a quantitative and qualitative proliferation of institutions concerned with human rights, from the more

---

[78] *Report of the International Law Commission on the Work of its 55th Session*, UN doc. A/58/10 (2003), chap. IV, para. 41.　　　　　　　　　　　　　　　　　　　　[79] Ibid., para. 12.

[80] Ibid., para. 13.

[81] August Reinisch, 'The Changing International Legal Framework for Dealing with Non-State Actors' at p. 42.

traditional treaty-based bodies to internal review mechanisms such as the World Bank's Inspection Panel.[82]

Reinisch highlights the increased interest over the last twenty years in using voluntary codes of conduct as a means of regulating corporations. He notes, however, that United Nations efforts to formulate a comprehensive set of principles failed in the early 1980s, and that in more recent years organizations such as the OECD and the ILO have developed codes relevant to their areas of activity. A novel development has been work on codes of conduct applying to international organizations themselves and to their operations in the field, as well as to codes governing NGOs. Reinisch argues that the heightened interest in codes of conduct emerged out of the increased demands for 'good governance' made on states,[83] which ultimately spilled over into a concern for good governance on the part of non-state actors. The key difficulty is that codes of conduct for both corporations and international organizations do not provide for strong supervisory or enforcement mechanisms. They do, however, offer a lightning rod for external pressure and scrutiny of conduct, and may engender such responses as consumer boycotts, negative publicity, and shareholder action if public opinion is mobilized around breaches of codes to which the non-state actor has professed adherence.[84]

Despite the fact that most codes lack enforcement mechanisms, there is a diverse range of national and regional laws which could be used to regulate the extraterritorial conduct of non-state actors in certain circumstances. Apart from the well known Alien Torts Claims Act in the United States,[85] there has been a revival of extraterritorial laws within the EU legal framework.[86] To the extent that there is a genuine effort by states to enforce international law through extraterritorial legislation, this may be a promising mechanism for the decentralized enforcement of international law. One dimension of this trend is a willingness to treat transnational corporations (TNCs) as 'accomplices' to human rights violations committed by states in which they operate subsidiaries.[87]

Reinisch traces the changing roles of international organizations and NGOs over the last thirty years, from a situation in which they were the 'good guys', and powerful states were the 'bad guys', to a context in which international organizations are increasingly challenged in terms of their own human rights performance.[88] Despite the intellectual energy now devoted to holding non-state actors accountable, Reinisch notes that international law still lacks an adequate conception of non-state actors as subjects.[89] There is some basis for the view that human rights obligations bind legal persons as well as states, but this is an implied rather than express consequence of existing human rights treaties.

The origins of the new preoccupation with non-state actors is argued to derive from a structural change in the international legal order, with a decrease in, and partial

---

[82] See p. 42.　　　[83] See p. 53.　　　[84] See pp. 55–6, 74–5.
[85] See Steinhardt for detailed discussion.　　　[86] Reinisch, see pp. 62–64.
[87] See pp. 71–2.　　　[88] See p. 69.　　　[89] See pp. 76–8.

disappearance of, the concept of the state as a mediating factor between international law and individuals.[90] Moreover, the state's role as regulator and guarantor of human rights is diminishing due to the pervasive privatization of state functions. Tendencies towards outsourcing state regulatory functions or permitting greater degrees of self-regulation of corporate entities dovetail with the hegemony of neo liberal economic doctrines and the accelerated mobility of finance capital.[91] The information revolution may also have increased the timeliness of information about the activity of non-state actors, making human rights violations more visible and better known in real time.

A promising development in the enforcement of human rights laws is an increased willingness for regional human rights courts such as the European Court of Human Rights to hold states responsible for non-state actors' conduct on their territory.[92] The direct accountability of non-state actors before international courts remains underdeveloped, something underlined by the International Criminal Court's lack of jurisdiction over legal persons.

B. Non-Governmental Organizations

Strong claims have been advanced in the past few years for the view that the role of NGOs, or more broadly of civil society, is indispensable in the building of a more equitable and effective international order. It has been argued, for example, that the active engagement of civil society, along with the corporate sector, 'is a critical if not imperative component in delivering policy outcomes that are timely, effective and legitimate. Creative institutional innovations are needed that connect governments, international organizations, civil society, and the corporate sector'.[93]

Menno Kamminga[94] traces the evolution of the one non-state actor which has long been recognized by international institutions: the non-governmental organization. He begins by noting the unease of many observers about the role which NGOs have come to play in certain important international contexts. He highlights the comments by the former President of the International Court of Justice, Gilbert Guillaume, who was highly critical of the fact that NGOs played important roles in relation to the Advisory Opinion on the legality of nuclear weapons and expressed the hope in response to an NGO letter-writing campaign to the Court that governments and inter-governmental institutions would be able to 'resist the powerful pressure groups which besiege them'.[95] Others have expressed similar concerns about the excessive influence wielded by NGOs, and the complaint has been expressed in strong terms by the Bush administration and its supporters in the United States.[96]

---

[90] See p. 77.   [91] See pp. 80–2.   [92] See pp. 83–5.

[93] Jan Martin Witte, Wolfgang H. Reinicke, and Thorsten Benner, 'Beyond Multilateralism: Global Public Policy Networks', at http://www.fes.de/IPG/ipg2_2000/artwitte.html.

[94] 'The Evolving Status of NGOs under International Law: A Threat to the Inter-State System?', Chapter 3 below.   [95] See p. 37.

[96] John Bolton, 'Should We Take Global Governance Seriously?', 1 *Chicago J. Int'l L.* (2000) 205 ('It is no exaggeration to say that, in United Nations circles, the demands of civil society to participate in

In an effort to clarify the focus of the Chapter, Kamminga seeks to define NGOs and, after noting that they are usually explained by reference to what they are not (governmental) rather than by what they are, explains the UN system for according certain degrees of status to such groups. He proceeds to see how NGOs measure up against the criteria proposed as traditional indicators of international legal personality. In relation to the capacity to conclude treaties he notes that any such right exists only under national law, if at all. His main focus is the International Committee of the Red Cross which, despite having the characteristics of a Swiss NGO, has been accorded international juridical capacity. In terms of the capacity to participate in international treaty-making he notes the case of the ILO, in which employers and workers' representatives participate in the negotiation of treaties, and then reviews the important drafting and lobbying roles that have been played by NGOs in various other treaty-drafting contexts. These include the UN Convention against Torture, the Framework Convention on Climate Change, the Landmines Convention, and the Statute of the International Criminal Court.

Under the heading of the capacity to bring international claims Kamminga notes that there are few if any pure cases of this sort but then reviews the rights accorded to NGOs and individuals enabling them to lodge complaints under various human rights treaties. Finally, he looks at liability under international law and concludes that there are rarely anything more than minor procedures for sanctioning them. In conclusion he observes that NGOs are certainly playing an increasingly prominent role in various international contexts. But while this role is sometimes reflected in their formal status, it remains generally 'extremely weak'.[97] Even if a set of proposals made by a panel of eminent persons in 2004 designed to enhance the role of civil society, and NGOs in particular, within the United Nations system were to be adopted, it is not clear that their roles would be greatly strengthened.[98] It should also be noted that Kamminga's analysis does not deal with NGOs in general and that the conclusions reached in relation to a chapter dealing with the role of business and other groups in the area of international economic law would differ in important respects.

C. International Organizations

While international organizations like the United Nations itself, the international financial institutions, or the World Trade Organization are regularly attacked for

---

decision-making on a level functionally equivalent to national governments are all but conceded'. Ibid., 216); Kenneth Anderson, 'The Limits of Pragmatism in American Foreign Policy: Unsolicited Advice to the Bush Administration on Relations with International Nongovernmental Organizations', 2 *Chicago J. Int'l L.* (2001) 371 ('[I]nternational organizations really do believe that they and international organizations ought to rule the world (with some help from Ottawa and Paris)'. Ibid., 388).

[97] See p. 109.

[98] *We the Peoples: Civil Society, the United Nations and Global Governance*, Report of the Panel of Eminent Persons on United Nations-Civil Society Relations, UN doc. A/58/817 (2004).

one or another of their policies they are nevertheless often overlooked in discussions of the role of non-state actors in relation to human rights. There are several plausible explanations for that neglect. The first is that they are not considered to be non-state actors, since they are effectively acting as surrogates for states in some of the things that they do, and in any event their 'lords and masters' are states. The second is that they are usually conceded to enjoy a degree of international personality and thus their status *vis-à-vis* states is not considered to be as dramatically different as is the case with other non-state actors. A third explanation is that most of their activities are considered, although not by a good many NGOs, to be essentially benign. And a fourth, closely related to the others, is that they don't seem to fit easily into the category of non-state actors since the latter is often assumed to consist of groups, albeit as diverse as corporations and terrorists, who don't have a natural affinity with human rights and cannot plausibly proclaim their adherence to the relevant norms.

Against that backdrop, François Gianviti[99] focuses on the three aspects of the relationship between the International Monetary Fund (IMF) and one of the principal international human rights treaties, the International Covenant on Economic, Social, and Cultural Rights. They are: do the provisions of the Covenant have some 'legal effect' on the IMF; is the IMF obligated to contribute to the achievement of the rights recognized in the Covenant; and to what extent can the Fund, acting in accordance with its Articles of Agreement, take account of the relevant rights?

This Chapter is of particular interest because it is the first time that a senior official of the IMF (its Legal Counsel) has addressed these issues in a systematic fashion in the context of a careful legal analysis of the various considerations. His analysis does not deal with the broader question of whether some of the rights contained in the Covenant are part of customary law, along with some or all of those recognized in the other Covenant—the International Covenant on Civil and Political Rights—and might thus be binding on that basis on an international organization such as the IMF.

In relation to the Covenant he emphasizes the fact that it is a treaty addressed to states, and an instrument to which they can become parties. But the relevant rights are neither addressed to an international agency such as the IMF nor is it permitted to become a party, even if it wished to do so. Moreover, the relationship agreement entered into between the UN and the Fund creates a relationship between 'sovereign equals', as a result of which the Fund is not required to give effect to resolutions of the General Assembly or to international agreements entered into by UN member states. He attaches considerable importance in his analysis to an otherwise little noted provision of the Covenant (Article 24), which in his words: 'explicitly recognizes that "[n]othing in the present Covenant shall be interpreted as impairing the provisions . . . of the constitutions of the specialized agencies which define the respective responsibilities . . . of the specialized agencies in regard to the matters dealt with in the present Covenant" '.[100]

---

[99] 'Economic, Social, and Cultural Rights and the International Monetary Fund', Chapter 4 below.
[100] Ibid., see p. 118.

In quoting this provision, however, he omits a reference after the first ellipsis to the Charter of the UN and after the second to the responsibilities 'of the various organs of the United Nations'. As a result he emphasizes that the IMF's Articles of Agreement could only be modified by a formal amendment, but does not address the argument that permitting the IMF to remain altogether aloof from the treaty regime might impair the provisions of the UN Charter and thus itself require a Charter amendment in order to be sustainable.

Gianviti concludes that the Fund can still contribute through its policies and programs to the realization of the objectives spelled out in the Covenant, even if it has neither a legal obligation nor a constitutional mandate to do so systematically. But the bottom line is that the Fund 'is not free to disregard its own legal structure for the sake of pursuing goals that are not its own mandated purposes',[101] even if those 'goals' are human rights. If a stronger involvement with human rights is desirable then the appropriate course is to seek an amendment to the Fund's Articles of Agreement.

D. Corporations

The question of terminology looms large in this respect with different authors opting to focus on 'transnational corporations', 'multinational corporations', or 'multinational enterprises'.[102] Similarly each international organization which addresses these issues—including the UN, the ILO, the Organization for Economic Cooperation and Development (OECD), and the EU—seems to have its own terminological preference and usually offers a variety of reasons why its choice is better than the alternatives. At the end of the day, the differences do not seem especially compelling and thus no attempt has been made in this volume to standardize the terminology. The phrase transnational corporations (TNCs) is used in the present Chapter primarily because it has long been the term of choice in the context of the United Nations' deliberations on the matter.

The picture that emerges from the Chapters in this volume that address corporate responsibility is that international law's capacity adequately to regulate the cross-boundary activity of TNCs lags considerably behind the social and economic realities of globalized production and trade. Existing domestic and international legal mechanisms are, to a considerable extent, unable to ensure that their enforcement of human rights obligations is effective when it comes to the activities of TNCs and other non-state actors. Partly as a result, the past decade has seen a proliferation of efforts to formulate codes of conduct, guidelines, ethical principles, and other voluntary and non-binding arrangements. They all attempt to provide a lightning rod for consumer and public awareness campaigns that endeavour to regulate

---

[101] 'Economic, Social, and Cultural Rights and the International Monetary Fund', Chapter 4 below, at p. 138.

[102] Multinational corporations are said to reproduce their activities in a range of different nations, primarily in order to overcome barriers to trade, while transnational corporations are single firms pursuing an international division of labour in different countries. See generally Higgott *et al.* note 36 above.

corporate conduct indirectly by threatening brand reputations or affecting investor confidence. Several of the contributions to this volume address different dimensions of these diverse efforts.

Ralph Steinhardt[103] argues that despite the fragmentary and seemingly weak regulatory structure that is emerging at the moment, there is a real potential for the slow crystallization of a new *lex mercatoria* governing the conduct of corporations. He locates the principal sources for this new *lex mercatoria* in four areas: market-based regimes, domestic regulation, civil liability, and international 'quasi-regulation'. Like Reinisch, Steinhardt highlights the important role of international public opinion, and corporations' exposure to campaigns against their brands on the basis of their conduct. He considers the mixed experience of voluntary codes of conduct embraced by TNCs operating in apartheid South Africa, and the newer phenomena of 'rights-sensitive' product lines.[104] Social accountability auditing and ethical investment organizations are relatively recent practices which attempt to link market incentives more directly with corporate social responsibility.[105] Some of these campaigns have had high profile successes in persuading countries to cease activities in countries where human rights violations are endemic, due in no small part to concerted NGO advocacy and activism.

Steinhardt discusses five instances of domestic legislation intended to restrain or discourage TNC involvement with human rights violations abroad.[106] The U.S. Foreign Corrupt Practices Act of 1977 (designed to prohibit bribery of foreign governments by U.S. corporations) has been an effective standard setter for U.S. business, and appears to have been influential in shaping similar laws in other countries. Some states, including France and the United Kingdom, use securities laws to require companies to report to the market on human rights and environmental compliance. Import and export control laws continue to be used as a means of discouraging involvement with human rights-abusing countries, and government procurement and public expenditure laws may include human rights conditionalities that require companies to meet certain standards in their foreign operations before they can be eligible for public monies. Finally, specific legislation has been introduced in the U.S. to penalize insurance companies that fail to pay valid claims by Holocaust survivors. As Steinhardt points out, laws such as these seek to create a nexus between market-based regimes and legislative regulation, by creating requirements that expose companies to market censure through exposure of human rights violations, or threatening companies' access to public financing and government contracts.

The Alien Tort Claims Act has become a primary vehicle in the U.S. for attempting to hold TNCs accountable for human rights violations abroad.[107] Despite considerable procedural hurdles, several civil claims against corporations

---

[103] 'Corporate Responsibility and the International Law of Human Rights: The New *Lex Mercatoria*', Chapter 6 below.   [104] See p. 183.
[105] See p. 184.   [106] See pp. 180–7.   [107] See pp. 194–6.

alleged to be complicit in grave human rights violations in foreign countries have survived strike-out motions. The cases have the potential to open up new understandings of corporate complicity in state human rights abuses, and Steinhardt summarizes the main kinds of wrongs which are actionable under ATCA.[108]

Finally, Steinhardt considers the regime of international 'quasi-regulation' that is emerging through international organizations. He points to bodies of principles promulgated by the ILO and OECD, and initiatives for a social clause under consideration by the WTO,[109] as evidence of an emerging 'cartel of values'. He then reviews some of the philosophical issues raised by imposing human rights obligations upon corporations, arguing that this imposition can be justified on a number of different grounds: deontological, utilitarian, and positivist.[110] There is no longer any basis for considering corporations to be the equivalent of purely private individuals, nor any convincing reason why a corporation should not be accountable for violations of international human rights law in the same way that it is liable for violations of domestic tort law or criminal law. Nevertheless, questions arise about how much corporate knowledge and involvement is required to hold a company responsible for human rights violations committed by a state in which it operates.[111]

Despite the limitations of existing mechanisms, Steinhardt is confident that together they promote the emergence of practices and habits that could form a new *lex mercatoria*: a body of law that is transnational in scope, grounded in good faith, reflective of market practices, and ultimately codified in the commercial law of nations and in international law. Codes of conduct, market-based regimes, civil litigation, and international principles reflect an intersection of the law and the marketplace.

David Weissbrodt and Muria Kruger[112] describe from the inside the process by which one of the most comprehensive attempts at formulating a corporate code of conduct was undertaken by the UN Sub-Commission for the Promotion and Protection of Human Rights, through its Working Group on the Working Methods and Activities of Transnational Corporations. Over a period of three years, the Working Group developed several drafts of what were initially called the Universal Human Rights Guidelines for Companies.[113] Weissbrodt himself was the key person in this endeavour and he and Kruger note that while there was a common desire to establish a binding code, the Working Group accepted the reality that political controversy would prevent the adoption of a treaty regulating TNCs and other businesses. Instead, the Working Group decided to implement the Guidelines as 'soft law' principles, and thereby introduce them into international law discourse and practice. In 2002 it adopted a revised draft entitled 'Norms on the Responsibilities of Transnational Corporations and Other Business Enterprises with Regard to Human

---

[108] See pp. 198–202.   [109] See pp. 202–12.   [110] See pp. 213–4.
[111] See pp. 215–7.
[112] 'Human Rights Responsibilities of Businesses as Non-State Actors', Chapter 8 below.
[113] See pp. 328–35.

Rights' ('the Norms'). Until such time as they are adopted by the Commission on Human Rights or another UN body such as the Economic and Social Council or the General Assembly, the document remains a draft, but it has been the subject of extensive consultations with human rights NGOs and companies.

The Norms seek to synthesize developments in treaty law which expressly or implicitly expand the scope of human rights obligations to non-state actors such as businesses, and clarify the extent of the obligations that apply directly to businesses.[114] The document pursues implementation through a number of avenues. First, it calls on businesses to adopt and implement the principles, and disseminate them amongst employees.[115] It also encourages businesses to conduct internal and external assessments of the extent to which current practices meet the standards in the Norms, and submit the assessment to an independent verification. Civil society entities, such as NGOs, trade unions, and business associations, are encouraged to take up the standards and use them as benchmarks for measuring performance, while intergovernmental organizations may also use them to inform the formulation of their own standards. States could use the Norms as a model for legislation, and domestic courts may also have regard to them. Thus, the hope is that the Norms will inform both business and state practice in setting standards and rules for business conduct, and so contribute to a harmonization of the substance of regulatory approaches.

Celia Wells and Juanita Elias[116] confront the difficulties inherent in attempting to hold corporations criminally liable for grave violations of human rights. The considerable barriers to enforcing the criminal liability of corporations in a domestic context are compounded internationally, not only due to the absence of an international criminal law specifically dealing with corporations, but also because of the complex corporate forms that are produced by relations of production in the age of globalization. Outsourcing, vertical disintegration, global commodity chains, and other production strategies complicate the legal attribution of responsibility where law (international and domestic) still largely presupposes discrete political communities defined in terms of territory.[117]

Wells and Elias review three different theories of corporate criminal responsibility: the agency principle, the 'controlling mind' approach, and the 'corporate culture' approach.[118] The first two theories seek to equate corporate responsibility with that of an individual actor, while the third takes a more holistic approach. The tendency to require an identification between the acts of an individual employee or manager and the corporation as a prerequisite to liability makes establishing an offence difficult in many common law countries. Within the EU there has been some convergence in corporate criminal liability frameworks,[119] and there appears to be a recent willingness among civil law countries to contemplate corporate criminal liability.

---

[114] See pp. 335–8.   [115] See p. 341.

[116] 'Catching the Conscience of the King: Corporate players on the International Stage', Chapter 5 below.   [117] See pp. 150–4.

[118] See pp. 156–57.   [119] See p. 159.

Wells and Elias then review the complicity principles that might be applied to corporations in international law, distinguishing between first order and second order direct complicity (where corporations either actively assisted in implementing policies that violate human rights or knew that their cooperation would result in human rights violations) and indirect complicity,[120] where a corporation's activities help maintain a regime's financial and commercial infrastructure. They argue that domestic criminal law concerning complicity should not be used too readily in the development of international criminal law, as the domestic law is uncertain and conflicted.[121] Wells and Elias also consider the complicity principles contained in Article 25 of the Rome Statute, which contain three routes to accessory liability: instigation, assistance, and joint enterprise. However, the Rome Statute does not apply to legal persons, so can best offer guidance to domestic courts applying international law to the conduct of TNCs. The present potential for applying international criminal law to companies remains limited, as the international enforcement of corporate responsibilities is secondary to the protection of the economic rights of corporations.[122]

Olivier De Schutter[123] reviews the European Union framework for the accountability of TNCs for human rights violations. He first considers the general international law principles governing state responsibility for the protection of individuals within their jurisdiction, and notes that in current international law there is no state responsibility for the private acts of nationals abroad.[124] As such, states are responsible for human rights violations committed by non-state actors on their own territory, but not for the extraterritorial conduct of TNCs domiciled in their territory. Nevertheless, in a context where developing nations compete for foreign investment from TNCs, states may not have the incentive properly to regulate TNC activity on their own territory, or may not have the means.[125]

De Schutter explores whether the European Convention on Human Rights provides any basis upon which developed states can be required to hold TNCs domiciled in their territory accountable for human rights violations committed abroad. Recent case-law appears to hold that states are not responsible for human rights violations committed by their nationals extraterritorially, unless that territory is under the effective control of the state (as was Iraq, for example, under the terms of the Coalition occupation).[126]

EU trade and development policies provide a means for the EU to provide uniform incentives for developing states to enforce human rights standards, but raise the concern that trade conditions may be perceived as a form of protection.[127] Moreover, De Schutter argues, the use of trade conditionalities is at best a clumsy and indirect means of regulating TNCs.[128]

---

[120] See p. 161.   [121] See p. 163.   [122] See p. 166.
[123] 'The Accountability of Multinationals for Human Rights Violations in European Law', Chapter 7 below.   [124] See p. 233.
[125] See pp. 235–6.   [126] See pp. 240–9.   [127] See pp. 253–60.   [128] See pp. 260–2.

In the realm of civil liability, De Schutter contends that there is some scope under the terms of European Community Law for a TNC domiciled in an EU country to be sued in the courts of that country for a tort committed outside the EU, creating a possible analogy with the ATCA.[129] It seems, however, that this possibility remains untested, and a number of complex doctrinal questions, such as *forum non-conveniens* and the problem of applicable law, would have to be clarified by EU national courts, before such a claim could proceed.[130] There is also the problem of attributing the acts of a non-EU located subsidiary to an EU-domiciled parent company. De Schutter shows that the applicable principles are not free from controversy in EU courts.[131]

There does not exist an EU-wide corporate criminal code governing extraterritorial TNC conduct, but De Schutter suggests that suitable models for the formulation for such a legal regime could be found in existing initiatives to criminalize the extraterritorial sexual exploitation of children, and in the Belgian universal jurisdiction laws.[132] He recommends that such legislation should be based on the active personality principle and should apply universally recognized principles of international human rights law, rather than domestic standards.[133]

Finally, De Schutter reviews the EU experience with codes of conduct, particularly the attempt to apply a code of practice to EU companies dealing with the apartheid regime in South Africa, and the 1998 code of conduct concerning arms exports. These experiences suggest that in order for codes of conduct to be effective, two conditions must be met: the codes should impose clearly verifiable obligations on companies and violations should be sanctioned, and the standards set should be as uniform as possible.[134] He notes that the EU Green Paper on Corporate Social Responsibility stresses the importance of monitoring compliance with codes of conduct, and that some steps have been taken to create a European Monitoring Platform.[135] There would also appear to be considerable potential for the EU to set procurement and export credit conditions which require TNC compliance with human rights principles or codes of conduct, subject to the non-discrimination requirements of EU economic law.[136]

7. CONCLUSION

This Introduction sets the scene for the various analyses that follow. In particular, it has sought to shed some light on the approaches advocated by mainstream international lawyers to the challenges presented by the emergence of an important, and in many contexts powerful or at least influential, array of non-state actors.

The received wisdom that emerges very clearly from the analyses of most international lawyers may be summarized in the following terms: (i) the international

---

[129] See pp. 262–7.   [130] Discussed at pp. 267–72.   [131] Discussed at pp. 272–6.
[132] Discussed at pp. 283–6.   [133] See p. 286.   [134] See p. 299.   [135] See pp. 301–2.
[136] See pp. 304–5.

legal framework is and will remain essentially state-centric; (ii) there is a very limited formal role for other international actors, although their participation in international decision-making processes is often desirable; (iii) transnational corporations should perhaps accept some moral obligations; but (iv) they have no clear legal obligations in respect to human rights apart from compliance with the law of the particular country in which they are operating. This is hardly a clarion call for reform, and it certainly has limited potential for responding effectively to the widely held perception that new approaches are indispensable if the accountability of non-state actors is to be promoted, thus ensuring that the international human rights regime is able to come to grips with one of the most pressing challenges confronting it.

For most international lawyers the assumption would be that it is possible within the confines of the existing system to do what needs to be done. That might include, for example, regulating transnational corporations, taking much more systematic account of the views of civil society, regulating the activities of private actors in cases where human rights values are otherwise left in jeopardy, and achieving these objectives by working through the state-centred mechanisms of international law. Whether this is in fact possible is a question to which many of the contributors in this volume address themselves. By way of conclusion it is striking to note how frequently notions of sovereignty, and of the prerogatives that are perceived to attach to it, are invoked within international settings to prevent developments which seek to adapt the overall system in order to enable it to respond adequately, or even just plausibly, to the new challenges.

2

The Changing International Legal Framework for Dealing with Non-State Actors

AUGUST REINISCH[*]

1. INTRODUCTION

Individuals are held civilly liable before national courts for genocide and human-itarian law violations.[1] Transnationally operating corporations may equally be held liable for human rights abuses by courts in various countries.[2] Firms are boycotted by consumers because they or their subsidiaries or even contractors do not comply with basic labour standards in foreign production sites.[3] The acts of international organizations are annulled by international courts for infringing human rights guarantees of individuals.[4] Lending decisions of international financial institutions are reconsidered if they would have a demonstrable negative human rights impact.[5]

These examples are evidence of a radical change of the way we are dealing with human rights issues today. Human rights seem to be everywhere. But are we still talking about traditional 'human rights law'? Where are the good old days when everyone knew that human rights violations can only be committed by states against individuals? Do 'human rights' provide the correct conceptual framework for the problem areas outlined above?

These questions are intrinsically linked to the fact that international as well as national lawyers have traditionally been trained to conceive of human rights as

---

[*] Participants at the Academy of European Law session at which these lectures were originally given were very helpful. I am further grateful for the comments made to an earlier version of this paper by Hanspeter Neuhold and Karl Zemanek. I am also very much indebted to Solveig Kaspar who provided valuable research assistance. This Chapter was finalized in autumn 2002.

[1] See the US civil action of *Kadic v. Karadzic, infra* note 255.

[2] See the human rights cases brought, in particular, before US, UK and other Common Law courts. For a discussion see Ralph G Steinhardt, Chapter 6 in this volume.

[3] See the consumer boycotts referred to *infra* at note 162.

[4] See the fundamental rights case-law developed by the ECJ *infra* note 236.

[5] See the reports of the Word Bank Inspection Panel *infra* at note 77.

fundamental guarantees and standards of legal protection for individuals against the power, and particularly, against the abuse of power, of states. Over the last half-century, human rights lawyers have fought for and have largely attained general acceptance that these guarantees are not merely contingent rights conferred by the goodwill of sovereign states (with the implication that they can always be taken away again). Instead, a shared understanding has developed that they are inherent and inalienable rights which, leaving aside all the philosophical problems of this concept, at least means that they are no longer at the disposal of states, but form part of international law giving rights and entitlements directly to individuals.[6] However, these developments have not affected the basic conceptual premise that human rights are limitations of state power, that they apply in the public sphere, and that they protect the (weak) individual against the (strong) state.

The introductory examples seem to indicate, however, a radical conceptual change in the way we use and think about human rights. Immediately, a number of theoretical and practical trends come to mind as possible causes of this change: the questioning of the public/private divide,[7] the debate on 'third-party effects' or *Drittwirkung* of human rights,[8] the 'good governance' discussion,[9] and the transfer of powers from states to non-state actors, be it through privatization or by shifting powers to international organizations.[10] All these are interrelated developments on the level of legal doctrine, of social conditions, of political realities, and the like. They seem to have contributed to a new awareness of the need to protect human rights, beyond the classic paradigm of the powerful state against the weak individual, to include protection against increasingly powerful non-state actors.

2. WHAT IS A 'LEGAL FRAMEWORK'?

What do we mean when we talk about a 'legal framework'? Are we talking about rules, about norms, laws, treaties, ethical standards, morality? Does it make sense to conceive of a legal framework as different sources of law? Or should we look at procedures and forums wherein we make legal arguments? Are we talking about political or legal processes? Is the framework defined by national or international courts, political bodies in international organizations, special accountability mechanisms, NGOs, the public, and/or the press?

Probably, all of these elements constitute a 'legal framework' in a broad sense wherein we have to come to terms with non-state actors and their human rights

---

[6] See only Rosalyn Higgins, *Problems and Process: International Law and How We Use it* (1994) 96.

[7] For a feminist critique, see Catherine MacKinnon, 'On Torture: A Feminist Perspective on Human Rights', in Kathleen Mahoney and P. Mahoney (eds), *Human Rights in the Twenty-First Century* (1993) 21.

[8] See Ingo von Münch, Pablo Salvador Coderch, and Josep Ferrer i Riba (eds), *Zur Drittwirkung der Grundrechte* (1998). See also *infra* text at note 169.   [9] See *infra* text at note 70.

[10] See *infra* text at note 195.

'performance'. Without entering a deeper debate about how to understand, to define and construct, or even deconstruct the notion of a legal framework, I propose to look at a number of elements that are generally considered to form, at least part of, a legal framework:

(1) the standards or behavioural rules themselves, substantive rules in an old-fashioned diction;
(2) the procedures used in discussing, supervising, and maybe even enforcing compliance with standards; and finally
(3) the institutions, forums, networks, etc. within which procedures are activated to invoke the standards.

The traditional instruments under international law, setting standards for human rights protection, were treaties binding the respective contracting parties.[11] This standard-setting was accompanied by an increased concerted effort on the part of international organizations and human rights bodies to develop the concept of unwritten human rights law (via customary law or general principles). Under the so-called 1235 and 1503 procedures[12] the UN ECOSOC (and thereby the Human Rights Commission) has assumed powers with regard to 'a consistent pattern of gross and reliably attested' human rights violations even in the absence of any treaty violations.[13] The International Court of Justice (ICJ) has held that the Universal Declaration of Human Rights constitutes at least partly customary international law.[14] By and large the human rights discourse was based on the traditional sources of international law as referred to in Article 38(1) of the Statute of the ICJ.[15]

---

[11] Standard-setting via treaty law led, on the universal level, to the two 1966 UN Covenants and to a number of special UN human rights treaties: International Covenant on Civil and Political Rights (ICCPR), G.A. Res. 2200A (XXI), 16 December 1966, 21 U.N. GAOR Supp. (No.16) at 52, U.N. Doc. A/6316 (1966), 999 U.N.T.S. 171; the International Covenant on Economic, Social, and Cultural Rights (ICESCR), G.A. Res. 2200A (XXI), 21 U.N. GAOR Supp. (No. 16) at 49, U.N. Doc. A/6316 (1966), 993 U.N.T.S. 3; the International Convention on the Elimination of All Forms of Racial Discrimination, G.A. Res. 2106 (XX), Annex, 20 U.N. GAOR Supp. (No.14) at 47, U.N. Doc. A/6014 (1966), 660 U.N.T.S. 195; the Convention on the Elimination of All Forms of Discrimination Against Women, G.A. Res. 34/180, 34 U.N. GAOR Supp. (No. 46) at 193, U.N. Doc. A/34/46 (1979), 1249 U.N.T.S. 13; the Convention Against Torture and Other Cruel, Inhuman, or Degrading Treatment or Punishment, G.A. Res. 39/46, Annex, 39 U.N. GAOR Supp. (No. 51) at 197, U.N. Doc. A/39/51 (1984), 1465 U.N.T.S. 85; the Convention on the Rights of the Child, G.A. Res. 44/25, Annex, 44 U.N. GAOR Supp. (No. 49) at 167, U.N. Doc. A/44/49 (1989), 28 ILM (1989) 1448 corrected at 29 ILM (1990) 1340.   [12] See *infra* text at note 22.

[13] In addition to the fact that under both procedures UN organs investigate the human rights record of states in the absence of any submission by these states to the supervisory mechanism.

[14] In the *Tehran Hostages* case the Court held '[w]rongfully to deprive human beings of their freedom and to subject them to physical constraint in conditions of hardship is in itself manifestly incompatible with the principles of the Charter of the United Nations, as well as with the fundamental principles enunciated in the Universal Declaration of Human Rights'. *United States Diplomatic and Consular Staff in Tehran (United States of America v. Iran)*, ICJ Reports (1980) 3, 42.

[15] See, however, the scholarly debates about the nature of human rights obligations as customary law and/or general principles of law: See Theodor Meron, *Human Rights and Humanitarian Norms as*

Today's human rights discourse is far more diverse.[16] We are using national law, voluntary codes of conduct, ethical standards, etc.[17] to discuss and analyse state, but increasingly also non-state, behaviour. International organizations[18] and NGOs[19] are expected more and more not only to advocate human rights compliance by states, but also to abide by these same rules themselves. The same expectation arises *vis-à-vis* TNCs.[20]

The traditional procedures by which human rights issues were addressed were based on treaty obligations by which states agreed to have their human rights record debated,

---

Customary Law (1989); Martti Koskenniemi, 'The Pull of the Mainstream', 88 *Michigan Law Review* (1989/90) 1952; Bruno Simma and Philip Alston, 'The Sources of Human Rights Law: Custom, Jus Cogens, and General Principles', 12 *Australian Year Book of International Law* (1992) 88.

[16] In this context Henry Steiner speaks of 'an expanding framework of relevant norms': Henry Steiner, *Business and Human Rights* (1999) 11.   [17] See *infra* text starting at note 29.

[18] International organizations are understood as inter-governmental organizations created by states (or other international organizations) usually on the basis of a treaty, endowed with a minimum of permanent organs, for the purpose of fulfilling certain common tasks. See C.F. Amerasinghe, *Principles of the Institutional Law of International Organizations* (1996), 8. For present purposes, 'international organisations' includes the group of highly integrated supranational organizations such as the EC and Euratom.

[19] NGOs are usually formed by private persons (individuals, bodies corporate) operating on a transnational level, but regularly associated under a domestic system of law. NGOs are frequently defined negatively by the fact that they are not established by states through a governmental agreement under international law. Cf. ECOSOC Res. 31, UN ESCOR, 49th Sess., Supp. No. 1, at 54, U.N. Doc. E/1996/96 (1996), stating that '[a]ny such [. . .] international governmental organization that is not established by agreement shall be considered a non-governmental organization for the purpose of these arrangements'. In addition to the requirements of private foundation, international scope, and independence from state influence, there are further typical features of NGOs, such as the requirement of a minimal organizational structure, of established headquarters, and a non-profit purpose.

[20] There are no generally accepted definitions of TNCs (transnational corporations), MNCs (multinational corporations), or MNEs (multinational enterprises). Various attempts have been made. According to the UN Draft Code of Conduct on TNCs, a TNC is an enterprise 'comprising entities in two or more countries, regardless of the legal form and fields of activity of these entities, which operate under a system of decision-making, permitting coherent policies and a common strategy through one or more decision-making centres, in which the entities are so linked, by ownership or otherwise, that one or more of them may be able to exercise a significant influence over the activities of others and, in particular, to share knowledge, resources and responsibilities with the others': Code of Conduct on Transnational Corporations, UN ESCOR, U.N. Doc. E/1988/39/Add. 1 (1988). In the more recent Sub-Commission on the Promotion and Protection of Human Rights, 'Norms on the Responsibilities of Transnational Corporations and Other Business Enterprises with Regard to Human Rights', E/CN.4/Sub.2/2003/12/Rev.2, Sec. 20, the term TNC 'refers to an economic entity operating in more than one country or a cluster of economic entities operating in two or more countries—whatever their legal form, whether in their home country or country of activity, and whether taken individually or collectively'.

The ILO Tripartite Declaration of Principles concerning Multinational Enterprises and Social Policy defines multinational enterprises as 'enterprises, whether they are of public, mixed or private ownership, which own or control production, distribution, services or other facilities outside of the country in which they are based': International Labour Organisation, Tripartite Declaration of Principles concerning Multinational Enterprises and Social Policy (1977), 17 ILM (1978) 422, para. 6. The OECD used the term MNEs in a similar way. See also P.T. Muchlinski, *Multinational Enterprises and the Law* (1995) 13.

discussed, maybe scrutinized, and ultimately even held unlawful.[21] This is accompanied by a gradual development of procedures: from 'weak' forms, such as an obligation to file state reports with a treaty body or to accept that individuals complain by way of 'communications', to a full-fledged judicial system with a direct right for victims to bring claims against states. In addition, some international organizations were able to develop non-treaty based methods of exercising at least some form of human rights supervision (e.g. ECOSOC 1235[22] and 1503[23] procedures) by publicly or confidentially discussing human rights problems with states. The 'mobilization of shame' has also worked in other international organizations, such as the ILO.[24]

Today, the human rights compliance of non-state actors such as TNCs may be the subject of litigation before national courts, it may be a topic at shareholder meetings, or it may be extensively discussed in the media or addressed by NGOs in a campaign to stop certain labour practices.

A far as the institutional framework is concerned, human rights issues were traditionally debated by the political bodies of international organizations. The development of more and more independent institutions, from expert organs, such as the Human Rights Committee[25] or the Committee on Economic, Social, and Cultural Rights,[26] to veritable international tribunals, such as the European Court of Human Rights or the Inter-American Court of Human Rights, was a clear advance in strengthening human rights protection against states.

---

[21] See for the UN system Philip Alston and James Crawford (eds), *The Future of UN Human Rights Treaty Monitoring* (2000).

[22] Economic and Social Council Resolution 1235 (XLII), 42 U.N. ESCOR Supp. (No. 1) at 17, U.N. Doc. E/4393 (1967). According to this resolution ECOSOC '[a]uthorize[d] the Commission on Human Rights and the Sub-Commission on Prevention of Discrimination and Protection of Minorities [. . .] to examine information relevant to gross violations of human rights and fundamental freedoms', and to 'make a thorough study of situations which reveal a consistent pattern of violations of human rights'.

[23] Economic and Social Council Resolution 1503 (XLVIII), 48 U.N. ESCOR (No. 1A) at 8, U.N. Doc. E/4832/Add 1 (1970). In this resolution ECOSOC '[a]uthorize[d] the Sub-Commission on Prevention of Discrimination and Protection of Minorities to appoint a working group consisting of not more than twenty-five members, with due regard to geographical distribution, to meet once a year in private meetings [. . .] to consider all communications [. . .] together with replies of Governments, if any, which appear to reveal a consistent pattern of gross and reliably attested violations of human rights and fundamental freedoms within the terms of reference of the Sub-Commission'. On the two procedures see Philip Alston, 'The Commission on Human Rights', in Philip Alston (ed), *The UN and Human Rights: A Critical Appraisal* (2nd ed. 2004).

[24] James Avery Joynce, 'Mobilization of Shame', in *The New Politics Of Human Rights* (1978) 79. See also Peter R. Baehr, 'Mobilization of the Conscience of Mankind: Conditions of Effectiveness of Human Rights NGOs', in *Reflections on International Law from the Low Countries in Honour of Paul de Waart* (1998) 135.

[25] Set up in accordance with Arts. 28 *et seq.* ICCPR, *supra* note 11. See Dominic McGoldrick, *The Human Rights Committee* (1991).

[26] The Committee on Economic, Social, and Cultural Rights was not set up through the ICESCR, rather it was established by ECOSOC resolution in 1985, Res. 1985/17 (28 May 1985). See Matthew C.R. Craven, *The International Covenant on Economic, Social, and Cultural Rights: A Perspective on its Development* (1995); and Philip Alston, 'The Committee on Economic, Social and Cultural Rights', in Philip Alston (ed), *The UN and Human Rights: A Critical Appraisal* (2nd ed. 2004).

Today we are confronted with a far wider panoply of institutions concerned with human rights, from national and international courts sitting in judgment over human rights violations committed by corporations or individuals, to accountability mechanisms, such as Inspection Panels of the World Bank and other international financial institutions (IFIs),[27] scrutinizing the human rights performance of international organizations, political bodies in international organizations, NGOs and their advocacy networks, the media, and the public at large.

Change lies in broadening the legal framework, both in the sense of a wider scope of application of substantive norms of behaviour and in the sense of more and more diverse procedures and institutions available where substantive norms can be challenged. This also has repercussions on the way we practise and think about human rights law. Human rights is no longer the arcane sub-field of specialists of public international law, frequently even from other fields of the law such as (domestic) constitutional law. Rather, it has not only become a subject rooted firmly in international law but it has also developed into an increasingly densely interwoven part of international law which can no longer be theoretically or practically separated from the rest of international law.[28]

3. THE CHANGING FRAMEWORK

I propose a rather modest start by trying to search for empirically observable elements of change. What kind of changes can be readily ascertained with regard to human rights and non-state actors? What are the most visible elements of human rights protection against infringements by non-state actors? This inquiry involves only the surface of change. I revert to deeper structural causes later.

Let us first focus on two very visible developments:

A. The more frequent and increasingly diverse use of codes of conduct addressed directly to non-state actors and
B. The increased use of extraterritorial regulation by states of the behaviour of non-state actors.

A. Increased Use of Codes of Conduct

The increased use of codes of conduct applicable to non-state, and especially corporate, behaviour could be seen as a new form of 'privatization' of human rights. Of course, the term 'privatization' is used here not in the sense of *Drittwirkung* or 'third-party effect',[29] but rather as an allusion to the increased self-regulation instead

---

[27] See *infra* text at note 77.

[28] See also on the 'intrusion' of human rights law into international law text *infra* at note 184.

[29] As used by Andrew Clapham, *Human Rights in the Private Sphere* (1993); Andrew Clapham, 'The Privatisation of Human Rights', 1 *European Human Rights Law Review* (1995) 20. See also *infra* note 169.

of state regulation. In this sense, 'privatization' of human rights means adopting human rights norms in the form of voluntary codes of conduct without state fiat.

With codes of conduct we normally associate legally non-binding rules, usually adopted voluntarily by corporations in order to guide their operations. Their substance is not limited to human rights, where they may focus on labour and social rights. Rather, they may extend to environmental issues[30] and shareholder interests.[31] But codes of conduct are not only addressed to TNCs: there is a recent trend to extend this type of self-regulation to other non-state actors. The following discussion is structured according to different non-state addressees of codes of conduct.

1. Corporate Codes of Conduct

Codes of conduct intended to regulate corporate, in particular TNC, behaviour are not a new phenomenon. In the 1970s, as a response to increased concerns over TNC interference with host state affairs, a first wave of codes of conduct was elaborated in the framework of various international organizations.[32] The UN set up a Commission on TNCs, the UNCTC, which was mandated to draw up a comprehensive code of conduct for TNCs.[33] A draft code was made public in 1984.[34] However, due to intense controversy surrounding the project, which in many respects suffered from the ideological controversy concerning the New International Economic Order, the UN abandoned its efforts to create such a code of conduct in 1993. In 1994 the Commission on Transnational Corporations became the Commission on International Investment and Transnational Corporations.[35] The OECD was more successful and produced a code of conduct in 1976[36] which was revised

[30] Valerie Ann Zondorak, 'A New Face in Corporate Environmental Responsibility: The Valdez Principles', 18 *Boston College Environmental Affairs L. Rev.* (1991) 457.

[31] Disclosure and transparency requirements in codes of conduct are typically aimed at protecting shareholder interests.

[32] See on these early codes: Baade, 'Codes of Conduct for Multinational Enterprises: An Introductory Survey', in N. Horn (ed), *Legal Problems of Codes of Conduct for Multinational Enterprises* (1980) 407; Jonathan I. Charney, 'Transnational Corporations and Developing Public International Law', *Duke Law Journal* (1983) 748; Norbert Horn, 'International Rules for Multinational Enterprises: The ICC, OECD, and ILO Initiatives', 30 *American University Law Review* (1981) 923; Seymour J. Rubin, 'Transnational Corporations and International Codes of Conduct: A Study of the Relationship Between Legal Cooperation and Economic Development', 30 *American University Law Review* (1981) 903.

[33] ECOSOC Res. 1913, UN ESCOR, 57th Sess., 5 December 1974, Supp. No. 1, 3, U.N. Doc. 5570/Add. 1 (1975).

[34] See United Nations Draft International Code of Conduct on Transnational Corporations, 23 ILM 626 (1984).

[35] See ECOSOC Res 1994/1, Integration of the Commission on Transnational Corporations into the institutional machinery of the United Nations Conference on Trade and Development, 14 July 1994, available at http://www.un.org/documents/ecosoc/res/1994/eres1994–1.htm.

[36] Cf. Organization for Economic Cooperation and Development (OECD), Guidelines for Multinational Enterprises, 21 June 1976, reprinted in 15 ILM (1976) 969.

in 2000.[37] In 1977, the ILO adopted a 'Declaration of Principles' addressing labour rights and TNCs.[38] Traditionally, these codes of conduct were formulated in the framework of international organizations by state representatives or at least under the control of states and were addressed to non-state actors, primarily to corporations. The UNCTC, OECD, and ILO codes are examples of this approach.

This international organization-driven formulation and adoption of codes of conduct was succeeded by a generation of private-initiative codes such as the Sullivan[39] and the MacBride Principles,[40] the Slepak Principles,[41] the Miller Principles,[42] the Maquiladora Standards of Conduct,[43] and others.[44] Most of these codes, that were very specifically tailored for specific countries and situations, were promoted by highly visible political figures. Trade unions also became more and more involved in the production of such codes. The 1997 'Basic Code of Conduct covering Labour Practices' of the International Confederation of Free Trade Unions[45] is an example.

Today we are witnessing a trend towards self-regulation, largely motivated by the wish of TNCs to escape the defensive position in which they found themselves after consumer boycotts and litigation. Many recent corporate codes of conduct have been adopted by TNCs themselves,[46] frequently with the collaboration of NGOs.

---

[37] OECD, Guidelines for Multinational Enterprises, Revision 2000, http://www.oecd.org/daf/ investment/guidelines/index.htm; see Steinhardt, *supra* note 2, [34–35].

[38] International Labour Organization (ILO) 'Tripartite Declaration of Principles Concerning Multinational Enterprises and Social Policy' 16 November 1977, reprinted in 17 ILM (1978) 423. See also the ILO Declaration on Fundamental Principles and Rights at Work and its Follow-Up, adopted by the International Labour Conference at its 86th session, Geneva, 18 June 1998, analysed by Steinhardt, *supra* note 2, at 203–204.   [39] See Steinhardt, *supra* note 2.

[40] The MacBride Principles are nine principles named after the late Sean MacBride in November 1984, aimed at eliminating anti-Catholic discrimination via U.S. companies doing business in Northern Ireland: http://www1.umn.edu/humanits/links/macbride.html. On both the Sullivan and the MacBride Principles see Christopher McCrudden, 'Human Rights Codes for Transnational Corporations: What Can the Sullivan and MacBride Principles Tell Us?', 19 *Oxford Journal of Legal Studies* (1999) 167.

[41] The Slepak Principles are named after the Soviet emigré and human rights activist Vladimir Slepak, a member of the original Moscow Helsinki Monitoring Group. They were developed for American companies doing business in the former Soviet Union. See Jorge F. Perez-Lopez, 'Promoting Respect for Worker Rights Through Business Codes of Conduct', 17 *Fordham International Law Journal* (1993), 13.

[42] The Miller Principles were developed by U.S. Representative John Miller (R-WA), aimed at encouraging political freedom and liberalization with the People's Republic of China and Tibet.

[43] The Maquiladora Standards of Conduct are directed at US TNCs operating production facilities in Mexico along the U.S.-Mexico border. See http://enchantedwebsites.com/maquiladora/cjm.html.

[44] See Lance Compa and Tashia Hinchliffe-Darricarrere, 'Enforcing International Labor Rights Through Corporate Codes of Conduct', 33 *Columbia J. Transnat'l L.* (1995) 663; see also Steinhardt, *supra* note 2 at [5].

[45] Adopted by the ICFTU Executive Board (Brussels, December 1997). Available at http:// www.icftu.org/displaydocument.asp?Index=991209513&Language=EN and at http://www.itcilo.it/ english/actrav/telearn/global/ilo/guide/icftuco.htm.

[46] See the list of 'Self-Imposed Company Codes' in Proposed draft human rights code of conduct for companies, Working paper prepared by Mr David Weissbrodt, Addendum, List of the principal source

This corresponds with a declining role for international organizations. Sometimes the self-regulation is also carried out within the framework of more or less formal business organizations. The International Chamber of Commerce guidelines are an early example of this,[47] the Caux Round Table Principles for Business are a more recent one.[48] The UN has also shown renewed interested, with initiatives such as the Global Compact and the Working Group on the Activities of Transnational Corporations.[49]

On the regional level, too, international organizations have rediscovered codes of conduct. For instance, in the EU, under the label 'corporate social responsibility', the European Commission reacted to the European Parliament's call for a code of conduct for European Multinationals[50] by adopting a Green Paper on a European framework for 'corporate social responsibility',[51] defined as 'a concept whereby companies integrate social and environmental concerns in their business operations and in their interaction with their stakeholders on a voluntary basis'.[52] One of the purposes of such EU action is to develop a legally binding framework to address issues of verification and monitoring. It is exactly such problems of the supervision of compliance and enforcement of codes of conduct which have brought back the governments, at least as facilitators or negotiators. For instance, the US Fair Labor Association includes NGOs, lawyers, and government representatives.[53] In the UK,

---

materials for the draft code of conduct for companies, U.N. Doc. E/CN.4/Sub.2/2000/WG.2/WP.1/Add.2 (25 May 2000).

[47] *International Chamber of Commerce* (ICC) 'Guidelines for International Investment', ICC Pub. No. 272 (1972).

[48] The Caux Round Table Principles for Business were issued in 1994 by senior business leaders from Europe, Japan, and North America 'to express a world standard against which business behavior can be measured.' See http://www.cauxroundtable.org/ENGLISH.HTM.

[49] The *Global Compact* was launched by Secretary-General Kofi Annan in 1999, Address at the World Economic Forum in Davos, Switzerland (31 January 1999), U.N. Doc. SG/SM/6448 (1999). Information on *The Global Compact* is available at http://www.unhchr.ch/global.htm and http://www.unglobalcompact.org./.

On 13 August 2003 the UN Sub-Commission on the Promotion and Protection of Human Rights approved and transmitted for adoption to the UN Human Rights Commission the Norms on the Responsibilities of Transnational Corporations and Other Business Enterprises with Regard to Human Rights, E/CN.4/Sub.2/2003/12/Rev.2, available at http://www.unhchr.ch/pdf/55sub/12rev2_AV.pdf. See Weissbrodt and Kruger, *infra* Chapter 8.

[50] European Parliament (EP), Resolution on EU standards for European Enterprises operating in developing countries: towards a European Code of Conduct, adopted on 15 January 1999, Resolution A4-0508/98 of 1998, OJ C 104/180, 14 April 1999. http://europa.eu.int/eur-lex/pri/en/oj/dat/1999/c_104/c 10419990414en01800184.pdf.

[51] Commission of the European Communities, Green Paper: Promoting a European Framework for Corporate Social Responsibility, COM (2001) 366 final, 18 July 2001. http://europa.eu.int/eur-lex/en/com/gpr/2001/com2001_0366en01.pdf. See also in more detail Olivier De Schutter, 'The Accountability of Multinationals for Human Rights Violations in European Law', *infra* Chapter 7.

[52] Green Paper, *supra* note 51, para. 20.

[53] See http://www.fairlabor.org/. Cf. David Kinley, 'Human Rights as Legally Binding or Merely Relevant?', in Stephen Bottomley and David Kinley, *Commercial Law and Human Rights* (2002) 25, at 34.

the 'Ethical Trading Initiative'[54] is 'supporting collaboration between business and the voluntary sector in promoting ethical business, including the development of codes of conduct and ways of monitoring and verifying theses codes'.[55]

Modern codes of conduct clearly focus on TNCs. They have received most public attention and they form the majority of the proliferating field of codes of conduct. Less noticed is the fact that other non-state actors also seem to have been addressed by codes of conduct.

2. Codes of Conduct for International Organizations

Though not usually called 'codes of conduct', international organizations have also increasingly been addressed by (strictly not legally binding) codes that include human rights norms. At first sight, this may seem an odd development. International organizations have now clearly been accepted as subjects of international law.[56] Thus, one would rather expect a discussion on whether, in the absence of any treaty law obligation, unwritten human rights norms are legally binding on them. This question has indeed been at the centre of the discussion about the human rights obligations of international organizations for quite some time.[57] It was most prominently addressed in the context of the question whether the European Communities are legally bound to respect fundamental rights. It also played an important role with regard to the issue whether UN forces had to comply with the humanitarian rules enshrined in the Geneva Conventions. The underlying tenor of recent developments appears to be that international organizations, as a result of their international legal personality, are considered to be bound by general international law, including any human rights norms, that can be viewed as customary law or as general principles of law. Still, there seems to be enough uncertainty in this area to leave room for voluntary guidelines.

The UN's 'voluntary' adoption of its own humanitarian law rules, applicable in UN military operations, may be regarded as an example of human rights-relevant self-regulation by an international organization. In 1999 the UN Secretary-General unilaterally promulgated 'fundamental principles and rules of international humanitarian law applicable to United Nations forces conducting operations under United Nations command and control.'[58] This initiative followed years

---

[54] The Ethical Trading Initative was formed in 1997 as an alliance of companies, NGOs, and trade unions operating in the UK, whose aim is to improve labour conditions in the global supply chains which produce goods for the UK market. See http://www.ethicaltrade.org/ and http://www.eti.org.uk.

[55] White Paper, Eliminating World Poverty: A Challenge for the 21st Century, Cmnd 3789 at 64 (1997), http://www.dfid.gov.uk/PoliceAndPriorities/files/whitepaper1997.pdf, cited in McCrudden, *supra* note 40, 169.   [56] See only Malcolm N. Shaw, *International Law* (4th ed., 1997), 190.

[57] Cf. August Reinisch, 'Securing the Accountability of International Organizations', 7 *Global Governance* (2001) 131.

[58] Observance by United Nations forces of international humanitarian law, United Nations, Secretary-General's Bulletin, ST/SGB/1999/13, 6 August 1999, reprinted in 81 *Int'l Rev. Red Cross*, No. 836, December 1999, 812; 36 ILM 1656 (1999). See, on the bulletin in general, Daphna Shraga, 'UN

of legal uncertainty about the relevance of the Geneva Conventions for UN operations.[59]

Though being a very special case, one might also draw a parallel to the development of human rights protection within the European Union. In the early stages of human rights protection against the acts of the supranational European Communities one finds the voluntarily adopted 1977 joint declaration by the European Parliament, the Council, and the Commission to respect human rights in any legislative act.[60] By this declaration the three institutions pledged to respect these rights in the exercise of their powers under the EC Treaty.[61] Much of the need to guarantee fundamental rights against Community action was accommodated by the judicially developed human rights protection of the ECJ. However, to some extent the recent, voluntary, 'solemn' declaration of the EU Fundamental Rights Charter in 2000 may also be regarded as an example of a self-regulatory human rights code.[62]

Another example of a voluntary code for international organizations which includes human rights norms can be found in the standards for the 'Accountability of International Organisations' currently elaborated by the International Law Association (ILA), a private association of international lawyers.[63] It is the ILA Committee's understanding of accountability to focus not only on the issue of

Peacekeeping Operations: Applicability of International Humanitarian Law and Responsibility for Operations-Related Damage', 94 *AJIL* (2000) 406.

[59] The Red Cross has repeatedly called for formal adherence by the United Nations to the Geneva Conventions. The UN's official view, however, has always been that 'the United Nations is not substantively in a position to become a party to the 1949 Conventions, which contain many obligations that can only be discharged by the exercise of juridical and administrative powers which the Organization does not possess, such as the authority to exercise criminal jurisdiction over members of the Forces, or administrative competence relating to territorial sovereignty. Thus the United Nations is unable to fulfil obligations which for their execution require the exercise of powers not granted to the Organization, and therefore cannot accede to the Conventions': Legal Opinion of the Secretariat of the United Nations, 'Question of the Possible Accession of Intergovernmental Organizations to the Geneva Conventions for the Protection of War Victims', *UN Juridical YB* (1972) 153.

[60] Joint Declaration by the European Parliament, the Council, and the Commission on Fundamental Rights of 5 April 1977, OJ C 103, 27 April 1977. Available at http://europa.eu.int/eur-lex/en/treaties/selected/livre602.html.

[61] The declaration contains the following two operative paragraphs:

  1 The European Parliament, the Council and the Commission stress the prime importance they attach to the protection of fundamental rights, as derived in particular from the constitutions of the Member States and the European Convention for the Protection of Human Rights and Fundamental Freedoms.

  2 In the exercise of their powers and in pursuance of the aims of the European Communities they respect and will continue to respect these rights.'

[62] The Charter of Fundamental Rights of the European Union was solemnly proclaimed at the meeting of the European Council held in Nice from 7 to 9 December 2000. Available at http://ue.eu.int/df/default.asp?lang=en.

[63] See the ILA Committee on Accountability of International Organisations which first met at the 68th ILA Conference 1998 in Taipei, ROC, in International Law Association (ed), *Report of the 68th Conference* (1998), 584; ILA Committee on Accountability of International Organisations, Second Report, in

securing accountability by way of procedures and remedies. Rather, the Committee has initiated its work by drafting a set of recommended rules and practices applicable to international organizations in general.

3. Codes of Conduct for NGOs

Some NGOs have come under public pressure for their activities. Criticism has been voiced with regard to conduct—sometimes violent street protests—attributable to or at least sponsored and advocated by some NGOs during world economic summits, WTO, World Bank, and IMF meetings, and on other occasions.[64] As a response, some NGOs have not only publicly distanced themselves from such acts of violence, but have also adopted codes of conduct as evidence of their adherence to non-violent protests. For instance, the New Economics Foundation (NEF) adopted a code of conduct after the violent protests surrounding the G7 Genoa summit.[65] According to the central provision of this 'code of conduct' the NGO pledges to set its 'actions within a framework of non-violence at all times'.

A different background for a more critical attitude towards NGOs stems from sometimes questionable advocacy campaigns. NGOs may occasionally, with differing degrees of culpability, make inaccurate or even outright false statements about a potential environmental harm or social damage which, coupled with a threat of inciting consumer boycotts or the like, causes their targets to change behaviour in ways that are sometimes very costly. The controversy surrounding the *Brent Spar* is a case in point.[66] Various environmental NGOs, among them Greenpeace, had claimed that scuttling an oil rig owned by Shell in the North Sea posed a serious ecological threat to the region. Despite the company's assurances to the contrary they demanded an expensive alternative of disposing of the oil platform. Subsequently, it turned out that most of the NGO allegations were incorrect. Shell did not recover the additional costs incurred. Incidents like *Brent Spar* raise a number of troubling questions concerning the accountability of NGOs. In particular, advocacy

International Law Association (ed), *Report of the 69th Conference* (2000), 875. See also Karel Wellens, 'ILA Committee on Accountability of International Organisations', 1 *Int'l L. Forum* (1999) 107.

[64] 'Luddites, extremists and the "leftover left"; unaccountable interest groups that undermine the authority of elected officials; armchair radicals from the rich world who have no right to speak for the Third-World poor. Reactions to the recent Prague street protests confirmed that NGO bashing has become a favourite sport for government officials, business and the Press': Mike Edwards, Time to put the NGO House in Order, *Financial Times*, 6 June 2000. Available at http://fpc.org.uk/hotnews/writes. See also Lisa Jordan and Peter van Tuijl, Political Responsibility in NGO Advocacy Exploring Emerging Shapes of Global Democracy, Europe's Forum on International Cooperation (April 1998) available at http://www.globalpolicy.org/ngos/role/globdem/credib/2000/1117.htm.

[65] Available at http://www.neweconomics.org/default.asp?strRequest=newsarchive&strNewsRequest=newsitem&intNewsID=116.

[66] Elizabeth A. Kirk, 'The 1996 Protocol to the London Dumping Convention and the Brent Spar', 46 *ICLQ* (1997) 957; Peter J. Spiro, 'New Global Potentates: Nongovernmental Organizations and the "Unregulated" Marketplace', 18 *Cardozo Law Review* (1996) 957, at 964.

NGOs have an immense interest in keeping and protecting their credibility, which is one of their most precious assets, comparable to the goodwill and reputation of business firms.

Some NGOs have taken up the challenge and voluntarily adopted their own codes of conduct. To date, NGOs express 'codes of conduct' focus on conduct relevant in the course of their advocacy. In the field of service provision too, equivalents of codes of conduct have been used.[67] One only has to think of the legion of NGOs active in the field of emergency and disaster relief.[68] In the course of UN and other international organizations subcontracting[69] they have partly taken over official tasks such as administrative functions. It is not difficult to imagine that in the course of such activities their actions may constitute what would be called a human rights violation if committed by a state.

4. Common Background and Motivation for Codes of Conduct

Some tentative conclusions as to the origin and shared background of these ethically inspired codes of conduct may be drawn. It appears that all these codes are to some extent a result of the 'good governance' debate which appeared under different guises on different levels but which still seems to have enough in common to be identified as a single phenomenon. Similar developments have taken place at different levels, which enable us to identify certain core elements of any good governance debate, such as the emancipation of the governed, accountability, transparency, and participation.

The demand for good governance was initially made of states, calling for open and transparent administration, accountability, and the rule of law.[70] Under the auspices of the international financial institutions, 'good governance' was demanded of borrowing governments. The underlying idea was a growing awareness that a stable and functioning framework would be a crucial element for enhancing

---

[67] See the Codes of Conduct of the International Red Cross (Principles of Conduct for The International Red Cross and Red Crescent Movement and NGOs in Disaster Response Programmes) or the Australian Council for Overseas Aid (Code of Conduct for Non Government Development Organisations). Available at http://www.ifrc.org/publicat/conduct/code.asp. and http://www.acfoa.asn.au/code/code.PDF.

[68] See Ralph Wilde, '*Quis Custodiet Ipsos Custodes?* Why and How UNHCR Governance of "Development" Refugee Camps Should be Subject to International Human Rights Law', 1 *Yale H.R. & Dev. L.J.* (1998) 107, at 109.

[69] Cf. Thomas G. Weiss (ed), *Beyond UN Subcontracting: Task-sharing with Regional Security Arrangements and Service-providing NGOs* (1998).

[70] The ILA Committee on Accountability of International Organisations, Second Report, lists the following characteristics as elements of good governance: 'transparency in both the decision-making process and the implementation of the ensuing institutional and operational decisions; a large degree of democracy in the decision-making process; access to information open to all potentially concerned and/or affected by the decisions at stake; the well-functioning of the international civil service; sound financial management; and appropriate reporting and evaluation mechanisms': *supra* note 63, at 878.

long-term development, as well as repayment capabilities.[71] Thus, the IMF and the World Bank started to advocate certain non-economic reforms, initially with a narrower focus, such as the development of an independent judiciary and the fight against corruption,[72] then more broadly demanding modernization of the state, consolidation of democratic institutions, protection of human rights and the environment, and social policy reform.[73] By the mid-1990s 'good governance' had become an important area of attention for the IMF.[74] At the regional level, the debate about EU accession and its political preconditions, as laid down in the 'Copenhagen criteria',[75] can also be viewed as a 'good governance' issue.

Once the 'good governance' box was opened, its demands could not be limited to states. Increasingly, international organizations were also confronted with requests for 'good governance'.[76] As institutional responses, again under the guidance of the international financial institutions, Inspection Panels were set up, first by the World Bank and subsequently by other development banks.[77] Other organizations, such as the EU, created ombudsman offices[78] in order to rectify instances of maladministration, the opposite of 'good governance'. Also at the universal level, organizations can no longer avoid being questioned about their governance. In the wake of the report of the UN Commission on Global Governance,[79] the UN has undertaken

[71] Michel Camdessus, 'Toward a Second Generation of Structural Reform in Latin America', Presentation at the *Annual Conference of the National Banks Association*, Buenos Aires (1997), http://www.imf.org/external/np/speeches/1997/mds9706.htm. See also Diana Tussie and Maria Pia Riggirozzi, 'Pressing Ahead with New Procedures for Old Machinery: Global Governance and Civil Society', in Volker Rittberger (ed), *Global Governance and the United Nations System* (2001) 158, at 168.

[72] See World Bank, *Helping Countries Combat Corruption: The Role of the World Bank* (1997), http://www1.worldbank.org/publicsector/anticorrupt/corruptn/coridx.htm. See also Carlos Acuña and M. Fernanda Tuozzo, 'Civil Society Participation in World Bank and Inter-American Development Bank Programs: The Case of Argentine', 6 *Global Governance* (2000) 443.

[73] See K. Ginther, E. Denters, and Paul J.I.M. de Waart (eds), *Sustainable Development and Good Governance* (1995).

[74] International Monetary Fund, Good Governance: The IMF's Role (1997). Available at http://www.imf.org/external/pubs/ft/exrp/govern/govern.pdf.

[75] The 1993 Copenhagen criteria require, *inter alia*, stability of institutions guaranteeing democracy, the rule of law, human rights, and respect for and protection of minorities; the existence of a functioning market economy as well as the capacity to cope with competitive pressure and market forces within the Union; the ability to take on the obligations of membership including adherence to the aims of political, economic, and monetary union. See http://europa.eu.int/comm/enlargement/intro/criteria.htm.

[76] World Bank, *Wapenhans Report* (1992).

[77] The World Bank Inspection Panel was set up in 1993 to provide an independent forum to private citizens who believe that they or their interests have been or could be directly harmed by a project financed by the World Bank. See Steinhardt, *supra* note 2 at [32–33].

[78] See Katja Heede, *European Ombudsman: Redress and Control at Union Level* (2000). See also Linda C. Reif (ed), *The International Ombudsman Anthology: Selected Writings from the International Ombudsman Institute* (1999).

[79] The Commission on Global Governance was established in 1992 and produced its main report entitled 'Our Global Neighborhood' in 1995. For information on the Commission see http://www.cgg.ch/.

a number of *ad hoc* reports to scrutinize its own governance record, for instance, in the field of peacekeeping.[80]

Most directly linked to the issue of codes of conduct for TNCs is the 'corporate governance' debate,[81] nowadays, partly filled with new content, frequently termed as 'social responsibility' discussion.[82] The debate on the role of corporations and their ethical standards has clearly gone beyond the famous Milton Friedman assertion that the 'only social responsibility of business [is] to increase profits'.[83] Even if the 'generation of long-term economic profit' is still considered to be a 'corporation's primary objective',[84] corporate 'good governance' clearly requires the balancing of all stakeholders' interests, 'stakeholders' being understood as all those who may affect and be affected by a corporation, including investors, employees, creditors, customers, and suppliers.[85] But the question remains, if one enlarges the group of stakeholders in corporations beyond the narrow confines of shareholders, how the

[80] See The Fall of Srebrenica, U.N. Doc. A/54/549 (15 November 1999), Report of the Secretary-General Pursuant to General Assembly Resolution 53/35; available at http://www.un.org/peace/srebrenica.pdf. Report of the Rwanda Genocide (15 December 1999); available at http://www.un.org/Depts/dpko/dpko/reports.htm. See also the Brahimi report, Report of the Panel on United Nations Peace Operations, U.N. Doc. A/55/305–S/2000/809 (21 August 2000); available at http://www.un.org/peace/reports/peace_operations/.

[81] See generally the journal *Corporate Governance: An International Review* and Daniel Fischel, 'The Corporate Governance Movement', 35 *Vanderbilt Law Review* (1982) 1259.

[82] See only the EU Commission Green Paper Promoting a European Framework for Corporate Social Responsibility, *supra* note 51. See also United Nations Conference on Trade and Development, The Social Responsibility of Transnational Corporations, U.N. Doc. UNCTAD/ITE/IIT/Misc.21 (1999) at 6. See also Editorial, Corporate Governance, 'Institutional Investors and Socially Responsible Investment', 10 *Corporate Governance: An International Review* (2002) 1; John Parkinson, 'The Socially Responsible Company', in Michael K. Addo, (ed), *Human Rights Standards and the Responsibility of Transnational Corporations* (1999) 49.

[83] The entire quotation is, of course, more encompassing: 'One and only one social responsibility of business [is] to increase profits so long as it stays within the rules of the game, which is to say, engages in open and free competition without deception or fraud': Milton Friedman, *Capitalism and Freedom* (1962) 133; see also Milton Friedman, 'The Social Responsibility of a Business is to Increase Profits', *N.Y. Times*, 13 September 1970 (Magazine) at 32; cited in UN Sub-Commission on the Promotion and Protection of Human Rights, Sessional working group on the working methods and activities of transnational corporations, Transnational Corporations and Other Business Enterprises, E/CN.4/Sub.2/2002/WG.2/WP.1/Add. 1, 24 May 2002, 15.

[84] I. Millstein *et al.* (OECD Report), *Corporate Governance: Improving Competitiveness and Access to Capital in Global Markets* (1998) 27.

[85] Michael K. Addo, 'Human Rights and Transnational Corporations: An Introduction', in Michael K. Addo (ed), *Human Rights Standards and the Responsibility of Transnational Corporations* (1999) 3, at 19; Robert McCorquodale, 'Human Rights and Global Business', in Bottomley and Kinley, *supra* note 53, 89, at 108. See also the wide definition in Sub-Commission on the Promotion and Protection of Human Rights, Norms on the Responsibilities of Transnational Corporations and Other Business Enterprises with Regard to Human Rights, E/CN.4/Sub.2/2003/12/Rev.2, Sec. 22, including 'stockholders, other owners, workers, and their representatives, as well as any other individual or group that is affected by the activities of transnational corporations or other business enterprises', mentioning, *inter alia*, 'consumer groups, customers, governments, neighbouring communities, indigenous peoples and communities, non-governmental organizations, public and private lending institutions, suppliers, trade associations, and others'.

diverse and sometimes contradictory interests of different stakeholders should be reconciled with each other. And surely, as long as ethically responsible behaviour can be translated into long-term profitability, it will be difficult to see whether TNCs are really willing to 'regard ethical and social values as possessing independent value.'[86] The good news for human rights is, of course, that—regardless of whether TNCs comply with them as a result of more or less enlightened self-interest—a higher degree of compliance will follow.

5. Problems with Codes of Conduct: The Supervision and Enforcement Deficit

It came as no surprise that the self-regulation of non-state actors, in particular of TNCs, entails serious problems. Some codes have been criticized for being more protective of the companies that adopted them than of the people they were intended to protect.[87] The supervisory and/or enforcement structures of many TNC-adopted codes are either non-existent or very weak. Thus, mere voluntary codes are frequently perceived to be insufficient to increase TNC human rights accountability effectively.[88] It is therefore not surprising that steps 'beyond voluntarism' are demanded.[89] The weak structure of codes of conduct is not limited to guidelines adopted by companies. Codes of conduct adopted under the auspices of international organizations also rarely provide for strong supervisory mechanisms. Frequently, they envisage no procedures or institutions at all. Some have adopted weak informal procedures such as the OECD guidelines with their National Contact Points[90] or the ILO with its Subcommittee on Multinational Enterprises with regard to the ILO Declaration on Fundamental

---

[86] Parkinson, *supra* note 82, at 62.

[87] According to Lena Ayoub, 'Nike Just Does It—and Why the United States Shouldn't: The United States' International Obligation to Hold MNCs Accountable for Their Labor Rights Violations Abroad', 11 *DePaul Bus. L.J.* (1999) 395, at 405, '[w]hile publicized codes of conduct impress consumers and the media, they have been largely ineffective at realizing the goals they purport to represent [. . .] due in large part to the lack of any legal enforcement mechanism upon these codes'. See also McCrudden, *supra* note 40, 168, on the controversy surrounding the Nike and Shell Codes.

[88] See UN Sub-Commission on the Promotion and Protection of Human Rights, Sessional working group on the working methods and activities of transnational corporations, Transnational Corporations and Other Business Enterprises, E/CN.4/Sub.2/2002/WG.2/WP.1/Add. 1, 24 May 2002, 17: 'The use of an entirely voluntary system of adoption and implementation of human rights codes of conduct, however, is not enough. Voluntary principles have no enforcement mechanisms, they may be adopted by transnational corporations and other businesses enterprises for public relations purposes and have no real impact on the business behavior, and they may reinforce corporate self-governance and hinder efforts to create outside checks and balances.'

[89] See International Council on Human Rights (ed), *Beyond Voluntarism: Human Rights and the Developing International Legal Obligations of Companies* (2002), available at http://www.cleanclothes.org/ftp/beyond_voluntarism.pdf.

[90] The OECD has demanded the establishment of National Contact Points for handling inquiries and contributing to the solution of problems that may arise in connection with the OECD Guidelines. It has also set up a Committee on International Investment and Multinational Enterprises (CIME) that can periodically or at the request of a member country hold an exchange of views on matters related to the Guidelines. See http://www.oecd.org/daf/investment/guidelines/faq.htm. See also Joachim Karl, 'The

Principles and Rights at Work.[91] In this context, it should be noted that, on the EU level, the European Parliament has at least expressed its wish that the planned code of conduct for European Multinationals[92] should constitute a legally binding standard whose implementation should be ensured by a monitoring mechanism.

These developments, however, are the exceptions rather than the rule. The rule still is the weakness of supervisory and enforcement elements in codes of conduct. It is a fascinating phenomenon that they are nevertheless not wholly ineffective. It would not be surprising to find that codes of conduct are regularly ineffective because no enforcement mechanism exists. What is far more astonishing is the fact that, broadly speaking, codes of conduct are often relatively effective in spite of the absence of any legally enforceable obligations under the codes themselves. A 'realist' answer may be readily available, arguing that all depends upon external pressure: TNCs are willing to abide by human rights standards only if threatened by 'sanctions', such as consumer boycotts, costly litigation (maybe involving class actions and punitive damages), or other economic disadvantages as a result of negative publicity in the media. Similarly, NGOs would only abide by ethical codes if they would otherwise lose contributions; and international organizations would only do so if they were likely to lose the support (including financial and political support) of their member states. While such a 'realist perspective' is surely helpful in explaining much of corporate and other non-state behaviour, it remains an interesting aspect of these developments that the extra-legal 'enforcers' (consumers, contributors, member states, etc.) have been willing to use their leverage. The fact that such pressure has been successfully mobilized shows that ethics are not irrelevant.

B. A Revival of Extraterritoriality

One way to secure human rights against non-state activities is for states, as primary addressees of international human rights law, to legislate and thus to 'translate' international human rights guarantees into the domestic legal order.[93] Primary

OECD Guidelines for Multinational Enterprises', in Michael K. Addo (ed), *Human Rights Standards and the Responsibility of Transnational Corporations* (1999) 89.

[91] ILO Declaration on Fundamental Principles and Rights at Work and its Follow-Up, adopted by the International Labour Conference at its 86th session, Geneva, 18 June 1998. The ILO Declaration is monitored through a quadrennial survey and through interpretations rendered by the Subcommittee on Multinational Enterprises. As of 15 November 1999, the Subcommittee had received over 23 requests for interpretations with very few passing the test of receivability so that an interpretation has been issued. Follow up and Promotion March 2000 by Subcommittee on Multinational Enterprises, ILO Doc. GB.277/MNE/1 (2000). http://www.ilo.org/public/english/standards/relm/gb/docs/gb277/pdf/mne-1.pdf.   [92] European Parliament Resolution, *supra* note 50.

[93] This is most clearly expressed in Art 2(2) ICCPR, *supra* note 11, providing: 'Where not already provided for by existing legislative or other measures, each State Party to the present Covenant undertakes to take the necessary steps, in accordance with its constitutional processes and with the provisions of the present Covenant, to adopt such legislative or other measures as may be necessary to give effect to the rights recognized in the present Covenant.'

legislative tools for this purpose are criminal law provisions protecting life, liberty, property, etc. of individuals against intrusion by other private parties. States may thereby fulfil their obligation under various international instruments, not only 'to respect', but also 'to ensure' or 'to secure' human rights.[94] Where states create domestic legal frameworks which are similar, or at least of a comparable quality, the ensuing level playing field for non-state actors should prevent them from human rights 'forum', or rather 'jurisdiction', shopping.

1. Different National Legal Standards

A general and broad assimilation of this human rights-relevant national legislation is, however, far from being realized. Instead, domestic legal guarantees and the effective levels of protection are highly diverse. They range from countries which have legislated in a way which broadly requires private parties also to comply with certain human rights norms, such as non-discrimination obligations,[95] to states which still have a culture of impunity, leaving unpunished violations of rights of individuals both by the state and by non-state actors. At the far end of this scale one would probably have to list so-called failed[96] or rogue states[97] which are no longer able or willing to ensure the minimum of legal security demanded from a state. However, even at the other end, at the high level of legal protection, the differences in national legislation and practice relevant for the enjoyment of human rights are significant. Thus, non-state actors may deliberately assess regulatory differences and choose specific countries for their operations in order to reduce their legal burdens. This type of calculation may be made primarily by business entities such as TNCs, but it could apply equally to other non-state actors: international organizations will be induced to establish their headquarters and to operate in countries where they will be offered the widest range of privileges and immunities isolating them from the otherwise applicable and enforceable national law. It is said that some countries engage in a veritable 'immunity dumping' in order to attract international organizations. After all, such an approach is nothing but rational behaviour which—if translated into economics—means that TNCs will seek to reduce regulatory costs. This type of cost-reduction by regulation-avoidance has frequently been described when 'forum shopping' by TNCs with regard to social or environmental regulations

---

[94] Cf. Art 2(1) ICCPR, *supra* note 11, Art 1 ECHR, Art 1 AmCHR, *infra* note 209, and the relevant case-law starting *infra* text at note 211.

[95] See the equal treatment legislation in some states, such as the UK Disability Discrimination Act 1995 (c. 50); French Articles 225-1 to 225-4 *Code Pénal*, or the Irish Employment Equality Act 1998.

[96] See Daniel Thürer, 'The "Failed State" and International Law', *International Review of the Red Cross* No. 836 (1999) 731; Matthias Herdegen, 'Der Wegfall effektiver Staatsgewalt im Völkerrecht: "The Failed State"', 34 *Berichte der Deutschen Gesellschaft für Völkerrecht* (1996) 68.

[97] See Thomas H. Henriksen, 'The Rise and Decline of Rogue States', 54 *Journal of International Affairs* (2001) 349; Petra Minnerop, 'Rogue States: State Sponsors of Terrorism?', 3 *German Law Journal* (1 September 2002). http://www.germanlawjournal.com/past_issues.php?id=188#fuss1.

is analysed. However, it equally occurs with respect to national legislation intended to protect human rights. The proximity of national labour and social security law to social human rights is an obvious example.

It is worth reflecting on the possible responses to reduce or at least mitigate such 'human rights forum shopping' by TNCs. The straightforward and ideal answer would clearly lie in increasing coherence between the diverse national legal frameworks. Legislative harmonization or regulatory assimilation, a process called 'approximation of the law' in the EC context,[98] eliminates the incentive for forum shopping. This is as true of human rights as it is of biodiversity, pollution control, or any other legislation. However, it is also a truism that we are currently very far from achieving such an approximation of human rights-relevant national legislation.[99]

2. US and Other Common Law Human Rights Litigation

Thus it is not surprising that, at least sometimes, an alternative option is pursued in order to make TNCs as well as other non-state actors comply with domestically translated human rights obligations. This alternative avenue lies in extending the application of national law to domestic and partly even foreign non-state actors operating abroad.[100] In other words, the extraterritorial application of human rights-relevant legal provisions is used to prevent regulatory avoidance strategies of non-state actors. Recent litigation in the US, involving corporations such as Unocal, Shell, Chevron, Texaco, ExxonMobil, and Coca Cola, bears witness to this trend. All these cases are legally based on the Alien Tort Claims Act (ATCA) of 1789.[101]

There is also some movement in other common law jurisdictions.[102] In the UK tort cases have been filed against British corporations, such as Rio Tinto,[103] Thor

---

[98] Art 94 (ex Art 100) TEC, the central authorization for harmonization measures entitled 'approximation of the laws', gives the European institutions wide-ranging powers of harmonization in areas directly affecting the establishment of the common market. See K. Armstrong and S. Bulmer, *The Governance of the Single European Market* (1998); G. Majone, *Regulating Europe* (1996).

[99] On second thoughts, this is less self-evident than it may seem. More and more states are adhering to the relevant human rights treaties and there is probably an increasing role for customary international law. These developments should contribute to a harmonized body of international human rights law.

[100] See Mark Gibney and R. David Emerick, 'The Extraterritorial Application of United States Law and the Protection of Human Rights: Holding Multinational Corporations to Domestic and International Standards', 10 *Temple International and Comparative Law Journal* (1996) 123; Gregory G.A. Tzeutschler, 'Corporate Violator: The Alien Tort Liability of Transnational Corporations for Human Rights Abuses Abroad', 30 *Columbia Human Rights L. Rev.* (1999) 359.

[101] See generally Steinhardt, *supra* note 2 [19–28].

[102] See Richard Meeran, 'The Unveiling of Transnational Corporations: A Direct Approach', in Michael K. Addo (ed), *Human Rights Standards and the Responsibility of Transnational Corporations* (1999) 161.

[103] Employee of a UK firm in Namibia brought compensation claim for contracting cancer while working at defendant's uranium mine with insufficient heath safeguards: *Connelly v. RTZ Corporation plc* [1996] 2 WLR 251; [1997] 3 WLR 373.

Chemicals,[104] and Cape Asbestos[105] for their activities abroad. Australian litigation against the Australian firm BHP Mining Company[106] led to an out-of-court settlement. In Canada a case was brought against Cambior[107] before the courts of Quebec which follows a civil law tradition. The common feature of these tort actions lies in the fact that they are based on a tort theory which recognizes that human rights violations, wherever committed, may trigger legal responsibility. The major (procedural) obstacles to recover damages have been rather technical doctrines, such as *forum non conveniens* (questioning whether the extraterritorial litigation is appropriate)[108] and the separate legal status of corporations (questioning the appropriateness of piercing the corporate veil in order to hold parents, or sometimes, subsidiaries, liable for the actions of related companies).[109]

3. Extraterritoriality and International Law

It is interesting to compare this recent 'revival' of extraterritoriality with earlier examples of extraterritoriality, considering that extraterritorial jurisdiction of any kind—whether to prescribe, to adjudicate, or to enforce[110]—always requires a specific justification in order to be considered lawful under international law.

The first wave of extraterritoriality focused on technical, corporate, and business law aspects such as competition law, corrupt practices, accounting, tax law, export controls, etc. In particular, US anti-trust law was at the forefront of using domestic law to take action against anti-competitive behaviour taking place abroad but having

[104] Personal injury claims brought by South African workers against UK firm for negligent failure to take protective measures against mercury poisoning at factory in South Africa: *Ngcobo and Others v. Thor Chemicals Holdings Ltd*, TLR 10 November 1995; *Sithole and Others v. Thor Chemicals Holdings Ltd and Another*, TLR 15 February 1999.

[105] Tort action by South African victims of asbestos mining by defendant company: *Lubbe v. Cape plc* [2000] 1 WLR 1545; *Adams v. Cape Industries plc* [1990] Ch. 433; [1991] 1 All E.R. 929.

[106] For environmentally harmful activities in Papua New Guinea. The settlement agreement again reached the courts in *Gagarimabu v. Broken Hill Proprietary Co Ltd and Another* [2001] VSC 517 (21 December 2001). See http://www.austlii.edu.au/au/cases/vic/VSC/2001/517.html.

[107] For environmental damage through mining activities in Guyana. See http://www.business-humanrights.org/Guyana.htm.

[108] Cf. for the English courts *Spiliada Maritime Corporation v. Cansulex Ltd* [1987] AC 460. The *forum non conveniens* argument was rejected by the House of Lords both in *Connelly v. RTZ Corporation plc* and in *Lubbe, supra* notes 103 and 105. For the US see the Bhopal case: *In re Union Carbide Corp Gas Plant Disaster*, 809 F. 2d 195 (1986). See also Andrew S. Bell, 'Human Rights and Transnational Litigation: Interesting Points of Intersection', in Stephen Bottomley and David Kinley (eds), *Commercial Law and Human Rights* (2002) 115; Malcolm J. Rogge, 'Towards Transnational Corporate Accountability in the Global Economy: Challenging the Doctrine of forum non conveniens in In re: Union Carbide, Alfaro, Sequihua, and Aguinda', 36 *Texas International Law Journal* (2001), 299.

[109] See Stephen Bottomley, 'Corporations and Human Rights', in Stephen Bottomley and David Kinley (eds), *Commercial Law and Human Rights* (2002) 47; Meeran, *supra* note 102.

[110] Cf. American Law Institute, *Restatement (Third) Foreign Relations Law of the United States* (1986) § 401. See also Shaw, *supra* note 56, 456.

a substantial, direct, and foreseeable effect within the US.[111] The *Alcoa* case[112] from the 1940s is the early leading decision establishing the use of the effects doctrine in this field of commercial law. Initially, extraterritoriality was fiercely opposed by the Europeans, in particular by Britain, as an unlawful extension of jurisdiction.[113] This even led to anti-suit injunctions between English and American courts as well as to blocking and claw-back legislation.[114] The *Fruehauf* affair[115] in the 1960s and the Siberian pipeline dispute[116] in the early 1980s are also examples demonstrating the underlying clash of interests about whether the home state of the parent company may compel the subsidiary to act in a particular way abroad. While the Europeans stressed territoriality to fend off any intrusion of US influence on 'their' companies, the Americans invoked personality, control, and effects theory to exercise extraterritorial jurisdiction. With the effects doctrine remaining controversial in a number of areas, it is remarkable that the European Commission, the 'anti-trust enforcement agency' within the EU, and backed by the ECJ,[117] has meanwhile adopted the effects principle *de facto*. It did so by exercising extraterritorial jurisdiction in order to extend the application of EC competition law to include conduct taking place outside the territory of the EU member states.[118]

These traditional examples of extraterritoriality basically involved a clash of national policy goals (securing fair competition law, fighting corrupt practices, etc.) with international law principles of jurisdiction emphasizing territoriality over any form of extraterritoriality. This has to do with the traditional function of international law as a law of co-ordination, separating spheres of competence of states and allocating spheres of jurisdiction within which states are free to act in their national

[111] See the formula used in US anti-trust legislation, *infra* note 122.

[112] *United States v. Aluminum Co of America*, 148 F.2d 416 (2d Cir. 1945).

[113] Andrea Bianchi, 'Extraterritoriality and Export Controls: Some Remarks on the Alleged Antinomy Between European and U.S. Approaches', 35 *GYIL* (1992) 366.

[114] For instance the British Protection of Trading Interests Act 1980, ch. 11, reprinted in 21 ILM (1982) 834; the Canadian Foreign Extraterritorial Measures Act, 33 Eliz. II, reprinted in 24 ILM (1985) 794; or the Australian Foreign Proceedings (Excess of Jurisdiction) Act 1984, No. 3 of 1984, reprinted in 23 ILM (1984) 1038.

[115] A jurisdictional dispute arose between France and the US over whether a French company had to comply with US export control legislation against China: *Fruehauf v. Massardy* (1964–65), [1968] D.S.Jur. 147, [1965] J.C.P. II 14274 bis, [1965] Gaz. Pal. See Andreas Lowenfeld, *Trade Controls for Political Ends* (2nd ed., 1984) 90.

[116] See A. Vaughan Lowe, 'The Problems of Extraterritorial Jurisdiction: Economic Sovereignty and the Search for a Solution', 34 *ICLQ* (1985) 724.

[117] The ECJ was initially reluctant to affirm extraterritorial jurisdiction. In the *Wood Pulp* case, the Court basically relied on a territorial principle finding that anti-competitive agreements entered into abroad were in fact 'implemented . . . within the common market'. See *Ahlström Osakeyhtiö v. Commission*, Joined Cases 89, 104, 114, 116–117, and 125–129/85, [1988] ECR 5193.

[118] See *ICI v. Commission*, Case 48/69, [1972] ECR 619, [1972] CMLR 557 and the so-called *Wood Pulp* cases, *supra* note 117. See also P.J. Kuyper, 'European Community Law and Extraterritoriality: Some Trends and New Developments', 33 *ICLQ* (1984) 1016.

interest.[119] In order to avoid conflicting jurisdictions, and based on the Westphalian and post-Westphalian concept of the territorial nation state, a state's territory was traditionally regarded as the basic unit for jurisdiction. Any extension of territorial jurisdiction had to be justified by other jurisdictional links, such as the personality principle or the effects doctrine or, in the field of criminal law, the protective as well as the universality principles. Jurisdictional conflicts were traditionally solved by recourse to these more or less technical principles without having regard to the content of the extraterritorial legislation.[120]

4. Can Shared International Interests Justify Extraterritoriality?

With the current 'new wave' of extraterritoriality, it is no longer purely national policy interests that are pursued by extending the borders of national jurisdiction. Rather, states are using their extraterritorial jurisdiction in order to enforce not (only) their own policy goals, but also international ones. Of course, one has to be very careful in assessing whether states truly enforce international law or whether they use this as a pretext to pursue their own national policies.[121] If we can take it as a valid assumption—at least for the sake of the argument—that states are increasingly using their extraterritorial jurisdiction in order to enforce human rights concerns, they could be seen as utilizing their national legal system to enforce international law. From this perspective, extraterritorial human rights litigation can be viewed as a form of decentralized enforcement of international law. This would, of course, also mean that the issue is no longer a clash between effective (extraterritorial) national policy enforcement *versus* neutral international law principles of jurisdiction, but rather a clash of substantive international law principles, i.e. human rights, with formal international law principles, i.e. territorial jurisdiction. Under these changed parameters, there is a possibility that 'substance' might override 'form'. Thus, there are new chances for extraterritoriality since affected states will have a hard time justifying their disregard of human rights in rejecting the extraterritorial acts of others. While international law only provided a value-neutral framework within which states were free to adopt and pursue their own policy through legislation, each state could easily defend its own sovereign right to determine its own policies and thus to legislate and remain unaffected by the legislation of other states. The growing convergence of policies, or at least the increasing substantive determination of national policy choices through international law, for

---

[119] 'There is no more important way to avoid conflict than by providing clear norms as to which state can exercise authority over whom, and in what circumstances. Without that allocation of competences, all is rancour and chaos': Higgins, *supra* note 6, 56.

[120] Except insofar as international law might provide recourse to a particular type of jurisdictional link, e.g. competition rules—effects doctrine; counterfeiting money—protective principle, etc. See also Shaw, *supra* note 56, 458.

[121] See the Helms-Burton debate where the US intention to portray its action as decentralized enforcement of the human right to property was contested by other states, *infra* text at note 132.

our purposes the increasing pressure to fulfil human rights obligations by enacting implementing legislation, has weakened the shield of national sovereignty and territorial jurisdiction.

The traditional approach of international law to allocate jurisdiction between the traditional subjects of international law, the states, was fairly straightforward— nowadays one would probably say 'user-friendly'—based on territoriality and nationality: states have jurisdiction over persons and things located within their territory and, to some extent, over persons and things, such as ships and aircraft, outside their territories if there is a special ('genuine') link to them such as citizenship or the like. Only very reluctantly, international law has recognized additional justifications for the exercise of extraterritorial jurisdiction. The objective territoriality principle or effects doctrine, according to which any conduct that has, for instance, a 'direct, substantial and reasonably foreseeable effect'[122] on a state's territory may be subject to that state's extraterritorial jurisdiction, is one example, by now largely accepted in the context of anti-trust/competition law. Whether it could be developed into a more general principle according to which any 'substantial or effective connection' with a state would give that state a legitimate basis for extra territorial jurisdiction remains to be seen.[123]

As already indicated, it is worth considering whether, in addition to these 'formal' jurisdictional principles, issues of substance, of the content of legislation, may have an impact on the legality of the exercise of extraterritorial jurisdiction. In this regard, it is useful to look to other fields of extraterritorial jurisdiction, such as humanitarian law and other forms of international criminal law providing for universal jurisdiction of contracting parties over very serious crimes. The Geneva Conventions give all Contracting States the right—some argue even the obligation—to prosecute war crimes committed by anyone, anywhere, without the need for any territorial or personal link to the crimes.[124] The traditional connecting factor is no longer required, but is replaced by the shared interests of the international community in

---

[122] See e.g. 1982 Foreign Antitrust Improvements Act, Public Law 97–290, Title IV, Section 402; 96 Stat. 1246; 15 USC Section 6a.

[123] See K.M. Meessen (ed), *Extraterritorial Jurisdiction in Theory and Practice* (1994); Werner Meng, *Extraterritoriale Jurisdiktion im öffentlichen Wirtschaftsrecht* (1994).

[124] According to Arts 49 *et seq*. Convention (I) for the Amelioration of the Condition of the Wounded and Sick in Armed Forces in the Field. Geneva, 12 August 1949, 75 UNTS 31; Arts 50 *et seq*. Convention (II) for the Amelioration of the Condition of Wounded, Sick, and Shipwrecked Members of Armed Forces at Sea, Geneva, 12 August 1949, 75 UNTS 85; Arts 129 *et seq*. Convention (III) relative to the Treatment of Prisoners of War, Geneva, 12 August 1949, 75 UNTS 135; Arts 146 *et seq*. Convention (IV) relative to the Protection of Civilian Persons in Time of War, Geneva, 12 August 1949, 75 UNTS 287, the Contracting Parties are under a special duty to prosecute and try persons alleged to have committed 'grave breaches' regardless of their nationality and regardless of the place where such 'grave breaches' occurred (principle of universality) or at least to extradite such persons. See Antonio Cassese, 'On the Current Trends towards Criminal Prosecution and Punishment of Breaches of International Humanitarian Law', 9 *EJIL* (1998) 2 at 5; Michael P. Scharf, 'Application of Treaty-Based Universal Jurisdiction to Nationals of Non-Party States', 35 *New England Law Review* (2001) 363.

preventing certain acts. The history of legal steps against bribery and corruption in general also provides an interesting lesson with regard to the gradual acceptance of extraterritoriality. The initial unilateral approach of the US in passing the 1977 Foreign Corrupt Practices Act[125] met with considerable disfavour and was rejected by some countries 'affected' by the extraterritorial application of this legislation.[126] The 1997 OECD Anti-Corruption Convention[127] broadly prohibits bribery both at home and abroad and permits the use of extraterritorial legislation. This has largely eliminated the controversy.[128] Parties to the OECD Convention would hardly be in a convincing position to complain about extraterritorial anti-corruption enforcement by other states if that action were prompted by their own inactivity contrary to their obligations under the convention.

At this point one could draw a parallel with the extraterritorial 'prosecution' of human rights violations as exemplified by current human rights litigation before US and other mostly common law jurisdictions. Whether they use traditional criminal law instruments or civil liability there is also a shared interest in preventing human rights infringements, not only by states but also by non-state actors. The prime instrument of national legislation is the incrimination of certain acts leading to criminal or civil responsibility regardless of whether they were committed within or outside the territory of the forum state. If the territorial state is bound by international agreements to ensure human rights, any opposition to extraterritorial enforcement would be hard to justify. In such a case the territorial state would be obliged to take action itself. If it refused to do so and coupled this refusal with a rejection of action by other states to enforce the same treaty rights extraterritorially, this non-co-operation could be qualified as an act of bad faith.

The common rationale would be that the defence of shared substantive interests, protecting human rights, gives additional weight to the exercise of extraterritorial jurisdiction.[129] Of course, behind such a model always lurks the danger of a unilateral assessment of what are human rights, which types of human rights deserve extraterritorial protection, etc. This, in turn, is related to the question who determines substance. The Helms-Burton controversy may serve as a useful illustration of the problem. This 1996 US legislation[130] provides, *inter alia*, for a cause of action before US courts against investors from anywhere in the world who happen to invest in property in Cuba formerly belonging to persons expropriated by the Castro

---

[125] 15 U.S.C. § 78dd, http://www.usdoj.gov/criminal/fraud/fcpa/fcpastat.htm.

[126] See P.M. Nichols, 'Regulating Transnational Bribery in Times of Globalization and Fragmentation', 24 *Yale Journal of International Law* (1999) 257.

[127] OECD Convention on Combating Bribery of Foreign Public Officials in International Business Transactions, adopted 21 November 1997, entered into force 15 February 1999. http://www.imf.org/external/np/gov/2001/eng/091801.pdf.

[128] It has also eliminated the competitive disadvantage for American companies *vis-à-vis* others which were 'lawfully' bribing abroad.   [129] See McCorquodale, *supra* note 85, at 101.

[130] Cuban Liberty and Democratic Solidarity (LIBERTAD) Act of 1996, Public Law 104–114, H.R. 927; reprinted in 35 ILM (1996) 357–78.

regime.[131] Among many other issues, one of the problems concerned the weight of the US claim that this legislation was in essence a measure permitting human rights enforcement by US courts.[132] For the US, the protection of private property against unlawful expropriation constitutes a general international law standard which they felt entitled to enforce even against private 'accomplices',[133] those who 'traffick' in former US property by purchasing land from the Cuban government today, in the governmental human rights violation, the discriminatory and uncompensated expropriation of American property in the 1960s. For the Europeans and many other affected countries, the Helms-Burton Act amounted to an impermissible extension of American values by prohibiting non-American companies from investing in Cuba.[134] Leaving many other technical aspects aside, one of the central issues in the Helms-Burton controversy was whether the right to property belongs to a core of customary international law principles which merit not only universal respect but also enforcement even by other states. It is obvious that the national interest and perspective of legislators and courts will play a great role in this issue. The same is true for litigation under the ATCA (which in a way served as a model for the Helms-Burton Act) where a national interpretation of what is to be considered international human rights law may depart from the *communis opinio scholarum*, the general opinion of international lawyers. This problem is related to the larger issue of the universality debate of human rights, to the question of which human rights call for universal respect and which may be regionally divergent. As with the question of universal human rights, so also in the context of Helms-Burton: hypocrisy appears to be the true problem.

The entire issue of extraterritorial human rights enforcement also displays interesting parallels to the debate currently taking place within the WTO with regard to the controversial insertion of a 'social clause' into the WTO legal order.[135]

---

[131] See Clagett, 'Title III of the Helms-Burton Act Is Consistent with International Law', 90 *AJIL* (1996), 435; Vaughan Lowe, 'US Extraterritorial Jurisdiction: The Helms-Burton and D'Amato Acts', 46 *ICLQ* (1997), 378; Andreas Lowenfeld, 'Congress and Cuba: The Helms-Burton Act', 90 *AJIL* (1996), 419–35; Brigitte Stern, 'Vers la mondialisation juridique? Les lois Helms-Burton et D'Amato-Kennedy', 100 *Revue Générale de Droit International Public* (1996) 979.

[132] See August Reinisch, 'Widening the US Embargo Against Cuba Extraterritorially. A few public international law comments on the "Cuban Liberty and Democratic Solidarity (LIBERTAD) Act of 1996"', 7 *EJIL* (1996), 545–62.

[133] In relation to the concept of complicity in human rights violations see Celia Wells, 'Catching the Conscience of the King: Corporate Players on the International Stage', *infra* Chapter 5.

[134] See European Union: Démarches Protesting the Cuban Liberty and Democratic Solidarity Act, reprinted in 35 ILM (1996) 397; Inter-American Juridical Committee, Opinion of 23 August 1996, CJI/SO/II/doc.67/96 rev 5; adopted by CJI/RES.II-14/96; reprinted in 35 ILM (1996) 1322.

[135] See Christopher McCrudden and Anne Davies, 'A Perspective on Trade and Labour Rights', in Francesco Francioni (ed), *Environment, Human Rights and International Trade* (2001), 179; Friedl Weiss, 'Internationally Recognised Labour Standards and Trade', in Friedl Weiss, Erik Denters, and Paul de Waart (eds), *International Economic Law with a Human Face* (1998), 79; Erika de Wet, 'Labor Standards in the Globalized Economy: The Inclusion of a Social Clause in the General Agreement On Tariff and

4. COMMON FEATURES

At this point, let me try to draw a few preliminary conclusions relating to the broader picture of the changing legal framework set out above. The common features I present in the following part are not an exhaustive description. Rather, they serve to illustrate and partly to explain some of the new approaches to non-state actors and human rights.

A. New Positions and New Alliances of Non-State Actors

Under traditional human rights law, the roles were clearly distributed among the main players. NGOs and international organizations were keeping an eye on the human rights performance of states and increasingly also of TNCs.[136] International organizations and NGOs were the 'good guys' and it was their role to advocate and promote human rights, to campaign for human rights observance, and to supervise compliance and find violations. The 'bad guys', powerful states or even less powerful ones which in relation to individuals always had a threatening potential of power, were the primary targets of human rights scrutiny.

These roles have been partially reversed today: international organizations are now increasingly questioned about their human rights performance. A prime example lies in the EU/EC, where a human rights case-law has been developed by the European Court of Justice,[137] but other international organizations, such as the UN with regard to its activities (or rather failure to act) in situations like

---

Trade/World Trade Organization', 17 *Human Rights Quarterly* (1995) 443. See also discussion in Steinhardt, *supra* note 2 at [35–37].

[136] See Felice D. Gaer, 'Reality Check: Human Rights NGOs Confront Governments at the UN', in Thomas G. Weiss and Leon Gordenker (eds), *NGOs, the UN and Global Governance* (1996) 51; Margaret E. Keck and Kathryn Sikkink, *Activists beyond Borders: Advocacy Networks in International Politics* (1998); Dianne Otto, 'Nongovernmental Organizations in the United Nations System: The Emerging Role of International Civil Society', 18 *Human Rights Quarterly* (1996) 107; Peter Willets (ed), *The Conscience of the World: The Influence of Non-Governmental Organizations in the U.N. System* (1996).

In its 1998 annual report, Amnesty International criticized not only individual governments and militant groups for human rights violations, but also businesses and international financial institutions, including Royal Dutch Shell, the World Bank, the International Monetary Fund, and the World Trade Organization. The report is available at http://amnestyusa.org/scripts/exit.cgi?www.amnesty.org/ailib/index.html.

See also the mission statement of 'CorpWatch. Holding Corporations Accountable': 'CorpWatch counters corporate-led globalization through education and activism. We work to foster democratic control over corporations by building grassroots globalization—a diverse movement for human rights, labor rights and environmental justice.' And see its report on the Nike lawsuit, available at http://www.corpwatch.org/trac/nike/lawsuit.html. Similarly, Human Rights Watch has gone beyond criticizing only states. In a 1999 report it was highly critical of Enron's activities in the course of a controversial electricity project in India where local opposition was harshly repressed. See Human Rights Watch, The Enron Corporation: Corporate Complicity in Human Rights Violations (1999), available at http://www.hrw.org/reports/1999/enron.   [137] See *infra* note 236.

Srebrenica[138] or with regard to its economic sanctions policy,[139] are becoming the subject of scrutiny by NGOs, affected states, and the public. A similar development can be witnessed in the context of international financial institutions: the IBRD and the IMF are questioned increasingly about the human rights compatibility of their development policies, in particular, in their lending practices.[140] NGO accountability is another new topic: their activities are subject to intensified scrutiny, and they are attacked for their lack of democratic structures and transparency. In some instances they are even accused of acting contrary to human rights.[141] In addition, the human rights implications of TNC activities have received renewed attention. TNCs as potential perpetrators of human rights violations have become the focus of much recent human rights discourse. But this is not the only aspect of human rights and TNCs. There is also the positive story about TNCs and human rights: TNCs may induce change and contribute to an enhanced human rights environment in the states where they operate.[142] On the macro level, the foreign investment they contribute to a national economy may raise living standards and create better social and economic conditions in the host countries. On the micro level, TNCs may act as promoters, serving as role models in adopting human rights (labour rights) standards

[138] This involved the failure of UN peace-keeping forces to protect civilians in the UN-declared 'safe areas' of former Yugoslavia, particularly, in and around Srebrenica where a massacre was carried out by Serb forces on Muslim civilians in summer 1995. The widespread criticism and allegations of responsibility prompted the General Assembly to commission an investigation which resulted in the Secretary-General's report on Srebrenica, *supra* note 80, which acknowledged that 'There is an issue of responsibility, and we in the United Nations share in that responsibility, as the assessment at the end of this report records': ibid., para. 5.

[139] See Hans-Peter Gasser, 'Collective Economic Sanctions and International Humanitarian Law: An Enforcement Measure Under the United Nations Charter and the Right of Civilians to Immunity: An Unavoidable Clash of Policy Goals?', 56 *Zeitschrift für ausländisches öffentliches Recht und Völkerrecht* (1996) 871; August Reinisch, 'Developing a Human Rights and Humanitarian Law Accountability of the UN Security Council for the Imposition of Economic Sanctions', 95 *AJIL* (2001), 851; W. Michael Reisman and Douglas L. Stevick, 'The Applicability of International Law Standards to United Nations Economic Sanctions Programmes', 9 *EJIL* (1998) 86.

[140] See François Gianviti, 'Economic, Social, and Cultural Human Rights and the International Monetary Fund', Chapter 4 *infra*; and Philip Alston, 'Can the International Human Rights Regime Accommodate Non-State Actors', Chapter 1, *supra*. See also Patricia Armstrong, 'Human Rights and Multilateral Development Banks: Governance Concerns in Decision Making', 88 *American Society of Int'l Law Proc.* (1994) 271; Daniel D. Bradlow, 'The World Bank, the IMF, and Human Rights', 6 *Transnat'l Law and Contemp. Problems* (1996) 47; Sabine Schlemmer-Schulte, 'The World Bank and Human Rights', 4 *Austrian Review of International and European Law* (1999) 230; Sigrun Skogly, *The Human Rights Obligations of the World Bank and the International Monetary Fund* (2001).

[141] Michael Edwards/David Hulme (eds), *Non-Governmental Organisations Performance and Accountability in the Post-Cold War World: Beyond the Magic Bullet* (1995); Ian Smillie, *The Alms Bazaar: Altruism Under Fire—Non-Profit Organizations and International Development* (1995).

[142] See Deborah Spar, 'The Spotlight and the Bottom Line: How Multinationals Export Human Rights', 77 *Foreign Affairs* (1998) 7; Jennifer Johnson, 'Public-Private Convergence: How The Private Actor Can Shape Public International Labor Standards', 24 *Brook. J. Int'l L.* (1999) 291; W.H. Meyer, 'Human Rights and MNCs: Theory versus Quantitative Analysis', 18 *Human Rights Quarterly* (1996) 368.

that should be copied by other firms. This concept of the alternative role of TNCs is a clear reversal of the 'stay out' policy advocated after heavy criticism of the involvement of some TNCs in the domestic affairs of host states, such as ITT in the overthrow of the Allende regime in Chile in 1973 and Elf Aquitaine's role in the ousting of the Congo-Brazzaville government in 1997.[143]

These changes, among others, witness that the roles have been, at least partly, reversed. There is a greater number of potential human rights violators, but there are also more potential human rights promoters and defenders and they may enter into new alliances with each other. Traditionally, international organizations could count on the support of NGOs in advocating human rights, in exposing state practices in violation of human rights, etc. Today, NGOs sometimes antagonize international organizations by severely criticizing the latter.[144] On the other hand, TNCs are trying to get NGOs on board in their human rights code of conduct campaigns to enhance their own standing; they have realized that 'human rights are good business'.[145] They are relying, *inter alia*, on NGO and other independent professional expertise for 'social accounting'.[146] Furthermore, international organizations partly try to co-opt NGOs. In particular, the International Financial Institutions (IFIs) such as the IMF, the World Bank Group, and regional development banks, as well as the WTO, have learned their lessons from Seattle and Genoa by creating NGO links.[147] The UN has tried to get NGOs 'on board' by changing the system of NGO consultative status,[148] by using their aid delivery services through UN subcontracting,[149] etc.

---

[143] See Menno T. Kamminga, 'Holding Multinational Corporations Accountable for Human Rights Abuses: A Challenge for the EC', in Philip Alston (ed), *The EU and Human Rights* (1999), 553, at 554.

[144] See the NGO criticism of the IMF and IBRD as well as the EU by 'statewatch' (http://www.statewatch.org/) and of the UN by 'unwatch' (http://www.unwatch.org/).

[145] Cf. Kinley, *supra* note 53, 26.

[146] Social Accountability 8000, for instance, is a monitoring and certification standard mainly for labour standards at factories. Modelled on the auditing process developed by the International Standards Organization, such as ISO 9000 and ISO 14000, it relies on certified monitors to verify compliance. SA 8000 was first issued in 1998 and revised in 2001. See http://www.cepaa.org/SA8000/SA8000/htm.

[147] See WTO Guidelines for Arrangements on Relations with Non-Governmental Organizations, WTO, WT/L/162, 23 July 1996. See also Steve Charnovitz, 'Participation of Nongovernmental Organizations in the World Trade Organization', 17 *U. Penn. J. Int'l Econ. L.* (1996) 331; Daniel C. Esty, 'Non-Governmental Organizations at the World Trade Organization: Cooperation, Competition, or Exclusion', 1 *J. Int'l Econ. L.* (1998) 123; Wolfgang Benedek, 'Developing the Constitutional Order of the WTO: The Role of NGOs', in *Development and Developing International and European Law: Essays in Honour of Konrad Ginther on the Occasion of his 65th Birthday* (1999) 228; Ibrahim F.I. Shihata, 'The World Bank and Non-Governmental Organizations', 25 *Cornell Int'l L. J.* (1992) 623.

[148] According to Art 71 UN Charter, the UN 'Economic and Social Council may make suitable arrangements for consultation with NGOs which are concerned with matters within the [Council's] competence'. Based on this Charter authorization, ECOSOC adopted Res. 288 B (X) (27 February 1950), Res. 1296 (XLIV) (23 May 1968), and Res. 1996/31 (25 July 1996), laying down the specific requirements for NGO accreditation. See http://www.un.org/documents/ecosoc/res/1996/eres1996-31.htm.

[149] See Leon Gordenker and Thomas G. Weiss, 'Devolving Responsibilities: A Framework for Analysing NGOs and Services', in Thomas G. Weiss (ed), *Beyond UN Subcontracting: Task-Sharing with Regional Security Arrangements and Service-Providing NGOs* (1998) 30.

The reversal of roles is also nicely encapsulated in the classical 'Who guards the guardians?'.[150] After the recent Enron disaster this could be rephrased into a more current 'who accounts for the accountants?' In any event, accountability is no longer a one-way exercise. Rather, it has become a multi-faceted issue.

B. Indirect Human Rights Enforcement—'Going After the Accomplices'

On a fairly general and abstract level another common attribute may be identified from recent trends in dealing with the human rights performance of non-state actors: a growing tendency to turn against 'accomplices' in case the main perpetrators cannot be held accountable. The underlying rationale and message of the (legal) accountability of companies complicit in direct human rights violations is clear: ultimately, TNCs will be deterred from investing in countries where they might be held responsible for acts of that state.

More and more frequently, legal devices are chosen to induce compliance via indirect sanctioning. The combination of extraterritoriality and vicarious liability has produced some remarkable examples, based on the philosophy: 'if you can't get the direct perpetrators, put pressure on those who collaborate with them or profit from their acts'. Examples are the *Unocal* litigation where direct action against Myanmar (Burma), the alleged direct human rights violator, appears unfeasible because, on the traditional inter-state plane, there is not sufficient leverage and because state immunity would prevent a direct claim against Myanmar in US courts.[151] Even if jurisdiction were upheld by national courts, the chances of enforcing an eventual judgement would be very low. Thus, it makes sense to seek redress against corporate accomplices to state action.

Corporate complicity is, of course, a very complex issue and it is useful to differentiate between various degrees of involvement and 'culpability' of corporate behaviour.[152] There is an obvious distinction between a company investing or otherwise doing business in a country with a questionable human rights record and actively supporting forced population transfers or using slave labour provided by government units. It has thus been suggested that different categories of 'complicity' be applied, such as actively assisting in human rights violations by others, benefiting from the opportunities created by human rights violations, or silence and inactivity in the face of human rights violations.[153]

---

[150] '*Quis Custodiet Ipsos Custodes*' ('But who guards the guardians?'), *Decimus Junius Juvenal*, Satires VI, 347. See also Ralph Wilde, 'Quis Custodiet Ipsos Custodes? Why and How UNHCR Governance of "Development" Refugee Camps Should be Subject to International Human Rights Law', 1 *Yale H.R. & Dev. L.J.* (1998) 107.

[151] In *Doe v. Unocal Corp*, 963 F. Supp. 880 (C.D. Cal. 1997) the claim against the State Law and Order Restoration Council of Myanmar and the Myanmar Oil and Gas Enterprise was dismissed for state immunity reasons.

[152] See Steven R. Ratner, 'Corporations and Human Rights: A Theory of Legal Responsibility', 111 *Yale Law Journal* (2001) 443, at 497. See also Celia Wells, *supra* note 133.

[153] See International Council on Human Rights (ed.) *Beyond Voluntarism: Human Rights and the Developing International Legal Obligations of Companies* (2002) 126. See also Human Rights Watch,

Some aspects of the Holocaust litigation before US courts follow this pattern. The *Princz* case is a pertinent example: an action for slave labour against the Federal Republic of Germany failed before US federal courts because of the immunity of the defendant.[154] Subsequent cases were instituted against companies which profited from slave labour either in a direct way, such as industrial firms,[155] or in a less direct way, such as banks and insurance companies.[156] In all these cases it is clear that the primary target of the US litigation is the atrocious policy of forced and slave labour organized by the Third Reich. The corporate defendants did not plan or institute this exploitative programme, but some may have willingly benefited from it. And because the direct perpetrator is unavailable as a defendant, the indirect 'beneficiaries' which may be subject to the jurisdiction of US courts today are named as defendants now.

The above examples all relate to US civil actions based on a concept of corporate liability for complicity in human rights violations perpetrated by governments. This appears to be by far the most likely situation when one is confronted with corporate human rights violations, although it may also happen that TNCs themselves engage in human rights violations. The precise legal standards for civil liability for such corporate complicity in human rights violations is, however, as unexplored as standards for their criminal responsibility.[157] Some tentative guidelines can be found in some of the codes of conduct mentioned above, although they are usually not helpful to the search for precise standards. The UN Global Compact, for instance, demands that businesses 'make sure they are not complicit in human rights abuses'.[158] The Commentary to the Norms on the Responsibilities for Transnational Corporations and Other Business Enterprises with Regard to Human Rights provides that '[t]ransnational corporations and other business enterprises shall have

---

The Enron Corporation: Corporate Complicity in Human Rights Violations (1999), available at http://www.hrw.org/reports/1999/enron.

[154] *Princz v. Federal Republic of Germany*, 813 F. Supp. 22 (1992), 26 F.3d 1166, 1180 (D.C. Cir. 1994).

[155] See e.g. *Iwanowa v. Ford Motor Co*, No. 98-CV-959, 1999 WL 719888 (D.N.J. 14 September 1999); *Gross v. Volkswagen*, No. 98-CV-4104 (D.N.J. filed 31 August 1998). See also the list of known World War II and National Socialist era cases against German companies pending in U.S. courts, at http://www.stiftung-evz.de/doku/stiftunginitiative/statement_english_annex_c.html.

[156] See among others the complaints filed in US federal courts *Duveen v. Deutsche Bank AG*, No. 99-CV-0388 (S.D.N.Y. filed 19 January 1999); *Watman v. Deutsche Bank*, No. 98-CV-3938 (S.D.N.Y. filed 3 June 1998); *Bodner v. Banque Paribas*, No. 97 Civ. 7433 (E.D.N.Y. filed 20 March 1998).

[157] Cf. Andrew Clapham and Scott Jerbi, 'Categories of Corporate Complicity in Human Rights Abuses', 24 *Hastings Int'l & Comp. L. Rev.* (2001) 339, who suggest a differentiation between direct corporate complicity, requiring intentional participation; beneficial or indirect corporate complicity, merely requiring knowledge of human rights violations from which companies will benefit; and silent complicity, where companies may be faulted for not acting or speaking out against systematic human rights abuses of host states. See also Celia Wells, 'Corporate Criminal Liability in Europe and Beyond', 39 *New South Wales Law Society Journal* (2001) 62.

[158] UN Global Compact, *supra* note 49; see Steinhardt, *supra* note 2 at 206.

the responsibility to use due diligence in ensuring that their activities do not contribute directly or indirectly to human rights abuses, and that they do not directly or indirectly benefit from abuses of which they were aware or ought to have been aware'.[159] Similar demands are formulated in a number of voluntary human rights codes of conduct and they are also expressed in the guidelines of ethical investments etc. This shows that, although no clear rules have yet crystallized with regard to this form of indirect human rights enforcement, the idea of putting (even just economic) pressure on non-state actors to improve human rights situations has gained broad support.

The idea of holding accountable those who are subject to accountability mechanisms even if they are only indirectly responsible for human rights infringements has also received renewed attention in the context of the European system of human rights protection. It lies at the heart of a new trend in the case-law of the European Court of Human Rights, marked by the Gibraltar voting case,[160] holding states accountable for human rights violations of international organizations of which they are members.

One could even draw an (admittedly rather far-fetched) parallel to recent US action against states harbouring terrorists. Although the roles are reversed here, it follows a similar pattern insofar as the US tries to hold governments accountable not for directly perpetrating terrorist acts or directly engaging in state-sponsored terrorism, but rather for aiding, supporting, not preventing, and not co-operating in the fight against, terrorism.[161]

This latter example may be evidence of a general theme of a changed international environment willing to enforce human rights, whether directly or not, against accomplices. It is, in any event, probably more than just the result of a growing frustration over the ineffectiveness of human rights protection against states.

C. Increasing Use of Non-Legal Means of Enforcing Human Rights Compliance of Non-State Actors

Recent developments with regard to TNCs and human rights may teach another interesting lesson. Legal enforcement techniques, holding human rights

[159] Sub-Commission on the Promotion and Protection of Human Rights, Commentary on the Norms on the Responsibilities of Transnational Corporations and Other Business Enterprises with Regard to Human Rights, E/CN.4/Sub.2/2003/38/Rev.2, Commentary (b) to Sec. 1.

[160] See *infra* note 219.

[161] This logic was first relied upon by the US against Sudan and Afghanistan. See Jules Lobel, 'The Use of Force to Respond to Terrorist Attacks: The Bombing of Sudan and Afghanistan', 24 *Yale J. Int'l L.* (1999) 537; Ruth Wedgwood, 'Responding to Terrorism: The Strikes Against bin Laden', 24 *Yale J. Int'l L.* (1999) 559. For post-11 September 2001 action see Antonio Cassese, 'Terrorism is also Disrupting Some Crucial Legal Categories of International Law', 12 *EJIL* (2001) 993; Jost Delbrück, 'The Fight Against Terrorism: Self-Defense or Collective Security as International Police Action? Some Comments on the International Legal Implications of the "War Against Terrorism"', 44 *German Yearbook of International Law* (2001) 9.

violators legally accountable before international or national tribunals, may become less central as a mechanism to protect human rights effectively. More 'non-legal' enforcement techniques are used to induce human rights compliance.

Consumer boycotts are now almost a classical 'non-legal' enforcement technique to induce human rights compliance by TNCs.[162] The threat of lost sales of products produced in an environmentally harmful way, by disregarding core labour standards, or otherwise having negative human rights implications has proven to be a highly effective deterrent against such activities. This effectiveness is, in turn, predicated and depends upon a growing awareness and sensitivity of consumers. The goodwill, reputation, and publicity attaching to a company's human rights performance has become an important intangible business asset which is vigilantly guarded.

The non-legal enforcement mechanisms are not exhausted with the 'stick' of consumer boycotts. 'Socially responsible investing' has developed from an initial policy of excluding investments in certain sectors (such as arms production, genetically modified organisms, tobacco, etc.) into a positive pro-investment choice concerning businesses that conform to certain standards.[163]

One of the reasons for this development may be the simple legal impossibility of using the 'normal' human rights enforcement mechanism of human rights scrutiny by international human rights monitoring bodies, courts, and tribunals. Non-state actors are not subject to the relevant human rights protection systems under various universal and regional human rights conventions. This is as true for TNCs as it is for international organizations and NGOs.[164] However, may be it is less the non-availability of legal means than their non-effectiveness, or at least their lesser degree of effectiveness, which has induced the turn towards non-legal means of enforcement. The far more compelling force of the non-legal mechanisms mentioned above—consumer boycotts and ethical investment strategies—can be directly translated into costs and gains for companies. This economic argument has not fallen on deaf ears on the part of some non-state actors, particularly TNCs.

---

[162] An early well known consumer boycott arose from the controversy about the marketing of infant formula in developing countries. See Nancy E. Zelman, 'The Nestlé Infant Formula Controversy: Restricting the Marketing Practice of Multinational Corporations in the Third World', 3 *Transnat'l L.* (1990) 697. A list of currently enforced boycotts is available at http://www.ethicalconsumer.org/boycotts/boycotts_list.htm. See also Kenneth A. Rodman, ' "Think Globally, Punish Locally": Nonstate Actors, Multinational Corporations, and Human Rights Sanctions', 12 *Ethics & International Affairs* (1998) 19. See further Steinhardt, *supra* note 2 at 185–6.

[163] See www.neweconomics.org as well as www.socialinvest.org. See also the Sustainable Investment Research International Group (SIRI) a coalition of 12 research organizations aiming to provide and promote high quality social investment research products and services: http://www.sirigroup.org. See generally Steinhardt, *supra* note 2 at 181 and 184 for a discussion of 'rights sensitive' products and socially responsible investment.

[164] See, however, *infra* text starting at note 225, for the potential of future development.

D. Enforcing Human Rights Compliance of Non-State Actors Regardless of Whether they are Strictly Bound by Human Rights Obligations

Another common feature of recent developments in the field of non-state actors and human rights seems to be the decreasing relevance of the legal quality of the standards invoked. Apparently, it is becoming less and less important whether the human rights standards sought to be enforced are legally binding or not. Regardless of whether a strict obligation to respect human rights exists *de lege lata*, many of the current 'enforcement' measures are used in order to induce compliance. This is true not only of the 'non-legal' means of consumer boycotts *vis-à-vis* TNCs and 'socially responsible' investments, but it also applies to the recent surge of suing TNCs before national courts as long as they are 'doing business' within the forum state.[165]

Of course, consumers and investors are free to choose where to buy or to invest. They may rely on moral or ethical choices when making their business decisions. If it comes, however, to holding business entities civilly liable (as in many of the ATCA actions before US courts) the question of legal responsibility arises. This clearly presupposes that obligations legally binding on TNCs have been breached. Findings of liability in the absence of a legal obligation would be irreconcilable with fundamental notions of the rule of law. One need not even invoke the *nulla poena sine lege* analogy of criminal law.[166]

There is another risk involved in the increasing demand for accountability regardless of whether those held accountable are legally bound by certain standards. It creates a danger of blurring the line between legal obligations and *de lege ferenda* standards which might ultimately backfire by weakening the obligatory character of human rights law.[167]

E. The Issue of Non-State Subjects of International Law: A Fresh Start or a Cul de Sac?

The question of personality or subjectivity under international law has fascinated generations of international lawyers and it has remained a precarious and complicated one.[168] It also arises in the context of non-state actors and human rights. The precise question is whether non-state actors are more than just indirect addressees of human rights norms which are directly addressed to states. We have seen that, at

---

[165] According to many US 'long arm' statutes, foreign defendants may be subject to the jurisdiction of US courts if they are considered to be 'doing business' within the US. See *Restatement (Third)*, *supra* note 110, § 421.   [166] Art 15(1) 1st Sentence ICCPR, *supra* note 11.

[167] See also UN Sub-Commission on the Promotion and Protection of Human Rights, Sessional working group on the working methods and activities of transnational corporations, Transnational Corporations and Other Business Enterprises, E/CN.4/Sub.2/2002/WG.2/WP.1/Add. 1, 24 May 2002, 17, noting the concerns expressed that 'that universal principles [for transnational corporations] will only dilute already established more specific standards focused on particular issues facing an industry, a transnational corporation, or other business enterprise'.   [168] Shaw, *supra* note 56, at 137 *et seq.*

least *prima facie*, non-state actors are increasingly the direct addressees of human rights standards. Numerous voluntary codes of conduct clearly formulate direct obligations for companies. Does that mean that they have become, at least partially, subjects of international law?

To some extent this discussion relates back to the *Drittwirkungs* debate of past decades.[169] However, one should clearly recognize that in German doctrine and jurisprudence, where the theory of 'third-party effect' was most intensely debated, *Drittwirkung* really dealt with the private law repercussions of fundamental rights norms, with the effect on the legal relationship between private parties. It did not elevate private, non-state actors to the level of direct addressees of constitutional rights and obligations.

In a traditional international law understanding, only subjects of international law can be addressees of international obligations. If one narrowly defines subjects of international law as comprising states, international organizations, as creatures of states, and a few historic subjects of international law, such as the Holy See and the Sovereign Order of Malta,[170] most non-state actors relevant for our purposes would be excluded from the outset. However, if one follows a more 'liberal' delimitation of subjects of international law, for instance, one that would hold that an entity can be considered a subject of the international legal system if it has rights and/or obligations under that system, then a closer examination of the relevant human rights standards appears to be necessary in order to find out which non-state actors may qualify.

The underlying rationale of considering certain non-state actors as subjects of international law is usually that international law directly endows them with certain rights and obligations. For instance, the ICRC enjoys partial international legal personality because the Geneva Conventions directly confer certain (international law) rights on it;[171] individuals are considered to be, at least partly, subjects of international law because they enjoy human rights directly as a result of international law and because they are directly obliged by international law not to commit certain internationally criminal acts such a genocide, crimes against humanity, and war crimes.[172] In all these cases the international legal order wants to confer a certain status upon non-state actors by directly giving them rights and/or obligations. If the international legal personality of non-state actors really depends upon international law then it seems appropriate to take a closer look at the meaning of international law in order to find out whether non-state actors really are direct addressees of human rights obligations.

Today, there is renewed interest in the question whether there are real direct legal obligations for non-state actors contained in international human rights

[169] See A. Drzemczewski, 'The European Human Rights Convention and Relations between Private Parties', 26 *NILR* (1979) 163; Andrew Clapham, 'The *Drittwirkung* of the Convention', in R.St.J. MacDonald *et al.* (eds), *The European System for the Protection of Human Rights* (1998) 22; M. Hunt, 'The Horizontal Effect of the Human Rights Act', *Public Law* (1998) 423; Ingo von Münch *et al.*, *supra* note 8.   [170] Shaw, *supra* note 56, at 171.

[171] Ibid., at 192.   [172] Ibid., at 182.

instruments. In this context one point of departure is the fact that, while states are clearly the primary addressees of human rights obligations, the language of core human rights instruments does not narrowly restrict itself to states. The 1948 Universal Declaration of Human Rights and the two 1966 UN Human Rights Covenants stipulate that '[n]othing in this Declaration may be interpreted as implying for any State, group or person any right to engage in any activity or to perform any act aimed at the destruction of any of the rights and freedoms set forth herein.'[173] Similarly, the idea of 'private' duties with regard to human rights[174]—in addition to the traditional, exclusive 'public' duties of states—finds some support in positive law. The Universal Declaration speaks of a duty of 'every individual and every organ of society' to 'strive to [...] promote respect'[175] and the two UN Covenants even of a 'responsibility' 'to strive for the promotion and observance' of human rights.[176] Although this development may not yet lead to the availability of adequate procedural remedies, it has now been reaffirmed by various human rights bodies that the core of human right obligations are binding on all parts of society including the non-state actors. For instance, the CESCR stated in its General Comment No. 14 that '[w]hile only States are parties to the Covenant and thus ultimately accountable for compliance with it, all members of society—individuals, including health professionals, families, local communities, intergovernmental and non-governmental organizations, civil society organizations, as well as the private business sector—have responsibilities regarding the realization of the right to health. State parties should therefore provide an environment which facilitates the discharge of these responsibilities.'[177] With respect to TNCs the recently adopted Norms on the Responsibilities of Transnational Corporations and Other Business Enterprises with Regard to Human Rights of the UN Sub-Commission on the Promotion and Protection of Human Rights similarly provide that '[w]ithin their respective spheres of activity and influence, transnational corporations and other business enterprises have the obligation to promote, secure the fulfilment of, respect, ensure respect of and protect human rights recognized in international as well as national law [...].'[178]

---

[173] Art 30 Universal Declaration of Human Rights, UN G.A. Res. 217 (1948). Similar language can be found in Art 5(1) of the two 1966 UN Covenants as well as in Art 17 ECHR.

[174] Chris Jochnick, 'Confronting the Impunity of Non-State Actors: New Fields for the Promotion of Human Rights', 21 *Human Rights Quarterly* (1999), 56; Jordan J. Paust, 'The Other Side of Right: Private Duties Under Human Rights Law', 5 *Harv. Hum. R. J.* (1992), 51.

[175] Preamble, Universal Declaration of Human Rights, *supra* note 173.

[176] The last preamble paragraph of both Covenants reads in full: '*Realizing* that the individual, having duties to other individuals and to the community to which he belongs, is under a responsibility to strive for the promotion and observance of the rights recognized in the present Covenant'.

[177] UN Committee on Economic, Social, and Cultural Rights, General Comment No. 14: 'The right to the highest attainable standard of health', 11 August 2000, U.N. Doc. E/C.12/2000/4, para. 42.

[178] UN Sub-Commission on the Promotion and Protection of Human Rights, Norms on the Responsibilities of Transnational Corporations and Other Business Enterprises with Regard to Human Rights, E/CN.4/Sub.2/2003/12/Rev.2, Sec. 1 2nd sentence.

This trend has also manifested itself in the privately endorsed, legally non-binding Asian Human Rights Charter 1998 which confirms the 'primary responsibility' of states for the promotion of human rights but declares in paragraph 2.8: 'The capacity of the international community and states to promote and protect rights has been weakened by processes of globalization as more and more power over economic and social policy and activities has moved from states to business corporations. States are increasingly held hostage by financial and other corporations to implement narrow and short sighted economic policies which cause so much misery to so many people, while increasing the wealth of the few. Business corporations are responsible for numerous violations of rights, particularly those of workers, women and indigenous peoples. It is necessary to strengthen the regime of rights by making corporations liable for the violation of rights.'[179]

All these developments point in a similar direction. It can be credibly asserted that a contemporary reading of human rights instruments shows that non-state actors are also addressees of human rights norms. If this interpretation is supported by the adoption of legally binding codes of conduct in the future, for instance via treaties, there remains no serious obstacle to considering non-state actors, in this context most likely TNCs, to have gained, at least to some extent,[180] international legal personality.[181]

As convincing as this reasoning may appear, it still has not wholly rid itself of a certain feeling of circularity.[182] Why would we want to show that non-state actors are subjects of international law? To demonstrate that they may be direct addresses of human rights obligations. How do we try to show that they are subjects of international law? By asserting that they are direct addressees of human rights obligations under international law. Truly, the suspicion that the whole matter of international legal personality forms a vast intellectual prison and that 'the whole notion of subjects and objects has no credible reality and [. . .] no functional purpose'[183] is sometimes hard to suppress.

F. Human Rights and General Public International Law: New Intersections Instead of Fragmentation

Nowadays, the fragmentation of international law into special sub-fields, maybe sub-systems, or even self-contained regimes, is frequently deplored as threatening

---

[179] Asian Human Rights Charter, declared in Kwangju, South Korea, 17 May 1998. Available at http://www.ahrchk.net/charter/pdf/charter-final.pdf.

[180] As early as *Reparation for Injuries Suffered in the Service of the United Nations*, Advisory Opinion, ICJ Reports (1949), 174, 178 the ICJ held that '[t]he subjects of law in any legal system are not necessarily identical in their nature or in the extent of their rights, and the nature depends on the needs of the community'.

[181] See Nicola Jägers, 'The Legal Status of the Multinational Corporation Under International Law', in Michael K. Addo (ed), *Human Rights Standards and the Responsibility of Transnational Corporations* (1999) 259, at 270.

[182] See Derek W. Bowett, *The Law of International Institutions* (4th ed., 1982) 337.

[183] Higgins, *supra* note 6, 49.

the coherence and unity of international law. Remarkably, this concern apparently prompted the UN's International Law Commission to create a working group to study the phenomenon.[184] It has also led other institutions to pay attention to the various aspects of fragmentation such as the Project on International Courts and Tribunals,[185] focusing on the proliferation of specialized international courts which, institutionally, may also contribute to the fragmentation of international law.

With all due respect for the perceived and actual risks of fragmentation in international law, it appears that with regard to human rights law and non-state actors this danger has not materialized, quite the contrary. Whereas human rights law may traditionally have been regarded as a rather arcane sub-field of international law where only specialists had a say, something outside of the international law mainstream, today's human rights law seems to have entered the broader international law arena. The changing framework under which human rights are no longer relevant not only *vis-à-vis* states but also with regard to non-state actors may have contributed considerably to this situation. Business and trade lawyers have to deal with human rights issues today. In the past, lawyers advising TNCs or international organizations could probably state confidently that they did not have to care about human rights law because it had no practical relevance for them. With increasing demands for human rights compliance by these non-state actors, they are forced to deal with human rights. Human rights law appears to 'encroach' upon all other fields of law, including trade and investment, commercial law, etc.[186] One might even speak of a slow human rights 'intrusion'. Hardly any field of international law remains unaffected by human rights. At a minimum, it seems that the inter-relatedness of human rights and other parts of international law is increasingly recognized.[187] One also witnesses such cross-fertilization of sub-fields of international law in other areas. The traditionally separate areas of GATT and EC law have increasingly become interrelated, and

[184] See Report of the Study Group on the Fragmentation of International Law, A/CN.4/L.628, 1 August 2002, available at http://daccess-ods.un.org/doc/UNDOC/LTD/G02/632/93/PDF/G0263293.pdf? OpenElement.

The original title of the subject of the ILC Working Group was 'The risks ensuing from the fragmentation of international law', a topic included in the ILC's programme of work. Subsequently, the title of the topic was changed to 'Fragmentation of international law: difficulties arising from the diversification and expansion of international law'. See http://www.un.org/law/ilc/sessions/54/54sess.htm.

[185] See http://www.pict-pcti.org/home.html.

[186] See also recent academic literature, for instance, Stephen Bottomley and David Kinley, *Commercial Law and Human Rights* (2002); Janet Dine, 'Human Rights and Company Law', in Michael K. Addo (ed), *Human Rights Standards and the Responsibility of Transnational Corporations* (1999) 209. See also the report of the UN High Commissioner for Human Rights, *Business and Human Rights: A Progress Report*, available at www.unhchr.ch/business.htm; Amnesty International (Dutch Section) and Pax Christi International, *Multinational Enterprises and Human Rights* (1998) available at http://www.paxchristi.nl/mne.html.

[187] See Philip Alston, 'The Myopia of the Handmaidens: International Lawyers and Globalisation', 8 *EJIL* (1997), 435, at 447, who, in 1997, was not convinced that the 'compartmentalization' of human rights values within a small part of the discipline of international law had been overcome.

while lawyers could once specialize in one field, totally ignoring the other, such isolation is no longer feasible.[188]

5. UNDERLYING CAUSES OF THE PERCEIVED CHANGES

Once we try to look beyond certain trends and features describing the changing framework of dealing with non-state actors by trying to explain it, or (more appropriately) trying to identify possible underlying causes of the perceived changes, we are entering highly speculative grounds. Nevertheless, I would like to put the phenomena observed into a broader context and offer some possible partial explanations.

A. Demise of the Nation State; Rise of Non-State Actors

The trend towards viewing non-state actors as direct addressees of human rights and other norms of international law may have to do with a major structural change in the international legal order: the decrease and partial disappearance of the concept of the state as a 'mediating'[189] factor between the international law level and the rights and duties of non-state actors. The 'waning', 'retreat', or 'demise' of the sovereign state, the centrepiece of the Westphalian concept of the international legal order, has been described, denied, deplored, and applauded for some time in the discourses of international relations and international law, history and sociology, and other disciplines.[190]

The declining role of states, manifested through their declining power, leads to the attempt to address non-state actors directly and goes hand in hand with the increase of power and influence of the latter. If it is true that 'with power comes

---

[188] Cf. J.H.H. Weiler, 'Cain and Abel: Convergence and Divergence in International Trade Law', in J.H.H. Weiler (ed), *The EU, the WTO and the NAFTA* (2000) 3.

[189] German international law doctrine uses the term *Mediatisierung* of non-state actors through states to describe the fact that international law norms are addressed to states only. Even if they ultimately intend to regulate non-state behaviour, states have to come in as 'intermediaries' in order to translate the international law norms into domestic ones. See Karl Zemanek, 'Verantwortlichkeit und Sanktionen', in Hanspeter Neuhold, Waldemar Hummer and Christoph Schreuer (eds), *Österreichisches Handbuch des Völkerrechts* (3rd ed., 1997) 463.

[190] See Joseph A. Camilleri and Jim Falk, *The End Of Sovereignty? The Politics Of A Shrinking And Fragmenting World* (1992); Martin van Creveld, *The Rise and Decline of the State* (1999); Kenichi Ohmae, *The End of the Nation State* (1995); Vivien A. Schmidt, 'The New World Order, Incorporated: The Rise of Business and the Decline of the Nation-State', *Daedalus* (1995) 75; Oscar Schachter, 'The Decline of the Nation-State and its Implications for International Law', 36 *Colum. J. Transnat'l L.* (1997) 7; Christoph H. Schreuer, 'The Waning of the Sovereign State: Towards a New Paradigm for International Law?', 4 *EJIL* (1993) 447; Susan Strange, *The Retreat of the State: The Diffusion of Power in the World Economy* (1996); Serge Sur, 'The State between Fragmentation and Globalization', 8 *EJIL* (1997) 421.

responsibility'[191] then it is only logical to demand human rights observance by those non-state actors which are now as powerful as some states and may thus violate human rights in the same way as states.[192]

B. The Retreat of the State as Human Rights Addressee and as Human Rights Guarantor

In the current discourse states appear to be no longer the sole addressees of human rights obligations. Attention has shifted to a large degree to non-state actors. But states have also retreated as prime guarantors of human rights. Non-state actors have taken over to set standards, to secure compliance, and to enforce human rights expectations. NGOs, trade unions, church groups, and others no longer rely on the willingness of states and governments to regulate TNC behaviour. Rather, they increasingly put direct pressure on companies and international organizations by mobilizing public opinion.[193] This can already be viewed as another form of the 'privatization' of human rights through 'privatized' standard setting, 'privatized' supervision, and 'privatized' enforcement.[194]

C. Global Trends Toward Privatization

If one reflects upon the changing legal framework of dealing with non-state actors and upon the question why non-state actors are more and more conceived as addressees of human rights norms, potential causes for this change come to mind. One very tempting explanation lies in the fact that non-state actors become more and more powerful and increasingly take over hitherto state functions. This development is, in turn, closely linked to the dual trends of shifting governmental tasks to international organizations on one hand and to private entities on the other.[195] 'Privatization' has not stopped at making inefficient state-owned enterprises more competitive. TNCs have entered what used to be in many countries 'reserved' state businesses in the 'public service' fields, through the privatization of electricity, gas, and other energy supply services.[196] But they have not halted there. Private

[191] UN Sub-Commission on the Promotion and Protection of Human Rights, Sessional working group on the working methods and activities of transnational corporations, Transnational Corporations and Other Business Enterprises, E/CN.4/Sub.2/2002/WG.2/WP.1/Add. 1, 24 May 2002, 5.

[192] See Ratna Kapur, 'From Human Tragedy to Human Rights: Multinational Corporate Accountability for Human Rights Violations', 10 *Boston College Third World L.J.* (1990) at 2.

[193] See McCrudden, *supra* note 40, 172.

[194] See *infra* text at note 195, for the consequences of traditional 'privatization' in the sense of delegating or outsourcing hitherto state functions to private non-state actors.

[195] See August Reinisch, 'Governance without Accountability?', 44 *German Yearbook of International Law* (2001), 270. See also Wilde, *supra* note 68, at 113.

[196] Where non-state actors, usually TNCs, enter the public service-providing industry the traditional sphere of the *Drittwirkungs* debate comes into play. It may limit party autonomy and thus the providers' contractual freedom by an obligation to contract with private consumers, etc. In addition, competition

companies are now even running prisons and detention centres for immigration services.[197] It is obvious that this requires additional checks and controls on these private actors in the public field. The security forces in 'private prisons' may treat the inmates as badly as public police forces have done. This danger of the privatization of public functions has been clearly recognized by human rights bodies. For instance, in its Comment on the UK's state report under the ICCPR, the Human Rights Committee stated that it was 'concerned that the practice of the State party in contracting out to the private commercial sector core State activities which involve the use of force and the detention of persons weakens the protection of rights under the Covenant'.[198]

At the same time states are increasingly transferring large areas of public functions to international organizations. It is the combined pressure of 'out-sourced' activities that makes human rights protection against non-state behaviour such an urgent task for the future, because only an effective system of dealing with non-state actors will prevent a situation of unaccountability.

D. Globalization

Not surprisingly, since all the above reasons are already pointing towards it, globalization is also a prime suspect giving rise to many of the changes perceived in dealing with non-state actors and human rights. Of course, one should be very careful when talking about 'globalization' which means too many different things to different people. Pointedly, 'globalization' has been called 'the most overused and underspecified concept in the lexicon of the social sciences and policy sciences since the end of the cold war'.[199] It is not intended to develop a new theory or even a new definition of globalization here. However, building on a commonly shared understanding of some of the characteristic elements of globalization, it is interesting to see how many of the changes observed may be nicely explained. For our purposes, we can take 'globalization' to mean an increasing process of cross-border societal exchanges and transactions, not limited to economic ones, but including among others communication, security, culture, mobility, and environment, or, as it has been termed, the 'widening, deepening and speeding up of worldwide interconnectedness in all types of contemporary social life, from the cultural to the criminal, the financial to the spiritual'.[200] But 'globalization' did not just 'happen', it

---

law devices, similar to the prohibition against abusing a dominant position under Art 82 TEC, may help to tame the free play of market forces to the detriment of consumers through discriminatory pricing, etc.

[197] According to Kamminga, *supra* note 143, at 559, in the US 5% of prison capacity is run by private companies. The largest of these, Corrections Corporation, also operates overseas in the UK and Australia. See www.correctionscorp.com.

[198] Comments of the Human Rights Committee, U.N. Doc. CCPR/C/79/Add. 55, 27 July 1995.

[199] Richard Higgott, 'Economic Globalization and Global Governance: Towards a Post-Washington Consensus?', in Rittberger, *supra* note 71, 127, at 128.

[200] David Held, Anthony McGrew, David Goldblatt, and Jonathan Perraton, *Global Transformation: Politics, Economics and Culture* (1999) 2.

is also, to an important degree, the result of deliberate political choices. The neo-liberal credo of 'Reaganomics' and 'Thatcherism,' advocating economic liberal-ization, deregulation, and privatization,[201] subsequently espoused by the IFIs as Washington Consensus,[202] contributed largely to the 'retreat of the state'.[203]

If we identify as products of 'globalization' the increased influence of TNCs and other non-state actors, the role of global communications and the media, the enormously enhanced interdependence of states in the fields of trade and investment, services, and finance[204] we can observe the preconditions for some of the perceived changes described above. The way we deal with human rights and non-state actors can be seen both as a response to globalization and as a way of using the vehicles of globalization. Demands for human rights accountability on the part of non-state actors is in many respects a consequence of the fall-out, the negative spill-over, of an increasingly globalized economy. The loss of state control over TNCs, and the promotion of liberalization, privatization, and deregulation by IFIs, contributed to a situation where human rights, particularly social and labour rights, but also the environment and other societal goods, are increasingly threatened by non-state actors.[205] Codes of conduct may be regarded as the self-regulatory (or market-induced) approach to the loss of control over powerful non-state actors. Whereas increased resort to extraterritorially, feasible only for the few remaining powerful state or quasi-state actors such as the US and the EU, demonstrates the resolute will of the main international actor, the sovereign state, not to give in.

At the same time, the human rights response to globalization relies on the advances of globalization. Global consumer boycotts require an effective flow of information between activist NGOs and the media in order to convey their mes-sages. They rely on the internet as a crucial vehicle of communication and have on various occasions masterfully employed modern technology for their purposes.[206] The information revolution makes corporate wrong-doing more rapidly and more broadly visible. At the same time, the enhanced information flow created by globalization has also contributed to a strengthening of the notion of truly universal and indivisible human rights, to what could be called a 'globalization of human

---

[201] See Christoph Scherrer, *Globalisierung wider Willen? Die Durchsetzung liberaler Außenwirtschafispolitik in den USA* (1999). [202] See Higgott, *supra* note 199, 127.

[203] See Susan Strange, *The Retreat of the State* (1996).

[204] See Andrew Clapham, 'Globalization and the Rule of Law', *The Review: International Commission of Jurists* No. 61 (1999) 17.

[205] See also UN Sub-Commission on the Promotion and Protection of Human Rights, Sessional working group on the working methods and activities of transnational corporations, Transnational Corporations and Other Business Enterprises, E/CN.4/Sub.2/2002/WG.2/WP.1/Add. 1, 24 May 2002, 3.

[206] The International Campaign to Ban Landmines, the NGO Coalition for an International Criminal Court, and the Anti-MAI campaign during the 1990s are impressive examples of the ability of non-state actors to influence political decisions of states. See Tanja Brühl and Volker Rittberger, 'From International to Global Governance: Actors, Collective Decision-Making, and the United Nations in the World of the Twenty-First Century', in Rittberger, *supra* note 71, at 8. See also Margaret E. Keck and Kathryn Sikkink, *Activists beyond Borders: Advocacy Networks in International Politics* (1998).

rights',[207] although one should not overlook the fact that this may be a one-sided Western view whose universality is denounced elsewhere as 'cultural imperialism'.

6. INSTEAD OF A CONCLUSION—OUTLOOK: WHAT CAN BE DONE TO SAFEGUARD HUMAN RIGHTS AGAINST INFRINGEMENTS BY NON-STATE ACTORS?

Where non-state actors replace states in the exercise of public functions, where states are no longer directly responsible for those activities, there is an apparent need to devise systems of accountability, including legal responsibility, for non-state behaviour, particularly, of behaviour that may infringe upon human rights. We are currently witnessing a very dynamic evolution of accountability mechanisms ranging from a more structured form of economic pressure, such as consumer boycotts and ethical investing, to legal liability enforced by national courts. All these are expressions of changes in legal thinking, in the conceptualization of the content and safeguarding of human rights. New frontiers are explored in theory and practice, by doctrine and litigation, and it is hard to predict which trends might ultimately crystallize into a new framework of human rights law relevant to non-state actors.

The following section focuses on the *lex lata* as well as the future potential for legal responsibility for non-state behaviour. Such responsibility systems could be located either on the level of international law or on the level of national law. The following section addresses these two options in turn. It starts by describing the growing perception that states may continue to be held responsible for non-state activities, including those of international organizations, TNCs, and NGOs. Still on the international law level, the question of direct responsibility of non-state actors and the concomitant issue of the availability of procedures and institutions is then addressed. Finally, the very lively development with regard to liability under domestic law before national courts is analysed and its potential for the future is addressed.

A. State Responsibility for Non-State Activities

In the traditional concept of human rights, only states were considered to be bound by human rights law and thus only state behaviour could lead to its responsibility in international law. However, we are now witnessing a clear departure from this purely state-centred approach. It has become more and more evident that even existing international human rights instruments could be interpreted so as to lead to state responsibility for non-state activities. This awareness has found its expression not only in legal doctrine,[208] but also in a number of decisions by international bodies.

---

[207] McCorquodale, *supra* note 85, at 91.

[208] See Clapham, *supra* note 29; Kamminga, *supra* note 143; Kinley, *supra* note 53, at 38; Peter T. Muchlinski, 'Human Rights and Multinationals: Is There a Problem', 77 *Foreign Affairs* (2001) 31.

The basic theoretical premise for 'vicarious' or 'indirect' human rights liability of states for non-state activities is deduced from various human rights instruments, which demand that states not only 'respect' human rights, but also 'ensure', 'protect', or 'secure' them.[209] If there is an obligation on states to ensure human rights for 'all individuals' then this obligation can be understood to imply that such duty may be violated if states fail effectively to protect against human rights infringements by non-state parties. Building on the traditional 'due diligence' requirement under customary international law,[210] human rights bodies have interpreted obligations to 'ensure' as state obligations to take measures to prevent non-state violations of human rights. As a consequence, the UN Human Rights Committee held states responsible for failing to do so adequately.[211] Also in its General Comments the Committee has used a concept of the 'horizontal effect' of human rights provisions. In its General Comment on the ICCPR's torture prohibition it stated: 'It is the duty of the State Party to afford everyone protection through legislative and other measures as may be necessary against the acts prohibited by Article 7, whether inflicted by people acting in their official capacity, outside their official capacity or in a private capacity'.[212] This idea of a vicarious state responsibility for non-state acts was formulated even more expressly by the UN

---

[209] For instance, Art 2(1) ICCPR, *supra* note 11, provides that 'each State Party [...] undertakes to respect and to ensure to all individuals within its territory and subject to its jurisdiction the rights recognized in the present Covenant [...]' Similarly, Art 1 of the American Convention on Human Rights provides that 'The States Parties to this Convention undertake to respect the rights and freedoms recognized therein and to ensure to all persons subject to their jurisdiction the free and full exercise of those rights and freedoms [...]' According to Art 1 ECHR 'The High Contracting Parties shall secure to everyone within their jurisdiction the rights and freedoms defined in Section I of this Convention'.

[210] See Shaw, *supra* note 56, at 556. See also Giuseppe Sperduti, 'Responsibility of States for activities of private law persons', in Rudolf Bernhardt (ed), IV *Encyclopedia of Public International Law* (2nd ed., 2000) 216; Astrid Epiney, *Die völkerrechtliche Verantwortlichkeit von Staaten für rechtswidriges Verhalten im Zusammenhang mit Aktionen Privater* (1992).

See also the reasoning of the *Velásquez Rodríguez* case, *infra* note 214.

There is a clear tendency by international courts to interpret this due diligence requirement broadly. In 1997 the ECJ stunned many observers by holding France responsible for a violation of the free movement of goods provisions under the EC Treaty resulting from a failure by French officials to take all necessary measures to prevent private parties, French farmers, from obstructing the free movement of Spanish agricultural products: Case C-265/95, *Commission v. France* [1997] ECR I-6959.

[211] For instance, in *Delgado Paéz v. Colombia*, No. 195/1985, the Human Rights Committee found a violation of the right to personal security under Art 9(1) ICCPR because the respondent government had failed to take appropriate measures to protect the applicant. In *Santullo v. Uruguay*, No. 9/1977, a case involving torture by unidentified persons, the same Committee held that Arts 2 and 7 ICCPR had been violated because the government had failed to ensure the applicant's physical integrity with an official investigation.

[212] General Comment No. 20 (44) 1992 Art 7, CCPR/C/21/Rev. 1/Add.3. This broad view clearly contrasts with the restrictive notion used in the Convention against Torture, G.A. Res. 46 (XXXIX) (1984) Art 1 defines torture as: 'any act by which severe pain or suffering, whether physical or mental, is intentionally inflicted on a person for such purposes as obtaining from him or a third person information

Committee on the Elimination of Discrimination against Women, which stated that: 'discrimination under the Convention is not restricted to action by or on behalf of Governments...Under general international law and specific human rights covenants, States may also be responsible for private acts if they fail to act with due diligence to prevent violations of rights or to investigate and punish acts of violence, and for providing compensation.'[213]

Regional human rights institutions have also espoused this reasoning in their case-law. In its well known *Velásquez Rodríguez* judgment, the Inter-American Court of Human Rights held in the case of disappearances that 'an illegal act which violates human rights and which is initially not directly imputable to a State (for example, because it is the act of a private person or because the person responsible has not been identified) can lead to international responsibility of the State, not because of the act itself, but because of the lack of due diligence to prevent the violation or to respond to it as required by the Convention'.[214]

The Strasbourg Court has also adopted a similar reasoning with regard to human rights violations by non-state actors. In *Costello-Roberts*, a case concerning corporal punishment in a privately run school in the UK, the European Court of Human Rights held that 'the State cannot absolve itself from responsibility by delegating its obligations to private bodies or individuals'.[215] Though a majority found that the treatment did not amount to a violation of the Convention's prohibition of inhuman or degrading punishment, the Court's minority view expounded on the potential liability of the UK by adding that '[a] State can neither shift prison administration to the private sector and thereby make corporal punishment in prisons lawful, nor can it permit the setting up of system of private schools which are run irrespective of Convention guarantees'.[216] The European Court of Human Rights continues to rely on the underlying rationale of the *Costello-Roberts* case that states parties to the Convention cannot absolve themselves from their human rights obligations by delegating their tasks to non-state actors. It has also applied it with regard to acts of international organizations. In *Waite and Kennedy*, a case more narrowly dealing with the human rights compatibility of wide-ranging grants of

---

or a confession, punishing him for an act he or a third person has committed or is suspected of having committed, or intimidating or coercing him or a third person, or for any reason based on discrimination of any kind, when such pain or suffering is inflicted by or at the instigation of or with the consent or acquiescence of a public official or other person acting in an official capacity. It does not include pain or suffering arising only from, inherent in or incidental to lawful sanctions.'

[213] UN Committee on the Elimination of Discrimination against Women, *General Recommendation 19, 'Violence against women'*, 30 January 1992, U.N. Doc. A/47/38, para. 9.

[214] *Velásquez Rodríguez v. Honduras*, Inter-American Court of Human Rights, 29 July 1988, Ser. C, No. 4, 9 HRLJ 212 (1988), para. 172.

[215] *Costello-Roberts v. United Kingdom*, European Court of Human Rights, 1993, Series A, No. 247-C, para. 27.

[216] Ibid., Joint Partly Dissenting Opinion of Judges Russdal, Thór Vilhálmsson, Matscher, and Wildhaber, 64.

jurisdictional immunity to international organizations,[217] the Strasbourg Court stated very broadly that '[i]t would be incompatible with the purpose and object of the Convention, however, if the Contracting States were thereby [i.e. by establishing international organizations in order to pursue or strengthen their cooperation in certain fields of activity and by attributing to these organizations certain competencies and according them immunities] absolved from their responsibility under the Convention in relation to the field of activity covered by such attribution'.[218] Most recently, in the *Matthews* case, also known as the Gibraltar voting case,[219] this reasoning was re-confirmed. There the European Court of Human Rights found a human rights violation on the part of the UK stemming from an act of the international organization, the European Community. In the Court's view the violation of the Convention by the EC member state resulted from the member's failure to ensure that its obligations under EC law did not violate the ECHR. This case is also remarkable in respect of the procedural issue of bringing a complaint against an international organization's behaviour. For a long time it was well settled case-law of the European Commission of Human Rights that it would not allow claims against an organization's member states, either individually or collectively, for human rights violations attributable to the organization.[220]

The policy rationale underlying such 'vicarious' or 'subsidiary' liability is clear: to increase pressure on states by continuing to hold them responsible for 'out-sourced' or 'delegated' activity in order to make sure that they have a direct interest in regulating the behaviour of non-state actors to whom they have transferred state tasks. This idea was clearly expressed by the UN Human Rights Committee which, after displaying its concern about 'the practice of [a] State party in contracting out to the private commercial sector core State activities which involve the use of force and the detention of persons weakens the protection of rights under the Covenant',[221] underlined that a 'State party remains responsible in all circumstances for adherence to all articles of the Covenant'.[222] This reasoning applies to both international

---

[217] *Case of Waite and Kennedy v. Germany*, Eur. Court H.R., Judgment of 18 February 1999; available at http://ww.dhcour.coe.fr/hudoc. See August Reinisch, '*Case of Waite and Kennedy v. Germany*, Application No. 26083/94; *Case of Beer and Regan v. Germany*, Application No. 28934/95, European Court of Human Rights, 18 February 1999', 93 *AJIL* (1999) 933.

[218] *Waite and Kennedy v. Germany, supra* note 217, para. 67.

[219] *Denise Matthews v. United Kingdom*, ECtHR, Application No. 24833/94, Feb. 18, 1999; available at http://ww.dhcour.coe.fr/hudoc. See Henry G. Schermers, 'European Court of Human Rights: Matthews v. United Kingdom, case note concerning the decision of the European Court of Human Rights', 18 February 1999, 36 *Common Market L. Rev.* (1999), 673.

[220] Concerning the European Communities see *M(elchers) & Co. v. Federal Republic of Germany*, ECommHR, Application No. 13258/77, 9 February 1990, 64 Decisions and Reports (1990), 138; concerning the European Patent Organization see *Heinz v. Contracting Parties who are also Parties to the European Patent Convention*, ECommHR, Application No. 12090/92, 10 January 1994, 76-A Decisions and Reports (1994), 125.

[221] Comments of the HR Committee, U.N. Doc. CCPR/C/79/Add. 55, 27 July 1995.

[222] Ibid.

organizations and TNCs as well as to other non-state actors. States cannot 'absolve' themselves from their human rights obligations by delegating their tasks to private parties, individuals, or international organizations. The privately sponsored Maastricht Guidelines on Violations of Economic, Social, and Cultural Rights of 1997, going beyond the idea of continuing responsibility of states even for delegated activities, revert back to the original core of the responsibility of states to protect human rights by insisting that 'The obligation to protect includes the State's responsibility to ensure that private entities or individuals, including transnational corporations over which they exercise jurisdiction, do not deprive individuals of their economic, social and cultural rights'.[223]

Clearly this reasoning has a great potential for the future. States, by becoming indirectly responsible for non-state human rights violations, will have a strong incentive to prevent such non-state behaviour. They can do so either by reducing the scope of delegated activities—a rather unlikely scenario given the present trends of privatization, outsourcing, and empowering of international organizations[224]—or by strengthening the legal framework calling for the observance of human rights by non-state actors.

B. Direct Accountability of Non-State Actors under International Law and before International Tribunals?

Direct accountability of non-state actors is underdeveloped in human rights instruments, and in international law in general, but it is not wholly excluded, either on the level of substance or that of procedure. At present one certainly cannot speak of any established system of international mechanisms whereby non-state actors are held directly accountable for human rights violations, even though one might recognize an increasing awareness that they are considered to be directly bound by human rights obligations.[225] However, a number of recent developments may lead to a profound change in how we conceptualize human rights obligations and the human rights accountability of non-state actors. It is not sur-prising that these are most advanced with regard to international organizations which have been considered to enjoy subjectivity or personality under international law for some time. Thus, the basic idea that they may be directly obliged under international law to respect human rights no longer meets major objections as a matter of principle. But we still seem to be far from establishing the 'jurisdiction' of international bodies to scrutinize the human rights performance of international organizations.[226]

International organizations are most likely to be considered potential 'objects' of human rights complaints before international human rights forums. Nevertheless,

[223] Maastricht Guidelines on Violations of Economic, Social, and Cultural Rights of 1997, reprinted in 20 *Human Rights Quarterly* (1998) 691.   [224] See *supra* text at note 195.
[225] See *supra* text at note 173.   [226] See Reinisch, *supra* note 57.

even in the most 'progressive' human rights forums, including the Strasbourg institutions, it is well settled case-law that human rights bodies generally do not consider themselves competent to decide upon human rights complaints against international organizations which are not parties to the relevant treaty instrument, even if all or some of its member states are.[227] The *Matthews* case suggests that the European Court of Human Rights might be willing to hear complaints against member states of international organizations with regard to activities attributable to those international organizations[228] but that does not appear to change the basic premise that international organizations, not parties to the ECHR, are not subject to the Court's jurisdiction. In the view of the European Court of Human Rights its jurisdiction is strictly limited to Contracting Parties.

However, insisting on such a formal requirement is not an absolute legal necessity in order to exercise jurisdiction. It would be possible to transfer the idea of a 'functional treaty succession' for these purposes. A 'functional treaty succession' of the EC into the legal position of the EC member states was assumed in the framework of the GATT.[229] When the EC had taken over all the relevant foreign trade powers from the member states it was treated as a member of the GATT without ever formally adhering to the agreement.[230] Conceivably, such a functional succession could be pertinent with regard to states which have transferred their human rights-sensitive tasks to international organizations.[231]

In the EU context, the *via regis* appears to be accession to the ECHR on the part of either the Union or at least the supranational organizations, EC and EURATOM. Such accession, rejected by an advisory opinion of the ECJ in the early 1990s,[232] would eliminate the procedural dilemma by directly subjecting the organization to the jurisdiction of the European Human Rights Court. It is interesting to note that, maybe partly as a result of the *Matthews* case,[233] the EU member states are

---

[227] See *Confédération Française Démocratique du Travail v. European Communities, alternatively their Member States (a) jointly and (b) severally*, European Commission on Human Rights, Application No. 8030/77, 10 July 1978, 13 DECISIONS AND REPORTS 231.　　[228] See *supra* note 219.

[229] Cf. Ernst-Ulrich Petersmann, 'The EC as a GATT Member: Legal Conflicts between GATT Law and European Community Law', in Hilf/Jacobs/Petersmann (eds), *The European Community and GATT* (1986) 23, at 73.

[230] The ECJ held in this regard that '[. . .] in so far as under the EEC Treaty the Community has assumed the powers previously exercised by Member States in the area governed by the General Agreement, the provisions of that agreement have the effect of binding the Community': *International Fruit Company v. Produktschap voor Gruenten en Fruit*, Joined Cases 21–24/72, [1972] ECR 1219, 1227.

[231] See the argument advanced by the European Commission in *Watson and Belmann* that '[f]ollowing its ratification by [all] the Member States, the Convention is now legally binding upon the Community': Case 118/75, [1975] ECR 1185, at 1194.

[232] *Accession of the Community to the European Convention for the Protection of Human Rights and Fundamental Freedoms*, Opinion 2/94, 28 March 1996, ECR I-1753. See also J. Kokott and F. Hoffmeister, 'Opinion 2/94, Accession of the Community to the European Convention for the Protection of Human Rights and Fundamental Freedoms', 90 *AJIL* (1996) 664.

[233] See *supra* note 219.

reconsidering this option.[234] Apparently they dislike being held accountable for acts of international organizations which they cannot fully control. If this motive can be verified it demonstrates that the indirect enforcement of human rights obligations of non-state actors by holding states liable in a 'vicarious' or 'subsidiary' fashion may prove effective.

To remain with the special case of the EU, one must also mention the possibility of bringing a human rights challenge against acts of the EC and EURATOM, and to a limited extent now also of the EU, before the ECJ. Though not originally provided for in the 1957 Treaty of Rome and never expressly included in any of the subsequent amendments, the fundamental rights challenge has been developed by the ECJ as one of the grounds for annulment,[235] thus opening up the procedural avenue of annulment actions for human rights complaints.[236] From a traditional international law perspective one could say that in such a case an international court scrutinizes the human rights performance of an international organization. Without entering into the debate about whether the European supranational organizations fit into the traditional category of international organizations,[237] one has to acknowledge that at present the fundamental rights jurisprudence of the ECJ more closely resembles the task of judicial/constitutional review of a national supreme or constitutional court than an outside human rights body assessing the human rights

---

[234] See Working Group on Incorporation of the Charter/Accession to the ECHR, Modalities and consequences of incorporation into the Treaties of the Charter of Fundamental Rights and accession of the Community/Union to the ECHR, CONV 116/02, WG II 1, Brussels, 18 June 2002, at 21, available at http://register.consilium.eu.int/pdf/en/02/cv00/00116en2.pdf. Meanwhile the Draft EU Constitution provides in Art 7 para. 2 first sentence that 'The Union shall seek accession to the European Convention for the Protection of Human Rights and Fundamental Freedoms', Draft Treaty establishing a Constitution for Europe, Brussels, 18 July 2003, CONV 850/03, available at http://european-convention.eu.int/docs/Treaty/cv00850.en03.pdf.

[235] According to Art 230 (ex 173) EC Treaty, the ECJ is competent to annul any 'act' of the EC institutions if its adoption constituted an 'infringement of the treaty or any rule of law relating to its application'.

[236] The early leading cases are Case 29/69, *Stauder v. City of Ulm* [1969] ECR 419; Case 11/70, *Internationale Handelsgesellschaft v. Einfuhr- und Vorratsstelle für Getreide und Futtermittel* [1970] ECR 1125; Case 4/73, *Nold v. Commission* [1974] ECR 491; Case 44/79, *Hauer v. Rheinland-Pfalz* [1979] ECR 3727. This judicial approach was 'codified' in Art 6(2) (ex F(2)) EU Treaty: 'The Union shall respect fundamental rights, as guaranteed by the European Convention for the Protection of Human Rights and Fundamental Freedoms signed in Rome on 4 November 1950 and as they result from the constitutional traditions common to the Member States, as general principles of Community law'.

See also B. De Witte, 'The Past and Future Role of the European Court of Justice in the Protection of Human Rights', in Philip Alston (ed), *The EU and Human Rights* (1999) 883; Antonio Cassese/Andrew Clapham/Joseph Weiler (eds), *European Union: The Human Rights Challenge* (1991); M. Dauses, 'The Protection of Fundamental Rights in the Community Legal Order' (1985) 10 *European Law Rev.* 398; J. Weiler and N. Lockhart, ' "Taking Rights Seriously" Seriously: The European Court and its Fundamental Rights Jurisprudence', 32 *CMLRev.* (1995) 51 and 579; N. Neuwahl and A. Rosas (eds), *The European Union and Human Rights* (1995).

[237] Since its 1964 landmark case *Costa v. ENEL*, Case 6/64 [1964] ECR 585, the ECJ asserted that the EC stands for a 'new autonomous legal order'.

conformity of an international organization. Apart from such doctrinal difficulties with the possibility of generalizing from the EU example one has to recognize that the fundamental rights protection within the EU legal order is unique and has not (yet) been followed by other international organizations.

It is unclear whether the potential for human rights scrutiny of the acts of international organizations can be extended to other non-state actors, such as TNCs or NGOs. On the international level there is a definite lack of procedures and/or institutions available for this task. The question is whether it is still convincing to attribute this accountability gap to the lack of international legal personality of these non-state actors. International law provides many examples where non-state actors, particularly TNCs, have direct access to international dispute-settlement procedures and where they are considered to enjoy rights directly under international law.[238] TNCs appear as plaintiffs against states in various *ad hoc* and institutionalized arbitration systems, such as that under the ICSID Convention.[239] One could thus argue that they should have not only rights but also obligations. If one remains with the ICSID Convention as a point of reference, one can see that the reciprocal element of direct obligations is already included there. The investors as non-state parties may not only institute arbitration, they may also be sued before an ICSID panel. Thus, one might argue that it would be a progressive next step to establish judicial or quasi-judicial forums competent to hear human rights complaints against TNCs. The problem in the human rights field is, of course, that we would be dealing with complaints by non-state actors, the victims of human rights violations, against other non-state actors: private actors against private actors. This is different from the mixed arbitration in the area of investment law. Nevertheless, the broadening of the spectrum of entities considered to be in a position to enjoy rights and obligations, including procedural standing before international dispute-settlement systems, demonstrates that human rights mechanisms for non-state actors are no longer wholly inconceivable on the international level.

It would appear, though, that such a major structural change required action by states to create such mechanisms. One would expect that states could decide to establish human rights institutions competent to deal with violations by non-state actors by treaty law. Given the reluctance of human rights bodies to extend their jurisdiction even with regard to international organizations, it appears unlikely that existing institutions would be willing to do so with regard to other non-state actors. However, one should not underestimate the possibility of a progressive case-law that may at least provide fertile ground for enlarging the circle of human rights obligees. It is perfectly possible that human rights institutions may become more assertive in

---

[238] Mixed arbitration is evidence that TNCs may have direct access to dispute settlement on the international level. See Peter Malanczuk, *Akehurst's Modern Introduction to International Law* (1997) 101.

[239] Convention on the Settlement of Disputes between States and Nationals of Other States, 18 March 1965, reprinted in 4 ILM (1965) 532. See Christoph C. Schreuer, *The ICSID Convention: A Commentary* (2001).

the exercise of their jurisdiction. While at present one could hardly conceive of, for example, the UN Human Rights Committee entertaining a communication complaining of TNC or NGO behaviour,[240] there are already indications in the current practice of adopting General Comments on provisions of the ICCPR and the ICESCR by the two Committees that they are willing to express their view on the human rights conformity of non-state behaviour. A pertinent example can be found in General Comment No. 8 on economic sanctions and respect for economic, social, and cultural rights[241] of the UN Committee on Economic, Social, and Cultural Rights. In this Comment the Committee, on the one hand, carefully stated that it did not in any way call into question the necessity for the imposition of sanctions in appropriate cases in accordance with Chapter VII of the UN Charter; on the other hand, it went on to assert that the Charter's human rights provisions 'must still be considered to be fully applicable in such cases'.[242] Thus, it did—though only incidentally—pronounce on the human rights obligations of an international organization, the UN. In its General Comment No. 14 on the right to the highest attainable standard of health[243] the CESCR also went beyond reaffirming an indirect human rights obligation on states to ensure that non-state actors do not violate human rights. It broadly asserted that '[w]hile only States are parties to the Covenant and thus ultimately accountable for compliance with it, all members of society—individuals, including health professionals, families, local communities, intergovernmental and non-governmental organizations, civil society organizations, as well as the private business sector—have responsibilities regarding the realization of the right to health'.[244] Similarly, the UN Human Rights Commission has indicated its willingness to consider non-state human rights violations under the 1235 and 1503 procedures.[245] The examples of the ILO and OECD supervision mechanisms[246] may also be worth considering. Although both codes are also legally non-binding, they provide for standardized reporting obligations and for systematic periodic review by an independent body.

---

[240] This is suggested by UN Sub-Commission on the Promotion and Protection of Human Rights, Sessional working group on the working methods and activities of transnational corporations, Transnational Corporations and Other Business Enterprises, E/CN.4/Sub.2/2002/WG.2/WP.1/Add. 1, 24 May 2002, 26, as the 'creation of additional reporting requirements by States' which would 'request States to include reports about the compliance of business enterprises' or even the power 'to receive [individual] communications regarding States that have failed to take effective action in response to businesses that have violated the respective treaties'.

[241] UN Committee on Economic, Social, and Cultural Rights, General Comment No. 8: 'The relationship between economic sanctions and respect for economic, social and cultural rights', 5 December 1997, E/C.12/1997/8.   [242] Ibid., para. 1.

[243] UN Committee on Economic, Social, and Cultural Rights, General Comment No. 14: 'The right to the highest attainable standard of health', 11 August 2000, U.N. Doc. E/C.12/2000/4.

[244] Ibid., para. 42.

[245] At least with regard to irregular armed groups and drug traffickers. See U.N. Doc. E/CN.4/1990/ SR.54.   [246] See *supra* notes 90 and 91.

On the EU level, the plans of the European Parliament go even further. It has recommended that a 'code of conduct for European Multinationals'[247] should comprise the establishment of a European Monitoring Platform. While no legislative action has been taken yet, the European Parliament decided to set up its own monitoring mechanism comprising public hearings with TNC representatives 'in order to discuss specific cases, of both good and bad conduct'.[248]

Another potential for a truly international human rights scrutiny of non-state actors may lie in the development of international criminal procedures. The example of the Nuremberg Tribunal already shows that it is not only individuals whose activities may be investigated, but also corporations. There was also some debate about including a provision enabling the new ICC to exercise criminal jurisdiction over legal persons.[249] Although no such provision was eventually included in the Rome Statute, it demonstrates that there is potential for corporate criminal responsibility for human rights violations before international institutions.

If even criminal responsibility under international law is no longer wholly excluded for non-state actors this demonstrates that there is a clear potential for direct human rights accountability under international mechanisms to be created if the necessary political will exists. Though the formation of such political will may be a formidable task, the important point is that it should be no longer possible to object to it on the basis of theoretical conceptions about the structure of international law. To put it differently and more simply: as long as states do not want non-state actors to be directly accountable for human rights violations, they will not become accountable. When states want them to become accountable, they can achieve this by establishing the required institutions and procedures.

C. Direct Human Rights Accountability Before National Courts

We have seen that national courts play an increasingly important role in forcing non-state actors to respect human rights standards. Of course, one has to differentiate between the various types of non-state actors. Domestic courts generally lack jurisdiction over international organizations. Whether as a result of constituent treaties, headquarters agreements, or customary international law, courts in virtually all countries respect the functional—and as a matter of practice largely

---

[247] EP Resolution *supra* note 50.

[248] Ibid., para. 20. Such hearings took place in October 2001 concerning European oil companies in Burma. See De Schutter, *supra* note 51.

[249] Cf. Art 23 para. 5 Draft Statute of the International Criminal Court, A/CONF.183/2/Add.1 (1998). See Andrew Clapham, 'The Question of Jurisdiction Under International Criminal Law Over Legal Persons: Lessons from the Rome Conference on an International Criminal Court', in Menno T. Kamminga and Saman Zia-Ziarifi (eds), *Liability of Multinational Corporations Under International Law* (2000) 139. See also Theodor Meron, 'Is International Law Moving Towards Criminalization?', 9 *EJIL* (1998) 18, at 19.

absolute—immunity of international organizations.[250] There is no noticeable trend yet that, in the aftermath of the *Pinochet* decisions,[251] the jurisdictional immunity of international organizations would be narrowed by carving out a *jus cogens* or human rights exception, although that may be an option. Even where plaintiffs have asserted claims phrased as human rights violations national courts have not pierced the immunity shield of international organizations.[252]

The role of national courts *vis-à-vis* TNCs and NGOs is quite different. These non-state actors do not enjoy any privileged standing. As legal persons constituted under the laws of a particular state, or in the case of TNCs and international NGOs frequently under the laws of a number of states, they are subject to the law and jurisdiction of (all) these states. The 'only' jurisdictional problems that may arise are those stemming from the extraterritoriality issue often involved.[253] In this context the open questions are mainly: whether national courts may lawfully (from an international law perspective) extend their jurisdiction over foreign non-state entities; whether they may hold non-state actors which are clearly subject to their jurisdiction liable for acts of other non-state actors, such as foreign subsidiaries or foreign parent companies; and whether (probably least controversially) they may extend their jurisdiction over their own non-state entities for activities abroad. Of course, this entails some very precarious issues and it will be difficult to find the right balance in each case. To the critics of extraterritorial human rights litigation this legal tool sometimes amounts to 'legalized coercion' by putting pressure upon domestic subsidiaries (or parents) of TNCs. By this type of litigation, foreign parents may be compelled to act or refrain from acting in a particular way. Similarly pressure may lie upon domestic parent companies in order to force foreign subsidiaries to behave in a certain way.

The currently booming transnational tort litigation in the US and elsewhere displays remarkable parallels to the 'vicarious liability' concept pursued before

---

[250] See August Reinisch, *International Organizations Before National Courts* (2000). See also Karel Wellens, *Remedies against International Organizations* (2002).

[251] See Andrea Bianchi, 'Immunity Versus Human Rights: The Pinochet Case', 10 *EJIL* (1999) 237; Jürgen Bröhmer, 'Diplomatic Immunity, Head of State Immunity, State Immunity: Misconceptions of a Notorious Human Rights Violator, Case Note concerning the Decision of the House of Lords, 9 December 1998', 12 *Leiden Journal of International Law* (1999) 361; Curtis A. Bradley and Jack L. Goldsmith, 'Pinochet and International Human Rights Litigation', 97 *Michigan Law Review* (1999) 2129; Ruth Wedgwood, 'International Criminal Law and Augusto Pinochet', 40 *Virginia Journal of International Law* (2000) 829.

[252] In *Abdi Hosh Askir v. Boutros Boutros-Ghali, Joseph E. Connor, et al.*, 933 F.Supp. 368 (S.D.N.Y. 1996) plaintiff tried to recover damages for unauthorized and unlawful possession of his property in Somalia, making a quasi-expropriation claim, and thereby implicitly challenged the legality of the UN's peace-keeping activities. The court, however, dismissed the case for lack of jurisdiction because the defendant organization enjoyed immunity from suit. See Reinisch, *supra* note 250, at 200 and 206. See also Michael Singer, 'Jurisdictional Immunities of International Organizations: Human Rights and Functional Necessity Concerns', 36 *Virginia Journal of International Law* (1995) 53.

[253] See *supra* text starting at note 93.

various human rights bodies.[254] But these national court decisions may also provide a fertile ground for the growing acceptance of direct human rights obligations on non-state actors.[255]

Finally, and here the discussion of extraterritoriality in pursuit of human rights completes the circle to the re-emergence of codes of conduct for the same purpose, this type of direct accountability before national courts appears to be the most efficient legal tool in securing human rights *vis-à-vis* corporate activities. The reason for this success can probably be found in the fact that the specific characteristics of human rights litigation in common law countries have effectively incorporated the economic arguments in favour of human rights compliance into legal ones. With the cost of the negative publicity surrounding such high-profile cases, and the threat of punitive damages at the end of an already very damaging process, TNCs have realized that respecting human rights makes good business sense. When courts no longer accept the TNC argument that human rights are 'none of their business', this will become costly. It is thus not surprising that prudent corporations make provisions for this eventuality by adopting their own codes of conduct in order to forestall any cases of potential liability. With all the problems of supervision and enforcement surrounding purely voluntary codes, the ultimate threat of costly legal liability remains a valuable counterpart to them.

---

[254] See *supra* text starting at note 209.

[255] Cf. *Kadic v. Karadzic*, 70 F.3d 232, 239 (2d Cir. 1995): 'We do not agree that the law of nations, as understood in the modern era, confines its reach to state action. Instead, we hold that certain forms of conduct violate the law of nations whether undertaken by those acting under the auspices of a state or only as private individuals.'

Part Two

Non-Governmental Organizations and International Organizations as Non-State Actors

3

The Evolving Status of NGOs under International Law: A Threat to the Inter-State System?

MENNO T. KAMMINGA*

1. INTRODUCTION

Non-governmental organizations (NGOs) appear to be subjected to increasing criticism. Unlike comments made in the past, the criticism is now coming from sources that deserve to be taken seriously.

In 1996 Judge Gilbert Guillaume, the then President of the International Court of Justice, took the unusual step of publicly criticizing the role played by NGOs, in the context of the Court's advisory opinion on the legality of nuclear weapons. In an individual opinion, he expressed his unease about the role played by the International Association of Lawyers against Nuclear Arms (IALANA) and other groups bringing pressure to bear on the Assemblies of the United Nations and the World Health Organization in order to induce them to refer a request for an advisory opinion to the Court. He also criticized these groups for organizing letter-writing campaigns aimed at the judges of the Court.[1] He posed the question whether under such circumstances the requests for opinions emanating from the Assemblies could still be regarded as coming from the bodies that had adopted them or whether the Court should not have dismissed them as inadmissible. He expressed the hope 'that Governments and inter-governmental institutions [would] still retain sufficient independence of decision to resist the powerful pressure groups which besiege them today with the support of the mass communication media'.[2]

* This is an updated version of an article that appeared in G. Kreijen *et al.* (eds.), *State, Sovereignty, and International Governance* (2002) 387–406. The author gratefully acknowledges the research assistance provided by Tania van Dijk.
[1] In his dissenting opinion, Judge Weeramantry reported that the Court had received well over three million signatures from NGOs and individuals in connection with this case: The Legality of the Threat or Use of Nuclear Weapons, advisory opinion [1996] ICJ Rep. at 216, dissenting opinion of Judge Weeramantry, text accompanying n. 3. [2] Ibid., individual opinion of Judge Guillaume, para. 2.

Serge Sur, Professor at the University of Paris II, expressed similar concern at the 'excessive' role played by NGOs at the Rome Conference which in 1998 adopted the Statute of the International Criminal Court. He pointed out that at the Conference NGO representatives were true partners in the negotiations, either indirectly by putting pressure on delegations or directly by being members of governmental delegations and being allowed to speak on their behalf. According to Professor Sur, in Rome States in effect abandoned their monopoly on inter-State negotiations.[3] The influence exerted by NGOs is also reflected in the Statute of the International Criminal Court itself. Under Article 15(2), the Court's Prosecutor may 'seek additional information from States, organs of the United Nations, inter-governmental or non-governmental organizations, or other reliable sources that he or she deems appropriate'. Professor Sur expressed his astonishment at the fact that NGOs are thereby put on the same level as states and inter-governmental organizations. He wondered whether, by allowing NGOs to put pressure on the International Criminal Court in this way, the Court does not risk being reduced to a People's Tribunal.[4]

The journal *The Economist* recently asked the question whether citizens' groups really are the first steps towards an 'international civil society' or whether they represent a dangerous shift of power to unelected and unaccountable special-interest groups. The journal posed this question in direct response to the mayhem caused by NGOs at the World Trade Organization summit meeting in Seattle in 1999. But it also pointed to the important role played by NGOs in pushing through the climate convention at the Earth Summit in Rio de Janeiro in 1992, and the convention banning landmines in 1997, and in sinking the Multilateral Agreement on Investment (MAI) in 1998.[5]

What these critics seem to be saying is: that the influence of NGOs on the international plane has been growing out of all proportion; that special interest groups cannot be expected to balance all relevant interests; that only States can be relied upon to do so; that while it may be right for pressure groups to exercise their influence within States they should not be allowed to do so on the international plane; and that unlike States (democratic States that is) NGOs are accountable to no one. In sum, the fear expressed by these observers is that NGOs have become so effective that they are beginning to present a threat to the Westphalian inter-State system.

While some of these complaints belong to the realm of political science, some of the points made by Guillaume and Sur appear to be suitable for legal scrutiny. Is it true, as Judge Guillaume seems to suggest, that NGOs are now in a position to manipulate the International Court of Justice for their own ends? Is it correct, as Professor Sur seems to imply, that international standard-setting conferences these days are at the mercy of NGOs? This raises familiar but rarely systematically addressed questions about the status of NGOs in international law. Brownlie lists

---

[3] S. Sur, 'Vers une Cour pénale internationale: la Convention de Rome entre les ONG et le Conseil de sécurité' (1999) 103 *RGDIP* 29 at 35–6. [4] Sur, above n. 3, at 37–8.

[5] 'The Non-Governmental Order: Will NGOs Democratise, or Merely Disrupt, Global Governance?', *Economist*, 11 Dec. 1999, 18–19.

the following traditional indicators of legal personality in international law: capacity to make claims in respect of breaches of international law; capacity to make treaties and agreements valid on the international plane; and the enjoyment of privileges and immunities from national jurisdictions.[6] Following a slightly different subdivision, we will consider the capacity of NGOs to conclude treaties (including treaties conferring privileges and immunities), their capacity to participate in treaty-making, their capacity to bring international claims, and their capacity to incur liability under international law. But first we need to define the subject of our enquiry, for it is not at all self-evident what an NGO is.

2. WHAT IS AN NGO?

Despite the increasing importance of NGOs in international law-making and enforcement, international law does not offer an authoritative definition of a non-governmental organization. Much confusion surrounds the subject. For example, a frequently quoted article in the Encyclopedia of Public International Law suggests that the concept of NGOs may encompass multinational corporations and even national liberation movements.[7] This appears to confuse NGOs with the wider concept of non-State actors.

The only relevant treaty in this area is the European Convention on the Recognition of the Legal Personality of International Non-Governmental Organizations, adopted by the Council of Europe in 1986.[8] In spite of its promising title, the Convention does not establish a procedure for the recognition of the international legal personality of NGOs on the international plane. It merely provides that the legal personality acquired by an NGO in the State Party in which it has its statutory office shall also be recognized in the other States Parties.[9] The Convention therefore does not alter the fact that NGOs, if they have any legal status at all, have such status only under domestic law.[10] Significantly, NGOs themselves were not consulted during the drafting of this treaty. A questionnaire was distributed to NGOs in 1976, with a view to identifying any problems experienced by them.[11] But it remains unclear what problems the respondents identified and therefore precisely which

---

[6] I. Brownlie, *Principles of Public International Law* (1998) 57.

[7] H.H.-K. Rechenberg, 'Non-Governmental Organizations' in R. Bernhardt (ed.), 3 *Encyclopedia of Public International Law* (1997) 612.

[8] ETS No. 124, entered into force 1 Jan. 1991. Only 9 of the 46 Member States of the Council of Europe have become parties so far: Austria, Belgium, France, Greece, Macedonia, Portugal, Slovenia, Switzerland, and the UK.   [9] Ibid., Art. 2.

[10] N. Rodley, 'Human Rights NGOs: Rights and Obligations (Present Status and Perspectives)' in T. van Boven *et al.* (eds.), *The Legitimacy of the United Nations: Towards an Enhanced Legal Status of Non-State Actors* (1997) 45.

[11] M.O. Wiederkehr, 'La Convention européenne sur la reconnaissance de la personnalité juridique des organisations internationales non gouvernementales du 24 avril 1986' (1995) 47 *Transn'l. Ass'ns* 181.

defects the Convention was trying to remedy. The Convention's Explanatory Report refers to problems caused by activities in several countries, meetings being held in diverse places, and personnel being employed of various nationalities[12] but it is difficult to see how this would be sufficient justification for the adoption of a Convention, particularly within Western Europe.

NGOs are most easily defined by explaining what they are not. First and foremost, NGOs are private structures in the sense that they are not established or controlled by States. This distinguishes NGOs from inter-governmental organizations (IGOs).[13] Secondly, NGOs do not seek to overthrow governments by force. This distinguishes them from liberation movements and armed opposition groups. Thirdly, while NGOs may seek to change government policies they do not aim to acquire State power themselves. This distinguishes NGOs from political parties. Fourthly, while NGOs may be engaged in fund-raising and merchandizing activities they do not seek financial profit for their own sake. This distinguishes NGOs from companies. Fifthly, while some NGOs may occasionally engage in civil disobedience, they are generally law-abiding. This distinguishes NGOs from criminal organizations.[14]

Any attempt to define NGOs in positive rather than negative terms is problematic, beyond the observation that they tend to be private citizens' groups established to further certain common objectives of their members.[15] The objectives pursued by NGOs differ considerably. Examples range from groups working for the common good, such as environmental and human rights groups, to special interest groups, such as trade unions and business associations. In terms of strategies employed by NGOs, a distinction may be made between organizations engaged in advocacy or campaigning, such as Greenpeace and Human Rights Watch, and organizations engaged in relief and assistance, such as CARE and Save the Children. Some organizations, such as Oxfam, combine the two functions. In practice, there appears to be a tendency for NGOs to become more involved in advocacy. Médecins sans

[12] Explanatory Report on the European Convention on the Recognition of the Legal Personality of International Non-Governmental Organizations (1986), para. 1.

[13] There are, however, some hybrid NGOs, such as the ICRC and IUCN, that include States or State agencies among their members or as members of their governing councils. See below n. 15.

[14] On the difference between NGOs and criminal organizations see A. Schmid, 'Non-State Actors: Organized Crime, Human Rights NGOs and the United Nations' in van Boven *et al.* (eds.), above n. 10, 125. Art. 2(a) of the UN Convention against Transnational Organized Crime, adopted on 15 Nov. 2000, defines an 'organized criminal group' as 'a structured group of three or more persons, existing for a period of time and acting in concert with the aim of committing one or more serious crimes or offences established in accordance with this Convention, in order to obtain, directly or indirectly, financial or other material benefit': UN Doc. A/55/383.

[15] Even this modest description is not entirely correct. Some organizations, such as the International Union for the Conservation of Nature (IUCN), the International Committee of the Red Cross (ICRC), and the International Federation of Red Cross and Red Crescent Societies, accept governmental authorities as members of their highest bodies. Under para. 12 of ECOSOC Resolution 1996/31 on the consultative relationship between the United Nations and non-governmental organizations, these organizations are nevertheless regarded as NGOs.

Frontières, initially set up as an aid agency, after some soul-searching a few years ago decided also to engage in advocacy under certain circumstances. Even a typical aid organization such as the Red Cross Movement has been debating whether to get involved in advocacy.[16]

NGOs are usually thought of as having an international character, with members and branches in more than one country and with objectives that are not limited to one State. This is the approach underlying the European Convention on the Recognition of the Legal Personality of International Non-Governmental Organizations and ECOSOC Resolution 1296 (XLIV) of 23 May 1968 on consultative relations between the United Nations and NGOs. However, ECOSOC Resolution 1996/31 of 25 July 1996, which replaces Resolution 1296, specifically provides that consultative relations may also be established with national organizations.[17] In that case, the views of the Member State in question must first be sought before they may be admitted to consultative status.[18] ECOSOC has thereby belatedly brought its relations with NGOs in conformity with UN Charter Article 71, which provides that consultative arrangements of ECOSOC with NGOs may, where appropriate, include relations with national organizations.

It is sometimes assumed that NGOs are a recent invention, emerging after the Second World War. In fact, the history of NGOs stretches back more than 200 years, starting with associations established at the end of the eighteenth century in the United States, France, and the United Kingdom to bring an end to the slave trade. Anti-Slavery International, which is still active today, was established in the United Kingdom in 1839 as the Anti-Slavery Society. It has been suggested that the role of NGOs may be cyclical, with reductions in importance during the two World Wars and a resurgence after each of these. The role of NGOs appears to have reached new heights during the 1990s, *inter alia* because of the many new issues (environment, development, international criminal law) appearing on the international agenda on which governments require input and support from NGOs.[19]

In terms of the resources available to them the significance of NGOs is now certainly on the increase. More than 2,500 NGOs currently have consultative status with ECOSOC. But this is only one indicator. The number of domestic NGOs probably runs into the millions. NGOs have also grown considerably in size, in terms of both their membership and their budgets.

Globalization has clearly been one of the main factors contributing to this growth. NGOs engaged in campaigning have greatly benefited from the sharply increased popularity of the Internet. This has helped to undermine the governmental monopoly on information. It has also made it much easier to mobilize people across the globe in favour of or against certain causes,[20] as was demonstrated for example

---

[16] P. Nobel, 'The Role of the International Red Cross and Red Crescent Movement in Promoting Respect for Human Rights' (1993) 293 *Int'l Rev. Red Cross* 146.   [17] Above n. 15, para. 5.

[18] Ibid., para. 8.

[19] S. Charnovitz, 'Two Centuries of Participation: NGOs and International Governance' (1997) 18 *Mich. J Int'l L* 183 at 268–70.   [20] See J. Matthews, 'Power Shift' (1997) 76 *Foreign Aff.* 51.

by the scuppering of the MAI. NGOs engaged in aid and relief have benefited from the currently prevailing view that such assistance can often more effectively be distributed through private agencies. As a result, many States have re-routed their aid and relief flows to NGOs. NGOs collectively now deliver more aid than the entire United Nations system does.[21]

3. CAPACITY TO CONCLUDE TREATIES

NGOs, if they have any legal status at all, tend to enjoy such status under domestic law only. It follows that they generally have no capacity to perform legal acts on the international plane. In particular they do not have the capacity to conclude treaties with States. This distinguishes NGOs from other non-State actors, such as inter-governmental organizations and multinational corporations, which do enjoy (limited) treaty concluding capacity. There are, however, notable exceptions.

Switzerland, as a host State for numerous international organizations, both inter-governmental and non-governmental, has adopted an interesting practice of defining the international status of NGOs in agreements with them that are sometimes indistinguishable from treaties under international law. These agreements demonstrate a flexible and pragmatic approach on the part of the Swiss authorities. No doubt underlying this practice has been their desire to maintain the attractiveness of the country as a seat for international institutions.

A prime example is the headquarters agreement concluded in 1993 between Switzerland and the International Committee of the Red Cross (ICRC), an association established under Swiss law.[22] This agreement explicitly recognizes the international juridical capacity of the ICRC and grants it privileges and immunities very similar to those enjoyed by IGOs. Accordingly, it provides that the ICRC and its staff are immune from legal process and that the ICRC's premises are inviolable. It also contains provisions on the settlement of disputes by way of arbitration, with the President of the International Court of Justice appointing a chairperson if the arbitrators appointed by the two parties are unable to agree on such an appointment between themselves. The ICRC has concluded comparable agreements with more than sixty States in which its delegations are located.[23] The International Federation of Red Cross and Red Crescent Societies has concluded similar headquarters agreements with more than thirty States, including Switzerland.[24] There can be little

---

[21] L. Gordenker and T. Weiss, 'NGO Participation in the International Policy Process' (1995) 16 *Third World Q.* 543 at 554.

[22] Agreement between the International Committee of the Red Cross and the Swiss Federal Council to determine the legal status of the Committee in Switzerland, 19 Mar. 1993 (1993) 293 *Int'l Rev. of the Red Cross* 152.　　　　　　　　　　[23] ICRC Annual Report 1998, available at www.icrc.org.

[24] See P. Gautier, 'O.N.G. et personnalité internationale: à propos de l'Accord conclu le 29 novembre 1996 entre la Suisse et la Fédération internationale des Sociétés de la Croix-Rouge et du Croissant-Rouge' (1997) 30 *Revue belge de droit international* 172.

doubt that all these agreements qualify as treaties under international law.[25] There are two main reasons for the unusual facilities enjoyed by the ICRC and the Federation. First, the ICRC has been provided with special responsibilities under Articles 9 and 10 of the First, Second, and Third Geneva Conventions and under Articles 10 and 11 of the Fourth Geneva Convention. Furthermore, States Parties to the Geneva Conventions participate in the International Red Cross Conference, the highest Red Cross organ.

The special status of the Red Cross organizations has also been recognized by the UN General Assembly. The Assembly granted observer status to the ICRC in 1990[26] and to the International Federation of Red Cross Societies in 1994.[27] The ICRC and the Federation are the only NGOs enjoying this status and the General Assembly clearly intends to keep it that way. During the same session in which it granted observer status to the Federation it decided that 'the granting of observer status in the General Assembly should in the future be confined to States and to those inter-governmental organizations whose activities cover matters of interest to the Assembly'.[28]

Some other NGOs based in Switzerland at first sight appear to qualify for similar status because of their special character. However, they have benefited from considerably less privileged treatment. The International Union for the Conservation of Nature is an unusual NGO that counts sixty-eight States and ninety-two government agencies among its members. More than 80 per cent of its budget derives from governments and IGOs. Nevertheless, the agreement Switzerland concluded with the IUCN in 1986 cannot be regarded as a proper headquarters agreement: it merely covers freedom of taxation for the IUCN and its foreign staff.[29] The International Olympic Committee is an association under Swiss law.[30] It counts no States among its members. In the early 1980s, attempts were made by the IOC to have its international legal personality recognized by the Swiss authorities and even by the UN General Assembly.[31] These efforts were not successful. The Swiss Federal Council adopted a mere decree (not an agreement) noting the importance for

[25] C. Dominicé, 'La personnalité juridique internationale du CICR' in C. Swinarski (ed.), *Studies and Essays on International Law and Red Cross Principles in Honour of Jean Pictet* (1984) 663 at 668–9. In the same vein see P. Reuter, 'La personnalité juridique internationale du Comité international de la Croix-Rouge', ibid. 783 at 790–1.

[26] GA Res. 45/6 (1990). See C. Koenig, 'Observer Status for the International Committee of the Red Cross at the United Nations: A Legal Viewpoint' (1991) 280 *Int'l Rev. Red Cross* 37.

[27] GA Res. 49/2 (1994). See W. Remans, 'The Granting of Observer Status by the General Assembly of the United Nations to the International Federation of Red Cross and Red Crescent Societies' in K. Wellens (ed.), *International Law: Theory and Practice. Essays in Honour of Eric Suy* (1998) 347–62.

[28] GA Res. 49/426 (1994).

[29] R.S. Imhoof, 'La personnalité juridique et le statut des institutions de caractère international: exemples tirés de la pratique suisse' (1989) 46 *Annuaire suisse de droit international* 93 at 107–8.

[30] Art. 19 of the Olympic Charter.

[31] D.J. Ettinger, 'Comment: The Legal Status of the International Olympic Committee' (1992) 4 *Pace YB Int'l L* 108–9. Surprisingly, however, the author concludes that the Committee does have international legal status.

Switzerland of having the IOC within its borders but confirming the organization's status under Swiss rather than international law.[32]

It may be deduced that States are willing to conclude treaties on an equal footing with NGOs if this suits their interests. This occurs on an *ad hoc* basis if the NGO in question resembles an IGO by having States among its members or because it resembles a State by having State-like functions. Clearly, such agreements bind only the parties, they do not create entitlements *vis-à-vis* third States.

4. CAPACITY TO PARTICIPATE IN TREATY-MAKING

At inter-governmental conferences NGOs generally do not enjoy the capacity to participate in the drafting of international instruments. Law-making on the international plane is a privilege that tends to be reserved for States. In line with this principle, ECOSOC Resolution 1996/31, the key UN resolution on consultative relations between ECOSOC and non-governmental organizations, specifically prohibits NGOs from engaging in 'negotiations'.[33]

A major exception to this rule, however, is the role played by workers' and employers' representatives in the International Labour Organization. Unlike in other IGOs, in the ILO workers' and employers' representatives participate on an equal footing with representatives from States. Under the ILO's tripartite system, each State is represented by four delegates, of whom two are government representatives and one each represents the employers and the workers of that State. This means that at the ILO employers' and workers' representatives have the same capacity as government representatives to participate in the drafting of conventions and other international instruments adopted by the ILO. This facility has certainly enabled these organizations to leave their mark on standard-setting within that organization.[34]

It is nevertheless doubtful whether the ILO presents an attractive model for the integration of NGOs into international law-making.[35] First, under Article 3(5) of the ILO Constitution, employers' and workers' delegates are selected by the governments of the States in question. This power obviously creates possibilities for abuse because many States lack employers' and workers' organizations that are independent of the government. Under Article 3(9) of the ILO Constitution the credentials of delegates at the Conference may be challenged, but this happens very rarely.[36] Secondly, while the ILO is very welcoming to workers' and employers' organizations, it is most inaccessible to other NGOs that have an interest in its

---

[32] Unpublished decree of 8 July 1981, referred to by Imhoof, above n. 29, 104 and quoted by Ettinger, above n. 31, 103–4.

[33] 'In recognition of the intergovernmental nature of the conference and its preparatory process, active participation of non-governmental organizations therein, while welcome, does not entail a negotiating role': ECOSOC Res. 1996/31, para. 50.   [34] Charnovitz, above n. 19, 216–19.

[35] See V. Leary, 'The ILO: A Model for Non-State Participation?' in van Boven *et al.* (eds.), above n. 10, 60.   [36] Leary, above n. 35, 71.

activities, such as human rights organizations.[37] Interestingly, it is not so much the government representatives at the ILO that resist participation from NGOs but the workers and the employers, for the apparent reason that broadening access to the ILO might undermine their own privileged position. As a result, the ILO runs the risk of becoming a rather inward-looking organization that excludes perspectives from the non-corporate world.

In spite of their limited formal status at IGO meetings, in practice NGOs often play a key role in creating awareness of the need to adopt international instruments and even in the drafting of such instruments. This is not a new development. The role of NGOs in international standard-setting stretches back to the role of the Anti-Slavery Society and other anti-slavery organizations in the nineteenth century in pressing for the adoption of treaties for the suppression of the slave trade.[38] But it seems fair to say that this role has continuously increased since the Second World War. It is no exaggeration to suggest that some of the most important international legal instruments of recent years would not have seen the light without the input of NGOs. This role may range from a mere stimulating role to the participation in drafting exercises as full participants with a right to make proposals on an equal footing with States. As the subject matter of multilateral treaties is becoming more and more complex, States depend on NGOs to provide information and expertise, which they or the Secretariats of IGOs may not have readily available themselves. States may also use NGOs to try out certain ideas that they are not yet prepared to defend themselves, or they may employ NGOs to help break a deadlock. NGO input into the drafting of international instruments has been especially crucial in the fields of human rights,[39] the environment,[40] and, more recently, disarmament. In furthering their international law-making objectives, NGOs have developed three broad strategies that may be labelled as high level approaches, campaigning, and coalition building. Combinations of these strategies have become routine features at international standard-setting conferences.

The International Commission of Jurists (ICJ), a small Geneva-based NGO consisting of senior judges and lawyers from different parts of the world, is a good example of an organization that has very effectively employed high-level approaches aimed directly at State representatives. The adoption in 1981 of the African Charter on Human and Peoples' Rights can clearly be attributed to the ICJ.[41] Seminars for African jurists convened by the ICJ in Lagos in 1961 and in Dakar in 1977

---

[37] I speak from my own experience as a representative of Amnesty International at International Labour Conferences. [38] Charnovitz, above n. 19, 191–2.

[39] See, generally, T. van Boven, 'The Role of Non-Governmental Organizations in International Human Rights Standard-Setting: A Prerequisite of Democracy' (1990) 20 *Cal. W Int'l LJ* 207; and C. Chinkin, 'The Role of Non-Governmental Organisations in Standard Setting, Monitoring and Implementation of Human Rights' in J.J. Norton, M. Andreas, and M. Footer (eds.), *The Changing World of International Law in the Twenty-First Century: A Tribute to the Late Kenneth R. Simmons* (1998) 51.

[40] See, generally, D. Tarlock, 'The Role of Non-Governmental Organizations in the Development of International Environmental Law' (1992) 10 *Chi.-Kent L. Rev.* 61.

[41] African Charter on Human and Peoples' Rights, Nairobi, 1981, 21 ILM 58 (1982).

recommended the creation of an African convention on human rights. Approaches to African heads of State by senior participants of the latter seminar resulted in a decision by these heads of State to appoint a drafting committee to prepare an African human rights instrument. Keba Mbaye, President of Senegal's Supreme Court and President of the ICJ, was appointed as its rapporteur.[42]

A different convention, the European Convention for the Prevention of Torture, adopted in 1987, was a joint initiative of the ICJ and another NGO, the Swiss Committee against Torture.[43] The idea behind this Convention—routine visits to places of detention by independent international observers in order to prevent the occurrence of torture—was conceived by Jean-Jacques Gautier, the President of the Swiss Committee. The text of the Convention adopted by the Council of Europe was closely based on a draft prepared at the Council of Europe's request by the ICJ and the Swiss Committee.[44]

The 'elitist' strategy followed by the ICJ was highly effective in these two instances because that was all that was required to convince key government representatives of the need to adopt these new international instruments. Such a strategy would probably have been insufficient to secure the adoption of a strong UN Convention against Torture in 1984.[45] The role of Amnesty International and the International Commission of Jurists in the negotiations themselves was clearly important.[46] However, because of its sensitive subject matter, it is unlikely that a decent Convention would have been adopted without the simultaneous campaigning of Amnesty International sections around the world. They drew attention to the widespread character and brutal nature of torture and the need recognize torture as a crime under international law.

Partly overlapping with the drafting of the Convention against Torture was the drafting of the UN Convention on the Rights of the Child.[47] Apparently because governments regarded its subject matter as less sensitive, the drafting of this Convention permitted more room for input by NGOs. In order to maximize their impact, NGOs interested in this Convention adopted a technique that has since become a virtual tradition at international standard-setting exercises: the creation of an NGO coalition. In 1983, twenty-three NGOs established the Informal NGO

---

[42] See H. Tolley, 'Popular Sovereignty and International Law: ICJ Strategies for Human Rights Standard Setting' (1989) 11 *HRQ* 561 at 578–9; and N. MacDermot, 'Le rôle des organisations non gouvernementales dans l'élaboration des normes relatives aux droits de l'homme' (1992) 90/1 *Bull. des droits de l'homme* 44 at 44–5.

[43] European Convention for the Prevention of Torture and Inhuman or Degrading Treatment or Punishment, Strasbourg, (1987) 27 ILM 1152 (1988).

[44] See above n. 42, Tolley, 571–2; and MacDermot, 46.

[45] UN Convention against Torture and Other Cruel, Inhuman or Degrading Treatment or Punishment, New York, 1984, 23 ILM 1027 (1984).

[46] On the role played by Amnesty International see V. Leary, 'A New Role for Non-Governmental Organizations in Human Rights: A Case Study of Non-Governmental Participation in the Development of International Norms on Torture' in A. Cassese (ed.), *UN Law/Fundamental Rights* (1979) 197–206.

[47] Convention on the Rights of the Child, 1989, 18 ILM 1448 (1989).

Ad Hoc Group on the Drafting of the Convention of the Rights of the Child.[48] The Group developed detailed textual proposals that were laid down in reports which were highly influential during the negotiations. Governments frequently turned to the Group for drafting assistance on difficult aspects of the text. It has been suggested that the imprint of the NGO Group can be found in almost every provision of the Convention.[49] Following the adoption of the Convention, the Group reconstituted itself into the NGO Group for the Convention on the Rights of the Child. This new Group has a more formal structure with several thematic subgroups. Its activities include various types of assistance to the Committee on the Rights of the Child established under the Convention to monitor its implementation.[50]

In the environmental field, NGOs played a crucial role in the adoption of the 1992 Framework Convention on Climate Change.[51] During the drafting of this Convention in Rio de Janeiro and also at subsequent follow-up meetings, NGOs contributed very effectively by using their expertise in direct contacts with delegates and by addressing the plenary session from the floor.[52] Environmental NGOs that were particularly involved in this forum include the World Wildlife Fund (WWF), Greenpeace, the Environmental Defence Fund, the Sierra Club, Ozone Action, and the WorldWatch Institute.[53] Some of these organizations co-ordinated their positions in an umbrella organization called Climate Action Network, currently encompassing more than 160 NGOs. An equally important role, however, is being played by business organizations such as the Climate Council, the Global Climate Coalition, and the World Business Council for Sustainable Development. Despite their promising names, these are umbrella organizations for fossil fuel extractors and related industries.[54]

Another example of a highly successful NGO coalition is the International Campaign to Ban Landmines (ICBL). The ICBL was created in 1992 by six NGOs: Handicap International, Human Rights Watch, Medico International, Mines Advisory Group, Physicians for Human Rights, and the Vietnam Veterans of America Foundation.[55] It currently has more than 1,200 member organizations. Until the ICBL began its activities, it was little known that anti-personnel mines kill or maim hundreds of innocent civilians, especially children, every week. The ICBL managed to put the phenomenon on the international map as a global crisis requiring a radical but simple response: a comprehensive ban on landmines.

---

[48] C. Price Cohen, 'The Role of Nongovernmental Organizations in the Drafting of the Convention on the Rights of the Child' (1990) 12 *HRQ* 137.   [49] Price Cohen, above n. 48, 142.

[50] C. Price Cohen, 'The United Nations Convention on the Rights of the Child: Involvement of NGOs' in van Boven *et al.* (eds.), above n. 10, 181–4.

[51] Framework Convention on Climate Change, New York, 1992 31 ILM 849 (1992).

[52] C. Giorgetti, 'The Role of Nongovernmental Organizations in the Climate Change Negotiations' (1998) 9 *Colo. J Int'l Envtl. L & Pol'cy* 115 at 126.   [53] Giorgetti, above n. 52, 127.

[54] Ibid., 130–3.

[55] J. Williams and S. Goose, 'The International Campaign to Ban Landmines' in M. Cameron *et al.* (eds.), *To Walk Without Fear: The Global Movement to Ban Landmines* (1998) 20 at 22; R. Price, 'Reversing the Gun Sights: Transnational Civil Society Targets Landmines' (1998) 52 *Int'l. Org.* 613 at 620.

No doubt the horrific character of its message and the simplicity of the proposed remedy were essential elements of the Campaign's success. A Convention providing for a total ban on the use, stockpiling, production, and transfer of anti-personnel mines was duly adopted in 1997 and entered into force in 1999.[56] The Convention was arrived at in a highly innovative way. The usual method of international standard-setting employs consensus as the method of decision-making and tends to be dominated by the great powers. In 1996, Canada took the lead in adopting a new approach involving 'like-minded States' and working closely with NGOs.[57] This method of avoiding the slowest-boat rule obviously allows considerably more scope for input by NGOs.[58]

The 'like-minded States' approach to standard-setting was also adopted at the 1998 Rome Conference on the Statute of an International Criminal Court.[59] The Like Minded Group included over sixty States that were committed to a strong Court. They worked closely with the NGO Coalition for an International Criminal Court.[60] The NGO Coalition, founded in 1995, eventually grew to a movement of more than 800 organizations, of which Amnesty International, Human Rights Watch, the Lawyers Committee for Human Rights, and the Women's Caucus for Gender Justice in the ICC were among the most active, not only in Rome but also during the three years of preparations for this Conference.[61] During the five weeks of the Rome Conference, the Coalition and its individual member organizations prepared detailed briefing papers, divided into thirteen working groups on the 128 Articles of the Statute, held regular meetings with governments and weekly meetings with the Conference Chair, provided expert advice and translations to governments, convened regional and sectoral caucuses, provided the Conference's only two daily newspapers, and organized media briefings.[62] The role played by NGOs in support of a strong International Criminal Court was therefore of a more sophisticated nature than the role of NGOs during the negotiations of the Landmines Convention. Unlike the Landmines Convention, the Rome Statute is a highly complicated legal instrument that required considerable technical drafting skills that many governmental delegates did not possess. Rome therefore represented yet another milestone in the contribution of NGOs to international law-making.

An analysis of the text of these conventions does not reveal any apparent resentment on the part of States of the role played by NGOs in the adoption of these

---

[56] Convention on the Prohibition of the Use, Stockpiling, Production, and Transfer of Anti-Personnel Mines and on their Destruction, Oslo, 1997, 36 ILM 1507.

[57] K. Anderson, 'The Ottawa Convention Banning Landmines, the Role of International Non-governmental Organizations and the Idea of International Civil Society' (2000) 11 *EJIL* 91–120, at 107.

[58] See M. Dolan and C. Hunt, 'Negotiating in the Ottawa Process: The New Multilateralism' in Cameron *et al.* (eds.), above n. 55, 392.

[59] Statute of the International Criminal Court, Rome, 17 July 1998 (1998) 37 ILM 999.

[60] P. Kirsch, 'Introduction' in H. von Hebel *et al.* (eds.), *Reflections on the International Criminal Court* (1999) 1 at 3.

[61] W. Pace, 'The Relationship between the International Criminal Court and Non-Governmental Organizations' in ibid., 200–5.   [62] Ibid.

instruments. On the contrary, in an apparent acknowledgement of the importance of NGO input, the conventions often provide NGOs with a formal role in their implementation and follow-up. The Convention on the Rights of the Child provides that its supervisory body may invite 'competent bodies' to provide expert advice on the implementation of the Convention.[63] The Climate Convention contains a remarkably liberal admissions policy for follow-up conferences. It provides that any non-governmental body 'which is qualified in matters covered by the Convention, and which has informed the secretariat of its wish to be represented at a session of the Conference of the Parties as an observer, may be so admitted unless at least one-third of the Parties present object'.[64] The Landmines Convention provides that NGOs may be invited to attend meetings of the States Parties and Review Conferences.[65] The Statute of the International Criminal Court provides that the Prosecutor may seek additional information, *inter alia* from NGOs.[66]

5. CAPACITY TO BRING INTERNATIONAL CLAIMS

NGOs do not generally have legal capacity to bring international claims against States alleging a breach of obligations owed to them. The first reason for this is of course that States tend not to owe any international legal obligations at all to NGOs. But even if such obligations exist, they cannot usually be enforced on the international plane. For example, the headquarters agreement concluded in 1947 between the United Nations and the United States provides that the authorities of the United States 'shall not impose any impediments to transit to or from headquarters district of . . . representatives of . . . non-governmental organizations recognized by the United Nations for the purpose of consultation under Article 71 of the Charter'.[67] However, in case of non-compliance on the part of the United States (something which has occurred from time to time[68]) the agreement does not enable NGOs to take legal action against the USA on the international plane.

There are nevertheless some instances in which States have accepted international obligations towards NGOs that are enforceable in this way. As we saw above, representatives of the ICRC enjoy significant privileges and immunities on a par with representatives of IGOs, which may be enforced through international arbitration.[69] Furthermore, under Article 34 of the European Convention on Human Rights NGOs have a right to lodge petitions to the European Court of Human Rights claiming to

---

[63] Art. 45(a), UN Convention on the Rights of the Child.

[64] Art. 7(6), UN Framework Convention on Climate Change.

[65] Arts. 11(4) and 12(3), Landmines Convention.

[66] Art. 15(2), Rome Statute of the International Criminal Court.

[67] S. 11, Agreement between the United Nations and the United States of America regarding the Headquarters of the United Nations, Lake Success, 26 June 1947, 147 UNTS 11 at 20.

[68] H. Schermers and N. Blokker, *International Institutional Law* (1995) 242.

[69] Text accompanying n. 22 above.

be victims of violations of the rights set forth in the Convention. A wide range of associations has submitted applications under this provision.[70]

Moreover, some international mechanisms of a semi-judicial nature permit NGOs to lodge complaints even if they themselves have not been victims of a violation. Accordingly, under the ILO's freedom of association procedure, complaints may be lodged not only by workers' or employers' organizations directly interested, but also by any international workers' or employers' organization having consultative status with the ILO. Complaints are considered by the Committee on Freedom of Association, which reports to the ILO's Governing Body.[71]

Comparable to this mechanism is the procedure established by the Additional Protocol to the European Social Charter Providing for a System of Collective Complaints. Pursuant to this Protocol, NGOs are entitled to bring 'complaints alleging unsatisfactory application of the Charter'.[72] Such complaints are considered by a Committee of Independent Experts, which may draw up a report for the Council of Europe's Committee of Ministers. The right to lodge such complaints is restricted to employers' and workers' organizations and certain other NGOs that have been put on a special list. The first complaint after the entry into force of the Protocol, alleging child labour in Portugal, was filed by the International Commission of Jurists. A more liberal regime creating access for a wider range of NGOs is offered by the American Convention on Human Rights. Under its Article 44, an NGO 'legally recognised in one or more Member States of the organisation, may lodge petitions with the [Inter-American Commission on Human Rights] containing denunciations or complaints of violation of this Convention by a State Party'.

Under some international mechanisms NGOs enjoy the possibility of third-party intervention. This does not amount to the ability to bring international claims, but it may offer important possibilities for influencing the development of international law.[73] Accordingly, while NGOs cannot be parties to contentious proceedings before the International Court of Justice, under Article 66 of the Court's Statute they may receive permission to submit relevant information to the Court in connection with requests for advisory opinions. In practice, however, the Court has been extremely reluctant to permit NGOs to take advantage of this facility.[74] The International League for Human Rights in 1950 received such permission in connection with the South-West Africa advisory proceedings but the League's subsequent submissions were declared inadmissible by the Court for various procedural reasons.[75]

---

[70] See P. van Dijk and G. van Hoof, *Theory and Practice of the European Convention on Human Rights* (3rd ed., 1998) 46.   [71] See the website of the ILO: www.ilo.org.

[72] Art. 1, Additional Protocol to the European Social Charter Providing for a System of Collective Complaints, 9 Nov. 1995 (1995) 34 ILM 1453.

[73] See D. Shelton, 'The Participation of Nongovernmental Organizations in International Judicial Proceedings' (1994) 88 *AJIL* 611.   [74] Ibid., 619–28.

[75] Roger S. Clark, 'The International League for Human Rights and South West Africa 1947–1957: The Human Rights NGO as Catalyst in the International Legal Process' (1981) 3 *HRQ* 101 at 116–21.

Regional human rights courts have been more forthcoming.[76] Under Article 36(2) of the European Convention on Human Rights (until recently Article 36(2) of the Rules of Court) the President of the European Court of Human Rights may invite 'any person concerned who is not the applicant to submit written comments or take part in hearings'. *Amicus curiae* briefs have so far been filed in dozens of cases, mostly by NGOs based in the United Kingdom, such as Amnesty International, Article 19, INTERIGHTS, and Justice. The information and arguments included in these briefs usually play an important role in the Court's proceedings.[77] NGOs may also submit *amicus curiae* briefs to the Inter-American Court of Human Rights both in contentious cases and with regard to requests for advisory opinions. The Inter-American Court has generally been more welcoming towards NGOs than has the European Court.[78]

Finally, and lowest in the legal hierarchy but not necessary lowest in terms of practical importance, NGOs often also play an essential role in more informal ways, by bringing relevant information to the attention of (members of) international monitoring bodies.[79] This possibility may be specifically provided for in the relevant treaty or resolution, or it may be contained in the monitoring body's rules of procedure, or it may not be based on any formal rule at all.

6. LIABILITY UNDER INTERNATIONAL LAW

Since NGOs, even international NGOs, tend to be established merely under domestic law, they can generally be held accountable only under domestic law. Accordingly, NGOs may be sued under domestic law for libel or for damage caused, for example by having published erroneous reports. Moreover, organizations such as Greenpeace are frequently sued for their acts of civil disobedience.

Can an NGO also be held liable under international law if it acts contrary to an international obligation incumbent upon it? This raises the question whether international law imposes any obligations at all on NGOs.

The Declaration on the Right and Responsibility of Individuals, Groups, and Organs of Society to Promote and Protect Universally Recognized Human Rights and Fundamental Freedoms, adopted by the UN General Assembly in 1999, in spite

---

[76] See, generally, M. Ölz, 'Non-Governmental Organizations in Regional Human Rights Systems' (1997) 28 *Colum. Hum. Rts. L Rev.* 307.

[77] M. Nowicki, 'NGOs before the European Commission and Court of Human Rights' (1996) 14 *NQHR* 239 at 297. Shelton, above n. 73, 638, finds the significance of *amicus* briefs 'difficult to evaluate'.

[78] See D. Padilla, 'The Inter-American Commission on Human Rights of the Organization of American States: A Case Study' (1993) 9 *Am. U J Int'l. L & Pol'y* 95 at 111; and Shelton, above n. 73, at 638–40.

[79] See P.H. Kooijmans, 'The Non-Governmental Organizations and the Monitoring Activities of the United Nations in the Field of Human Rights' in *The Role of Non-Governmental Organizations in the Promotion and Protection of Human Rights: Symposium Organized on the Occasion of the Award of the Praemium Erasmianum to the International Commission of Jurists* (1989) 15–22.

of the expectations created by its title, does not contain any significant obligations on NGOs.[80] The Declaration merely provides that NGOs have 'an important role to play and a responsibility' in promoting human rights and the right of everyone to a social and international order. It is unlikely that any liability under international law could ever be based on these provisions, even if it were assumed that they contain binding obligations.

Some UN resolutions appear to assume that NGOs are bound by the purposes and principles of the UN Charter. The Declaration and Programme of Action adopted at the Vienna World Conference on Human Rights provides that NGOs may not exercise the rights and freedoms of the Universal Declaration of Human Rights contrary to the purposes and principles of the United Nations.[81] ECOSOC Resolution 1996/31 on the consultative relationship between the United Nations and non-governmental organizations similarly provides that an NGO may be deprived of its consultative status if it abuses its status by engaging in 'a pattern of acts contrary to the purposes and principles of the Charter of the United Nations including unsubstantiated or politically motivated acts against Member States of the United Nations incompatible with those principles and purposes'.[82] A comparable provision was included in its predecessor resolution, ECOSOC Resolution 1296.[83]

It is difficult to see, however, how an NGO could breach a purpose or a principle contained in the UN Charter. The only principle of the Charter that could conceivably be infringed by an NGO is the prohibition of intervention in internal affairs contained in Article 2(7). However, Article 2(7) is addressed to the United Nations. While it is generally assumed that a similar obligation rests on individual States,[84] there is no authoritative evidence of a similar obligation on NGOs.[85]

On the basis of the penalty provisions contained in ECOSOC Resolutions 1296 and 1996/31, several NGOs have nevertheless been deprived of their consultative status so far. The International Lesbian and Gay Association (ILGA) had its Roster status suspended in 1994 after the United States had complained that one of its US affiliates was advocating paedophilia.[86] The United States may not have realized that this decision might open a Pandora's box. Christian Solidarity International (CSI) had its consultative status revoked in 1999 at the insistence of Sudan because it had been represented by a Sudanese rebel leader, John Garang, at a session of the UN Commission on Human Rights.[87] This decision was taken in spite of the fact that Resolution 1996/31 requires a pattern of violations as a condition for the withdrawal of status. The decision was not, as is usually the case in ECOSOC, taken

---

[80] GA Res. 53/144 (1999).

[81] Vienna Declaration and Programme of Action, 1993, 32 ILM 1673 (1993).

[82] Above n. 15, para. 57(a).   [83] Para. 36(b).   [84] See e.g. GA Res. 2625 (XXV) (1970).

[85] It has been suggested that Charter Art. 71 prevents Art. 2(7) from being invoked against NGOs: A. Drzemczewski, 'The Role of NGOs in Human Rights Matters in the Council of Europe' (1987) 8 *Hum. Rts. LJ* 273 at 274. However, this seems like a redundant and in any case not very convincing argument.   [86] ECOSOC Res. 1994/50.

[87] Press Release ECOSOC/5876.

by consensus but by a majority (twenty-six in favour to fourteen against, with twelve abstentions).[88]

These decisions by ECOSOC appear to mark a significant change in its attitude towards NGOs. They seem to indicate a greater willingness on the part of Sates to assume that NGOs may be held accountable and that they should pay a heavy price even for minor transgressions. During the 1970s and 1980s States accused by NGOs of human rights abuses at the UN Commission on Human Rights frequently complained about alleged abuses of consultative status. Some of these complaints were similar to those being made against CSI. For example, in 1977 Argentina complained about a representative of a 'terrorist' organization being allowed to make statements on behalf of the International Commission of Jurists and Pax Romana. However, neither on that occasion nor on other occasions in that period was there any significant support among States for the withdrawal of consultative status of the NGOs in question.[89]

7. CONCLUSIONS

NGOs play an increasingly important role on the international plane, and to some extent this is being reflected in their formal status. Some 'hybrid' NGOs have concluded treaties with States and they enjoy privileges and immunities similar to those of IGOs. In some instances, NGOs are also able to bring international claims against States. Perhaps most spectacularly, NGOs more and more play a crucial role in the drafting of international instruments and in the follow-up and monitoring of those instruments. This latter role has frequently been enshrined in treaties and other formal arrangements.

However, the extent of these developments should not be exaggerated. The formal status of NGOs under international law is still extremely weak. At the United Nations, NGOs can still only have consultative relations with ECOSOC and not with bodies that matter, such as the Security Council and the General Assembly. Discussions on the involvement of NGOs in international economic forums such as the World Trade Organization (WTO) are still in their infancy.[90] Moreover, States

---

[88] Ibid. Since then several NGOs have had their consultative status suspended by ECOSOC by a majority vote, apparently on political grounds.

[89] M. Kamminga and N. Rodley, 'Direct Intervention at the UN: NGO Participation in the Commission on Human Rights and its Sub-Commission' in H. Hannum (ed.), *Guide to International Human Rights Practice* (1984) 186 at 189 and 192–7.

[90] See e.g. S. Charnovitz, 'Participation of Nongovernmental Organizations in the World Trade Organization' (1996) 17 *Un. Pa. J Int'l Econ. L* 331; D. Esty, 'Non-Governmental Organizations at the World Trade Organization: Cooperation, Competition, or Exclusion' (1998) 1 *J Int'l Econ. L* 123; W. Benedek, 'Developing the Constitutional Order of the WTO: The Role of NGOs' in W. Benedek, H. Isak, and R. Kicker (eds.), *Developing and Development of International and European Law: Essays in Honour of Professor Konrad Ginther* (1999) 313; G. Marceau and P. Pedersen, 'Is the WTO Open and Transparent? A Discussion of the Relationship of the WTO with Non-governmental Organisations and Civil Society's Claims for More Transparency and Public Participation' (1999) 33 *J World Trade* 5.

are still in full control of access to the international system. NGOs may at any time be deprived of their right to act on the international plane if they are perceived, rightly or wrongly, to have misbehaved. States appear to be increasingly willing to invoke this sanction. After decades in which no NGO was deprived of its consultative status with ECOSOC, since 1996 several NGOs have been stripped of this status, on highly arbitrary grounds and with scant respect for the procedures laid down for this purpose by ECOSOC itself.

There is therefore little evidence that States will ever allow NGOs to become a serious threat to the inter-State system. NGOs would in any case begin to present such a threat only if their role were increasing at the expense of the role played by States or if they set out to establish a rival system of world government. There is simply no indication that this is happening. The mayhem caused by demonstrators at WTO conferences may look threatening but as long as the participants do not have a clear vision of an alternative international system the worry seems rather misplaced.

If and when NGOs are permitted to participate in international decision-making, they are allowed to do so because they help to strengthen rather than weaken the inter-State system. By contributing the views of civil society, they confer badly needed legitimacy on the international system. International decisions taken without the input of NGOs risk remaining unimplemented because they lack the required degree of public support. By contributing expertise, NGOs also help to improve the quality of international decisions. Many subjects of international conferences have become so technical that numerous States, not only the smaller ones, find it hard to muster the necessary specialist knowledge. Furthermore, by providing their information and expertise for free, NGOs offer significant savings to the inter-State system. Many underfunded IGO programmes would not be able to carry out meaningful activities without the substantive input received from NGOs.

Important decisions affecting the daily lives of citizens around the world are made at international meetings by faceless bureaucrats and representatives of highly undemocratic nations.[91] Giving NGOs a role in international governance may not, at first sight, be a satisfactory remedy for this unsatisfactory state of affairs. To begin with, it should be frankly admitted that not all NGOs are by definition praiseworthy. NGOs may serve special and limited interests that are not laudable. The objectives of some groups are excessively narrow or even discriminatory or racist.[92]

Moreover, anyone can establish an association and call it an NGO. The claim to be non-governmental should therefore not be accepted at face value: there are numerous subtle and less subtle ways in which States may influence individual NGOs. For example, in order to operate NGOs often require official registration by the authorities of the States in which they are located. This means they must meet

---

[91] Van Boven, above n. 39, 223.

[92] O. Schachter, 'The Decline of the Nation-State and its Implications for International Law' (1997) 36 *Colum. J Transnat'l L 7* at 14.

the criteria laid down by the authorities. Or they may acquire tax-exempt status only if they meet certain criteria established by the host State. Furthermore, many NGOs depend on government funds even for their core activities.

Finally, many NGOs, even those committed to promoting democracy and good governance, are far from democratic themselves. Few NGOs have regular internal elections and fewer still have policies that are determined democratically by their members. Some consist of only one or two people. As a result, the representatives of many NGOs at international conferences may be expected to push their own agendas rather than those of their constituents. Their claims to represent civil society should be taken with a considerable pinch of salt.[93]

However, reality is not as depressing as might seem to follow from such a recital of the failings of NGOs. Unlike States, NGOs derive their authority not simply from their existence but from their individual qualities. NGOs that are not perceived as working for the common good, that are not entirely independent of governments, or that have no mechanisms for internal accountability will attract few individual supporters and little funding and will have little impact on the international plane. Of course, this does not prevent such NGOs from being vocal, but volume should not be confused with influence. NGO coalitions, an instrument created by NGOs themselves, also have an important moderating effect. They are unlikely to endorse sectarian positions from marginal groups because this would risk undermining their own credibility. On the other hand, positions that manage to become part of an NGO platform—especially when it is a platform shared by a varied group of hundreds of NGOs—may legitimately be regarded as the views of civil society.

In sum, there is still much more reason for concern about the negative impact of 'irresponsible' governments than about 'irresponsible' NGOs. The formal and informal checks on the influence of NGOs on the international plane are such that there is no need for a general system of *appellation contrôlée* under international law.

---

[93] Gordenker and Weiss, above n. 21, 553. See also P.J. Simmons, 'Learning to Live with NGOs' (1998) 120 *Foreign Pol'y* 82 at 83.

4

Economic, Social, and Cultural Human Rights and the International Monetary Fund

FRANÇOIS GIANVITI*

1. INTRODUCTION

This Chapter explores the relationship between economic, social, and cultural human rights and the activities of the International Monetary Fund (the Fund). More specifically, it examines: to what extent the provisions of the International Covenant on Economic, Social and Cultural Rights (the Covenant) have legal effect on the Fund; to what extent the Fund is obliged to contribute to the achievement of the objectives of the Covenant; and to what extent it may do so under its Articles of Agreement.

The Covenant was adopted by the United Nations General Assembly in 1966 and came into force among the countries that had become party to it in 1976. It is presently in force among 145 States, most of which are Fund members.[1] Under the Covenant, the parties undertake to implement its substantive provisions within their own territories, to cooperate internationally towards the progressive full achievement of the substantive rights contained in the Covenant, and to participate in the reporting mechanism established to monitor the implementation of the Covenant.

The Covenant is part of a wide network of international instruments, which includes United Nations General Assembly resolutions and declarations and a number of other treaties. On one hand, the Covenant is linked to the 'obligation of States under the Charter of the United Nations to promote universal respect for, and observance of, human rights and freedoms'.[2] Together with the Universal Declaration of Human Rights and the International Covenant on Civil and Political

---

* The opinions expressed in this article are those of the author and not necessarily those of the International Monetary Fund.

[1] It may be noted, however, that some 18 Fund members, including Indonesia, Malaysia, Pakistan, Saudi Arabia, and the United States, are not parties to the Covenant. The United States signed the Covenant in 1977, but has not ratified it.   [2] Covenant, Preamble, fourth paragraph.

Rights, it forms the International Bill of Rights. The Universal Declaration of Human Rights states that 'everyone, as a member of society [. . .] is entitled to realization [. . .] of the economic, social and cultural rights indispensable for his dignity and the free development of his personality'.[3] On the other hand, the Covenant is linked to the right to development, proclaimed at the 1993 World Conference on Human Rights in Vienna, as this right is defined as the right by virtue of which 'every human person and all peoples are entitled to participate in, contribute to, and enjoy economic, social, cultural and political development'.[4] Thus, the Covenant is integrated in a wide web of other instruments, and it could be argued that it should not be considered by itself. Nevertheless, the Covenant is also the one global instrument in which economic and social rights have been crystallized in a treaty that is legally binding on the parties to it. For this reason, it is the Covenant that is considered here in its relations to the Fund.

The Fund was established in 1946 and had been functioning for a number of years when the United Nations' Commission on Human Rights started work on the Covenant. During the elaboration of the Covenant, the Fund was invited to participate and to comment on draft clauses, but it declined the invitation. In its response, the Fund expressed interest in the work of the Commission on Human Rights, but stated that 'the limits set on our activities by our Articles of Agreement do not appear to cover this field of work'.[5] It is worth noting that the World Bank also declined the invitation to participate in the elaboration of the Covenant. The Bank's response to the invitation was that 'since the activities of the International Bank do not bear directly upon the work of the Commission, the Bank does not plan to send a representative to attend the Commission's forthcoming meeting'.[6] By contrast to other specialized agencies whose mandates explicitly or implicitly included the promotion of human rights,[7] the Fund took the position that the

---

[3] Universal Declaration of Human Rights, Article 22.

[4] Declaration on the Right to Development, adopted by GA res 41/128 (1986), Article 1, para. 1.

[5] UN Economic and Social Council, *Co-operation Between the Commission on Human Rights and the Specialized Agencies and other Organs of the United Nations in the Consideration of Economic, Social and Cultural Rights*, UN Doc. E/CN.4/534 (1951), Annex, p. 5.

[6] *Ibid*, p. 4. The United Nations Secretariat seems to have acquiesced to these positions. A report prepared by the Secretary-General contained the following statement in connection with the right to work and the question of full employment: 'Although the activities of both the [. . .] Fund and the [World] Bank are aimed at making a contribution to the general economic well-being of the world and so to the achievement of full employment, the basic instruments of these bodies have not been drawn up in such a way as to permit any direct connection between their activities and the effective recognition of human rights'. UN Commission on Human Rights, *Activities Of The United Nations And Of The Specialized Agencies In The Field Of Economic, Social And Cultural Rights, Report Submitted By the Secretary General*, UN Doc. E/CN.4/364/Rev.1 (1952), UN Sales No. 1952.IV.4, para. 30 (1952).

[7] The International Labor Organization (ILO), the World Health Organization (WHO), the United Nations Educational, Scientific and Cultural Organization (UNESCO), and the Food and Agriculture Organization (FAO) participated actively in the elaboration of the Covenant. The mandates of the first three contain specific references to the promotion of human rights; the constitution of the FAO makes no specific reference to rights, but refers to the promotion of 'common welfare' through higher nutrition

questions raised in the elaboration of the Covenant were outside its own mandate. Thus in the early 1950s neither the Fund nor the Bank saw the links between their respective activities and the economic, social, and cultural rights that would become part of the Covenant.

A number of factors, common to the Fund and the Bank, contributed to this view.

First, at the most general level, the Fund and the Bank saw themselves (and continue to see themselves) as international organizations separate from their members, governed by their respective charters. Unlike States, international organizations are established to achieve limited objectives and they are equipped with financial and human resources to achieve only the objectives assigned to them. This division of labour among international organizations is required not only for reasons of efficiency but also because the members of international organizations have agreed to cooperate within the framework of their respective charters without necessarily sharing other objectives or values outside these charters. And, in the event that some or all members of an international organization adhere to a treaty containing such other objectives or values, this in itself does not result in these objectives or values becoming part of the organization's mandate unless and until agreement is reached to amend the organization's charter.[8]

Secondly, and more specifically, the Fund and the Bank saw themselves as purely technical and financial organizations, whose Articles of Agreement prevented them (explicitly in the case of the Bank, implicitly in the case of the Fund) from taking political considerations into account in their decisions. Their role as financial institutions was to provide economic assistance, not to dictate political changes.

Thirdly, as was the case of the Bank, but unlike the United Nations, decision-making power in the Fund was vested in organs whose decisions were taken by weighted voting, rather than on a one-country, one-vote basis. These factors led to concerns over the possibility of inconsistent decisions between the United Nations and the Fund or the Bank.

Fourthly, the importance of maintaining the independence of the two Bretton Woods organizations was further highlighted by the provisions of their respective Articles of Agreement which required that they cooperate with what became the United Nations. The Articles made it clear, however, that arrangements for such

---

levels and standards of living. *See* Philip Alston, 'The United Nations' Specialized Agencies and Implementation of the International Covenant on Economic, Social and Cultural Rights', 18 *Colum. J. Transnt'l. Law*, 79 at 81, note 12 (1979).

[8] For instance, the European Community is not bound by the provisions of the European Convention on Human Rights, although its members are party to the Convention (*see* the advisory opinion of 28 March 1996 of the European Court of Justice on Accession by the Community to the European Convention for the Protection of Human Rights and Fundamental Freedoms, reviewed by Giorgo Gaja in *Common Market Law Review*, 1996, p. 973; Jean-FranHois Renucci, *Droit européen des droits de l'homme*, 2nd edition, 2001, p. 339; *see also* decision of 20 February 2001 of the EC Court of first instance, reviewed by J.C. Fourgoux in *Gazette du Palais*, 25–26 April 2001).

cooperation could not indirectly amend the Articles. Any such arrangement that would involve a modification of any provision of the Articles would be effected only after amendment in accordance with the Articles.[9]

Fifthly, the Relationship Agreements that the Fund and the Bank had entered into with the United Nations in 1947 stated clearly the need, based on their respective Articles of Agreement, for the Fund and the Bank to function as independent international organizations.

In addition to these common elements, the Fund's own mandate was even more remote than the Bank's from the issues which the Commission on Human Rights would debate. The Fund was not a project lender, and was not involved in sectoral activities; it did not finance health or education. It was a monetary agency, not a development agency. Its financial role was limited to providing foreign exchange to help its members overcome temporary balance of payments problems. In a formal interpretation of its Articles of Agreement in 1946, the Fund's Executive Board had interpreted them 'to mean that the authority to use the resources of the Fund is limited to use in accordance with its purposes to give temporary assistance in financing balance of payments deficits on current account for monetary stabilization operations'.[10] The Fund had no authority over its members' domestic policies, and economic growth was not a recognized factor in the Fund's decisions. Moreover, the Fund's Articles did not authorize any distinction between the members of the Fund based on their status as developing or otherwise, and access to the Fund's resources was a matter of entitlement, subject to conditions specified in the Articles, leaving little scope for introducing differentiation between members based on economic or social rights considerations.

Since the 1950s the purposes of the Fund have not changed, but its practice and its mandate under the Articles of Agreement have evolved to meet the changing needs of its members. The Fund is still a monetary agency, not a development agency. It does not fund projects, but still provides only balance of payments support, although the concept of balance of payments need is now more flexible than in the past for the use of resources earmarked for developing countries. Also, the Fund now exercises surveillance over certain policies of its members, and the special needs of developing countries, particularly the poorest of them, have received recognition.

This evolution has been gradual, with the Second Amendment of 1978 being the most important milepost. Beginning in the 1960s the principle of uniformity of treatment of members did not prevent the Fund from adopting different policies on its financial assistance, with specified different types of conditions for different types

[9] Article X of the Articles of Agreement of the Fund, and Article V, Section 8(a) of the Articles of Agreement of the IBRD. As it was finally adopted in 1966, the Covenant contains a 'symmetrical' provision to the effect that 'nothing in the present Covenant is to be interpreted as impairing the provisions [. . .] of the constitutions of the specialized agencies [. . .] in regard to the matters dealt with in the [. . .] Covenant'.

[10] Decision No. 71–2, 26 September 1946, *Selected Decisions and Selected Documents of the International Monetary Fund* (25th Issue, 31 December 2000) (hereafter: *Selected Decisions*), p. 129.

of balance of payments problems, some of which could be specific to developing countries, such as the stabilization of prices of primary products (Buffer Stock Financing Facility) or export shortfalls due to variations in world market conditions (Compensatory Financing Facility). In 1974, the Fund established the Extended Fund Facility (EFF) as a vehicle for long-term balance of payments assistance (repayable over ten years) to countries whose balance of payments problem required major structural reforms; it was noted in the decision creating the facility that it was 'likely to be beneficial for developing countries in particular'. Gradually, as industrial countries have 'graduated' from Fund assistance, more and more attention has been given in the design of Fund facilities to the needs of developing countries.

Among developing countries, those with low per capita incomes require particular attention. They need either concessional loans or outright grants. Until the second amendment of its Articles of Agreement, the Fund was not allowed to provide this type of assistance. However, the appreciation of its gold holdings made it possible to organize a system of sales of gold at the official price, followed by contributions of capital gains generated by the purchases to a Trust Fund managed by the Fund for concessional loans to developing countries with low per capita incomes. With the second amendment, the Fund was authorized to achieve the same result without going through the complicated procedure of sales followed by contributions. Moreover, it was allowed to use capital gains on gold sales also for grants. The resources generated by sales of gold have been supplemented by various contributions from donor countries. The Poverty Reduction and Growth Facility has benefited from this dual financing (gold sales and contributions) and extends concessional loans. The Facility for Heavily Indebted Poor Countries provides grants to enable recipient countries to discharge their indebtedness to the Fund; it is an indirect form of debt forgiveness.

Not only has the Fund become more receptive to the needs of developing countries but its role as guardian of the international monetary relations has substantially expanded to include overseeing its members' domestic economic and financial policies. With the second amendment of the Articles of Agreement, Fund members undertook new obligations that go beyond the conduct of their exchange rate policies. Each member is now required, under the amended Article IV, to 'endeavor to direct its economic and financial policies toward the objective of fostering orderly economic growth with reasonable price stability, with due regard to its circumstances'.

While the Fund remains a monetary institution responsible for maintaining orderly exchange rates and a multilateral system of payments free of restrictions on current payments and whose financial assistance is only for balance of payments purposes, the cumulative effect of changes in its practice and in its Articles of Agreement has introduced new elements to the relationship between the Fund and the Covenant. There are two aspects to this question. The first is whether the Fund is legally bound to give effect to the provisions of the Covenant in its decisions. The second is whether, and to what extent, the Fund's own Articles of Agreement allow or require the Fund to achieve objectives that are similar (even though not identical) to those of the Covenant. These two aspects are discussed in turn.

2. APPLICABILITY OF THE COVENANT TO THE FUND

There are three reasons for concluding that the Covenant does not apply to the Fund: the Fund is not a party to the Covenant;[11] the obligations imposed by the Covenant apply only to States, not to international organizations; and the Covenant, in its Article 24, explicitly recognizes that '[n]othing in the present Covenant shall be interpreted as impairing the provisions [. . .] of the constitutions of the specialized agencies which define the respective responsibilities [. . .] of the specialized agencies in regard to the matters dealt with in the present Covenant'.

Nevertheless, a number of arguments have been put forward to justify the applicability of the Covenant to the Fund. Two main lines of argument have been advanced. Under one approach, the Fund as a subject of international law and a specialized agency within the UN system would be bound by general norms of international law, particularly those adopted pursuant to the UN Charter. The conclusion would be that the Covenant has a direct effect on the Fund, which is bound to implement its provisions. Under a second approach, the Covenant would not apply directly to the Fund but it would have an indirect effect on the Fund through its members. The members of the Fund that are parties to the Covenant must, within the Fund, discharge their obligation of cooperation with other States, whether those other States are parties to the Covenant or not. Moreover, if these other States are parties to the Covenant, there is an additional duty not to induce them to breach their obligation under the Covenant by adopting measures inconsistent with those obligations. These two, substantially different, approaches are now examined in turn.

A. Direct Effect of the Covenant

Two arguments have been advanced to support the claim that the Covenant has a direct effect on the Fund. One argument is based on the relationship of the Fund with the United Nations. The other is that the obligations set forth in the Covenant are mandatory provisions of general public international law, and thus binding on all subjects of international law, including international organizations. Both arguments would lead to the conclusion that the Fund's Articles of Agreement should be interpreted in a manner consistent with the objective of promoting the rights contained in the Covenant, or deemed to be amended if this was necessary to achieve these objectives. The implications of a positive view of such a direct effect could be far-reaching.

---

[11] Similarly, the European Community, not being a party to the European Convention on Human Rights, is not bound by its provisions (*see* footnote 8, above).

Would it mean that the obligations set out in the Covenant would apply to the Fund as if it were a party to the Covenant? For example, would the Fund be required to finance health and education projects while its mission is only to provide balance of payments assistance? Would the Fund have to disregard the principle of uniform treatment, which still governs its general resources (i.e. resources not generated by capital gains on gold sales) to provide special assistance to developing countries? Would the United Nations Committee on Economic, Social and Cultural Rights exercise jurisdiction over the Fund's activities and the decisions of its organs? Once the principle is admitted that the Covenant takes precedence over the Articles, the whole institutional and legal structure within which the Fund operates can be questioned.

B. The Link with the United Nations

It has been stated that 'there are strong legal arguments to support the position that the IMF is obligated in accordance with international law, to take account of human rights considerations. The first is that the Fund is a United Nations body and must therefore be bound by the principles stated in the U.N. Charter. Among those principles and purposes of the organization is the promotion of respect for human rights. It is not therefore a political objective, but a legally mandated one.'[12] A number of comments may be made on this statement. First, the Covenant itself reserves the position of the constitutions of the specialized agencies. The parties agree that 'nothing in the [. . .] Covenant shall be interpreted as impairing the constitutions of the specialized agencies which define the respective responsibilities of the various organs of [. . .] the specialized agencies in regard to the matters dealt with in the [. . .] Covenant'.[13] Thus the Covenant does not affect the Articles of Agreement of the Fund, including its mission and governance structure. Neither does it affect the rights and obligations of its members set out in the Articles of Agreement.

Secondly, the Fund is not a 'United Nations body', but a specialized agency within the meaning of the Charter of the United Nations, which means that it is an intergovernmental agency, not an agency of the United Nations. In accordance with Article 57 of the Charter, the Fund was brought into relationship with the United Nations by a 1947 agreement in which the United Nations recognizes that, 'by reason of the nature of its international responsibilities and the terms of its Articles of Agreement, the Fund is, and is required to function as, an independent organization'.[14] Furthermore, Article X of the Fund's Articles of Agreement, while requiring the Fund to cooperate with 'any general international organization' [i.e. the United Nations], specifies that 'Any arrangements for such cooperation which would

---

[12] Philip Alston, 'The International Monetary Fund and the Right to Food', 30 *How. L.J.*, 473 at 479 (1987). [13] Covenant, Article 24.

[14] Agreement Between the United Nations and the International Monetary Fund, 15 November 1947, Article I, para. 2, reprinted in *Selected Decisions*, p. 651.

involve a modification of any provision of [the Articles of Agreement] may be effected only after amendment to [the Articles]'. Thus the relationship established by the 1947 Agreement is not one of 'agency'[15] but one of 'sovereign equals'.[16] It follows that the Fund's relationship agreement with the United Nations does not require it to give effect to resolutions of the United Nations, such as the resolutions under which the members of the General Assembly adopted the Universal Declaration or the Covenant, or to international agreements, such as the Covenant, entered into by the members of the United Nations.

C. General Principles of International Law, Obligations *Erga Omnes*, and *Jus Cogens*

Commentators have mentioned a number of legal bases for the proposition that the Covenant, or the norms included in it, are applicable to the Fund directly as a subject of international law.[17]

1. Customary International Law

One such basis would be the view that the norms contained in the Covenant are now part of general or customary international law. It has been argued that, even in the absence of any consent on the part of an international organization, its freedom to act in the pursuit of its mandated objectives may be constrained by international law norms. Under this argument, such norms would not operate to change the objectives of the international organization set out in its constituent instrument, but to limit in some way the actions that the organization could legitimately take in pursuit of such objectives.[18] It has been suggested that a similar reasoning should be applied to

---

[15] In order to avoid any ambiguity on this point, a statement was placed in the record of the negotiations stating that 'it was understood [. . .] that the statement in Article I, paragraph 2, that the Bank (Fund) is a Specialized Agency established by agreement among its member governments carries with it no implication that the relationship between the United Nations and the Bank (Fund) is one of principal and agent'. Committee on Negotiations with Specialized Agencies, *Report on Negotiations with the International Bank for Reconstruction and Development and the International Monetary Fund*, United Nations document E564, at 3 (16 August 1947), quoted in William E. Holder, 'The Relationship Between the International Monetary Fund and the United Nations', in Robert C. Effros, ed., *Current Legal Issues Affecting Central Banking*, vol. 4, IMF, p. 16, at p. 18. (1997).

[16] Leland M. Goodrich, Edvard Hambro, and Anne Patricia Simons, *Charter of the United Nations, Commentary and Documents*, Columbia University Press, New York, p. 421 (1969).

[17] On this question *see generally* Jean-François Flauss, 'La Protection des Droits de l'Homme et les Sources du Droit International, Rapport général', in Société Française pour le Droit International, *Colloque de Strasbourg, La Protection des Droits de l'Homme et l'Évolution du Droit International*, Pédone, Paris, p. 11, especially pages 48–71 (1998).

[18] For example, with respect to the use of force by the United Nations, it has been suggested that: '*dès l'instant où l'on admet que l'Organisation, comme telle, a le pouvoir d'utiliser la force [. . .] il faut nécessairement en déduire que l'Organisation comme telle a la capacité d'être le destinataire des règles de droit destinées à réglementer l'usage de la force, pour autant que ces règles soient compatibles avec les buts et les*

human rights generally, and that the international financial organizations have in this respect a 'duty of vigilance' to ensure that its actions do not have negative effects on the human rights situation in its borrowing members.[19]

The applicability of this line of reasoning to the Covenant (or the rights set out in it) would depend initially on a finding that the norms it contains are part of general international law.[20] It has been stated that the Universal Declaration 'is now part of the customary international law of nations and therefore binding on all States'.[21] Others have gone only so far as to state that *some* human rights have attained such status, and the examples they give are in the area of political and civil rights.[22]

principes de l'Organisation et ne soient pas contredites par des dispositions spécifiques de la Charte'. Paul De Visscher, 'Les conditions d'application des lois de la guerre aux opérations militaires des Nations Unies', Institut de Droit International, 54-I *Annuaire*, p. 34 (1971) quoted in Pierre Klein, *La Responsabilité des organisations internationales dans les ordres juridiques internes et en droit des gens*, Brussels, p. 346 (1998).

[19] Pierre Klein, 'La responsabilité des organisations financières internationales et les droits de la personne', 1999 *Revue Belge de Droit International*, 97, at 113.

[20] In addition, if the norms of customary law were to have effect on an international organization, it would be necessary to establish that the activities of the organization overlap with the content of the norms. Given the conclusion reached in this Chapter on the first point, it is not necessary to discuss this second point.

[21] Humphrey, 'The International Bill of Rights and Implementation', 17 *Wm. & Mary L. Rev.* 259 (1976), cited in Schachter, 'International Law in Theory and Practice', Hague Acad. Int'l L., 178 *Recueil des Cours*, 9, at 340 (1982). Schachter comments: 'I would not go that far[...]'. *See* Judge Schachter's views in the next footnote. *See also* Marc Cogen, 'Human rights, prohibition of political activities and the lending policies of Worldbank and International Monetary Fund' in Chowdhury, Denters, and de Waart, eds., *The Right to Development in International Law*, 379, at 387 (1988): 'the Universal Declaration and the International Covenants represent minimal standards of conduct of all people and all nations. Intergovernmental organizations are inter-state institutions and they too are bound by the generally accepted standards of the world community'.

[22] *See* for example Schachter, footnote 21 above: '[Only] some of the rights recognized in the Declaration and other human rights texts have a strong claim to the status of customary law'. Schachter mentions as examples slavery, genocide, torture, mass murders, prolonged arbitrary imprisonment, and systematic racial discrimination. *See also* Jean-François Flauss, 'La Protection des droits de l'homme et les sources du droit international', Rapport général, in Société Française pour le Droit International, *Colloque de Strasbourg, La Protection des droits de l'Homme et l'Évolution du Droit International*, Paris, p. 11 (1998). Professor Flauss concludes his survey of positive law of human rights by stating that: *'on ne peut pas ne pas être frappé par la très large correspondance de substance existant entre les normes de protection des droits de l'homme reconnues avec certitude par le droit international général et les règles de protection résultant de l'article 3 commun aux quatre Conventions de Genève applicables aux conflits armés internationaux. En d'autres termes, le droit international des droits de l'homme coïncide matériellement, pour l'essentiel, voire pour sa presque totalité, avec les 'principes généraux de base du droit humanitaire''* (*ibid*, p. 59). Under Article 3 of each of these Conventions, '[civilians and other non-participants in the hostilities] shall in all circumstances be treated humanely, without any adverse distinction founded on race, colour, religion or faith, sex, birth or wealth, or any other similar criteria. To this end, the following acts are and shall remain prohibited at any time and in any place whatsoever with respect to the above-mentioned persons: (a) Violence to life and person, in particular murder of all kinds, mutilation, cruel treatment and torture; (b) Taking of hostages; (c) Outrages upon personal dignity, in particular humiliating and degrading treatment; (d) The passing of sentences and the carrying out of executions without previous judgment pronounced by a regularly constituted court, affording all the judicial guarantees which are recognized as indispensable by civilized peoples'.

The various pronouncements of the International Court of Justice on human rights seem to support this second view.[23] The most that can be said in this regard is that it is not generally accepted that the Covenant (or the norms contained in it) form part of general or customary international law.

Since the norms contained in the Covenant have not reached the status of norms of general international law, it would be difficult to sustain that they impose themselves on the Fund in some other fashion, either as obligations *erga omnes*, or as part of *jus cogens*. Nevertheless, it may be useful to consider these two points briefly.

2. *Obligations* Erga Omnes

Under this heading, the view would be taken that certain obligations, including certain human rights obligations, would be owed 'to the entire international community'.[24] The origin of this theory is to be found in the *Barcelona Traction* case and the distinction the International Court of Justice drew, *obiter dictum*, between the obligations a State owes to the international community as a whole and those arising *vis-à-vis* another State.[25] A discussion of this complex topic would be well beyond the scope of this Chapter. Suffice it to state that the scholarly opinion does not seem to have reached a consensus around the idea that human rights other than those enumerated by the International Court of Justice have attained the status of obligations *erga omnes*.[26] The reservation in Article 24 of the Covenant concerning the charters of the specialized agencies would support this conclusion.

3. Jus Cogens

'A treaty is void if, at the time of its conclusion, it conflicts with a peremptory norm of general international law.'[27] As in the case of obligations *erga omnes*, there is no evidence that economic and social rights have reached the status of norms of *jus cogens*.[28] Article 24 of the Covenant leads to the same conclusion.

---

[23] Professor Flauss writes that, read together, the advisory opinions and cases in which the ICJ has considered human rights as part of general international law would lead to the conclusion that the ICJ explicitly identifies four human rights: the right not to be held in slavery, the right to be protected from racial discrimination, the right not to be subject to inhuman treatment in case of deprivation of liberty, and the right not to be abusively deprived of liberty. To which Professor Flauss adds, in view of the Advisory Opinion on the Genocide Convention, the right to life, and that the interdiction of inhuman treatment includes acts of torture. Flauss, *Rapport Introductif, op. cit.*, p. 57, footnote 266.

[24] John C. Ciorciari, 'The Lawful Scope of Human Rights Criteria in World Bank Decisions: An Interpretative Analysis of the IBRD and IDA Articles of Agreement', 33 *Cornell Int'l L. J.* 331 at 357 (2000).

[25] *Barcelona Traction, Light & Power Co. Ltd (Belg. v. Spain)*, 1970 I.C.J. 3. 'Such obligations derive, for example, in the contemporary international law, from the outlawing of acts of aggression, and of genocide, as also from the principles and rules concerning the basic rights of the human person, including protection from slavery and racial discrimination'.

[26] Maurizio Ragazzi, *The Concept of Obligations Erga Omnes*, p. 144 (1997).

[27] Vienna Convention on the Law of Treaties, Article 53.

[28] *See* Schachter, 'International Law in Theory and Practice', Hague Acad. Int'l L., 178 *Recueil des Cours*, 9, at 340 (1982); for a more recent discussion, *see* Ragazzi, footnote 26 above, who writes: 'Except

In any event, Article 24 of the Covenant shows that the Covenant was not intended to supersede the charters of the specialized agencies. In order for any norm of the Covenant to become binding on an international organization, the organization would in effect need to modify its constituent instrument. To the extent that the international organization could not give effect to the norm without doing violence to its constituent instrument, the norm would not prevail over the constituent instrument. With respect to the Fund, the social rights to health or education, for example, lie outside its mandate. Finally, questions would also arise concerning the contents of such an obligation. This issue is discussed below in the context of the possible obligation on the Fund not to hinder the implementation of its members' own international obligations. It may thus be concluded that the Covenant is not a treaty that is binding on the Fund, and thus it has no direct effect on the Fund.

D. Indirect Effect of the Covenant

Under this view, the members of the Fund that are party to the Covenant would have an obligation to seek the implementation of the Covenant not only in their bilateral relations with other parties, but also through their actions in international organizations. The terms of the Covenant do not limit the duty to cooperate internationally to cooperation with other States Parties or with States in general. The duty is general and, if the interpretation made of it by the Committee on Economic, Social and Cultural Rights is shared by the States Parties, the duty would include cooperation both with and within international organizations. The Committee appears recently to have taken the view that States Parties to the Covenant have a duty to ensure that the policies and decisions of the international financial organizations of which they are members are in conformity with the obligations of States Parties to the Covenant.

The manner in which this indirect effect would affect an international organization may vary depending on the country involved. First, all States Parties would be under a general obligation to seek, in the international organizations in which they are members, the adoption of policies conducive to the achievement of the rights set out in the Covenant in the territories of all States Parties. Such a duty would fall particularly on those States Parties that are thought to have some influence on the policies of the international organizations.[29] Secondly, a State Party

---

for the general acceptance of the peremptory character of the prohibition of aggression and the protection of some, but not all, human rights, the definition of the precise content of *jus cogens* is still uncertain'. He adds (p. 50) that the examples given of norms of *jus cogens* 'largely coincide with those of obligations *erga omnes* given in the *Barcelona Traction* case'.

[29] *See* for example the Committee's Concluding Observations on Belgium: 'The Committee encourages the Government of Belgium, as a member of international organizations, in particular the International Monetary Fund and the World Bank, to do all it can to ensure that the policies and decisions of those organizations are in conformity with the obligations of States parties to the Covenant, in particular the obligations contained in article 2.1 concerning international assistance and cooperation'.

receiving technical or financial assistance from an international organization would be under a separate duty to ensure that the programme it undertakes with such assistance is consistent with its obligations under the Covenant. Conversely, the international organization would have a duty to ensure that it did not hinder the State Party's ability to implement the Covenant. In a few recent instances, the Committee has commented on the need to ensure that a country's obligations under the Covenant 'be taken into account' in all aspects of the country's negotiations with international financial institutions 'to ensure that economic, social and cultural rights, particularly of the most vulnerable groups of society, are not undermined'.[30] These two aspects of the question are next examined in turn.

1. States Parties' Actions Through the Decision-Making Organs of the Fund

It is of course for States Parties to ascertain the extent of their obligations of international cooperation, and to decide what action they need to take as members of international organizations to discharge them. Nevertheless, two general comments may be made in this respect. First, a State Party's obligation with respect to international cooperation within international organizations is no greater than its obligation to cooperate on a bilateral basis with other States Parties. As the State Party's obligation under the Covenant is stated in general terms, without any quantified or other criteria,[31] its obligation to cooperate within international

(E/C.12/1/Add.54, 1 December 2000, para. 31). Similar observations have been made with respect to Italy (E/C.12/1/Add.43, 23 May 2000, para. 20). Since these countries do not make use of the Fund's resources, there is no conditionality to which questions related to human rights could be attached.

[30] *See* for example the Committee's Concluding Observations on Morocco: 'The Committee strongly recommends that Morocco's obligations under the Covenant be taken into account in all aspects of its negotiations with international financial institutions, like the International Monetary Fund, the World Bank and the World Trade Organization, to ensure that economic, social and cultural rights, particularly of the most vulnerable groups of society, are not undermined'. E/C.12/1/Add.55, 1 December 2000, para. 38.

[31] *See* for example Philip Alston and Gerard Quinn, 'The Nature and Scope of States Parties' Obligations Under the International Covenant on Economic, Social and Cultural Rights', 9 *Hum. Rts. Q.* 156, at (1987): 'on the basis of the preparatory work it is difficult, if not impossible, to sustain the argument that the commitment to international cooperation contained in the Covenant can accurately be characterized as a legally binding obligation upon any particular State to provide any particular form of assistance'. *See also* Mathew C. R. Craven, *The International Covenant On Economic, Social And Cultural Rights, A Perspective On Its Development*, Oxford, p. 149 (1995): '[During the drafting of the Covenant,] the general consensus was that developing States were entitled to ask for assistance but not claim it as a legal right. The text of article 11 bears out this conclusion. In recognizing the role of international co-operation in the realization of the rights, it stipulates that it should be based on "free consent"'. The Committee on Economic, Social, and Cultural Rights has also stopped short of finding a specific content to the obligation to cooperate. In its General Comment No. 3, the Committee stated: 'The Committee wishes to emphasize that in accordance with Articles 55 and 56 of the Charter of the United Nations, with well-established principles of international law, and with the provisions of the Covenant itself, international cooperation for development and thus for the realization of economic, social and cultural rights is an obligation of all States. It is particularly incumbent upon those States which are in a position to assist others in this regard. The Committee notes in particular the importance of the Declaration on the Right

organizations and in their relations with international organizations is also a general one, not one that is defined in terms of quantitative or other criteria.[32] Secondly, the fact that the parties have undertaken certain obligations under the Covenant does not authorize them to disregard their other treaty obligations, including the obligations they have undertaken as members of the relevant international organizations. In their participation in international organizations, the parties must abide by: the rules of the organization with regard to its decision-making processes; the limits on the use it may make of its resources; and the factors it may take into account in deciding on the uses of its resources.

This principle has a number of consequences with respect to the Fund. First and foremost, the governing organs of the Fund are not free to impose conditions on the members' access to the Fund's resources if these conditions exceed the Fund's powers. Under the Fund's Articles of Agreement, its members are entitled to have access to its general resources, provided that their use of these resources is in accordance with the Articles of Agreement and the policies adopted under them.[33] The Fund is not free to deny access to its general resources on the part of a member if the member meets the conditions stated in the Articles of Agreement and the policies adopted under them.

Secondly, in the formulation of its policies on the use of its general resources, the Fund must be guided by the criteria set forth in the Articles of Agreement. The relevant provision is Article V, Section 3(a), which requires the Fund to 'adopt policies on the use of its general resources [. . .] that will assist members to solve their balance of payments problems in a manner consistent with the provisions of this Agreement and that will establish adequate safeguards for the temporary use of the general resources of the Fund'. These are the only considerations that may be taken into account by the Fund in the design of its policies on the use of its general resources.

Thirdly, the key condition of access of members to the Fund's general resources is that the member represents that it has a 'balance of payments need' for such

---

to Development adopted by the General Assembly in its resolution 41/128 of 4 December 1986 and the need for States parties to take full account of all of the principles recognized therein. It emphasizes that, in the absence of an active programme of international assistance and cooperation on the part of all those States that are in a position to undertake one, the full realization of economic, social and cultural rights will remain an unfulfilled aspiration in many countries. In this respect, the Committee also recalls the terms of its General Comment 2 (1990).' (UN Committee on Economic, Social and Cultural Rights, *The nature of States parties obligations (Art. 2, para. 1), General Comment No. 3*, Fifth session, 1990).

[32] It has been suggested, however, that States Parties whose own resources are insufficient to implement the rights set out in the Covenant in their territories have a duty to request international assistance. *See* Eric M.G. Denkers, 'IMF Conditionality: Economic, Social and Cultural Rights, and the Evolving Principle of Solidarity', in Paul de Waart, Paul Peters, and Erik Denters, eds., *International Law and Development*, Nijhoff, p. 238 (1988).

[33] Article V, Section 3 (b)(i). Although the entitlement ceases when the Fund's holdings of the member's currency reach 200% of the member's quota, access beyond that limit may be permitted by the Fund under its policies. This access remains subject to the other rules of the Articles, including Article V, Section 3(a).

resources, which means that the member has a need for the resources because of its balance of payments, its reserve position, or developments in its reserves. Other resources administered by the Fund are also subject to a similar limitation.[34] The members of the Fund are not free to give access to its resources for uses not permitted by the Fund's Articles of Agreement, nor to divert resources entrusted to the Fund by some of its members to uses other than those stipulated by the donors.

Fourthly, members of the Fund must take into account the requirement that the members' temporary use of the Fund's general resources is granted 'under adequate safeguards', to protect the Fund from misuse of those resources and to ensure that they are repaid.[35]

Fifthly, States Parties must take into account that the Fund plays a catalytic role in the flow of funds to its developing and transition-economy member countries, and that this requires the Fund to consider the effect of the programmes it supports on other member countries. In particular, this requires that the programmes that the Fund supports are credible, i.e. capable of being successfully implemented, and likely to be implemented, so as to generate the confidence of other sources of funds on which the economy is dependent.

Thus, in their actions in the governing organs of the Fund, the officials selected by the States Parties to the Covenant are not free to disregard the provisions of the Articles of Agreement of the Fund, and, in particular, may not divert its resources to uses that are not provided for in the Articles.

2. Obligations of States Receiving Fund Assistance, and
   Indirect Obligations of the Fund

If the obligations of the Covenant rest on the parties to it, and these obligations include a duty to ensure that the economic programmes they undertake with international financial assistance are consistent with their undertakings under the Covenant, there remains to discuss whether there exists any concomitant obligation on the part of the organizations. The duty in question would not be a direct one, stemming from the Covenant, but would be derived from the State Party's obligation to implement the Covenant in its territory. Under the terms of the Covenant itself, such a duty would not affect the constituent instrument of the specialized agencies. It would thus leave intact the rights and obligations of the organization and its members as stated in the constituent instrument. It is therefore within the

---

[34] Resources under the Fund's Extended Structural Adjustment Facility (ESAF) and now the Poverty Reduction and Growth Facility (PGRF) are separate from the Fund's general resources and access to them is conditioned on the member experiencing a 'protracted balance of payments problem', which is defined in a more flexible way than the 'balance of payments need' of the Articles of Agreement, but shares with the latter the fact that it is a macroeconomic test, not one that considers the needs of particular sectors of the economy.

[35] Article V, Section 3(a) of the Articles of Agreement. This requirement does not apply to resources other than the general resources; for instance, grants for debt reduction are made to heavily indebted poor countries under the HIPC Initiative (cf. pp. 134–36 below).

framework of these rights and obligations that the Covenant could have an indirect impact on a specialized agency.

For the Fund, these considerations would limit the possible obligation to one that would not do violence either to its mandate or to the respective rights and obligations of the Fund and its members as stated in its Articles of Agreement. It would also exclude a positive duty to engage in a specific action or activity, or to provide a specific amount of financial resources to any member or group of members. What then would be the remaining contents of such an obligation? Commentators have suggested various definitions of such a duty. For example, it has been suggested that they have a 'duty of vigilance' to ensure that their actions do not produce negative human rights effects,[36] or a duty to 'pay due regard' to the Covenant.[37] Others have put the obligation in negative terms, as a duty 'not to undermine' the borrowing country's efforts to abide by the human rights conventions to which they are parties.[38] However, there are serious impediments to defining a specific duty of the

[36] Pierre Klein, 'Les Institutions Financières Internationales et les Droits de la Personne', 1999 *Revue Belge de Droit International*, p. 97 at 111–14. Klein finds the source of this obligation in the *Corfu Channel* case, and, extending the principle to international organizations, suggests that they 'impose on international financial institutions the duty to ensure that their decisions do not produce negative consequences on the human rights situation in the borrowing States'.

[37] Michael Lucas, 'The International Monetary Fund's Conditionality and the International Covenant on Economic, Social and Cultural Rights: An Attempt To Define The Relations', 1992 *Revue Belge de Droit International*, p. 104 at 122. The obligation is based on the author's views of the 'general prosperity' clause of Article I, paragraph (v) of the Fund's Articles of Agreement and the relationship between the Fund and the United Nations.

[38] With respect to the World Bank, Bradlow has written: 'at least in those countries that are signatories to human rights conventions, the Bank may have an obligation to ensure that its operations do not undermine the country's efforts to abide by these conventions'. He added in a footnote: 'Applying this standard will not be easy given the differing interpretations States may have about how to implement their human rights obligations. A satisfactory outcome to this problem would be facilitated by an explicit Bank human rights policy'. Bradlow recognizes that the Fund's influence over human rights is more limited than the Bank's, because (i) it is a monetary, not a development, institution; and (ii) it operates in a much shorter time horizon. But he adds that the Fund has 'some' responsibility to help protect the citizens of its member countries from human rights abuses. 'It cannot be indifferent to situations in which human rights abuses have become so serious as to cause monetary consequences'. But he acknowledges that there are limits to the Fund's ability to act in this respect: 'It should be noted that the Fund faces a more difficult situation in this regard than the Bank. There are three reasons for this. First, as the manager of the international monetary system, the IMF must balance its responsibilities to the citizens of the violating State against its responsibilities to the other stakeholders in the international monetary system. Consequently, it cannot easily impose sanctions on a State that violates human rights if this would have substantial adverse effect on the international monetary system. Second, the IMF has fewer options than the Bank for dealing with human rights abuses. Because the IMF provides financing for general balance of payments support rather than for specific projects, it cannot easily direct the flow of the financing. Consequently, its only option when faced with a serious human rights problem is to either deal with the State purely on the basis of its monetary situation or to impose sanctions on the State. Third, the Articles of Agreement constrain the IMF's ability to use sanctions. The Articles require the IMF to make its financing facilities available to any Member State in "good standing" who is suffering from the type of balance of payments problem that the facility was established to help correct. A member is in "good

Fund with regard to the Covenant. These impediments can be seen from the perspective of the country involved, and from that of the Fund.

With respect to the country itself, it must first be acknowledged that it is the responsibility of each country to make sure that its policies are consistent with its international commitments and, for this purpose, to ascertain the extent of those commitments and the manner in which it will discharge them. This is particularly the case with respect to undertakings that are progressive in nature and broad in scope, such as many of the undertakings set out in the Covenant. Given the considerable discretion States Parties have in assessing the efforts they can make at any point in time in gradually achieving economic and social rights under the Covenant, it is the responsibility of the authorities in the country to decide how to include considerations related to the implementation of such rights in the design of the country's economic plans and policies. It follows that it is for the member to bring up such considerations in its relations with the Fund.

It may be noted that the ability of many countries which desire to make progress in this field may be constrained. First, if one considers only the question of the budgetary allocations that can be made in a crisis situation, it quickly becomes apparent that the choices of the government may be extremely limited. In the face of a shortfall in income, a government may face a number of conflicting claims on what few resources are available, and may not be in a position, in spite of its best efforts and with all the external assistance available, to insulate the poorest segments of its population from the effects of the crisis. Thus there may be significant limits to the ability of a State Party to devote resources to the promotion of the social rights set out in the Covenant, and some temporary regression in the achievement of these rights may be unavoidable.

Secondly, the achievement of improvements in the social conditions called for in the Covenant is not exclusively a matter of increasing government social expenditures. Economic growth, or growth-oriented adjustment, is an indispensable precondition of the redistribution of wealth implied in the Covenant. In turn, economic growth needs to be fostered by a judicious mix of policies involving many different facets of the economy, including, in particular, fostering private investment, both domestic and foreign. In this sense, to judge a country's performance under the Covenant exclusively from the perspective of its spending on social programmes would be inappropriate.

Thirdly, in assessing the effects of a particular programme or policy adopted by a State Party against the State's international commitments, it is important to compare the outcome of the programme or policy with the alternative of the lack of a programme and the lack of external support to the country. Even allowing for the difficulty of making such comparisons, it is possible that, in many cases, lack of

standing" if it is performing all the obligations of membership in the IMF. These obligations, as stipulated in the Articles of Agreement, do not include human rights performance.' Daniel D. Bradlow, 'Symposium: Social Justice and Development: Critical Issues Facing the Bretton Woods System: the World Bank, the IMF and Human Rights', 6 *Transnt'l Law and Contemp. Probs.*, 47, at 72–3 (1996).

a Fund-supported programme would have resulted in worse outcomes for the poorest segments of the population than the Fund-supported programme provided. While no claim is made that all Fund-supported programmes are necessarily the best ones that could be devised under the circumstances, it must be acknowledged that a number of constraints limit the ability of member countries to develop programmes that respond adequately to the crisis situation in which the programme is developed while at the same time fully protecting the poorest segments of the population.

With respect to the Fund, it must first and foremost be emphasized that the Fund has no general mandate to ensure that its members abide by their international obligations. The extent to which the Fund may consider the international under-takings of its members is defined by the Fund's own purposes. The Fund may view the discharge by its members of certain international obligations as particularly significant. This is the case of the member's financial obligations to the Fund itself, and the Fund has adopted detailed policies to deal with its members' arrears to it [39] The Fund also considers a member's arrears to other lenders as relevant, and has adopted policies in this regard.[40] Beyond such financial obligations, however, the Fund has neither the mandate nor the capacity to consider all of a member's international commitments. As mentioned above, it is up to each member to decide for itself which of its international commitments are significant in the design of its programmes of adjustment, and how these international commitments are to be interpreted and applied. In particular, it is up to each member to decide how its international commitments regarding economic and social rights, as well as con-stitutional or other legal requirements, may affect its adjustment programme. The Fund cannot substitute itself to the member for this purpose.

Moreover, the Fund must also take other considerations into account. In its own decisions to support member country's adjustment programmes, the Fund must act in conformity with its Articles of Agreements. In its surveillance activities, the policies it adopts must 'respect the domestic social and political policies of members',[41] which constrains the Fund's ability to raise social development issues in this context. While this constraint does not apply to the Fund's policies with respect to the use of its resources, other provisions of the Articles must be taken into account. In particular, in its decisions on the use of its resources, the Fund must take into account a number of factors that are not covered as such by the Covenant, and indeed, that are not related directly to human rights, but which are required to be taken into consideration by its Articles of Agreement. For example, the Fund must be mindful of the effects of a crisis in a particular country, not only on the country itself, but also on its neighbours in and possibly beyond the region. The sudden devaluation of a currency may produce an artificial advantage in terms of price of the concerned country's exports that is not welcomed by other Fund members. It may

---

[39] *See Selected Decisions*, pp. 140–6 and 548–67.

[40] Decision No. 3153-(70/95) dated 26 October 1970, *Selected Decisions*, p. 197, and Chairman's summings up at pp. 198 and 199. [41] Article IV, Section 3(b).

also render a country's imports more expensive, and reduce the export opportunities of its trading partners. Also, a sudden flight of capital from one country may trigger a similar outflow from other countries unless it is remedied early. Similarly, the Fund must bear in mind that it acts as a catalyst in the transfer of resources to the members making use of its resources. To enhance the flow of funds to its members, the Fund must ensure that the programmes it supports are realistic and can reasonably be expected to be completed successfully. Also, the Fund must, under its Articles of Agreement, make its resources available to its members under 'appropriate safeguards', intended to provide assurance that the funds will be used as intended, and that they will be repaid on schedule.

While the States Parties to the Covenant have undertaken certain obligations, in particular the obligation to achieve progressively certain social rights for their population, the practical implementation of these obligations is subject to a number of constraints that are particularly difficult to overcome for developing countries. For its part, within its mandate and resources, the Fund provides technical assistance and financial resources intended to help its members overcome the balance of payment difficulties that hamper their development efforts. It does so on the basis of its own Articles of Agreement.

E. Conclusion

The Fund is a specialized agency. The *raison d'être* of a specialized agency is to enable countries that may have different political systems and do not necessarily share all the same economic, social, and cultural values to cooperate together in well defined areas. The question is whether it is better for the international community to allow this kind of cooperation to continue or whether adherence to common political, economic, social, and cultural values should be a condition for membership in specialized agencies. Until now the former approach has prevailed, and it may be expected to prevail as long as the benefits of cooperation outweigh those of exclusion.

3. CONSIDERATIONS RELATED TO ECONOMIC AND SOCIAL HUMAN RIGHTS UNDER THE FUND'S ARTICLES OF AGREEMENT

While the Covenant has no legal effect on the Fund, it does not follow that the Fund may not, on the basis of its Articles of Agreement, take into account the relationship between its activities and the achievement of the social rights contained in the Covenant. The contribution of the Fund to the economic preconditions for the achievement of the rights contained in the Covenant is discussed in this section. However, before discussing this topic, it may be useful to consider more fully the broader context in which the rights contained in the Covenant may be achieved.

This broader context includes a wider set of economic rights than those contained in the Covenant, and it involves economic considerations as well as legal ones.

It may be noted first that the Covenant does not contain all the important rights that need to be exercised in order for individuals to enjoy the social progress that is the objective of the Covenant. There are a number of rights that are essential for the achievement of the social rights set out in the Covenant but which are not stated in the Covenant. For example, the right to own property is stated in the Universal Declaration, but it is not included in either of the two Covenants, and thus has remained outside the scope of the human rights monitoring system. Similarly, workers' rights are expressed in the Covenant in terms reflecting the situation of wage-earners who work in their own country and do not have family abroad. Other rights, such as the rights to engage in economic activity and to trade, are as important to the realization of the rights specified in the Covenant. These rights provide the very basic tools that all people, including the poor, can use to engage in economic activity and to improve their economic condition. Also, in today's open economy, the right to work in other countries (incomplete as it is) and to remit one's earnings to one's family at home are equally important to a large number of workers. While the provisions of the Covenant may represent a common ground around which members of the United Nations found agreement at a certain point in time, they now appear somewhat removed from the realities of today's internally and externally open economy.

Moreover, the social rights set out in the Covenant will not be realized unless certain economic preconditions are met. These preconditions include economic growth, without which no significant redistribution of wealth can take place. Also, the structural reforms and policies that need to be put in place are not limited to spending on social services. As the Fund's contribution to the 1995 World Summit for Social Development stated:

Social development requires a strategy of high-quality economic growth, macroeconomic stability, which generates low inflation, and promotion of the agricultural sector, where many of the poor work. A strategy of high-quality growth comprises a comprehensive package of policies encompassing four elements: (i) macroeconomic policies aimed at a stable and sustainable macroeconomic environment; (ii) structural policies aimed at a market-based environment for trade and investment; (iii) sound social policies, including social safety nets to protect the poor during periods of economic reform, cost-effective basic social expenditures, and employment-generating labor market policies; and (iv) good governance through accountable institutions and a transparent legal framework.[42]

Within this broad framework, however, the appropriate mix of policy to be applied at any given time by any given government is an elusive matter. Continuous adjustment of policies is an inescapable requirement, and results are never assured.

---

[42] International Monetary Fund, *Social Dimensions of the IMF's Policy Dialogue, prepared by the Staff of the International Monetary Fund for the World Summit for Social Development, Copenhagen, March 6–12 1995*, IMF Pamphlet Series No. 47, p. 1.

In this context, what the international financial institutions can provide is advice and financial assistance intended to help countries establish (or re-establish, as the case may be) and maintain the economic basis without which the States Parties to the Covenant are not in a position to fulfil their undertakings. For its part, the Fund is contributing to the objective of maintaining an international monetary system which provides a framework that facilitates economic growth. It is also pursuing certain economic rights which have a bearing on the achievement of social rights in an open economy, such as unrestricted payments for current international transactions, including family remittances. In providing financial assistance, the Fund has increasingly taken into account the special needs of developing countries, which are those States Parties to the Covenant that need international assistance to achieve their commitments under the Covenant.

Within this broader framework, certain aspects of the Fund's Articles of Agreement and activities are of special importance to the achievement of the rights set out in the Covenant. These appear under the Fund's responsibilities towards the international monetary system and its surveillance function (A), as well as under the financial assistance it provides to its members (B).[43]

A. Economic Growth as an Objective of Fund Surveillance

Economic growth is a necessary precondition for raising the standards of living of peoples, as States Parties to the Covenant have undertaken gradually to achieve.[44] Without growth, the right to health, food, or education cannot be further achieved. In this context, the inclusion of references to economic growth in the provisions of the Fund's Articles dealing with the objectives of the international monetary system and the Fund's surveillance responsibilities is significant.

Under the second amendment of the Fund's Articles of Agreement, the par value system was abandoned, and under Article IV Fund members were authorized to establish the exchange arrangements of their choice but undertook to collaborate with the Fund and other members to assure orderly exchange arrangements and to promote a stable system of exchange rates. More specific obligations with respect to economic, financial, and exchange rate policies were set forth in the same provision. For its part, the Fund was given responsibility for overseeing both the international monetary system in order to ensure its effective operation and the compliance of each member with its obligations under Article IV. In particular, the Fund was given the obligation to exercise 'firm surveillance' over the exchange rate policies of members. Also with the second amendment, growth appears in the Articles of Agreement, both as a purpose of the international monetary system, and as an objective of each member's economic and financial policies.

---

[43] Another aspect, not discussed here, is the Fund's technical assistance to its members.

[44] Good governance may be seen as another precondition, or even as a condition of growth itself. Poor governance (including corruption) may lead to the capture of the fruits of growth by those in power, and it may act as an obstacle to growth itself, in particular by stifling investment.

Article IV contains an introductory paragraph in which the objectives of the international monetary system are set out as follows:

Recognizing that the essential purpose of the international monetary system is to provide a framework that facilitates the exchange of goods, services, and capital among countries, *and that sustains sound economic growth*, and that a principal objective is the continuing development of the orderly underlying conditions that are necessary for financial and economic stability, each member undertakes to collaborate with the Fund and other members to assure orderly exchange arrangements and to promote a stable system of exchange rates (emphasis added).

It is at the request of Executive Directors of the Fund elected by developing countries (supported by others) that the expression 'sustains sound economic growth' was added to Section 1. As one commentator has noted, by the introduction of this expression into Article IV, the Articles 'explicitly recognized economic growth as one of the criteria for judging the successful functioning of the international monetary system'.[45]

Each Fund member undertakes to 'endeavor to direct its economic and financial policies toward the objective of fostering orderly economic growth with reasonable price stability, with due regard to its circumstances'.[46] In exercising its surveillance over the members' exchange rate policies, the Fund's appraisal 'shall take into account the extent to which the policies of the member, including its exchange rate policies, serve the objectives of the continuing development of the orderly underlying conditions that are necessary for financial stability, the promotion of sustained sound economic growth, and reasonable levels of employment'.[47] Thus, the Fund's surveillance covers the policies of its members to serve sustained sound economic growth and, in that context, the Fund assesses not only specific policies of its members but also, more generally, their observance of certain standards of 'good governance'.[48] However, the scope of the Fund's surveillance is limited by the Articles, which provide that the principles adopted by the Fund for the guidance of its members 'shall respect the domestic social and political policies of members'.[49] Although issues of social policy often come up in discussions of budget equilibrium, this provision restricts the ability of the Fund to extend its surveillance to deal directly with issues of social policy.

B. Financial Assistance

The Fund may provide financial assistance to its members, either directly out of its general resources (held in the Fund's General Resources Account) or from other resources.

---

[45] Margaret Garritsen de Vries, *The International Monetary Fund 1972–1978, Cooperation on Trial, volume II, Narrative and Analysis*, IMF, p. 754 (1985).   [46] Article IV, Section 1(i).

[47] Surveillance Over Exchange Rate Policies, Fund Executive Board Decision No. 5392-(77-63), 29 April 1977, as amended, *Selected Decisions*, p. 10.

[48] Guidance Note of 2 July 1997 (EBS/97/125), *Selected Decisions*, p. 31.

[49] Article IV, Section 3(b).

C. From the Fund's General Resources

The financial assistance the Fund provides through its general resources is rooted in the provision of the Articles of Agreement which states that a purpose of the Fund is 'to give confidence to members by making the general resources of the Fund temporarily available to them under adequate safeguards, thus providing them with opportunity to correct maladjustments in their balance of payments without resorting to measures destructive of national or international prosperity'.[50] In addition, Article V, Section 3 requires the Fund to adopt policies on the use of its general resources, including policies on stand-by arrangements, and authorizes it to adopt special policies for special balance of payments problems 'that will assist members to solve their balance of payments problems *in a manner consistent with the provisions of this Agreement*' (emphasis added).[51]

Conditionality is the 'explicit link between the approval or continuation of the Fund's financing and the implementation of certain specified aspects of the government's policy program'.[52] The conditionality attached to the use of the Fund's resources has to be consistent with the provisions of the Articles of Agreement. This limits the types of conditions that may be included to those that can be accommodated under the Articles. A recent survey shows that, while the scope of structural conditionality has been expanded, the majority of structural conditions are concentrated in a relatively small number of sectors that are at the very core of the Fund's involvement in its member countries: exchange and trade systems, and fiscal and financial sectors.[53] Even within this range, there is often tension between 'ownership' of the programme and policies that make up the reform programme the Fund supports, and the sovereignty of the Fund members. The 1979 Guidelines on Conditionality underscored the principle of parsimony and the need to limit the performance criteria to the minimum number needed to evaluate policy implementation. They also stressed that the Fund should pay due regard to the country's social and political objectives, economic priorities, and circumstances.[54]

Within this broad framework, what is the possible link between Fund conditionality and economic, social, and cultural rights? Two legal bases can be found. The first is in the purposes of the Fund, which apply to its financial assistance: one of the Fund's purposes is '(v) To give confidence to members by making the general resources of the Fund temporarily available to them under adequate safeguards,

---

[50] Article I(v).

[51] Article V, Section 3. By contrast, Article V, Section 12(f), which applies to the Special Disbursement Account resources, and Article V, Section 2(b), which is applicable to the administered accounts (ESAF, PRGF), only require that the use of these resources be 'consistent with the purposes of the Fund'.

[52] International Monetary Fund, *Conditionality in Fund-supported Programs: Policy Issues*, 16 February 2001, paragraph 10 (available through the Fund's Internet site). [53] *Ibid*, paragraph 50.

[54] *See* International Monetary Fund, *Conditionality in Fund-Supported Programs, Overview*, 20 February 2001, paragraph 3 (available through the Fund's Internet site).

thus providing them with opportunity to correct maladjustments in their balance of payments *without resorting to measures destructive of national or international prosperity*' (emphasis added). Under this provision, the Fund has taken the view that its conditionality could include the removal of exchange and trade restrictions, but also the avoidance of measures that may be damaging to the environment or to the welfare of the population. For instance, attention may be given to health and education budgets, safety nets, and good governance, including avoidance of corruption. However, this does not mean that the Fund sees itself as trying to substitute itself for the national authorities in determining national priorities. In particular, military expenditures are outside the scope of Fund conditionality pursuant to a decision of the Executive Board.[55] More recently, there has been a discernible trend towards reducing the Fund's involvement in domestic policies through conditionality. The general criteria would be that the Fund should limit its conditionality to macroeconomic variables and to those structural elements that are critical to macroeconomic stability. The World Bank would be expected to strengthen its role in the other areas where structural adjustment is needed.[56]

Another basis for Fund involvement is its assessment, as a condition for its assistance, that the member's programme is viable and likely to be implemented. This means that, if a programme is so strict that it is likely to generate strong popular opposition, it may not be implemented, and the Fund should not support it. It also means that, if egregious or systematic violations of human rights lead foreign governments or creditors to suspend their financial assistance or other forms of external financing, the programme may not be implemented, and the Fund should not support it. Clearly this does not establish a direct link with the objectives of the Covenant. However, to the extent that major violations of economic and social human rights would trigger civil unrest or a lack of foreign financing, there would be at least an indirect link. Whether or not a programme may create such problems is a matter of judgment for the Managing Director when transmitting the member's request to the Executive Board and for the Executive Board when deciding on the request.

D. Special Facilities for Developing Countries

Because of the principle of uniform treatment among members, the Fund's general resources must be made available to all members, whether developed or developing,

---

[55] Concluding Remarks by the Acting Chairman, 2 October 1991, *Selected Decisions*, p. 447, at p. 448.

[56] Erik Denters has suggested that the Fund has a duty to 'heed requests by members to avoid, as far as possible, "measures destructive of national prosperity" and to safeguard socioeconomic standards as long as balance of payments support is provided under adequate safeguards'. Erik Denters, *Law and Policy of IMF Conditionality*, Kluwer, p. 183 (1996). Denters, while recognizing that the Fund is not bound by the Covenant, suggests that Article I, para. (v) and its reference to the correction of maladjustments of balance of payments 'without resorting to measures destructive of national or international prosperity' provides the legal basis for this duty.

for balance of payments assistance. Other resources of the Fund, however, may be earmarked for balance of payments assistance to developing countries. There are two categories of such resources: (a) capital gains on sales of the Fund's gold, once transferred to the Special Disbursement Account, may be used for 'balance of payments assistance [. . .] on special terms to developing members in difficult circumstances' taking into account 'the level of per capita income' (Article V, Section 12(f)(ii)); and (b) contributions may be made to the Fund, in the form of loans or grants, for financial or technical assistance consistent with the purposes of the Fund to specified countries or groups of countries (Article V, Section 2(b)). On the basis of these provisions, certain resources have been generated or contributed for financial assistance to developing countries. This financial assistance is provided by the Fund through concessional lending under the Poverty Reduction and Growth Facility (PRGF) and through debt relief under the Heavily Indebted Poor Countries (HIPC) Initiative.

The Fund supports the economic adjustment and reform efforts of its low-income members through the PRGF, which provides loans at an annual interest rate of $\frac{1}{2}$ of 1 per cent with repayment periods of 5½–10 years. The PRGF, which incorporates recommendations from past evaluations of the Fund's concessional lending facility, is designed to make poverty-reduction programmes a key element of a growth-oriented strategy. Programmes supported by the PRGF are framed around a comprehensive, nationally owned poverty-reduction strategy, the costs of which are fully incorporated into the macroeconomic framework. In the case of HIPC-eligible members, this tightens the link between resources made available by debt relief and additional poverty reduction efforts.

The HIPC Initiative is designed to reduce the external debt burden of eligible countries to sustainable levels, enabling them to service their external debts without the need for further debt relief and without compromising growth. Launched in 1996, the Initiative marked the first time that multilateral, Paris Club, and other official and bilateral creditors united to take this kind of comprehensive approach to debt relief. Assistance under the HIPC Initiative is limited to countries that are eligible for PRGF and International Development Association (IDA) loans and that have established strong track records of policy performance under PRGF- and IDA-supported programs but are not expected to achieve a sustainable debt situation after full use of traditional debt-relief mechanisms.

A strong track record of policy implementation is intended to ensure that debt relief is put to effective use. Currently, seventy-seven members of the Fund are eligible to receive PGRF loans. While the qualification of these members for the HIPC Initiative is determined on a case-by-case basis, the enhancements to the Initiative could allow as many as forty-one Fund members to qualify for assistance.[57]

---

[57] *See* International Monetary Fund, *Financial Assistance for the IMF's Poorest Members: An Update*, 2 May 2001, para. 3.

4. CONCLUSIONS

This Chapter has considered the relationship between the Fund and the Covenant. The following points have been made regarding the nature and role of the Fund.

The Fund is a monetary agency, not a development agency. While its mandate and policies have evolved over time, it remains a monetary agency, charged with the responsibility to maintain orderly exchange rates and a multilateral system of payments free of restrictions on current payments.

The Fund functions essentially at the macroeconomic level, not at the level of individual sectors; its responsibilities in this respect are different from those of the development banks.

The Fund's resources (including those entrusted to it by donors) can be used for balance of payments purposes, not for project financing.

For its part, the Covenant is a treaty between States which contains obligations addressed to States. Neither by its terms nor by the terms of the Fund's relationship agreement with the United Nations is it possible to conclude that the Covenant is applicable to the Fund. Moreover, the norms contained in the Covenant have not attained a status under general international law that would make them applicable to the Fund independently of the Covenant.

The fact that the Covenant does not apply to the Fund does not mean that the Fund does not contribute to the objectives of the Covenant. The Fund's contribution to economic and social human rights is essential but indirect: by promoting a stable system of exchange rates and a system of current payments free of restrictions, and by including growth as an objective of the framework of the international monetary system, as well as providing financial support for balance of payment problems, the Fund helps provide the economic conditions that are a precondition for the achievement of the rights set out in the Covenant.

Should the Fund do more to assist its member countries in achieving the objectives of the Covenant? The participation of the Fund in the HIPC Initiative and in the PRSP process clearly shows that the Fund has adapted its activities to the needs of its poorest member countries. However, in the final analysis, what it can do is determined by its Articles of Agreement, itself a treaty among its 183 member countries. As has been aptly written: 'there is a limit to "institutional elasticity", i.e., the extent to which institutions created and still used for other purposes can be "stretched" in order to get them to perform human rights functions when those functions are accomplished *at the expense* of their manifest functions'.[58]

In a time when the Cold War is over, and the wide ideological divide that had dominated the post-World War II period has all but disappeared, it is tempting to brush aside the principle of specialization that has governed the establishment of the specialized agencies and their relationships with the United Nations and between

---

[58] W. Michael Reisman, 'Through or Despite Governments: Differentiated Responsibilities in Human Rights Programs', 72 *Iowa L. Rev.* 391, at 395 (1987) (emphasis in the original).

themselves. However, States continue to have differing (and sometimes divergent) views on a number of topics, many of them with human rights implications. The principle of specialization continues to permit States with different views to cooperate among themselves on matters of common interest to them in spite of these differences.

In the end, the question may be raised: just how important are these institutional rules that limit the extent to which the Fund can take the Covenant into account? Should they not be bent, or ignored entirely, to put the Fund fully at the service of the higher cause of human progress that the Covenant represents? The answer to this question is to be found in the nature of the Covenant itself. The Covenant is a treaty, a set of legal rules binding on the parties to it. In selecting this form, the drafters of the Covenant relied on the rule of law as the vehicle to bring about more fully the human progress expressed in the Universal Declaration of 1948. International organizations are also subject to the rule of law. Their members, their debtors, and their creditors all expect them to carry out their activities at all times in conformity with the rules that apply to them. However, the international financial organizations, including the Fund, are helping their member countries in developing sound frameworks for governance and better legal and judicial systems, all of which highlights the rule of law as a central element of development. If the international organizations are to be successful in this task, they must be credible. To be credible, they must apply the rule of law to their own situation, just as they encourage others to apply it to theirs.

Hence, legal considerations do matter, and the Fund is not free to disregard its own legal structure for the sake of pursuing goals that are not its own mandated purposes. If the members of the Fund believe that it should adopt a more direct approach to the integration of human rights considerations in its decisions, they may of course propose an amendment to the Fund's Articles of Agreement. It is the theme of this Chapter that the Fund already contributes significantly to the achievement of the objectives of the Covenant, while discharging all of its responsibilities towards all of its members.

Part Three

Corporations

5

Catching the Conscience of the King: Corporate Players on the International Stage

CELIA WELLS AND JUANITA ELIAS*

A touch of cynicism is perhaps no bad thing. It is hard enough to conceptualize the 'corporation' for the purposes of developing legal and moral accountability at the best of times. The fate of some of the world's largest corporations underlines that difficulty in a stark way. Revelations of corporate fraud on a grander scale than even the most committed corporate critics might have imagined triggered a serious slide in share values in 2002. In what senses did Enron and WorldCom exist? One day (year) Enron was the subject of the biggest investigation undertaken by Human Rights Watch,[1] the next it had 'disappeared' in a cloud of debts, almost taking its auditors Arthur Andersen with it.[2] Investment analysts, accountants, and now bankers came under a searching spotlight.[3] In a symbolic display calculated to emphasize their betrayal of decent corporate values but also likely to undermine any faith in them, executives of WorldCom, the second largest communications company in the US, were handcuffed and marched into

* We have been assisted in the preparation of this paper by Lisa Carson and Louise Obara of the ESRC Centre for Business Relationships Accountability Sustainability and Society, Cardiff University. Their help has been invaluable. We also thank those who have commented on the paper in draft: Robin Churchill, Bob Lee, Derek Morgan, and Oliver Quick.

[1] Human Rights Watch 'The Enron Corporation: Complicity: The Dabhol Power Corporation' (January 1999) www.hrw.org/reports/1999/enron/, accessed 28 October 2002.

[2] Andersen was fined US$500,000 and given 5 years' probation and a fine after being found guilty of obstructing justice: http://www.chron.com/cs/CDA/story.hts/business/1620528/ accessed 18 September 2003.

[3] Enron, Tyco, Global Crossing, Martha Stewart, ImClone, and AOL Time Warner were all accused or charged with deceiving investors: *The Independent* 28 July 2002. Enron's Treasurer was given a 5-year prison sentence after pleading guilty to conspiracy charges: http://news.findlaw.com/business/s/20030910/enronpleadc.html, accessed 18 September 2003. Ten other executives pleaded not guilty; for information on Enron investigations and litigation see http://news.findlaw.com/legalnews/lit/enron, accessed 18 September 2003.

court.[4] These corporate scandals highlight two important distinctions: that between corporate and white collar offending and that between corporate and directorial responsibility. As to the first, the Enron and other scandals disclose some white collar (that is offending against the company itself) as well as corporate crime (that is crime affecting consumers, employees, and others). The second distinction subdivides the field of corporate crime into the accountability of the *corporate entity* and the accountability of individual directors and officers for that crime.

While this essay is concerned with human rights violations rather than fraud by multinational corporations,[5] similar lessons emerge.[6] Many corporations, like states, have the resources and power both to perpetrate and to escape responsibility for abuse. This explains the air of scepticism pervading this contribution. The subject is one that benefits from a huge and expanding literature, including scholarly legal writing, governmental and intergovernmental outputs, as well as the work of campaigning groups such as Amnesty International and Human Rights Watch.[7] From this mass we have attempted to distil an essence, and three core questions emerge in relation to multinational corporations: what legal avenues are possible? what principles of accountability can be used? and what models of complicity can be applied? Beneath these core issues lurk many undercurrents and it has not always been possible to keep their warring ways under control. If we are to address the question of *how* corporate complicity might be introduced then it is necessary to suspend judgement on *whether* corporate complicity is likely to be an effective mechanism for regulating multinational corporations. It is not possible to write simply about structures and rules without thinking both about the legal and political contexts in which they might operate and about the efficacy of an international regime of corporate liability. If sometimes in what follows we seem to be very cynical, while at others on the side of the angels, this accurately reflects our ambivalence.[8] While most of us would like to sign up to reduce human rights violations, the means of achieving that reduction remain elusive.

---

[4] Worldcom incorrectly accounted for $3.8bn in operating expenses purely to meet profit targets promised to Wall St. *The Guardian* 2 August 2002; for up to date news see http://news.findlaw.com/legalnews/lit/worldcom/index.html, accessed 27 October 2002.

[5] We have used the term multinational corporation interchangeably with multinational enterprise (MNE) and transnational corporation (TNC). For a discussion of the distinctions drawn between these terms, see *infra*, text accompanying note 41.

[6] Some argue that one strategy is to bring actions for misleading advertising against corporations that make false claims about their human rights credentials.

[7] Amnesty International, www.amnesty.org; Business and Human Rights www.business-humanrights.org/; Human Rights Watch www.hrw.org; Business-Human Rights Watch, www.Corporate-responsibility.org; www.accountability.org.uk; www.accaglobal.com/sustainability; www.neweconomics.org.

[8] Capturing the angelic side, Mason notes that 'the ideology of human rights has become so influential that it has attained the status of a religion': 'Comment on Papers Presented at the Commercial Law and Human Rights Conference' in S. Bottomley and D. Kinley (eds), *Commercial Law and Human Rights* (2002), 1 at 4.

In the first two sections we explain the background and context of the contemporary debate about the role of multinational corporations in human rights abuses, including an outline of some of the strategies already attempted to hold corporations to account. National jurisdictions either are reluctant to or encounter difficulty in applying criminal sanctions to corporations. For most, criminal law applied to individual human agents is altogether a more attractive enterprise. The reasons for this are both conceptual and (broadly) political. We explore those difficulties in the third section below. Multinational corporations are accused both of direct human rights abuses and of colluding in various ways with repressive states. Because of the normative implications of this task many writers have drawn on complicity, a notion widely recognized in systems of criminal law. Indeed it has been claimed that complicity is 'an essential concept in the context of international efforts to ensure a higher standards [sic] of corporate social responsibility'.[9] In the fourth section therefore we examine the concept of complicity and explore the ways in which it might be used to hold multinational corporations to account in international law. As we argue, however, it is not the marriage of criminal law principles and international law[10] but the adoption of the corporation as a fully accepted member of the 'legally responsible' family that presents the greatest obstacle here.[11]

While many national laws have only recently begun to address the corporation as the potential subject of criminal law, so too international law attracts its own sceptics, those who believe it to have a limited role in sanctioning or preventing human rights abuses. Many of the arguments run parallel in these two fields and are rooted in (often submerged) assumptions about the functions and purposes of law. This will be the subject of the final section below, a broad evaluation of the roles that law is capable of performing.

1. CONTEXT: CORPORATE REGULATION IN AN ERA OF GLOBALIZATION

A. Transformations in Power

Issues of corporate accountability need to be considered in the light of the changing nature of state power and influence in the international system and the rising power of multinational corporations, whose involvement in human rights violations has a long history. In particular, firms operating in primary sector extractive industries, because of their dependence on fixed geological factors, are more likely to collude with repressive regimes in setting up and protecting their production sites. United Fruit in Guatemala (1954) and ITT in Chile (1973) co-operated with the American

---

[9] Clapham, 'On complicity', in M. Henzelin and R. Roth (eds), *Le Droit penal a l'epreuve de l'internationalisation* (2000), 241.

[10] War Crimes Tribunals and the International Criminal Court have yet to regard corporations as within their jurisdiction.   [11] See the discussion *infra* in section 4.

government in the overthrow of the pro-labour rights governments of Arbenz (Guatemala) and Allende (Chile). Royal Dutch Shell co-operated closely with the Nigerian military government in suppressing local resistance to oil extraction policies and practices in Ogoniland. Shell made it possible, at company expense, for the military regime violently to suppress environmental campaigners.[12] More recent is the evidence of multinational corporate involvement in human rights violations in Sudan's oil fields, in the form of support of the military regime through provision of infrastructure and foreign revenues.[13] And BP, regarded as one of the more socially responsible companies, is part of a consortium whose agreement with Turkey to build the Baku-Tblisi-Ceyahn oil pipeline suspends environmental and other laws except the constitution itself.[14]

But human rights abuses are not confined to these sectors alone. In the manufacturing sector (where multinational corporations account for almost all of the world's manufactured exports)[15] there are numerous examples of firms or their suppliers taking advantage of local workforces, through low pay, long hours, and poor working conditions as well as suppressing trade union rights. Some have even suggested that manufacturing multinational corporations have an interest in supporting authoritarian regimes (such as that of Suharto in Indonesia) where human rights are routinely violated.[16] States are unlikely to take action against multinational corporations in order to protect labour standards and human rights because of fears of losing much needed foreign investment. Multinational corporations tend to establish subsidiaries in countries where conditions are favourable to their business. In their negotiations with the governments of host countries their ability to pick up and leave provides them with a great deal of leverage over states dependent upon the jobs that they provide. Development strategies by international financial institutions such as the World Bank and IMF, alongside programmes of deregulation and privatization, render states even less willing to frighten off foreign investors; they are more dependent upon them than ever before.

Corporate complicity emerged as a possible mechanism of regulation when it was recognized that corporations and states may be equally implicated in human rights abuses. To expand this further, two interconnected developments help to understand why many people believe it is necessary to bring multinational corporations under the

[12] D. Forsythe, *The Political Economy of Human Rights: Transnational Corporations*, Human Rights Working Papers (University of Denver) http://www.du.edu/humanrights/workingpapers/papers/14-forsythe-03-01.pdf No. 14, posted 26 March 2001, accessed 6 August 2002, at 6.

[13] Christian Aid, *The Regulatory Void: EU company involvement in human rights violations in Sudan* http://www.christian-aid.org.uk/indepth/0105suda/sudan.htm, accessed 28 October 2002.

[14] Monbiot 'Trouble in the Pipeline' *The Guardian* 3 September 2002, http://politics.guardian.co.uk/columnist/story/0,9321,785316,00.html accessed 24 September 2002. The consortium includes two American companies Unocal and Delta Hess, which may be vulnerable to litigation under the Alien Tort Claims Act, discussed *infra* in section 2. For a description of the project, see Socor 'You can't call this pipeline a Pipedream now' *Wall Street Journal Europe*, 27–29 September 2002.

[15] D. Held *et al.*, *Global Transformations* (1999), at 254.

[16] J. Pilger, *The New Rulers of The World* (2002); Suharto's government was overthrown in May 1998.

authority of international human rights frameworks: the changing international legal system and the effect of economic globalization in undermining the significance of the state. Traditionally international law conforms largely to a state-centric view of world politics. In this conceptualization, states are viewed as the primary actors in the international system, with international law acting to regulate relations between states.[17] This hinges on the idea that humankind is organized into discrete, political communities defined in terms of their territory. Within their territories nation states—or their national governments—claim total and exclusive authority over (and allegiance from) their peoples. As well as being defined in terms of territory and sovereignty, the state in the international system is often viewed as an autonomous actor in the sense that fixed borders delineate its domestic political, social, and economic activities from the world outside. The sovereign nation-state therefore takes responsibility for ensuring the security and well-being of its citizens, protecting them from external interventions.[18] 'What a State did inside its borders in relation to its own nationals remained its own affair, an element of its autonomy, a matter of its "domestic jurisdiction".'[19] Many of the early examples of individual rights in international law were confined to the protection of a State's own citizens while abroad: in other words the motivation for it was politico-economic rather than humanitarian.[20]

International law was not about individuals or classes of people, but a mechanism for maintaining stable international relations in an 'anarchic' international system (one in which there is no central sovereign authority). Challenges to the role and primacy of the state in world politics has, however, fundamentally altered the role and function of international law, and it is to these challenges that we now turn. In recent years the role and function of international law has expanded, concerning itself with relations not only between states but also, through concerns about human rights, with the individual. For example, the recognition in international law of war crimes, crimes against humanity, and genocide makes clear that acting in accordance with domestic legal frameworks or acquiescing to the commands of national leaders is not an adequate ground for absolving individual guilt.[21] The application of these principles of international law (established at Nuremberg) was seen most recently in the establishment of war crimes tribunals for the former Yugoslavia (1993) and Rwanda (1994). Although these tribunals experienced real problems in bringing the key accused to trial, 'both have taken important steps toward implementing the law

---

[17] A. Cassese, *International Law* (2001), at 3.

[18] McGrew, 'Power shift: from national governance to global governance?' in D. Held (ed), *A Globalizing World* (2000), at 133.

[19] Henkin, 'International Law: Politics, Values and Functions', *216 Collected Courses of Hague Academy of International Law* 13 (vol IV, 1989) at 208. [20] Ibid.

[21] Held, *Violence, Law and Justice in a Global Age* (2001), Social Science Research Council Essays on Globalization after September 11, Nov 5, http://www.ssrc.org/sept11/essays/held.htm accessed 6 August 2002. And see Clapham, 'Globalization and the Rule of Law', paper prepared for International Commission of Jurists' Triennial Meeting, Cape Town 1998, http://www.business-humanrights.org/Globalization-and-the rule-of-law.htm, accessed 1 September 2002.

governing war crimes and thereby, reducing the credibility gap between the promises of such law, on the one hand, and the weakness of its application, on the other'.[22] The establishment of an International Criminal Court is designed further to entrench the connection between international legal principles in relation to human rights violations and their enforcement.[23]

Held views this process of strengthening international legal commitments to human rights as another side to the multi-faceted nature of globalization:

> the story of globalization is not just economic: it is also one of growing aspirations for international law and justice. From the UN system to the EU, from changes to the laws of war to the entrenchment of human rights, from the emergence of international environmental regimes to the foundation of the International Criminal Court, there is also another narrative being told—a narrative which seeks to reframe human activity and entrench it in law, rights and responsibilities.[24]

States have lost authority to supranational bodies at the same time as they have privatized many of their domestic functions.[25] But it is economic globalization that is generally presented as the major challenge to state sovereignty. The idea of the unitary, autonomous, sovereign state has always been something of a fiction, but there are several ways in which the sovereignty of states has been undermined over the past two decades, with consequent implications for international law. Stubbs and Underhill suggest that global economic changes have significantly undermined state-centric conceptualizations of the global order:

> the growth of the global economy, especially during the 1980s, has created problems for the state. As the global economy has become more complex and the transnational political and economic linkages have expanded, seemingly exponentially, the state's tasks of monitoring and, where appropriate, attempting to control events and non-state actors have in many cases been made more difficult. The capacity of the institutional state, in terms of its resources, knowledgeable people, and legislative authority, has not always kept pace with the relatively rapid changes taking place in both the international and domestic political economies. State actors are finding themselves scrambling to keep up with events.[26]

B. Economic Globalization

The challenge to the economic sovereignty of states comes in particular from financial speculation in deregulated currency markets and the growing economic

---

[22] Held, *supra* note 21, at 3.

[23] Rome Statute of the International Criminal Court, adopted by the United Nations Diplomatic Conference of Plenipotentiaries on the establishment of an International Court on 17 July 1998, ratified and established 1 July 2002.   [24] Held, *supra* note 21, at 1.

[25] International Council on Human Rights Policy (ICHRP) *Beyond Voluntarism: Human Rights and the Developing Legal Obligations of Companies* (2002), at 10. See also Kamminga and Zia-Zarifi, 'Liability of Multinational Corporations under international law: An introduction' in Kamminga M. and Zia-Zarifi, S. (eds), *Liability of Multinational Corporations under International Law* (2000), at 5.

[26] Stubbs and Underhill, 'State Policies and Global Changes', in R. Stubbs and G.R.D. Underhill (eds), *Political Economy and the Changing Global Order* (1994), at 423.

power of multinational corporations. These processes make it much more difficult to regard countries as controlling their own separate economies. Writers place different degrees of emphasis on the processes; some (often labelled the 'hyperglobalists') talk about the end of the state,[27] whilst others talk more in terms of the changing role of the state in an era of globalization. States find that their role has become increasingly complex in a more highly interdependent world and take on the role of attempting to attract international capital rather than of regulating it.[28] A rather obvious point is that some states have greater levels of power and influence, and therefore ability, to regulate multinational corporations. However, in a globalized economy, firms (especially those in manufacturing) can move easily across borders and evade boycotts and sanctions.[29] Many of these writings also focus attention on the diminishing centrality of the state in world politics. Multinational corporations are viewed as rival sources of power and influence in the world.[30]

In terms of measuring the economic might of multinational corporations, it has become standard practice, of which Table 1 is an example, to present a comparison of the annual revenue of multinational corporations with country Gross Domestic Product (GDP).[31] It has been suggested that corporations make up 51 of the 100 world's largest economies and that the combined sales of the world's top 200 corporations are far greater than a quarter of the world's economic activity.[32] The same researchers also suggest that although there are now 40,000 corporations in the world whose activities cross national boundaries, the top 200 of these firms (largely comprising US and Japanese firms) account for a huge (and growing) share of the world's economic activity.[33]

It can be observed that these giants cover a broad range of economic activity from extraction to manufacturing to telecommunications. It is estimated that multinational corporations control 75 per cent of world trade and, significantly, over a third of this is intra-firm trade,[34] indicating the extent to which production lines have taken on a global and discursive character. Firms have become increasingly transnational or 'stateless'[35] at the centre of the emergence of a global economy, 'one in which the stress is placed

[27] For example, K. Ochame, *The Borderless World: Power and Strategy in the Interlinked Economy* (1990); also Ochame, *The End of the Nation State* (1996).

[28] For example, S. Strange, *States and Markets* (1988); P. Cerny, *The Changing Architecture of Politics: Structure, Agency and the Future of the State* (1990), at 237; and Roscrance, 'The Rise of the Virtual State', *Foreign Affairs*, July/Aug 1996.

[29] Willets, 'Transnational Actors and International Organizations in World Politics', in J. Baylis and S. Smith (eds), *The Globalization of World Politics: An Introduction to International Relations* (2001), at 364.

[30] For example Strange, *supra* note 28.

[31] See for example C. W. Kegley and E.R. Witkopf, *World Politics: Trend and Transformation* (2001).

[32] S. Anderson and J. Cavanagh, *Top 200: The Rise of Global Corporate Power*, Corporate Watch, 2000, available at http://www.globalpolicy.org/socecon/tncs/top200.htm, accessed 8 August 2002.

[33] Ibid.

[34] Stopford 1994, cited in Chang, 'Globalization, Transnational corporations and economic development', at 98.

[35] Higgott, Underhill, and Bieler, 'Introduction: Globalization and Non-state actors', in R. Higgott, G. Underhill, and A. Bieler (eds), *Non-State Actors and Authority in the Global System* (2000), at 1–2.

Table 1: *Corporate Revenues and Gross Domestic Product: Selected Companies and Countries*

Rank	Company	Revenue $ billions 1998	Country (Approximate GDP equivalent)
1	General Motors (US)	161.3	Denmark/Thailand
10	Toyota (Japan)	99.7	Portugal/Malaysia
20	Nissho Iwai (Japan)	67.7	New Zealand
30	AT&T (US)	53.5	Czech Republic
40	Mobil (US)	47.6	Algeria
50	Sears Roebuck	41.3	Bangladesh
60	NEC (Japan)	37.2	United Arab Emirates
70	Suez Lyonnaise des Eaux	34.8	Romania
80	HypoVereinsbank (Germany)	31.8	Morocco
90	Tomen (Japan)	30.9	Kuwait
100	Motorola (US)	29.4	Kuwait
150	Walt Disney (US)	22.9	Belarus
200	Japan Postal Service (Japan)	18.8	Tunisia
250	Albertson's (US)	16.0	Sri Lanka
300	Taisei (Japan)	13.8	Lebanon
350	Goodyear Tyre & Rubber (US)	12.6	Oman
400	Fuji Photo Film (Japan)	11.2	El Salvador
450	CSX (US)	9.9	Bulgaria
500	Northrop Grumman (US)	8.9	Zimbabwe

Source: United Nations Research Institute for Social Development.[36]

upon the erosion of national boundaries and the movement of economic activities across national boundaries'.[37] This trans-nationality in itself poses problems for national and international law.[38] Firms are no longer under the exclusive jurisdiction of single nation states, making them increasingly difficult to regulate.

C. Defining Multinational Corporations

The problems that international law is trying to address are those created by the global economic domination of multinational corporations (MNCs). But what is a multinational corporation? We cannot take the term 'MNC' as legally uncontested or unproblematic. The question cannot be answered without first considering the multinational company or enterprise (as is often the preferred term) as an organization.[39] Muchlinski charts the move from a simple definition of the MNC

[36] Visible Hands: Taking Responsibility for Social Development, UNRISD, January 2000 http://www.unrisd.org/unrisd/website/document.nsf/(httpPublications)/FE9C9439D82B525480256B670065EFA1?OpenDocument, accessed 13 August 2002, at 77.

[37] Allen, 'Crossing borders: footloose multinationals' in J. Allen and C. Hammnett (eds), *A Shrinking World?* (1995), at 59.

[38] Dubin, 'The Direct Application of Human Rights Standards to, and by, Transnational Corporations' 61 *The Review of the International Commission of Jurists* (1999), 35.

[39] Muchlinski, 'The Company Law Review and Multinational Corporate Groups' in de Lacy J., *The Reform of United Kingdom Company Law* (2002), 249, at 251; also Muchlinski 'Holding Multinationals

as a corporation with a home in one country but operating in and under laws of others as well, to a more economic conception emphasizing control through direct investment. The OECD Guidelines for Multinational Enterprises for example use the following definition:

companies or other entities established in more than one country and so linked that they may co-ordinate their operations in various ways. While one or more of these entities may be able to exercise a significant influence over the activities of others, their degree of autonomy within the enterprise may vary widely from one multinational enterprise to another. Ownership may be private, state or mixed.[40]

This reflects the more fluid organization and structure of many modern companies. They are as likely to be heterarchical as hierarchical, with strategic alliances with other producers, seeking economies of scale in manufacturing.[41] Some writers use the term MNC to describe the more traditional horizontally organized company which replicates its activities within different regions of the global economy, in contrast to the transnational company (TNC) which seeks to establish global operations, using an international division of labour with little regard for national boundaries.[42] Adopting a pragmatic approach, Kamminga and Zia-Zarifi suggest that 'Regardless of the terms used, it is the ability of MNCs to operate across national borders and outside the effective supervision of domestic and international law that makes them important actors ripe for greater investigation under international laws'.[43]

One way of measuring a firm's multinationality is its foreign direct investment (FDI): the extent to which it is investing capital offshore and establishing wholly or jointly owned subsidiary companies overseas rather than just sourcing goods via systems of international trade.[44] This is a process of internalizing markets.[45] The late 1980s and 1990s witnessed a significant rise in FDI in the manufacturing sector. Multinational corporations today account for almost all of the world's manufactured exports, in contrast to the early post-war years when multinational corporations were concentrated in the primary sector.[46] The combined effect of these trends is that more countries are being drawn into the global economy via the activities of multinational corporations. Growth in foreign direct investment (both in terms of FDI stocks and FDI flows) since 1986 has outstripped growth in world trade

to Account: Recent Developments in English Litigation and the Company Law Review' 23 *Company Lawyer* (2002) 168–79.

[40] As amended in 2000, www.oecd.org/daf/investment/guidelines/mnetext.htm.

[41] Muchlinski, 'The Company Law Review', *supra* note 39, at 252.

[42] Higgott, Underhill, and Bieler 'Introduction: Globalisation and Non-State Actors' in R. Higgott *et al.* (eds) *Non-State Actors in the Global System* (2000), at 1–2.   [43] Ibid. at 3.

[44] Hymer, *The International Operations of National Firms: A Study of Foreign Direct Investment*, 14 Monographs in Economics (1976).

[45] Caves, 'The Multinational Enterprise as an Economic Organisation', in R.E. Caves, *Multinational Enterprises and Economic Growth* (1982), reprinted in J.A. Friedan and D.A. Lake (eds), *International Political Economy: Perspectives on Global Power and Wealth*, 3rd edition (1997), at 139–53.

[46] Held *et al.*, *supra* note 15, at 254.

(measured in terms of exports). As Held writes, 'In the 1990s few economies are outside the reach of MNC activity and global production networks . . . all regions of the globe, to a greater or lesser extent are both the home and the host to multinational corporations or their foreign affiliates'.[47]

The nature of global production processes has changed significantly; firms engage in a variety of different offshore production strategies, including foreign direct investment, subcontracting, and outward processing trade (where manufacturers subcontract the most labour intensive sections of the production process to neighbouring low wage countries).[48] The multinational firms engaged in manufacturing are often regarded as efficiency seeking firms,[49] spreading their production processes worldwide in order to take advantage of lower production costs or particular competitive conditions of a national market. With intergovernmental aid now largely overtaken by foreign direct investment, the temptation for host countries to attract investors with minimal human rights standards is often difficult to resist.[50] Human rights abuses can occur whether the outsourcing takes place via wholly or partly owned subsidiary or through use of supply contracts.

While some specific questions arise in relation to the parent—subsidiary relationship, often a company will outsource via contracts rather than keep the whole chain of supply under its formal control. This is convenient for avoiding responsibility for human rights abuse in the host country and is one compelling reason to look for means of holding the company responsible for the indirect as well as the direct effects of its activities. As the next section discloses, there are numerous actual and potential legal responses to this modern phenomenon.

2. HOLDING CORPORATIONS TO ACCOUNT: THE FRAMEWORK

It is a mistake to think that multinational corporations are complete outlaws from the international arena. Aside from anything else they are pretty proficient at invoking its protection and facilities where it suits them.[51] Many commentators make the point that the United Nations Declaration of Human Rights applies to states, organizations, and individuals alike. In the words of its Preamble: 'every individual and every organ of society, keeping this Declaration in mind, shall strive

---

[47] Held *et al.*, *supra* note 15, at 244.

[48] The ILO Working Party on The Social Dimensions of the Liberalization of International trade, GB.273/WP/SDL/1(Rev 1) 273rd Session, Geneva 1998, para 2 refers to 'growing networks of enterprises operat[ing] across national boundaries in an astonishing array of contractual, equity and joint venture arrangements', quoted by McCorquodale, in Bottomley and Kinley, *supra* note 8, 89 at 90.

[49] J.H. Dunning, *Multinational Enterprises and the Global Economy* (Essex: Addison Wesley, 1993), at 79–80.   [50] Kamminga and Zia-Zarifi, *supra* note 25, at 2.

[51] Ibid. at 5. They point out that the drive through WTO and bilateral treaties has been to increase the protection of MNCS against the interference of states.

by teaching and education to promote respect for these rights and freedoms and by progressive measures, national and international, to secure their universal and effective recognition and observance'.[52] Henkin asserts that 'Every individual includes juridical persons. Every individual and every organ of society excludes no one, no company, no cyberspace'.[53] While it does not impose legally binding obligations on corporations, the UN Norms on Responsibilities of Transnational Corporations are an important restatement of existing international human rights law.[54]

Under international law natural persons have a duty not to violate fundamental norms (including piracy, aircraft hijacking, forced labour, genocide, war crimes, and crimes against humanity).[55] Ramasastry argues that wherever international law implicates individuals it also includes corporations: 'To the extent that individuals have rights and duties under customary international law and international humanitarian law, multinational corporations as legal persons have the same set of rights and duties'.[56] National courts in jurisdictions with developed systems of corporate criminal liability have begun to treat corporations in the same way as natural persons with regard to international customary law.[57] The suggestion that the movement is in the direction of imposing international legal obligations on corporations needs considerable qualification, however. Some international instruments, notably the Rome Statute establishing the International Criminal Court, exclude legal persons from their ambit.[58]

One of the main areas of human rights violations by multinational corporations to attract attention is what has come to be called 'militarized commerce'.[59] Companies engaged in mining and extraction industries retain local military forces, with known poor human rights records, to protect their operations. Amnesty International and Human Rights Watch have produced lengthy reports,[60] and numerous articles can

---

[52] Universal Declaration of Human Rights, 1948, G.A. Res. 217A (III).

[53] Henkin, 'The Universal Declaration at 50 and the Challenge of Global Markets' 25 *Brooklyn Journal of International Law* (1998), 17–25, at 25.   [54] UN Doc. E/CN.4/Sub2/2003/12/rev 2 (2003).

[55] Convention on the Prevention and Punishment of the Crime of Genocide, 1948, 78 UNTS 277—133 States parties; International Convention on the Elimination of All Forms of Racial Discrimination, 1965, 669 UNTS 195—162 States parties; Convention Against Torture and Other Cruel, Inhuman or Degrading Treatment or Punishment, 1984, GA Res. 39/46 (1984)—130 States Parties; Slavery Convention 1927, http://www.unhchr.ch/html/menu3/b/treaty3.htm; Convention on the Non-Applicability of Statutory Limitations to War Crimes and Crimes Against Humanity 1968, http://www.unhchr.ch/html/menu3/b/p_limit.htm.

[56] Ramasastry, 'Corporate Complicity: From Nuremberg to Rangoon, An Examination of Forced Labour Cases and their Impact on the Liability of Multinational Corporations' 20 *Berkeley Jnl of Int Law* (2002), 91 at 96.   [57] *Supra* note 56, at 101.

[58] Rome Statute of the International Criminal Court, adopted by the United Nations Diplomatic Conference of Plenipotentiaries on the establishment of an International Court on 17 July 1998, Article 25(1).   [59] Forcese, 'Deterring Militarized Commerce' 31 *Ottawa Law Review* (1999), 171.

[60] Prince of Wales Business Leaders & Amnesty International 2000, 'Human Rights: Is it any of your business?'; Prince of Wales Business Leaders & Amnesty International 2001, 'Business and Human Rights, A Geography of Corporate Risk' http://www.humanrightsrisk.org/csr/csrwebassist.nsf/content/b1f2.html; Avery, 'Business and Human Rights in a Time of Change' 2000: http://www.amnesty.org.uk/business/pubs.shtml;

be found in the North American law journals.[61] They describe the activities of mining, extraction, and power companies such as BP and Occidental Petroleum in Colombia, Nova Corporation in Chile, Unocal in Burma, Royal Dutch Shell and Chevron in Nigeria, and Enron in India. Forcese concludes that these case studies 'show, first, that militarized commerce, while perhaps not commonplace, is certainly extant among resource companies operating in the developing world and, second that security forces affiliated at some level have been implicated in serious human rights abuses'.[62]

While the most direct legal response would be through a criminal or civil action in the host country, it does not take much insight to see that it is unlikely that a state which itself abuses human rights would prosecute such cases or be receptive to civil litigation.[63] This has led to the pursuit of legal redress in the home country of the multinational corporation complicit in the host state's human rights abuses.[64] The main examples include actions based on domestic tort law and the inventive use of the US federal Alien Tort Claims Act. A further stage is the possibility of pursuing multinational corporations in international law. The main focus of this essay is on problems that are common to national and international law, difficulties arising from the nature of the corporation as a legal actor, and the concept of complicity. However, the changing and amoebic characteristics of the *multinational* corporation present further challenges that may be particularly amenable to international law.

Two examples of national jurisdictions responding to the challenge of MNC liability can be seen in the UK based litigation arising from the activities of Cape plc and Thor Chemical Holdings, and in the use of ATCA in the United States.[65] Both of these deploy the mechanism of tort law, although ATCA does so via international customary law. Muchlinski identifies two main issues: does the national court have jurisdiction, and is the company liable for the breach of care? In the cases against Cape plc and Thor Chemicals, both companies domiciled in the UK but operating

Human Rights Watch 1999, 'The Price of Oil: Corporate Responsibility and Human Rights Violations in Nigeria's Oil Producing Communities'; Human Rights Watch, 'The Enron Corporation: Corporate Complicity in Human Rights Violations': http://www.hrw.org/reports/1999/enron/.

[61] Forcese, *supra* note 59; Forcese, 'Achilles Heel: Corporate Complicity, International law and the Alien Tort Claims Act' *Yale Jnl of Intl Law* (2001), 487; Hall, 'Multinational Corporations' Post Unocal Liabilities for Violations of International Law' 34 *George Washington International Law review* (2002), 401; Ramasastry 2002, *supra* note 56; Stephens, 'Corporate Accountability: International Human Rights Litigation against Corporations in US courts' in Kamminga and Zia-Zarifi (eds), *supra* note 25, 209; Stephens, 'The Morality of Profit: Transnational Corporations and Human Rights' 20 *Berkeley J Int Law* (2002), 45.   [62] Forcese, *supra* note 59, at 184.

[63] The pros and cons of civil and criminal liability regimes are discussed in Forcese, ibid.

[64] See discussion of the home state options in McCorquodale, in Bottomley and Kinley, *supra* note 8, at 99–101.

[65] Stephens discusses jurisdictional issues in actions against multinational corporations in the US in 'Corporate Accountability', *supra* note 61, at 222–3. See generally Bell, 'Human Rights and Transnational Litigation: Interesting Points of Intersection' in Bottomley and Kinley, *supra* note 8, at 115.

in South Africa, the main issue was that of jurisdiction, while the ATCA cases are concerned with the substantive question. Cape was alleged to have exposed large numbers of employees and local residents to asbestos, while Thor exposed employees to highly toxic chemical processes. The English courts accepted jurisdiction against Thor,[66] but the issue of forum gave rise to protracted litigation in the cases against Cape.[67] After three appellate outings, this preliminary issue was eventually resolved in favour of the claimants and a settlement was reached.[68] Although, as Muchlinski argued, Cape was more typical of a hierarchical parent-subsidiary, the defendants maintained that they had devolved operations to their South African affiliates.[69] In terms of legal outcome the principle was accepted that an English based company can be sued in England for the acts of foreign based subsidiaries if it is shown that the foreign forum is unable to provide the environment to ensure that substantive justice can be done. Yet the tortuous nature of the Cape litigation on the issue of forum[70] may speak strongly to the desirability of clearer international forums for such cases.[71]

The Alien Tort Claims Act 1789 gave to US district courts 'original jurisdiction of any civil action by an alien for a tort only, committed in violation of the law of nations or a treaty of the United States'.[72] It converts a violation of international law of nations into a domestic tort actionable in federal courts. In its modern incarnation, ATCA has been held to apply to private actors in relation to international crimes of genocide, war crimes, and crimes against humanity.[73]

Given its territorial basis, deploying criminal law against multinationals for their activities abroad is even more fraught. True, there are exceptions to the territorial principle such as offences in relation to sexual exploitation of children, terrorism, and drug smuggling, but the principle of domestic sovereignty in relation to criminal law is well established. While states can prosecute their own nationals, including

---

[66] *Ngobo* et al. *v Thor Chemicals Holdings* [1995] TLR 579 (settled for £1.3 million in 1997), and *Sithole* et al. *v Thor Chemicals Holdings* [1999] TLR 110.

[67] *Lubbe v Cape plc* [1999] International Litigation Procedure 113 (CA) (UK proper forum); *Afrika* et al. *v Cape* 139 (CA) (South African forum); *Lubbe* et al. *v Cape* [2000] 1 WLR 1545 (HL: overturned these decisions and re-asserted UK as proper forum).

[68] Although settlement was reached in January 2002, when Cape agreed to place £21m in trust fund (£5,250 per employee), no money had been paid by October 2002, prompting fresh legal actions: http://www.business-humanrights.org/Asbestos.htm, accessed 27 October 2002.

[69] Muchlinski, *supra* note 41, at 253.   [70] Described in detail ibid. at 256–8.

[71] See the discussion of corporate nationality in Clapham, 'The Question of Jurisdiction under International Criminal Law over Legal Persons: Lessons from the Rome Conference on an International Criminal Court' in M. Kamminga and S. Zia-Zarifi (eds), *Liability for Multinational Corporations under International Law* (2000), 139 at 179 *et seq*; and see in the same collection Byers, 'English courts and serious human rights violations abroad: A preliminary assessment', 241.

[72] Now 28 USC #1350 1994. See See Ralph G Steinhardt, 'Corporate Responsibility and the International Law of Human Rights: The New *Lex Mercatoria*', Chapter 6 in this volume, at 19–27 for a discussion concerning ATCA and recent cases against Unocal and Shell. See also Stephens, 'Corporate Accountability', *supra* note 61, and Zia-Zarifi, 'Suing Multinational Corporations in the US for Violating International Law' 4 *UCLA J. Intl. & Foreign Aff.* (1999) 81.

[73] *Filartiga v Pena-Irala* 630 F. 2d 876 (2d Cir. 1980); *Kadic v Karadzic* 70 F.3d at 244 (2d Cir. 1995).

corporations, for serious offences committed abroad, and non-nationals for international crimes, this does not address the problem of their unwillingness to do so.[74] This is the background to the many calls, like this one from Richard Meeran, the British lawyer who acted successfully for South African asbestosis victims against Cape Plc, for a formal international framework to deal with MNC complicity: 'A legally binding convention that is enforceable in practice needs to be formulated to ensure proper multinational accountability, capturing the supply-chain, not just subsidiaries. This convention must be applied internationally and, in a development of international law, apply to corporations as well as states.'[75]

3. HOLDING CORPORATIONS TO ACCOUNT: GENERAL PRINCIPLES

The notion of corporate responsibility for crime is, however, far from universally accepted. Most non-common law jurisdictions in Europe resisted corporate criminal liability until recently. This is one of the reasons for the omission of corporations as potential defendants[76] from the Rome Statute establishing the International Criminal Court (ICC).[77] Given that the ICC is concerned with the most egregious of wrongful conduct (genocide, crimes against humanity, war crimes, and aggression[78]) this omission might be thought to be fatal to any proposal that corporations be liable in international law for lesser breaches of human rights. But there are several reasons why this would be too hasty a conclusion.

First, a cycle of national and transnational debates about the control and regulation of fraud, economic crime, corruption, health and safety, and environmental sustainability means that corporate liability for crime has increasingly appeared on the agenda in many jurisdictions over the last ten years. Secondly, although the jurisprudential rift that exists between common law and civil law jurisdictions may appear to suggest a fundamental difference in approaching corporate misbehaviour; in fact the differences in institutional arrangements for regulating corporations are more apparent than real. In all jurisdictions, and at the supranational level such as

---

[74] We are grateful to Robin Churchill for this point. Forcese discusses territoriality provisions in Canada, *supra* note 59, at 195. See also Gobert, 'Corporate Killings at Home and Abroad: Reflections on the Government's Proposals' 118 *Law Quarterly Review* (2002) 72; Mullan, 'The Concept of Double Criminality in the Context of Extraterritorial Crimes' *Crim LR* (1997) 17; and Alldridge, 'The Sexual Offences (Conspiracy and Incitement) Act 1996' *Crim LR* (1997) 30.

[75] *Mail & Guardian [South Africa]*, 19 April 2002. See also ICHRP, *supra* note 25; World Development Movement, London, *Making Investment work for People: An International Framework for Regulating Corporations* (1999); Christian Aid, *Need for Legally Binding Regulation of Transnational Corporations* www.christianaid.org.uk/indepth/0202tnc/transc.htm, accessed 21 August 2002. These organizations reported to the UN Sub-Commission on the Promotion and Protection of Human Rights working group on the working methods and activities of transnational corporations, UN Doc. E/CN.4/Sub.2/2002/13 (2002).

[76] Art. 25(1) Rome Statute states: 'The Court shall have jurisdiction over natural persons pursuant to this Statute'. [77] W. Schabas, *An Introduction to the International Criminal Court* (2001), at 80.

[78] Art. 5 Rome Statute.

the European Union, there already exist sanctions-backed provisions specifically to regulate business (health and safety at work, trading standards, control of financial institutions, and so on). What differs between jurisdictions is the legal mechanism selected. In some this is a branch of criminal law, perhaps enforced by a specialist agency but pursued through the regular criminal courts, or perhaps tried in separate courts but nonetheless criminal offences; while in others, the institutional sanctions are found in administrative codes. In those jurisdictions that have adopted the former solution, there has often been the parallel development that enterprises have been held liable for the 'classic' offences as well. Those that have adopted the administrative route do so in the main because liability of groups under their criminal codes has been historically unacceptable as a matter of principle. Criminal law in these jurisdictions addresses individual human agents. Nonetheless, it is not uncommon for individual directors of corporations to be held accountable for negligently caused deaths; Italy provides an example here. Whichever of these models—criminal, quasi-criminal, or administrative sanctions—is adopted it will also form part of a larger legal institutional structure.

Thirdly, it is not such an imaginative leap to conceive of a corporation as the subject of international law. While the mind-set of the criminal lawyer is to think about individuals, that of the international lawyer was, until the middle of the last century, to think about states. Yet the ICC and other war crimes tribunals finalize the break in that mould by addressing specifically the crimes of individual human agents. For the international lawyer to embrace a corporate entity is therefore less of a conceptual hurdle than for a domestic jurisdiction to move away from the individual. As people become more accustomed to conceiving of collective entities as wrongdoers, the conceptual gulf may become much less wide. Indeed the Rome Statute contained in its draft form a clause extending jurisdiction over legal persons:

Draft Art 23(5) The Court shall have jurisdiction over legal persons, with the exception of States, when the crimes committed were committed on behalf of such legal persons or by their agencies or representatives.

(6) The criminal responsibility of legal persons shall not exclude the criminal responsibility of natural persons who are perpetrators or accomplices in the same crimes.[79]

There are still many hurdles to be overcome. Those who advocate the accountability of multinationals in international law tend to be stronger in the arguments as to *why* this would be a good thing than in their solutions to *how* this might be achieved. In particular they tend to skate over problems of attributing mental elements to corporate entities.

A. Traditional Attribution Rules

It is in criminal law that many of the difficult questions arise as to how a legal entity such as a corporation can be responsible. Criminal law is pre-eminently concerned

---

[79] See Clapham, *supra* note 9.

with standards of behaviour enforced, not through compensation, but through a system of state punishment negotiated via standards of fault such as intention, knowledge, and subjective recklessness. Whether and how that system should be applied to corporations thus attracts more controversy than does the ascription of civil liabilities. Regulatory offences often do not use these culpability requirements.

Broadly, three different theories for attributing blame to corporations compete for attention. The first is based on the agency principle, in which the company is liable for the wrongful acts of all its employees. United States federal law employs a principle of this type (*respondeat superior*) for all offences, while English law limits its application to certain regulatory offences. The second theory of blame attribution, which English law utilizes for all other offences, identifies a limited layer of senior officers within the company as its 'brains' and renders the company liable only for their culpable transgressions, not for those of other workers. The third theory locates corporate blame in the procedures, operating systems, or culture of a company. 'Company culture theory' is deployed in the Australian Criminal Code Act 1995,[80] and is proposed in relation to a corporate homicide offence in the UK.[81]

The first two theories have in common that they seek in different ways to equate corporate culpability with that of an individual and both are therefore derivative forms of liability. Further, the second version adopts an anthropomorphic vision of company decision-making. The third theory, on the other hand, exploits the dissimilarities between individual human beings and group entities.

In private law, an employer or principal is vicariously liable for most of the acts of any employee or agent. Criminal law has generally accepted this avenue of blame attribution in a limited range of strict liability offences. A full-scale vicarious liability principle is endorsed in South Africa as well as in the federal law of the United States, thus confirming that there is no difficulty in applying the vicarious principle to offences both of strict liability and of subjective knowledge. Under the English binary scheme, vicarious principles apply to certain regulatory offences only. To render a corporation vicariously liable, the employee's conduct must be within the scope of the individual's employment or authority, although this is widely interpreted: the activity may be expressly forbidden but nonetheless be within the scope of employment. As long as the employee is acting in furtherance of the corporation's business she is acting within the scope of her employment.[82]

Vicarious liability has been criticized both for including too little in demanding that liability flow through an individual, however great the fault of the corporation, and for including too much in blaming the corporation whenever the individual employee is at fault, even in the absence of corporate fault.[83] This summary of the

---

[80] S. 12.

[81] Law Commission for England and Wales, *Involuntary Manslaughter*, Report 237 (1996); Home Office, *Reforming the Law on Involuntary Manslaughter: The Government's Proposals* (2000).

[82] C. Wells, *Corporations and Criminal Responsibility* (2001); Note, 'Corporate Crime: Regulating Corporate Behaviour Through Criminal Sanctions' 92 *Harvard Law Review* (1979) 1227, at 1250.

[83] Colvin, 'Corporate Personality and Criminal Liability' 6 *Criminal Law Forum* (1995) 8.

drawbacks of vicarious liability neatly encapsulates one of the major problems in any discussion of corporate responsibility: how to conceptualize 'corporate' fault. Vicarious liability attracts criticism as a mechanism for attributing fault because it is felt that there is some other way of measuring 'corporate culpability'. The key question is to establish what that way might be.

Few would recommend the 'identification' theory as it has developed in England in the last sixty years for serious offences such as fraud, theft, and manslaughter. One of the objections to finding corporations liable for such offences was that they required proof of a mental element of intention, recklessness, or negligence. For the purposes of corporate liability for this type of offence, courts developed the identification theory, under which certain key personnel are said to act as the company (rather than on behalf of it, as is the case with vicarious liability). The underlying theory is that company employees can be divided into those who act as the 'hands' and those who represent the 'brains' of the company.[84]

Thus, despite the radical decision to extend to corporations liability for traditional offences, there has for a long time been a clear reluctance to give the doctrine any bite. Identification theory also bears some relation to the vicarious or agency principle rather than an organic theory. However, if it were conceptualized as an organic theory where the director is seen to embody the company, the courts would be freed to extend liability if they were so inclined.

B. Holistic Theories

The emergence of corporate responsibility as a topic of debate reflects concerns about the safety of workers and of members of the public, and has led to doubts about the appropriateness of the two theories of corporate responsibility previously recognized by legal systems. Vicarious liability, as we have seen, is indeterminate in its sweep. It has rarely been applied to serious offences such as manslaughter (federal jurisdiction in the US does not include homicide offences). Identification liability regards the transgressions of only a limited number of people within the company as relevant to the attribution of culpability to the company itself. The underlying basis of the two principles, despite the rhetoric, is of less substance than at first appears. In both vicarious and identification liability the individual company employee can be prosecuted in her own right, and in each case, the company can only be liable if fault is found in one individual.

The ideas considered in this section (aggregation or collective knowledge, corporate culture, and due diligence) have in common an attempt to escape from company liability derivative on the wrongdoing of one individual. In other words, they aim to capture the 'corporateness' of corporate conduct.

In many large organizations, task specialization means that, even amongst officers senior enough to count for alter ego [identification] purposes, one individual

---

[84] *Tesco v Nattrass* [1972] AC 153, HL.

director will not have access to all the information on which to base a finding of knowledge or negligence. Aggregation of pockets of knowledge from a number of individual employees has been accepted in US federal courts, based on the idea that information known in part to multiple actors within the corporation but not known fully to one actor be aggregated and imputed to the corporation.[85] However, it has not been adopted in jurisdictions reliant on the more restrictive identification theory for knowledge-based offences. It is instructive to quote the US court:

> [K]nowledge acquired by employees within the scope of their employment is imputed to the corporation. In consequence, a corporation cannot plead innocence by asserting that the information obtained by several employees was not acquired by any one individual employee who then should have comprehended its full import. Rather, the corporation is considered to have acquired the collective knowledge of its employees and is held responsible for their failure to act accordingly.[86]

While radical in terms of traditional doctrine, aggregation of knowledge is an incomplete solution. A scheme of corporate liability has to look further than individuals (atomized or aggregated) to the corporation's structure itself.

A developing theory for attributing fault to a corporation is based on corporate culture or management systems. The Australian Criminal Code Act 1995, applying to federal offences, contains one of the most detailed modern restatements of organizational liability. For offences of intention, knowledge, or recklessness, the 'fault element must be attributed to a body corporate that expressly, tacitly or impliedly authorized or permitted the commission of the offence'.[87] Authorization or permission can be shown in one of three ways. The first echoes the *Tesco v Nattrass* version of identification liability, and the second extends the net wider to 'high managerial agents'. The third represents a clear endorsement of an organizational or systems model, based on the idea of 'corporate culture'. 'Corporate culture' can be found in 'an attitude, policy, rule, course of conduct or practice within the corporate body generally or in the part of the body corporate where the offence occurred'. Evidence may be led that the company's unwritten rules tacitly authorized non-compliance or failed to create a culture of compliance.

The Australian Code has been in force for only a brief period and its interpretation is in its infancy. The proposed offence of corporate killing in England and Wales also includes a management-based attribution principle based on 'management failure . . . conduct falling far below what can reasonably be expected of the corporation in the circumstances'.

If the role of liability is to induce the corporation as principal to monitor its agents, then what should happen to a corporation which does so diligently, yet still fails? The US federal regime does not provide an affirmative defence but the very broad liability regime is softened by its relationship with prosecution and sentencing policies, creating a strong incentive for monitoring compliance. Counter indicators

---

[85] *US v T.I.M.E.-D.C., Inc* (1974) 381 F. Supp.730 (WD Va.).   [86] At 738–9.
[87] S. 12.3.

for corporate prosecution include the existence of a generally effective compliance programme; where the offence is committed by a 'rogue' employee; the corporation's past history; co-operation; and voluntary disclosure.[88] Prosecution discretion thus fits with the philosophy of the federal sentencing guidelines for corporate offenders in rewarding prevention and compliance.[89] Sentencing credit is given for effective compliance plans and for self-reporting.

C. International Convergence

The Council of Europe accepted in 1988 the recommendation of its select committee that member states consider the promotion of corporate liability.[90] The guiding principles state that liability should attach irrespective of whether a natural person can be identified but that the enterprise should be exonerated where its management is not implicated and has taken all necessary steps to avoid the offence. Three Council of Europe treaties, dealing with corruption, environmental crimes, and cybercrime, include corporate criminal liability. Each recommends the introduction of corporate criminal liability, but leaves up to the signatory states to decide whether criminal penalties or other effective measures against legal entities should be imposed.[91]

Other than via the Corpus Iuris project,[92] there has not been a move towards standardization in the EU, despite the divergent national developments described above. The Convention on the Protection of the European Communities' Financial Interests requires member states to provide for various forms of liability on the part of legal persons, including liability for active corruption involving the financial interests of the Community.[93] This leaves the signatory states with no discretion, members would have to introduce criminal liability for enterprises in cases of government fraud concerning subsidies and similar crimes. A similar provision is incorporated in the recent OECD Convention, discussed below. The EU's own Convention on Corruption does not, however, deal directly with the liability of legal persons.[94]

[88] Federal Principles of Prosecution of Corporations, US Department of Justice, 1999.

[89] US Sentencing Guidelines Manual, ch 8.   [90] Recommendation No. R (88) 18.

[91] See Clapham 2000, *supra* note 9, at 172–8. Criminal Law Convention on Corruption, ETS no. 173, in force July 2002. Neither the Convention on the Protection of Environment through Criminal Law ETS no. 172 (1998, to date one ratification) nor the Convention on Cybercrime ETS no. 185 (2001, to date three ratifications) is yet in force.

[92] While the status of the project is somewhat in doubt, it is useful to examine as a model for a pan-European set of principles. Art. 13 covers the criminal liability of organizations, discussed further below, text accompanying note 141. For a useful table on the legal position in the 15 member states, see M. Delmas-Marty and J. Vervaele, *The Implementation of the Corpus Iuris in the Member States* (2000), www.law.uu.nl/wiarda/corpus/, Annex II.

[93] Convention on the Protection of the European Communities' Financial Interests 1995, Second Protocol, 1997, Article 3.

[94] Convention on the Fight against Corruption involving Officials of the European Communities or Officials of Member States of the European 1998.

The OECD Convention on Bribery and Corruption, signed by twenty-nine members and a further five non-members, has a wider reach than the EU or the Council of Europe treaties, although it lacks the supra-national legislative or per-suasive effects of the former. Article 2 requires each party 'to take such measures as may be necessary, in accordance with its legal principles, to establish the liability of legal persons for the bribery of a foreign public official'. Although this does not require signatories to legislate for corporate criminal liability as such, Article 3 obliges them to introduce effective, proportionate, and dissuasive criminal penalties for those who bribe foreign public officials. Those countries where criminal responsibility does not apply to legal persons 'shall ensure that they are subject to effective, proportionate and dissuasive non-criminal sanctions, including monetary sanctions'.[95] The OECD is actively monitoring the implementation of the Convention in member states and considering adding more specificity to Article 2.[96]

In combination, these international instruments have begun to exert powerful pressure on states to introduce or refine existing corporate liability provisions. While most code based continental legal systems long eschewed corporate liability,[97] the debate is perhaps no longer whether to have corporate liability but what form it should take.[98] Not that the aversion was ever shared by all European jurisdictions; it was strongest amongst Germany, Italy, and Spain. Jurisdictions across Northern Europe such as the Netherlands and Denmark have adopted a pragmatic approach for some considerable time.[99] The traditional objection to penal responsibility of legal persons in German criminal law culture has begun to crumble.[100] In most jurisdictions administrative sanctions are gradually being replaced by direct criminal provisions. In the 1980s and '90s Norway, France, and Finland all incorporated criminal punishments against enterprises in their new penal codes, and Denmark consolidated its existing negligence based standard.[101] The French Penal Code was amended in 1991 to remove the general principle that liability could not attach to *personas morals* (i.e. non human entities).[102] In Germany (and countries such as Italy, Spain, Portugal, Greece, and Poland inspired by German doctrines) this has been under active debate in many and Portugal introduced a limited

---

[95] OECD Convention on Combating Bribery of Foreign Public Officials in International Transactions, 1997. This came into force in 1999.

[96] See Laufer, 'Corporate liability, risk shifting, and the paradox of compliance' 52 *Vand. L. Rev.* (1999) 1343.

[97] See for example Mueller, 'Mens Rea and the Corporation' 19 *University of Pittsburgh Law Review* (1957) 21.

[98] Coffee, 'Corporate Criminal Liability: An Introduction and Comparative Survey' in A. Eser, G. Heine, and B. Huber *Criminal Responsibility of Legal and Collective Entities* (1999) at 9.

[99] The best general comparative collection is Eser, Heine, and Huber, ibid.; on Europe see Heine, 'New Developments in Corporate Criminal Liability in Europe: Can Europeans Learn from the American Experience—or Vice Versa?' *St Louis—Warsaw Transatlantic Law Journal* (1998) 173.

[100] Eser, 'Opening Address' in Eser, Heine, and Huber, *supra* note 98, at 2.

[101] See Heine, *supra* note 99.   [102] Jeandidier, *Droit Penal Général* (1991) 341.

exception to this in the new Penal Code of 1983,[103] as did Italy in 2001.[104] Even in Germany fewer theorists now subscribe to the view that the social and ethical disapproval inherent in criminal punishment makes no sense when applied to a corporation.[105]

These European civil law developments display a new willingness to move towards corporate liability and reflect cultural shifts in jurisdictions which have until recently been extremely reluctant to contemplate group liability because of its historical association with repressive regimes. (A somewhat ironic reluctance in the context of this paper's concerns with abuses of human rights.) We have also witnessed cultural changes in perceptions of corporate responsibility. Because of differences in legal and political background, these changes have had disparate impacts in individual jurisdictions. Those jurisdictions that have come late to corporate liability are in a position to develop principles that are less hide-bound than those in the common law countries.

Breaches of human rights obligations do not necessarily have to be characterized as crimes but, as argued earlier, the normative nature of the standards makes crime the closest analogy. Some clear lessons emerge from this account of corporate liability principles. The notion of corporate responsibility for crime is not universally accepted.[106] Even in jurisdictions where it exists, its theoretical and doctrinal development is immature and quite varied. Applying these developments to multinational corporations will present further difficulties of course, even if the question were their direct responsibility for offences committed by their subsidiaries or contractors further down increasingly diffuse supply chains. Those arguing for a more developed doctrine of complicity often fail to consider this problematic foundation. Principles of complicity are drawn mostly from criminal law and, as we will see below, are generally based on proof of knowledge, something that has proved difficult in the development of corporate liability. It is to these we now turn.

4. HOLDING CORPORATIONS TO ACCOUNT: DEVELOPING COMPLICITY PRINCIPLES

A. Taxonomy of Corporate Complicity

The word [complicity] has its origins from com-plicare, a 'picture folding together', an entwining; but it is also an intricacy, a complexity; and finally, and more conventionally, it is being party to or involved in wrongdoing, as an accomplice, in a 'bad confederacy'.[107]

---

[103] Portugal Penal Code 1983, Art. 11.   [104] Law of 8 June 2001 no. 231.

[105] Heine 1998, *supra* note 99.

[106] Stephens, *supra* note 61, notes that the extension of ATCA jurisdiction to corporations is undoubtedly a reflection of the 'common acceptance of the concept of corporate crime [in the US]', at 220.

[107] Veitch, 'Complicity' 5 *Res Publica* (1999), 227.

It is worth thinking about the types of corporate conduct that might give rise to complicity responsibility. As with corporate liability generally there may be *individuals* within the corporate structure who act unlawfully and the Rome Statute can of course be applied to individual directors.[108] The violations may be a direct result of a corporate policy or decision, rather than attributable to any one individual. An example would be where a company enters into a contract with a state to build a pipeline, or a dam, and negotiates the suspension of human rights laws as part of its terms (as appears to have occurred with the consortium constructing the Baku-Tblisi-Ceyahn pipeline and the Turkish government).[109] It is this type of corporate participation that may prove the harder to capture.

Andrew Clapham has developed the argument for corporate complicity, emphasizing: 'For some in the human rights movement it made no sense to talk of "corporate violations" when the violations of international law were actually being committed by the state'.[110] Complicity therefore comprises not only direct involvement in the immediate execution of the abuse but includes benefiting from abuses committed by someone else.[111]

Forcese's case studies suggest that multinational companies involved in militarized commerce can be implicated in several types or layers of complicity.

First, companies providing revenue to human rights abusing regimes or militaries can be accused of a form of 'financial complicity' [for example financial support for units of the Colombian military]. Second, companies providing material support to a regime or military that enhances its human rights-abusing capacity can be accused of a form of 'material complicity' [for example permitting Indonesian troops to use company infrastructure or equipment]. Last, companies that call upon the services of human rights-abusing militaries for immediate security support, resulting in human rights abuses, can be accused of 'incitement complicity' [for example the behaviour of oil companies in Nigeria].[112]

Commonly a taxonomy of three types of involvement is used to describe corporate complicity with abusive states: direct complicity, indirect complicity, and beneficiary complicity.[113] The South African Truth and Reconciliation Commission uses a similar but not entirely congruent scheme of first-, second-, and third-order involvement in sustaining apartheid policies.[114] The Truth Commission's first- and second-order categories appear to represent two different ways of being *directly* complicit: 'a corporation which knowingly assists a state in violating customary international law principles in the UN Declaration of Human Rights could be viewed as directly complicit in such a violation.'[115]

---

[108] Schabas, *supra* note 77, at 439.   [109] See discussion above, text accompanying note 14.

[110] Clapham, *supra* note 9, at 242.   [111] Ibid. at 245.   [112] Forcese, *supra* note 59.

[113] Danish Human Rights and Business Project, *Defining the Scope of Business Responsibility for Human Rights Abroad* (2001) www.humanrights.dk.

[114] South African Truth and Reconciliation Commission Report, volume Four, ch 2, Business and Labour 1998.

[115] Clapham and Jerbi, 'Categories of Corporate Complicity in Human Rights Abuses' Background Paper for Global Compact Dialogue on the Role of the Private Sector in Zones of Conflict (2001), at 3.

First-order complicity covers the specific case of those who assist in the design or implementation of human rights-violating policies. A question might arise as to the role of lawyers whose clients participate in such negotiations.[116] Second-order complicity appears to encompass those who knew that their products would be used to assist in repression, such as the manufacture of torture instruments.

Indirect complicity comprises those situations where the multinational corporation's activities help to maintain a regime's financial and commercial infrastructure. Human Rights Watch suggests that corporate complicity covers: 'Situations in which [a] corporation facilitates or participates in government human rights violations. Facilitation includes the company's provision of material or financial support for states' security forces which then commit human rights violations that benefit the company'.[117] One writer describes this as 'collapsing' the distinction between direct and indirect complicity.[118]

Beneficiary or third-order involvement describes the way that businesses silently exploit the regime, benefiting from lower wage costs because of poor conditions or discriminatory practices, for example. This would appear to be a form of 'continuing act' liability. It could be that the company is unaware of the type of regime with which it is dealing, or perhaps that the regime itself becomes less respectful of human rights over a period of time. Ramanastry argues that if a multinational corporation, after learning of human rights violations linked to its investment, continues to do business with the host country it should give rise to accomplice liability. Her proposal for ATCA liability is that it is incurred when there is proof of an international crime, and that the corporation has contributed in a material way, and that it intended or was reckless as to its commission.[119]

What about the multinational corporation that condones through its continuing presence in the face of known human rights abuses by the state? A number of nongovernmental organizations endorse the proposition that inaction on the part of a multinational corporation once it is aware of systematic human rights abuses can amount to complicity. This may be difficult to sustain as a legal standard, although there is a moral obligation.[120] Much depends on how much of the so-called regulative gap can be appropriately or effectively filled. What is needed is a model of complicity that is not so restrictive as to be ineffective except against the most egregiously bad multinational corporations but neither so inclusive that it will be politically unacceptable except to the most ethically compliant states.

B. Complicity in Criminal Law

Nearly all conceptions of complicity have requirements of knowledge and awareness. We showed in section 3 that some national systems do not recognize corporations

---

[116] Kamminga and Zia-Zarifi wryly comment that they could attract no lawyers representing major MNCs to participate in the Colloquium on which their book is based: *supra* note 25, at 15.

[117] In the Enron report, *supra* note 1.   [118] Ramasastry, *supra* note 55.   [119] Ibid.
[120] Ibid.

as potential criminals at all, and others have had difficulties with a concept of corporate knowledge. Some have narrow approaches to finding corporations guilty of offences requiring proof of knowledge. We also suggested that the difference between jurisdictions that recognize full blown corporate liability and those that do not can be exaggerated. Similarly, the rhetorical claim that criminal law is pre-dominately concerned with the individual wrongdoer can also be overstated. Here the comparison is not so much between the individual and an abstract entity such as the corporation, as between the treatment of the criminal actor and the individual as a member of a group of actors.

Criminal law has the individual actor at its ideological forefront.[121] But in the shadows, behind the doctrinal curtains, is the spectre of group liability. While criminal law (in its doctrinal clothes) has remained uncomfortable with group liability, criminological studies have long reflected the group basis of much 'criminal' activity, the literature abounds with gangs, criminal associations, organ-ized crime, and criminal sub-cultures. Within criminal law, complicity or accessorial liability was until recently under-theorized,[122] and even now its place in the wider picture of criminal theories of responsibility is uncertain.

Our argument then is not that criminal law has failed altogether to accommodate groups. It is rather that we have to penetrate the layers of opacity in doctrinal criminal law to reveal, under the individual robes, the underlying 'groupness' of criminal law and practice. It is relatively easy to point to the preoccupation with individual liability and individual responsibility in traditional conceptions of criminal law. Group based liability is uncomfortably accommodated rather than clearly embraced. Yet in practical terms its significance is hard to overstate. It is not just aiding and abetting or participatory liability that we need to include here, but inchoate forms such as incitement and conspiracy which assume more than one 'player'. In regulatory law corporations are often prosecuted and competition law seeks to control cartels. There is a centrality to groups in criminal law practice that is denied by its relative marginality in theoretical accounts.

Complicity is similarly central to the International Criminal Court. The major criminals brought before it 'will not be the actual perpetrators of the crimes, soiling their hands with flesh and blood'.[123] They will be those who organize, plan, and incite offences.[124] It seems accepted in international war crimes tribunals that the principles of accessorial liability are relatively uniform across jurisdictions.[125] In what follows we first give a brief account of complicity doctrine in English law, followed by an analysis of the provisions of the Rome Statute and other international instruments. This stage setting will allow a more informed discussion of the applicability or adaptability of these principles in order to hold human rights-violating corporations to account.

---

[121] This section draws on C. Wells, 'Girls, Gangs and Fears' in L. Bibbings and D. Nicolson (eds), *Feminist Perspectives on Criminal Law* (2000) 123–37.

[122] See K. Smith, *A Modern Treatise on the Law of Complicity* (1991).

[123] Schabas, *supra* note 77, at 81.   [124] Art. 25(3).   [125] ICHRP, *supra* note 25, at 62.

Participation in crime as a 'secondary party' can take many different forms, including giving advice, material assistance, equipment, or encouragement. It can take place before the principal offence (when it will often be described as counselling or procuring) or at the same time (when it is usually described as aiding and abetting). It can cover unforeseen results where the parties are carrying out a 'joint enterprise'. And it leads to full criminal liability for the principal offence which is punishable as severely as principal liability.

The *mens rea* requirement for participation consists in intent to assist or encourage and/or in knowledge or awareness that one is doing so.[126] Participatory liability is one of those areas of criminal law that has an in-built tendency to get out of hand, especially if the foundational picture has been painted from the individualized 'every *actus reus* accompanied by a concurrent *mens rea*' standpoint. Assistance at the time of a crime is less problematic in this regard than encouragement or help beforehand. Turning prior help into liability runs counter to criminal law's espousal of knowledge-based intention. The classic example is that of a shopkeeper who sells an item to another person (P) knowing that P intends to use it in crime. According to *NCB v Gamble*,[127] the shopkeeper is an accomplice in every case where the customer's intention to commit that kind of offence is known. But, following *Gillick*,[128] this will ensnare the shopkeeper only where this is the shopkeeper's purpose. This converts knowledge-based intention (the bedrock of most criminal law) into purpose–based intention. Purpose is not usually admitted as an exculpatory factor because it comes dangerously close to admitting that motive counts. Criminal doctrine, Norrie convincingly argues, is forced to eschew motive in order to maintain its even-handedness between subjects, rich and poor.[129] Participatory liability is one of those areas where motive forces its way to the surface. As Norrie says. 'Motive could not so easily be expunged from the law or legal process. Suppressed, it persistently irrupts within legal discourse.'[130]

In addition, the joint enterprise doctrine of 'common purpose' extends as much as it limits liability, for it is premised on the assumption that the person will be liable for some unintended consequences of the agreed plan. If there were to be rigid adherence to the principle of 'subjective' *mens rea*, as doctrine would prescribe, failure to contemplate another's actions should circumscribe liability. But in joint enterprise cases the general rule is that a participant in an unlawful (but not murderous) enterprise, who realizes that the accomplice *might* kill or cause grievous bodily harm in the cause of the enterprise, will be liable if the accomplice *does* kill, unless the killing was carried out with a wholly unexpected weapon.[131] Participatory liability thus extends 'subjective' doctrinal principles of personal responsibility to

---

[126] *Gillick v West Norfolk & Wisbech Area Health Authority* [1986] AC 112.

[127] [1959] 1 QB 11; [1959] 3 WLR 434.   [128] *Supra* note 126, at 122.

[129] A. Norrie, *Crime Reason and History; a Critical Introduction to Criminal Law* (2001) at 39–40.

[130] Ibid. at 40.

[131] *Powell and English* [1997] 3 WLR 959, 981 (HL); see also *Uddin* [1998] 3 WLR 1000.

cover a range of activities at various degrees of distance from the perpetration of the *actus reus* of criminal offences.

This brief excursus into complicity law should caution against too ready a reliance on domestic law for the development of international principles. A leading commentator notes that 'the English law of complicity is replete with uncertainties and conflicts'.[132] Despite this, considerable weight appears to have been given to cases such as *NCB v Gamble* in the development of war crimes jurisprudence as encapsulated in the Rome Statute.[133]

C. Complicity under the Rome Statute

The Rome Statute sets out its complicity stall in Article 25(3).[134] Provision for a more expansive liability for military commanders and other superiors is made in Article 28. (See the Appendix to this Chapter for the text of these two provisions.) Indeed, commander liability, which is discussed in more detail below, may well prove the most appropriate model for the development of corporate complicity. The three routes to liability under the general principles of Article 25 roughly cover instigation, assistance, and joint enterprise. The terms used are as follows:

1. ordering, soliciting, or inducing the crime [Article 25(3)(b)];
2. aiding, abetting, or otherwise assisting, including providing the means for its commission, for the purpose of facilitating the commission of an offence [Article 25(3)(c)]; and
3. where the person is acting as part of a group with a common purpose, any contribution to the offence will lead to liability provided that the contribution is intentional, and is either made with the aim of furthering the criminal activity or purpose of the group, or is made with knowledge of the intention of the group to commit the crime [section 25(3)(d)].

Although Schabas argues that the second route effectively incorporates the first,[135] others distinguish between activity *before* the offence in the form of instigation (in classic terms the accessory before the fact) and assistance of a more practical kind.[136] Eser argues that the inclusion of 'ordering' alongside 'soliciting or inducing' is inappropriate. Someone who orders a crime is more than complicit: they are a principal or perpetrator.[137] As it is difficult to demarcate between soliciting and inducing,

---

[132] A. Ashworth, *Principles of Criminal Law* (1999), at 456.

[133] The War Crimes tribunals are discussed by Schabas in 'Enforcing International Humanitarian Law: Catching the Accomplices' 83 *International Review of the Red Cross* (2001) 439.

[134] Legislated specifically in England and Wales in International Criminal Court Act 2001, s. 65; see May and Powles, 'Command Responsibility: A New Basis of Criminal Liability in English Law' *Crim LR* [2002] 363.   [135] Schabas, *supra* note 77, at 81.

[136] Eser, 'Individual Criminal Responsibility' in Cassese, Gaeta, and Jones (eds), *The Rome Statute of the International Criminal Court: A Commentary* (2002), ch 20 at 795.   [137] Ibid. at 797.

inducing could be used as an 'umbrella term'.[138] No mental requirement is specified for the instigator leaving it subject to the general provision in Article 30; this provides for liability only if the material elements of an offence are committed with intent or knowledge. Intent in relation to conduct where 'that person means to engage in the conduct; and in relation to a consequence, that person means to cause that consequence or is aware that it will occur in the ordinary course of events' (Article 30(2)). 'Knowledge' means awareness that a circumstance exists or a consequence will occur in the ordinary course of events (Article 30(3)). The instigator needs both to intend that the principal commit the crime and to realize that the principal has the relevant mental element for that crime (for example, intention). The overall effect is that the instigator needs a 'double intent' with regard to his own conduct and that of the principal.[139]

When it comes to assisting, under Article 25(3)(c), there is no requirement that the assistance be substantial or material.[140] However, this objective breadth may be mitigated by the subjective requirement that the assistance be given 'for the purpose of facilitating the commission' of the crime.[141] Such a term can of course be subject to restrictive or expansive interpretation.[142] How, if at all, does it differ from the word 'aim' used in Article 25(3)(d)?

This brings us to the third route for the accomplice in another's wrongdoing: that of joint enterprise, a provision relying on the inherently tricky concept of 'group intent'. It might be thought that the doctrinal objections to 'group intent' raised in relation to corporate liability are shown to be somewhat shallow by the apparent ease with which the concept is accepted in complicity doctrine. A number of questions arise. Can a 'group' consist of only two persons? Eser suggests not, but English complicity law has no problems with such an idea.[143] Is a common purpose any more than a conspiracy (agreement) put into action? Again, English law would suggest that this is exactly what is covered by the term. In the vast majority of cases liability will be as easy to found under the second route, aiding, abetting, or assisting. In two respects, however, the joint enterprise route is perhaps wider. First, it does not actually require proof that the person has the purpose of facilitating the crime; it allows the alternative mental element of knowledge of the intention of the group. And secondly, it can be argued that there is an evidential advantage for the prosecution where it can show there is a joint enterprise. It is then easier to argue by inference that any accomplice is responsible for the unintended (but 'contemplated') consequences of the group's intended enterprise.

---

[138] Ibid. at 796.   [139] Ibid. at 797.

[140] Cf. 'Report of the International Law Commission on the Work of Its Forty-Eighth Session, 6 May–26 July 1996' UN Doc. A/51/10, at 24, as discussed by Schabas, *supra* note 77, at 82. Eser notes that both the ICTY and ICTR read such a requirement into their respective statutes, *supra* note 136, at 800.   [141] In addition to the general intention and knowledge implied in Art. 30.

[142] English courts generally reject arguments from motive and have sometimes equated 'purpose' with 'intention', see text above accompanying note 127.   [143] Eser, *supra* note 136, at 802.

How might this be applied to a corporation? Supposing that a provision such as that in Corpus Iuris were adopted, then offences could be committed by corporations 'provided the offence is committed for the benefit of the organisation by some organ or representative of the organisation, or any person acting in its name and having power, whether by law or merely in fact, to make decisions'.[144] Overall, Article 25 sets out a relatively narrow range of laibility requiring proof of active assistance and knowledge.

In the context of this paper, commander or superior liability provides a significant line of analogous argument. Corporations could be regarded as responsible for the activities of their employees and agents.[145] Under the Rome Statute the rules are slightly different for civilian than for military commanders but in both cases they are wider than the general complicity principles in Article 25 because they include liability for failure to act. In the case of civilians this failure to exercise control leads to liability only where:

(i) the superior *either knew, or consciously disregarded information which clearly indicated,* that the subordinates were committing or about to commit such crimes;

(ii) the crimes concerned activities that were within the effective responsibility and control of the superior; and

(iii) the superior failed to take all necessary and reasonable measures within his or her power to prevent or repress their commission or to submit the matter to the competent authorities for investigation and prosecution.

For military commanders the provision does not require proof of knowledge or wilful blindness, it is enough that the defendant 'knew or, *owing to the circumstances at the time, should have known* that the forces were committing or about to commit such crimes . . .' (Article 28, emphasis added). This introduces a new basis of liability in English law[146] insofar as it covers *failure to prevent* an offence as well as active participation under normal aiding and abetting rules.

All this is developed in considerably more depth in the Rome Statute than in Corpus Iuris, which merely defines accomplice liability as knowingly helping a natural person or organization to commit the illegal act.[147]

Corporate complicity attempts to bridge two divides: that between states and individuals in international law, and that between individuals and group entities in national laws. Clapham notes that complicity in international law has arisen in two different contexts: individual criminal responsibility and state responsibility.[148] However, he both over- and under-states the difficulties in holding multinational

---

[144] Art. 13; see *supra* note 92.

[145] Zia-Zarifi, *supra* note 71, argues that this principle was invoked, albeit implicitly, in *John Doe v Unocal* 963 F.Supp.880 (C.D. Cal. 1997), *supra*, text accompanying note 74; he describes this as a 'potentially revolutionary step in international law', in text of fn. 101.

[146] International Criminal Court Act 2001, s. 65.   [147] Corpus Iuris, *supra* note 92, Art. 11.

[148] Clapham, *supra* note 9, at 249.

corporations responsible for complicity in human rights violations when he argues:

> To invoke the complicity of states in the wrongful acts of other states one does not need to show an essential contribution to a wrongful act. Nor does one have to show that the assisting state shared the intention of the assisted state. What is required is knowledge of the circumstances of the internationally wrongful act. By analogy one would not have to prove the intent of a company (a difficult and perplexing task in national criminal law), nor would one have to show that but for the contribution the crime would not have been committed.[149]

It overstates the problem because for example the ICC already incorporates these wider forms of participation (it does not require the causal link of essential contribution for example; there is no reason for this to alter if the Rome Statute were extended to corporations.). It understates the problem because the 'perplexing issues' in corporate liability are still there so long as proof of knowledge is required.[150] The ICC provides a useful template in contrast to the jurisprudence of ATCA which is still under debate.[151] Conflicting District Court decisions evidence the difficulty in establishing workable principles of corporate complicity with courts unsure whether direct involvement is required to trigger liability.

5. REGULATORY REGIMES RECONSIDERED

The cultural, social, and political changes associated with the development of highly interdependent global economies help to explain the rise in debate about corporate liability but do not necessarily justify its adoption. Arguments about the justness of holding corporations to account are sometimes confused with arguments that corporate accountability would lead (without more) to the world being a safer place or one that is more respectful of human rights. And, as McCorquodale notes, the concept of human rights has also been globalized.[152] Yet of course legal control comes in many forms from outright prohibitions to complex layers of regulation. Responsibility and accountability are terms that cannot be taken as self-defining. Ratner poses the broad question underlying this essay in a concise form:

> If a MNC making shoes in Vietnam hires a contractor to make the cotton laces, who hires a subcontractor to provide the cotton cloth, who hires a subcontractor to grow the cotton, who hires a subcontractor to actually pick the cotton, and this last actor uses forced labour in his practices, can the corporation be said to be responsible for his activities?[153]

---

[149] Ibid. 260.
[150] This is not a problem for US federal law, which attributes knowledge of any employee to the corporation, but it is in most common law states.   [151] *Supra* note 72.
[152] McCorquodale, in Bottomley and Kinley, *supra* note 8, 89 at 91.
[153] Ratner, 'Corporations and Human Rights: A Theory of Responsibility' 111 *Yale Law Journal*, 443, at 521.

In principle the answer is simple:

The human rights obligations assumed by each government require it (or should require it) to use all appropriate means to ensure that actors operating within its territory or otherwise subject to its jurisdiction comply with national legislation designed to give effect to human rights.[154]

International law can effect change through demands on states to regulate corporations. Some of the problems in asking states to control multinational corporations were rehearsed above. They include the reluctance of host states to cut off the hand that feeds them, problems of jurisdiction in home state litigation, and more generally the difficulty in pinning down the legal personality of a multinational corporation. But there are also problems in asking international law to step in more directly. On its website, the International Criminal Court is said to be needed '. . . to take over when national criminal justice institutions are unwilling or unable to act'.[155] If states are unable or unwilling to act against multinational corporations, then there also lies a case for extending the powers of the ICC to cover them. However, worries exist about granting multinationals the same effective legal status as states in international law. 'In parallel with national legislation, we need international standards that are directly binding on multinational corporations. States have long resisted these, because imposing such obligations would give companies status in international law, which they felt was dangerous.'[156] A number of questions are raised: to what extent are multinational corporations like states? Is there more danger in the potential for collusion between those multinationals and states? What are the limitations of law in controlling the political and economic force of globalized business?

It is important not to overstate the similarities between states and multinational corporations. Corporations are powerful, but unlike states they have no obligation to ensure the well-being of their employees and stakeholders. They may be somewhat akin to diplomatic actors in that they bargain with states and often even shape state policies. Yet some assert that 'The most fundamental *raison d'être* of the transnational corporation is precisely economic self-interest, not to be a human rights actor'.[157] Despite their 'transformative capacity',[158] their power to change things for the better based upon their ability to stimulate and control the flow of investment, technology, profits, and more, multinationals do not usually demonstrate loyalty to, or responsibility for, the citizens of the countries in which their subsidiaries reside.

---

[154] H. Steiner and P. Alston, *International Human Rights in Context* (2nd ed., 2000), at 1349.

[155] http://www.un.org/law/icc/general/overview.htm, accessed 28 October 2002.

[156] International Restructuring Education Network (IRENE) 'Controlling Corporate Wrongs: The Liability of multinational Corporations: Legal Possibilities, Initiatives and Strategies for Civil Society (2000), http://www.cleanclothes.org/publications/corp-1.htm. accessed 1 August 2002.

[157] Forsythe, *supra* note 12. See also Mander, 'The Rules of Corporate Behaviour' in E. Goldsmith and J. Mander (eds), *The Case Against the Global Economy: And a Turn towards Localization* (2001), at 85–6.

[158] Elson and Pearson, 'Introduction: Nimble Fingers and Foreign Investments' in D. Elson and R. Pearson (eds), *Women's Employment in Multinationals in Europe* (1989), at 1.

However, a more fundamental barrier to the development of international legal codes to regulate the behaviour of multinational corporations, is that the human rights agenda is perceived as secondary (or even contradictory) to the protection of the economic rights of corporations. The omission of human rights from the WTO's international legal codes committed to the principle of maintaining and enhancing global free trade is evidence of this. As one of the most powerful international bodies, the WTO has avoided questions of human rights. Attempts to attach a social clause have failed. With a few exceptions (notably in ILO, UNESCO, and WHO rules) human rights are not effectively integrated into the law of most worldwide organizations.[159] This despite the fact that most of the 144 member states of the WTO have ratified or signed the 1966 UN Human Rights Covenants as well as regional and bilateral treaties on the protection of human rights.[160] The WTO's power is reflected in the trade sanctions at its disposal. Yet it is also a non-democratic organization making its rulings largely in private and with very little involvement by the less developed countries.[161] One writer has suggested that 'The new WTO established by the Uruguay Round of GATT is designed, in effect, to serve as a governing body for transnational corporate interests'.[162]

The desire to create a liberal trading system in which the rights of multinational corporations are fully protected (by the WTO) is not mirrored by the protection of the economic and social rights of individuals. An example is the way in which rules on intellectual property were invoked to protect multinational corporations in the pharmaceutical sector from the manufacture of generic anti-AIDs medication. Multinational corporations have also benefited from international law through access to international commercial dispute mechanisms.[163] Similarly the impact of the UN Global Compact has been limited by two key shortcomings: the lack of any system for monitoring corporate compliance and the failure of the UN to apply these same standards to its own agencies and their procurement.

The suggestion that international legal accountability would hinder commercial effectiveness has been countered with the observation that 'there is no question that corporations thrive in the highly regulated, highly litigious environments of North America and Western Europe'.[164] This possibly underestimates the extent to which

---

[159] Petersmann, 'Time for a United Nations "Global Compact" for Integrating Human Rights into the Law of Worldwide Organizations: Lessons from European Integration' 13 *European Journal of International Law* (2002) 62.

[160] The Covenants are the binding treaties developed from the Universal Declaration of Human Rights and together the three instruments form the International Bill of Human Rights. International Covenant on Civil and Political Rights, 1966, G.A. Res. 2200A (XXI)—148 states parties; International Convention on Economic, Social, and Cultural Rights, 1966, G.A. Res. 2200A (XXI)—145 states parties; European Convention for the Protection of Human Rights and Fundamental Freedoms, 1950, 213 UNTS 221, ETS 5—41 states parties.

[161] J. Richter, *Holding Corporations Accountable: Corporate Conduct, International Codes and Citizen Action* (2001) at 12.

[162] Clarke, 'Mechanisms of Corporate Rule', in Goldsmith and Mander (eds), *supra* note 157.

[163] ICHRP, *supra* note 25, at 12.   [164] Kamminga and Zia-Zarifi, *supra* note 25, at 8.

corporations can and do use this litigious environment to their advantage. What can be said is that (large and powerful) corporations are currently able to exploit the present international regime in order to protect their competitive interests (through the WTO and OECD in particular), while avoiding or evading responsibility for non-economic abuses.[165]

Even where human rights are on their agenda, international agreements are not necessarily effective guardians of such rights. The OECD Guidelines on Multinational Enterprises are underpinned by contradictory premises: recognition of the relative power of multinationals over their host states (particularly where a developing country) running parallel with the desire of some states to protect multinationals from national intervention.[166] The 2000 revision acknowledges the human rights obligations of multinationals in somewhat qualified terms: they should 'respect the human rights of those affected by their activities consistent with the host government's international obligations and commitments'.[167] It is wise to acknowledge the large number of difficulties that lie in the way of implementation of such guidelines. Murray notes some of these:[168] governments are loath to take measures to ensure compliance especially in relation to labour matters; measures are costly and beyond the resources of governments in developing countries; the increasing global mobility of capital ('the race to the bottom') discourages regulatory initiatives that may drive up labour costs; the complexity of multinational supply chains leads to endless debates about where responsibility lies; and difficult issues persist of universal versus particular standards.[169] The argument for international human rights standards is that they *are* universal. It is then a moral argument rather than one grounded in effectiveness.

In general, international regulation is conducted through the medium of non-binding codes, guidelines, charters, and so on.[170] Codes of conduct and international standards can lead to better practice. State regulatory policies are as much constituted *by* as constituted *of* private regulation, argue Braithwaite and Drahos.[171] A linear relationship can be observed between industry self-regulation and the development of Codes through the work of NGOs and mass publics.[172] In its paper 'Beyond Voluntarism', the International Council on Human Rights Policy makes a powerful argument for the capacity of law to encourage a 'culture of compliance'.[173] And it is important to remember the role of reporting facts in

---

[165] Kamminga and Zia-Zarifi, *supra* note 25, at 8.

[166] Murray, J., 'A New Phase in the Regulation of Multinational Enterprises: The Role of the OECD', *International Law Journal* (2001), vol. 20, no. 3, pp. 255–270.

[167] OECD Guidelines for Multinational Enterprises, para 11.2, 2000.   [168] Ibid.

[169] Dickerson, 'Transnational Codes of Conduct through Dialogue: Leveling the Playing Field for Developing Country Workers' 53 *Florida Law Review* (2001), 611. But see Vienna Declaration and Programme of Action, UN World Conference on Human Rights, Vienna, 1998, para 5.

[170] McCorquodale, in Bottomley and Kinley, *supra* note 8, at 95; and Johns, 'The Invisibility of the Transnational Corporation: An Analysis of International Law and Legal Theory' 19 *Melbourne University Law Review* (1995), 893.   [171] J. Braithwaite and P. Drahos, *Global Business Regulation* (2000), at 481.

[172] Ibid. at 497.   [173] ICHRP, *supra* note 25, at 10.

promoting change.[174] The idea that businesses might have a legitimate role in advancing human rights is a relatively new one. It has been fuelled by the proactivity of non-governmental organizations such as Amnesty International. They argue that the business community has a wider responsibility—both moral and legal—to use its influence to promote respect for human rights. Since large companies regularly try to influence governments' tax and trade policies, their labour laws, and environmental rules, their silence in the face of injustice is not neutral. Few would argue with Amnesty's Human Rights Principles for Companies:

All companies have a direct responsibility to respect human rights in their own operations. Their employees and other people with whom they work are entitled to rights such as freedom from discrimination, the right to life and security, freedom from slavery, freedom of association . . . and fair working conditions.[175]

Multinational corporations can promote human rights through a number of activities, suggest Amnesty: by developing an explicit company policy on human rights; by providing effective training in international human rights standards; by consulting non-governmental organizations on the level and nature of human rights abuses in countries in which they operate; and by establishing a clear framework for assessing the potential impact on human rights of all the company's and its sub-contractors' operations. The primary responsibility for implementation and monitoring should lie with the company but should be independently verifiable. This approach will be assisted as the UN Norms on the Responsibilities of Transnational Corporations are promulgated.[176]

Others are sceptical: at worst codes are 'figleaves for exploitation'[177] and at best largely ineffective.[178] Voluntary codes are selective and few cover the same ground.[179] Few would disagree that the climate of opinion has moved towards demanding greater accountability of multinational companies, an accountability that should be enforced through international mechanisms.[180] Nor would many disagree that most people welcome the adoption of human rights policies by companies but are sceptical about their follow-through.[181]

Our task in this essay has been to explore ways in which multinational corporations could be brought to account for human rights violations in which they are complicit. It is clear that such a task cannot be approached in isolation. In their magisterial study of global business regulation Braithwaite and Drahos point to the complex plurality of actors involved in business regulation, the power of the nation

---

[174] M. Keck and K. Sikkink, *Activists Beyond Borders: Advocacy Networks in International Politics* (1998).   [175] January 1998, AI index: ACT 70/01/98.

[176] Sub-Commission for the Protection and Promotion of Human Rights 2003, *supra* note 54.

[177] Kearney, 'Corporate Codes of Conduct: The Privatized Application of Labour Standards' in S. Picciotto and R. Mayne (eds), *Regulating International Business: Beyond Liberalisation* (2000), at 208.

[178] Kamminga and Zia-Zarifi, *supra* note 25, at 9.   [179] ICHRP, *supra* note 25, at 15.

[180] Ibid.

[181] Avery, 'Business and Human Rights in a Time of Change' in Kamminga and Zia-Zarifi, *supra* note 25, 17 at 31.

state, in particular the US, the growth of international organizations, and the importance of epistemic communities.[182] It is worth restating the obvious point that corporations owe their status in law *to law*. From this it follows that they should be challengeable in law,[183] through revocation of their status, through claims for false advertising, or actions against individual directors. Before an effective regime can be developed it will be necessary to drive through a company culture or organizational principle of attribution. This would then need to be supplemented by complicity rules that reflect the reality of state and corporate structures of decision-making. But is also necessary to adhere to another sense of 'reality': the capacity of corporations to reinvent themselves. Not only are corporations adept at protecting their own interests through entrenched human rights codes,[184] they are good at staying one step ahead of the game. Law does not easily provide answers to complex and uncertain political and economic challenges.

APPENDIX

Rome Statute of the International Criminal Court, adopted by the United Nations Diplomatic Conference of Plenipotentiaries on the establishment of an International Court on 17 July 1998, Article 25(3) provides that:

...a person shall be criminally responsible...within this jurisdiction of the Court if a person:

(a) commits such a crime, whether as an individual, jointly with another or through another person, regardless of whether that other person is criminally responsible;

(b) orders, solicits, or induces the commission of such a crime which in fact occurs or is attempted;

(c) for the purpose of facilitating the commission of such a crime, aids, abets or otherwise assists in its commission or its attempted commission, including providing the means for its commission;

(d) in any other way contributes to the commission or attempted commission of such a crime by a group of persons acting with a common purpose. Such contribution shall be intentional and shall either:

    (i) be made with the aim of furthering the criminal activity or criminal purpose of the group, where such activity or purpose involves the commission of a crime within the jurisdiction of the Court; or

    (ii) be made in the knowledge of the intention of the group to commit the crime;

---

[182] *Supra* note 171.   [183] IRENE, *supra* note 156.

[184] Ewing, 'Human Rights, Social Democracy and Constitutional Reform' in C. Gearty and A. Tomkins (eds), *Understanding Human Rights* (1996) 40.

(e) in respect of the crime of genocide, directly and publicly incites others to commit genocide;

(f) attempts to commit such a crime by taking action that commences its execution by means of a substantial step, but the crime does not occur because of circumstances independent of the person's intentions. However, a person who abandons the effort to commit the crime or otherwise prevents the completion of the crime shall not be liable for punishment under this Statute for the attempt to commit that crime if that person completely and voluntarily gave up the criminal purpose.

Article 28 provides:

Responsibility of commanders and other superiors

(a) A military commander or person effectively acting as a military commander shall be criminally responsible for crimes within the jurisdiction of the Court committed by forces under his or her effective command and control, or effective authority and control as the case may be, as a result of his or her failure to exercise control properly over such forces, where·

   (i) that military commander or person either knew or, owing to circumstances at the time, should have known that the forces were committing or about to commit such crimes; and

   (ii) that military commander or person failed to take all reasonable measures within his or her power to prevent or repress their commission within the matter to the competent authorities for investigation and prosecution.

(b) With respect to superior and subordinate relationships not described in paragraph (a), a superior shall be criminally responsible for crimes within the jurisdiction of the Court committed by subordinates under his or her effective authority and control, as a result of his or her failure to exercise control properly over such subordinates, where:

   (i) the superior either knew, or consciously disregarded information which clearly indicated, that the subordinates were committing or about to commit such crimes;

   (ii) the crimes concerned activities that were within the effective responsibility and control of the superior; and

   (iii) the superior failed to take all necessary and reasonable measures within his or her power to prevent or repress their commission or to submit the matter to the competent authorities for investigation and prosecution.

6

Corporate Responsibility and the International Law of Human Rights: The New *Lex Mercatoria*

RALPH G. STEINHARDT

Corporate law and international human rights law have historically evolved in isolation from one another. In practice, the transnational corporation has remained relatively immune from effective international regulation of any variety, let alone the obligation to protect human rights, and human rights lawyers have traditionally considered governments—not private companies—to be the principal targets for concern. With a handful of exceptions, international human rights instruments have traditionally addressed the conduct of governments, and instruments treating the transnational corporation, when they exist at all, have addressed restrictive or corrupt business practices and neglected any obligation a corporation might have to protect the civil and political rights of individuals in the society at large.

In part, the distance between these two legal cultures reflects matters of apparent principle: one received orthodoxy locates rights in a 'public' realm, binding only on governments in their dealings with individuals, and corporate profits in a 'private' realm, governed only by the rules of the marketplace. Certainly, the state-centeredness of international law, though qualified constantly, has never been so compromised as to equate the corporation with the state that gives it existence or to trigger state-like obligations to respect human rights standards. A separate orthodoxy, grounded in the bedrock conception of an 'exclusive domestic jurisdiction', treats the protection of human rights as properly within the reach of modern international law and the regulation of corporate conduct as a matter of domestic law.

As a result of these lawyerly habits of mind, the distinction between corporate practice and international human rights law may have come to seem both inevitable and proper. In its received form, however, it has become dysfunctional. Over the last decade, prominent transnational companies have adopted codes of conduct which make the protection of at least some human rights an explicit corporate objective. Coalitions in apparel, textiles, and footwear have adopted standards industry-wide to govern international labour practices. A global standard for social accountability—SA8000—has been created to guide and assess corporate compliance with international human rights norms across industrial and geographical boundaries. Many companies now advertise their international human rights policies. Corporate officers periodically gather at human-rights roundtables and affirm the strategic value of a public commitment to such rights, even as a self-styled 'progressive' stream of corporate and management scholarship offers a theoretical foundation for understanding the economic self-interest of corporate social responsibility.

These developments may simply reflect a new way in which one corporation chooses to compete with another, but entrepreneurialism alone is inadequate to account for the sea change in the corporate culture: national, state, and municipal legislation increasingly regulates the market through 'human rights conditionality', barring corporate presence in certain countries where human rights are not respected, or requiring certain corporate practices, or linking government contracts and other benefits to a corporation's compliance with international human rights norms. And now overarching those regulatory initiatives is the prospect of civil liability, as various domestic courts have ruled that corporations may in principle be obliged to pay substantial awards of damages for their complicity in abuses by the governments with which they do business. On the international plane, multilateral and bilateral investment agreements increasingly oblige transnational corporations to protect the human rights of workers and other citizens, even as international financial institutions, like the World Bank and the regional development banks, episodically adopt rights-based policies with consequences for the transnational corporation.

The rough coherence of these developments with one another and within the larger framework of international law suggests that corporate counsel and management, not to mention scholars of international law and corporate law, ignore this recent history at their peril. But it is a mistake to assume that change is occurring only within the corporate world. In fact, the international human rights movement is in a reciprocal process of transformation. A movement that has focused almost exclusively on state actors must now grapple with the range of complex relationships among governments, people, and organizations. Human rights advocacy, which has traditionally emphasized such rights as bodily integrity and political expression, has broadened its focus to include economic concerns like the rights of labour, the transparency of government operations, and the protections of private property. The 'good politics/bad economics' that has occasionally characterized the recommendations of human rights advocates and non-governmental organizations has begun to give way to sophisticated economic models of advocacy, explicitly defending the long-term profitability of human rights protection and unifying the rights of political dissidents with the interests of transnational corporations under the rubric of 'the rule of law'.

This article explores this emerging, controversial order and the legal premises on which it rests. Part I demonstrates that the corporate human rights movement consists of four separate but compatible regimes, each grounded in well established principles of international and domestic law: (i) a market-based regime, under which corporations compete for consumers and investors by attempting to conform to international human rights standards or a substantial subset of them; (ii) a regime of domestic regulation, exemplified by directives and legislation in the United States which, through human rights conditionality, recruit the transnational corporation as an instrument of foreign policy; (iii) a regime of civil liability, enforced through private lawsuits in domestic courts and exemplified by *Doe v. Unocal, Presbyterian Church v. Talisman*, and the Holocaust litigation; and (iv) a regime of international regulation and quasi-regulation by intergovernmental organizations, which have attempted to channel corporate conduct in ways that are thought to be socially responsible. Part II explores the most pointed objections to these developments: that social responsibility movements subvert the implicit promise of corporations to their shareholders or require expertise that corporations cannot be expected to have; that none of the four regimes is conspicuously successful in protecting human rights, and none adequately distinguishes degrees of corporate culpability or gives adequate notice of the corporation's human rights responsibilities *ex ante*; that *Unocal* and its progeny impose a uniquely American form of liability that disadvantages U.S. corporations in the global marketplace; and that imposing greater human rights obligations just as corporations are voluntarily beginning to undertake them demonstrates the truism that no good deed goes unpunished. The article also responds to potential objections from the human rights perspective, especially the argument that the current body of corporate human rights concerns is pretextual, unambitious, skewed towards labour rights, and unenforceable. Many human rights advocates resist any argument to the effect that a corporate human rights agenda is 'good business' because that argument commodifies basic principles of human dignity and thus surrenders the moral high ground. In this view, corporations should protect human rights because it is the right thing to do, whether it is profitable or not. Moreover, critics argue, shifting the focus to economic rights or forcing all human rights under the 'rule of law' rubric undermines whatever coherence the human rights movement has achieved over the last half-century.

These objections are far from trivial, though in my view they are ultimately insufficient to derail the corporate human rights initiative altogether. Instead, they define and illuminate a middle path, maintaining the general impetus towards corporate responsibility in the human rights field but justifying a global standard that is so grounded in international law as to offer corporations a measure of protection from aggressive or idiosyncratic approaches to human rights. The article concludes by suggesting that the corporate responsibility initiative shares some essential characteristics with the ancient *lex mercatoria*: a set of good mercantile practices, growing out of the needs and customs of the marketplace, that ultimately gave rise to law in more recognizable and more enforceable form. In short, if a new law of corporate human rights responsibility emerges from this 'buzzing, blooming confusion' of developments and initiatives, it would not be the first time that law had gradually crystallized from commercial practices that were grounded in what the entrepreneurial class considered to be its own long-term self-interest.

Part I. Regimes of Corporate Responsibility

1. A MARKET-BASED REGIME: HUMAN RIGHTS ENTREPRENEURIALISM

The record of transnational corporations' commitment to human rights is distinctly mixed. On one hand are periodic reports of corporate complicity in (or profits from) human rights abuses in a variety of states around the world, suggesting that there is no shortage of targets for those who consider corporations an essential partner in the way human rights get abused in the modern world. A contemporaneous school of management theory has challenged the notion that these corporations owe anything other than legal, profitable operations to anyone other than stockholders, noting in the words of Milton Friedman that 'the social responsibility of business is to increase its profits'. On the other hand, prominent transnational corporations have increasingly adopted statements of general business principles, which typically include the protection of at least some human rights, especially of workers, and industry-wide coalitions have committed themselves to similar precepts. Because they are defended in part as attempts to attract both customers and investors, these statements of principle implicitly repudiate the assumption that social responsibility is inherently unprofitable, but, for that reason, they also provoke the suspicion that the corporate commitment to human rights is neither altruistic nor particularly credible.

The recent effort to compete for sales and capital through a public commitment to international human rights—'human rights entrepreneurialism' as it were—had its precursors in the anti-apartheid and pro-environment movements. The Sullivan Principles, first articulated in 1977, amounted to a voluntary code of conduct for companies doing business in South Africa under the apartheid regime. The principles required integrated workplaces, fair employment practices, and affirmative action, and a signatory company's compliance with these principles was assessed by independent auditors. The Sullivan Principles not only offered an alternative to divestment, as urged by some stockholders and activists, it also blunted the periodic efforts to impose economic sanctions on South Africa or to ban foreign companies from doing business there.[1] The principles also gave companies an objective, common standard under which their presence in South Africa might be defended in

---

[1] Daniel Pink, 'The Valdez Principles: Is What's Good for America Good for General Motors?', 8 *Yale L. & P. Rev.* (1990) 180, at 189 (footnotes omitted) ('Congressional sanctions often loomed in the background for Sullivan companies. Since these sanctions threatened to disrupt their ability to do business, many companies signed the Sullivan Principles to quell legislative action.')

the competition for a good corporate image. In 1984, with some 125 signatories, the principles were expanded to require companies to take more aggressive action against apartheid, tantamount to corporate civil disobedience. The principles provided a benchmark for the managers of municipal pension funds and university endowments and were ultimately incorporated in an executive order adopted by President Reagan. They also served as the model for the MacBride Principles, which articulated a code of conduct for companies doing business in Northern Ireland. But by 1987, with only glacial change in South Africa, even the drafters of the Sullivan Principles considered them a failure and urged corporations to withdraw from South Africa altogether.

The political and economic value of the Sullivan Principles—such as it might have been—was not lost on advocates in the environmental movement, who recognized that a limited and relatively well defined set of norms, combined with some objective measure for assessing compliance, could promote competition for customers and investors and allow companies to avoid more stringent forms of regulation or liability. Despite their uncertain impact in South Africa, the Sullivan Principles thus served as a model for the Valdez Principles, adopted by the Coalition for Environmentally Responsible Economies, which required signatory companies *inter alia* to protect the biosphere, use renewable resources, dispose of wastes properly, disclose environmental risks, and submit to an annual environmental audit. Anecdotal evidence suggests that management in some corporations has taken the principles seriously, at least when stockholders do, and the principles ultimately contributed to a marketplace in which companies are expected to be environmentally conscious. The appearance of specialized products on the mass market, like shade-grown coffees, recycled-paper products, and dolphin-safe tuna, is a response to consumers who are motivated in part by environmental concerns, even as 'green portfolios' attest to the existence of environmentally conscious investors.

The evidence of a similar market-driven commitment to human rights takes many forms, as illustrated in the following.

A. 'Rights-Sensitive' Product Lines and Branding

Many market-leading transnational companies have determined that a profitable contingent of consumers will pay a premium for some assurance that the goods they purchase are not produced or marketed in violation of the rights of workers and communities. Starbucks offers 'fair trade' coffees, noting in print on every cup that the production and marketing of its products harm neither coffee workers nor the environment. Chiquita, having adopted an independently verifiable social and environmental standard for its banana farms in Latin America, has begun to market an 'Ethical Banana' in response to consumer demand, especially in Europe.[2] And, in

---

[2] The standard is administered by the Rainforest Alliance, an international non-profit organization responsible for certifying farms under its Better Banana Project (BBP). Complying with the BBP

response to the problem of 'conflict diamonds', the World Diamond Council has developed a protocol for assuring that the profits from the sale of gems do not support governments or paramilitary groups that abuse civilians[3] and has promoted the 'Kimberley Process'[4]—international negotiations on the creation of a more reliable and permanent system of combatting the illicit trade in diamonds.[5] Similarly, the apparel industry, often in partnership with human rights NGOs, has adopted various workplace codes of conduct and principles of monitoring in order to eliminate sweatshop practices.[6] The awareness that rights-sensitive product lines and branding offer a competitive advantage is thus widespread in the business community, across industry types and political borders, even if its translation into corporate practice is episodic at best.[7]

reportedly cost Chiquita more than US$20 million in capital expenditure, and millions more in annual operating costs, but Chiquita's quality director in Europe has judged the money to have been well invested: 'Many of our retail customers would not be doing business with us unless we had a really thorough and deeply rooted programme like this' *quoted at* http://www.ethicalperformance.com/best_practice/archive/1001/case_studies/chiquita.html.

[3] World Diamond Council, Joint Resolution of the World Federation of Diamond Bourses and the International Diamond Manufacturers Association (19 July 2000).

[4] *See* Testimony of Loren Yager, Director, International Affairs and Trade, United States General Accounting Office, *International Trade: Significant Challenges Remain in Deterring Trade in Conflict Diamonds*, before the Subcommittee on Oversight of Government Management, Restructuring and the District of Columbia, Committee on Governmental Affairs, U.S. Senate (13 February 2002), at 5–6: 'In May 2000, African diamond producing countries initiated the Kimberley Process in Kimberley, South Africa, to discuss the conflict diamond trade. Participants now include states and countries of the European Union involved in the production, export, and import of rough diamonds; as well as representatives from the diamond industry, notably the World Diamond Council, and nongovernmental organizations. The goal is to create and implement an international certification scheme for rough diamonds, based primarily on national certification schemes and internationally agreed minimum standards for the basic requirements of a certificate of origin. The scheme's objectives are to (1) stem the flow of rough diamonds used by rebels to finance armed conflict aimed at overthrowing legitimate governments; and (2) protect the legitimate diamond industry, upon which some countries depend for their economic and social development.'

[5] *See* U.N. Res. 56/263 (13 March 2002) ('the opportunity for conflict diamonds to play a role in fueling armed conflict can be seriously reduced by introducing a certification scheme for rough diamonds and that such a scheme would help protect the legitimate trade and ensure the effective implementation of the relevant resolutions of the United Nations Security Council containing sanctions on the trade in conflict diamonds'.) *See also* U.N. Res. 55/56 (1 December 2000) (calling on the international community to develop detailed proposals for a simple and workable international certification scheme for rough diamonds based primarily on national certification schemes and on internationally agreed minimum standards).

[6] *See, e.g.* in Europe, the Clean Clothes Campaign, *Code of Labour Practices for the Apparel Industry Including Sportswear*, available at <http://www.cleanclothes.org/codes.htm>; in the United States, the Fair Labor Association, *Workplace Code of Conduct* and *Principles of Monitoring*, available at <http://www.fairlabor.org/>.

[7] *See generally* Robert J. Liubicic, 'Corporate Codes of Conduct and Product Labeling Schemes: The Limits and Possibilities of Promoting International Labor Rights Standards Through Private Initiatives', 30 *Law & Pol'y Int'l Bus.* (1998) 111.

B. Unilateral Codes of Conduct

Beginning in the early 1990s, a handful of companies began unilaterally to adopt statements of general business principles, which purported to institutionalize the company's commitment to good practices. In 1991, for example, Levi Strauss adopted its 'Global Sourcing and Operating Guidelines', which declared that 'we will favor business partners who share our commitment to contribute to improving community conditions' and 'may withdraw production from [any factory that violates these standards] or require that a contractor implement a corrective action plan within a specified time period'. The company also adopted 'Country Assessment Guidelines' to enable it to assess the possibility of harm to its reputation from doing business in a particular country. Among the criteria used in the Guidelines is 'whether the [h]uman rights environment would prevent us from conducting business activities in a manner that is consistent with the Global Sourcing Guidelines and other company policies'. The company's well publicized decision to withdraw from Myanmar in 1992 gave effect to these policies.[8] Similar statements of policy followed from Reebok and The Body Shop, though these were considerably more specific in articulating the rights to which the company was committing itself.[9] Whether these initial, unilateral corporate commitments made any immediate or verifiable difference in the lives of workers or of citizens is inevitably a matter for speculation. But the fact that other companies, such as Royal Dutch Shell, Exxon-Mobil, Nike, Liz Claiborne, and many others, have adopted similar policies suggests that the advantages of human rights entrepreneurialism were not lost on competitors or the commercial world generally, even if the means of enforcing the codes remain obscure.[10]

---

[8] 'Under current circumstances, it is not possible to do business in Myanmar without directly supporting the military government and its pervasive violations of human rights': quoted in T. Smith, 'Transnational Influence: The Power of Business', *Human Rights: The New Consensus* (1994) at 151.

[9] For example, the 'Human Rights Production Standards', adopted by Reebok in 1992, declared that the company's 'devotion to human rights worldwide is a hallmark of our corporate culture', and focused on a range of employee rights in the workplace, including the rights to non-discrimination, fair wages, reasonable hours and overtime policies, freedom of association, and occupational safety, as well as the prohibition of child labour and forced or compulsory labour of any sort. In 1994, The Body Shop adopted its 'Trading Charter', which went well beyond these workplace rights and incorporated the Universal Declaration of Human Rights as corporate policy. The Body Shop subsequently expanded this commitment, in terms strongly reminiscent of traditionally governmental obligations and well beyond the rights of workers, in its 'Statement of Human Rights Principles': 'While we respect cultural differences, and are aware of the economic disparities that exist within and between countries, we believe that the civil, political, economic, social, and cultural rights outlined in the Universal Declaration of Human Rights (UDHR) are universal, indivisible, interdependent and inter-related. Our goal is to encourage the creation of working and living conditions where people can fulfil their potential, where their human rights are respected without prejudice, and where they can determine their own destiny. We will seek business partners who share this commitment.'

[10] See section 1(C), *infra*, suggesting the litigation uses of these unilateral codes.

C. Social Accountability Auditing and Certification

In an effort to standardize the various corporate codes and to define corporate social responsibility across firms and across industry sectors, some multinational companies—often in partnership with human rights organizations and trade unions—have adopted verifiable standards governing conditions in the workplace. Social Accountability (SA) 8000, for example, offers a voluntary process under which independent auditors may certify that a company complies with standards in nine essential areas: child labour, forced labour, health and safety, freedom of association, freedom from discrimination, disciplinary practices, work hours, compensation, and management systems to assure compliance.[11] The standards themselves are drawn from conventions of the International Labour Organization, the Universal Declaration on Human Rights, and the U.N. Convention on the Rights of the Child, *inter alia*. Like other auditable standards, including ISO 9000 (establishing quality control standards) and ISO 14001 (establishing environmental management standards), SA 8000 and similar standards[12] allow companies to differentiate themselves from their uncertified competitors. Admittedly, the Arthur Andersen scandal in 2002 undermined the independent accounting profession, and SA 8000 may be objectionable on the additional ground that it purports to quantify the unquantifiable or requires for its success a consumer who is both insensible to price and in possession of perfect information. But the practical value of SA 8000 may lie in its potential to alter the commercial relationship between a company and its suppliers, who, because the standards apply upstream, have a clear competitive incentive to seek, receive, and advertise certification.

D. Ethical Investment Organizations and Shareholder Pressure

Human rights concerns are present in the investment market as well as the consumer market. Individual and institutional investors have increasingly followed 'social' or 'ethical' criteria, both in screening their initial investments and—perhaps more effectively—in voting their shares as stockholders, with the result that management must increasingly respond to investors' calls for 'sustainable business', *i.e.* business 'that enhances long-term shareholder value by addressing the needs of all relevant stakeholders and adding economic, environmental, and social value through its core

---

[11] SA 8000 was developed by the Council on Economic Priorities Accreditation Agency, now Social Accountability International. The text of SA 8000 is available at www.cepaa.org/sa8000_review.htm (visited 8 November 2002). As of this writing, some 162 firms, in 27 countries and representing 30 industries, have been certified under SA 8000, including Avon Products, Toys 'R' Us, and Otto-Versand. Factory certification is valid for three years, with surveillance audits at six-month intervals.

[12] In the United Kingdom, the Institute of Social and Ethical AccountAbility has introduced AccountAbility (AA)1000, which, like SA 8000, offers objective criteria for measuring the social and ethical achievements of companies. The Dutch Association of Investors for Sustainable Development has adopted standards that appear to be the basis for an emerging Europe-wide accreditation standard, approved by the European Commission.

business functions'.[13] Major stock markets have developed social indices for the guidance of investors,[14] major investment houses have developed ethical-investment mutual funds (*e.g.* Dreyfus' Third Century Fund and Merrill Lynch's Ecological Trust), and an ethical consulting industry has emerged to assist companies manage risk by adhering to the norms of corporate citizenship.[15]

The profitability and the effectiveness of socially responsible investing ('SRI') are inevitably difficult to measure. Some recent data suggest that the corporate scandals of 2002 led to an increase in SRI and that socially responsible mutual funds significantly outperformed diversified funds.[16] Growth in SRI since 1995 has been substantial.[17] But the anecdotal evidence that pension fund managers exert ethical leverage is also compelling. In 2002, for example, the largest pension fund in the United States decided to pull out of four East Asian countries—Thailand, the Philippines, Malaysia, and Indonesia—despite the fact that these countries had some of the best performing economies in Asia, and it did so primarily because of its human rights concerns in those nations, especially reports of forced labour, discrimination, and interference with the freedom of association.[18] 'Conscientious proxy statements' led to substantial corporate pullouts from Burma in the 1990s and from South Africa in the 1980s, and high-profile investigations of child labour practices led to a restructuring of supply chain relationships in many industries explicitly in order to maintain share value.[19]

E. The Rise and Convergence of NGOs

An integral part of human rights entrepreneurialism has been the rise of non-governmental organizations that are specifically devoted to assuring that human rights norms are respected in the marketplace. Some NGOs have developed standard reporting guidelines,[20] and others have emerged to report on companies' social

---

[13] Tim Dickson, 'The Financial Case for Behaving Responsibly' *Financial Times* (19 August 2002) 5.

[14] *See e.g.* the Dow Jones STOXX Sustainability Index (<http://www.sustainability-indexes.com>), and the FTSE4Good index (<http://www.ftse4good.com>). These indices are necessarily partial, because they include only 'high impact' and only particular areas of corporate responsibility, some of which have little to do with human rights.

[15] *See e.g.* Financial Times-Prentice Hall, *Visions of Ethical Business* (2002). *See generally* Louisa Wah, 'Treading the Sacred Ground', 87 *Management Review* (1998) at 18–22.

[16] Social Investment Forum, *Market Slump Providing Unexpected Boost to Socially Responsible Mutual Funds* (30 July 2002), available at <http://www.socialinvest.org/areas/news/020730.htm>.

[17] *See* Dickson, note 13 above; and Wah, note 15 above.

[18] *See* Lesley Curwen and Manuela Saragosa, 'Major Pension Fund Quits Asian Countries: Malaysia's Human Rights Record Prompted Calpers Exit', *BBC World Business Report* (21 February 2002).

[19] Elizabeth Larson and Bonnie Cox, 'Social Accountability 8000: Measuring Workplace Conditions Worldwide', *Quality Digest* (1998) 28.

[20] In August 2002, for example, the Global Reporting Initiative (GRI) released a set of public reporting guidelines to help companies and other organizations disclose performance beyond the financial bottom line. *See* 2002 Sustainability Reporting Guidelines, available at <http://www.globalreporting.org>.

performance.[21] Non-governmental organizations with traditional human rights mandates have increasingly criticized private companies for their role in human rights abuse,[22] as have consumer, labour, religious, and cultural NGOs. These groups may be especially effective in organizing publicity campaigns and boycotts in response to perceived instances of corporate irresponsibility.[23] Perhaps more telling are the non-adversarial relationships that have developed between human rights NGOs and business leadership NGOs, which have jointly engaged in public information and outreach campaigns.[24] Even before the traditional human rights NGOs focused on the issue, business groups were developing norms of corporate citizenship and modes of implementation. The Caux Roundtable, comprised of senior business leaders from Europe, Japan, and North America, was one of the first organizations of any sort to articulate *Principles for Business*: an aspirational set of recommendations covering a wide range of corporate behaviour.[25]

These market-based initiatives have provoked their share of cynicism not least because the companies alleged to be complicit in abuses are frequently the very companies that adopt human rights principles with the greatest public fanfare, and there is nothing other than the market to 'enforce' these various standards. But, even if accurate, the critique misses the essential characteristic of the market-based regime, namely that it is compelled not so much by law as by potentially powerful commercial incentives. As articulated by the U.N. High Commissioner for Human Rights, the commercial advantages of corporate compliance with human rights standards include: (1) ensuring compliance with local and international laws; (2) satisfying consumer concerns; (3) promoting the rule of law, by contributing to 'the development of legal systems in which contracts are enforced fairly, bribery and corruption are less prevalent and all business entities have equal access to legal process and equal protection under law'; (4) building community goodwill; (5) improving supply chain management by selecting business partners that are

---

[21] *See e.g.* CorpWatch, at <http://wwwcorpwatch.org>; The Investor Responsibility Research Center, at <http://www.irrc.org>; the Social Investment Forum, at <http://www.socialinvest.org>; and the Shareholder Action Network, at <http://www.shareholderaction.org>. A coalition of investor responsibility groups has developed a comprehensive set of global corporate responsibility criteria. *See* the Ecumenical Council for Corporate Responsibility (ECCR), Interfaith Center on Corporate Responsibility (ICCR), and the Canadian Taskforce on Churches and Corporate Responsibility (TCCR), *Principles of Global Corporate Responsibility: Bench Marks for Measuring Business Performance* (2003).

[22] *See e.g. Human Rights are Everybody's Business* (January 2002), available at <http://web.amnesty.org/web/web.nsf/pages/ec_home>; Human Rights Watch, *Without Remedy: Human Rights Abuse and Indonesia's Pulp and Paper Industry* (January 2003), available at <http://hrw.org/reports/2003/indon0103/>.

[23] *See* Steven Greenhouse, 'A Weapon for Consumers: The Boycott Returns', *New York Times* (26 March 2000).

[24] *See e.g.* Amnesty International and the Prince of Wales International Business Leaders Forum, *Business and Human Rights: A Geography of Corporate Risk*, available at <http://www.iblf.org/csr/csrwebassist.nsf/content/b1f2.html#2>.

[25] The Principles were adopted in 1994, for the purpose of 'express[ing] a worldwide standard for ethical and responsible corporate behavior and...offered as a foundation for dialogue and action by business and leaders worldwide', available at <http://www.cauxroundtable.org>.

well managed and reliable; (6) enhancing risk management by assuring more stable and productive business operations; (7) keeping markets open; (8) increasing worker productivity and retention; and (9) applying corporate values in a way that maintains 'the faith of employees and external stakeholders in company integrity'.[26] The UNHCHR is no market consultant of course, but the dynamic she articulated is confirmed by the emergence of best practices adopted by the market players themselves.[27]

2. A REGIME OF DOMESTIC REGULATION

Supplementing (and perhaps provoking) the market-based, self-regulating mechanisms just described are domestic regulatory initiatives which require or encourage the protection of human rights in the marketplace. In a variety of countries, the last decade has seen the proliferation of legislation that attempts to recruit the transnational corporation as an instrument of foreign policy, by barring any corporate presence in, or transactions with, certain countries where human rights are not respected, or requiring certain corporate practices (especially with respect to workers' rights), or conditioning government contracts, market access, and other benefits on a corporation's compliance with international human rights norms. But, as the following examples suggest, this domestic legislation is typically episodic and limited either geographically to particular countries (like Burma or South Africa under apartheid) or substantively to particular human rights violations (like forced labour). There is no domestic legislation defining a comprehensive, enforceable code of human rights conduct for multinational corporations, though it is possible to identify common themes or approaches in this body of law and to mark its slow evolution towards breadth and definition.

One statutory precedent in the United States offers an instructive if cautionary tale in the move towards legislating corporations' human rights responsibilities: the Foreign Corrupt Practices Act of 1977 ('FCPA'),[28] which *inter alia* prohibits any publicly traded company in the United States from paying bribes to a foreign official. Growing out of a series of bribery scandals that had compromised U.S.

---

[26] U.N. High Commissioner for Human Rights, *Business and Human Rights: A Progress Report*, <available at http://www.unhchr.ch/business.htm#I1>.

[27] *See* comments of the President of the American Chamber of Commerce in Hong Kong, J. Kamm, 'The Role of Businesses in Promoting Respect for Human Rights', *quoted in* M. Daly, 'The New Joint Venture: Human Rights and Business' *Human Rights Solidarity* (1997) at 7 ('while it might not always be the case that trade and business are good for human rights, it most certainly is the case that a good human rights environment is always good for business. Businesses are acting in their own self-interest when they actively promote respect for human rights in countries where they operate.')

[28] Pub. L. 95-213, §§ 101–104, Dec. 19, 1977, 91 Stat. 1494 (codified at 15 U.S.C. § 78m, § 78dd-1 & 2, and §§ 78ff), as amended by the Foreign Corrupt Practices Act Amendments of 1988, Pub. L. 100-418, Title V, § 5003(a) *et seq.*, 102 Stat. 1107, and the International Anti-Bribery and Fair Competition Act of 1998, Pub. L. No. 105-366, §§ 1–4.

foreign relations with Chile, Italy, the Netherlands, and Japan, the FCPA was initially resisted by American businesses on the ground that it would subject them to a unique form of liability and thereby put them at a distinct competitive disadvantage. But by the early 1990s attitudes began to change:

> It was becoming increasingly clear that the dimensions of the bribery problem were much greater than many thought. In addition to recognizing the debilitating effect on government and on public trust in government, widespread bribery came to be seen as leading itself to a serious misallocation of resources. Developing nations in particular could ill afford such waste. The adverse effect of official corruption on investments was also becoming increasingly apparent. An IMF study suggested that there was a demonstrable inverse relationship between the level of corruption prevalent in a country and the level of investment as a percent of domestic product.[29]

In quick succession, public and private actors embraced the principles (if not the details) of the FCPA.[30]

Thus, instead of illustrating the tendency of the United States to legislate morality extraterritorially, hurting only U.S. companies in the process, the FCPA offered an organizing principle for a new business culture; indeed, the FCPA is now routinely cited by U.S. firms as the exemplar of progressive legislation, protecting them from the importuning of foreign officials and improving the quality of competition in the global marketplace. Certainly issues of interpretation and application persist, and what change has occurred took a generation to achieve, but the FCPA does provide a striking example of how domestic legislation can give rise to a consensus for change and international standard-setting, so long as it is grounded in both moral and economic principle and so long as it is not persistently overbroad.

The preliminary outlines of a similar legislative and cultural dynamic are discernible with respect to human rights in the marketplace; as suggested by the following.

A. Securities Regulation and Disclosure

Nations with strong capital markets have experimented with requiring social disclosure as a way of promoting corporate responsibility. In February 2002, for example, France adopted legislation that requires all French companies to report on

---

[29] Alan Swan & John Murphy, *Cases and Materials on the Regulation of International Business and Economic Relations* (2nd ed. 1999) 831.

[30] For example, the International Chamber of Commerce issued Rules of Conduct to Combat Extortion and Bribery (1996); the Organization of American States concluded the Inter-American Convention Against Corruption (1996); the United Nations General Assembly adopted a Declaration Against Corruption and Bribery in International Commercial Transactions (1996); the European Union offered its Convention on the Fight Against Corruption Involving Officials of the European Communities or Official States of the European Union (1997); the Council of Europe adopted a Criminal Law Convention which included provisions on criminalizing corrupt payments (1999); the Organization of Economic Cooperation and Development adopted the Convention on Combating Bribery of Foreign Officials in International Business Transactions (1999); and the World Bank issued anti-bribery Guidelines for Procurement under IBRD and IDA Credits.

the 'sustainability' of their practices, including human rights compliance and environmental impacts. No enforcement measures are specified in the French legislation, but other nations have experimented with social disclosure as a way of bringing market pressure to bear on corporate decision-making. In 2000, the United Kingdom amended its Pension Act to require fund trustees to disclose their policy on social, environmental, and ethical issues, and, in 2001, the United States Commission on International Religious Freedom endorsed the use of disclosure statements to help investors decide if they wished to purchase the securities of companies thought to be complicit in the violation of religious freedoms in Sudan.[31]

The legal infrastructure for requiring corporate disclosure is already in place in the leading capital markets of the world. The U.S. Securities and Exchange Commission ('SEC'), for example, is authorized by statute to issue disclosure regulations as 'necessary or appropriate in the public interest for the protection of investors'. If companies wish to raise capital in U.S. markets, they must file a disclosure statement for investors, and false or incomplete disclosure can lead to substantial penalties and criminal proceedings against the company and its directors and managers, as well as civil liability. The legislative history of the Securities Act of 1933 provides for the 'use of disclosure as a regulatory means to foster greater public accountability in the corporate enterprise'. As investors begin to care more about the human rights records of public companies, the SEC may find an opening for exercising its regulatory powers and expanding the requirements for 'social disclosure', including information on the countries in which a company does business, information on its domestic and global labour practices, and information on its domestic and global environmental effects.[32] Because contingent liabilities must be disclosed, the securities laws also leverage the rise of civil lawsuits against corporations for human rights abuse (as described below), and the financial impact of investor consciousness may therefore be greater than the effects of an actual award of damages to particular plaintiffs.

B. Transactional Controls: Imports, Exports, and Sanctions

Legislation and executive regulation clearly provide for the imposition of trade sanctions on particular countries where human rights abuses are profound and widespread, as in Burma and apartheid South Africa.[33] During the Cold War,

---

[31] *Report of the United States Commission on International Religious Freedom* (1 May 2001) 155.

[32] *See* Cynthia Williams, 'The SEC and Corporate Social Transparency' 112 *Harvard L. Rev.* (1999) 1197.

[33] *See e.g.* Exec. Order 12532, 50 *Fed. Reg.* 36861 (Sept. 9, 1985) (imposing sanctions on South Africa), *revoked by* Exec. Order 12769, 56 *Fed. Reg.* 31855 (July 10, 1991); Exec. Order 13047, 62 *Fed. Reg.* 28301 (May 20, 1997) (banning new investment in Burma); Sudan Peace Act of 2002, 50 U.S.C. 1701 note; Executive Order 13213, 66 *Fed. Reg.* 28829 (May 22, 2001) (banning all rough diamond shipments from Sierra Leone for an indefinite period). Sanctions may of course be imposed to advance national security and foreign policy interests to which human rights are secondarily related to human rights, including the effort to combat terrorism and the proliferation of weapons of mass destruction.

especially after 1974 when the Jackson-Vanik Amendment was adopted,[34] the United States could use human rights concerns, especially emigration, to restrict trade with Communist countries. The sanctions for these pervasive violations generally run state-to-state, but multinational corporations are clearly affected by them, and they may even be complicit in the conditions that trigger the sanctions in the first place. When the commerce is itself a form of human rights abuse, as in human trafficking, a range of trade sanctions may be imposed.[35] Congress has also linked trade preferences[36] with the protection of 'internationally recognized worker rights'[37] which corporations no less than governments must respect. Executive regulation has similarly targeted the importation of goods that are 'mined, produced, or manufactured wholly or in part by forced or indentured child labor'.[38]

When they are implemented, these restrictions may be challenged as a form of protectionism and therefore incompatible with the trade liberalization regime of the World Trade Organization.[39] But human rights conditionality may actually reinforce WTO principles by reducing the trade-distorting economic advantages of 'social dumping': the lowering of production costs not through competition and efficiency but through the violation of international labour standards. In certain economic circumstances, human rights abuses committed by governments might even qualify as an export subsidy that is subject to countervailing duty laws. But even if that hypothetical possibility is never pursued, the existing import controls and sanctions legislation offer a powerful illustration of how domestic law channels market conduct towards the protection of certain human rights and the penalization of abuses.

See e.g. Iran and Libya Sanctions Act of 1996, 50 U.S.C. § 1701 note; Exec. Order 13088, 64 *Fed. Reg.* 24021 (June 9, 1998) (prohibiting new investment in the Republic of Serbia in response to the situation in Kosovo).

[34] Trade Act of 1974, §§ 401–406, 19 U.S.C. §§ 2431–36, as amended, *e.g.* with respect to China by Pub. L. No. 106-286, 114 Stat 880, and the Republic of Georgia by Pub. L. No. 106-476, 114 Stat 2101.

[35] *See e.g.* Victims of Trafficking and Violence Protection Act of 2000, 22 U.S.C. § 7108.

[36] The Generalized System of Preferences for example grants duty-free status to imports from developing countries that 'take steps to' respect such rights, 19 U.S.C. 2461-66 (2000). *See also* The Caribbean Basin Trade Partnership Act, 19 U.S.C. 2701-06 (2000). The 2000 Sanders Amendment to Section 307 of the Trade Act of 1930 clarified that the statutory ban on the importation of products made with 'forced' labour includes products made with 'forced or indentured child labor'. 19 U.S.C. 1307 (2000). The Omnibus Trade and Competitiveness Act of 1988 made the failure to comply with 'internationally recognized worker rights' an unfair trading practice, potentially triggering trade sanctions. 19 U.S.C. 2411 (2000).

[37] These rights include: (a) the right of association; (b) the right to organize and bargain collectively; (c) a prohibition on the use of any form of forced or compulsory labour; (d) a minimum age for the employment of children; and (e) acceptable conditions of work with respect to minimum wages, hours of work, and occupational safety and health: 19 U.S.C. 2462(a)(4).

[38] Exec. Order 13126, 'Prohibition of Acquisition of Products Produced by Forced or Indentured Child Labor,' 64 *Fed. Reg.* 32383 (1999).

[39] *See* Part I, section 1(D) above. *See generally*, Frank Garcia, 'The Global Market and Human Rights: Trading Away the Human Rights Principle', 25 *Brooklyn J. Int'l L.* (1999) 51.

C. Administrative Law: Linking Government Benefits to Social Performance Criteria

One way that domestic legislation can induce compliance with human rights standards is to ensure that no public money is spent facilitating or enabling human rights violations, even if that effect is achieved indirectly through the operations of private companies. For example, certain provisions of U.S. law make workers' rights relevant to government decision-making, especially in foreign aid[40] and public sector financing,[41] and incentives for the development of a private sector in former Communist states have similarly been made contingent on the protection of international recognized workers' rights.[42] But other specific categories of human rights abuse are also targeted: the President of the U.S.A. may use his considerable administrative authority under the International Emergency Economic Powers Act[43] for example to combat trafficking in persons,[44] and countries that violate international religious freedom may find that their companies are denied U.S. government contracts and a comprehensive range of other benefits.[45]

Legislation linking government decision-making to human rights more broadly conceived is rare, but it exists.[46] One example is the statute governing the Export-Import Bank of the United States ('Eximbank'), which generally requires that the decision to extend credit to a particular applicant or to finance a particular transaction abroad be guided by exclusively commercial considerations and good banking practice.[47] Politics and ideology are to be irrelevant, suggesting that human rights norms—with their political overtones—are to be avoided. But the statute also provides:

Only in cases where the President, after consultation with [certain congressional committees], *determines that such action would be in the national interest where such action would clearly and importantly advance United States policy in such areas as* international terrorism, nuclear

---

[40] Amendments to the Foreign Assistance Act of 1961 bar funding any programme of the Agency for International Development which contributes to the denial of 'internationally recognized worker rights', 22 U.S.C. 2151 *et seq.* (1992), and require executive officers 'to use the voice and vote of the United States to urge [international financial institutions] . . . to adopt policies to encourage borrowing countries to guarantee internationally recognized worker rights'. 22 U.S.C. 1621 (1996).

[41] The Overseas Private Investment Corporation can provide insurance to U.S. companies only if the countries in which they propose to operate complies with the regime of internationally recognized workers' rights. 22 U.S.C. 2191 (1986).

[42] *See e.g.* Support for East European Democracy Act of 1989, Pub. L. No. 101–179, 22. U.S.C. 5421 (1989).   [43] 50 U.S.C. 1701 *et seq.*

[44] Victims of Trafficking and Violence Protection Act of 2000, 22. U.S.C. 7108.

[45] International Religious Freedom Act of 1998, 22 U.S.C. 6401, 6445.

[46] *See e.g.* Human Rights and Security Assistance, 22 U.S.C. § 2304 (a)(2) (' . . . no security assistance may be provided to any country the government of which engages in a consistent pattern of gross violations of internationally recognized human rights. . . . [T]he term "gross violations of internationally recognized human rights" includes torture or cruel, inhuman, or degrading treatment or punishment, prolonged detention without charges and trial, causing the disappearance of persons by the abduction and clandestine detention of those persons, and other flagrant denial of the right to life, liberty, or the security of person.')

[47] Eximbank was established 'to aid in financing and to facilitate exports and imports and the exchange of commodities and services between the United States . . . and any foreign country or the agencies or

proliferation, environmental protection and *human rights* (including child labor), *should the Export-Import Bank deny applications for credit for nonfinancial or non-commercial considerations.*[48]

Known as the 'Chafee Amendment', this provision is hardly a model of clarity, but it assures at a minimum that Eximbank does not subsidize or underwrite egregious departures from the international law of human rights: an application for credit may be denied on otherwise impermissible non-commercial grounds if the President determines that such action 'would clearly and importantly advance' the human rights policy of the United States. The legislative history of the Chafee Amendment offers little guidance in the interpretation of this language, though it does nothing to cut back the apparent breadth of the President's authority. Similarly, the few administrative decision in the public record reveal little of the State Department's internal criteria in these matters,[49] though there is also no support for the proposition that the President's authority will be narrowly construed.

Clear cases under the Chafee Amendment might involve a hypothetical Eximbank loan to a company that engages in the slave trade or manufactures gas for the mass extermination of a people. Doubtless in such a case the President would determine that the United States should not subsidize or facilitate any activities that constitute crimes against humanity or which fall within the universal criminal jurisdiction of states. There is reason to believe that the Chafee Amendment will also be invoked when potential Eximbank financing is linked to violations of international humanitarian law. In December 1999, the White House overrode the decision of Eximbank and denied the application of a Russian firm, Tyumen Oil Company, for approximately US$500 million in loan guarantees. Although the government was not obliged to publish the reasons for its decision, the continuing violations of international humanitarian law in Chechnya certainly framed its deliberations.

D. Holocaust Restitution

Over the last decade, in both Europe and the United States, legislation has proliferated for the purpose of assuring that survivors of the Nazi Holocaust are offered compensation from the companies that were complicit in genocide, crimes against humanity, war crimes, and other egregious violations of human rights. Some of these laws require disclosure of business in Europe during the Nazi regime, especially in the insurance sector.[50] Some allow the state insurance commissioner to suspend the operating licence of any insurer that fails to pay any valid claim from a Holocaust

---

nationals thereof'. In the United Kingdom, the Export Credit Guarantees Department has adopted a set of business principles that include the protection of human rights, available at <http://www.ecgd.gov. uk/index/pi_home/pi_bp.htm>.

[48] 12 U.S.C. § 635(b)(1)(B) (emphasis supplied).

[49] *See e.g. In re Cameroon*, 59 *Fed. Reg.* 16254 (1994).

[50] *See e.g.* Holocaust Victims Insurance Relief Act, Wash. Rev. Code § 48.104.060 (1999) (requiring any insurer who sold policies in Europe between 1933 and 1945 to disclose all records and information regarding those policies to the Washington state insurance commissioner).

survivor until that claim is paid.[51] The broadest provide a cause of action to recover damages from corporations for the violation of a human rights standard, typically the use of slave labour.[52] The constitutionality of state and local statutes with foreign policy implications remains contested, though they may survive challenge to the extent that they conform to federal legislative and executive policy [53]

Although the evolving regime of domestic regulation can only be suggested by these examples, certain themes emerge. First, domestic legislation creates an increasingly dense regulatory environment in which corporate operations in violation of at least some human rights standards pose legal risks to the company itself. The laws establishing U.S. import controls for example adopt a meaningful form of 'human rights conditionality' in the international marketplace, even though they target only specific labour practices used in the production of particular goods introduced into the American market. Rights-sensitive export controls by contrast are not necessarily limited to labour rights, but they tend to be limited geographically and politically, targeting only the most offensive states that also happen to have weak import markets (*e.g.* Sudan and Burma but not China and Russia). Nor is broader-gauged legislation linking trade and human rights likely to emerge until there is consensus on two recurring issues: whether human rights conditions are better advanced by 'constructive engagement' with an abusive government or by its economic isolation, and whether human rights conditionality can be squared with the trade liberalization regime of the World Trade Organization. On the other hand, the trade statutes are clearly useful as a means of advancing an important if limited subset of human rights in an important if limited subset of states. And the disclosure provisions of national and state securities laws offer an untested but powerful vehicle for improving corporate compliance with a broader range of human rights norms, driven by the markets' demand for information and transparency. Moreover, the statutory linkage between governmental decision-making and international human rights offers episodic but unprecedented opportunities for recourse to equally broad conceptions of human rights, not necessarily as trumps but as relevant considerations in complex administrative (and therefore corporate) decision-making. There is in addition this crucial historical perspective: experience with the FCPA and with the

---

[51] *See e.g.* Holocaust Victim Insurance Act, Cal. Ins. Code § 790-790-15 (Deering 1998).

[52] California law, for example, allows anyone who was forced into labour without pay by the Nazis, their sympathizers, or allies, for any period of time between 1929 and 1945, the right to recover compensation from the entity, or its successor in interest, for whom the labour was performed. The suit may be brought directly against the entity or through its subsidiary or affiliate, and the statute of limitations is suspended if the action is commenced on or before 31 December 2010. Cal. Civ. Code § 354.6 (Deering 1999). *See generally* Michael J. Bazyler, 'Nuremberg in America: Litigating the Holocaust in United States Courts', 34 *U. Rich. L. Rev.* 1 (2000) at annex.

[53] *See* the Supreme Court's decisions in *Crosby v. National Foreign Trade Council*, 530 U.S. 363 (2000) (invalidating a state law sanctioning state contractors that work in Burma), and *American Ins. Ass'n v. Garamendi*, 539 U.S. 396 (2003) (invalidating a state law requiring disclosure of Holocaust-era insurance policies).

Depression era securities laws suggests that the time lag between the adoption of legislation and the evolution of a responsive business culture can be measured in decades, and progress is almost never linear. But if the economic health of the market improves as that culture evolves, the stimulus provided by the threat of public enforcement of domestic law is gradually internalized by the corporate actors themselves: the market regime and the regime of domestic regulation are in that sense mutually reinforcing.

3. A REGIME OF CIVIL LIABILITY

Now overarching and perhaps propelling the market and regulatory initiatives is a third regime of corporate responsibility: the prospect of civil liability, as various domestic courts have ruled that corporations may in principle be obliged to pay substantial damage awards for their complicity in abuses by the governments with which they do business. In a series of cases arising out of World War II, for example, survivors have sued companies that relied on slave labour[54] or seized the property of Jews during the Nazi Holocaust[55] or manufactured goods the sole purpose of which was the destruction of the Jews.[56] Some of these cases have been settled through the payment of compensation to the plaintiffs.[57] But the majority of these private initiatives have nothing to do with the Holocaust: companies that pursue 'human rights entrepreneurialism' and proclaim a commitment to human rights as part of their marketing campaigns could face liability for deceptive advertising if that commitment is violated in fact,[58] and a company that attempted to raise capital in U.S. markets without disclosing human rights practices—or the contingent liabilities they entail—could similarly face liability under the securities laws. But, in the United States at least, these are specialized forms of liability arising under state

---

[54] *See e.g. In re World War II Era Japanese Forced Labor Litigation*, 164 F.Supp. 2d 1160 (N.D. Cal. 2001), *aff'd sub nom.; Deutsch v. Turner Corp.*, 2003 WL 139746 (9th Cir. Jan. 21, 2003), *opinion amended and superseded on denial of rehearing by Deutsch v. Turner Corp.*, 324 F.3d 692 (9th Cir. Mar 06, 2003); *Iwanowa v. Ford Motor Co.*, 67 F.Supp. 2d 424 (D.N.J. 1999).

[55] *See e.g. Bodner v. Banque Paribas*, 114 F. Supp. 2d 117 (E.D.N.J. 2000). *Cf. American Ins. Ass'n, supra* note 53.

[56] *Burger-Fischer v. Degussa AG*, 65 F.Supp. 2d 248 (D.N.J. 1999). *Cf. Abu-Zeineh v. Federal Laboratories Inc.*, 975 F. Supp. 774 (W.D. Pa. 1994) (challenging one company's production of riot control gas used by Israeli security forces against Palestinians).

[57] Volkswagen AG agreed to compensate survivors of the concentration and labour camps for the abuse they suffered at its plants during World War II, after a German court allowed Auschwitz survivors to sue for compensation. In 1998, Switzerland's two biggest banks agreed to pay Holocaust survivors US$1.25 billion in compensation for wartime losses. *In re Nazi Era Cases Against German Defendants Litigation*, 129 F.Supp. 2d 370 (D.N.J. 2001). *See also Doe v. The Gap*, 2002 WL 1000073 (D.N.J. May 10, 2002).

[58] *Kasky v. Nike, Inc.*, 119 Cal. Rptr.2d 296 (Cal. 2002), *cert. granted*, 123 S.Ct. 817 (2003), *cert. dismissed as improvidently granted*, 123 S.Ct. 2554 (2003). In September 2003, Nike agreed to pay US$1.5 million to settle the case.

or federal substantive law, in contrast to the comprehensive range of abuses challengeable under the Alien Tort Statute ('ATS'),[59] which provides that 'the district courts shall have original jurisdiction of any civil action for a tort only, committed in violation of the law of nations or a treaty of the United States'. ATS actions have been filed in a U.S. federal court against some of the largest multinational companies for their alleged complicity in human rights violations around the world.[60] Some of these cases have been dismissed on *forum non conveniens*, jurisdictional, political, or factual grounds, but none has been dismissed on the ground that private companies are *in principle* immune from liability under international law.[61] To the contrary, in *Doe v. Unocal*,[62] the most prominent of these cases to date, the court of appeals ruled that the plaintiffs were entitled to try to prove their case, implicitly rejecting the prophylactic rule proposed by the defendants to the effect that private corporations do not act under colour of law and therefore cannot violate the law of nations or a treaty of the United States.

In *Unocal*, a group of Burmese villagers sued the U.S. corporation, Unocal, and Total, S.A., a French company, for a range of human rights abuses allegedly committed in the course of a pipeline project undertaken by a joint venture between those two companies and the Burmese government. The gravamen of the complaint was that Unocal conspired with the other defendants to conduct the

---

[59] 28 U.S.C. § 1350 (also occasionally referred to as 'Section 1350' or 'the Alien Tort Claims Act'). The ATS was adopted as part of the First Judiciary Act (1789). The first Congress evidently intended to empower the national courts of the United States to hear tort cases that implicate the fundamentally federal interests in foreign nationals and the interpretation of international law. The ATS was probably intended to assure that pirates found in the United States could be sued by their foreign victims to recover damages, and foreign diplomats assaulted in the United States could similarly use the federal courts to recover damages. The statute became a vehicle for the protection of human rights in 1980 with the decision of the Second Circuit Court of Appeals in *Filartiga v. Pena-Irala*, 630 F.2d 876 (2d Cir. 1980). *See generally* Ralph G. Steinhardt, 'The Internationalization of Domestic Law,' in *The Alien Tort Claims Act* (Steinhardt and D'Amato, eds., 1999).

[60] Cases have been brought for example against the world's largest pharmaceutical company, Pfizer, for injuries suffered by Nigerian citizens injured by an experimental antibiotic administered without their informed consent, in violation of treaty and customary international law, *Abdullahi v. Pfizer*,___F.Supp. 2d__, 2002 Dist. Lexis 17436 (17 Sep. 2002), *vacated and remanded*, 77 Fed. Appx. 48 (2d Cir. 2003); against Unocal Corporation for its complicity in slave-like practices and other human rights violations through a joint venture with the government of Burma, *see below*; against Royal Dutch Shell and Chevron for abuses in Nigeria, *Wiwa v. Shell*, 2002 WL 319887 (S.D.N.Y. 28 Feb. 2002) and *Bowoto v. Chevron*, 312 F.Supp.2d 1229 (N.D. Cal. 2004); against Talisman for its alleged abuses in Sudan, *Presbyterian Church of Sudan v. Talisman Energy*, 244 F. Supp. 2d 289 (S.D.N.Y. 2003); and against Texaco for its environmental wrongs in Ecuador. *Aguinda v. Texaco, Inc.*, 945 F. Supp. 625 (S.D.N.Y. 1996). *See Aguinda v. Texaco*, 303 F.3d 470 (2d. Cir. 2002).

[61] *See e.g. Abdullahi v. Pfizer*, and *Aguinda v. Texaco*, note 60 above.

[62] 963 F.Supp. 880 (C.D. Cal. 1997) (*Unocal I*), 110 F. Supp. 2d 1294 (C.D. Cal. 2000) (*Unocal II*), *on appeal*, 2002 WL 31063976 (9th Cir. 2002). As of this writing, although the Ninth Circuit Court of Appeals had decided to rehear the case *en banc*. *Doe v. Unocal, reh'g en banc granted, opinion vacated*, No. 00-56603, 00-56628, 2003 WL 359787 (9th Cir. 14 Feb. 2003), the parties have apparently agreed to settle the case. *See* Lisa Girion, *Los Angeles Times*, 'Unocal to settle Rights Claims' (14 Dec. 2004).

affairs of the joint venture through a pattern of human rights violations. By allegation, Unocal knew at the time of its joint venture that the Burmese government had a history of human rights abuses (including forced relocation, forced labour, and torture), that it understood that those violations would be continued in order to make the pipeline operational, and that the company actually benefited from those violations. Liability did not rest on the assertion that the corporate defendants merely maintained some arms-length business relationship with a state that had committed human rights violations, nor was there any allegation that the corporation was vicariously liable for the action of its state-owned joint venture partner.

Rather, in rejecting the defendant's motion to dismiss, overturning the defendant's summary judgment, and allowing the plaintiffs to prove their case, the district court in *Unocal I* articulated two distinct circumstances under which a nominally private actor might nonetheless bear international responsibility: when the corporation—like any individual—commits one of that narrow class of wrongs identified by treaty and custom as not requiring state action to be considered wrongful, and those more general circumstances in which the offensive conduct is sufficiently infused with state action to engage international standards. These two categories of liability are entirely consistent with other decisions under the Alien Tort Statute involving 'proto-states' and paramilitary groups and their leaders, including *Kadic et al. v. Karadzic*, in which the Second Circuit Court of Appeals ruled that the former leader of the Bosnian Serb faction could in principle be liable for genocide, war crimes, rape, and other torture, among other abuses, even if he were not acting in concert with, or under official authority of, any state.[63]

A. Per Se Wrongs: Conduct Requiring No State Action as a Matter of Law

The first category of wrongs recognized by these courts prohibits certain conduct regardless of whether the actor is a state or not. This should be non-controversial, because the treaties defining these human rights violations explicitly override the requirement of state action. Article IV of the Genocide Convention for example requires that persons committing genocide be punished, 'whether they are constitutionally

---

[63] *Kadic et al. v. Karadzic*, 70 F.3d 232 (2d Cir. 1995), *cert. denied*, 116 S.Ct. 2524 (1996). In doing so, the court of appeals rejected the lower court's ruling that Karadzic, having never acted under colour of law, could not have international obligations. *Accord Trajano v. Marcos*, 978 F.2d 493 (9th Cir. 1992), *cert. denied*, 113 S.Ct. 2960 (1993). Similarly, in *Carmichael v. United Technologies Corp.*, 835 F.2d 109, 113–14 (5th Cir. 1988), the Court of Appeals assumed without deciding that the Alien Tort Claims Act confers jurisdiction over private parties who conspire in, or aid or abet, official acts of torture. *Cf. Tel-Oren v. Libyan Arab Republic*, 726 F.2d 774 (D.C.Cir. 1984) (Edwards, J., concurring), *cert. denied*, 470 U.S. 1003 (1985) (deciding that terrorism by an organization without evidence of state participation is not actionable under the Alien Tort Claims Act); *Sanchez-Espinoza v. Reagan*, 770 F.2d 202, 206–07 (D.C. Cir. 1985) (deciding that neither treaty nor custom reaches the private, non-state conduct at issue in the case).

responsible rulers, public officials or private individuals'.[64] Similarly, certain provisions of the Geneva Conventions on the laws of war, in particular common Article 3, bind all parties to an armed conflict, even if they are non-states. These examples hardly erase the distinction between state and non-state actors for all purposes, but they clearly support the *Karadzic* court's modest conclusion that 'certain forms of conduct violate the law of nations whether undertaken by those acting under the auspices of a state or only as private individuals'[65] and the *Unocal I* court's decision that 'this action involves allegations of forced labor and . . . slave trading is included in that "handful of crimes" for which the law of nations attributes individual responsibility'.[66]

The customary status of these liability principles rests in part on the endorsement by consensus of the decision of the military tribunal at Nuremberg, which found private actors guilty of such international crimes as economic plunder and enslavement, and the mistreatment of civilians and prisoners of war, many of whom were forced to work under inhumane conditions in the defendants' private mines and factories. In the cases against *Flick, Krupp,* and *Krauch,* for example, the tribunal made its now-famous declaration that the application of international law to individuals rests upon no revolutionary principle, and forty-three private German citizens were convicted for committing crimes against humanity, the Tribunal finding explicitly that the defendants' actions had been independent of the government. The International Law Commission, directed by the United Nations General Assembly to codify the Nuremberg principles, has never required state action for wrongs of this type; indeed, in 1985, the ILC rejected a draft which would have limited liability to 'State authorities' in favour of a draft making all '[i]ndividuals who commit an offence against the peace and security of mankind' liable. The Statute of the International Criminal Tribunal for the Former Yugoslavia similarly sets no *per se* limit on the types of individuals who may be liable.[67]

From this perspective, the least controversial aspect of *Unocal* and *Karadzic* is that private individuals (whether natural or juristic) who commit torts in the course of violating international law fall squarely within the reach of the Alien Tort Statute. Pirates, the very exemplar of intended defendants under the Act, were not always or necessarily considered 'state actors', and there was never any question that their depredations were in violation of the law of nations.[68] Nor was there any

---

[64] Convention on the Prevention and Punishment of the Crime of Genocide, 9 Dec. 1948, Art. IV, 78 U.N.T.S. 277, 280.   [65] 70 F.3d at 239.

[66] 963. F. Supp. at 891. The court elides forced labour and slave-trading despite the fact that older international authorities define and criminalize them separately. *Id.,* at 892. A panel of the Ninth Circuit Court of Appeals agreed. 395 F.3d 932; 945–47 (9th Cir. 2002), but, after the full court decided to rehear the case *en banc. Doe v. Unocal, reh'g en banc granted, opinion vacated,* No. 00-56603, 00-56628, 2003 WL 359787 (9th Cir. 14 Feb. 2003) the parties apparently agreed to settle the case. *See* note 60, *supra.*

[67] For other examples of international legal responsibilities being imposed on non-state actors, *see* David Weissbrodt and Maria Kruger, 'Human Rights Responsibilities of Businesses as Non-State Actors', Chapter 8 in this volume.

[68] One of the earliest exercises of jurisdiction under the Act involved an unlawful seizure of property by a non-state actor. *Bolchos v. Darrell,* 3 F. Cas. 810 (D.S.C. 1795).

doubt that private citizens who infringed the rights of ambassadors or diplomats could be sued under § 1350, and the statute clearly provided jurisdiction over a child custody dispute that involved a breach of the law of nations.[69] In its occasional interpretations of the Act, the executive branch has endorsed the proposition that private actors can be proper defendants and therefore must in principle be capable of violating the law of nations or a treaty of the United States.[70]

It therefore involves no radical expansion of either international principles or domestic jurisdiction to conclude that private entities, including corporations, bear a measure of international liability enforceable in the courts of the United States, at least for a narrow class of extraordinary wrongs.

B. Contextual Wrongs: Conduct that is Sufficiently State-Like or State-Related to Trigger Liability for Human Rights Violations

Routine commercial activity by transnational corporations does not typically fall into Category I of course. But there will be cases in which plaintiffs can prove that the defendants' corporate conduct involved sufficient state action to satisfy the broader requirements of international liability and therefore expose the corporation to a much stricter set of human rights standards. There can certainly be no rule that corporations, regardless of their relationship with a government, are immune from liability for their state-like or state-related activities. The *Unocal I* court for example noted by allegation that:

SLORC and MOGE are agents of the private defendants; that the defendants are joint venturers, working in concert with one another; and that the defendants have conspired to commit the violations of international law alleged in the complaint in order to further the interests of the Yadana gas pipeline project. . . . Plaintiffs have alleged that the private . . . defendants were and are jointly engaged with the state officials in the challenged activity, namely enforced labor and other human rights violations in furtherance of the pipeline project.[71]

In determining whether these allegations were sufficient in principle to trigger a finding of state action, the *Unocal* court, like the *Karadzic* and *Marcos* courts before it, ruled that the plaintiffs were entitled to prove such a relationship using the ' "color of law" jurisprudence' adopted by U.S. courts under Section 1983 of the federal antidiscrimination statutes.[72]

---

[69] *Adra v. Clift*, 195 F. Supp. 857 (D. Md. 1961).

[70] In 1907, for example, Attorney General Bonaparte opined that foreign citizens injured by a private company's diversion of water in violation of a bilateral treaty between Mexico and the United States could sue under the Alien Tort Claims Act. 26 *Op. Att'y Gen.* 250 (1907).

[71] 963. F. Supp. at 891.

[72] 42 U.S.C. 1983. *See Wiwa v. Royal Dutch Petroleum*, 2002 WL 319887, at *13 ('a private individual acts under color of law within the meaning of section 1983 when he acts together with state officials or with significant state aid. The relevant test . . . is the "joint action" test, under which private actors are considered state actors if they are "willful participants" in joint action with the state or its agents.

Unfortunately, according to the Supreme Court itself, those cases 'have not been a model of consistency'.[73] The courts have portrayed the requisite relationship between the state and the private actor in a variety of ways, and at such a high level of abstraction as to be of limited predictive value in either the courtroom or the boardroom. In one seminal decision, the Supreme Court concluded unhelpfully that a nominally private actor acts under color of law if 'he has acted with or has obtained significant aid from state officials, or because his conduct is otherwise chargeable to the State'.[74] Elsewhere, the Supreme Court has rested § 1983 liability only on a nexus 'sufficiently close' that the state's exercise of 'coercive power' or its 'significant encouragement, either overt or covert' necessitates that the private actor's conduct 'must in law be deemed to be that of the state'.[75] Courts sometimes look to determine whether there is 'a substantial degree of cooperative action' between the state and the private actor in effecting the deprivation of rights,[76] or whether the state and private actors 'share a common, unconstitutional goal'.[77] Some consider a close financial relationship between the private party and the state sufficient to satisfy the 'color of law' requirement.[78] Some require a 'symbiotic relationship', or a 'close nexus', or a 'conspiracy' between them.[79] When the Ninth Circuit Court of Appeals attempted to summarize the law, it declared that '[t]he Supreme Court has articulated four distinct approaches to the state action question: public function, state

Where there is a substantial degree of cooperative action between the state and private actors in effectuating the deprivation of rights, state action is present'); *Kadic v. Karadzic*, 70 F.3d 232, 245 (2d Cir. 1995), *cert. denied* 116 S.Ct. 2524 (1996) ('"color of law" jurisprudence under 42 U.S.C. Sec. 1983 is a relevant guide to whether a defendant has engaged in official action for purposes of jurisdiction under the Alien Tort Act'). *Accord Hilao v. Marcos*, 25 F.3d 1467, *cert. denied*, 115 S.Ct. 934 (1995); *Abdullahi v. Pfizer*, 2002 WL 31082956 (S.D.N.Y., 17 September 2002). *See also Carmichael v. United Technologies Corp.*, 835 F.2d 109, 113 (5th Cir. 1988) (assuming without deciding 'that the Alien Tort Statute does confer subject matter jurisdiction over private parties who conspire in or aid and abet, official acts of torture'.)

[73] *George v. Pacific-CSC Work Furlough*, 91 F.3d 1227, 1230 (9th Cir. 1996) (citing *Leebron v. National R.R. Passenger Corp.*, 513 U.S. 374, (1995)), *cert. denied*, 519 U.S. 1081 (1997).

[74] *Burton v. Wilmington Parking Authority*, 365 U.S. 715, 725 (1961) ('the State has so far insinuated itself into a position of interdependence with [the private party] that it must be recognized as a joint participant in the challenged activity'). *Accord, NCAA v. Tarkanian*, 488 U.S. 179, 192 (1988) (declaring that 'the question is whether the State was sufficiently involved to treat that decisive conduct as state action. This may occur if the State creates the legal framework governing the conduct; if it delegates its authority to the private actor; or sometimes if it knowingly accepts the benefits derived from unconstitutional behavior'). [75] *Blum v. Yaretsky*, 457 U.S. 991 (1982), at 1004.

[76] *Gallagher v. Neil Young Freedom Concert*, 49 F.3d 1442, 1453 (10th Cir. 1995).

[77] *Cunningham v. Southlake Ctr. for Mental Health, Inc.*, 924 F.2d 106, 107 (9th Cir. 1991). *Accord, Fonda v. Gray*, 707 F.2d 435, 437 (9th cir. 1983) ('A private party may be considered to have acted under color of state law when it engages in a conspiracy or acts in concert with state agents to deprive one's constitutional rights').

[78] *Jatoi v. Hurst-Eutess-Bedford Hosp. Auth.*, 807 F.2d 1214, 1221–22, *modified on denial of reh'g*, 819 F.2d 545 (5th Cir. 1987), *cert. denied*, 484 U.S. 1010 (1988).

[79] *Lugar v. Edmondson Oil*, 457 U.S. 922, 941 (1982) (private actor, in attaching property through self-help, found to be a state actor).

compulsion, nexus, and joint action'[80] but it was unable to clarify whether these were necessary factors to be considered in every case or independent criteria with varying thresholds or burdens of proof.

The relationships between transnational corporations and governments can assume each of these forms[81] or indeed none of them, as when the company simply operates in the country without any governmental participation in the commercial enterprise. As a consequence, until the nexus standards are unified domestically or accepted internationally,[82] and unless the analogy between alien tort claims and the federal anti-discrimination statutes is fully defended in principle, the applicable standards may offer insufficient guidance to corporations attempting in good faith to avoid liability under the Alien Tort Statute: the Section 1983 analogy—however defensible in cases like *Unocal* or *Wiwa* or *Talisman*—cannot tell the court how to handle the intermediate case where a corporation simply benefits, without contractual nexus, from a generalized system of abuse or dismisses an employee because he is a target of persecution by a government unconnected by contract or otherwise to the enterprise.

There are moreover certain predictable obstacles to alien tort litigation as a means of enforcing the human rights obligations of corporations. The inconvenient forum doctrine (*forum non conveniens*) for example may require a court to dismiss or suspend an action in the United States if an adequate alternative foreign forum is available and if the plaintiff's decision to sue in the United States choice of forum must be trumped by an amalgam of public and private considerations.[83] Some recent ATS litigation against corporations has also been derailed by the political question doctrine, under which certain issues are deemed inappropriate for judicial

---

[80] *George v. Pacific-CSC Work Furlough*, 91 F.3d 1227, 1230 (9th Cir. 1996). Thus for example, '[u]nder the joint action approach, private actors can be state actors if they are "wilful participant[s] in joint action with the state or its agents." An agreement between government and a private party can create joint action.' *Id.*, at 1231.

[81] *See e.g. Sarei v. Rio Tinto et al.*, 221 F. Supp. 2d 1116, 1148 (C.D.Cal.2002) ('whether examined in terms of "joint action", or the control necessary to support a finding of "proximate cause", plaintiffs have adequately alleged that [the government's] actions are "fairly attributable" to Rio Tinto. Specifically, they have alleged that [the government] acted as Rio Tinto's agent, that Rio Tinto "controlled" its actions and that Rio Tinto was a "willful participant/conspirator" in them'); *Iwanowa v. Ford Motor Co.*, 67 F.Supp. 2d 424 (D.N.J. 1999), at 445–46 ('the complaint alleges that defendants acted in close cooperation with Nazi officials in compelling civilians to perform forced labor').

[82] One potential source of overlap is the continental notion of *Drittwirkung*, under which private parties may be found to have violated certain constitutional rights of citizens, even if the constitution primarily limits the conduct of the state and its actors. *See generally* Andrew Clapham, *Human Rights in the Private Sphere* (1993), at 179–82; *Case of X and Y v. The Netherlands*, Judgment of 25 Mar. 1985, Ser. A, vol. 91.

[83] *Compare* decisions in which an adequate alternative forum was held to exist, *e.g. Aguinda v. Texaco*, 303 F.3d 470 (2d Cir. 2002) and *Abdullahi v. Pfizer*, __F. Supp. 2d__, 2002 Dist. Lexis 17436 (Sep. 17, 2002), *vacated and remanded*, 77 Fed. Appx. 48 (2d Cir. 2003), *with* decisions in which either no alternative forum was found adequate, *e.g. Eastman Kodak v. Kavlin*, 978 F. Supp. 1078 (S.D. Fla. 1997), or the U.S. interest in hearing alien tort claims *inter alia* weighed in favour of hearing the case, *e.g. Wiwa v. Dutch Petroleum Co.*, 226 F.3d 88 (2d Cir. 2000), *cert. denied*, 2001 U.S. Lexis 2488 (2001).

resolution, especially to the extent that they implicate the executive branch's authority over foreign affairs.[84] It is also conceivable that a corporation will enjoy sovereign immunity as an 'agency or instrumentality' of the foreign state by virtue of its incorporation and ownership structure, and in that case no U.S. court will have jurisdiction unless the case falls within one of the statutory exceptions to immunity.[85] But decisions under both the Foreign Sovereign Immunities Act[86] and § 1983[87] suggest that sovereign immunity for corporations is exceptional and highly fact-dependent. For that reason, it can pose no *per se* barrier to cases of this type. It is also possible that the act of state doctrine will derail an ATS case to the extent that it requires a U.S. court to judge the validity *vel non* of a foreign sovereign's public act within its own territory. The State Department has a privileged voice in this assessment and has filed various statements in ATS litigation, in some cases supporting[88] and in other cases undermining[89] the case. But the act of state doctrine should be no more of a prophylactic barrier to ATS litigation than the political question doctrine, foreign sovereign immunity, or *forum non conveniens*: the courts have limited the act of state doctrine to shield only official acts, by a government in power, in pursuit of a public purpose[90] or 'in the public interest'[91] and the politics of human rights are such that governments routinely avoid claiming abuses as policy or viewing them as expressions of sovereignty. Nor should the doctrine apply when

---

[84] *See e.g. Sarei v. Rio Tinto*, note 81 above. *See generally, Baker v. Carr*, 369 U.S. 186, 217 (1962). Advocates can avoid the political question if they can prove that there is law for the court to apply or, in the words of *Baker*, that there are 'judicially manageable standards' and no textual commitment of the issue 'to a coordinate branch of government'. *Committee of United States Citizens Living in Nicaragua v. Reagan*, 859 F. 2d 929, 941 (D.C. Cir. 1989) (the political question doctrine, with its 'shifting contours and uncertain underpinnings' and its 'susceptibility to indiscriminate and overbroad application', should not displace whatever legal standards applied).

[85] Foreign Sovereign Immunities Act, 28 U.S.C. 1330, 1602 *et seq*. ('FSIA'). On the statutory criteria for extending foreign sovereign immunity to a corporation, see FSIA, § 1603(b). Immunity would not extend to any human rights violation that fell within the terms of the FSIA's exceptions (*e.g.* waiver, commercial activity with a nexus to the United States, unlawful takings, torts in the United States, certain acts of terrorism). FSIA, § 1605(a)(1)-(7).

[86] *First National City Bank v. Banco Para el Comercio Exterior de Cuba*, 462 U.S. 611 (1983).

[87] Under § 1983, private actors do not get the immunity of a state simply by acting under colour of state law: the immunity enjoyed by a state official does not attach to a private conspirator. *See e.g. Wyatt v. Cole*, 504 U.S. 158, 166 (1992) (private parties in conspiracy with state officials to violate constitutional rights do not qualify for good faith immunity); *Dennis v. Sparks*, 449 U.S. 24, 31–32 (1980) (judge's absolute immunity does not extend to private party conspirator acting with state judge under colour of law); *Goldschmidt v. Patchett*, 686 F.2d 582, 585 (7th Cir. 1982) (immunity of prosecutor does not extend to parties who conspire with him or her to violate the civil rights of others).

[88] *See e.g. Filartiga v. Pena Irala*, 630 F.2d 876 (2d Cir. 1980).

[89] *See e.g.* letter from William H. Taft, Legal Adviser to Judge Louis Oberdorfer, *Doe et al. v. Exxon-Mobil, et al.*, No. 01-CV-1357 (DDC) (29 July 2002) (copy on file with author).

[90] *W.S. Kirkpatrick v. Environmental Tectonics Corp.*, 493 U.S. 400, 406–10 (1990); *Alfred Dunhill of London, Inc. v. Republic of Cuba*, 425 U.S. 682, 695–705 (1976); *Republic of the Philippines v. Marcos*, 862 F.2d 1355, 1360–61 (9th Cir. 1988) (*en banc*), *cert. denied*, 490 U.S. 1035 (1989); *Forti v. Suarez-Mason*, 672 F. Supp. 1531, 1545–46 (N.D. Cal. 1987).

[91] *Liu v Republic of China*, 892 F.2d 1419, 1432 (9th Cir. 1989).

there are clear rules of international treaty law and custom that provide judicially manageable standards for the resolution of the case.[92] The high jurisdictional showing required to prove a violation of 'the law of nations or a treaty of the United States' screens out frivolous cases against private corporations, assuring that the courts enforce only those norms that clear the high threshold for proving customary international law and that, at least with respect to Category II wrongs, clearly require state action.[93]

Alien tort litigation is not a seamless or cost-free means of enforcing the human rights obligations of corporations. The apparent threat that it represents to the corporate world is nonetheless counterbalanced by the fact that not a single one of the forty or so cases filed against corporate defendants to date has resulted in a single final judgment, and the great majority of suits have been dismissed on pre-trial motions. But the principal defence of the act does not lie in its ineffectiveness. To the contrary, its continued utility is illuminated by a simple observation: if a multinational corporation were today conducting the slave trade or manufacturing gas for a concentration camp, there is no doubt that it would and should face civil and criminal sanctions. Although there may be disagreement about the extent of liability for less egregious wrongs, there clearly can be no doctrinal firebreak that insulates private corporations from responsibility in principle under international human rights law. The regime of civil liability offers a 'stick' that, in appropriate but extraordinary circumstances, reinforces the 'carrot' of the marketplace.

4. A REGIME OF INTERNATIONAL REGULATION: TOWARDS A TRANSNATIONAL CARTEL OF VALUES

Despite the historical failure of intergovernmental organizations to adopt a comprehensive code of conduct for multinational corporations,[94] some prominent multilateral organizations have found human rights increasingly relevant to their mandates. As a consequence, they may prove to be an effective forum for developing a unified front on matters of human rights—a 'cartel of values' as it were—to assure that corporations and governments do not engage in a perpetual race to the bottom in the protection of international human rights. The argument is not that the major intergovernmental institutions, such as the World Trade Organization and the World Bank, are inevitably forces for good in the protection of human rights: on the

[92] *See* comment (c) to § 443 of the *Restatement (Third) of U.S. Foreign Relations Law* ('a claim arising out of an alleged violation of fundamental human rights . . . would . . . probably not be defeated by the act of state doctrine, since the accepted international law of human rights is well established').

[93] *See e.g. Bigio v. Coca-Cola Co.*, 239 F.3d 440, 447 (2d Cir. 2000) (ATS claims of religious discrimination require proof of state action); *Mendonca v. Tidewater, Inc.*, 159 F.Supp.2d 299 (E.D. La. 2001). *See generally Sosa v. Alvarez-Machain*, 124 S. Ct. 2739 (2004).

[94] *See e.g.* the abortive U.N. Draft International Code of Conduct for Transnational Corporations, 23 *Int'l Leg. Mats.* 626 (1984), which after many years of drafting and negotiation within the U.N. Commission on Transnational Corporations was never adopted.

contrary, a powerful critique rests on their sins of commission (like promoting the liberalization of trade at the expense of human rights, or imposing structural adjustment policies that promote political repression, or allowing a democratic deficit in their own decision-making) and sins of omission (like remaining 'apolitical' as required by their articles of association and thereby ignoring human rights abuses of member governments). But there is a marked and increasing tendency within these organizations to link commerce and human rights through international regulation and soft law instruments, which—taken together—define a fourth regime of principle and practice.

A. International Labour Organization and the Tripartite Declaration of Principles concerning Multinational Enterprises and Social Policy

The International Labour Organization ('ILO') was established because its founders agreed that workers faced conditions which, if unattended, could create social unrest and provoke revolution on a global scale.[95] But they also realized that each government had a short-term economic incentive to let someone else go first: the needed social reform inevitably raised the costs of production, and any industry or government that unilaterally improved labour conditions would find itself at a steep competitive disadvantage. If each government could attract foreign capital investment by suppressing wages and impoverishing its own people, only an enforced cartel of values could accomplish the reform that all agreed was necessary. In the words of the Preamble to the ILO Constitution, 'the failure of *any* nation to adopt humane conditions of labour is an obstacle in the way of *other* nations which desire to improve the conditions in their own countries' (emphases added). The ILO offered a forum for agreeing on minimum protections for workers, and its tripartite structure among governments, employers, and labour organizations assured a measure of legitimacy among the relevant constituencies and, as a consequence, a measure of effectiveness. The clear objective was to allow a humane comparative advantage to prevail in international markets by unifying and harmonizing labour rights, and through a series of conventions and recommendations, the organization attempted to set minimum standards *inter alia* for the freedom of association, the right to organize and to bargain collectively, the abolition of forced labour, and the rights to equality of opportunity and treatment.

The centrepiece of the ILO's corporate responsibility agenda remains the Tripartite Declaration of Principles concerning Multinational Enterprises and Social Policy,[96] adopted over twenty-five years ago and revised periodically ever since. In addition to the conventions and recommendations incorporated into the original

---

[95] The Preamble of the ILO Constitution declares that 'conditions of labour exist involving such injustice, hardship, and privation to large numbers of people as to produce unrest so great that the peace and harmony of the world are imperilled'.

[96] ILO, Tripartite Declaration of Principles concerning Multinational Enterprises and Social Policy, 17 *Int'l Leg. Mats.* 422 (1978).

instrument, the Tripartite Declaration now includes the Declaration on Fundamental Principles and Rights at Work (and its Follow-Up programme),[97] which expands the obligation to protect labour rights and attempts to strengthen the means of implementation and enforcement. But the Tripartite Declaration remains non-binding by its terms: implementation has been constrained by its dependency on domestic incorporation by states and on promotion and publication campaigns by non-governmental entities like Sweatshop Watch, the Campaign for Labor Rights, and the Maquila Solidarity Network. The direct obligations of multinational enterprises under the Declaration have remained implicit at best, with the ILO concluding meekly that 'the contribution of multinational enterprises to its implementation can prove an important element in the attainment of its objectives'.[98]

But to focus on the Declaration and its discontents (or the dysfunction of the ILO generally) is to miss the broader significance of the ILO's contribution to a regime of best practices with respect to corporate social performance. The ILO has been instrumental for example in identifying the overlap between labour concerns and the unique vulnerabilities of particular populations (such as women, indigenous minorities, and children) with the consequence that the intellectual apartheid that has separated international labour law from international human rights law can no longer be maintained, suggesting in turn a broader range of human rights concerns in the marketplace. ILO standards have also become the touchstone in domestic litigation challenging corporate labour practices around the world,[99] giving them an effectiveness beyond the ILO mechanisms themselves. In addition, labour standards have become intrinsically entwined with international trade negotiations, especially on a bilateral and regional basis,[100] reinforcing the relevance (if not necessarily the effectiveness) of human rights standards in the global marketplace.

Perhaps the best example of these developments and their interrelationship is the ILO's continuing campaign against child labour. The International Programme on the Elimination of Child Labour (IPEC) has established a critical empirical link between the violation of children's rights and the perpetuation of poverty and inequitable development:

The inclusion of the effective abolition of child labour in the ILO Declaration on Fundamental Principles . . . highlighted the growing consensus across the world that child labour

[97] ILO, Declaration on Fundamental Principles and Rights at Work, 86th Session, Geneva, 18 June 1998, *available at* http://www.ilo.org/public/english/standards/decl/declaration/text/index.htm.

[98] Addendum to the Tripartite Declaration of Principles concerning Multinational Enterprises and Social Policy, adopted by the Governing Body of the International Labour Office, Subcommittee on Multinational Enterprises, ILO Doc. GB.277/MNE/3 (6 March 2000).

[99] *See e.g.* in the United States, litigation under the Alien Tort Claims Act, notably *Estate of Rodriquez v. Drummond Co., Inc.*, 2003 WL 1889330 (N.D. Ala., 14 April 2003); *Presbyterian Church of Sudan v. Talisman Energy, Inc.*, 244 F. Supp. 2d 289 (S.D.N.Y. 2003). The German Forced Labour Compensation Programme similarly draws on ILO standards in establishing a compensation fund for the survivors of forced and slave labour during the Holocaust.

[100] *See e.g.* the Free Trade Agreement between the United States and Jordan, signed on 24 October 2000, which, for the first time, included enforceable labour and environmental standards, as defined in

represents a serious threat to sustainable economic and social development everywhere. The unanimous adoption, the following year, of the Worst Forms of Child Labour Convention, 1999 (No. 182), and its subsequent unprecedented rate of ratification, attest to the strength of the political will among ILO member states to tackle, with employers' and workers' organizations and all partners in civil society, these most extreme forms of child labour.[101]

The complexity of child labour (and the instinct to avoid any cure that is worse than the disease) led the ILO to distinguish the categories of child labour that must be abolished, including: labour performed by a child who is under a minimum age specified in national legislation; labour that jeopardizes the physical, mental, or moral well-being of the child, denominated 'hazardous work'; and 'the unconditional worst forms of child labour', meaning slavery, trafficking, debt bondage, and other forms of forced labour, forced recruitment for use in armed conflict, prostitution, and pornography, and illicit activities.[102] The problem of child labour is worst in the unregulated economy that characterizes much of the world, but corporations in the formal economy that benefit from supply-chain violations in the informal economy, and *a fortiori* who commit them directly, face unprecedented scrutiny as a consequence of the ILO's cartel of values and the structured vigilance of civil society.

B. The United Nations Sub-Commission on Human Rights

In comparison to the *lex lata* status of many ILO conventions, the Sub-Commission on Human Rights for many years negotiated and in August 2003 adopted a set of principles governing corporate human rights standards, entitled 'Norms on the Responsibilities for Transnational Corporations and Other Business Enterprises with Regard to Human Rights'.[103] The Norms draw on a variety of treaties, resolutions, and declarations, but they also rest on a somewhat expansive theory of corporate responsibility, linking it not to the company's control but to its 'influence'[104] and 'benefit'.[105] It also conceives the transnational corporation broadly,

the ILO Declaration on Fundamental Principles, in the body of a trade treaty, *available at* <www. sice.oas.org/tradee.asp#usjor>.

[101] International Labour Organization, *A Future Without Child Labour* ix-x (May 2002).

[102] *Id.*, at x.

[103] United Nations Economic and Social Council, Commission on Human Rights, Fifty-Fifth Session of the Sub-Commission on the Promotion and Protection of Human Rights, *Norms on the Responsibilities of Transnational Corporations and Other Business Enterprises*, E/CN.4/Sub.2/2003/12/Rev.2 (2003) (*'Norms'*). For an analysis of the Norms co-written by one of its drafters, *see* Weissbrodt and Kruger, Chapter 8 below.

[104] *Norms*, at 1:

Within their respective spheres of activity and *influence*, transnational corporations and other business enterprises have the obligation to respect, ensure respect for, prevent abuses of, and promote human rights recognized in international as well as national law, including the rights and interests of indigenous peoples and other vulnerable groups (emphasis added).

[105] *Id.*, at 3:

Transnational corporations and other business enterprises shall not engage in *nor benefit from war crimes*, crimes against humanity, genocide, torture, forced disappearance, forced or compulsory labour,

referring not to its legally defined structure nor to that of its subsidiaries and contractors, but to an 'economic entity' or indeed a 'cluster of economic entities' operating in two or more countries. Until these terms are defined legally and not just economically, the Norms are likely to remain *lex ferenda* at best. The adopted document is also overly progressive, because it obliges corporations to respect and promote economic, social, and cultural rights, like adequate food, health, housing, and education. And the fact that bribery and fair business practices are included suggest that the Sub-Commission's Norms offer the broadest-gauged standards currently in contemplation. On the other hand, an expansive approach is possible primarily because implementation rests on internalization by the multinational corporations themselves, 'subject to periodic monitoring and verification by United Nations, other international and national mechanisms already in existence or yet to be created, regarding application of the Norms'.[106] It is premature to assume that governments will embrace the Norms, which were after all negotiated and promulgated by experts and not state representatives, but, as an indication of the underlying trajectory of developments at the international level, the Norms are indicative.

C. The United Nations Secretary-General: the Global Compact

Announced by U.N. Secretary-General Kofi Annan in January 1999 and formally launched at U.N. Headquarters in July 2000, the Global Compact articulates nine principles in the areas of human rights, labour standards, and the environment, designed to assure that the fragile process of globalization is not derailed by the concentration of economic power, the degradation of the environment, or the perpetuation of poverty and human rights abuses. Under the Compact, companies may voluntarily commit to protecting internationally proclaimed human rights and eliminating all forms of forced or compulsory labour and discrimination. But the Compact is clearly not a regulatory instrument, and it articulates no binding code of conduct. Nor does it offer any forum for policing a company's compliance, other than a minimal annual self-reporting requirement. But it does offer a concrete setting for what was previously called 'human rights entrepreneurialism', means by which one company can distinguish itself from its competitors in the market, and to the extent that the Global Compact is integrated into corporate development and training programmes, it can contribute towards the coalescence of voluntary standards into meaningful and practical norms of behaviour. It is well to remember that the Universal Declaration of Human Rights—now routinely considered the

hostage-taking, extrajudicial, summary or arbitrary executions, other violations of humanitarian law, and other international crimes against the human person as defined by international law, in particular human rights and humanitarian law (emphasis added).

[106] *Id.*, at 16. In addition, under 17:

States should establish and reinforce the necessary legal and administrative framework for ensuring that the Norms and other relevant national and international laws are implemented by transnational corporations and other business enterprises.

authoritative interpretation of States' human rights obligations under the U.N. Charter—began life as an entirely aspirational document, and there is some doubt that states would have voted for it had they predicted its legal trajectory.

D. The Bretton Woods System

Intergovernmental institutions devoted to economic development or monetary stability, notably the World Bank and the International Monetary Fund, long thought themselves constrained by an obligation in their mandates to make decisions apolitically, with the result that human rights concerns were traditionally considered out of bounds. Article IV of the Bank's Articles of Agreement for example provides in pertinent part that:

the Bank and its officers shall not interfere in the political affairs of any member; nor shall they be influenced in their decisions by the political character of the member or members concerned. *Only economic considerations shall be relevant to their decisions*, and these considerations shall be weighed impartially in order to achieve the [Bank's] purposes stated in Article 1.[107]

Designed to be non-ideological tools for the achievement of exclusively 'economic' ends, the Bank and the Fund rarely structured their activities either to facilitate the protection of human rights or to prevent and punish abuses. Gradually, however, the development consequences of the Bank's disregard of human rights conditions in recipient countries[108] and the human rights consequences of some IMF structural adjustment policies[109] induced both institutions to expand what was meant by the term 'economic considerations'. And today, though it cannot be said that the international financial institutions are especially vigilant or consistent in making decisions that are sensitive to human rights concerns,[110] the current work of the Bretton Woods institutions is by historical standards more constrained by objectives like democratization, good governance, the rule of law, and the protection of indigenous peoples' and women's rights.[111]

---

[107] Articles of Agreement of the International Bank for Reconstruction and Development, *opened for signature*, Dec. 27, 1945, 60 Stat. 1440, T.I.A.S. No. 1502, 2 U.N.T.S. 134, *as amended*, Dec. 16, 1965, 16 U.S.T. 1942, T.I.A.S. No. 5929, at § 10, Art. IV (emphasis supplied). *See generally* Ibrahim Shihata, 'The World Bank and Human Rights: An Analysis of Legal Issues and the Record of Achievements' 17 *Den. J. Int'l L. & Pol'y* 39 (1988).

[108] Elizabeth M. King and Andrew D. Mason, *Engendering Development through Gender Equality in Rights, Resources, and Voice* (World Bank Report No. 21776, 2001). The potential scope of the Bank's human rights concerns is suggested by its decision that female genital mutilation is an economic issue within its mandate. George Graham, 'Pledge over Female Mutilation: World Bank and IMF Win Commitment by Burkina Faso', *Financial Times* (22 April 1994) A6.

[109] *See generally* Daniel Bradlow, 'Symposium: Social Justice and Development: Critical Issues Facing the Bretton Woods System' 6 *Transnat'l L. & Contemp. Probs.* (1996) 47.

[110] For a defence of the IMF's position in this regard see François Gianviti, 'Economic, Social, and Cultural Rights and the International Monetary Fund', Chapter 4 above.

[111] *See e.g.* World Bank Operational Manual, Operational Directive (OD) on Indigenous Peoples 4.20 (September 1991); *id.*, Operational Policy (OP) on Involuntary Resettlement 4.12 (December 2001)

This is not the result of some sudden and irrepressible altruism at these institutions. Following controversial funding decisions at the Bank, for example, some major donors made their willingness to contribute to the development effort contingent on the establishment of an independent inspection function by the Bank. This was accomplished by creating an Inspection Panel designed 'to provide a formal mechanism for receiving complaints from people directly affected by Bank-supported projects on the grounds of [its] failure to abide by its own policies, including environmental and social policies, when designing, appraising, and supervising the implementation of projects'.[112] The panel process offers a transparent accountability mechanism for the Bank itself, but it creates no liability and invests individuals with no substantive rights that might be enforced against the Bank. Nor does it create social responsibility obligations for multinational corporations that may be involved. Nor has the panel process met with unqualified support within the Bank itself, especially after its criticism of the Bank's dam project in Tibet.

But the panel process does offer evidence of a glacial change in the legal and commercial environment. Specifically, it suggests three layers (or generations) of human rights concerns within the Bank that have emerged over time: (i) initially, the Bank's support for physical infrastructure projects in education, health care, housing, and sanitation enabled a variety of recipients to begin to exercise certain economic and social rights; (ii) more recently, the Bank's focus on pragmatic abstractions like good governance, the rule of law, independent judiciaries, and transparency has brought a greater range of rights, including political rights, within reach of beneficiaries; and (iii) most recently, the Bank has articulated the understanding that sustainable development requires at a minimum the institutionalization of concern for particularly vulnerable populations, notably children, indigenous peoples, and women,[113] as well as broader commitments to democracy, social justice, transparent and accountable governance, and universal human rights.[114]

('Bank experience indicates that involuntary resettlement under development projects, if unmitigated, often gives rise to severe economic, social, and environmental risks'); *id.*, World Bank Operational Policy (OP) on Gender and Development 4.20 ('The objective of the Bank's gender and development policy is to assist member countries to reduce poverty and enhance economic growth, human well-being, and development effectiveness by addressing the gender disparities and inequalities that are barriers to development').

With respect to the IMF, Professor Bradlow argues that the collapse of the par value system in 1971 'expanded the range of issues that the IMF needed to address in its Article IV consultation with its Member States. ... [B]ecause such issues as labor, health, and agricultural policies can directly affect the value of a country's currency and its ability to adjust to changes in its balance of payments, the IMF needs to consider all these issues in its surveillance of its Member State's monetary policy.' Bradlow, note 109 above, at 69–70.

[112] Sabine Schlemmer-Schulte, 'The World Bank Inspection Panel: A Record of the First International Accountability Mechanism and Its Role for Human Rights' 6 *Human Rights Br.* (1999) 1.

[113] The International Bank for Reconstruction and Development, *Development and Human Rights* (1998) 20.

[114] *See e.g.* 'Copenhagen Declaration on Social Development' in *Report of the U.N. World Summit for Social Development*, U.N. Doc. A/CONF.166/9 (1995) at 26.

The IMF's capacity to affect human rights conditions is perhaps more modest than the Bank's, given its institutional concern with macroeconomic, particularly monetary, policies, instead of discrete development projects. And the means at its disposal—financing the general balance of payments *vel non*—is too blunt an instrument to address specific human rights violations. But, as the Fund's experience with apartheid South Africa demonstrated, systematic human rights violations can have a macroeconomic and particularly monetary impact, affecting a member state's ability to meet its obligations to the Fund.[115] The Fund seems also to have understood that its conditionality and structural adjustment policies have human rights consequences that can be severe and for which the Fund itself is responsible.[116] Of course, the Fund's decisions create no direct legal obligations for multinational corporations, but they do establish an environment in which the corporation must act.

E. The Organization for Economic Cooperation and Development

The OECD Guidelines for Multinational Enterprises comprise recommendations by governments to multinational enterprises that operate in or from their territories. Though the Guidelines are entirely voluntary, they offer one of the few examples of government representatives (as distinct from the experts in the U.N. Sub-Commission or an international secretariat or advocates or NGOs) addressing the management of multinational companies directly in a multilateral setting through the expression of shared expectations. The states obligate themselves to implement the Guidelines and to promote compliance with them by all enterprises that operate in or from the member state's territory. Several areas of business conduct are covered, but it was not until 2000 that the Guidelines expressly included human rights, providing that 'enterprises should . . . [r]espect the human rights of those affected by their activities consistent with the host government's obligations and commitments'. In other words, rather than imposing obligations on the companies, the revised Guidelines enjoin corporations to act consistently with the host state's international human rights obligations, presumably including the Universal Declaration of Human Rights and the human rights treaties to which the host state is a party. Earlier versions of the Guidelines focused on labour rights on the rationale that labour conditions were within the innermost circle of corporate control and that going beyond human rights concerns within the company's control was neither politic nor effective. But the most recent iteration of the Guidelines and the recent set of concerns within the OECD itself suggest that the body of relevant human rights norms is not inert but is in a steady state of evolution: since 2001, the OECD

[115] Daniel Bradlow, 'Debt, Development and Democracy: Lessons from South Africa' 12 *Mich. J. Int'l L.* (1991) 647.

[116] Michael Lucas, 'The International Monetary Fund's Conditionality and the International Covenant on Economic, Social, and Cultural Rights: An Attempt to Define the Relation' 25 *R. Bel. D. Int'l* (1992) 104.

and its staff have addressed as human rights concerns a wide variety of business problems, including working conditions in the supply chain, multinational enterprises in situations of violent conflict and widespread human rights abuses, management control systems, and bribery.

The institutional enforcement of the Guidelines consists in 'follow-up', soft procedures such as consultations, good offices, mediation, conciliation, as well as 'clarifications' of the guidelines themselves, none of which qualifies as a judicial or even a quasi-judicial proceeding. Implementation necessarily rests on the will of governments through their National Contact Points, as specified in the Guidelines; non-governmental organizations have been especially critical of that process, especially after the failure of the OECD's Multilateral Agreement on Investment (MAI). From one perspective, the MAI negotiations failed because no consensus emerged on the contours of a social clause, provisions protecting environmental, cultural, indigenous, and social rights. But here too there is a certain naïvety that dismisses the exercise because it is not yet fully effective, missing the degree to which governments, businesses, trade unions, and non-governmental organizations have committed to the process as a whole and the steady accumulation of heightened expectations by the governments of the most powerful economies in the world.

F. The World Trade Organization

The WTO occupies at best ambiguous space in the emerging international regime of corporate responsibility. Its predecessor organization, the General Agreement on Tariffs and Trade, emerged in isolation from other multilateral institutions of global governance such as the United Nations and the World Bank, and its body of norms was considered largely *sui generis*. Its purpose, like that of the WTO, was trade liberalization and the reduction of tariffs and other barriers to trade, which seemed separate from, indeed irrelevant to, the protection of human rights.[117] But irrelevance turned to incompatibility during the Uruguay Round of trade negotiations (from which the WTO eventually emerged) when negotiators considered and rejected a 'social clause' which would have assured that international trade standards were interpreted consistently with other standards protecting the rights of labour and the environment. After sustained opposition from the governments of developing nations and some business interests, all that remains of the social clause is a provision in the Preamble, urging in vague and unenforceable terms that economic relations be conducted in a way that raises standards of living, ensures full employment, and

[117] The primary objective of the WTO is to 'liberalise international trade and place it on a secure basis' which will 'thereby contribut[e] to the economic growth, development, and welfare of the world's people'. Final Act Embodying the Results of the Uruguay Round of Multilateral Trade Negotiations, Agreement Establishing the Multilateral Trade Organization, 33 *International Legal Materials* (1993) 13. *See generally* Frank J. Garcia, 'The Global Market and Human Rights: Trading Away the Human Rights Principle' 25 *Brook. J. Int'l L.* 51 (1999).

increases real income in an environmentally sustainable way.[118] Screening trade according to more robust human rights criteria potentially offered a pretext for protectionism and was therefore not adopted. There was moreover an institutional concern: the WTO would have enough difficulty enforcing internationally accepted trade rules, especially early in its history, and could not be expected to condition trade liberalization on compliance with an additional layer of human rights standards whose normative status may be contested and which were beyond the organization's expertise in any event. Nor could the WTO be expected to play the human rights enforcer when the profit motive had historically submerged States' criticism of their trading partners' human rights abuses.

Nevertheless, in ways that are characteristic of the age, states and civil society gradually understood an episodic and partial linkage between human rights protections and the quality of the international market: labour abuses could depress export prices below fair market value and amount to a form of 'social dumping'; certain forms of trade, like the sale of conflict diamonds, would not be entitled to the benefits of trade liberalization; and the prospect of admission to the organization could induce non-member states to accede to human rights treaties and become part of a broader 'cartel of values' in the promotion of the rule of law and transparent, accountable governance. The WTO's dispute settlement mechanism also offered human rights advocates a potential technique for making human rights protections part of every state's economic self-interest: the threat of retaliatory sanctions, approved by a quasi-judicial panel subject to appellate review, for violations of international norms, has generated an admirable if imperfect record of compliance.

Admittedly, the law that is enforced and respected within the WTO is generally divorced from norms protecting human rights, and the rules on most favoured nation treatment or the reduction of trade barriers suggest that the WTO is more likely to invalidate unilateral trade sanctions intended to punish a state's human rights abuses than it is to facilitate them. Under Article XX of the WTO agreement, states may adopt measures that restrict trade if these are 'necessary' to achieve a narrow class of social objectives,[119] including the protection of public morals, or the protection of human life and health, or relating to the products of prison labour. But the potential power of Article XX to reconcile trade liberalization with other goals of the international community has never been fully realized,[120] in part because the WTO's Appellate Body and its GATT predecessor have traditionally defined 'necessity' narrowly, rarely allowing trade restrictions under Article XX and then only when no less restrictive alternative was available. As the international regulatory environment becomes more dense in the protection of the environment or human rights, it may be possible to argue that compliance with international obligations is

---

[118] Agreement Establishing the World Trade Organization, signed at Marrakesh, 15 April 1994.

[119] Steve Charnovitz, 'The Moral Exception in Trade Policy' 38 *Va. J. Int'l L.* 689 (1998).

[120] *See* International Council on Human Rights Policy, *Beyond Voluntarism: Human Rights and the International Legal Obligations of Companies* (2002) at 112–16.

also 'necessary'[121] and that the WTO cannot carve out an immunity for itself or its members from the body of human rights norms, and the fight will then be about which universal human rights are within the WTO's mandate and which ones are not. Until those arguments are fully addressed and resolved, perhaps the best that can be expected of the WTO is that it will abide by the precautionary principle and 'first do no harm'.

To these international initiatives, one might add the public–private partnership implicit in the Voluntary Principles on Security and Human Rights, developed in December 2000 by the governments of the United States and the United Kingdom in cooperation with multinational companies in the extractive industries and human rights NGOs, as a means of establishing common principles governing corporate human rights responsibilities. One might add the regional development banks, notably the European Bank for Reconstruction and Development and the Asian Development Bank, which have incorporated social concerns into their projects, linking the objective of poverty reduction to the means of judicial reform and the protection of indigenous minorities. The Commission on the European Communities has disseminated its Green Paper 'Promoting a European Framework for Corporate Social Responsibility' and developed its underlying principles through its July 2002 'Communication concerning Corporate Social Responsibility: A Business Contribution to Sustainable Development'.[122] The European Union as whole might be the model of how intergovernmental organizations initially devoted to economic concerns gradually expand their understanding of the linkages between economics and human rights; indeed, the court of the European Court of Justice now routinely interprets economic or commercial disputes in the light of international human rights obligations of the member states and the EU itself.[123] Although none of these international standards imposes obligations directly on multinational corporations, they clearly contribute to a dense regulatory environment that undermines the received distinctions between state and non-state actors, between profit and altruism, and between commercial standards and human rights law.

Part II. An Initial Response to Objections

The above analysis suggests that the corporate human rights initiative is a pastiche of developments across international, industrial, and institutional boundaries. The four regimes, compatible with one another at a high level of abstraction, are also readily distinguishable, combining voluntary market-driven commitments undertaken by private actors themselves, tightly targeted obligations imposed by governments *ex ante*, cartels of values articulated by intergovernmental actors, and principles of liability imposed *ex post* by the courts in extraordinary circumstances. The prior

---

[121] *See e.g.* Report of the Appellate Body, *Import Prohibition of Certain Shrimp and Shrimp Products*, WT/DS58/AB/R (1998) 1634.   [122] COM (2002) 347 (final).

[123] Jurgen Schwarze, *European Administrative Law* (1992).

analysis does not, however, fully convey the controversy that surrounds each of these regimes nor the reasons not to be particularly optimistic that the corporate human rights initiative is linear or progressive, as though it consisted of phenomena that are inevitably coalescing into law. This section briefly explores these objections and concludes that they compel, not the reversal or abandonment of the corporate human rights initiative, but an international process of standard-setting to address three recurring questions: (i) which human rights is the corporation obliged to respect? (ii) What kind of relationships between corporations and governments will trigger the fullest range of obligations? And (iii) what remedies are most appropriate when violations occur?

1. THE NORMATIVE PROBLEM AND FRIEDMAN'S CRITIQUE

One fundamental objection to the development of a corporate human rights regime requires its proponents to articulate, explain, and defend the principle on which a corporation *should* be obliged to meet human rights standards in the first place. As noted above, Milton Friedman among others has pointed out that social responsibility movements subvert the shareholder primacy principle, which 'mandates that management—the corporation's directors and senior officers—devote its energies to the advancement of shareholder interests. If pursuit of this objective conflicts with the interests of one or more of the corporation's nonshareholder constituencies, management is to disregard such competing considerations'.[124] The objection is grounded in the legally enforceable obligation requiring management to maximize the return on the shareholders' investment[125] and the assertion that the introduction of human rights criteria subverts that promise by requiring expertise in human rights monitoring and *de facto* control over abuses that corporations do not have and cannot be expected to have.

There are several possible responses to the demand for a normative principle-of-justification for the extension of human rights obligations to private corporations. The first is classically consequentialist and might be characterized as the 'market reliability rationale'. As the market regime suggests (see above), it is in the long-term

---

[124] David Millon, 'Communitarianism in Corporate Law: Foundations and Law Reform Strategies', *Progressive Corporate Law* (Mitchell ed., 1995) 1.

[125] *Dodge v. Ford Motor Corp.*, 170 N.W. 668 (Mich. 1919) ('A business corporation is organized and carried on primarily for the profit of the stockholders. The powers of the directors are to be employed for that end'). *See also*, American Law Institute, *Principles of Corporate Governance: Analysis and Recommendations* (1994) Section 2.01, Rep. Note 1: 'Some cases, mostly arising before the turn of the century, applied the concept reflected in *Dodge v. Ford*, a strict notion of *ultra vires*, or both, to strictly preclude the utilization of corporate resources, either by way of donation or otherwise, for humanitarian, educational, philanthropic, or public welfare activities'.

self-interest of the corporation to conform to at least some subset of human rights standards, because the company may pay a price in capital markets if its shares lose value by virtue of socially conscious investment decisions by potential shareholders, or it may lose in the consumer market by virtue of boycotts or market choices, and increasingly it may lose in the court-room. Moreover, respect for human rights tends to correlate to a commitment to the rule of law, and a corporation can clearly operate more profitably in a more ordered environment. The business judgment rule, far from requiring management to ignore human rights concerns, would at least allow and arguably require management to maintain the corporate reputation by adhering to best practices in the protection of human rights. The shareholder primacy principle, to the extent that it rested on the assumption that corporate altruism is unprofitable, has clearly undergone a fundamental transformation over the last century.[126]

Another possibility is classically deontological and reminiscent of the natural law approaches to rights: rights are primary; human beings have rights by virtue of being human; and those rights are not dependent on a government's willingness to recognize them. Indeed, in this view, governments exist and are legitimate only to the extent that they protect the human rights of its citizens. In this view, no one and nothing is immune from the obligation to respect those rights, so that the burden rests on those who would carve out an exception to human rights obligations rather than on those who would extend them to corporations. The fact is that many multinational corporations are more powerful economically than many governments, and it is perverse in this view to immunize the stronger entity, with unprecedented resources at its command, and in many cases vastly greater impact on the daily lives of people, and free them of human rights obligations. This is especially true as more government operations (such as the running of prisons) are privatized: no government can avoid its international human rights obligations by delegating them to a private corporation. Both must be held accountable if human rights are abused in the exercise of government functions, no matter who or what is actually performing them.

A third possible rationale is positivistic, at least as that term is understood at international law to refer to the practice of states, including the adoption of treaties. This too shifts the burden of proof: because the law treats both human beings and corporations as individuals, it falls to those who would carve out the exception for

---

[126] Section 2.01 of the American Law Institute's *Principles of Corporate Governance: Analysis and Recommendations* (1994) provides:

    (a) ...a corporation should have as its objective the conduct of business activities with a view to enhancing corporate profit and shareholder gain.

    (b) Even if corporate profit and shareholder gain are not thereby enhanced, the corporation, in the conduct of its business: (1) is obliged, to the same extent as a natural person, to act within the boundaries set by law; (2) may take into account ethical considerations that are reasonably regarded as appropriate to the responsible conduct of business; and (3) may devote a reasonable amount of resources to public welfare, humanitarian, educational, and philanthropic purposes.

companies to justify an international exemption, given that companies can plainly violate domestic criminal law and tort law and be held accountable. A somewhat different positivist rationale would look, not to the practice of states internationally, but to the standard company law of most municipal legal systems, where there is an important *quid pro quo* in operation: companies receive from the state the benefit of incorporation, meaning the right to exist and to limit the liability of stockholders to the extent of their investment, and, in exchange for that considerable and profitable right, they can be expected to serve the public interest and not abuse their privileges. From this perspective, the premise that corporations are exclusively private is fundamentally inaccurate: 'corporations really are both private and public simultaneously... [C]orporations are not purely private individuals. They are institutions that sometimes act as quasi-governments and, even when they do not, they take actions that affect every aspect of people's lives, including people who have no formal contractual relationship with them.'[127] From this perspective has grown a communitarian or progressive stream of corporate law scholarship, articulating a 'concern about the harm to nonshareholders that can occur as a result of managerial adherence to the shareholder primacy principle. Efforts to maximize shareholder wealth are often costly to nonshareholders and often come at the expense of particular nonshareholder constituent groups'.[128]

The common philosophical denominator in these approaches is the understanding that international law is not different in kind from other sources of obligation for the modern corporation. It is well established that a corporation might be liable in tort for damages caused by the negligence or intentional acts of its employees. A corporation can violate the property rights of others and be required to pay damages or obey an injunction. A corporation can be guilty of criminal offences including conspiracy and aiding and abetting. Nothing in the four regimes suggests that the human rights norms imposed on or undertaken by the corporation are intrinsically incompatible with their juristic status.

2. THE PROBLEM OF NOTICE: WHICH RIGHTS AND WHICH PUBLIC–PRIVATE RELATIONSHIPS?

A separate class of objections demands not philosophical justification but pragmatic clarity in the articulation of human rights norms for corporations. At base, runs this critique, none of the four regimes adequately distinguishes degrees of corporate

---

[127] Alan Wolfe, 'The Modern Corporation: Private Agent or Public Actor?', 50 *Wash. & Lee L. Rev.* (1993) 1673, at 1692.

[128] Millon, note 124 above, at 1. *See also* Ariane Berthoin Antal, *Corporate Social Performance: Rediscovering Actors in Their Organizational Contexts* (1992) 11: 'This body of literature provides theoretical access to the concept of corporate social responsibility, it offers models for the process of corporate social responsiveness, and it suggests factors influencing corporate social performance'.

culpability or gives adequate notice of the corporation's human rights responsibilities. The objection rests on a central and reasonable question: is it possible for a corporation acting in good faith to know in advance which rights it must respect and which relationships with governments it must avoid in order to escape complicity-based liability, or is this a body of law in such a constant state of evolution that no company can have notice of its responsibilities and potential liabilities? The most specific objection rests on the assumption that the corporation will be responsible merely for operating in a country where human rights violations occur, even if the corporation has no control over the abuses: can liability be premised on the corporation's knowledge that abuses occur and the benefits it may derive—even indirectly—from the abuse?

But the legal elements are not in place for such a sweeping and ill defined liability. Consider first the body of *per se* violations that are wrongful with or without state action (previously labelled 'Category I' norms): piracy, slavery, genocide, certain war crimes, *etc.* Every corporation must be considered on notice that conduct that falls within this extraordinary category will be wrongful, and they may face a variety of sanctions for engaging in it. If at the margins there may be controversy case-by-case about what qualifies as 'slavery' or 'war crimes' or the rest, there is considerable practical guidance in the treaties defining these wrongs and in the practice of states and tribunals interpreting them. In addition, *outside* of Category I wrongs, it is possible that certain conduct will be a violation of the corporation's voluntary code or some industry standard or SA 8000, but these violations are likely to trigger market sanctions (or conceivably legal sanctions under false advertising laws) but not legal sanctions under the assertedly more inchoate law of nations. In either event, the corporation will have the notice that comes of voluntarily undertaking (and defining) a human rights commitment with its eyes open. By contrast, Category II wrongs—wrongs that do require state action and that apply to a corporation only by virtue of its relationship with a state actor—are necessarily more complicated. But the guidance offered by Section 1983 of the antidiscrimination statutes, *supra*, offers at least preliminary guidance: a 'dense relationship' is not enough. As noted above, the U.S. Supreme Court has articulated four distinct approaches to the state action question: public function, state compulsion, nexus, and joint action,[129] and, though it has not yet articulated the relationship between the four tests, these four standards could form the basis of an international agreement defining the requisite relationship required to trigger corporate liability for Category II wrongs. Why exactly would standards deemed to provide adequate if limited guidance in the context of domestic civil rights enforcement be inadequate if imported into international human rights enforcement? If the only reason for rejecting the extension is that Section 1983 is domestic

---

[129] *See e.g. George v. Pacific-CSC Work Furlough*, 91 F.3d 1227, 1230 (9th Cir. 1996). Thus for example, '[u]nder the joint action approach, private actors can be state actors if they are "wilful participant[s] in joint action with the state or its agents." An agreement between government and a private party can create joint action.' *Id.*, at 1231.

law of the United States alone, then it could form the basis for the negotiation of a common, practical standard to be internationalized by treaty.

Another, somewhat more theoretical, approach to the problem of definition is to begin with the axiom of moral agency that no one can be held responsible for acts beyond his or her control. The modern corporation is a complex entity with varying forms of control in different places and times. For that reason, it may be best to correlate its human rights obligations to 'concentric circles of control', which reflect the varying degrees of the corporation's effectiveness and impact. In the closest circles of control, the corporation has the greatest obligation, so that the closer the violation is to the corporation's work, the greater is its level of responsibility. If, for example, an oil corporation places a pipeline along a route it knows the host government will clear of indigenous peoples by force, that is obviously distinct from a company that happens to do business in a place where the human rights violations are unrelated to the corporation's work. Or if that company offers its helicopters to transport government soldiers for an abusive raid on a tribal village that is complicating the corporation's work, the company would bear a measure of aiding-and-abetting responsibility. By contrast, if an insurance company has no relationship economically or operationally with the government's human rights violations or the operations of the oil company, it is attractive to conclude that no responsibility should arise in these circumstances. In the latter case, the human rights violations are in a concentric circle around the corporation that is too far removed from its essential work and mission. By contrast, a corporation's benefit from a generalized system of human rights violations might again trigger market sanctions or, as in South Africa, it might subject the corporation to a generalized regime of domestic and international sanctions, but it would probably not ground tort liability under the Alien Tort Statute. The question of 'which rights' is thus intrinsically linked to the question of 'which relationships': internationally-defined labour rights on working hours and remuneration will be directly relevant to a large manufacturing operation, rights of physical integrity will be directly relevant to a company providing security consulting services to a government, and the international rules governing the treatment of detainees will be directly relevant to any newly privatized prison operation.

But a corporation cannot be held liable for a host government's systemic violations of civil, political, economic, social, and cultural rights, unless the corporation contributes to the violation: certainly nothing in the regime of civil liability, *supra*, overrules the established standards of tort or delictual liability, including the standards of responsibility and proximate cause. A corporation's 'mere benefit' from a government's abuses of human rights is not enough to trigger liability.[130]

---

[130] *See e.g. Doe v. Unocal*, 395 F.3d 932; 947–55 (9th Cir. 2002) ('[W]e may impose aiding and abetting liability for *knowing practical assistance or encouragement* which has a substantial effect on the perpetration of the crime', emphasis supplied). *See* note 60, *supra*.

3. THE PROBLEM OF AMERICAN EXCEPTIONALISM

Critics have occasionally opposed the corporate human rights initiative, especially the *Unocal* litigation and its progeny, to the extent that it imposes a uniquely American form of liability that disadvantages U.S. corporations in the global marketplace.[131] The concern is that exposure under the Alien Tort Statute imposes a risk of adjudication of tort liability that is poorly defined substantively, unevenly enforced, potentially uninsurable, and geographically unlimited. The risk is exacerbated by the alleged manipulability of 'the law of nations', the prospect of abusive or politically motivated lawsuits, and the impropriety of U.S. judges issuing decisions that trench on executive and congressional prerogatives in foreign relations.

But the argument fails in its premises: the litigation 'stick' is not a uniquely American phenomenon. Pending actions in the United Kingdom, Belgium, France, and Japan similarly test the civil and criminal exposure of companies to liability for their complicity in egregious human rights violations in various parts of the world. Nor is the Alien Tort Statute (ATS) the only or necessarily the predominant vehicle for imposing liability: as human rights entrepreneurialism expands and domestic regulation increasingly reflects human rights concerns, the failure to live up to announced commitments may violate not so much the law of nations as domestic laws prohibiting false advertising or requiring transparency in the securities market or prohibiting certain practices or transactions with certain governments. Nor is the law of nations infinitely malleable: on the contrary, the law of nations consists in the generalized, nearly universal practice of states to which governments conform out of a sense of legal obligation (*opinio juris*). In the face of this high evidentiary standard, the allegation that the 'law of nations' will be interpreted to impose international liability for garden-variety fraud, or for the human rights violations of arms-length suppliers or regulators, or under merely emerging standards of human rights law (*lex ferenda*) is radically overstated. Nor, as shown above, are the courts powerless to protect defendants from political or abusive lawsuits. But even if—as some critics assert—the statute should be repealed because abusive lawsuits were occasionally filed under it, certain staples of American legal practice, like the Sherman Antitrust Act, the Racketeer Influenced and Corrupt Organizations Act, the class action rules, and the Administrative Procedure Act, would be vulnerable long before the Alien Tort Statute.

4. THE PROBLEM OF MEANS: ASPIRATIONS *VERSUS* OBLIGATIONS

An additional constellation of objections questions the propriety of imposing human rights obligations just as corporations are beginning to undertake them voluntarily. Hidden in the adage that 'no good deed goes unpunished' is the insight

---

[131] *See e.g.* Elliot Schrag, 'The Long Way to Find Justice: What Are Burmese Villagers Doing in a California Court?', *Washington Post* (14 July 2002) at p. B2.

that a salutary development can be derailed by the effort to accelerate or over-interpret it, and efforts to make voluntary codes the basis for liability will assure that the corporations will stop adopting them. From this perspective, it is essential to the success of the codes that they remain legally unenforceable: preference should be given to the regime of market-induced and market-enforced human rights aspirations.

Without denying the value of the market regime, these objections rest on a caricature of the market itself, as though markets were necessarily hostile to legal frameworks and enforceable norms. As Professor Coase and others have demonstrated, however, markets work best, not when there are no liability rules, but when those rules are clearly articulated and fairly applied. In other words, the market should work and be allowed to work, but litigation *ex post* and standard setting *ex ante* will define the minimum beneath which the market will not be allowed to operate, and the clearer those standards are—and the more impartial their application—the more efficient the marketplace will be.

There is moreover an important historical connection between the emergence of law and the undertakings of commercial actors. As shown in Part III, *infra*, commercial law has characteristically emerged in ways that undermine the distinction between voluntary aspiration and legal obligation. Contemporary commercial law frequently arises out of the custom of merchants in a particular trade, for example, even though the custom began not as an obligation but as a voluntary practice. The significance of the code movement is thus not as a force in opposition to the emergence of legally obligatory norms but as a potential reinforcement of it, an assurance that norms do not radically outpace the voluntary aspirations of the corporations themselves. This is not to say that the corporate codes place a ceiling on the eventual scope and content of enforceable standards, but it does suggest that the choice of proceeding by means of aspirational codes rather than obligatory standards rests on a misleading and unstable distinction.

5. THE PROBLEM OF REMEDIES: WHAT BEST PROTECTS RIGHTS?

Closely related to the preference for voluntary codes instead of obligatory instruments is the conviction that human rights are better protected by engagement, even with an abusive government, than by divestment and quarantine. In this view, the creation of an upwardly mobile middle class that insists upon a government that is responsive to the citizenry, transparent, and faithful to the rule of law does more for the cause of human rights than economic and cultural isolation. The corporate human rights regimes, to the extent that they penalize the presence of corporations in less developed countries with governments that violate human rights standards, ultimately lead to the perpetuation of poverty and autocracy. They may also interfere with local, home-grown techniques for accountability, which better reflect the mores of that society than does the international articulation of human rights standards or the adjudication of corporate liability in a foreign court. At base, this is an empirical claim about the impact of the corporate presence, drawing on examples like Burma and Iraq, where international isolation has assertedly perpetuated abusive governments, in contrast to South Africa, where 'constructive engagement' assertedly hastened the demise of apartheid.

But history rarely yields its lessons without a fight. Perhaps the revolution in South Africa was attributable to the sheer moral power of Nelson Mandela. Perhaps it was the mixture of divestment by some corporations and constructive engagement by others. Perhaps the demographics of power and legitimacy would not allow the permanent suppression of a large majority race by a small minority race. Perhaps the corporations helped to perpetuate apartheid for decades, but under international scrutiny their support weakened sufficiently in the 1980s to allow the majority to seize power. Perhaps every assessment of the multinational corporations' role in ending apartheid—or in the protection and violation of human rights generally— says more about the interpreter than about the raw data. The evidence on all sides of the question is anecdotal.

As a consequence, the empirical defence of the multinational corporation as a force for good in the protection of human rights cannot be directly tested and confirmed. But even if it were, it would not support a generalized critique of the emerging regimes outlined above. After all, the regimes do not by themselves compel (or necessarily even complicate) the decision to invest or not to invest. A company might adopt a voluntary code or adhere to the Voluntary Principles in order to protect its market or brand, and nothing in that decision requires divestment or avoidance of economic opportunity. And its legal vulnerability under the Alien Tort Statute depends on that company's complicity in egregious violations, not its presence *vel non* in a country with an abusive government. Indeed, the only part of the emerging regimes to constrain corporate presence are domestic and international sanctions, and then at least the decision to pursue investment is essentially made for the corporation. As suggested in Part I, the four regimes offer a measure of redundancy that is generally coherent with other developments in international and domestic law.

6. COMMODIFICATION AND OTHER OBJECTIONS FROM THE HUMAN RIGHTS PERSPECTIVE

Not all objections to the corporate human rights initiative come from the corporate world. Some human rights advocates also offer a pointed critique, noting that none of the four regimes has been conspicuously successful in protecting human rights; that the emerging corporate human rights norms are pretextual, unambitious, skewed towards labour rights, and largely unenforceable; that the market sanctions in particular presume an implausibly well informed consumer or investor who is in the luxurious position to pay a premium for the assurance that human rights have been respected, and its civil liability regime depends on the rare coincidence of finding a willing plaintiff with standing, access to U.S. courts, and the resources to sue, plus a proper defendant within the personal jurisdiction of those courts. Nor is it a congenial concession to assume that the best argument for a corporate human rights agenda is that it is 'good business': that argument commodifies basic principles of human dignity and thereby surrenders the moral high ground. In this view, corporations should protect human rights because it is the right thing to do, whether it is profitable or not.

Although these objections represent the minority view among large human rights NGOs, they are serious. They also illustrate how the best can be the enemy of the good. Taken with the other objections outlined above, they illuminate a middle path, a consultative and inclusive process for articulating a global standard to offer corporations a measure of protection from aberrational local approaches to human rights. But even if that international standard setting exercise is much delayed or even abandoned altogether, there is precedent—as shown next—for believing that a more coherent and stable system of norms may emerge from the four regimes of principle: that there is forest here and not just trees.

Part III. Towards a Modern Reconception of the *Lex Mercatoria*

In the sources and the content of norms governing corporate responsibility, it is possible to see the emergence of a new *lex mercatoria*: a contemporary variant of the medieval law merchant. The *lex mercatoria* was developed and enforced as a tool to promote better business practices through offers of security to consumers and other merchants, and it also served an interstitial role, filling the gaps of each jurisdiction's commercial law and harmonizing disparate approaches in different markets and nations. The law's genesis in the customs of the marketplace:

was by far the most decisive factor in its development: it made the law eminently a practical law adapted to the requirements of commerce; and as trade expanded and new forms of commercial activity arose—negotiable paper, insurance, etc.—custom everywhere fashioned and framed the broad general principles of the new law. Custom is alike the ruling principle and the originating force of the Law Merchant.[132]

In this way, the *lex mercatoria* became one model for innovation in the introduction of new legal principles and doctrines, originating and evolving from the initiative of merchants motivated by a long-term, sophisticated, and mutual self-interest. As a result, key entrepreneurial concepts and practices found their way into the commercial law of states[133] and ultimately into contemporary international trade

---

[132] William Mitchell, *An Essay on the Early History of the Law Merchant* (1904, reprinted 1969) 12.

[133] Harold J. Berman and Colin Kaufman, 'The Law of International Commercial Transactions (*Lex Mercatoria*)', 19 *Harv. Int'l L. J.* (1978) 221 (noting that certain widespread similarities in legal doctrines governing the allocation of risk of loss or damage to goods, standard clauses in bills of lading or letters of

law and the U.N. Convention on Contracts for the International Sale of Goods.[134] The international legal order thereby replicated and formalized the ethical business order, rather than displacing, coercing, or pre-empting it.[135]

But there were more than utilitarian reasons for the emergence and the stability of *lex mercatoria*: the influence of canon law tended to inject transnational standards of good faith and equity into commercial dealings as well. 'Canon law, the body of universal law and procedure developed by the [Roman Catholic] Church for its own governance *and to regulate the rights and obligations of its communicants* had from the beginning its own sphere of application and separate courts, . . . [but] there was a tendency towards overlapping jurisdiction, and before the Reformation it was common to find ecclesiastical courts exercising civil jurisdiction' (emphasis added).[136] For that reason, it was perhaps inevitable that jurisprudence of the Church would converge with (and to some extent displace) the Roman civil law:[137] the pragmatic need for cooperation, combined with the 'spiritual jurisprudence' then ascendant, assured that merchants would act with some sense of mutual restraint in their dealings with one another.[138]

credit, and arbitration clauses are 'due in part to common commercial needs shared by all who participate in international trade transactions'.) *See also* Wyndham A. Bewes, *The Romance of the Law Merchant* (1923) 28–62, 77–9 (demonstrating that certain doctrines of contemporary commercial law can be traced through the law merchant and ultimately to medieval business customs, including the enforceability of informal agreements, the rights of a possessor of a bearer bill of exchange, the protection of the good faith purchaser of stolen goods even against the original owner when the goods were bought in 'open market', the right of a seller to stop the transit of goods if the buyer defaults after shipment, and the right of partners to an accounting). *Accord*, Leon E. Trakman, *The Law Merchant: The Evolution of Commercial Law* (1983) 225–6 and 33 (describing similarities between the ancient *lex mercatoria* and the modern Uniform Commercial Code in the United States).

[134] John Honnold, 'The Influence of the Law of International trade on the Development and Character of English and American Commercial Law', in *Colloquium on the Sources of the Law of International Trade* (Schmitthoff ed., 1964) 76. *See also* Trakman, note 133 above, at 7: '[Contemporary] international trade has been motivated by the inspiration of need, mutual interest, and a fear of suffering business sanctions. . . . Just as the medieval merchants relied upon trade codes to govern their adventures, modern merchants rely on international codification to facilitate conventional trade. . . . Just as medieval merchants devised their own institutional means of allocating the risks of nonperformance, merchants today rely upon a combination of contract negotiations, industry custom and inter-party practice to resolve impediments to their performance.'

[135] *Compare* INCOTERMS, a source of international uniform definitions for commercial delivery terms, which defines the obligations of sellers and buyers regarding shipment and receipt of goods. Because its publisher, the International Chamber of Commerce, is a non-governmental entity, INCOTERMS does not have the legally binding effect of an international treaty. But it does provide a written expression of custom and usage, or best practice, in the industry. Parties to international transactions often expressly incorporate INCOTERMS into their contracts, and even when they do not, courts will occasionally incorporate it for them. Ralph Folsom, Michael Gordon, John Spanogle, *International Business Transactions* (2001) at 72.

[136] J.F. O'Connor, *Good Faith in International Law* (1991) 25–6.

[137] *Id. See also* Frederick Pollock and Frederic Maitland, *The History of the English Law Before the Time of Edward I* (1959), 190 (demonstrating that, in the early medieval period, a 'new and Christian tinge' came to colour contractual obligations and commercial law generally).

[138] Trakman, note 133 above, at 7.

As a result, 'the merchant was entitled to rely upon standards of fairness which evolved in light of commercial practice'.[139] By the sixteenth century, for example, virtually every commercial nation in Europe had altered prior doctrine and, in response to the usages of the merchant class, recognized the enforceability of a bona fide purchaser's rights, the validity of sales confirmed by the payment of earnest money, the validity and enforceability of formless contracts, the negotiability of bills of exchange, the obligations of partners and agents, and the necessity of swift justice *ex aequo et bono*.[140] In each of these respects, commercial habits and practices were transformed into legal institutions, doctrines, and codes, with the result that the law was increasingly uniform even as it became increasingly cosmopolitan and equitable.

The *lex mercatoria* was also distinguished by the ways in which its norms were enforced and commercial disputes were resolved. The dominant mode of enforcement was the internalization of norms by entrepreneurs themselves.[141] One determinant of a merchant's sustained prosperity was his ability to conform to the expectations of the market, which were formalized only over time into law: there were concrete commercial consequences for any merchant insufficiently committed to the abstract standards of good faith that underlay the pragmatic doctrines in the law merchant. When internalization failed and disputes did arise, they were typically resolved not by professional judges in the formal setting of a courtroom but by the merchants themselves, sometimes through mercantile councils and guilds, or through informal, expeditious forms of mediation and arbitration. When a dispute became sufficiently serious or prolonged that the local courts became involved, the law that governed was—directly or indirectly—what the merchants had adopted to facilitate ethical and uniform trade practices.[142]

It will be noted that the *lex mercatoria*, in its original form, effectively blurred the received distinction between self-interest and altruism (*pace* Ayn Rand and Milton Friedman). Adam Smith fully understood the reinforcing dynamic between these two forces. Smith of course is commonly invoked by advocates of *laissez-faire* capitalism who stress those passages in the *Wealth of Nations* that find the 'invisible hand' in rational economic actors' pursuing their self-interest. But this ignores the balance at work in Smith's philosophy, especially in *The Theory of the Moral Sentiments*, which focuses on the innate sense of empathy with which human beings regulate their instinct for acquisitive self-interest.[143] It radically oversimplifies

---

[139] Mitchell, note 132 above, at 11.   [140] *Ibid.*, at 93, 157–8.

[141] *Cf.* Harold H. Koh, 'The 1994 Roscoe Pound Lecture: Transnational Legal Process', 75 *Nebraska L. Rev.* (1996) 181, at 203–6.

[142] Mitchell, note 132 above, at 156; Berman and Kaufman, note 133 above, at 226–7: 'Through the decisions of Lord Mansfield and his successors, there was created a body of judicially declared English commercial law which incorporated and refined rules developed in earlier times throughout Europe. The incorporation of the law merchant added a cosmopolitan dimension to the English common law, without which the common law courts could hardly have served the needs of British commerce.'

[143] Adam Smith, *The Theory of the Moral Sentiments* (1759) 1: 'How selfish soever man may be supposed, there are evidently some principles in his nature, which interest him in the fortune of others, and render their happiness necessary to him, though he derives nothing from it except the pleasure of seeing it'.

Smith's theory of capitalism to suggest that individuals in natural or juristic form are exempt from the dictates of conscience or equity; indeed (and perhaps counter-intuitively), the distinction between altruism and self-interest cannot account for the variance in commercial decision-making by individuals, by firms, and by nations. If it did, the rational breach of contracts would be nearly universal, and *pacta sunt servanda* would become the relic of a naïve age.

In sum, *lex mercatoria* comprised a body of authority that was (and remains to this day) transnational in scope, grounded in good faith, reflective of market practices, and codified ultimately in the commercial law of the various nations and in inter-national law. Because these features reappear in some emerging forms of commercial law in the twentieth and twenty-first centuries, these new pockets of law have been described as 'a' or 'the' new *lex mercatoria*.[144] But with consequences not yet fully appreciated by either the corporate community or the human rights community (let alone the academic community) the corporate human rights standards described above offer fertile ground for the emergence of a similarly stable and significant body of commercial standards.

It is clear at the threshold that the market-based initiatives described above reflect the apparent competitive advantages of establishing and projecting a reputation for equitable conduct and a measure of transparency in corporate decision-making. The Kimberley Plan governing the sale of conflict diamonds, the evolution of SA 8000, and the sale of rights-sensitive product lines, *inter alia*, suggest that the market ultimately gives new relevance to international human rights standards in the global economy. Similarly, corporate codes of conduct have become common in the extractive, apparel, and footwear industries, especially among those accused of profiting from human rights abuses, indicating that the rise of accountability standards is attributable to the companies themselves, as they attempt publicly to capitalize on consumers' and investors' sense of responsibility. Motivated at least in part by long-term and sophisticated self-interest rather than by statute or decree or judgment, these may be viewed as mere marketing techniques, but they work to the extent that they blur the received distinction between an entrepreneur's self-interest and her altruism. Thus, while it may be true that states have historically failed to define the obligations of transnational corporations in any setting, companies have chosen to do so and remain free to do so within the protected sanctuary of the business judgment rule. The central point remains: it would be neither unprecedented nor illegitimate if what began as the articulation and internalization of best business practices became enforceable legal standards over time, either through domestic regulation, international standard-setting, or in extraordinary circumstances the prospect

---

[144] Examples include *inter alia* the law of cyberspace, Aron Mefford, 'Note: *Lex Informatica*: Foundations of Law on the Internet,' 5 *Ind. J. Global Leg. Stud.* (1997) 211; David Johnson and David Post, 'Law and Borders—The Rise of Law in Cyberspace,' 48 *Stanford L. Rev.* (1996) 1367; and the norms adopted in transnational arbitration panels. Harold J. Berman and Felix J. Dasser, *The 'New' Law Merchant and the 'Old': Sources, Content, and Legitimacy in Lex Mercatoria and Arbitration* (Carbonneau ed., 1990).

of civil liability. There is in short a critical historical connection between best practices in the market and the rules of law: 'In all great matters relating to commerce, the legislators have copied, not dictated'.[145]

But, it may be objected, this analysis fails because human rights standards are not yet common business conventions, let alone universal norms. Nor are they conspicuously successful. Nor do they cement the relationship among merchants through reciprocal assurances of commercial good faith. On the contrary, the principal beneficiary of these standards (and the 'altruism' behind them) is not the mercantile community itself: it is a labour force or a society or even an idea. But the genetic marker of the *lex mercatoria* was that seemingly soft notions like good faith evolved into widely accepted standards that became some of the hardest commercial law there is and that a merchant's self-interest depended on his or her respect for the interests of others. At the substantive core of this supposedly private law in other words were public values, and at the core procedurally of what became commercial law were voluntary undertakings of the merchant class.[146]

It is in addition ahistorical to require that so new a development be wholly formed before it can be taken seriously: in the synergistic dynamic that was the *lex mercatoria*, practices affected rules which affected practices which refined rules, and so on, over centuries. The key lay in the dynamic that allowed a communal sense of fairness or equity to emerge and get transformed into doctrinal form. That dynamic is again on display as the business and legal culture changes in response to the four regimes of principle and practice described above. It also suggests that the business community and the human rights community might assist one another in the articulation of a common sense of justice and the development of legal standards in order that the benefits of compliance might be maximized at decreasing marginal cost.

In short, human rights entrepreneurialism, the codes of conduct, the *Unocal* litigation and its progeny, the work of groups like the Investor Responsibility Research Center, and the adoption of domestic and international legal norms reflect a partial but real development at the intersection of the law and the marketplace. Indeed, the corporate human rights initiative mirrors the two dominant faces of globalization: the expansion of international trade and commerce without regard to boundaries, and the universalizing effects of the human rights movement—the only global ideology to survive the twentieth century. Without suggesting at all that the corporate culture is about to enter some millennial Age of Aquarius, we will see the continued development of broad-based organizations specifically devoted to bringing human rights issues into the corporate boardroom, the modest growth of a consumer- and investor-driven market dynamic that embraces

---

[145] 1 Goldschmidt, *Handbuch des Handelsrechts* 378–79 (1891), *cited in* Trakman, note 133 above, *at* 10.

[146] *See Bank of Conway v. Stary*, 200 N.W. 505 (N.D. 1924) (declaring that the law merchant was 'a system of law that [did] . . . not rest exclusively on the institutions and local customs of any particular country, but consisted of certain principles of equity and usages of trade which general convenience and a common sense of justice have established to regulate the dealings of merchants . . . in all commercial countries of the civilized world'.)

human rights concerns, the imposition of civil and criminal liability in appropriate circumstances, and a continuing transformation in the work of human rights advocates, all of which reinforces the insight that we must not think too simply about corporate decision-making, nor too simply about human rights law, nor in the end too simply about the received distinction between so-called public and so-called private law.

7

The Accountability of Multinationals for Human Rights Violations in European Law

OLIVIER DE SCHUTTER

Multinational enterprises (MNEs) domiciled in the Member States of the European Union may generally be said to benefit from complete impunity when they commit human rights violations abroad. This is especially true in the typical situation in which they invest in developing countries, either by extending their activities to those countries or by creating subsidiaries with a distinct legal personality, because of the lack of interest of local governments in the protection of human rights or, more often, because of their inability to ensure that protection effectively. The impunity of MNEs is a reality, whether these enterprises are directly responsible for human rights violations or whether their responsibility is more indirect, such as when their presence in certain jurisdictions facilitates or encourages human rights abuses by governments.[1]

The main focus of this Chapter is the progress achieved by the European Union law to date and how it might develop in future to put an end to this element of practical impunity. To a large extent, the problems faced by EU law are not specific to that legal order. EU law faces the same dilemmas as those with which lawyers working on the accountability of multinationals for human rights violations, at the intersection of international economic law and international human rights law, are so familiar. Should this increased accountability rely on the mechanisms of the

---

[1] This study focuses on the liability of multinationals, i.e. corporations the economic activities of which develop in different countries, either directly or by the creation of subsidiaries having a distinct legal personality but which are *de jure* or *de facto* under the control of the parent corporation. It should be emphasized, though, that, however difficult it may appear to impose on MNEs obligations in the field of human rights, the difficulties we face in that respect are even more insuperable when human rights violations appear in the course of economic activities developed in a number of States, when different corporations, at different stages of the production and marketing of a good, cooperate in the international division of labour. MNEs are, relatively speaking, easy targets for regulation, because of the centralized control the parent company exerts on a chain of activities; but the impunity of economic actors operating transnationally is even more difficult to challenge when there is no such central locus of control, and where the different entities are bound by exclusively contractual relationships.

market, for example by introducing ethical or social criteria in public procurement policies or by encouraging social labelling so as to facilitate the sanction by the consumers of unethical practices, or should legally binding solutions be preferred? If the latter, should we prefer civil liability, and thus privilege the objective of compensating the victims of human rights violations, or criminal liability, with its sometimes more efficient tools for repression by involving the state apparatus in the investigatory process? And what division of tasks should we favour, in this progress towards more accountability on the part of MNEs for human rights violations in foreign jurisdictions, between international law and municipal law? Should we confine international law to imposing on States a duty to protect the human rights of those whom the activity of the MNE affects, by regulating this activity? Or should international law directly impose obligations on the MNEs, as it already does, with respect to some international crimes, on individuals?[2] If this latter option is preferred, should we count on voluntary initiatives by the MNEs, albeit encouraged perhaps by the definition of large frames like, in the United Nations, the 'Global Compact' initiative or, in the European Union, the notion of 'Corporate Social Responsibility'? Or should we focus rather on harder norms of international law, imposing on MNEs obligations to respect human rights just as these obligations have been traditionally imposed on States?

We shall discover that not only the questions are familiar. The answers, too, point in the same direction: just like general public international law or the law of international organizations (e.g. the International Labour Organization or the Organization for Economic Cooperation and Development) European Union law is reluctant to impose overly strict requirements on multinational enterprises operating from within one of its Member States; except for a still vague emphasis on the voluntary contribution corporations should make towards 'a better society and a cleaner environment' as it appears in the definition of corporate social responsibility, a concept as promising for the future as it is underdeveloped in the present.[3] Control of the activities of MNEs in third countries is still essentially left to the States acting individually: the prisoner's dilemma situation in which this leaves us, in which no State dares to move forward out of fear that the enterprises will leave its national

---

[2] On the promises of this line, see the International Council on Human Rights Policy, _Beyond Voluntarism. Human Rights and the developing international legal obligations of companies_ (2002).

[3] 'Corporate social responsibility is essentially a concept whereby companies decide voluntarily to contribute to a better society and a cleaner environment. At a time when the European Union endeavours to identify its common values by adopting a Charter of Fundamental Rights, an increasing number of European companies recognise their social responsibility more and more clearly and consider it as part of their identity. This responsibility is expressed towards employees and more generally towards all the stakeholders affected by business and which in turn can influence its success' (Commission of the European Communities, Green paper: Promoting a European framework for corporate social responsibility (COM(2001) 366 final, 18.7.2001, para. 8). This definition of corporate social responsibility is essentially unchanged in the Communication from the Commission concerning Corporate Social Responsibility: A business contribution to Sustainable Development (COM(2002) 347 final, 2.7.2002), which built upon the reactions received on the presentation of the Green Paper.

territory once they feel the threat becomes too imminent to be ignored, is again an all too well known consequence of this state of matters, just compounded perhaps within the EU by the degree to which free movement of investments in capital has been achieved.

Before detailing this diagnosis and the possible avenues for overcoming its unsufficiencies, however, European Union law must be located in a more general context. The first part of this Chapter analyzes the two components of the regulative gap already alluded to: first, still very much indebted to its stato-centrist origins (international law as obliging *States*, its primary subjects) the international legal order fails to impose obligations directly on MNEs as such; secondly, the ability of individual States, acting separately, to regulate the activities of multinationals remains limited, because of 'the ability of multinationals to move capital between different countries, to create flexible structures, and exploit the legal fiction that subsidiaries are independent from their parents'.[4] The second part of this Chapter examines whether the European Convention on Human Rights, one of the remarkable features of which, indeed, is the extent to which it has imposed on its Contracting States an obligation to prevent violations committed by private parties, distinguishes itself from this general picture of public international law, including international human rights law. The answer, we shall see, is a disappointing one: beyond certain exceptional circumstances to which the activities of their MNEs abroad do not belong, the States Parties to the Convention are under no obligation to protect the fundamental rights of persons whose situation, perhaps, they may influence, but who live outside their 'jurisdiction', understood essentially as referring to the national territory of the Contracting States.

The following parts of this Chapter focus more specifically on the European Union. In Section 3, I locate the question of the accountability of multinationals in the broader framework of the attitude of the European Union towards the promotion of global labour standards, as it influences its trade and development co-operation policies. In Section 4, I detail under which conditions MNEs domiciled in the EU could be civilly liable for human rights violations outside the EU, committed either in the course of their activities or by their subsidiaries. In Section 5 the focus is on criminal liability, and on the respective roles of the EU and its Member States in adopting extra-territorial criminal legislation prohibiting certain violations of human rights. In Section 6, I comment on the voluntary contribution of MNEs to the promotion of human rights: corporate social responsibility, indeed, refers to voluntary initiatives by which corporations go beyond the legal requirements imposed upon them to meet the expectations of all the stakeholders, and some of these initiatives, especially the adoption of codes of conduct, may serve to improve the observance by the business community of fundamental rights. Finally, in Section 7, I comment briefly on one important lever which the EU Member States have at their disposal to encourage corporations fully to respect human rights: besides acting as

---

[4] Council on Human Rights Policy, *supra* note 2, at 12.

regulators, States act as economic actors on the market. Public procurement policies and public credits to exports, especially, could take better account of human rights concerns, and the EU may have a role to play in encouraging such inclusion by its Member States.

This Chapter is a study of the tools available in European Union law to ensure that multinational enterprises respect their human rights obligations. I focus on mechanisms, rather than on substantive norms. I discuss issues such as the the civil liability of multinationals domiciled in the EU for human rights violations committed abroad; the imposition of criminal liability on corporations in such a situation; the potential of codes of conduct and the notion of corporate social responsibility; and the linkage of access to export credits or public contracts to the human rights obligations of the companies applying for such credits or contracts. On the other hand, I do not discuss the extent of human rights obligations of corporations: for example, what should be considered the 'sphere of influence' of a corporation, in which it has to promote human rights, or which notion of complicity we should adhere to when a corporation is accused of encouraging, or even not denouncing, violations committed in the States where they invest. Although they are separated for the sake of this analysis, the two questions, procedural and substantive, are closely connected. For instance, it is obvious that the extent of the obligations which may be imposed on companies on the basis of a code of conduct they voluntarily adopt is larger than the extent of the obligations which may be imposed by criminal legislation targeting the same actors, especially if that legislation extends its geographical scope of application beyond the national territory of the State which adopts it, or even confers a universal jurisdiction to the courts of that State. This interrelationship will be explored, I hope, elsewhere.

1. THE IMPUNITY OF MULTINATIONAL ENTERPRISES

The reasons why violations by MNEs of internationally recognized human rights generally remain unpunished are relatively easy to comprehend.[5] International law is classicly addressed to States. Only in exceptional cases does it hold individuals directly responsible for violations. Even when international law does impose obligations on individuals directly, the liability of corporations will depend on the procedures set up by the States, in the absence of adequate institutional mechanisms in the international legal order for imposing such obligations on legal persons rather than natural persons (A). States, in principle, are under an obligation not only to respect the internationally protected human rights by which they agreed to abide,

---

[5] For a lucid analysis, see Joseph, 'Taming the Leviathans: Multinational Enterprises and Human Rights', 46 *N.I.L.R.* (1999), at 171–203. For an attempt to define the regime of the legal responsibility of corporations for human rights abuses which they commit or of which they are complicits, see Ratner, 'Corporations and Human Rights: A Theory of Legal Responsibility', 111 *Yale L.J.* (2001) at 443. See also N. Jägers, *Corporate Human Rights Obligations: In Search of Accountability* (2002), esp. chap. VI.

but also to protect these rights from violations which would be committed by private persons on whom they can exercise control (B). However, the international law on State responsibility does not support the assertion that all the acts of a State's nationals, even committed abroad, would be imputable to the State, because the jurisdiction of the State could extend to those acts under the active personality principle (C). On the other hand, the States in whose territory foreign corporations conduct their activities will often be unwilling to impose that these activities fully respect the human rights of the persons whom they affect, or will be unable to so do effectively (D). In sum, although international human rights law contains norms which could easily lend themselves to being imposed on private corporations, the enforcement mechanisms are still inadequate (E).

A. Individual Responsibility Under International Law

In the famous words of the International Military Tribunal of Nuremberg, which revived for the modern era the notion of direct responsibility of individuals under international law, 'Crimes against international law are committed by men, not by abstract entities, and only by punishing individuals who commit such crimes can the provisions of international law be enforced'.[6] But even in the restricted field of crimes against international law which may be committed by individuals who are then responsible directly under international law (genocide, crimes against humanity, and war crimes,[7] which together represent but a small subset of human rights violations) the enforcement mechanisms of international law have as yet reached not legal persons, but natural persons: 'men' indeed, 'not abstract entities'. Even the International Military Tribunal of Nuremberg, although it could declare an organization criminal,[8] which meant that membership of such an organization or

---

[6] International Military Tribunal for the Trial of Major War Criminals, judgment of 1 October 1946, repr. 41 *A.J.I.L.* (1947) 172, at 221. It is also as individuals acting in their private capacity, and not solely as agents of the State, that natural persons may commit international crimes. A. Clapman cites the following passage of the *Flick* case, a trial concerning the head of a group of industrialists found guilty of war crimes for employment of slave labour and spoliation of public and private property. The defendant, Friedrich Flick, did not belong to the apparatus of the Nazi State. The US Military Tribunal said in that circumstance: 'It is asserted that international law is a matter wholly outside the work, interest and knowledge of private individuals. The distinction is unsound. International law, as such, binds every citizen just as does ordinary municipal law. Acts judged criminal when done by an officer of the Government are criminal also when done by a private individual. . . . There is no justification for a limitation of responsibility to public officials' (Case 48, *Trial of Friedrich Flick and Five Others* [1947], 9 Law Rep. of the Trials of War Criminals 1, at 18, reproduced in 14 *International Law Rep.* (1947), at 266, and also cited by Clapham, 'The Question of Jurisdiction Under International Criminal Law Over Legal Persons: Lessons from the Rome Conference on an International Criminal Court', in M.T. Kamminga and S. Zia-Zarifi (eds), *Liability of Multinational Corporations under International Law* (2000) 139, at 166).

[7] See on the definitions of these crimes against international law the Statute of the International Criminal Court adopted on 17 July 1998 in Rome, Articles 6 to 8.

[8] Charter of the International Military Tribunal (Annex to the 8 August 1945 London Agreement establishing an ad hoc International Military Tribunal, 28 UNTS 284), Arts. 9 and 10.

financial support in knowledge of its criminal activities could lead to the conviction of an individual, only had jurisdiction over natural persons. Like the IMT itself, the various Allied tribunals created under Article 10 of the Control Council Law, although they did hold certain corporate officials criminally responsible for the acts of the company, still excluded finding the corporation as such, the 'instrumentality' of the individuals, criminally liable.[9]

The Rome Conference of the Summer of 1998, which would lead to the adoption of the Statute of the International Criminal Court, represents the latest attempt to move international criminal law in the direction of identifying criminal liability in legal persons. Although the draft statute presented at the beginning of the Rome Conference did provide that the International Criminal Court would have jurisdiction over legal persons 'when the crimes committed were committed on behalf of such legal persons or by their agencies or representatives',[10] this possibility was removed during the last stage of the negotiations. Under the Statute finally adopted, only natural persons may be tried before the ICC, although the crimes of which they may be convicted include those crimes committed 'by a group of persons acting with a common purpose'.[11] The final suggestion to confer to the Court jurisdiction over 'juridical persons' when the natural person charged with having committed genocide, a crime against humanity, or a war crime, was both 'in a position of control within the juridical person under the national law of the State where the juridical person was registered at the time the crime was committed' and was acting 'on behalf of and with the explicit consent of that juridical person and in the course of its activities', was not retained, not because of insuperable objections of principle, but rather because of the technical complexities raised by the suggested innovation and the time constraints the participants in the Conference were facing.[12]

Of course, the lack of an institutional mechanism in international human rights law authorizing legal persons other than States to be sued directly can by no means be interpreted as meaning that the international law of human rights does not at present impose obligations on legal persons, and in particular corporations. Indeed, even in the restricted field of international criminal law, there is no reason why the criminal liability of juridical persons should not be affirmed in the future, perhaps in 2009 when, seven years after the entry into force of the Statute, the Review Conference will have to decide on amendments to the Statute. This development

---

[9] The US Military Tribunal stated, in the *Flick* case, *supra* note 5, that 'the corporate defendant, Farben, is not before the bar of this Tribunal and cannot be subjected to criminal penalties in these proceedings. We have used the term Farben as descriptive of the instrumentality of cohesion in the name of which the enumerated acts...were committed. But corporations act through individuals...' see I.D. Seiderman, *Hierarchy in International Law: The Huam Rights Dimension* (2001), at 228.

[10] Article 23 para. 5 of the draft Statute (UN Doc. A/CONF.183/2/Add.1, at 49), cited by Clapham, *supra* note 6, at 143–4.   [11] Article 25(3)(d) of the Statute.

[12] Clapham, *supra* note 6, at 157. See, however, on the difficulties resulting during the drafting of the Rome Statute from the fact that 'the very principle of corporate criminal responsibility is not recognized in some domestic systems, and, in respect of those jurisdictions where such a principle is accepted, there is no commonly accepted means of application', Seiderman, *supra*, note 9, at 229.

would not be unprecedented in international criminal law: as A. Clapham reminds us,[13] the war trials held after the Second World War led to the conviction of certain German industrialists, notably the directors of I.G. Farben, whose criminal liability was based on the finding that *the company* had committed war crimes. And it was for purely jurisdictional reasons, rather than substantive ones, that the corporation I.G. Farben was not convicted as such by the US Military Tribunal in Nuremberg which convicted its directors.[14] It nevertheless remains true that, under international criminal law, the jurisdictional obstacle remains to this day. Should that obstacle be removed, it would still concern only a limited domain of the human rights internationally protected.

B. The Obligation of States to Protect Individuals under their Jurisdiction

Perhaps it may be requiring too much of international law, at the present stage of its development, to affirm the direct liability of corporations in the international legal order and institute the mechanisms adequate to impose it. In most cases where international law will impose on companies an obligation to respect the internationally recognized fundamental rights, it will do so *indirectly*, through the mediation of the international responsibility of the State. As a party to international treaties in the field of human rights or as bound, in any event, by the peremptory norms of international law[15] (which include the prohibition of slavery and slave trade, genocide, racial discrimination, apartheid, and torture[16]) States are

[13] See also Ratner, *supra* note 5, at 477–9 and Lippman, 'War Crimes Trials of German Industrialists: The "Other Schindlers"', 9 *Temp. In'l & Comp. L.J.* (1995), at 173.

[14] Clapham, *supra* note 6, at 166–71.

[15] According to Article 53 of the Vienna Convention on the Law of Treaties of 23 May 1969 (1155 UNTS, at 331), a norm has that status if it is a norm 'accepted and recognized by the international community of States as a whole as a norm from which no derogation is permitted and which can be modified only by a subsequent norm of general international law having the same character'. See esp. Wolfke, '*Jus Cogens* in International Law', 6 *Polish Yearbook of International Law* (1974), at 145; Simma and Alston, 'The Sources of Human Rights Law: Custom, Jus Cogens and General Principles', 12 *Australian YB of International Law* (1992), at 82; M. Raggazi, *The Concept of International Obligations* (1997); and I.D. Seiderman, *Hierarchy in International Law: The Human Rights Dimension* (2001).

[16] In the *Case Concerning Barcelona Traction, Light & Power Co. Ltd. (Belgium v. Spain)*, ICJ Reports (1970) 3, at 32, the International Court of Justice mentioned that the obligations *erga omnes* which 'are the concern of all States' include 'the outlawing of the act of aggression, and of genocide, as also from the principles and rules concerning the basic rights of the human person, including slavery and racial discrimination'. Although it is doubtful that all human rights impose obligations *erga omnes* on States, the prohibition of torture has certainly acquired the status of a peremptory norm of international law. See Human Rights Committee, General Comment no. 24 (52), UN Doc. CCPR/C/21/Rev.1/Add.6 (1994); International Criminal Tribunal for the Former Yugoslavia, *Prosecutor v. Furundzija*, 10 December 1998, Case no. IT-95-17/I-T, (1999) ILM 317, para. 153 ('Because of the importance of the value it protects, this principle [proscribing torture] has evolved into a peremptory norm or *jus cogens*, that is, a norm that enjoys a higher rank in the international hierarchy than treaty law and even "ordinary" customary rules'); *Regina v. Bow Street Metropolitan Stipendiary Magistrate and Others*, ex parte *Pinochet Ugarte (No. 3)* judgment by the

under an obligation, not only to *respect* the human rights binding upon them by abstaining from taking any action through their organs which could lead to a violation of these rights, but also to *protect* these rights from violations which could be committed by other private parties and would lead to the same practical effect for the individual victim. It sometimes happens that international treaties specifically affirm such an obligation, and they may even add that the States Parties must adopt measures against organizations or corporate entities which commit such acts which, if adopted by State organs, would constitute a violation by the State of its international obligations. A good example is the International Convention on the Elimination of All Forms of Racial Discrimination, whose Articles 2(1)(d) and 4(b) impose on the Contracting Parties an obligation to 'prohibit and bring to an end, by all appropriate means, including legislation as required by circumstances, racial discrimination by any persons, group or organisation', and an obligation to 'declare illegal and prohibit organisations . . . which promote and incite racial discrimination'.[17] But the ICERD is not isolated in that respect. The Convention against Torture,[18] the Convention on the Elimination of All Forms of Discrimination Against Women,[19] and the Convention on the Rights of the Child[20] all contain provisions obliging the States Parties to take measures against private parties whose activities could threaten the rights these instruments seek to guarantee. A last example, immediately relevant for corporate conduct, is that of the 1997 OECD Convention on Combating Bribery of Foreign Public Officials, Article 2 of which provides that 'Each Party shall take such measures as may be necessary, in accordance with its legal principles, to establish the liability of legal persons for the bribery of a foreign public official'.[21]

In all these situations, international law in effect imposes obligations indirectly on private parties, including legal persons, by imposing directly on the States, its primary subjects, an obligation to protect the rights of individuals from interference by others. Even without a specific provision relating to that obligation of the State in an international human rights treaty, however, it is today generally agreed

---

House of Lords of 24 March 1999, [1999] 2 W.L.R. 827, [2000] AC 147; Eur. Ct. H. R. (GC), *Al-Adsani v. United Kingdom* (Appl. no. 35763/97), judgment of 21 November 2001, para. 61. See also the sources cited in J. Crawford, *The International Law Commission's Articles on State Responsibility: Introduction, Text and Commentaries* (2002), at 246.

[17] International Convention on the Elimination of All Forms of Racial Discrimination, UNTS No. 195.   [18] See CAT, Art. 4.

[19] See CEDAW, Art. 2(e) (States Parties are under an obligation to 'take all appropriate measures to eliminate discrimination against women by any person, organisation or enterprise').

[20] See CRC, Arts. 2(2), 3(3), and 19(1).

[21] Art. 2 of the OECD Convention on Combating Bribery of Foreign Public Officials in International Business Transactions, 17 December 1997 thereby obliges States Parties to exercise jurisdiction in respect of bribery offences committed abroad by their nationals (see also Art. 4 of the Convention). See Joseph, *supra* note 5, at 184, and Nichols, 'Regulating Transnational Bribery in Times of Globalisation and Fragmentation', 24 *Yale Journ. of Int'l Law* (1999), at 257.

that what States may not do directly (infringing human rights they are bound to respect) they will not be authorized to do indirectly (by remaining passive in the face of comparable violations committed by private persons).

The consequences flowing from the essentially stato-centric character of public international law would therefore be lessened if the obligation of States under international law to protect internationally recognized human rights by regulating the activities of MNEs were fully respected: indeed, in its broadest understanding, the obligation of the States to protect the human rights they have undertaken to guarantee would include not only an obligation on the host States where MNEs develop their activities (usually by setting up a subsidiary having a distinct legal personality) to protect human rights on their own national territory, but also an obligation on the home State, of which the MNE has the nationality, to regulate its activity wherever it takes place, because of the effective control it may exercise on that company. Let us briefly consider this latter obligation, before examining the usefulness of affirming the former.

C. The Absence of an Obligation on Home States to Control their Nationals Abroad

Except in certain limited fields such as the prohibition of bribery[22], international law has been reluctant to impose such a far-reaching obligation as the one just stated on the home States of multinational enterprises. It is true that, in principle, the national of a State remains under the control of the State of which he is a national even after entering another State, although he then also falls under the jurisdiction of that other State.[23] It has been argued on that basis that, at least with respect to *jus cogens* norms, home States should be under an obligation to exercise that control to prohibit their nationals, whether real or corporate, from violating peremptory norms of international law even when abroad—the 'meaningfulness of *erga omnes* obligations', indeed, resting 'on the idea that state responsibility exists for the violation of any of those obligations which can be directly or indirectly traced to the acts or omissions of the state'.[24] According to this thesis, 'the conduct of the national is assimilated to that of the state itself by not seeking to prevent that conduct where the state had knowledge of it nor punish the national once the

---

[22] See *supra*, note 21.

[23] *Skirotes v. Florida*, 313 U.S. 69 (1941) (stating that the United States 'is not debarred by any rule of international law from governing the conduct of its own citizen upon the high seas or even in foreign countries' (Hughes, CJ)).

[24] See Sornarajah, 'Linking State Responsibility for Certain Harms Caused by Corporate Nationals Abroad to Civil Recourse in the Legal Systems of Home States', in C. Scott (ed.), *Torture as Tort: Comparative Perspectives on the Development of Transnational Human Rights Litigation* (2001), chap. 18, esp. at 502. For another argument in favour of that position, de Arechega and Tanzi, 'International State Responsibility', in M. Bedjaoui (ed.), *International Law: Achievements and Prospects* (1991), at 359, cited by M. Sornarajah.

harm was caused'.[25] In fact, such an obligation to control the national abroad may be seen as the correlative to the right of the State, under international law, to protect its nationals by exercising its diplomatic protection[26]—a rule whose practical operation has often been connected to the colonial enterprise and the need for the colonial powers to guarantee the foreign investments of their corporations, but which still seeks its counterpart in a postcolonial regime on State responsibility. This could be defended on two grounds. First, if a State claims a right to *protect* its nationals from injuries suffered in another State, must the home State not itself exercise *control* on its nationals abroad, insofar as the threat of the exercise of diplomatic protection diminishes, in effect, the control which may be exercised on those persons by the States which host their activities? Secondly, if a foreign corporation violates the rights of citizens of a State hosting its activities, should this State not be authorized to exercise protection of its own nationals (as a form of diplomatic protection) by invoking the responsibility of the home State of the corporation?

Such a thesis does not describe adequately the present status of the law of State responsibility. According to the International Law Commission's Articles on State Responsibility, 'The conduct of a person or group of persons shall be considered an act of a State under international law if the person or group of persons is in fact acting on the instructions of, or under the direction of control of, that State in carrying out the conduct' (Article 8). In other situations than those listed, the acts of private individuals, whether or not they are nationals of the State, will not be attributable to the State. Even when a private individual is 'highly dependent' on the State for, e.g., the subsidies granted by the State or other forms of support received from it, his/her acts will not for that sole reason be considered to be those of the State. This was the principle affirmed in the *Military and Paramilitary Activities in and against Nicaragua* case, where the International Court of Justice held with respect to the alleged responsibility of the United States for the violations of human rights and humanitarian norms by the *contras* that:

even the general control by the respondent State over a force with a high degree of dependency on it, would not in themselves mean, without further evidence, that the United States directed or enforced the perpetration of the acts contrary to human rights and humanitarian law

---

[25] Scott, 'Introduction', in Scott, *supra* note 24, at 21. M. Sornarajah defines his position slightly otherwise: according to him, State responsibility must be recognized in respect of violations of *jus cogens* principles in two situations: where a State 'knowingly permits its nationals to engage in violations of *jus cogens* principles whilst abroad', and where 'a State gives active assistance to those who are known to violate or are seen as capable of violating such *jus cogens* principles' (Sornarajah, *supra* note 24, at 504).

[26] F. Amerasinghe, *State Responsibility for Injuries to Aliens* (1965). After quoting from the *Mavromattis Palestine Concession Case*, 1924 PCIJ Series A, No. 2, at 12 (in which the Court said: 'By taking up the case of one of its subjects and by resorting to diplomatic action or international judicial proceedings on his behalf, a State is in reality asserting its own rights—its right to ensure, in the person of its subjects, respect for the rules of international law'), M. Sornarajah comments: 'The converse of this is that a developing state should be able to assert its rights of protection of its nationals when an alien causes damage in its state and its nationals are not provided relief in the home state of the alien in which his assets are situated and to which he has repatriated profits of his operations in the host state' (Sornarajah, *supra* note 24, at 497).

alleged by the applicant State. Such acts would well be committed by members of the contras without the control of the United States. For this conduct to give rise to legal responsibility of the United States, it would in principle have to be proved that that State had effective control of the military or paramilitary operations in the course of which the alleged violations were committed.[27]

With respect to the operation of MNEs in foreign countries and the violations it commits there of international human rights, this lack of imputability to the State of the acts of private individuals, including legal persons, not acting on its instructions or under its direction or control could only be met (compensated for) by insisting that the positive obligation of a State, under international human rights law, to 'protect' these rights against the acts of private parties should extend beyond borders of the national territory, to all situations to which the State may indeed extend its protection without violating the principles of international law, including the principle of comity with other nations. These situations would include those where the threath to human rights emanates from its own nationals, whose activities, indeed, the State has the competence to control under the active personality principle. However desirable this may be, it does not represent the contemporary extension of a State's international responsibility.

D. The Obligation on Host States to Regulate the Conduct of MNEs Operating within their National Territory

Should one then turn to the other branch on the alternative, and be satisfied with the obligation on the host State in which the MNE conducts its activities to protect internationally recognized human rights under its jurisdiction? The difficulty here is not in the theoretical existence of such an international legal obligation, quite apart from the consideration that not all international treaties in the field of human rights have benefited the quasi universal ratification of the Convention on the Rights of the Child, for example, a fact for which the growth of customary international law does not wholly compensate. The problem is really elsewhere. It lies in the incentives the States may have fully to respect these obligations, not only by the adoption of legislative measures, but also by investing sufficient means in their effective monitoring and implementation.

First, one cannot of course count on the host State to ensure that human rights will be respected on its territory if the State itself is the prime violator of these rights, and when the violations committed by the MNE either are imposed by the host State (whose domestic laws, for instance, require discriminatory practices in recruitment), or consist in the support the MNE lends to those violations by the State (in which case the MNE may be said to be complicit in the governmental abuses). Secondly, even when the host State is not deliberately engaged on a path of

---

[27] *Military and Paramilitary Activities in and against Nicaragua (Nicaragua v. United States of America), Judgment of 27 June 1986 (Merits)*, ICJ Reports (1986), para. 115.

human rights violations, its authorities may lack the means or the political will to enforce its domestic legislation which, for instance, imposes certain health and safety conditions in the working environment, prohibits discrimination based on union membership, or would protect, in theory, against threats to physical integrity by private security services of the firms operating within the national territory.[28] In a situation where many developing states urgently need foreign investment as a condition for economic growth, 'some governments may have neither the interest nor the resources to monitor corporate behavior'.[29] Foreign Direct Investment (FDI) represented half the level of official development aid in 1990; ten years later, it represented three times that level. This gives an idea of the growing dependency of developing countries on FDI: not only is FDI a condition of economic growth and of the enhancement of the export capacities of the developing countries in a context where they often have to face very important debt burdens, but moreover, as it involves a long-term relationship between the parent company and the subsidiary it controls, it may favour technology transfer and develop human resources.[30] This dependency in fact places the developing States in a prisoner's dilemma, in which, whilst *all* States may have preferred to be presented with a different set of options, no State *individually* wishes to impose too heavy a burden on the corporations investing in its territory, out of fear that these corporations might choose to shift their activites to less restrictive locations.[31] One might think that the developing States which can attract foreign investment by their natural resources in the oil or mining industries would constitute an exception, as potential investors have nowhere to go except where such resources can be found; but these States are in other ways even more dependent on the presence of MNEs on their territory, because of the technology they require to have access to and to exploit these mineral resources.

The competition which exists between developing States seeking to attract foreign investments is a difficulty not to be underestimated. Although it would be extremely costly for *each State individually* to take steps towards the imposition of highly requiring standards on MNEs operating within its territory, it would benefit *all the developing States*, not only to impose on MNEs globally uniform standards but

---

[28] Joseph, *supra* note 5, at 176–7; J.A. Paul and J. Garred, *Making Corporations Accountable: A background paper for the United Nations Financing for Development Process* (2000); K. De Feyter, *World Development Law* (2000), at 182.   [29] Ratner, *supra* note 5, at 462.

[30] Commission of the European Communities, Communication from the Commission to the European Parliament, the Council, the Economic and Social Committee and the Committee of the Regions, 'Towards a global partnership for sustainable development', COM(2002) 82 final, Brussels, 13.2.2002, at 5 and 18.

[31] According to S.R. Ratner, 'Host states have adjusted domestic laws to make them more attractive to corporations, handed over tracts of land to *de facto* control by corporations, or simply turned a blind eye to violations of domestic law' (Ratner, *supra* note 5, at 460). The notion of a 'global "prisoner's dilemma"' is put forward by Benvenisti, 'Exit and Voice in the Age of Globalization', 98 *Mich. L. Rev.* (1999), at 167. See also van Wezel Stone, 'Labor and the Global Economy: Four Approaches to Transnational Labour Regulation', 16 *Mich. J. of Int'l L.* (1995), at 987; and Lippman, 'Transnational Corporations and Repressive Regimes: The Ethical Dilemma', 15 *Calif. Western Int'l L. J.* (1985), at 542.

also to subject them to effective surveillance: indeed, the imposition of such uniform standards would make developing States less vulnerable to the threat by an MNE that it will leave the territory if the local regulations become more demanding or costly to comply with. However, this competition between developing States is not the only problem. Another, no less serious, obstacle to effective regulation of MNEs by the host States is that, when these are developing States, they are also in competition with developed States, especially the Member States of the OECD, in globalized markets in which, in some cases, the goods they produce are competitive precisely because of the lack of stringent environmental, social, or ethical standards, facilitating low-cost production. It is well known that developing States opposed increased recognition by the WTO of environmental, health, and social concerns, as advocated by the international NGO movement and by the European Union, because of their fear that the imposition of such standards—at least if defined at the level of those prevalent in developed countries—might endanger the comparative advantage they enjoy.[32] To these developing States, the insistence on production processes which respect labour rights, environmental standards, and the interests of the local communities, may be resented as economic protectionism veiled behind the rhetoric of universal human rights. This view may be criticized as relying on a narrow definition of human development, focused exclusively on economic growth rather than, as Amartya Sen has most eloquently advocated, on an expansion of the basic freedoms of the individual.[33] It may also be denounced as adopting an overly short-term perspective on the protection of basic rights such as the right to education (as opposed to child labour[34]), the right to health (as opposed to environmental pollution), or the right to fair remuneration (as opposed to the competitive advantage gained by low salaries in developing countries) which, indeed, although costly in the short term, may appear in the longer term as highly rewarding investments.[35] Whatever the usefulness of these critiques in the global discussion on the universalization of ethical, social, and environmental standards, they do not address the immediate needs of developing States which have no choice but to seek to attract foreign investment in their territory, either for macro-economic reasons or because this is the only way for them to gain access to the updated technology necessary for the exploitation of their natural resources.

We are thus confronted with a void: international law does not directly reach the corporate actor; it does not impose an obligation on the home State to control

[32] De Feyter, *supra* note 28, at 99. On this debate, see O. Mehmet, E. Mendes, and R. Sinding, *Towards a Fair Global Market. Avoiding a new slave trade* (1999); Thwaites, 'La "clause sociale": Protection des droits humains ou protectionnisme économique?', in J.D. Thwaites (ed.), *La mondialisation, Origines, développement et effets* (2000), at 261; Scherrer, 'The Pros and Cons of International Labour Standards', in N. Malanowski (ed.), *Social and Environmental Standards in International Trade Agreements: Links, Implementations and Prospects* (1997). [33] A. Sen, *Development as Freedom* (1999).

[34] See e.g. De Feyter, 'The prohibition of child labour as a social clause in multilateral trade agreements', in E. Verhellen (ed.), *Monitoring Children's Rights* (1996).

[35] See esp. UNDP, *Human Rights and Human Development: World Report on Human Development 2000* (2000).

the activities of corporations of its 'nationality' abroad, not even when these activities are conducted directly, without any creation of a subsidiary company or by sub-contracting; finally, even when international law imposes on the State hosting the investment to protect its population from human rights violations, and thus to oblige all actors operating within its national territory to respect these rights, the host State will typically lack the incentive or the resources to adopt effective measures in that respect.

One could have hoped that the European Convention on Human Rights would have offered a remedy to that situation. Indeed, perhaps in no other inter-national or regional instrument for the protection of human rights has an obliga-tion to protect been extended more fully than in the Convention, imposing on the Contracting States far-reaching duties to adopt measures to prevent violations committed by private parties. However, despite its remarkable achievement in this respect, the European Convention on Human Rights presents a limitation which makes it essentially useless as a tool to compensate for the deficiencies of general public international law with regard to the imposition of human rights obligations on corporations operating transnationally. Indeed, although it has been interpreted for over twenty years as obliging its Contracting States not only to abstain from violating the rights and freedoms it recognizes but also to adopt measures to protect these rights and freedoms from violations committed by others, it by no means derogates from the classical framework of public international law, with the limitation I have just emphasized: although the States Parties to the Convention must control private individuals acting under their jurisdiction, when these individuals appear to threaten the rights of others with whom they interact they are under no obligation to control their nationals operating outside the national territory.

2. THE EUROPEAN CONVENTION ON HUMAN RIGHTS

A. The 'Essentially Territorial' Notion of Jurisdiction

In an inadmissibility decision of 12 December 2001, the Grand Chamber of the European Court of Human Rights unanimously rejected the application of citizens of the Federal Republic of Yougoslavia, who had been injured or had lost relatives in the bombing of the Serbian Radio and Television (RTS) buildings in Belgrade, on 23 April 1999, during the air strikes campaign of the NATO forces which lasted from March to June 1999. Notwithstanding the wording of Article 1 of the Con-vention,[36] the applicants submitted that the impugned acts of the respondent States, which were located either in the FRY or in their own territories but producing

---

[36] According to which 'The High Contracting Parties shall secure to everyone *within their jurisdiction* the rights and freedoms defined in Section I of [the] Convention' (emphasis added).

effects in the FRY, brought them and their deceased relatives within the jurisdiction of those States. The Court rejected that presentation. It held that:

the case-law of the Court demonstrates that its recognition of the exercise of extra-territorial jurisdiction by a Contracting State is exceptional: it has done so when the respondent State, through the effective control of the relevant territory and its inhabitants abroad as a consequence of military occupation or through the consent, invitation or acquiescence of the Government of that territory, exercises all or some of the public powers normally to be exercised by that Government.[37]

In this view, 'jurisdiction' is seen as the exercise of powers normally at the disposal of the government over a particular geographical area. Although the European Court of Human Rights states that this 'geographical' understanding of the notion of jurisdiction may be extended in exceptional cases recognized in customary international law or in treaties,[38] and although it presents its judgment as interpreting the Convention in conformity with general public international law,[39] its identification of the imputability of certain situations to the Contracting States is in fact more restrictive than what general public international law would imply—not considering, at least, the fact (heavily insisted upon by the European Court) that the European Convention on Human Rights is a *regional* instrument for the protection of human rights, constituting a specifically *European* public order.[40] The generally accepted rules of public international law on the scope of State responsibility consider as an act of the State the conduct of any State organ acting in that capacity;[41] this rule, as recognized by the International Court of Justice, has a customary character.[42] The International Law Commission observed in 1975 that 'Such conduct [by a State organ] is and remains an act of the State to which the organ belongs, by virtue of draft articles 5 et seq[43] which set no territorial limitation on the attribution of the State of the acts of its organs'.[44] No developments since in its codificatory enterprise suggest that this view would now be invalid.

[37] Eur. Ct. H.R. (GC), *Bankovic et al. v. Belgium and 16 other States* (Appl. no. 52207/99), dec. of 12 December 2001, para. 71.

[38] See para. 73 of the *Bankovic* decision: 'the Court notes that other recognised instances of the extra-territorial exercise of jurisdiction by a State include cases involving the activities of its diplomatic or consular agents abroad and on board craft and vessels registered in, or flying the flag of, that State. In these specific situations, customary international law and treaty provisions have recognised the extra-territorial exercise of jurisdiction by the relevant State.'

[39] See para. 57 of the decision and, on the relationship between the *Bankovic* decision and general public international law, N. Riou, *L'Europe des libertés*, January 2002, no. 7, at 18; and Cohen-Jonathan, 'La territorialisation de la juridiction de la Cour européenne des droits de l'homme', *Revue trimestrielle des droits de l'homme* (2002), at 1069, esp. at 1074–82.   [40] See para. 80 of the *Bankovic* decision.

[41] See Article 4 ('Conduct of organs of a State') of the ILC's Articles on State Responsibility.

[42] *Difference Relating to Immunity from Legal Process of a Special Rapporteur of the Commission on Human Rights*, ICJ Reports (1999), 62, at 87, para. 62.

[43] These articles correspond to Articles 4 et seq. of the Articles on State Responsibility adopted by the International Law Commission on 9 August 2001, constituting chap. II ('Attribution of conduct to a State') of the final text.   [44] 2 *Yearbook of the ILC* (1975), at 83.

Perhaps the most convincing argument in favour of the decision of the *Bankovic* Court, therefore, is not to be found in the compatibility this holding maintains between the European Convention on Human Rights and general public international law, but rather in the rules specific to the Convention and, more precisely, in the intent of the Contracting States when they inserted the expression 'everyone within their jurisdiction' in Article 1 of the Convention, to designate *vis-à-vis* whom the States were undertaking to secure the rights and freedoms set forth in that instrument. Although, admittedly, this expression replaced the more restrictive initial draft provision ('the Member States shall undertake to ensure to *all persons residing within their territories*') with an amended formulation adopted with the intention to 'widen as far as possible the categories of persons who are to benefit by the guarantees contained in the Convention', this expansion was never meant to extend to persons found beyond the territories of the Contracting States: the preparatory works show beyond any doubt that the Convention was drafted to benefit all persons residing, living, travelling through, or remaining either legally or illegally on their territories, but it was not intended to impose obligations on States Parties beyond that closed circle of persons.[45]

Whichever the firmness of its basis in the preparatory work of the Convention, it may nevertheless be asserted that the inadmissibility decision in the case of *Bankovic* constitutes a retreat from the previous case-law, both of the European Commission on Human Rights and of the Court itself.[46] The European Commission of Human Rights has always stipulated that when agents of the States (not only diplomatic or consular agents[47] but also armed forces) act outside the national territory, 'not only do they remain under its jurisdiction when abroad but [they also] bring any other persons or property "within the jurisdiction" of that State, to the extent that they exercise authority over such persons or property. Insofar as, by their acts or

---

[45] On the debates surrounding the wording of the provision which has now become Article 1 of the European Convention on Human Rights, see Lawson, 'The Concept of Jurisdiction and Extra-territorial Acts of State', in *Liber Amicorum Peter Kooijmans* (2001). In this excellent study, the author (a counsel for the applicants in *Bankovic*, but writing before the admissibility decision was known in that case) arrives, however, at a different conclusion than my own on the lessons to be drawn from the genesis of Article 1 ECHR.

[46] See generally on this question, Decaux, 'Le territoire des droits de l'homme', in *Liber amicorum Marc-André Eissen* (1995), at 65; O. De Schutter, *Fonction de juger et droits fondamentaux* (1999), at 315–18; Giakoumopoulos, 'L'étranger en "zone internationale" et les garanties de la Convention européenne des droits de l'homme', in *Frontières du droit, Frontières des droits*, (1993), at 211; E. Wyler, *L'illicite et la condition des personnes privées, La responsabilité internationale en droit coutumier et dans la Convention européenne des droits de l'homme* (1995), at 105–8.

[47] See already Eur. Commiss. H.R., *X v F.R.G.*, decision of 26 September 1965, 8 *Yearbook of the ECHR* (1965), at 158 (recognizing that the Federal Republic of Germany may violate the Convention thorough the acts adopted by its Embassy in Morocco, *vis-à-vis* German nationals). This hypothesis in which the acts of State organs may be imputed to that State even if occuring outside the national territory and even if that territory is not covered by the Convention is not put into question by the *Bankovic* decision: the acts of consular or diplomatic authorities are, as we have seen, one of the exceptions recognized by para. 73 of the decision.

omissions, they affect such persons or property, the responsibility of the State is engaged.'[48] This case-law has been adopted by the Court from the Commission in *Drozd and Janousek v. France and Spain.* In that case, the European Court of Human Rights had to decide whether the situation complained of, the alleged violation of Article 6 of the Convention (fair trial) by the Andorran courts at a time when Andorra was not covered by the Convention, was imputable to either France or Spain, because of the very specific status of Andorra in public international law and because its relationships with Spain or France may not be assimilated to relationships between two sovereign States. The Court held in its judgment of 26 June 1992 that in the situation complained of the applicants were not 'within the jurisdiction' of either France or Spain. Indeed, while agreeing with the applicants that 'The term "jurisdiction" is not limited to the national territory of the High Contracting Parties; their responsibility can be involved because of acts of their authorities producing effects outside their own territory'[49], the Court noted in paragraph 96 of its judgment that:

Whilst it is true that judges from France and Spain sit as members of Andorran courts, they do not do so in their capacity as French or Spanish judges. Those courts, in particular the Tribunal de Corts, exercise their functions in an autonomous manner; their judgments are not subject to supervision by the authorities of France or Spain. Moreover, there is nothing in the case-file which suggests that the French or Spanish authorities attempted to interfere with the applicants' trial . . .

This passage from the *Drozd and Janousek* judgment[50] illustrates that, at that time at least, the European Court of Human Rights fully agreed with the pre-existing case-law of the European Commission according to which, even when they act outside the national territory of the State party, the official organs of a Contracting Party to the Convention may engage the responsibility of that State.[51] It is only

---

[48] Eur. Commiss. H.R., *Cyprus v. Turkey* (Appl. no. 6780/74 and 6950/75), decision of 26 May 1975, 2 *D.R.*, at 136. See also, *inter alia*, Eur. Commiss. H.R., *Ilse Hess v. the United Kingdom* (Appl. no. 6231/73), decision of 28 May 1975, 2 *D.R.*, at 73 (concerning the detention of the husband of the applicant in the Spandau Prison in Berlin, under the joint authority of the four allied powers (France, the USSR, the United Kingdom, and the USA), the Commission notes: 'a State is under certain circumstances responsible under the Convention for the actions of its authorities outside its territory'). See also the other examples cited in the *Drozd and Janousek* judgment of 26 June 1992, at para. 91 (see *infra*).

[49] Eur. Ct. H.R., *Drozd and Janousek v. France and Spain* judgment of 26 June 1992, Series A no. 240, para. 91.

[50] The *Drozd and Janousek* doctrine was confirmed with respect to the Principality of Andorra: Eur. Commiss. H.R , *Albert Llovera v. Andorra and subsidiarily France and Spain* (Appl. no. 18582/91, decision of 30 November 1992; and Eur. Commiss. H.R., *Francisco Iribarne v. France* (Appl. no. 16462/90), decision of 19 January 1994 (see also the judgment of the European Court of Human Rights in that case, of 24 October 1995, Series A no. 325-C). This doctrine was also extended to violations alleged to have taken place in the Principalty of Monaco: Eur. Commiss. H.R., *Jacques Meignan v. France* (Appl. no. 21392/93), decision of 28 June 1993.

[51] This is already implicated by the very structure of the judgment, in the part relating to the preliminary objections raised by the French and Spanish governments. The Court considers first whether the

because the judges from France and Spain sitting in the Andorran courts did not do so 'in their capacity as French or Spanish judges' and because the French or Spanish authorities did not attempt to 'interfere with the applicants' trial' that these applicants were not considered to be, *ratione personae*, under the jurisdiction of either France or Spain. In fact, in at least two cases still pending before the European Court of Human Rights at the time of writing, the Court has declared admissible applications directed against States Parties to the Convention for acts of their organs committed not only outside their national territory but also outside a territory otherwise covered by the Convention, in situations where they were not exercising total *de facto* control of a particular geographical zone, as in the *Loizidou* case, with respect to the occupation of Northern Cyprus by the armed forces of Turkey:[52] in the case of *Öcalan*, the leader of the PKK who was arrested and abducted from Kenya and from there brought to Turkey where he now faces trial, the Court did not in principle exclude that the circumstances of the initial deprivation of liberty of Öcalan and of his abduction could trigger the international responsibility of Turkey;[53] in the case of *Issa and others*, the Court declared admissible an application by Iraqi sheperds complaining of the acts of Turkish forces in Northern Iraq.[54] The *Bankovic* decision recognizes the tension with these previous cases, where it says that 'in any event the merits of those cases remain to be decided'.[55] Respectfully, this may be considered a strange way to draw a convincing distinction.

B. The Link with the Obligation to Prevent Violations by Private Actors

After the inadmissibility decision in *Bankovic*, the European Court of Human Rights may be said to have adopted a position retreating from general public international law on the basis of a professed fidelity to the original understanding of the Convention. It may also be safely asserted that this position, far from being dictated by its previous case-law, in fact constitutes an unavowed overruling of its own precedents. It would be vain, if facile, to speculate on the motives which could have led the Court in that direction. Far more interesting (and, for the purposes of this study, relevant) is the link between this position of the Court and its important case-law obliging on the States Parties to the Convention to protect the rights of individuals

applicants, when tried by the Andorran courts, could be said to fall under the jurisdiction *ratione loci* of France or Spain, a question which the Court answers in the negative; it then considers whether, *alternatively*, the applicants fall under the jurisdiction *ratione personae* of either of the defending States. The very separation of these two questions illustrates that the notion of 'jurisdiction', as it appears in Article 1 of the Convention, may not be reduced to the national territory of the States parties to the Convention.

[52] Eur. Ct. H.R., *Loizidou v. Turkey*, judgment of 18 Dec. 1996, *Rep.* 1996-I, at 2235–6, §56. See also Eur. Ct. H.R., *L. Christodoulidou v. Turkey* (Appl. no. 16085/90), admissibility decision of 7 December 1999.

[53] Eur. Ct. H.R. (1st sect.), *Abdullah Öcalan v. Turquie* (Appl. no. 46221/99), admissibility decision of 14 December 2000.

[54] Eur. Ct. H.R., *Issa and others v. Turkey* (Appl. no. 31821/96), decision of 30 May 2000.

[55] Para. 82.

under their jurisdiction, i.e. to take measures to prevent other private parties from violating the rights and freedoms of the individual which the State organs may not violate directly. The 'all-or-nothing' approach adopted by the *Bankovic* decision with respect to the notion of 'jurisdiction' may have been guided by the idea that, because the obligation of the Contracting States goes beyond a simple obligation to 'respect' the rights and freedoms set forth in the Convention and extends to an obligation to 'protect' these rights and freedoms from the threats of other private individuals, it would be unworkable to consider that the 'jurisdiction' of a State, defining the set of situations in which the State is bound by the Convention, extends not only beyond its national borders but also beyond those situations in which the State exercises a control as effective as that which it exercises on its national territory, for example[56] in cases of military occupation. In finding that the 'jurisdiction' of Turkey extends to the Northern part of Cyprus, occupied since 1974 by the Turkish military forces, the Court noted that, notwithstanding the establishment of the 'Turkish Republic of Northern Cyprus', Turkey could be held responsible for the acts of the authorities of this entity. The effective control over the territory implied, in the view of the Court, that the acts of the 'TRNC' could be imputed to Turkey:

It is not necessary to determine whether . . . Turkey actually exercises detailed control over the policies and actions of the authorities of the 'TRNC'. It is obvious from the large number of troops engaged in active duties in northern Cyprus that her army exercises effective overall control over that part of the island. *Such control, according to the relevant test and in the circumstances of the case, entails her responsibility for the policies and actions of the 'TRNC'.* Those affected by such policies or actions therefore come within the 'jurisdiction' of Turkey for the purposes of Article 1 of the Convention. Her obligation to secure to the applicant the rights and freedoms set out in the Convention therefore extends to the northern part of Cyprus.[57]

This may be analogized with the acts of private parties under the jurisdiction of a State Party to the Convention. 'Jurisdiction' must mean 'effective control', because a State bound by the Convention must 'secure' the rights and freedoms of all persons under its jurisdiction, not only by not violating these rights or freedoms directly through the activities of its organs, but also by not remaining passive in the face of violations committed by private persons whom the State, therefore, should

---

[56] It is also obvious that, if the notion of 'jurisdiction' were to be restricted to the national territory of the State, defined as the geographical area on which the State *declares* that it exercises its sovereignty, it would be possible for a State to exclude certain situations from the scope of applicability of the Convention simply by defining as 'extra-territorial' certain zones, even when such zones are under the effective control of the State. See e.g. Eur. Ct. H.R., *Amuur v. France* judgment of 25 June 1996, note De Schutter, 'Privation de liberté et maintien en zone internationale', 89 *Rev. dr. étr.* (1996), at 341. At § 52 of its *Amuur* judgment, the Court notes that 'even though the applicants were not in France within the meaning of the Ordinance of 2 November 1945, holding them in the international zone of Paris-Orly Airport made them subject to French law. Despite its name, the international zone does not have extraterritorial status'. The effective control exercised by the French authorities on the applicants, Somali asylum-seekers detained in the so-called 'international zone' of a French international airport, therefore places them under French 'jurisdiction', notwithstanding the definition by French law of that zone as 'extraterritorial'.

[57] Eur. Ct. H.R., *Loizidou v. Turkey*, judgment of 18 Dec. 1996, *Rep.* 1996-I, at 2235–6, § 56.

effectively coerce. The analogy remains limited however, because, when—as under the Convention—a State is bound by an obligation to prevent,[58] it does not mean that, *as such*, the conduct of private individuals will be imputable to the State: indeed, it is only *in combination with a failure to act* by the State organs (the legislator has failed to make certain conduct punishable, the executive has failed to prosecute, the judge has failed to grant reparation) that the responsibility of the State will be affirmed.[59] The European Convention on Human Rights remains in that respect within the orthodoxy of international law, which does not consider that may *directly* be attributed to the State, and perhaps trigger its international responsibility, all the acts by private persons which the State may have prevented. It is one thing for the State organs to be obliged to prevent certain events from occuring under the jurisdiction of the State; it would be quite another to impute directly to the State—whether or not these preventive measures have indeed been adopted—acts committed by private individuals under its jurisdiction, and to find the State internationally responsible simply because the preventive measures it has adopted have failed to achieve the intended result.

The latter regime would move international law in a direction which, ultimately, may have the dangerous consequence of obliging a State to exercise a much more extensive control on events occuring under his jurisdiction than is now usually the case.[60] As explained in the Commentaries of the International Law Commission's codification of a list of Articles on State Responsibility, although such a large notion of imputability to the State could have been theoretically imagined, this approach is rejected in international law, 'both with a view to limiting responsibility to conduct which engages the State as an organization, and also so as to recognize the autonomy of persons acting on their own account and not at the instigation of a public authority'.[61] Therefore the general regime in international law (leaving aside certain rules concerning more specific situations which do not lend themselves to being easily summarized) is that particular conduct may be attributed to the State either (1) when it constitutes the conduct of a person or entity which, according to the

---

[58] The notion of an obligation to prevent was defined in Article 23 of the Draft Articles on State Responsibility provisionally adopted by the International Law Commission on first reading (1999). The Articles on State Responsibility adopted by the International Law Commission in 2001 do not include, unlike the preceding drafts, a typology of the international obligations of States, such a classification being considered unnecessarily complicated and doctrinal, and entailing limited consequences. However, Article 14 of the Articles adopted, which deals with the extension in time of the breach of an international obligation, does allude to the specificity of the obligation to prevent. This specificity consists in that, when it is bound by such an obligation, the State must prevent a particular event from occuring, whichever the means chosen by the State to that effect: see Art. 14(3).

[59] See e.g. Eur. Ct. H.R., *A. v. the United Kingdom*, judgment of 23 September 1998, *Reports of Judgments and Decisions* 1998-VI, § 22; and De Schutter, 'L'intervention de l'Etat dans les relations familiales: droit au respect de la vie familiale et droit à la protection de l'enfant dans la jurisprudence de la Cour européenne des droits de l'homme', *Rev. trim. dr. fam.* (1999), at 427.

[60] See generally A. Clapham, *Human Rights in the Private Sphere* (1993).

[61] Crawford, *supra* note 16, at 91.

internal law of the State, is an organ of a State, or (2) when the conduct is that of a person or entity exercising powers constitutive of certain elements of the governmental authority which have been delegated to that person or entity by the State, or (3) when the conduct is that of certain private persons or groups of persons who are 'in fact acting on the instructions of, or under the direction or control of, that State in carrying out the conduct'.[62]

C. The Absence of an Obligation of Contracting States to Control the Activities of their Nationals Abroad

As a result of the restriction imposed on the extra-territorial scope of the Convention in *Bankovic*, it would clearly be impossible today to rely on that instrument to oblige a Contracting State to exercise control over the conduct of its nationals acting outside the national territory, or over the conduct abroad of enterprises incorporated within the concerned State or having established in that State their headquarters, even when these persons' conduct leads to the violation of the fundamental rights of those with whom they interact.

Prior to *Bankovic*, such a hope could have been entertained. The European Commission on Human Rights has on at least one occasion noted that not only the 'acts' by the public authorities of a State party abroad, but even their 'omissions' could lead to a finding of violation of the Convention[63]—although it appears, from the very case in which that statement was made, that the conduct of a private individual occuring outside the national territory would trigger the international responsibility of the Contracting State only insofar as it could be proven that the individual acted under the instructions, direction, or control of the State.[64] Perhaps more importantly, some members both of the Court and of the Commission had made clear in the pre-*Bankovic* era that the responsibility of the State under the Convention could be based not only on the exercise of 'enforcement jurisdiction' abroad by a State Party to the Convention (i.e. the acts of State agents abroad or of

---

[62] The latter formulation is that of Article 8 of the Articles on State Responsibility adopted by the International Law Commission on 9 August 2001. Chapter II of these Articles constitutes the latest and most authoritative statement on the situations in which conduct may be attributed to the State in general public international law.

[63] Eur. Commiss. H.R., *Stocké v. Germany* (Appl. no. 11755/85), Rep. of 12 October 1989 (Series A, 1999, at 24), § 166.

[64] This condition was not satisfied in *Stocké*. The applicant, a German national who had fled his home country, where he was suspected of tax offences, to France, was induced under a false pretext by a private police informer, Mr Köster, to board a plane which ended up landing in Germany, where he was arrested. Neither the Commission nor the Court, however, considered it established that the private informant acted under the direction of the German police, rather than upon his own initiative. The Court considered in § 54 of its judgment 'that it has not been established that the cooperation between the German authorities and Mr Köster extended to unlawful activities abroad. Accordingly, it does not deem it necessary to examine . . . whether, if it had been otherwise, the applicant's arrest in the Federal Republic of Germany would have violated the Convention' (Eur. Ct. H.R., *Stocké v. Germany*, judgment of 19 March 1991, Series A no. 199, § 52).

private persons acting under the instruction, direction, or control of the State), but also on the exercise of 'prescriptive jurisdiction' (i.e. the exercise by a State of its power to apply its regulations to persons or activities outside its own national territory),[65] even in cases where the alleged violation would have resulted from an unwillingness to act rather than from the adoption of a particular legislation. This appears from certain isolated opinions formulated in the case of *Drozd and Janousek*, on which I have already relied. In that case, the European Court of Human Rights alluded to the fact that, if the French and Spanish magistrates sitting the Andorran courts had been acting 'in their capacity as French or Spanish judges', the applicants (who complained about the conditions in which they were convicted by the Andorran courts) would be under the 'jurisdiction' of either France or Spain (indeed, probably of both States jointly). On the other hand it clearly did *not* consider sufficient for the situation complained of to fall under the 'jurisdiction' of France (in the meaning of Article 1 of the Convention) that France could have influenced the norms under which the applicants were convicted. In a joint dissenting opinion, however, five judges of the Court[66] quoted approvingly from the dissenting opinion of J. Frowein, one of the most eminent members of the Commission, in whose view

France's responsibility could [only] be excluded if France had no real power to guarantee observance of the rights set out in the Convention (no. 6231/73, *Ilse Hess v. the United Kingdom*, decision of 28 May 1975, DR 2, pp. 72–75). As its competence to legislate and its appointment of judges show, France does have the power to ensure that the Convention is respected.

Considering the unchallenged rule according to which the State may impose obligations on its nationals even when they are abroad (active personality principle of jurisdiction), such an opinion would have had potentially far-reading consequences, making it an obligation for the States Parties to the Convention not only to guarantee the rights and freedoms of the Convention to all the persons within their national territory, but also to adopt legislation obliging their nationals abroad not to act in violation of the rights and freedoms listed in the Convention, for example by committing torture, restricting the freedom of association rights of their employees, or committing sexual abuses. This view, however, has not prevailed. Under *Bankovic*, the Contracting States do not owe the benefit of the European Convention on Human Rights to persons found outside their national territory,

---

[65] On this distinction, see Scott, 'Translating Torture into Transnational Tort: Conceptual Divides in the Debate on Corporate Accountability for Human Rights Harms', in Scott, *supra* note 24, at 45, 54.

[66] Judges Pettiti, Valticos, Lopes Rocha, approved by judges Walsh and Spielmann. Laying the accent on the participation of France and Spain in the administration of the entity of Andorra, the dissenting opinion concludes: 'It must thus be considered that the [French and Spanish Co-Princes of the Principality of Andorra] should even now use their authority and influence in order to give effect in Andorra to the fundamental principles of the European Convention on Human Rights, which has the force of law or even overrides national law in their own countries, and more generally is a basic element of the rule of law in Europe'.

even where the source of the violation of which these persons are victims is located within that territory: in a situation where the violation of rights protected under the Convention were committed abroad, say, by the subsidiary of a parent corporation domiciled in a State Party to the Convention, but with the parent corporation exercising a direct control on the activities of its subsidiary, a literal reading of *Bankovic* would imply that the victims of this violation could not trigger the international responsibility of that State, even though it could easily have regulated the activities of the parent company; even though, in other words, the author of the violation clearly is under the 'jurisdiction' of the State.

D. A Two-Tiered Approach to the Relationship between 'Jurisdiction' and National Territory

The consequences of the position defended by Jochen Frowein within the European Commission of Human Rights may be far-reaching. Such extreme consequences, however, would not necessarily have followed from a different holding in *Bankovic*, more in line with the previous case-law of the Convention. Rather than adopting the 'all-or-nothing' approach of the notion of 'jurisdiction' which characterizes that case, it would have been perfectly defensible to settle for a two-tiered solution according to which, whilst the States Parties to the Convention would have been under an obligation to *protect* the Convention rights and freedoms of all persons on their national territory, they would only be obliged to *respect* those rights and freedoms when acting, through their organs, outside the national territory. This would have meant that, whether they acted within the national territory or abroad, the organs of the States would remain under an obligation to respect the Convention, but that their obligation to adopt positive measures to prevent certain violations from occuring, when these violations have their source in the acts of private parties, would only be imposed in situations where they exercise effective control, i.e. in situations either located on their national territory or over which (as Turkey does in Northern Cyprus) it exercises a *de facto* control of equivalent scope. In this system, the national territory would serve to ground a *presumption of effective control* by the Contracting State.[67] But the notion of effective control is only useful when one has to decide on the extent of the obligation of a State to take measures to protect individuals from the acts of other private parties: no 'effective control' is required when all that is required of the State is not to violate the rights and freedoms of the Convention through the acts of its organs.

The main advantage of such a regime of extraterritoriality of the Convention, based on this two-tiered distinction between the obligation to 'respect' (an obligation *not to interfere with* the rights protected under the Convention) which would be imposed on the organs of the Contracting State wherever they act, and the obligation to 'protect' (an obligation to *take measures* effectively to prevent violations of the

---

[67] On such a presumption, see Ch. de Visscher, *Les effectivités du droit international public* (1967), at 119 and 157; Lenoble, 'Responsabilité internationale et contrôle territorial', *R.B.D.I.* (1981–1982), at 95.

Convention having their immediate source in the acts of private parties) which would only extend to situations in which the State may effectively exercise control, i.e. its own territory or the geographical zones over which the State exercises comparable authority, would therefore be to justify limited extraterritorial applicability of the Convention, whilst avoiding imposing on the Contracting States obligations with which they will not be able to comply.

The case of *Al-Adsani v. the United Kingdom* serves as an illustration of the usefulness of such a distinction, precisely for the sake of proposing a realistic approach to the extraterritoriality of the European Convention on Human Rights.[68] In this case the applicant, who had both British and Kuwaiti nationality, claimed to have been tortured by an influential Sheikh related to the Emir of Kuwait, and by Kuwaiti state officials. He had instituted civil proceedings in England but, because of the immunity granted to the Kuwaiti government from civil suit, had failed to obtain compensation against the Sheikh and the Government of Kuwait in respect of injury to his physical and mental health caused by these acts of torture. In his application lodged against the United Kingdom, Mr Al-Adsani alleged a violation of Article 3 of the Convention: according to him, the United Kingdom had failed to secure his right not to be tortured. The Court rejected the claim:

> The applicant does not contend that the alleged torture took place within the jurisdiction of the United Kingdom or that the United Kingdom authorities had any causal connection with its occurrence. In these circumstances, it cannot be said that the High Contracting Party was under a duty to provide a civil remedy to the applicant in respect of torture allegedly carried out by the Kuwaiti authorities.[69]

Leaving aside the question of the immunity of the foreign State which will arise each time compensation is sought from a foreign government[70] (as in *Al-Adsani*) it would be theoretically imaginable to oblige the States Parties to the Convention to offer a judicial remedy to all their nationals claiming to have suffered from a violation of the rights and freedoms guaranteed to them by the Convention, wherever that violation occurs. However, this would mean obliging those States to adopt extraterritorial legislation, on the basis of the passive personality principle (legislation prohibiting certain acts when the victim is a national), when this remains the most contested basis on which extraterritorial criminal legislation by a State may be justified under international law,[71] and when the question of whether States may

---

[68] Eur. Ct. H. R. (GC), *Al-Adsani v. the United Kingdom* (Appl. no. 35763/97), judgment of 21 November 2001. On the developments within English courts of the *Al-Adsani* litigation, see Byers, 'Al-Adsani v. Government of Kuwait and others', *British Yearbook of International Law* (1996), at 67. For a commentary on the outcome of the case, Zwanenburg, 'Het EVRM, staatsimmuniteit en jus cogens', 27 *NJCM-Bull.* (2002) 6, at 760.   [69] *Al-Adsani*, § 40.

[70] On this question, see Kloth, 'Immunities and the right of access to court under the European Convention on Human Rights', 27 *E.L.Rev.* (2002), at 33.

[71] See H. Steiner and Ph. Alston (eds), *International Human Rights in Context* (2000), at 1133 (citing the American Law Institute, *Restatement (Third), The Foreign Relations Law of the United States*, 1987, sect. 402). The 'passive personality principle' is defined in the Restatement as 'prescribing with respect to

authorize their courts to exercise their jurisdiction in actions claiming damages in respect to serious crimes of international law committed outside the territory of the forum State has proven to be so divisive at the Hague Conference on Private International Law.[72] Moreover, this would have the effect of imposing on the Contracting States an obligation to *remedy* a violation of the Convention rights which they are, in fact, not in a position to *prevent* from occuring. Affirming such an obligation could create the mistaken impression that the duty of the States under the Convention is, rather than not to violate the rights and freedoms they are bound to respect, simply to offer a form of compensation when such violations do occur. And such compensation is not even certain to be obtained, if the defendant (author of the violation for which the victim seeks a remedy) cannot be found on the territory of the forum State, and the judgement thus has to be given *in absentia*. Perhaps, despite these objections, the worst violatins of human rights, those which, universally condemned, are violations of *jus cogens* norms, should still be proscribed by extraterritorial legislation, opening a remedy to the victim either when the victim is a national of the forum state (passive personality principle) or whichever his nationality (universal jurisdiction) even when the author of the violation is not found in the forum state. However, this would be unworkable with respect to the whole set of rights protected under the European Convention on Human Rights.

In the two preceding parts of this Chapter I have sought to explain why there existed a regulative gap with respect to imposing on MNEs obligations to respect human rights, and why, regarding the European States bound by the European Convention on Human Rights, this instrument has proved unable to fill this gap: although they are the home States of many multinationals operating outside Europe, the States Parties to the European Convention on Human Rights are neither under an obligation to control the activities of their multinationals operating abroad (if any violations of the Convention occur in the course of these activities, they will be considered to fall outside the 'jurisdiction' of the States parties, in the meaning of Article 1 of the Convention) nor are they under an incentive to do so. As to the States in which multinationals invest, whether or not, under international law, they should protect the human rights of those affected by the acts of the MNEs on their territory, they will more often not be in a position to do so, even when they are not, themselves, the primary violators of those rights. In the absence of enforceable norms of international law directly imposing obligations on MNEs, therefore, their impunity remains essentially unchallenged.

---

acts committed outside a state by a non-national where the victim was a national'. See e.g. Article 689-1 of the French Criminal Code (*code de procédure pénale*), according to which any foreigner having committed a crime outside the French territory may be prosecuted and judged according to the French criminal legislation when the victim is of French nationality.

[72] Perhaps I may simply refer to Van Schaak, 'In defense of civil redress: the domestic enforcement of human rights norms in the context of the proposed Hague judgments convention', *Harvard Int'l L. J.* (2001), at 141.

3. THE EUROPEAN UNION AND HUMAN RIGHTS
IN THIRD COUNTRIES

Although neither the European Union nor the European Community has been given an explicit competence to fulfil fundamental rights, except in rather specific settings,[73] EU law does occupy a particularly advantageous position, which justifies seeking to rely on it to put an end to this state of practical impunity. A first advantage is too obvious and well known to require emphasis. A distinct feature of European Community law, which sets it apart from general public international law and may justify the (perhaps somewhat overblown) statement by the European Court of Justice that 'the Community constitutes a new order of international law for the benefit of which the states have limited their sovereign rights, albeit within limited fields, and the subjects of which comprise not only Member States but also their nationals',[74] resides in the combination of the doctrine of the direct effect of EC law and of the referral mechanism which, under Article 234 EC, in fact obliges the national jurisdictions to submit to the interpretation of the requirements of EC law by the European Court of Justice, by creating a direct channel of communication between the national courts of the Member States and the European Court of Justice.[75] The significance to us of this specificity of the legal order of the European Union cannot be overstated: in contrast to most international treaties, the European treaties not only confer rights on private individuals and impose obligations on them, but they do so *directly*, without having to rely on the fidelity with which the States (under the jurisdiction of which these individuals are situated) respect their international obligations.

Another advantage is more worthy of emphasis, because it is more recent and bears a more direct link to the topic of this study. It is that, at an accelerated pace since a few years, the Member States of the European Union and the institutions of the EU have adopted a number of initiatives by which they demonstrate their attachment to certain values in the social, environmental, and ethical fields and their intent to ground on these values the further stages of the construction of the European Union. Although the proclamation of the Charter of Fundamental Rights of the European Union on 7 December 2000[76] may be the best known example of that evolution, away from the initial goal restricted to economic integration and towards an integration driven by the pursuit in common of certain shared values,

---

[73] See generally Weiler and Fries, 'A Human Rights Policy for the European Community and Union: The Question of Competences', in Ph. Alston, M. Bustelo, and J. Heenan (eds.), *The EU and Human Rights* (1999), at 147.

[74] Case 26/62, *Van Gend en Loos v. Nederlandse Administratie der Belastingen*, [1963] ECR 3, 12.

[75] See also, under Title VI TEU, Art. 35 §5 (defining the conditions under which a referral may be made to the European Court of Justice). However, the decisions and framework decisions which are to be adopted under that Title of the Treaty of the European Union do not produce direct effects (see Art. 34 § 2(b) and (c)). See Monjal, 'Le droit dérivé de l'Union européenne en quête d'identité, à propos de la première décision-cadre du Conseil', *R.T.D.E.* (2001), at 335. [76] *OJ* 2000 C 364/1.

two other manifestations of this trend, of this new identity which the Union is seeking for itself, may be insisted upon. A first manifestation is the growing role of the values of human rights and democratization in the commercial and development cooperation policies of the European Union.[77] A second manifestation is the insistance on the responsibilities of corporations with respect to their environment, their employees, their clients, and the collectivity as a whole, which the concept of 'corporate social responsibility' purports to summarize.[78]

A. The Promotion of Human Rights, in particular Core Labour Standards, in the EU Trade and Development Cooperation Policies

I will devote little space to the first of these two developments which is, indeed, less directly related to the topic of this study. Of course, if third States, and especially developing countries, are given incentives to better respect human rights (in particular, the core labour standards) this may in time diminish the chances of MNEs disregarding these rights when operating in these countries, and it will reduce the risk that MNEs will make themselves complicit in human rights abuses, committed either by the host government or, with the passive tolerance of the government, by the MNEs' local sub-contractors. The link between the accountability of MNEs for human rights violations and the improvement of the record of the host State in the field of human rights would remain, in any event, an indirect one.

My second reason for devoting less space to the commercial and development cooperation policies of the European Union, although these policies do list human rights among their objectives, has to do with the substantive content of these policies. Indeed, these policies appear to be hostage to the fear regularly expressed by developing States that if a link were to be created between trade and fundamental rights, in particular social standards, it might be abused for protectionist purposes. This fear, as yet, has constituted the single most important obstacle to the introduction of social concerns in the agenda of the WTO. The following passage of the 1996 Singapore WTO Ministerial Declaration, in effect operating a clear division of tasks between the WTO and the ILO, the former concerning itself with free trade, the latter entrusted with the promotion of labour standards, clearly expresses this

---

[77] See generally Simma, Aschenbrenner, and Schulte, 'Human Rights Considerations in the Development Co-operation Activities of the EC'; and Riedel and Martin, 'Human Rights Clauses in External Agreements of the EC', both in Ph. Alston, M. Bustelo, and J. Heenan (eds.), *supra* note 73, at 571 and 723; M. Bulterman, *Human Rights in the Treaty Relations of the European Community, Real Virtues or Virtual Reality?*, Antwerpen-Groningen-Oxford, Intersentia-Hart, 2001. And European Commission, *Communication from the Commission to the Council and the European Parliament: The European Union's role in promoting human rights and democratisation in third countries*, COM(2001) 252 final, 8 May 2001.

[78] See esp. European Commission, *Communication from the Commission concerning Corporate Social Responsibility: A business contribution to Sustainable Development*, COM(2002) 347 final, Brussels, 2 July 2002. On this theme, see recently Gatto, 'The European Union and Corporate Social Responsibility: Can the EU Contribute to the Accountability of Multinational Enterprises for Human Rights?', 32 *Working Paper, K.U. Leuven, Faculty of Law, Institute for International Law* (2002), 97 pages.

difficulty where it states, in words which the Council of the European Union would repeat practically word by word three years later:[79]

We renew our commitment to the observance of internationally recognised core labour standards. The International Labour Organization (ILO) is the competent body to set and deal with these standards, and we affirm our support for its work in promoting them. We believe that economic growth and development fostered by increased trade and further trade liberalization contribute to the promotion of these standards. We reject the use of labour standards for protectionist purposes, and agree that the comparative advantage of countries, particularly low-wage developing countries, must in no way be put into question. In this regard, we note that the WTO and ILO Secretariats will continue their existing collaboration.

This fear can be met, to some extent, by progressing towards universally agreed definitions of the content of the core labour standards and of their precise requirements. The Copenhagen Declaration on Social Development and its accompanying Programme of Action, adopted on 12 March 1995 at the conclusion of the World Summit for Social Development, as well as, especially, the adoption on 18 June 1998 by the International Labour Conference of the Declaration on Fundamental Principles and Rights at Work, constitute important steps in that direction, insofar as they identify authoritatively the core labour standards of universal applicability.[80] The identification of such standards does not create the link between liberalization of trade and respect for labour standards which the EU, in particular, had been calling for since the initial Conference of Marrakech creating the WTO.[81] The two issues continue to be dealt with separately; a sanctions-based approach to the respect of the core labour standards, which would lead to imposing trade barriers against products originating from countries failing to meet these standards, is now unanimously rejected. And, although studies by the OECD have demonstrated that stronger labour standards improve efficiency and lead to faster economic growth, and have not damaged the export performances of the countries having

---

[79] See the Council Conclusions of October 1999 on trade and labour, adopted in preparation of the third WTO Ministerial Conference.

[80] In the Programme of Action adopted at the 1995 Copenhagen World Summit for Social Development, governments committed themselves to 'safeguarding and promoting respect for basic workers' rights, including the prohibition of forced labour and child labour, freedom of association and the right to organise and bargain collectively, equal remuneration for men and women for work of equal value, and non-discrimination in employment, fully implementing the conventions of the International Labour Organisation (ILO) in the case of States parties to those conventions, and taking into account the principles embodied in those conventions in the case of those countries that are not States parties to thus achieve truly sustained economic growth and sustainable development'. The Declaration on Fundamental Principles and Rights at Work, adopted by the International Labour Conference on 18 June 1998, identifies as the four core labour standards: freedom of association and the effective recognition of the right to collective bargaining; the elimination of all forms of forced or compulsory labour; the effective abolition of child labour; and the elimination of discrimination in respect of employment and occupation.

[81] On the position of the EU, see European Commission, Communication from the Commission to the Council, the European Parliament and the Economic and Social Committee, 'Promoting Core Labour Standards and Improving Social Governance in the Context of Globalisation', COM(2001) 416 final, Brussels, 18.7.2001.

adopted them,[82] it is considered nevertheless that the improvement of the core labour standards should result from a choice by the concerned State, rather than be imposed on it by the threath of commercial sanctions.

However, the stated rejection of a 'sanctions-based approach' does not seem to exclude the development of certain incentives, encouraging the adoption and effective implementation of the core labour standards by the developing countries with whom the EC enters into cooperation agreements. Since 1992, the agreements concluded between the EC and third countries are required to include a clause defining human rights as an essential element. In the 23 June 2000 Cotonou Agreement, which has taken the succession of the previously existing Lomé Agreements between the EC and the ACP States, the Parties 'reaffirm their commitment to the internationally recognised core labour standards, as defined by the relevant ILO Conventions, and in particular the freedom of association and the right to collective bargaining, the abolition of forced labour, the elimination of the worst forms of child labour and non-discrimination in respect of employment' (Article 50(1)). But this commitment translates into an undertaking by the parties to cooperate with a view to the promotion of core labour standards, *inter alia*, by exchange of information, education and awareness-raising programmes, enforcement of existing national legislation and strengthening of existing legislation (Article 50(2)), whilst 'The Parties agree that labour standards should not be used for protectionist trade purposes' (Article 50(3)).

The Community Generalised System of Preferences (GSP) scheme is another example of the rejection of a sanctions-based approach combined with the institution of a mechanism encouraging developing countries to adopt the core labour standards set universally. Under the GSP scheme, initially promoted by the UNCTAD after its creation in 1964, industrialized countries grant autonomous and non-reciprocal trade preferences to all developing countries. The EC implemented its own scheme in 1971, after the GATT Contracting Parties agreed on an 'enabling clause' allowing for an exception to the principle of the most-favoured-nation treatment in favour of developing countries, thus facilitating a form of positive discrimination in favour of developing countries. The current regime is the product of important evolutions since the original system was set up. One of the most remarkable of these evolutions is a change in the notion of development itself, which is not limited to economic growth, but should include the respect and improvement of environmental standards and fundamental social rights, an idea which is captured by the notion of 'sustainable development'. This results in the distinction of two different levels in the Regulations implementing the GSP scheme: alongside the 'general arrangements', which provide basic trade preferences aiming at the traditional objectives of economic development, with more or less important reductions of the duty rates according to the category to which a product belongs (from the

---

[82] Two OECD studies on International Trade and Core Labour Standards have been completed, in 1996 and in 2000 respectively.

most sensitive products to the least sensitive ones), and duty-free access for almost all the products originating from the least developed countries, other arrangements provide for incentives favouring the respect for fundamental social rights and the protection of the environment. Since 1995, countries which respect these environmental and social standards are rewarded by the granting of additional preferences.[83] Thus, under Article 14(2) of Regulation 2501/2001 of 10 December 2001, countries must prove that they comply with ILO Conventions Nos. 29 and 105 on forced labour, 87 on the freedom of association, 98 concerning the right to organize and to bargain collectively, Nos. 100 and 111 on non-discrimination in respect to employment and occupation, and No. 138 on child labour, to qualify under the social policy incentive clause.[84] Not only must the national legislation incorporate 'the substance' of these conventions; this legislation must also be 'effectively applied'. The countries which satisfy these conditions may obtain increases in preferential treatment,[85] but the request is only granted after an assessment by the European Commission not only on the regulatory measures adopted by the requesting country to satisfy these social standards, but also on the effective implementation of these standards and the monitoring procedures provided in the country. The examination of the request is preceded by the publication of a notice in the *Official Journal of the European Communities*, making it possible for all interested parties to make their views known in writing.[86]

The Community GSP scheme also provides for the possibility of temporary withdrawal of preferences, in the face of certain clearly unacceptable practices

[83] Until the entry into force of the current Regulation (covering the period from 1 January 2002 to 31 December 2004) the provisions relating to these incentives appeared under Title II (Articles 8–21) of the Council Regulation (EC) No 2820/98 of 21 December 1998, which entered into force on 1 July 1999 (Council Regulation (EC) No 2820/98 of 21 December 1998, OJ 1998 L 357/1, last amended by Regulation (EC) No 416/2001, OJ 2001 L 60/43); they now appear under Title III (Articles 14–20 (labour standards) and 21–24 (environmental standards)) of Council Regulation (EC) No 2501/2001 of 10 December 2001 (Council Regulation (EC) No 2501/2001 of 10 December 2001 applying a scheme of generalized tariff preferences for the period from 1 January 2002 to 31 December 2004, OJ 2001 L 346/1).

[84] This list is longer than the list of ILO instruments mentioned in Article 11 of Regulation No. 2820/98, which only mentioned ILO Conventions Nos. 87 on the freedom of association, 98 concerning the right to organize and to bargain collectively, and 138 on child labour. The new Regulation thus brings the special incentive arrangements into line with the concept of 'fair labour standards', as adopted at the level of the ILO. See Commission of the European Communities, Proposal for a Council Regulation applying a scheme of generalised tariff preferences for the period 1 January 2002 to 31 December 2004, COM(2001) 293 final, Brussels, 12.6.2001, para. 32 of the Explanatory Memorandum; and the position of the Commission as expressed in the Communication from the Commission to the Council, the European Parliament and the Economic and Social Committee, 'Promoting Core Labour Standards and Improving Social Governance in the Context of Globalisation', COM(2001) 416 final, Brussels, 18.7.2001, at 22.

[85] Special incentive arrangements are also provided for the protection of the environment. Under Article 21 of Regulation No. 2501/2001, they may be granted to the countries which apply the international standards on the sustainable management of tropical forests.

[86] At the beginning of 2002, only the Republic of Moldova appeared to benefit from the special incentives with respect to labour rights. See the Annex to Regulation No. 2501/2001.

among which the practice of any form of slavery or forced labour, serious and systematic violation of the freedom of association, the right to collective bargaining, or the principle of non-discrimination in respect of employment and occupation, the use of child labour, or the export of goods made by prison labour (Article 26).[87] When the Commission or a Member State receives information that may justify temporary withdrawal, the Commission may begin an official investigation on the alleged practices, if sufficient grounds exist for such an investigation (Articles 27 to 29). The investigation is confidential. However, the interested parties are invited to contact the Commission and their cooperation in the investigation is sought; the Commission seeks to collect all the available information in the most impartial way, including by consulting the findings of the ILO and economic actors operating within the country concerned by the investigation. The investigation leads either to a termination of the proceedings or to the submission of a proposal to the Council recommending the withdrawal of the preferential treatment; the Council decides on the proposal within thirty days, by a qualified majority (Article 29(4)). In the case of Burma, the systematic character of the violations in the form of forced labour and child labour led the EC to withdraw the additional preferential rights after an observation period of ten years.[88]

The combination of an official rhetoric denying that the violation of core labour standards may justify the imposition of commercial sanctions with a practice which, simply by resorting to 'incentives', both positive and negative, in fact does reward or penalize developing countries on the basis of their willingness to improve their social and environmental standards at home,[89] demonstrates the acuteness of the dilemma. The central question is whether developing countries may seek to ameliorate the position of their export products on the global markets by diminishing—or, more often, by not raising—the social and environmental standards at home, or not. There are at least three difficulties in this respect.

The first difficulty is in the identification of the labour standards which may be universally imposed. The reference to the 1998 ILO Declaration on Fundamental Principles and Rights at Work, even apart from the fact that it refers neither to environmental standards nor, more broadly, to ethical standards, may not wholly be up to the task, because, for example, it would be compatible with those principles for

[87] Here again, the list of the violations of core labour standards which may lead to the temporary withdrawal of preferential arrangements provided for in the GSP Community scheme is expanded in Regulation No. 2501/2001. Comp. Art. 26 of this Regulation with the corresponding provision (Art. 22) of Regulation No. 2820/98.

[88] See Council Regulation (EC) No. 552/97 of 24 March 1997 temporarily withdrawing access to generalized tariff preferences from the Union of Myanmar, OJ 1997 L 85/8.

[89] According to the Council Conclusions of October 1999 on trade and labour, the EU encourages 'further positive measures building on the incentives already applied by the EU for the enhancement of labour rights, in particular through additional improvements in market access for developing country exports, and not through trade-restrictive measures'. The distinction between a positive discrimination approach benefiting countries respecting labour rights and a sanctions-based approach appears rather formalistic.

a country to keep the wages at very low levels, even below minimal subsistence levels, to maintain the competitiveness of its products without making efforts to improve the productivity of its fabrication processes.[90] On the other hand, the heroic efforts to present the imposition of core labour standards in the agenda of trade negotiations as not constituting 'a protectionist policy on the part of the industrialized countries', because these are values which are genuinely sought after by these countries quite apart from the economic consequences of their promotion at a universal level, will not seem convincing to the impartial observer.[91]

The second difficulty is that there may be tension between insisting on the idea that respect for core labour standards represents an investment in future development and, in fact, an asset in globalized competitive markets, and at the same time using incentives (a euphemism to designate commercial sanctions) to coerce developing countries into the adoption and implementation of these standards. The following comment by the Economic and Social Committee expresses the dilemma explicitly, where the promotion of better labour standards is presented as being to the advantage of the developing countries themselves, as if they were to be rescued from their temptation, or that of their governments, to seek only immediate advantages in the growth of exports, whilst neglecting the future:

World trade must bring benefits for all. Every effort must be made to avoid fierce competition between developing countries using comparative advantages solely based on low wages and exploitation. In many cases, they cannot compete with the production quality of the industrialised countries. In order for the poorer countries to escape from this trap, the foundations must be laid for higher productivity and innovative capacity—and this begins with people in the workplace. Infringements of association and collective bargaining rights, along with child labour and forced labour, are not really comparative advantages for the developing countries.[92]

A third difficulty is that, while it insists on universal respect for core labour standards, the European Union remains largely passive in the face of the activities of multinational enterprises over which it may exercise control (because they are incorporated in a Member State of the Union or have their headquarters in a Member State) although one of the reasons why developing countries may maintain

---

[90] Of course, it could be argued that 'Association and collective bargaining rights enable workers to secure wage levels commensurate with the productivity of their labour. They do not eliminate worldwide differences in workers' incomes, but the gap may gradually be closed. To this extent a comparative advantage remains' (Opinion of the Economic and Social Committee on 'Human Rights in the Workplace' (2001/C 260/14), OJ 2001 C 260/79, 3.2.5).

[91] See the Opinion of the Economic and Social Committee on 'Human Rights in the Workplace' (2001/C 260/14), OJ 2001 C 260/79, 3.3.2: 'In the overall context of such a negotiating package it is clear that the core labour standards are not and must not be seen by developing countries as a protectionist policy on the part of the industrialised countries. If the European Union is making respect of the core labour standards a key part of its core political agenda, then it must obviously pursue a policy based on these principles and implement them itself and in its external relations.'

[92] Opinion of the Economic and Social Committee on 'Human Rights in the Workplace' (2001/C 260/14), 3.2.2.

labour and environmental standards at a low level is precisely to attract foreign direct investment on their territory. Indeed, the promotion by the EU of core labour standards in the context of globalization, which led the Commission of the European Communities to adopt an important communication on that subject on 18 July 2001, explicitly relies on a territoriality-based understanding of the protection of fundamental social rights. MNEs, whichever their State of origin, are to be regulated by the host States in which they invest, rather than by their home States of origin: the EU support of the initiatives by host States should encourage the implementation of national labour legislation 'that adapts the international consensus of the ILO conventions to local realities, thus facilitating ratification and implementation', and it should encourage the institution of 'realistic monitoring mechanisms likely to strengthen compliance with the legislation by domestic employers and MNEs'.[93]

On this third question, another route could be chosen. As the Commission of the European Communities recognizes in its recent communication 'Towards a global partnership for sustainable development', it should be part of any sustainable development strategy of the European Union—this 'sustainability' refers, in this context, to a development not reduced to economic growth, but which includes respect for the environment and core labour standards—to 'encourage European companies' commitment to corporate social responsibility'.[94] Indeed, the influence of multinational enterprises can be such that they should be invited to play a part in 'increasing respect for human rights world-wide' and in using 'their often considerable influence within a developing country to support rather than undermine that country's own efforts to achieve sustainable development'.[95] The assignment of a responsibility to multinational enterprises with such a role should be replaced in its larger framework: that of the emergence of a new discourse on the relationship of economic actors with their immediate environment and with the collectivity as a whole.

It is in this broader context, therefore, that the trend towards better accountability of MNEs should be understood. Indeed, one way to conceptualize the link between

---

[93] Communication from the Commission to the Council, the European Parliament, and the Economic and Social Committee, 'Promoting Core Labour Standards and Improving Social Governance in the Context of Globalisation', COM(2001) 416 final, Brussels, 18.7.2001, at 18.

[94] Commission of the European Communities, Communication from the Commission to the European Parliament, the Council, the Economic and Social Committee, and the Committee of the Regions, 'Towards a global partnership for sustainable development', COM(2002) 82 final, Brussels, 13.2.2002, at 9.

[95] Commission of the European Communities, Commission from the Commission to the Council and the European Parliament, 'The European Union's role in promoting human rights and democratisation in third countries', COM(2001) 252 final, Brussels, 8.5.2001, at 3. The communication goes on: 'It is in the interest of those companies [to contribute to an increasing respect for human rights]: stable countries and free societies are also the best places to invest and to do business. For that reason, the promotion of human rights and democracy is also an essential complement to the EU's support for multilateral trade and investment facilitation'.

the strong support of the EU for a universal respect of the core labour rights (which translates into both its trade policy and its development cooperation policy) on one hand, and the initiatives it may take in controlling MNEs operating from a Member State of the EU, is by analyzing the trend towards enhancing the accountability of MNEs as a way for the EU to accept its responsibilities in the promotion on human rights in third countries without making itself vulnerable to accusations of disguised protectionism or, even worse, of punishing the populations of third countries whose governments commit human rights abuses. With that view in mind I now turn to the notion of corporate social responsibility, the 'external dimension' of which offers a translation of the need for greater accountability of MNEs for human rights violations committed abroad. The notion imposes responsibilities on multinational actors operating, in coordinated fashion, under different jurisdictions, of both EU States and developing States. By focusing on private actors and their economic activities, rather than on States and their national territories, it facilitates the move beyond the dilemma, either not to contribute to the promotion of human rights (and especially labour standards) or to enter a spiral of incentive schemes which will be vulnerable to the accusation of protectionism.

B. Corporate Social Responsibility

The notion of corporate social responsibility (CSR) is defined by the European Commission as 'a concept whereby companies decide *voluntarily* to contribute to a better society and a cleaner environment', and thus go beyond legal compliance, for instance, to use more environmentally responsible technologies or to improve working conditions of management–employee relations. Why should the companies do so? Because CSR, we are told, improves competitiveness. Indeed, the positive impact of socially responsible practices is both direct (impact on productivity) and indirect (impact on business reputation):

Positive direct results may for example derive from a better working environment, which leads to a more committed and productive workforce or from efficient use of natural resources. In addition, indirect effects result from the growing attention of consumers and investors, which will increase their opportunities on the markets. Inversely there can sometimes be a negative impact on a company's reputation due to criticism of business practices. This can affect the core assets of a company, such as its brands and image.[96]

---

[96] Commission of the European Communities, Green Paper 'Promoting a European Framework for Corporate Social Responsibility', COM(2001) 366 final, Brussels, 18.7.2001, at 7. See also Commission of the European Communities, *Communication from the Commission concerning Corporate Social Responsibility: A business contribution to Sustainable Development*, COM(2002) 347 final, Brussels, 2 July 2002, at 6 and 9–10 (developing the same arguments). This latter Communication, however, confesses a certain uncertainty about the importance of CSR to 'long-term business success': the document notes that, although it has 'been argued that opportunities and advantages for enterprises stemming from complying with international social and environmental conventions, norms or "soft law" instruments can outweigh costs', and although 'most businesses support the assumption of a positive impact of CSR on competitiveness, particularly in the long run', 'they are however not able to quantify this effect' (at 9).

This does not mean, however, that any form of regulation or other form of public intervention would be made superfluous if more businesses were to turn to socially responsible practices, either because they would be enlightened about where their best interests lie, or because they are driven to such practices by the forces of the market, especially consumers and investors. Indeed, for the 'indirect' positive economic impact of CSR to occur, certain mechanisms should be put in place to facilitate the market incentives rewarding CSR. In many cases, except for the most flagrant situations where a company is publicly denounced for its practices, the ethical choices by consumers will only be possible if certain indicators help them make these choices. These indicators, sparing the public a very time-consuming search on which products it is 'ethical' to purchase, may take the form of social or ethical labelling or, under certain conditions, of codes of conduct backed by an independent and credible monitoring (see Section 6 of this chapter below). Although the searching capacities of large investors are much more important, they too may require to be guided in their options, if they wish to take into account those dimensions of the companies in which they invest which the market does not visibly sanction or reward, i.e. those which are distinct from the sheer profitability of the investment. As to the 'direct' positive economic impact of CSR for the companies who act responsibly, again a regulatory framework may usefully contribute to such an impact occuring. With respect to many socially responsible practices, companies will frequently find themselves in the familiar situation where what would be profitable in the long run if other competitors act similarly will be costly in the short run, where certain competitors, seeking an immediate return on the investment of the shareholders, will act otherwise. Corporate social responsibility is an investment, perhaps, but as such, its returns are not immediate. Therefore:

Corporate social responsibility should . . . not be seen as a substitute to regulation or legislation concerning social rights or environmental standards, including the development of new appropriate legislation. In countries where such regulations do not exist, efforts should focus on putting the proper regulatory or legislative framework in place in order to define a level playing field on the basis of which socially responsible practices can be developed.[97]

Is CSR, then, to be left to the voluntary initiatives of the companies who feel they should do more than simply obey the existing legislation? Or is it a pretext for imposing, by the adoption of regulations, new and further-reaching obligations on companies? Is it economically profitable, and should we count on the blind powers of the market to push in that direction? Or do the market forces, left to themselves, not suffice, and how then should they be helped to produce the effects we hope for? These elements already give us some understanding of the ambiguities of the notion of corporate social responsibility, of course, but also (and perhaps precisely *because of* these ambiguities rather than *despite* them) of the wealth of its potential.

[97] Commission of the European Communities, Green Paper 'Promoting a European Framework for Corporate Social Responsibility', *supra* note 96, at 7.

The business of business is not just to do business: it is to improve the quality of the workforce by providing training; it is to contribute to a cleaner environment by adopting less polluting production methods; it is to combat violations of labour standards not only by respecting these standards in its own production plants but also by refusing to deal with subcontractors who violate those standards or work with subcontractors who themselves commit such violations; it is to use its influence on governments which abuse human rights to promote a fuller respect for these rights. This new role for companies may translate into different methods of implementation. In the remainder of this Chapter, I analyze these methods as they relate to the activities of European MNEs in developing countries. Building on the simple finding that companies can no longer shield themselves behind their purely profit-seeking motive, I discuss four ways by which the human rights dimension of CSR has led, or may in the future lead, to initiatives in the European Union. I move from the most compulsory method, the imposition of legally binding obligations, to the least compulsory: codes of conduct, social labelling initiatives, and the introduction of incentives in public procurement policies or by other mechanisms making it profitable for business to respect human rights.

4. THE CIVIL LIABILITY OF MULTINATIONALS UNDER EUROPEAN UNION LAW

The imposition of legal obligations on MNEs domiciled in the European Union, to ensure that they respect fundamental human rights in their activities abroad, whether these are conducted directly or through a subsidiary company, could take essentially one of two forms. This section analyses the conditions under which European MNEs may be found civilly liable for human rights violations committed abroad, by the MNE itself or a subsidiary which is its 'alter ego', or even—when the MNE may be considered complicit in the violation—by the State hosting the investment. Section 5 of this Chapter, below, addresses the criminal liability of the MNE in the same circumstances.

A. A European ATCA?

Under European Community law, the national jurisdictions of the Member States of the European Union are in principle competent to accept service of civil proceedings against corporations based in the EU which (either directly or indirectly, through the control exercised on subsidiaries) are civilly liable for certain acts, wherever these take place, and even if the damage occurs or is caused outside the territory of the Member States. This results from the partial harmonization of the conditions of judicial competence in the European Union. The use of the rule in the context of human rights litigation, for violations committed abroad, especially in developing countries where European multinationals operate, has been explicitly envisaged by the European Parliament. On 15 January 1999, the European Parliament adopted a 'Resolution on EU standards for European enterprises operating in developing countries: towards a European Code of Conduct'.[98] In the Preamble, the Parliament mentions that the resolution is adopted 'having regard to Article 220 of the EC Treaty regarding reciprocal recognition of court judgments[99], to the 1968 Convention on jurisdiction and the enforcement of judgments in civil and commercial matters, usually known as the Brussels Convention, and to the Joint Action of 24 February 1997 adopted by the Council on the basis of Article K.3 of the Treaty on European Union[100] concerning action to combat trafficking in human beings and sexual exploitation of children'. The operative part of the Resolution does not mention these instruments, but the draft text (the Motion for a Resolution initially presented by Mr Richard Howitt, MEP) included a paragraph which stated that the European Parliament:

24. Request the European Council confirm the interpretation in the 1968 Brussels Convention that, for cases of basic duty of care, legal action may be taken against a company in the E.U. country where its registered office is, in respect of any third country throughout the world, and calls on the Commission to study the possibility of enacting legislation, which open European courts to lawsuits involving damage done by MNEs, thus creating a precedent for developing customary international law in the field of corporate abuse.

This passage was outvoted by ninety-six votes to eighty-nine, and thus does not appear in the text finally adopted. However, this should not distract from the fact that such a use of the 27 September 1968 Brussels Convention,[101] now consolidated as Community law in Council Regulation No. 44/2001 of 22 December 2000 on jurisdiction and the recognition and enforcement of judgments in civil and commercial matters[102] could be defended, and indeed appears to face no major

[98] A4-0508/1998, OJ 1999 C 104/176.   [99] Now renumbered as Art. 293 EC.
[100] Now renumbered as Art. 31 TEU.
[101] The European Community Convention on Jurisdiction and the Enforcement of Judgments in Civil and Commercial Matters of 27 September 1968 came into force in 1973; its principles were extended to EFTA countries by the Lugano Convention of 1988. For the last consolidated version of the Brussels Convention, see OJ 1998 C 27/1.
[102] OJ 2001 L 12/1. The Regulation entered into force on 1 March 2002. The subject of judicial cooperation in civil matters entered Community law with the changes brought to the Treaty of Rome by the Treaty of Amsterdam of 2 October 1997, which entered into force on 1 May 1999. On the relationship between the 1968 Brussels Convention and Regulation No. 44/2001, see Article 68 of the latter instrument. On Regulation No. 44/2001, see H. Gaudemet-Tallon, *Compétence et exécution des jugements en Europe* (2002); Kennet, 'The Brussels I regulation', *I.C.L.Q.* (2001), at 725; Droz and Gaudemet-Tallon, 'La transformation de la Convention de Bruxelles du 27 septembre 1968 en règlement du Conseil concernant la compétence judiciaire, la reconnaissance et l'exécution des décisions en matière civile et commerciale', *Rev. crit. de dr. int. privé* (2001), at 601; Nuyts, 'La communautarisation de la Convention de Bruxelles', *J.T.* (2001), at 913; Schmidt, 'De EEX-Verordening: de volgende stap in het Europese procesrecht', *N.I.P.R.* (2001), at 150; Watté, Nuyts, and Boularbah, 'Le règlement "Bruxelles I" sur la compétence judiciaire, la reconnaissance et l'exécution des décisions en matière civile et commerciale', *J.T.D.E.* (2002), at 161.

obstacle.[103] Under Article 2(1) of Regulation No. 44/2001, 'persons domiciled in a Member State shall, whatever their nationality, be sued in the courts of that Member State'. Article 2 of the Brussels Convention contained the same rule of *forum rei*. Article 60(1) of the Regulation simply adds to the rule of the 1968 Brussels Convention, for the sake of predictability with respect to the identification of what is understood by the 'domicile' of legal persons,[104] that for the purposes of the Regulation, 'a company or other legal person or association of natural or legal persons is domiciled at the place where it has its: (a) statutory seat, or (b) central administration, or (c) principal place of business'.

Regulation No. 44/2001 also provides for two alternative grounds for jurisdiction of the courts of one Member State, which the plaintiff may wish to rely on in certain circumstances. First, 'in matters relating to tort, delict or quasi-delict'[105] the plaintiff may sue 'in the courts for the place where the harmful event occurred or may occur'.[106] Importantly, the European Court of Justice has found that 'where the place of the *happening of the event* which may give rise to liability in tort, delict or quasi-delict and the place where that event *results in damage* are not identical, the expression "place where the harmful event occurred" in Article 5(3) of the Convention must be understood as being intended to cover both the place where the damage occurred and the place of the event giving rise to it, so that the defendant may be sued, at the option of the plaintiff, in the courts for either of those places'.[107] As a consequence, where a decision is taken, for instance by a board of directors, in a Member State other than the Member State where the company is domiciled, which causes the damage for which reparation is sought, the plaintiff should be able to sue in the first Member State where the decision was adopted: in certain (admittedly rather exceptional) cases, for instance if the plaintiff resides in the Member State where the decision was taken and would therefore more easily lauch his suit in that State, this basis of jurisdiction may be favourable to the plaintiff.

Secondly, 'A person domiciled in a Member State may, in another Member State, be sued . . . as regards a dispute arising out of the operations of a branch, agency or other establishment, in the courts for the place in which the branch, agency or other

---

[103] See esp. Betlem, 'Transnational Litigation Against Multinational Corporations Before Dutch Civil Courts', in M.T. Kamminga and S. Zia-Zarifi (eds.), *Liability of Multinational Corporations under International Law* (2000), at 283.

[104] For the determination of the domicile of the defendant, the private international law rules of each forum State should normally apply (Article 59(1) of Regulation No. 44/2001). This was also the case with respect to the determination of the domicile of legal persons in the Brussels Convention. The current Regulation considers that 'The domicile of a legal person must be defined autonomously so as to make the common rules more transparent and avoid conflicts of jurisdiction' (Preamble, Recital 11).

[105] In the framework of the 1968 Brussels Convention, the European Court of Justice considered that 'tort, delict or quasi-delict' was to be taken as an independent concept 'covering all actions which seek to establish the liability of a defendant and which are not related to a "contract" within the meaning of Article 5(1)' (Case 189/87 *Kalfelis v Schröder* [1988] ECR 5565, paragraph 18).   [106] Article 5(3).

[107] Case C-51-97, *Réunion européenne SA and others*, [1998] ECR I-6511, para. 28 (my emphasis). See earlier Case 21/76, *Bier v Mines de Potasse d'Alsace* [1976] ECR 1735, paras. 24–5.

establishment is situated'.[108] This means that a company domiciled in a Member State may be sued in another Member State where is has established a branch, agency, or establishment[109] in cases where, for instance, 'operations' of that subsidiary or branch have caused damage for which a tort action seeks compensation.[110] It appears from the case-law of the European Court of Justice on the notion of 'operations of a branch, agency or other establishment' that these include acts whose effects are not restricted to the territory of the forum State.[111] Therefore, 'if harm ensued from any operations of that branch, even where the damage occurred outside the forum State, its parent company can be sued' in the State where the branch is located.[112]

These provisions therefore recognize that the jurisdictions of the Member States are competent to hear tort actions based on the damage suffered by victims, wherever these are domiciled and whatever their nationality, caused by the activities of a multinational enterprise domiciled in a Member State or by any of its branches. The action will be lodged either in the State where the parent company is domiciled or, where a branch of that company has actually been at the basis of the act causing the damage, in the State where that branch is located.

Such a use of the 1968 Brussels Convention, and now of Regulation No. 44/2001, would be analogous to a European 'Foreign Tort Claims Act'. The expression refers of course, by modifying it, to the *Alien Tort Claims Act* (ATCA) initially in section 9 of the First Judiciary Act of 24 September 1789, conferring jurisdiction upon the United States federal courts on actions lodged by aliens claiming damages

---

[108] Article 5(5).

[109] The concept is interpreted to exclude the situation of an independant commercial agent who, although he/she represents a company domiciled in another Member State, 'merely transmits orders to the parent undertaking without being involved in either their terms or their execution' (Case 139/80, *Blanckaert and Willems PVBA*, [1981] ECR 819, para. 13).

[110] Article 5(5) of the Brussels Convention (now Art. 5(5) of the Regulation No. 44/2001) has been read by the European Court of Justice to give this provision an extended meaning. In a judgment of 9 December 1987, the Court agreed that, for reasons of legal certainty and because of the appearances created by such a situation in the eyes of other economic actors, the clause could apply to a case in which 'a legal entity etablished in [a Member State] maintains no dependant branch, agency or other establishment in another [Member State] but nevertheless pursues its activities there through an independent company with the same name and identical management which negotiates and conducts business in its name and which it uses as an extension of itself' (ECJ, 18 Dec. 1987, Case 218/86, *SAR Schotte GmbH*, [1997 ECR 4905, para. 17). Not only may the clause be invoked in the presence of two legally independant entities (rather than in the situation explicitly envisaged by Art. 5(5) where a single company creates a branch, an agency, or an establishment in another Member State) but it may even be invoked when the defending entity, domiciled in another Member State, is is fact a subsidiary of the entity situated in the Member State before the jurisdictions of which the action is lodged.

[111] See the discussion by Betlem, *supra* note 103, comparing Case 33/78, *Somafer SA v. Saar-Ferngas AG*, [1978] ECR 2183, at 2194, with the more recent Case C-439/93, *Lloyd's Register of Shipping v. Société Campenon Bernard*, [1995] ECR I-961, para. 20 ('undertakings may form part of the operations of an ancillary establishment within the meaning of Article 5(5) of the Convention even though they are to be performed outside the Contracting State where it is situated, possibly by another ancillary establishment'). [112] Betlem, *supra* note 103, at 288.

for torts committed in violation of the law of nations, wherever the harm occured.[113] The ATCA has been spectacularly revived since a decision of 30 June 1980 by the Court of Appeals of the Second Circuit in the case of *Filartiga v. Pena-Irala*[114] before being further extended to cover actions filed against multinational corporations domiciled in the United States for violations of universally recognized norms of international law committed outside U.S. territory.[115] In one respect at least, it could be said that the use of the 1968 Brussels Convention advocated by the rapporteur for the European Parliament on EU standards for European enterprises operating in developing countries would even expand the jurisdiction of European courts in comparison to that of the United States federal courts under ATCA.[116] Indeed, the ATCA may only be relied on by plaintiffs who are aliens; the scope of the jurisdiction conferred upon European courts by Regulation No. 44/2001 is not thus limited, so we may be justified in speaking of that Regulation as constituting, in part, a *Foreign* Tort Claims Act, rather than an *Alien* Tort Claims Act. However, this difference between the two instruments must not be exaggerated, and certainly should not lead us to dismiss the comparison between them. First, with respect to the crimes of torture or extra-judicial killing committed under authority or colour of law of a foreign nation, this limitation to the ATCA was removed by the Torture Victim Protection Act of 1991.[117] Moreover, in the kind of suits we are concerned with, lodged against MNEs for human rights violations committed abroad either

---

[113] First Judiciary Act 1789 (ch. 20, S. 9(b)), now codified as 28 U.S.C. S. 1350: 'The District Courts shall have original jurisdiction of any civil action by an alien for a tort only, committed in violation of the law of nations or a treaty of the United States'. There exists some controversy about the original intent behind the adoption of this section of the Act: cf. Burley, 'The Alien Tort Statute and the Judiciary Act 1789: A Badge of Honor', 83 *A.J.I.L.* (1989), at 461 (for an exapansive view), and Sweeney, 'A Tort Only in Violation of the Law of Nations', 18 *Hastings International and Comparative Law Rev.* (1995) at 445 (for a more restrictive view). See also Koh, 'Transnational Public Law Litigation', 100 *Yale L.J.* (1991), 2347, at 2353. See also the dissenting opinion of judge Edwards in *Tel-Oren v. Libyan Arab Republic*, 726 F.2nd 774 (D.C. Cir. 1984), at 782–3.   [114] *Filartiga v. Pena-Irala*, 630 F.2nd 876 (1980).

[115] See esp. the suits against the Californian corporation Unocal for the complicity of its subsidiaries in gross human violations committed the Myanmar military in ex-Burma: *Doe I v. Unocal Corp.*, 963 F.Supp. 880 (C.D. Cal. 1997); *National Coalition Government of the Union of Burma v. Unocal, Inc.*, 176 F.R.D. 329 (C.D. Cal. 1997); *Doe I v. Unocal Corp.*, 110 F. Supp. 2d 1294 (C.D. Cal. 2000). Another spectacular example is the suit lodged by relatives of Ken Saro-Wiwa and other activists of the Ogoni community in Nigeria after the execution of these activists in November 1995, which followed the repression by the Nigerian authorities of protests against the presence of Shell in the area of Nigeria where the Ogoni people reside: *Wiwa v. Royal Dutch Petroleum Co.*, 226 F.3d 88 (2d Cir. 2000); *Wiwa v. Royal Dutch Petroleum Co.*, No. 96 Civ. 8386 (KMW), 2002 WL 319887 (S.D.N.Y., Feb. 28, 2002). Both these suits are still currently pending before the U.S. federal courts.

[116] For a recent synthesis, Stevens, 'Translitigating Filartiga: A Comparative and International Law Analysis of Domestic Remedies for International Human Rights Violations', 27 *Yale J. Int'l L.* (2002), at 1.

[117] See the *Torture Victim Protection Act* of 1991, 28 U.S.C. S. 1350(2) (1994), Pub. L. No. 102-256, 106 Stat. 73: 'An individual who under actual or apparent authority, or color of law, of any foreign nation (1) subjects an individual to torture shall, in a civil action, be liable for damages to that individual, or (2) subjects an individual to extrajudicial killing shall in a civil action, be liable for damages to the individual's legal representative or to any person who may be a claimant in an action for wrongful death'.

directly or by subsidiaries, the limitation is of little practical importance: the vast majority of the victims, indeed, are nationals of the host States, where the violations produce their effects, rather than nationals of the State home to the MNE. On three other questions of major importance however, the European system based on the 1968 Brussels Convention now transformed into Regulation No. 44/2001 appears either more generous than the United States Alien Tort Statute, or at least potentially as generous.

B. The Question of the Forum Conveniens

First, the potential of the ATCA is to some extent limited by the *forum non conveniens* doctrine, developed with the objective of avoiding jurisdictional forum shopping in the United States by victims seeking redress who have other avenues open to them. According to the *forum non conveniens* doctrine, even when United States federal courts would formally have jurisdiction on a particular action brought to them, they may dismiss the action where there exists an alternative forum open to the plaintiffs and where the balancing of the public and private interests involved leads to the conclusion that turning to the alternative forum is preferable.[118] Although it was hardly even alluded to in *Filartiga*, because of the lack of any alternatives to the victims in that case,[119] the doctrine has played an important role, for example in *Wiwa v. Royal Dutch Petroleum Co. and Shell Transport*. In that case, the plaintiffs[120] sought reparation from Royal Dutch and Shell Transport, respectively incorporated and headquartered in the Netherlands and the United Kingdom. The plaintiffs alleged that Shell Nigeria, a subsidiary company jointly controlled by the two named defendants, planned and supported gross human rights abuses committed by the Nigerian government and military against the resistance movement to the destruction of the homeland of the Ogoni people by the oil exploration activities of Shell Nigeria. After the district court had considered that the suit should be dismissed because the plaintiffs could have sued in the courts of the United Kingdom, the United States Court of Appeals for the 2nd Circuit decided, on 14 September 2000, that 'in balancing the interests, the district court did not accord proper significance to a choice of lawful U.S. resident plaintiffs or to the policy interest implicit in our federal statutory law in providing a forum for adjudication of claims of violations of the law of nations'. The presumption that the

---

[118] See e.g. *Gulf Oil Corp. v. Gilbert*, 330 U.S. 501, 506–8 (1947); *Koster v. American Lumbermens Mut. Cas. Co.*, 330 U.S. 518 (1947).

[119] See *Filartiga v. Pena-Irala*, 577 F.Supp. 860, 865 (1984) ('The United States policy against forum shopping does not warrant a denial. Plaintiffs could get no redress in Paraguay and sued Pena where they found him').

[120] The plaintiffs were relatives of the writer and Ogoni activist Ken Saro-Wiwa, and of John Kpuinen, another member of the Movement of the Survival of the Ogoni People also executed by the Nigerian authorities on 10 November 1995 with eight other militants of the Ogoni resistance movement. On the background, see S.I. Skogly, 'Complexities in Human Rights Protection: Actors and Rights Involved in the Ogoni Conflict in Nigeria', 15 *Neth. Quar. H. R.* (1997), at 47.

choice of the forum by the plaintiff should normally be deferred to is based on a realistic reading of the difficulties faced by victims of officially sponsored torture. The Court of Appeals noted:

One of the difficulties that confront victims of torture under color of a nation's law is the enormous difficulty of bringing suits to vindicate such abuses. Most likely, the victims cannot sue in the place where the torture occurred. Indeed, in many instances, the victim would be endangered merely by returning to that place. Is it not easy to bring such suits in the courts of another nation. Courts are often inhospitable. Such suits are generally time consuming, burdensome, and difficult to administer. In addition, because they assert outrageous conduct on the part of another nation, such suits may embarrass the government of the nation in whose courts they are brought. Finally, because characteristically neither the plaintiffs nor the defendants are ostensibly either protected or governed by the domestic law of the forum nation, courts often regard such suits as 'not our business'.[121]

The question of whether the doctrine of *forum non conveniens* conflicts with the harmonization in civil jurisdiction and enforcement sought by the 1968 Brussels Convention (and, today, by Regulation No. 44/2001) has been hotly debated, in the context of the application of the criteria of these European instruments by the British and Irish courts.[122] The question is not of purely theoretical or academic import-ance, considering the large number of multinational corporations which have chosen to be incorporated in the United Kingdom, especially for fiscal reasons. To com-pensate for the very large attribution of jurisdiction to them even in the presence of an element of extraneity in the case, the courts in the United Kingdom have tra-ditionally exercised a relatively broad discretion on whether to continue proceedings or to suspend them, where an alternative forum was identified and appeared more closely linked to the dispute.[123] Soon after the High Court had decided that the very

---

[121] The *pro victima* reading of the *forum non conveniens* doctrine by the Court of Appeals has been implictly approved by the United States Supreme Court, which decided on 26 March 2001 to deny certiorari to appeal to the defendants (cert. denied, 00-1168). See on the developments of this case: http://www.earthrights.org/shell/.

[122] See esp. Collins, '*Forum non conveniens* and the Brussels Convention', 106 *L.Q.R.* (1990), at 535; Fentiman, 'Jurisdiction, Discretion and the Brussels Convention', *Cornell International Law Journal* (1993), at 73; Hartley, 'The Brussels Convention and *Forum Non Conveniens*', 17 *E.L. Rev.* (1992), at 553; Kennett, '*Forum non conveniens* in Europe', *Cambridge L.J.* (1995), at 555; Gaudemet-Tallon, 'Le *forum non conveniens*, une menace pour la Convention de Bruxelles?', *Rev. crit. dr. inter. privé* (1991), at 510; Marongiu Buanaitu, '*Forum Non Conveniens* Facing the Prospective Hague Convention and E.C. Regulation on Jurisdiction and the Enforcement of Judgments in Civil and Commercial Matters, *Riv. di. dir. eur.* (1999), at 3; North, 'La liberté d'appréciation de la compétence (jurisdictional discretion) selon la Convention de Bruxelles', *Mélanges François Rigaux* (1993), at 383; and A. Nuyts, 'L'exception de *forum non conveniens* (étude de droit international privé comparé)' (Ph.D. on file at the Faculté de Droit de l'Université libre de Bruxelles, Bruxelles, 2002, at 187 ff.).

[123] See *Sim v. Robinow* (1892), 19 R., 665 at 668, *per* Lord Kinnear: 'the plea can never be sustained unless the court is satisfied that there is some other tribunal, having competent jurisdiction, in which the case may be tried more suitably for the interests of all the parties and for the ends of justice'. And esp. *Spiliada Maritime Corporation v. Cansulex Ltd.* [1987] A.C. 460, at 476: 'The basic principle is that a stay will only be granted on the ground of *forum non conveniens* where the court is satisfied that there is some

purpose of the Brussels Convention—to harmonize the rules on jurisdiction in the European Community, so as to limit the potential for conflict between national courts of different Member States—would be defeated if the courts in the United Kingdom retained an element of discretion in situations where, according to the Brussels Convention, they would have jurisdiction as of right,[124] the Court of Appeal decided, in *Re Harrods*,[125] that *when third States are involved*[126] (the case involved a Swiss-owned company domiciled in the United Kingdom, but conducting all its activities in Argentina) this purpose of the Brussels Convention did not come into play anymore. Indeed, the Convention only seeks to avoid conflicts *between Member States of the European Community*, and moreover, it would be strange, from the point of view of public international law, to have the Brussels Convention extend its effects to third States, which are not parties to that treaty.[127] Although an interpretation of the requirements of the 1968 Brussels Convention on that point was requested from the European Court of Justice, the case referred to the Court was struck off after a friendly settlement was reached by the parties.[128] The compatibility of the *Harrods* judgment of the Court of Appeal with the Brussels Convention therefore remains a source of controversy to this date.

The case of *Lubbe v. Cape plc* is illustrative of the significance of the controversy with respect to the possibilities of acting against MNEs domiciled in the United Kingdom.[129] In February 1997, claims for compensation were lodged by five employees of an asbestos mine in the Northern Province of South Africa, which

other available forum, having competent jurisdiction, which is the appropriate forum for the trial of the action, i.e. in which the case may be tried more suitably for the interests of all the parties and the ends of justice'.

[124] See *S & W Berisford plc v. New Hampshire Insurance Co.* (1990) 2 QB 631; and *Arkwright Mutual Inc. Co. v. Bryanston Insurance Co. Ltd.* (1990) 2 QB 649.

[125] *Re Harrods (Buenos Aires) Ltd* (1991) 4 All ER 334, (1992) Ch. 72 (C.A.). See Diuntjer Tebbens, 'The English Court of Appeal in *Re Harrods*: an unwelcome interpretation of the Brussels Convention', in M. Sumampouw, *Law and Reality: Essays on national and international procedural law* (1992), at 60; and Beernaert and Coibion, 'La doctrine du forum (non) conveniens: Réconciliation avec le texte de la Convention de Bruxelles?', *Journal des tribunaux* (2000), at 409.

[126] See *Re Harrods (Buenos Aires) Ltd* (1991) 4 All ER 334, 339, on the distinction between the two situations. *Forum non conveniens* may not be invoked when the alternative forum to that designated by the Brussels Convention (in particular the domicile of the defendant) is a court of a Member State of the European Community.

[127] The position of the Court of Appeal in *Re Harrods* appears to have been heavily influenced by the thesis defended the previous year in the *Law Quarterly Review* by Collins, *supra* note 122, who expressed the opinion that 'The contracting states were setting up an intra-Convention mandatory system of jurisdiction. They were not regulating relations with non-contracting states' (at 539).

[128] Case C-314/92, *Lademinor v. Interconfinanz*, *OJ* 1992 C 219/4; and order of 21 February 1994, *OJ* 1994 C 103.

[129] Meeran, 'Liability of Multinational Corporations: A Critical Stage in the UK', in M.T. Kamminga and S. Zia-Zarifi, *supra* note 103, at 251, 258–61; Muchlinski, 'Corporations in international litigation: problems of jurisdiction and the United Kingdom asbestos cases', *I.C.L.Q.* (2001), at 1; Fentiman, 'Stays and the European Conventions: End-Game?', *C.L.J.* (2001), at 10.

was managed by a subsidiary wholly owned by Cape plc, a company domiciled in England. The plaintiffs suffered from asbestosis and an asbestos-related form of cancer. The liability of Cape plc was based on negligent control by the parent company over the operations of its subsidiary, which it should have obliged to limit exposure to asbestos to a safe level. The defendant company argued that, although it was domiciled in the United Kingdom and that, therefore, Article 2 of the Brussels Convention gave the English courts jurisdiction on the case, these courts should relinquish jurisdiction in favour of South African courts, to the jurisdiction of which Cape plc offered to submit. Cape plc also insisted that South Africa was the proper forum, as the injuries were suffered there, and as the factual allegations were based in that jurisdiction. A first decision favourable to that thesis, adopted on 12 January 1998 by the Queen's Bench Division, was reversed by the Court of Appeal on 30 July 1998;[130] on 14 December 1998 the House of Lords refused leave to appeal from that judgment. However, the decision on jurisdiction, favourable to the claimants, led a group of 1,539 new claimants to lodge another suit before the High Court,[131] leading the Court of Appeal to reverse its attitude in a second judgment on 29 November 1999.[132] In a judgment of 20 July 2000, after having granted leave to appeal from both judgments by the Court of Appeal, the House of Lords decided that the plaintiffs should be able to pursue the proceedings before the English courts, because returning them to the South African courts could lead to a denial of justice, because of the difficulties they would be facing in obtaining legal representation and because of the lack of experience of those courts in the handling of group actions.[133]

The leading opinion of Lord Bingham of Cornhill did not specifically adopt a position on the preemption of the *forum non conveniens* doctrine by Article 2 of the Brussels Convention.[134] Indeed, the House of Lords having concluded to the jurisdiction of the English courts, any answer to that question would have been of no practical relevance. However, the opinion does contain a suggestion that, in cases where the question of jurisdiction is governed by the Brussels Convention, the doctrine of *forum non conveniens* should not constitute an obstacle to the exercise of their jurisdiction by the English courts where the competing forum is a jurisdiction of another State Party to the Convention. The leading opinion introduces its discussion of the *forum non conveniens* doctrine by saying that 'the principles to be applied by the English court in deciding that application *in any case not governed by*

130   *Lubbe* et al. *v. Cape plc* (CA 30 July 1998) [1998] C.L.C. 1559.
131   *Group Action Afrika* et al. *v. Cape plc* (QBD 30 July 1999) [2000] 1 Lloyd's Rep. 139.
132   *Rachel Lubbe* et al. *v. Cape plc* (CA 29 Nov. 1999) [2000] 1 Lloyd's Rep. 139.
133   *Lubbe v. Cape plc* [2000] 1 W.L.R. 1545 (HL).
134   In the second judgment by the Court of Appeal (of 29 November 1999), Pill L.J. expressly noted that the plaintiffs—who, indeed, did not wish the proceedings to be delayed while a reference would be made to the European Court of Justice—had not pursued their contention that Article 2 of the 1968 Brussels Convention deprived the English court of any discretion to stay an action brought against a defendant domiciled in the United Kingdom (*Rachel Lubbe* et al. *v. Cape plc* (CA 29 Nov. 1999) [2000] 1 Lloyd's Rep. 139, at 164–5).

Article 2 of the Brussels Convention are not in doubt'.[135] The lengthy discussion of the *forum non conveniens* doctrine in the judgment seems to indicate that the House of Lords considers it is to follow the solution of the Court of Appeal in the above-mentioned *Harrods* case: where the competing forum is a third State rather than a Contracting State to the Brussels Convention, the question of jurisdiction should still be guided by the *forum non conveniens* doctrine.

Although it was not disapproved of by the House of Lords in *Lubbe*, the *Harrods* doctrine seems to be incompatible with recent developments within the case-law of the European Court of Justice.[136] In a judgment it delivered on 13 July 2000[137] the Court answered a concern expressed by a French judge that Community law would be applied in third States if the rules on jurisdiction established by the Brussels Convention could be invoked by a claimant domiciled outside the Community. The Court stated that 'the system of common rules on conferment of jurisdiction established in Title II of the Convention is based on the general rule, set out in the first paragraph of Article 2, that persons domiciled in a Contracting State are to be sued in the courts of that State, irrespective [either] of the nationality of the parties[138] [. . . or . . .] of the plaintiff's domicile or seat'[139] the rationale for that rule being that it is easier, in principle, for the defendant to defend him- or herself in the place where he or she is domiciled. Therefore, 'the Convention does not, in principle, preclude the rules of jurisdiction which it sets out from applying to a dispute between a defendant domiciled in a Contracting State and a plaintiff domiciled in a non-member country'.[140] According to the Court, the general rule of jurisdiction being conferred on the courts of the domicile of the defendant could be disapplied 'only in exceptional cases where an express provision of the Convention provides that the application of the rule of jurisdiction which it sets out is dependent on the plaintiff's domicile being in a Contracting State'.[141] The position thus expressed by the European Court of Justice seems to suggest that, if it had answered either the *Harrods* or the *Lubbe* courts on the interpretation of the 1968 Brussels Convention in those cases, it would probably have found the application of the *forum non*

---

[135] This formulation by Lord Bingham of Cornhill, although it seems to be inspired by the terms of the Civil Judgments Act 1982 which introduced the 1968 Brussels Convention into the UK national legal order (the Act mentions that 'Nothing in the Act shall prevent a court in the United Kingdom from staying, striking out or dismissing any proceedings on the ground of forum non conveniens or otherwise, where to do so is not inconsistent with the 1968 Convention' (s. 49)), in fact postulates that either the Brussels Convention will be applicable, or the doctrine of *forum non conveniens* will apply. But this delimitation of the respective scope of application of the two rules was not, in fact, what s. 49 of the Civil Judgments Act intended. Rather, this provision did not exclude that the Brussels Convention could refer back to the principles from national law (including the doctrine of forum non conveniens in the UK), on certain questions it did not rule on itself.   [136] See Muchlinski, *supra* note 129, at 12–13.

[137] But see also, in the previous case-law, Case C-190/89, *Rich*, (1991) ECR I-3855 (judgment of 25 July 1991).

[138] Case C-412/98, *Group Josi Reinsurance Company SA*, [2000] ECR, para. 34 (judgment of 13 July 2000).   [139] Ibid. para. 53.

[140] Ibid. para. 59.   [141] Ibid. para. 61.

conveniens doctrine, in situations where the United Kingdom has jurisdiction based on the domicile in that State of the defendant, to be incompatible with the requirements of the Brussels Convention, or, today, with those of Regulation No. 44/2001. This impression is further reinforced by the wording of recital 11 in the Preamble of this Regulation, which insists that 'the rules of jurisdiction must be highly predictable and founded on the principle that jurisdiction is generally based on the defendant's domicile and jurisdiction must always be available on this ground save in a few well defined situations in which the subject-matter of the litigation or the autonomy of the parties warrants a different linking factor'. Although this does not constitute an explicit condemnation of the preemption of the jurisdiction attributed by the Regulation by the *forum non conveniens* doctrine, that is clearly the spirit of the insistence of this recital on 'predictability'.[142]

C. The Question of the Applicable Law

It is on the question of the law applicable to the damage claim that the two systems seem to differ most strikingly. The Alien Tort Claims Act concerns only torts committed 'in violation of the law of nations', a restriction which the Court of Appeals for the 2nd Circuit in *Filartiga* justified by noting that 'Were this not so, the courts of one nation might feel free to impose idiosyncratic legal rules upon others, in the name of applying international law'.[143] In most of the cases presented to the federal courts of the United States under the ATCA, such a reference to the 'universally accepted norms of the international law of human rights' served not only to justify the exercise of their jurisdiction by those courts, but also to identify the rules applicable to the tort action, thus removing the choice of law question from the court.

It is true that some federal courts have chosen a different attitude, first very hesitatingly introduced by Judge Edwards in his opinion in the D.C. Court of Appeals judgment in *Tel-Oren v. Libyan Arab Republic*, in which the Palestine Liberation Organization (P.L.O.) was sued by the victims of an attack on a civilian bus in Israel.[144] The suggestion to grant jurisdiction once the plaintiff pleads a violation of international law, but then to turn either to municipal tort law or to the *lex loci delicti* for the identification of the standard of liability,[145] may indeed present the advantage of dispensating the judge from what Judge Edwards called her

---

[142] H. Gaudemet-Tallon bases on this argument her position that the *forum non conveniens* doctrine must certainly be considered inapplicable where jurisdiction is based on Regulation No. 44/2001 and where the competing forum is another Member State of the EC. She would be prepared to admit for more flexibility where third States are involved: see Gaudemet-Tallon, *supra* note 102, paras. 77 and 81.

[143] *Filartiga v. Pena-Irala*, 630 F.2nd 876, 881.

[144] *Tel-Oren v. Libyan Arab Republic*, 726 F.2d 774 (D.C. Cir. 1984), cert. denied, 470 U.S. 1003 (1985).

[145] See, for an approach which remained isolated in that respect, *In Re Estate of Ferdinand E. Marcos Human Rights Litigation/Trajano v. Marcos*, 978 F.2d 493 (9th Cir. 1992) (application of Philippine wrongful death statutes to a suit for torture, leading to the death of the victim, by Philippine intelligence officers).

'awesome duty ... to derive from an amorphous entity—i.e. the "law of nations"—standards of liability applicable in concrete situations'.[146] It may also end any confusion which may still be present about the consequences of a violation of international law by a private individual who is not in any way connected to the State. Indeed, some United States federal courts have taken the view that only torts committed by individuals in violation of international law 'under color of an official authority' may imply jurisdiction under the ATCA. Such a view appears to have a purely accidental origin in the *Filartiga* jurisprudence where, indeed, acts of *torture* were alleged against the defendant, Mr America Pena-Irala, a Paraguayan police officer found in the U.S. at the time the action was filed: as would be later confirmed in the 1984 Torture Convention, torture is only prohibited in international law when practised by a person acting in an official capacity or at the instigation, or with the consent or acquiescence of, a public official.[147] But the restriction of ATCA suits to violations committed either by agents of the State, or private persons closely connected to the State or acting under its instructions or effective control, is encouraged by the notion that international law is primarily directed to the States, and only exceptionally reaches directly the acts of the private individual, as with crimes of genocide, war crimes, or crimes against humanity.[148] Perhaps this restriction, which threatens severely to limit the reach of the ATCA,[149] would be more easily removed if the reference to the 'law of nations' in the Statute were seen as necessary to grant jurisdiction to the federal courts, whilst not determining the issue of the applicable standards of liability. These advantages, however, do not seem to compensate for what would be missed in such an understanding of ATCA suits: as eloquently expressed by a federal district court in the *Xuncax* litigation against a former Guatemalan Defence Minister:

reading the Alien Torts Claims Act as essentially a jurisdictional grant only and then looking to domestic tort law to provide the cause of action mutes the grave international law aspect of

---

[146] *Tel-Oren*, 726 F.2d at 781.

[147] The *Filartiga* decision relies on the Declaration on the Protection of All Persons from Being Subjected to Torture and Other Cruel, Inhuman or Degrading Treatment or Punishment, adopted by the United Nations General Assembly on 9 December 1975 (Res. 3452(XXX)). For another example of such a restriction with respect to acts of torture, see *In re Estate of Ferdinand E. Marcos Human Rights Litigation/ Trajano v. Marcos*, 978 F.2d 493, 501-502 (9th Cir. 1992).

[148] For an admission of individual liability for such crimes, see *Kadic v. Karadzic*, 70 F.3d 232, 242-243 (2d Cir. 1995).

[149] In the *Tel-Oren* litigation which has just been mentioned, the Court of Appeals of Washington, D.C., refused to accept jurisdiction in the suit brought against Libya and the PLO by victims of a terrorist attack in Israel, on the basis that the PLO is not a 'State' (Libya was judged to have immunity from the suit); the United States Supreme Court denied certiorari. *Tel-Oren v. Libyan Arab Republic*, 726 F.2nd 774 (D.C. Cir. 1984), *cert. denied*, 470 U.S. 1003 (1985). See, D'Amato, 'What Does Tel-Oren Tell Lawyers? Judge Bork's Concept of the Law of Nations is Seriously Mistaken', 79 *A.J.I.L.* (1985), at 92; and Koh, 'Civil Remedies for Uncivil Wrongs: Combatting Terrorism Through Transnational Public Law Litigation', 22 *Texas Int'l L.J.* (1987)169, at 202–8. Other decisions are less clear in this respect: see e.g. *Sanchez-Espinoza v. Reagan*, 770 F.2nd 202 (D.C. Cir. 1985).

the tort, reducing it to no more (or less) than a garden-variety municipal tort. This is not merely a question of formalism or even of the amount or type of damages available; rather it concerns the proper characterization of the kind of wrongs meant to be addressed under the Alien Torts Claims Act: those perpetrated by *hostis humani generis* ('enemies of all human kind') in contravention of *jus cogens* (peremptory norms of human rights law). In this light, municipal tort law is an inadequate placeholder for such values.[150]

It will therefore be easily explained that, in the context of the ATCA, the liability of the defendant will be identified on the basis of those norms of international law which will be considered at once specific, universal, and obligatory. It may be said that the form of extraterritoriality which victims relying on the ATCA invoke is both *adjudicative* and *prescriptive*:[151] not only are United States federal courts competent, they also will apply international norms, rather than refer back to the law of the place where the event took place of where the damage occured. In apparent contrast with the ATCA, the form of extraterritoriality we are led to by relying on the 1968 Brussels Convention to claim compensation against a MNE having its domicile in an EU Member State remains purely *adjudicative*, and leaves open the question of which law will be applicable to the liability claim. The law applicable to the tort action will generally be the *lex loci delicti*, the law of the jurisdiction where the harmful event took place. Although, in most cases, the applicable national law will identify serious human rights violations such as torture or forced labour as a tort or a delict, the reference to the *lex loci delicti* as the applicable law may create a difficulty where that law is unsufficiently protective of the victims, either because the national legislation designed as applicable by the rules of private international law of the forum State tolerates (or even imposes) certain practices like gender discrimination, violations of freedom of association, or environmental damage, or when certain amnesties are granted in the applicable national legal system to those having committed the tortious acts. In these cases, however, the application of the foreign law will face the obstacle of the public policy of the forum: British courts, for example, consider that although courts should be 'very slow to refuse to give effect to the legislation of a foreign State in any sphere in which, according to accepted principles of international law, the foreign state has jurisdiction', a law constituting a grave infringement of human rights (at issue was a Nazi nationality law that deprived Jews outside Germany of their nationality) should not be recognized 'as a law at all' by the courts in the United Kingdom.[152] It may also be argued that the application, by European courts, of a foreign law which would entail gross violations of human rights, would constitute a

---

[150] *Xuncax v. Gramajo*, 886 F. Supp. 162, 182–3 (D. Mass. 1995). Still, the reference only to *jus cogens* norms (whilst, in fact, all universally recognized norms of international law may be invoked in ATCA suits) alerts us to the price which is to be paid as we seek to rely on the substantive norms of international law in such suits: only those norms of international law which are sufficiently detailed and specific to function as defining a standard of liability will be usefully invoked in such a context.

[151] In the categories suggested by Scott, 'Translating Torture into Transnational Tort: Conceptual Divides in the Debate on Corporate Accountability for Human Rights Harms', in Scott, *supra* note 24, at 54.   [152] *Oppenheimer v. Cattermole*, [1976] AC 349.

violation of the obligations of the State of which these courts are organs under the European Convention on Human Rights.[153] At last, the principle of *lex loci delicti* may sometimes lead to the application of the law of the forum, even when victims of human rights violations seek to obtain damages from the parent company for having unsufficiently exercised control over the activities of its subsidiary operating abroad, by suing where the defendant company is domiciled. Indeed, although the damage was effected abroad, the violation of the duty, at the origin of the liability claim, occured in the forum State, where the parent company is domiciled.[154]

[153] On this question, see Cohen, 'La Convention européenne des droits de l'homme et le droit privé français', *Rev. critique de dr. inter. privé* (1989), at 451; Mayer, 'La Convention européenne des droits de l'homme et l'application des normes étrangères', *Rev. critique de dr. inter. privé* (1991), at 651; Van Loon, 'De wisselwerking tussen internationaal privaatrecht en rechten van de mens', in *Grensoverschrijdend privaatrecht: Een bundel opstellen over privaatrecht in internationaal verband, Mélanges J. Van Rijn van Alkemade* (1993); Courbe, 'Le droit international privé et les difficultés d'insertion de la Convention dans le système français', in P. Tavernier (ed.), *Quelle Europe pour les droits de l'homme? La Cour de Strasbourg et la réalisation d'une union plus étroite (1950-1995)* (1996); Herzog, 'Constitutional limits on choice of law', 234 *R.C.A.D.I.* (1992), at 249; Docquir, 'Le droit international privé à l'épreuve de la Convention européenne des droits de l'homme', 4 *Ann. Dr. Lv.* (1999), at 473. In a case concerning the recognition by the Italian courts of a judgment adopted by the courts of the Vatican in violation of the right to a fair trial and the rights of defence of the applicant, the European Court of Human Rights found the situation imputable to the Italian State (Eur. Ct. H.R. (2nd sect.), judgment *Pellegrini v. Italy* (Appl. no. 30882/96) of 20 July 2001). In *Gentilhomme* however, the applicants were complaining that their children, having both Algerian and French nationality (although Algeria does not recognize such situations of double nationality with respect to Algerian nationals) were denied access to French teaching institutions in Algeria after a unilateral decision in 1988 by the Algerian authorities to denounce a 1962 agreement between France and Algeria concerning cultural cooperation and providing for education in French public teaching institutions of children defined as binationals according to French law. The Court considered that the French authorities has merely submitted to a decision taken by Algerian authorities and applicable on the national territory of Algeria, although of doubtful validity in regard to public international law. By accepting that decision, France had not exercised its 'jurisdiction', in the meaning of Article 1 of the Convention; the situation complained of, therefore, could not be imputed to France: 'Les faits dénoncés en l'espèce, . . . sont . . . la conséquence d'une décision prise unilatéralement par l'Algérie. Quelle que soit la régularité de cette décision au regard du droit international public, elle s'analyse concrètement en un refus de l'Algérie de se conformer à l'accord du 19 mars 1962. Les autorités françaises, dont l'exercice en l'espèce de la "juridiction" sur le territoire algérien avait son seul fondement dans cet accord, n'ont pu qu'en tirer les conséquences quant à la scolarisation des enfants se trouvant dans la situation de ceux des requérantes. Bref, les faits dénoncés ont été causés par une décision imputable à l'Algérie, prise souverainement par elle sur son propre territoire et échappant au contrôle de la France. Autrement dit, dans les circonstances particulières de la cause, lesdits faits ne peuvent être imputés à la France' (Eur. Ct. H.R. (2nd sect.), judgment *Gentilhomme, Schaff-Banhadji and Zerouki v. France* (Appl. nos. 48205/99, 48207/99, and 48209/99) of 14 May 2002, § 20). The contrast between the two cases should not be exaggerated, however, as they can be distinguished on one crucial point: in *Gentilhomme*, the French authorities simply had no choice but to submit to the Algerian change of mood; in *Pellegrini*, instead, the Italian courts were left with the possibility of choosing to recognize the annulment of the marriage or not.

[154] Cf. the *Mines de Potasse* case-law of the European Court of Justice (Case 21/76 *Bier v Mines de Potasse d'Alsace* [1976] ECR 1735), with respect to the interpretation to be given to Article 5(3) of the 1968 Brussels Convention (now Article 5(3) of Regulation No. 44/2001): the Court considered that the expression 'where the harmful event occured' which appears in that provision refers either to the place where the damage occurred or to the place where the event causing the damage occured.

D. The Question of the Parent–Subsidiary Relationship and of the Corporate Veil[155]

In the context of legal suits alleging the civil liability of a EU-based corporation for acts committed outside the EU, one of the most difficult questions is that of the possibility of imputing the violation to that corporation, when it may have only an indirect relationship to the act causing the violation. The question of the imputability of the alleged violation committed abroad to the corporation domiciled in a Member State of the European Union will depend on the nature of the links which exist between the direct author of the violation and that corporation (whether the direct author of the violation is a branch of the abovesaid corporation, its subsidiary, or an autonomous entity enjoying variable degrees of independence) and the recognition given in doctrine to these links, when these are *de facto* rather than *de jure*.

The diversity of solutions may be summarized thus. The nature of the relationship between the direct author of the violation and the EU-based defendant corporation may be either (a) societal or (b) contractual. A societal relationship is obviously present where the direct author of the violation is a mere branch or agency of the defendant corporation. No problem of imputability exists in that case: the act will be directly imputed to the corporation which committed it, albeit in the course of business activities it leads outside the jurisdiction where it has its headquarters or where it is registered. Where the direct author of the violation and the EU-based defendant corporation have distinct personalities, however (and this will be the most frequent hypothesis) the issue is more complex. The parent–subsidiary relationship is still societal rather than contractual, but there may be differing degrees of control of the parent corporation on the activities of its subsidiary. Piercing the corporate veil may be possible in some cases, for instance where the parent corporation fully owns the subsidiary or possesses more than 50 per cent of the shares of the subsidiary company, so that it is in a position to control effectively its activities, or where the boards of directors of both companies are composed essentially or fully of the same individuals.

Where the link between the direct author of the violation and the EU-based defendant corporation is contractual rather than societal, this latter reasoning may still justify imputing the acts of the direct author of the violation to the corporation which, although it has no formal means of controlling the activity of that author, exercises a *de facto* influence on that activity, because of the economic dependancy of the direct author on the defendant corporation.[156] Here, piercing the corporate veil must be understood not as identifying the formally existing relationships between two corporate entitites having separate legal personalities, and thus going beyond reliance on the sole criterion of distinct legal personality: it must be understood,

---

[155] See esp. Meeran, 'The Unveiling of Transnational Corporations: A Direct Approach', in M.K. Addo (ed.), *Human Rights Standards and the Responsibility of Transnational Corporations* (1999), at 161; and by the same author, 'Liability of Multinational Corporations: A Critical Stage in the UK', in Kamminga and Zia-Zarifi, *supra* note 129, at 251.

[156] P. Muchlinski, *Multinational enterprises and the law* (1995), at 327.

rather, as taking into account *de facto* control which the defendant corporation could exercise over its sub-contractor, because of the economic pressure it would be capable of exercising on that sub-contractor. A last situation is that of an existing contractual relationship between the EU-based defendant corporation and a sub-contractor abroad, which allegedly violates human rights, but on which the former corporation is incapable of exercising influence: in this case, one probably has to exclude attributing the act of the latter to the former, and despite the business relationship between the EU-based defendant corporation and the foreign company, it will be very difficult to assert that the European corporation is civilly liable for the damage caused by the violations committed by the foreign company. This of course does not exclude that, where the EU-based defendant corporation participated in the decision directly causing the violation, or even did not react to information that such a decision would be taken when it would have been able to discourage it, the joint liability of the two companies may be asserted.

Of these four situations thus distinguished, two especially are problematic: those where, despite the distinct legal personalities of the EU-based corporation and the foreign corporation, the former exercises *de jure* or *de facto* control over the latter such that it may be justified, in some instances, to attribute the acts of the foreign corporation to the European corporation. Whether or not such an attribution can be made will depend not only on the reality of the control exercised *in general* on the activites of the foreign corporation by the EU-based corporation, but also on the implication of this latter corporation, if any, *in the specific activity or business decision* of the foreign corporation which has led to the violation complained of. Between these two elements, we may postulate a relationship in the form of communicating vases. If the general level of control exercised by the EU-based corporation over its subsidiary or its sub-contractor is sufficiently important, it will matter less if the particular act alleged against the foreign company was not adopted in the knowledge of the EU-based corporation: this corporation should have exercised due diligence on the activities of the foreign company, because of the *de facto* or *de jure* control it exerts over it. Conversely, if the control exercised by the EU-based corporation over its subsidiary or its sub-contractor is weak, the act of the latter will be attributable to the defendant corporation only if it can be shown that, in the particular circumstances, it took an active part in the decision which led to the human rights violation for which reparation is sought, or at least was informed of that decision when it was made and did nothing to prevent or discourage it. But we will then find ourselves in a classic case of joint liability, with two distinct liabilities of two separate actors which acted together.

The 'unity of concern' or 'enterprise' approach developed by the European Court of Justice in European Community competition law illustrates one route by which the corporate veil may be pierced where the corporation which is the direct author of the violation and the defendant corporation have distinct legal personalities, and where the latter seeks to shield itself from a legal suit by invoking that separation. But the doctrine also illustrates the communicating vases relationship (just alluded to above) between the degree of effective control exercised by one company over another, and the implication of the controlling company in the specific act which may trigger its civil liability. Of course, the context in which the European Court of Justice developed this approach is quite distinct from ours. The 'unity of concern' approach has led the European Court of Justice to consider that actions by subsidiaries could be imputed to the parent company if it appeared that the parent actually acted through its subsidiary. Following this approach, Articles 81 and 82 of the EC Treaty can reach certain undertakings, whether or not domiciled in the EU, which effectively control parties to an agreement impeding competition within the common market.[157] The question we are facing is not identical to that of the liability of the parent company domiciled outside the European Union for anti-competitive behaviour producing effects in the European Community.[158] In fact, ours is, to some extent, exactly the reverse question: it is whether the parent company domiciled within the European Union may be held liable for the acts committed abroad by its subsidiary, and, if the corporate veil may be pierced, under which conditions. In other words, which level of control by the parent company over the acts of its subsidiary will be considered sufficient for the unity of the enterprise to predominate on the distinctiveness of the separate legal personalities?

Despite the fact that the respective settings are clearly distinguishable, we may seek inspiration from the answer given to that question by the European Court of Justice. Consider, by way of example, the controversy which led to the *Stora* judgment of 16 November 2000. One of the submissions of Stora Kopparbergs Bergslags AB, the applicant company before the European Court of Justice, was that the Court of First Instance had erred in imputing to Stora the commercial policy of its wholly owned subsidiary, Kopparfors, on the market of cartonboard. In paragraph 80 of the contested judgment, the CFI had reasoned that:

80. In the present case, since the applicant has not disputed that it was in a position to exert a decisive influence on Kopparfors' commercial policy, it is, according to the case-law of the Court of Justice, unnecessary to establish whether it actually exercised that power. Since Kopparfors has been a wholly-owned subsidiary of the applicant since 1 January 1987, it has necessarily followed a policy laid down by the bodies which determine the parent company's policy under its statutes (see Case 107/82 *AEG* v *Commission* [1983] ECR 3151, paragraph 50). In any event, the applicant has not submitted any evidence to support its assertion that Kopparfors carried on its business on the cartonboard market as an autonomous legal entity

---

[157] Case 48/69, *ICI v. Commission* [1972] ECR 619, 692 ff. (Advocate General Mayras); Case 6/72, *Continental Can and Europemballage v. EC Commission* [1973] ECR 215, paras. 14–16; Joined Cases 6–7/73, *CSC and ICI v. Commission* [1974] ECR 223, paras. 26–31. See P.J. Kuyper, 'European Community Law and Extraterritoriality: Some Trends and New Developments', 33 *I.C.L.Q.* (1984), at 1013.

[158] The 'single economic unity' approach of the European Court of Justice is also used to exculpate companies from the accusation of violating the prohibition of agreements laid down in Art. 81 EC Treaty: where a subsidiary does not enjoy real autonomy, it cannot be said to have concluded an agreement with the parent company; the 'agreement' will be analysed, rather, as the division of tasks between a single economic group. In this respect the approach of the European Court of Justice is favourable to the companies of that group.

which determined its commercial policy largely on its own and had its own board of directors with external representatives.

The reasoning of the Court of First Instance, according to which a parent company holding 100 per cent of the shares of a subsidiary necessarily has the power to exercise a decisive influence over the policy of that subsidiary, so that there is a presumption of control which the parent company faces the burden of rebutting, was confirmed by the European Court of Justice in its judgment of 16 November 2000. It is useful, however, to locate this approach as an intermediate one on a scale of solutions. At one end of the scale, perhaps, would be the idea that the corporate veil may not be pierced: that the attribution to the subsidiary of a distinct legal personality excludes holding another economic actor liable for its acts, except in situations of joint liability where, for whatever reason, the acts of the parent company have joined their effects with those of the subsidiary entity in creating the damage. This solution would not be realistic, or rather its effect would be to ensure for parent companies complete impunity for acts which they could not only have avoided by exercising due control over their subsidiaries, but which, moreover, they could have explicitly approved or even instructed to commit. It would conflict with the classic statement according to which 'the fact that a subsidiary has separate legal personality is not sufficient to exclude the possibility of imputing its conduct to the parent company ... in particular where the subsidiary, although having separate legal personality, does not decide independently upon its own conduct on the market, but carries out, in all material respects, the instructions given to it by the parent company'.[159] At the other end of the scale would be the idea that once a parent company is in a position to exercise a decisive influence over its subsidiary (because it owns 50 per cent of the shares or more) then any act of the latter should be imputable to the former, without there being any need to show that, in the particular circumstances of each case, the parent company gave guidelines or instructions to the subsidiary. This would totally subordinate the legal organization of the group of companies in separate legal entities to the economic understanding of the power relationships within the group.

Between these extreme solutions, a number of intermediate positions may be preferred, even in the specific situation of a wholly owned subsidiary. For instance, one could consider that the effect of a 100 per cent shareholding in the subsidiary necessarily implies that the competent organs in the parent company also determine the subsidiary's policy, irrespective of any other specific indicia of effective control over a particular act. Such a position could be read into certain judgments of the European Court of Justice.[160] One could also consider that a 100 per cent

---

[159] Case 48/69, *International Chemical Industries* [1972] ECR 619; Case 6/72, *Europemballage and Continental Can v. Commission* [1973] ECR 215, para. 15.

[160] Case 107/82, *AEG v. Commission* [1983] ECR 3151, para. 50. After having recalled its previous case-law to the effect that 'the fact that a subsidiary has separate legal personality is not sufficient to exclude the possibility of imputing its conduct to the parent company ... in particular where the subsidiary, although having separate legal personality, does not decide independently upon its own conduct on the market, but carries out, in all material respects, the instructions given to it by the parent company'

shareholding must be combined with other elements: for instance the existence of the same management for both the parent company and its subsidiary, or that 'the parent company actually exercised the power to influence the conduct of the subsidiary which its control of the latter's shares conferred on it', for imputability to exist.[161] Or one could take the position that, although the acts of a totally owned subsidiary are presumptively attributable to the parent company, the presumption is not complete, in that other indicia should be put forward to buttress the presumption of control, and thus of imputability. This would appear to be the position of Advocate General J. Mischo in *Stora*: 'although the Commission has the burden of proving that the parent company in fact exercised decisive influence over its subsidiary's conduct, that burden is eased in the case of 100 per cent control. Something more than the extent of the shareholding must be shown, but it may be in the form of indicia'; indeed, 'When a parent company owns all the shares in another company, it can be assumed that it is much more probable that it will exercise tight control over the subsidiary in regard to strategic decisions on pricing, salaries and major investments than that the parent company is not interested in such matters and that the subsidiary enjoys complete autonomy'.[162] As already mentioned, the position of the European Court of Justice in *Stora*, supportive in that respect of the Court of First Instance, was that although 'a 100 per cent shareholding in itself [is not sufficient] for a finding that the parent company was responsible', nevertheless there may be circumstances where this situation operates to reverse the burden of proof, i.e. which may legitimately lead one to suppose 'that the parent company in fact exercised decisive influence over its subsidiary's conduct'.[163] This position is close to that of Advocate General Mischo, but not identifical: it seems that the European Court of Justice accepts that, in certain situations, the fact that the parent company wholly owns a subsidiary and does not deny that the subsidiary lacks decisional autonomy may lead to a reversal of the burden of proof.

Depending on where precisely the line is drawn (the special case of a wholly owned subsidiary is, of course, not the one fraught with the most difficulties) we will arrive at different understandings of the scope of the obligation of the parent company to exercise a form of due diligence on the acts of its subsidiary. The question of imputability to the parent company of the acts of the subsidiary is, indeed, not a question of fact, but a normative question. The question is not: typically,

---

(para. 49), the Court goes on to say that the check 'whether [the parent company] actually made use of this power' is superfluous in the case of a wholly owned subsidiary, which 'necessarily follows a policy laid down by the same bodies as [determine the parent company's policy]' (para. 50). In his opinion delivered on 18 May 2000 in the case of *Stora Kopparbergs Bergslags AB*, Advocate General J. Mischo summarizes this case-law as meaning that 'a wholly-owned subsidiary necessarily follows a policy laid down by its parent company, so that the parent may have the subsidiary's conduct imputed to it without the need to show in any way that it gave instructions or guidelines to its subsidiary' (para. 18).

[161] This seems to have been the position of Stora Kopparbergs Bergslags AB in Case C-286/98 P.
[162] Opinion of Advocate General J. Mischo, delivered on 18 May 2000, paras. 48–49.
[163] ECJ, 16 November 2000, *Stora*, paras. 28–29.

what influence *does* a parent company exercise over the operations of a subsidiary under specificied conditions? Rather, it is: which obligations, and of which reach, do we decide we *want* to impose on parent companies with respect to the acts of their subsidiaries? A presumption of control, and thus of imputability, in certain situations, translates into the imposition of a duty on the parent company to exercise due diligence: it will be under an obligation to protect the human rights of those whom, being affected by the acts of its subsidiary, are within the 'sphere of influence' of the parent company. The absence of any presumption of that kind, and the correlative requirement, in each case, to justify the imputability to the parent company of the acts of its subsidiary, will lead, conversely, to imposing on the parent company only an obligation to respect human rights in the course of its activities: as long as the violations committed (elsewhere) by its subsidiary cannot be traced back to initiatives the parent company has taken, it will escape liability, as the legal persons remain distinct.

E. The Future Use of Regulation No. 44/2001 Against MNEs Domiciled in the EU

It will be recalled that the Resolution on 'EU standards for European enterprises operating in developing countries: towards a European Code of Conduct' adopted by the European Parliament on 15 January 1999 does not mention, except for a vague passage in its Preamble, what was then the 1968 Brussels Convention. However, in the Resolution adopted on 29 May 2002 on the Commission Green Paper on promoting a European framework for corporate social responsibility, the European Parliament, again on the basis of a Report by R. Howitt:

Draws attention to the fact that the 1968 Brussels Convention [as consolidated in Regulation 44/2001 (OJ L 12, 16.1.2001, p. 1)[164]] enables jurisdiction within the courts of EU Member States for cases against companies registered or domiciled in the EU in respect of damage sustained in third countries; calls on the Commission to compile a study of the application of this extraterritoriality principle by courts in the Member States of the Union; calls on the Member States to incorporate this extraterritoriality principle in legislation.[165]

The passage is rather encouraging. It invites us to consider the 1968 Brussels Convention, now codified as Regulation 44/2001, as pregnant with an 'European ATCA', an evolution which it presents as being possible without further legislative

---

[164] This precision is lacking in the adopted resolution, although it figured in the proposed Motion for a Resolution included in the Draft Report on the Commission Green Paper on Promoting a European Framework for Corporate Social Responsibility (Committee on Employment and Social Affairs of the European Parliament, rapporteur: R. Howitt, 5 March 2002). I have no explanation for this change.

[165] Resolution on the Commission Green Paper on promoting a European framework for corporate social responsibility (COM(2001)366—C5-0161/2002—2002/2069(COS)), para. 50. The two last sentences of this paragraph were adopted as an amendment proposed by A. Van Lancker, MEP from the Socialist Group.

changes.[166] The time is ripe, it seems, for legal actions on that basis. That neither the European Commission, in its Communication of 2 July 2002 concerning Corporate Social Responsibility,[167] nor the Council of Ministers in its Resolution on Corporate Social Responsibility of 3 December 2002[168] allude to that possibility should not constitute an obstacle.

5. CRIMINAL LIABILITY OF MULTINATIONALS UNDER EUROPEAN UNION LAW

This section considers whether, and under which conditions, European Union law could encourage the development of the criminal liability of EU-based multinational enterprises in the most extreme cases of corporate misconduct. In some cases this route may be more promising than that of civil liability.[169] First, the state apparatus will be put in service of the fight against impunity of corporations for human rights violations, which may more efficiently deter corporate misconduct and facilitate the burden imposed on victims to prove the reality of that misconduct. Secondly, affirming the criminal liability of the corporation as such may be, in many cases, preferable to affirming the criminal liability of particular individuals, for instance the directors of the company or the executives more immediately involved in the alleged mispractices where these took place. Finding the legal person responsible will ensure more adequate compensation for victims. It may ensure that the same violations will not be repeated in the future, especially where the sanctions imposed on the

---

[166] Cf. the corresponding paragraph in an initial draft resolution on the Green Paper: the European Parliament in that first proposed motion for a resolution 'Calls for the 1968 Brussels Convention to be reviewed in order to clarify the possibility of legal jurisdiction within European Courts for cases of corporate criminal liability involving the worst (and exceptional) cases of corporate negligence in third countries, where access to justice is limited'. This much more hesitant wording, which suggested, indeed, that the present text would not suffice to evolve towards an European ATCA, moreover presented the disadvantage of including a form of the *forum non conveniens* doctrine in the application of the jurisdictional rules of the 1968 Brussels Convention. Although the resolution is more assertive, it should be noted that an amendment proposed by R. Howitt by which the E.P. 'furthermore calls on the Commission to explore the possibility of bringing forward a liability directive to address liability of those multinational corporate groups that are headquartered in one or more EU Member States for serious environmental damage or injury to the health of people in third countries' was not adopted.

[167] COM(2002) 347 final.

[168] Employment, Social Policy, Health and Consumer Affairs Council, 2470th Council Meeting, Brussels, 2–3 December 2002, 14892/02 (Presse 376).

[169] See esp. on these advantages the Preamble to Recommendation No. R (88) 18 of the Committee of Ministers to Member States concerning liability of enterprises having legal personality for offences committed in the exercise of their activities, adopted on 20 October 1988 at the 420th meeting of the Ministers' Deputies. The Recommendation of the Committee of Ministers encourages the Member States of the Council of Europe to apply criminal liability and sanctions to enterprises, 'where the nature of the offence, the degree of fault on the part of the enterprise, the consequences for society and the need to prevent further offences so require'.

corporation include not only fines but also confiscation of property or the closure of certain businesses. Finally, it may prove very difficult, if not impossible, to identify within a complex corporate structure, comprising multiple levels of decision, the individual directly responsible for the alleged violation, and whose criminal liability, therefore, could be engaged where the activities of the corporation lead to such a violation.

Of course, these reasons merely imply that extending the criminal liability of companies for human rights violations which may be imputed to them may be necessary for the effective protection against abuses from corporate conduct. It should not be seen as a substitute either for civil liability, which presents its own advantages,[170] or for the criminal liability of individuals directly responsible for violations which occured in the course of corporate activity, whenever these individuals can be identified.

A. The Example of Extraterritorial Criminal Legislation on Sexual Exploitation of Children

One of the instruments the Howitt Resolution of 15 January 1999 mentions in its Preamble is the Joint Action of 24 February 1997, adopted by the Council on the basis of Article K.3 of the Treaty on European Union (now Article 31 TEU) concerning action to combat trafficking in human beings and sexual exploitation of children.[171] With respect to trafficking in human beings, the Joint Action has been superseded since by the adoption of a normative instrument, in the form of a Framework Decision adopted on 19 July 2002.[172] The reference remains interesting as an example of an instrument adopted under Title VI of the Treaty on the European Union (now limited to police cooperation and judicial cooperation in criminal matters, previously more broadly concerning justice and home affairs) presenting three combined characteristics: it exemplifies the use of the competences of the European Union in the field of criminal judicial cooperation to ensure adequate protection of fundamental rights; it defines the conditions of criminal liability of legal persons; and it encourages each Member State to adopt criminal legislation extending its reach beyond the national territory.

First the Joint Action of 24 February 1997, and now the Framework Decision of 19 July 2002, were adopted with a view to guaranteeing fundamental rights: according to its Preamble, the Joint Action is adopted 'Recalling Article 34 of the Convention on the Rights of the Child of 20 November 1989. Whereas trafficking in human beings and sexual exploitation of children constitute serious infringements of fundamental human rights, in particular human dignity.'[173] Article 34 of the

---

[170] See Jägers, *supra* note 225, at 212–14.   [171] OJ 1997 L 63/2.

[172] Council Framework Decision (2002/629/JHA) of 19 July 2002 on combating trafficking in human beings, OJ 2002 L 203/1.

[173] See also the 3d Recital of the Preamble to the Framework Decision of 19 July 2002.

Convention on the Rights of the Child provides, indeed, that 'States Parties undertake to protect the child from all forms of sexual exploitation and sexual abuse. For these purposes, States Parties shall in particular take all appropriate national, bilateral and multilateral measures to prevent [three listed forms of sexual abuse]'. Harmonization of the Member States' criminal legislations is required because this will facilitate judicial cooperation between the Member States, and thus effective law enforcement. Secondly, the Joint Action obliges each Member State not only to ensure that certain defined forms of behaviour are made criminal offences punishable by 'effective, proportionate and dissuasive criminal penalties', but also that 'legal persons may, where appropriate, be held administratively liable in connection with the offences listed in [the Joint Action] or criminally responsible for such offences, committed on behalf of the legal person in accordance with modalities to be defined in the national law of the Member State. That liability of the legal person is without prejudice to the criminal responsibility of the physical persons who have been accomplices in or instigators of those offences'.[174] Sanctions against legal persons may include confiscation of property, or temporary or permanent closure of establishments which have been used or intended for committing such offences.

Thirdly, the Joint Action requires Member States to give extraterritorial effect to their national criminal provisions concerning trafficking in human beings and sexual exploitation of children.[175] With the exception of one of the offences listed in the joint action, the States must provide that their authorities will be competent not only when the offence is committed on their national territory, but also in cases where the person committing the offence is 'a national or a habitual resident of [the] Member State'.[176] Although the Member State may provide that the adoption or the exercise of such an extraterritorial competence will depend on whether the offence is also punishable under the law of the State where it was committed, this exception to the rule of extraterritorial jurisdiction will only be admitted where another solution, not including this exception, would be 'contrary to the established principles of [the concerned State's] criminal law relating to jurisdiction'. Moreover:

Where a Member State maintains the requirement of double criminality . . . it shall keep its law under review, with a view to ensuring that this requirement is not an obstacle to effective measures against its nationals or habitual residents who are suspected of engaging in such

---

[174] Title II, A, (c), of the Joint Action.

[175] See also Recommendation Rec(2001) 16 on the protection of children against sexual exploitation, adopted by the Committee of Ministers of the Council of Europe on 31 October 2001 at the 771st meeting of the Ministers' Deputies, encouraging the Member States of the Council of Europe to 'consider taking such measures as may be necessary in order to establish extra-territorial jurisdiction over the offences defined under article 2. *c*, *d* and *e* in cases where: *a*. these offences are committed by their nationals; *b*. these offences are committed by any person who has his/her habitual residence on their territory; and, as appropriate, *c*. the victim is one of their nationals'. The Member States are also requested to 'Consider the possibility of establishing jurisdiction over offences of sexual exploitation of children, also in cases where the facts are not punishable under the law of the state where they are committed in particular on account of the age of the victim' (§ 64).   [176] Title II, A, (f), of the Joint Action.

offences in jurisdictions which may not have taken adequate measures as referred to in Article 34 of the Convention on the Rights of the Child of 20 November 1989.

This requirement of extraterritorial incrimination, however, remains wholly within the boundaries which, arguably, are set by public international law to such an expanded prescriptive and adjudicative jurisdiction.[177] Indeed, although the definition of these boundaries remains a matter for controversy after the International Court of Justice failed to address this question in the case of the *Arrest Warrant of 11 April 2000* (*Democratic Republic of the Congo v. Belgium*[178]) it is undisputed that, aside from criminalizing certain forms of conduct which occur within its national territory (territoriality principle), a State may adopt legislation criminalizing certain types of conduct when adopted by its nationals, wherever that conduct takes place (active personality principle of jurisdiction); that it may extend the reach of its criminal legislation to acts committed outside the national territory when the victims are its nationals (passive personality principle of jurisdiction); and that it may enact criminal legislation intending to protect certain very important interests of the State (protective principle of jurisdiction).

Thus, the Joint Action of 1997 and the Framework Decision of 2002, which also contains such a principle of extraterritorial legislation,[179] are perfectly compatible even under the most restrictive reading of which territorial scope of application a State may give its criminal law. Not only is it normally admitted for a State to exercise a form of personal jurisdiction on its nationals even with respect to their activities outside the national territory (the Joint Action only slightly expands the

---

[177] I use here the term 'prescriptive jurisdiction', in conformity with the distinction C. Scott suggests between 'enforcement jurisdiction', 'prescriptive jurisdiction', and 'adjudicative jurisdiction', already mentioned above.

[178] In that case, one of the arguments initially put forward by Congo was that 'The universal jurisdiction that the Belgian State attributes to itself under Article 7 of the Law [of 16 June 1993]' constituted a 'violation of the principle that a State may not exercise its authority on the territory of another State and of the principle of sovereign equality among all Members of the United Nations, as laid down in Article 2, paragraph 1, of the Charter of the United Nations'. However, Congo dropped this argument in the later developments of the proceedings. In its judgment of 14 February 2002, the International Court of Justice therefore considers that 'in view of the final form of the Congo's submissions, the Court will address first the question whether, *assuming that it had jurisdiction under international law to issue and circulate the arrest Warrant of 11 April 2002* [delivered against the then Minister for Foreign Affairs, A. Yerodia], Belgium in so doing violated the immunities of the then Minister for Foreign Affairs of the Congo' (para. 46). In her dissenting opinion, the *ad hoc* Judge for Belgium Ms Van den Wyngaert vehemently criticized this methodology. In her view, not only should the International Court of Justice have addressed the question of whether or not Belgium was in violation of international law by recognizing for its courts a universal jurisdiction for certain crimes of international law; it should also have answered that question in the negative.

[179] Under Article 6(1) of the Framework Decision (*supra* note 172), 'Each Member State shall take the necessary measures to establish its jurisdiction over an offence referred to in Articles 1 and 2 where: (a) the offence is committed in whole or in part within its territory, or (b) the offender is one of its nationals, or (c) the offence is committed for the benefit of a legal person established in the territory of that Member State'. The latter two grounds of jurisdiction are optional, however, when the offence is committed outside the territory of the Member State concerned: see Art. 6(2).

traditional rule by including jurisdiction on 'habitual residents') but, moreover, the compulsory exercise of such competences by the authorities of the Member State is defined so as to make their intervention subsidiary to that of the authorities of the State where the offence was committed: the Member States having adopted the Joint Action may provide that double incrimination will be required, within the limits just mentioned, especially those imposed by the Convention on the Rights of the Child which requires effective protection of the child from sexual exploitation; further, they may decide that the extraterritorial jurisdiction will only be exercised 'if certain procedural conditions are fulfilled, or where the alleged offender cannot be extradited because of:—a refusal by the Member States concerned to comply with a request for extradition made by the State where the offence was committed, or;—confirmation by that latter State that it does not intend to request the extradition of the alleged offender, or;—failure by that State to request the extradition of the alleged offender within a reasonable time'.[180] Moreover, as the reference to the Convention on the Rights of the Child indicates, there exists on the question of combating 'sex' with children such a consensus worldwide that the extraterritoriality of the legislation may be easier to defend.[181]

B. The Added Value of Harmonization at the Level of the European Union

Notwithstanding the specificity of combating the sexual exploitation of children, it should be obvious that these different characteristic features of the Joint Action of 24 February 1997 could furnish the basis for a similar initiative with a view to harmonizing the criminal legislations of the Member States of European Union in the field of violations of human rights committed abroad by MNEs incorporated in the EU. Leaving aside here the state of public opinion, there are essentially two differences between the two issues. First, it is at best doubtful whether Article 31 TEU provides a legal basis for the adoption of an act (a framework decision probably) seeking to harmonize the criminal legislation of the Member States of the EU with respect to human rights violations committed by legal persons. Our question should be, therefore, not what we should do in the existing constitutional framework, but whether that framework should be changed to make such an initiative possible. Secondly, the adoption of such an instrument under Title VI of the TEU would lead the Member States to expand their criminal legislation much further than they were required to do after the adoption of the 1997 Joint Action on

---

[180] Title II, D, of the Joint Action.

[181] Craig Scott rightly notes that 'The more consensus there is of a common international interest in a specific form of legal sanction with respect to specific subject matter, the more that this will count in favour of the acceptability of extraterritorial regulation'. Referring to sexual exploitation of children, the author continues: 'The real question now is not whether states are permitted to regulate their nationals' conduct but whether they have a duty to do so as an extension of their duty to ensure human rights. The more debate focuses on this question, the more it is reasonable to assume that states at least have (prescriptive and adjudicative) jurisdiction over their nationals' behaviour'.

sexual exploitation of children, and perhaps, in some States, to adopt wholly new criminal provisions to target particularly egregious forms of corporate conduct. But this in fact pleads in favour, of, rather than against, such an initiative at the level of the European Union. Could it not be presumed that, if the Member States acting separately are slow to criminalize corporate conduct violating human rights, and even more so to adopt legislation having an extra-territorial scope to that effect, it is because it would be extremely costly for them to do so? Should they not act together, therefore, if acting alone they are paralyzed? Could it not be considered, moreover, that important differences of attitude between Member States with respect to human rights violations committed by companies domiciled under their jurisdiction may justify an initiative by the European Union because of the distortions of competition these differences may entail between these companies, according to the Member State where they are established, at least in a context where extraterritorial legislation is essentially based on the active personality principle rather than on a principle of universal jurisdiction?[182]

The Belgian example may serve to illustrate the added value which could result from the adoption of an instrument in the European Union. Between 1993 and 2003, there existed a law attributing 'universal' jurisdiction to the Belgian courts for war crimes.[183] Initially limited to war crimes, the law was further extended in 1999 to cover the crime of genocide, as defined by Article 2 of the Convention of 9 December 1948 and Article 6 of the Treaty of Rome containing the Statute of the International Criminal Court, and crimes against humanity, the definition of which is borrowed from Article 7(1) of the same Statute.[184] It was a procedure launched under this law against the then Minister for Foreign Affairs of Congo, A. Yerodia, which led the Democratic Republic of the Congo to file proceedings against Belgium before the International Court of Justice, in the *Arrest Warrant of 11 April 2000 Case* referred to above. The Law on serious crimes against international humanitarian law has been combined on two occasions with the Law of 4 May 1999

---

[182] Cf. the opinion of the European Parliament according to which 'the legal and tax provisions of certain Member States which allow tax deductibility for bribes paid in third countries are totally contrary to the Treaty, particularly as regards the provisions concerning aid granted by Member States, since they distort or threaten competition by favouring particular undertakings or products' (Resolution of 6 October 1998 on the communication from the Commission to the Council and the European Parliament on a Union policy against corruption (COM(97)0192—C4-0273/97) (A4-0285/98), Preamble, Recital N (OJ 1998 C 328/46)).

[183] Loi du 16 juin 1993 relative à la répression des infractions graves aux Conventions internationales de Genève du 12 aout 1949 et aux protocoles I et II du 8 juin 1977, additionnels à ces conventions, *M.B.*, 5 August 1993. See esp. Andries, David, Van den Wijngaert, and Verhaegen, 'Commentaire de la loi du 16 juin 1993 relative à la répression des infractions graves au droit international humanitaire', *Rev. dr. pén. et de crim.* (1994), at 1114; and David, 'La loi belge sur les crimes de guerre', *R.B.D.I.* (1995), at 668.

[184] Loi du 10 février 1999 relative à la répression des violations graves du droit international humanitaire, *M.B.*, 23 March 1999. See P. d'Argent, 'La loi du 10 février 1999 relative à la répression des violations graves du droit international humanitaire', *Journal des tribunaux*, 1999, at 549.

on the criminal liability of legal persons.[185] A first complaint was filed in October 2001 against the president of Congo-Brazzaville, Denis Sassou Nguesso, for crimes against humanity committed during and after the civil strife of 1997: the French company TotalFinaElf is mentioned as complicit, for the logistical support it is claimed to have offered to the main defendant. A second complaint was filed in May 2002, this time against unidentified authors of crimes against humanity, including acts of torture, arbitrary killings, and slavery, in Myanmar (ex-Burma), with TotalFinaElf and two of its executives designated as accomplices. These lawsuits, as well as a number of other legal actions based on the Law of 16 June 1993 which appeared politically motivated and were considered an embarrassment to the Belgian diplomacy, led to severe pressures being exercised for the revision of the 'universal jurisdiction' this legislation provided for. The world of business especially denounced the Law of 1993 as creating in Belgium a climate inhospitable to MNEs deploying activities in different parts of the world, including in countries and under regimes where, because of the abuses committed by the government or with its approval or tolerance, it would be very difficult to be an investor without facing the threath of being accused of complicity with these abuses.[186]

As a result of these pressures, the 1993 Law, expanded in 1999, was seriously restricted in 2003. Leaving the terrain of 'universal jurisdiction', the Law of 5 August 2003[187] modifies the Law of 1993 by introducing a requirement that some form of link must exist between the situation complained of and the Belgian legal order. Three alternative possibilities are now open: either the author of the violation is a Belgian national or resides in Belgium, legally or not, when the prosecution commences against him/her (active personality principle); or the victim is a Belgian national or resides in Belgium since three years at least at the moment the violations occur—but whether or not a complaint of the victim may lead to a criminal investigation will depend in this case on an appreciation by the prosecution authorities whether or not the complaint is admissible and whether there is no alternative forum available (passive personality principle); or the author of the violations is found on the Belgian territory, where a conventional or customary rule of international law admits of that ground of jurisdiction of Belgian courts. These modifications, restrict the scope of application of the Belgian Law on serious crimes against international humanitarian law, which in its present form does not provide for 'universal jurisdiction' at all. This is a step backwards in the fight against impunity for crimes of international law, which is hardly compensated by the almost simultaneous entering into force of the Rome Statute of the International Criminal

---

[185] Loi du 4 mai 1999 instaurant la responsabilité pénale des personnes morales, *M.B.*, 22 June 1999.

[186] See Wouters and De Smet, 'De strafrechtelijke verantwoordelijkheid van rechtspersonen voor ernstige schendingen van het internationaal humanitair recht in het licht van de Belgische Genocidewet', in E. Brems and P. Vanden Heede (eds.), *Bedrijven en mensenrechten. Verantwoordelijkheid en aansprakelijkheid* (2003) 309.

[187] Loi du 5 août 2003 relative aux violations graves du droit international humanitaire, M.B., 7 August 2003.

Court. By making these changes, Belgium wished to reassure certain countries whose officials had been threatened by the 1993 Law. But it also intended to protect its attractiveness to companies, which may have been discouraged from investing in Belgium or locating their domicile in Belgium, where they also conduct activities in foreign jurisdictions where they may be found to be complicit in human rights abuses. However, another route could have been followed. It would have been to insist on the adoption by the other Member States of the European Union of similar legislation, to share between European States the burden of offering a forum to the victims of the most serious human rights violations wherever they take place.

It is true that none of the relevant international instruments (the Geneva Conventions of 1949 and their additional Protocols of 1977, the 1948 Convention on the Prevention and Repression of Genocide, the 1984 Convention against Torture, or the 1998 Statute of the International Criminal Court) requires the States Parties to adopt the principle of a truly *universal* jurisdiction for the crimes they identify, although they may impose, to some extent, the extraterritorial application of the provisions in national legislation which criminalize these acts.[188] However, neither does Article 34 of the United Nations Convention on the Rights of the Child, which relates specifically to sexual exploitation of children, nor any other provision of that instrument, oblige States Parties to adopt extraterritorial legislation to combat specific forms of violations of the rights of the child, and the Joint Action of 24 February 1997 was nevertheless adopted with a view to giving effect to that provision. To move towards European harmonization, there is no need to have to fulfil an international obligation on the Member States: it is enough that the required legal basis exists and that the intervention of European Union law presents added value, in comparison to what Member States could achieve individually. As the Joint Action on trafficking in human beings and sexual exploitation of children shows, moreover, this added value may reside in facilitating fuller respect by the Member States for their international obligations.[189]

---

[188] Article 5(1)(b) of the Convention against Torture and other Cruel, Inhuman or Degrading Treatment or Punishment, adopted 10 December 1984, G.A. Res. 39/46, U.N. GAOR, 39th Sess., Supp. No. 51, U.N. Doc. A/39/51 (1985), 1465 UNTS, at 85, provides that each State party shall establish its jurisdiction over acts of torture 'when the alleged offender is a national of that State'.

[189] It is doubtful, but the possibility cannot be wholly excluded, that, in some future, the States Parties to the European Convention on Human Rights may be under an obligation to provide access to a court to victims of the most serious forms of human rights violations, constituting violations of peremptory norms of international law (*jus cogens*), including the prohibition of torture, when no rule of international law requires the recognition of an immunity to the defendant (see Clapham, 'Revisiting Human Rights in the Private Sphere: Using the European Convention on Human Rights to Protect the Right of Access to the Civil Courts', in Scott, *supra* note 24, at 513; as well as the 'Postcript' by the same author, esp. on *Al-Adsani*, at 721–722). Indeed, the judgment of the European Court of Human Rights in *Al-Adsani v. United Kingdom* leaves the question open. In that case, the Court declared that it had not been provided with 'a firm basis on which to conclude that the immunity of States *ratione personae* is no longer enjoyed in respect of civil liability for claims of acts of torture' – but this could be read to mean that, should an action be launched against an *individual* rather than a *State*, at least when the defendant enjoys no immunity imposed by public international law (see ICJ, Case *concerning the Arrest Warrant of 11 April 2000,*

In fact, Belgium offers a second example equally worthy of mention at this juncture. A Bill has been introduced in the House of Representatives, which, according to its title, seeks the 'universal criminalization of certain violations of fundamental social rights'.[190] The objective is to build on the emergence of certain norms considered of universal applicability in the field of social rights—the eight core conventions of the International Labour Organization, the essential content of which is reiterated in the Declaration on the Fundamental Principles and Rights at Work of 18 June 1998—to extend the notion of 'universal' jurisdiction to the violation of those norms—or to extend it, more precisely, to the violation of the Belgian national legislation which corresponds to these norms. The principle is that all persons, whichever their nationality, having violated these norms (including legal persons, after the entry into force of the previously mentioned Law of 4 May 1999) can be prosecuted in Belgium if they are found on Belgian territory. There is no requirement of double incrimination: the norms the violation of which is sanctioned are universally accepted by the international community, so that it would not constitute an encroachment on the sovereignty of other States to promote their universal respect.

What are the chances of such a Bill being adopted? It will immediately be seen that it faces two kinds of critiques, apparently in contradiction with one another, but in fact perfectly complementary. One critique would be that, by adopting such a law, Belgium would be choosing a protectionist attitude in the field of social rights: the law, disguised behind altruistic motives, would in fact be promoting the self-interest of the Belgian—or, more largely, the Northern—workers. Another critique would be that the adoption of such a law, especially if it leads to well publicized prosecutions, would scare a part of the business world away from Belgium; it would therefore not be in Belgium's interest to adopt it. Both these critiques in fact are directed at the falsely ingenuous departure point of the law, according to which any State may take it upon itself to promote the universal respect of certain norms the universal character of which is recognized. This position, which constitutes the most

judgment of 14 February 2002, *supra* note 178), the British courts should have declared themselves competent. The European Court of Human Rights itself suggests that this could be a valid distinction: it noted that the courts of the United Kingdom, in the *Pinochet* case, 'held that, after the Torture Convention and even before, the international prohibition against official torture had the character of *jus cogens* or a peremptory norm and that no immunity was enjoyed by a torturer from one Torture Convention State from the criminal jurisdiction of another. But...that case concerned the immunity *ratione materiae* from criminal jurisdiction of a former head of State, who was at the material time physically within the United Kingdom. As the judgments in the case made clear, the conclusion of the House of Lords did not in any way affect the immunity *ratione personae* of foreign sovereign States from the civil jurisdiction in respect of such acts' (para. 65, referring to the judgment of the House of Lords in *Regina v. Bow Street Metropolitan Stipendiary Magistrate and Others, ex parte Pinochet Ugarte (No. 3)* judgment of 24 March 1999 [2000] AC 147).

[190] Proposition de loi insérant un article 10 quinquies dans le titre préliminaire du Code de procédure pénale, en vue de l'incrimination universelle de certaines violations des droits sociaux fondamentaux, *Ch.*, sess. 1999-2000, doc. no. 0315/001, 9 December 1999.

obviously available answer to both critiques, in fact neglects the gap between the existence of universal norms such as freedom of association, non-discrimination in employment, prohibition of child labour and forced labour, and the rather diverse implementation of these norms in different parts of the world. Here, again, the promotion of such legislation at the level of the European Union would be much more favourable, both for reasons of efficacy (if the purpose is truly to deter, by imposing criminal liability on the offenders, certain acts constituting a violation of fundamental social rights as recognized by the ILO) and for policy reasons (if one wishes to avoid a single Member State attracting all the criticism generally addressed to extraterritorial legislation for the legal imperialism it manifests). Simply put: action may be required at the level of the Union, because a Member State acting individually, even if genuinely motivated by a wish to promote universal respect of an internationally recognized standard may simply not be in a position to do so.

C. Imposing Criminal Liability on Corporations for Human Rights Violations

If it is agreed that an initiative by the European Union would be desirable to encourage the Member States to adopt legislation imposing criminal liability on corporations for serious human rights violations committed either at home or abroad, which charactertistics should such an initiative present? Three questions are to be considered: the form of extraterritoriality which would be most desirable; the norms whose violation should lead to criminal sanctions; and the relationship between the criminal liability of the corporation and the criminal liability of the individuals within that corporation who are directly responsible for the violations committed.

The EU initiative called for should base the jurisdiction of the Member States, ideally, not only on the normal territoriality principle, but also on the active personality principle: the national courts should have jurisdiction over the nationals of the forum State, and over the corporations established in that State.[191] This form of extraterritoriality, short of universal jurisdiction, would nevertheless be 'pure' extraterritoriality, in that it would not require double incrimination.[192] Such a solution should be seen as a compromise between territoriality of the offence as the sole basis for jurisdiction and pure universal jurisdiction, whatever the place of the offence, the nationality of its author, and the nationality of the victim. It would avoid the hypocrisy of the first solution, in which our MNEs are authorized to inflict upon others what we refuse to allow them to do to our workers and communities at home. But it would also escape the accusation of protectionism and judicial imperialism so easily thrown at the second solution: in effect, by imposing extraterritorial jurisdiction based on the active personality principle, the European States would be imposing on 'their' MNEs an obligation to respect certain fundamental

---

[191] See Art. 6(1) of the Framework Decision (2002/629/JHA) of 19 July 2002 on combating trafficking in human beings, *supra* note 172.

[192] Van den Wijngaert, 'De toepassing van de strafwet in de ruimte. Enkele beschouwingen', in *Liber amicorum Frédéric Dumon* (1983), at 516.

rights when operating abroad, directly or through subsidiaries, without imposing the respect of these norms directly on third States; and an exception could be provided, with respect to fundamental rights which are neither part of peremptory norms of international law nor binding on the host State by virtue of the international conventions that State adhered to, when the national legislation of the host State requires that certain restrictions be brought to these rights. Such a conception of permissible extraterritoriality would appear to be compatible with the present state of international law, including the principle of comity between nations.[193]

A second question concerns the identity of the norms whose violation, by corporations operating from the EU and conducting activities abroad, could justify imposing on them criminal liability. Essentially the same criteria as have inspired the United States federal judiciary in interpreting the notion of 'law of nations' in the context of the Alien Tort Claims Act should be relied upon. First, the norms in question should enjoy almost universal recognition, and universal recognition should not be confused, of course, with universal obedience.[194] It would be both inadvisable and impractical to have the Member States impose on 'their' companies obligations which go beyond these universally recognized norms of international law. Indeed, at least in some extreme cases and with respect to certain environmental or social norms, this would put these EU-based corporations at a disadvantage in comparison with their competitors based in other, more tolerant, jurisdictions, with the implication that political support for the imposition of such extended obligations may be difficult to find, and that some corporations might even be tempted to delocalize their headquarters. Moreover, because of the impression of legal imperialism necessarily entailed by the adoption of an extraterritorial legislation, especially of a criminal sort, it may be opportune to base such legislation on

---

[193] In the context of the OECD, the Member States have agreed, under the 21 June 1976 Declaration on International Investment and Multinational Enterprises, to 'co-operate with a view to avoiding or minimising the imposition of conflicting requirements on multinational enterprises' (para. III). Under the General Considerations concerning conflicting requirements imposed on mutlinational enterprises, it is stated that 'In contemplating new legislation, action under existing legislation or other exercise of jurisdiction which may conflict with the legal requirements or established policies of another Member country and lead to conflicting requirements being imposed on multinational enterprises, the Member countries should [*inter alia*] have regard to relevant principles of international law', and 'endeavour to avoid or minimise such conflicts and the problems to which they give rise by following an approach of moderation and restraint, respecting and accommodating the interests of other Member countries'. It is further stated in a note that 'Applying the principle of comity, as it is understood in some Member countries, includes following an approach of this nature in exercising one's jurisdiction'. Although these considerations apply formally only between the Member States of the OECD, they may be seen as an interpretation of the relationship of extraterritorial jurisdiction with the principle of comity. The OECD Guidelines, esp. as revised in June 2000, are discussed further in broader detail below at text accompanying notes 227–233.

[194] An adequate starting point for the listing of such international norms, both enjoying almost universal recognition and relevant for the conduct of companies, may be found in the European Parliament's 15 January 1999 Resolution on EU standards for European enterprises operating in developing countries: towards a European Code of Conduct (rapporteur R. Howitt) (A4-0508/1998, OJ 1999 C 104/176), at para. 12.

universally recognized norms of international law, to escape the reproach of wishing to impose one's own values (for instance one's values as to how to conduct ethical business) on other States. Finally, the more universal the norms are which extra-territorial legislation adopted by the home State of a multinational enterprise seeks to impose wherever the activity takes, the less the risk of conflicting requirements being imposed on the same business activity.[195]

Secondly, the international norms on the basis of which the liability could be based would need to be implemented at a sufficient level of specificity to lend themselves to the imposition of criminal sanctions in cases of violation. It should be emphasized, however, that it is not the international norm which would need to be specific, as in the case of the ATCA where international law directly serves as a basis for a civil action in tort liability lodged with the United States courts. The suggestion here is, rather, that a right such as the right to health, although defined in relatively vague terms in the International Covenant for Economic, Social, and Cultural Rights, may by its very presence in the Covenant justify recognizing an extrater-ritorial reach to certain provisions from the criminal code of an EU Member State, for example with respect to marketing dangerous products or environmental pol-lution detrimental to the health of the population. What needs to be universal is the fundamental right the effective protection of which justifies the adoption of extra-territorial criminal legislation. What needs to be specific is the precise definition of the behaviour considered criminal, which will typically rely on norms more detailed and complete than the international norm itself, although rights such as those to respect for private or family life, freedom of expression, and freedom of association may well constitute exceptions.

A third question is that of the relationship between the criminal liability of the legal person for certain severe violations of human rights, and that of the natural persons who are the direct authors of the violation complained of. Any definition of this relationship should take into account two conflicting requirements: first, of course, to ensure that the criminal liability of the legal person serves a useful effect, i.e. is not so narrowly defined that it will be in most cases impossible to engage; secondly, however, there is a need to avoid any sense of collective punishment, where one individual uses his or her position within a company as a shield to escape his or her own liability, or uses the company apparatus and operational resources to commit offences for the purely private purposes he or she has.[196] The need to steer

---

[195] The risk should not be overestimated. The sheer lack of adequate protection of certain fundamental rights, in the legal system of certain jurisdictions, does not lead to conflicting requirements being imposed on economic actors conducting activities there: it is only if the law of the host State imposes certain violations that the conflict arises. In any event, the extraterritorial legislation envisaged could provide for an exception in such cases, unless the local rule is in violation of a peremptory norm of international law.

[196] It will be noted, in relation to the use of the expression 'collective punishment' in this context, that the sanctions usually imposed on legal persons found criminally liable, such as exclusion from entitlement to public benefits or aid, disqualification from the practice of commercial activities, or the temporary or permanent closure of an establishment used for committing the offence (see Art. 5 of the the Framework Decision (2002/629/JHA) of 19 July 2002 on combating trafficking in human beings, *supra* note 179)

away from collective responsibility justifies the principle, formulated for instance by the 1988 Recommendation of the Committee of Ministers of the Council of Europe to Member States concerning liability of enterprises having legal personality for offences committed in the exercise of their activities, according to which 'The enterprise should be exonerated from liability where its management is not implicated in the offence and has taken all the necessary steps to prevent its commission' (Principle I.4). Therefore, although criminal liability of the enterprise may help to attain certain objectives of the criminal law and augment both its dissuasive effect and the chances of reparation for the victims, which will even justify the imposition of a criminal liability of enterprises 'for offences committed in the exercise of their activities, even where the offence is alien to the purposes of the enterprise', not all faults of its employees can be imputed to the company: either the 'directing minds' of the company must have played a role in the commission of the offence (in the vocabulary of the common law[197]) or the company must have failed to exercise due diligence in monitoring the activities of its employees.

These principles have now gained common acceptance.[198] They clearly also guide Article 4 of the the Framework Decision of 19 July 2002 on combating trafficking in human beings, which states under the heading 'Liability of legal persons' that 'Each Member State shall take the necessary measures to ensure that legal persons can be held liable' for the offences identified in the Decision, 'committed *for their benefit* by any person, acting either individually or as part of an organ of the legal person, *who has a leading position within the legal person*, based on: (a) a power of representation of the legal person, or (b) an authority to take decisions on behalf of the legal person, or (c) an authority to exercise control within the legal person'. The Article then adds that, apart from that situation where the 'directing minds' of the enterprise have played a role in the offence, 'each Member State shall take the necessary measures to ensure that legal persons can be held liable where the lack of supervision or control' by a person having such a leading position in the company 'have rendered possible

will affect not only the legal person as such, but also, by definition, all its employees, who will suffer economic consequences of the losses entailed and may, for instance, be laid off as a consequence of a liability which is not theirs personally.

[197] G. Ferguson, 'Corruption and Corporate Criminal Liability', paper presented at the conference *Corruption and Bribery in Foreign Business Transactions: A Seminar on New Global and Canadian Standards*, 4–5 February 1999, Vancouver, Canada, at 6. Cited in M. Wagner, 'Corporate Criminal Liability: National and International Responses', International Society for the Reform of Criminal Law 13th International Conference, *Commercial and Financial Fraud: A Comparative Perspective*, Malta, 8–12 July 1999.

[198] See also e.g. Article 9(1) of Council of Europe Convention on the Protection of the Environment through Criminal Law of 4 November 1998 (E.T.S., no. 172), stating that 'Each Party shall adopt such appropriate measures as may be necessary to enable it to impose criminal or administrative sanctions or measures on legal persons on whose behalf an offence referred to in [the provisions of the Convention defining certain environmental offences] has been committed by their organs or by members thereof or by another representative'. On 1 June 2002, only one State (Estonia) has ratified the Convention, which should be ratified by at least 3 States before it may enter in force.

the commission of [the offence] for the benefit of that legal person by a person under its authority'.

In sum, there would be few difficulties if the choice was made by the European Union to invite the Member States to adopt certain measures to ensure that certain forms of corporate conduct, leading to severe violations of human rights, are made punishable by criminal legislation applicable not only in the territory of each Member State, but also to the conduct of corporations established in a Member State, even when the conduct takes place outside the territory. It is true that, in the present form of the treaties, an adequate legal basis may still be lacking. This should be remedied. But the questions of principle raised by such an initiative—to ensure the effectiveness of *which* norms, by *which* form of extra-territoriality, with *which* combination of individual and corporate responsibility—have met their answers in other contexts. None of the problems seem insuperable.

6. THE VOLUNTARY CONTRIBUTION OF MULTINATIONALS TO THE PROMOTION OF HUMAN RIGHTS: CODES OF CONDUCT

Codes of conduct have acquired, deservedly, a bad reputation in human rights circles. When they are designed by the companies concerned, when they lack any independent and public monitoring mechanism, they are indeed merely public relations exercises. Their sudden proliferation is suspicious: by adopting codes of conduct and presenting self-regulation as the most adequate way for them to accept social responsibility, are companies not avoiding the drive towards the regulation of their activities? However, although it is essentially well founded, the difficulty with an across-the-board condemnation of codes of conduct is that it fails to distinguish between different types of codes, and the different control mechanisms their adoption can be combined with to give them effect. It will be useful, then, to present the variety of techniques which fall under the notion of 'codes of conduct', so as to identify the conditions under which these may be said to serve a useful purpose, rather than simple window-dressing.

A. The 1977 Code of Conduct for EU Enterprises Operating in South Africa

An historical example offers a point of departure. After the United Kingdom joined the European Communities in 1973, the Community—inspired by the British example of the Code of Practice which was then being imposed on UK firms having subsidiaries operating in South Africa—adopted a Code of Conduct[199] (on 20 September 1977) with the same philosophy: under the growing pressure of public

---

[199] *Bull. EC*, 9-1977, at 50.

opinion to boycott South Africa or, at least, to stop investing there, the purpose was to guarantee that the economic actors operating under the regime of apartheid would respect certain principles and thus not become complicit in racial discrimination.[200] The Code was adopted under the European Political Cooperation (EPC), the predecessor of the Common Foreign and Security Policy (CFSP) introduced with the Maastricht Treaty. Given the extreme fragility of European foreign policy at the time, the adoption of the Code of Conduct was considered to be a success, notwithstanding its important limits. The Code, which was to be voluntarily adopted by European businesses operating in South Africa (although a minority of the Member States and the European Parliament strongly advocated a mandatory code) covered a number of employment practices, imposing, for example, freedom of association (including the recognition of black trade unions), desegregation in the workplace, and minimum wage levels. Under Article 7 of the Code, the firms agreeing to abide by the Code were to report annually on its application: the report was to mention the number of black Africans employed in the undertaking and comment on the progress made in each of the six fields covered by the Code. These reports were to be transmitted to the national governments. This implementation by the Member States, each government receiving reports from its own enterprises, soon appeared to constitute one of its main handicaps: Martin Holland notes that, behind the impression of a common uniform measure, 'there were serious discrepancies in application between member states resulting in superficial uniformity'.[201] A Resolution adopted soon after the Code of Conduct was first inaugurated mentions that a uniform application of the Code is required if distorsions in competition between European enterprises operating in South Africa are to be avoided.[202] Although improvements were brought to the system when the Code was revised in November 1985, by the introduction of a more detailed common reporting format to ensure uniformity in firm reporting, by involving the national parliaments, the European Parliament, and the Economic and Social Committee in the annual reporting process, and by providing for consultation between the diplomatic representations of the Member States in South Africa,[203] this remained a difficulty throughout the lifetime of the Code.

The creation of a transitional government in South Africa in 1993 led to the abandonment of the requirement of formal reporting under the Code of Conduct, which had by then outlived its purpose. The results of a decade and a half of implementation of the Code appeared to be extremely meagre. Not only did the number of employees covered by the Code diminish after 1985–86, when the

---

[200] On the context of the adoption of the Code, see M. Holland, *European Union Common Foreign Policy: From EPC to CFSP Joint Action and South Africa* (1995), at 36–9.

[201] Holland, *supra* note 200, at 39.

[202] Résolution sur la forme, le statut, le contexte et l'application du code de conduite pour les entreprises de la Communauté ayant des filiales, des succursales ou des représentations en Afrique du Sud, OJ 1979 C 127/56, para. 10 of the resolution.

[203] On these changes, Holland, *supra* note 200, at 42–3.

divestment policy was adopted, but also the objectives set by the Code were hardly met during the period: in 1990 still, 'universal recognition of black trade unions was absent; the use of migrant labour continued to represent 10 per cent of the Community's black workforce; 2 per cent of employees were still paid below the recommended minimum "supplemented living level (SLL)"; and "a small number of companies . . . had not yet achieved full desegregation" as required by section 6 of the Code'.[204] Almost from the start, the Code of Conduct was criticized by certain business circles and conservative political groups as impeding the competitiveness of European enterprises in South Africa; at the same time, it was dismissed by progressives as being inspired by an outmoded paternalism and as simply legitimating the businesses remaining in South Africa when the priority was to leave.

B. The 1998 Code of Conduct for Arms Exports[205]

The lessons from the Code of Conduct for European undertakings operating in South Africa were not wholly assimilated in 1991–1992, when the EU Member States for the first time agreed on a list of eight criteria governing arms exports, here again in the field of intergovernmental cooperation given the presence of an explicit clause in the Treaty of Rome reserving to the Member States the questions related to arms production and trade.[206] Indeed, although these criteria were common—they required, *inter alia*, to take into account the human rights record of the recipient, whether or not the export was to a region of tension, whether or not the recipient was at war or in a process of internal repression—they were interpreted in widely different terms by the EU countries, with little coordination between them as to, for example, how to judge the eligibility of a particular country in the face of human rights abuses committed by its government, or whether or not a particular region of the world should be defined as a 'region of tension'. The lack of uniform interpretation of the criteria prompted a coalition of NGOs led by Saferworld to propose a more detailed European Union Code of Conduct for arms exports, and a vast campaign for the adoption of such was launched during the period 1993–98. The United Kingdom presidency of the Union from the first semester 1998 represented a breakthrough. Early during that presidency, the European Parliament expressed its regret that 'the existing common EU criteria governing arms exports, agreed by the Council in 1991–1992, are being applied by each individual Member State according to its own interpretation and have not prevented the flow of arms from EU Member States to countries which violate human rights, to regions of instability and military aggressors'.[207] The newly elected Labour government, having secured

---

[204] Holland, *supra* note 200, at 50.

[205] I am basing my presentation on A. McLean, 'The European Union Code of Conduct on Arms Exports', in Addo, *supra* note 155, at 115.

[206] See Article 223 EEC Treaty (now, after modification, Article 296(1) EC).

[207] European Parliament, Resolution of 15 January 1998 on a European code of conduct on the export of arms (B4-0033, 0058, 0064, 0081, 0086, and 0104/98), OJ 1998 C 034/163.

the support of the French government, seized the occasion. It proposed a much more stringent Code, comprising a system of coordination between the attitudes of the Member States for its uniform implementation.

The resulting system is far from perfect, but it still represents a notable step forward in comparison with the 1991–92 criteria and their system of implementation. Among other criteria, the Code of Conduct on arms exports, adopted on 25 May 1998, stipulates that 'Member States will not issue an export licence if there is a clear risk that the proposed export might be used for internal repression', if the export is to a region of instability, or 'if there is a clear risk that the intended recipient would use the proposed export aggressively against another country or to assert a territorial claim'. It is of course essential for the effectiveness of the Code that denial by one Member State of an export licence will not be undercut by another. Therefore, the Member States are to inform one another when they refuse an export licence because it does not satisfy one of the listed criteria, and if a country wishes to take up the contract it must consult with the Member State which previously denied the licence. The system is only partly satisfactory because these consultations remain purely bilateral, thus not meeting the expectations of the European Parliament,[208] which according to A. McLean 'will inevitably lead to a lack of consistency in the implementation of the Code'.[209] This is only partially compensated by the annual reports Member States have to circulate on their national arms exports and implementation of the Code, as these reports are not made public—a measure which would facilitate parliamentary control—and in any case are only retrospective, and therefore can hardly serve the purpose of *a priori* coordination of policies. This lack of multilateral coordination is further accentuated by the absence of a common list of countries which, because of their human rights record, should not be issued licences.

Andrew McLean concludes from his presentation of the May 1998 Code of Conduct on Arms Exports that the decisions whether or not to grant export licences 'will continue to be made according to national discretion and the effectiveness of the Code is likely to depend on the extent to which the Member States consider themselves as being bound by export licence denials which are issued by other governments'.[210] This may be seen as a result of the conflicting needs of the arms industry in the EU, which requires common rules to ensure that the particular arms export policy of each national government will not put some companies at a competitive disadvantage in comparison to competitors in other Member States, but at the same time prefers the least stringent rules possible. By attempting to satisfy

---

[208] Prior to the adoption of the Code, the European Parliament called on the Council and the Member States 'to improve the prevailing situation by agreeing on consultation mechanisms which ensure that all Member States are swiftly informed of approvals and denials of export licences, and that any Member State intending to undercut a decision by another is obliged to inform and consult with all other Member States about its intention': see the Resolution on a code of conduct for arms exports (B4-0502, 0505, 0520, 0522, 0529, and 0546/98), OJ 1998 C 167/226, para. 2 of the resolution.

[209] McLean, *supra* note 205, at 120.   [210] McLean, *supra* note 205, at 121.

both needs, the compromise solution embodied in the 1998 Code of Conduct may end up meeting neither: the temptation of arms export policies to be guided by national economic interests remains present, and the victims of arms exports to repressive regimes in third countries remain insufficiently protected. In this context, it is regrettable that, just as it has not at yet affirmed the obligation of States Parties to the European Convention on Human Rights to offer a remedy against the most serious forms of human rights abuses either caused by their nationals or of which their nationals are victims (according to, respectively, the active and the passive personality principle in the exercise of jurisdiction), the organs of the Convention have considered that the decision of a State Party to authorize the selling of arms to an oppressive regime does not trigger the international responsibility of that State Party, even when this decision results in damage being caused to the victims of that regime, in the absence of a sufficiently direct link between the failure of the State to effectively control arms exports from its territory and the injury caused abroad.[211] A more extensive definition of the obligation of the States Parties to the Convention to protect the rights of individuals, even when the effects of the violation occur abroad, against the consequences of the decisions taken by their organs, may have provided the necessary incentive for Member States of the European Union to make further progress on this question.[212]

The experience of the Code of Conduct for European Community enterprises operating in South Africa shows that, for a code of conduct to be effectively implemented, two conditions should be fulfilled: first, the code of conduct should impose clearly verifiable obligations on the entreprises who decide to adopt them, and violations of the code should be sanctioned; and secondly, to ensure comparability between the undertakings, uniform standards should be set, although the concrete significance these standards will take may differ from sector to sector or from context to context. Codes of conduct, by definition, are voluntarily adopted; if

---

[211] Eur. Commiss. H.R., *Rasheed Tugar v. Italy* (Appl. no. 22869/93), decision of 18 October 1995, unpublished. The applicant, an Iraqi national, was employed as a mine-clearer in Iraq, when, in April 1993, he stepped on a mine and his lower right leg had to be amputated. In 1982 the Iraqi Ministry of Foreign Affairs had made a contract with the Italian company V.M., regarding the supply by V.M. to Iraq of 5,750,000 anti-personnel mines to be delivered before December 1983. Before 1990 there was no specific law in Italy regulating the export of weapons. The Italian Ministry of Foreign Trade enjoyed a wide margin of discretion in delivering export licences. The applicant alleged that he was a victim of the violation by Italy of the right to life protected under the Convention: Italy 'did not regulate the sale of anti-personnel mines not containing any self-detonating or self-neutralising mechanism, thus failing to secure his right to life as guaranteed by Article 2 of the Convention'. The Commission dismissed the application as manifestly ill founded, reasoning that 'the applicant's injury cannot be seen as a direct consequence of the failure of the Italian authorities to legislate on arms transfers. There is no immediate relationship between the mere supply, even if not properly regulated, of weapons and the possible "indiscriminate" use thereof in a third country, the latter's action constituting the direct and decisive cause of the accident which the applicant suffered.'

[212] It may not be purely coincidental that Ms Françoise Hampson (Essex University), who played a major role in the Saferworld-led campaign of 1993 in favour of a European Code of Conduct on Arms Exports, was during the same period representing M.R. Tugar before the European Commission on Human Rights.

they are imposed, there is nothing to distinguish them from regulation, and the expression then loses its specific meaning. This voluntary character of codes of conduct should not necessarily lead to the conclusion that they are useless: harmless to companies, of no help to their workers or the communities they affect by their activities. Not only are codes of conduct standards which companies proclaim to adopt and abide by, which implies that trade unions will be able to rely on these standards in the course of negotiating collective agreements[213] or that the content of the code of conduct may serve the purpose of identifying what constitutes a 'fault' in the context of civil liability proceedings against the company.[214] But, moreover, codes of conduct could, once they are voluntarily adopted or accepted by companies, impose on these certain obligations, either by the institution of independant monitoring mechanisms or by the use of the 1984 Directive concerning misleading and comparative advertising. Codes of conduct also facilitate the functioning of market mechanisms obliging a company to internalize, to some extent at least, the costs of violating social, ethical, or environmental standards, under pressure from consumers or investors.

C. The Code of Conduct as Misleading Advertising of a Company's Practices

In its May 2002 Resolution on the Commission Green Paper on promoting a European framework for corporate social responsibility, the European Parliament 'calls on the Commission to enforce strong consumer protection measures to uphold the credibility of corporate information in relation to environmentally and socially responsible business practice, in particular applying the provisions regarding misleading advertising'.[215] Codes of conduct, whether drafted by an enterprise to suit its own needs and specificities or adopted from a Model Code, primarily serve as a message to the consumers that the goods or services they are acquiring are produced in socially, ethically, or environmentally acceptable conditions. Codes of conduct, in that sense, advertise the practices of the company to its customers, whose choices are increasingly guided by principles other than purely economic considerations. The

---

[213] See e.g. the Code of Conduct adopted in September 1997 by the social partners in the European textile and clothing sector (European Apparel and Textile Organisation EURATEX (employers) and European Trade Union Federation of Textiles, Clothing, and Leather ETUF:TCL (workers)). As remarked in a Newsletter from the European Commission: 'Through the inclusion of its clauses in national collective agreements—which are negotiated and concluded at national level in the Member States of the European Union—the content of this code acquired legal status and binding force. It therefore constitutes a good example of how problems related to implementation and monitoring of codes of conduct can be tackled' (European Social Dialogue (Newsletter from the EC Employment & Social Affairs DG), May 1999, at 5–6).

[214] See e.g. McCrudden, 'Human Rights Codes for Transnational Corporations: What Can the Sullivan and MacBride Principles Tell Us?', 19 *Oxford J. Legal Stud.* (1999), at 167; or Betlem, *supra* note 103, at 294–5.

[215] Resolution, *supra* note 164, para. 33. Council Directive 84/450/EEC of 10 September 1984 relating to the approximation of laws, regulations and administrative provisions of the Member States concerning misleading advertising (OJ 1984 L 250/17) is mentioned in the Preamble of the Resolution.

Council Directive of 10 September 1984 concerning misleading and comparative advertising defines 'advertising' in the broadest fashion possible, as 'the making of a representation in any form in connection with a trade, business, craft or profession in order to promote the supply of goods or services . . .'[216] Codes of conduct are covered by this definition. The information misleading to the consumers which, 'by reason of its deceptive nature, is likely to affect their economic behaviour', includes the method of manufacture or the geographical origin:[217] thus, whenever codes refer to the working conditions in which the advertsised goods were produced, or—as may be justified when certain boycott campaigns are launched—to the countries in which the production took place, this information, if deceptive, should be sanctioned, and Member States are under an obligation ensure that adequate and effective means exist to combat advertising referring to it. The Directive details the procedural safeguards which must be provided by national legislations of the Member States, for the consumer to be effectively protected against misleading advertising. In particular, organizations regarded under national law as having a legitimate interest in prohibiting misleading advertising should be able to take legal or administrative action;[218] and, perhaps even more importantly, in such proceedings courts or administrative authorities should have the power 'to require the advertiser to furnish evidence as to the accuracy of factual claims in advertising if, taking into account the legitimate interest of the advertiser and any other party to the proceedings, such a requirement appears appropriate on the basis of the circumstances of the particular case', and 'to consider factual claims as inaccurate' if the evidence thus demanded 'is not furnished or is deemed insufficient by the court or administrative authority'.[219]

D. Monitoring Compliance with Codes of Conduct

By relying on the national legislations implementing the Directive of 10 September 1984 on misleading and comparative advertising, consumer organizations could therefore request from the competent national authorities that they become overseers of the practices of undertakings. According to the Directive, when these decide to publicize a Code of Conduct by which they present their methods of production as respecting certain social, ethical, or environmental standards, they must accept scrutiny of their activities. This illustrates that codes of conduct, whatever the initial purpose of the company adopting it, may lead to the imposition of new obligations on that company, because it binds itself by the code it adopts. Aside from the specific mechanism of the 1984 Directive on misleading and comparative advertising, a proposal has been made for systematic independent monitoring of the codes

---

[216] Article 2 of Council Directive 84/450/EEC of 10 September 1984 concerning misleading and comparative advertising, as amended by Directive 97/55/EC of European Parliament and of the Council of 6 October 1997, OJ 1997 L 290/18, corrigendum OJ 1998 L 194/54.

[217] Article 3 of Council Directive 84/450/EEC.

[218] Article 4(1) of Council Directive 84/450/EEC.

[219] Article 6 of Council Directive 84/450/EEC.

of conduct adopted by EU-based enterprises, as a condition of the credibility of these codes of conduct. The July 2001 Green Paper of the European Commission on corporate social responsibility notes that:

With respect to human rights there is a need for ongoing verification where the implementation and compliance with codes is concerned. The verification should be developed and performed following carefully defined standards and rules that should apply to the organisations and individuals undertaking the so-called 'social auditing'. Monitoring, which should involve stakeholders such as public authorities, trade unions and NGOs, is important to secure the credibility of codes of conduct. A balance between internal and external verification schemes could improve their cost-effectiveness, in particular for SMEs. As a result there is a need to ensure greater transparency and improved reporting mechanisms in codes of conduct.

The 1999 Howitt Resolution already called on the Commission to study the possibility of setting up a European Monitoring Platform, as an independant and impartial forum in which the social partners, NGOs from north and south and representatives of indigenous and local communities, would be represented, and one of its tasks would be to receive information about the voluntary initiatives and conduct of business and industry 'so that their compliance with . . . private voluntary codes of practice (if adopted) could be properly assessed'.[220] Such a mechanism would, in effect, oblige the enterprises to abide by their own, self-imposed, standards, by obliging enterprises to report on the implementation of their code of conduct and by providing for independent control of the compatibility of their conduct with the standards set forth in the code. In the 2001 Resolution on the Green Paper of the Commission on corporate social responsibility, based on the consultations and findings of the same rapporteur, the European Parliament calls for the creation of an 'EU Multi-Stakeholder CSR Forum, comprising representation from business, trade unions, non-governmental organizations and public authorities including from developing countries', and entrusted with the registration of voluntary codes of conduct and with their verification 'against minimum applicable international standards such as the OECD Guidelines for Multinationals and the ILO Core Labour Standards'.[221] The European Monitoring Platform called for by the European Parliament in its 15 January 1999 Resolution has been set up, as yet, only in a preliminary format. The Communication of the European Commission on Corporate Social Responsibility of 2 July 2002 merely states that codes of conduct should 'include appropriate mechanisms for evaluation and verification of their implementation, as well as a system of compliance', and it invites the EU Multi-Stakeholder Forum on CSR to 'consider the effectiveness and credibility of

---

[220] Resolution on EU standards for European enterprises operating in developing countries: towards a European Code of Conduct, adopted by the European Parliament on 15 January 1999, A4-0508/1998, OJ 1999 C 104/176, para. 17.

[221] Resolution on the Commission Green Paper on promoting a European framework for corporate social responsibility (COM(2001)366—C5-0161/2002—2002/2069(COS)), paras. 13–14.

existing codes of conduct and how convergence can be promoted at European level'.[222]

Especially for SMEs, the institution of such an independent monitoring body, publicly funded and working on a permanent basis, would present another advantage: it notably diminishes the costs of adopting a code of conduct made credible by the existence of such a control mechanism. And for all enterprises, it may limit the tension between their desire to reassure the buyers of their products or services as to the conformity of these with certain standards, and the need to avoid a too costly competitive disadvantage, in the presence of other enterprises competing on the same market but perhaps less scrupulous, either in the standards they adopt or in ensuring that their conduct corresponds to the norms to which they profess to adhere. In these two ways, the institution of a monitoring body at a European level, perhaps operating as a Commission Office, should be seen not as a further obstacle imposed on the economic activity of enterprises bases in the European Union, but as a public good furnished to these enterprises, facilitating their socially responsible conduct in a competitive environment which does not necessarily immediately reward such conduct.

However, the 1999 Howitt Resolution also recommended the regular organization of public hearings on specific cases of corporate conduct, both good and bad. The purpose is to put pressure on companies by the negative publicity which certain practices could receive through such hearings, the effectiveness of which in monitoring corporate conduct relies heavily on the interest the media could take in the public discussion of certain situations. The second of such hearings was held in October 2001, when a French company (TotalFinaElf) and a British company (Premier Oil) were questioned on allegations that, through their oil exploitation activities in Burma, they were complicit in wide-scale human rights abuses committed by the Burmese military.

In the context of such a procedure, too, the adoption by a company of a code of conduct may prove more compromising for the company than would initially have been imagined. Indeed, attendance by the company at the public hearing is voluntary, and the only sanction for a company refusing to attend (as Adidas chose to do in the first such public hearing, organized on the theme of the textile industry in Southeastern Asia and in which the CleanClothes campaign had a prominent role) will be a possible negative reaction from the public of consumers, at least if the media adverstise sufficiently widely the uncooperative attitude of the enterprise. But a company which has adopted a code of conduct will find it difficult to refuse even to discuss the conformity of its practices with the code. Such a refusal will immediately make the code of conduct appear as purely an exercise in public relations, and the negative impression created on the public will be important.

---

[222] Communication of the Commission on Corporate Social Responsibility, COM(2002) 347 final, at 8. See also on the missions of the CSR EMS Forum at 18 of the Communication. More should be known on the potential of that Forum in 2004, when it is to file a report with the Commission on its future role.

E. Model Codes of Conduct

As the recent Resolution of the European Parliament on the Green Paper on corporate social responsibility states in its findings, 'the broad diversity of voluntary codes of conduct and labels with very different standards and verification mechanisms makes comparison of effective performances problematic'.[223] Indeed, this diversity.[224] makes it very difficult for the consumer to distinguish between credible and less credible codes. This leads to an asymmetry of information between the enterprise and the consumer, for the enterprise may know what its self-adopted code is worth (according to both its standards and monitoring mechanisms) but this will be very difficult for the consumer to discover. As a result (as in Gresham's law revisited by G.A. Akerlof in his famous analysis of the market in used cars) if enterprises and consumers are left to themselves, the worst codes of conduct may drive out the better ones.[225] Whilst the existence of good codes of conduct benefits all the enterprises, by enhancing the reputation of a particular sector or market or of the act of adopting a code of conduct in general, it will be more advantageous for each individual enterprise to adopt a less stringent code of conduct, as the consumer will be unable to tell the difference: in the long run, the worst codes will dominate the market, as there will be no incentive for individual enterprises to accept the costs associated with the adoption of stricter codes which will bring rewards to the sector as a whole. It is therefore necessary to reduce the uncertainty, the asymmetry between the consumers (buyers) and the enterprises (sellers). Model codes serve precisely to counteract the uncertainty about the quality of codes of conduct.

The institution of a Model Code of Conduct for European businesses was perhaps the single most important proposal put forward in the 1999 Howitt Resolution, which, with that objective in view, listed the international standards which the drafting of such a code should take into account.[226] The focus seems now to have changed. Rather than drafting a new model code, the Commission is encouraged to ensure better compliance with existing codes and, in particular, to support the OECD Guidelines for Multinational Enterprises, which indeed present the advantage of being applicable in principle not only to European companies, but also to their most important competitors from other industrialized countries (including

---

[223] Preamble, I.

[224] It appeared from a review by the ILO of 233 codes of conduct and social label systems that many of these codes or labels were incomplete, when compared to the Core Labour Standards: see the Study Prepared by the Working Party on the Social Dimensions of the Liberalisation of International Trade, ILO, Governing Body, 273d session, Geneva, November 1998 (GB.273/WP/SDL/1(Rev.1)).

[225] See Akerlof, 'The Market for "Lemons": Quality Uncertainty and the Market Mechanism', 84 *Quarterly Journal of Economics* (1970), at 488; reproduced in G.A. Akerlof, *An Economic Theorist's Book of Tales* (1984, 2nd ed. 1993), chap. 2.

[226] See Resolution on EU standards for European enterprises operating in developing countries: towards a European Code of Conduct, adopted by the European Parliament on 15 January 1999, A4-0508/1998, OJ 1999 C 104/176, para. 12.

Canada, Japan, Korea, New Zealand, Turkey, and the United States). It is encouraged by the European Parliament to 'verify' the voluntary codes of conduct 'against minimum applicable international standards', which would in fact amount to a form of certification by the Commission—or, rather, by the EU Multi-Stakeholder CSR Forum which is currently being set up—of these codes, again so as to ensure that the consumer will not be misled by the presentation of codes which do not meet these minimum standards.

The promotion of the OECD Guidelines deserves an explanation.[227] The OECD Guidelines for Multinational Enterprises were adopted on 21 June 1976 by the OECD Member States (with the exception of Turkey), and were presented at the time as the necessary counterweight to the extensive protection granted during the same period to the rights of investors.[228] These Guidelines are recommendations made to the enterprises from the thirty Member States of the OECD, as well as to three non-Member States which have adopted them.[229] Revised OECD Guidelines were adopted in June 2000. These include a provision according to which enterprises should 'respect the human rights of those affected by their activities consistent with the host government's international obligations and commitments'.[230] As remarked by N. Howen and the other authors of the report of the International Council on Human Rights Policy on *Human rights and the developing international legal obligations of companies*, the phrase not only 'extends the responsibility of enterprises far beyond respect for the labour rights of their workers' to include, 'for example, ensuring that their activities do not harm the human rights of those in the communities in which they operate'; it also 'makes clear that multinational enterprises should measure their conduct against the international obligations of the host state and not merely national laws, especially if these are weaker than international standards'.[231] But the 2000 revision also sought the revitalize the monitoring process, based on the institution of National Contact Points, usually governmental offices, in each OECD country. These NCPs should promote the guidelines, handle enquiries about them, but also assist in the difficulties social partners may encounter in implementing them, by aiding in the interpretation of the Guidelines. NCPs may also receive complaints, when Member States, enterprises, trade unions, or 'other parties concerned' allege that a particular enterprise has violated the Guidelines, either on the territory of a Member State, or in its activities in a third State.[232] If no

---

[227] See esp. S.C. van Eyck, *The OECD Declaration and Decisions Concerning Multinational Enterprises: An Attempt to Tame the Schrew* (1995); J. Oldenziel, *The 2000 Review of the OECD Guidelines for Multinational Enterprises: A New Code of Conduct?* (2000); Jägers, *supra* note 5, at 101–9.

[228] See Karl, 'The OECD Guidelines for Multinational Enterprises', in Addo, *supra* note 155, at 89.

[229] Argentina, Brazil, and Chile.   [230] Para. II.2.

[231] International Council on Human Rights Policy, *supra* note 2, at 67.

[232] International Council on Human Rights Policy, *supra* note 2, at 100, referring to OECD, National Contact Points, Procedural Guidance, I.C.5. The original Declaration on International Investment and Multinational Enterprises (21 June 1976) mentioned, with respect to the Guidelines, that the Member States 'jointly recommend to multinational enterprises *operating in their territories* the observance of the Guidelines . . . '(I.). However, the Preamble of the Guidelines, in para. 3, noted that 'Since the operations

solution is found at the national level, or if the NCP considers there is a need to clarify a point of interpretation of the Guidelines so as to avoid differing readings from country to country, the situation may be referred to the Committee on International Investment and Multinational Enterprises (CIME) which is entrusted with the final responsibility for clarification of the Guidelines. Since the 2000 revision, the NCP, however, must issue a statement when no agreement is reached at the national level, which may include naming the denounced corporation, unless 'preserving confidentiality would be in the best interests of effective implementation of the Guidelines'.[233] Although the procedure could develop into a truly effective complaints mechanism, its efficiency is still limited at the present stage of its evolution: not only is compliance with the Guidelines totally voluntary, but also there is no enforcement procedure even for those companies which choose to abide by these Guidelines and are found to have violated them. However, the 2000 revision of the supervisory mechanism of the Guidelines may hold certain promise for the future. The confidential character of the proceedings before the NCP and the CIME, which previously in fact excluded pressure to comply by consumers, is not absolute anymore; and the *locus standi* of NGOs before the NCPs has been improved.

By calling on the Commission to implement contact points for the OECD Guidelines for Multinational Enterprises in 'all its delegations in third countries where EU-based companies operate', to staff these contact points with officers trained in CSR matters, and to ask for reports from the EU Delegations abroad on the result of the work of those contact points,[234] the European Parliament confirms

of multinational enterprises extend throughout the world, including countries that are not Members of the Organisation, international co-operation in this field should extend to all States. Member countries [will seek to cooperate with non-Member States, in particular developing countries] with a view to improving the welfare and living standards of all people both by encouraging the positive contributions which multinational enterprises can make and by minimising and resolving the problems which may arise in connection with their activities'. The OECD 1996 study on *Trade, Employment and Labour Standards* (OECD Publ., 1996) mentions that the Guidelines 'have a role to play as a voluntary instrument to promote responsible behaviour of MNEs. This role would be enhanced if home and host countries made it known that they expect foreign investors to follow the Guidelines worldwide and if non-Member countries were encouraged to endorse the Guidelines'. The 2000 revision of the Guidelines merely confirms that these Guidelines are binding upon multinational enterprises domiciled in the OECD countries, wherever they operate: this revision has removed any doubts as to the geographical scope of the Guidelines.

[233] OECD review June 2000, *Procedural Guidance*, C 4.(b).

[234] Resolution on the Commission Green Paper on promoting a European framework for corporate social responsibility (COM(2001)366—C5-0161/2002—2002/2069(COS)), para. 47. The Commission has not yet followed this suggestion. It did, however, state that it would seek to 'promote awareness and application of CSR abroad, including through its Delegations, by encouraging debate and exchange of good practice, between and among third country and European stakeholders', and that it would insist on the inclusion in EU external relations agreements of the phrase: 'The Parties (or the European Community and its Member States) remind their multinational enterprises of their recommendations to observe the OECD Guidelines for Multinational enterprises, wherever they operate' (see Communication of the Commission on Corporate Social Responsibility: A business contribtution to Sustainable Development, COM(2002) 347 final, at 26).

that these Guidelines should be chosen, above any other specifically 'European' Code of Conduct, as setting universally applicable standards for MNEs from industrialized countries. This choice will be followed by the European Commission in its Communication of 2 July 2002 on Corporate Social Responsibility.[235] It is coherent with the objective of limiting, in the interest of both business and consumers, the diversity of standards applicable to the activities of MNEs. As remarked by the European Parliament's Committee on Industry, External Trade, Research, and Energy in the short justification preceding its opinion on the Commission Green Paper on corporate social responsibility, the OECD guidelines are 'the only multilaterally endorsed comprehensive framework of rules governing the activities of multinational activities. . . . Rather than developing further codes of conduct, the EU should draw on initiatives such as these and the UN Draft Fundamental Human Rights Principles for Business Enterprises.'[236] This may also be understood in the context of the increasingly diverging representations the EU and the United States have of the social responsibility of corporations: the development of specifically European standards for MNEs operating in third countries could have adverse consequences on the competitiveness of European companies in comparison to their United States counterparts, a situation which, as illustrated by the experience of the Community Code of Conduct for enterprises operating in South Africa between 1977 and 1993, may in time undermine the effectiveness of the standards.[237]

F. Conclusion

In the synthesis paper of a conference held in November 2001 under the Belgian Presidency of the EU, 'The European Social Agenda and the EU's International Partners', we read that the European Social Model 'encourages the mobilisation of consumers and social NGOs in monitoring the implementation of these codes. However, it does not rely on these voluntary efforts by themselves: it holds regulation and legislation in reserve. It thereby distances itself from the neo-liberal position of those who would look to the market and consumer pressure to drive economic development and respect for social rights, with government playing only a

---

[235] See Communication from the Commission concerning Corporate Social Responsibility: A business contribution to Sustainable Development, COM(2002) 347 final, at 6: 'the OECD Guidelines for Multinational Enterprises are the most comprehensive, internationally endorsed set of rules governing the activities of multinationals. In promoting CSR in developing countries, EU businesses should demonstrate and publicise their world-wide adherence to them.' The CSR strategy of the Commission, it is stated, is based *inter alia* on 'support and compatibility with *existing* international agreements and instruments' (at 8, my emphasis).

[236] Annexed to the Report of the Committee on Employment and Social Affairs on the Commission Green Paper, 30 April 2002, A5-0159/2002, at 24–5.

[237] This is also why the European Parliament states the obvious when, in its 15 January 1998 Resolution on a European code of conduct on the export of arms, it says it is 'convinced that any such EU code of conduct will be all the more successful when the other main arms exporters, such as the USA, but also the Russian Federation and China, agree to similar rules'. The same conviction is expressed in the second resolution it adopted three months later on the same topic.

minimal role'.[238] Indeed, if codes of conduct are simply tools to guide the choice of consumers, leaving it to the market mechanisms not only to ensure the effective respect of their codes of conduct by the companies who publish them but also to define the content of these codes, the risk is real that these voluntarily adopted codes will mislead the consumers, will lack credibility in the absence of any form of independant monitoring, will settle on minimal standards, or would contain important lacunae in comparison with what internationally agreed standards would impose. It is as a basis for public action that voluntarily defined and adopted codes of conduct may present some utility. Absent these conditions, they will remain merely the result of window-dressing initiatives by companies who wish to satisfy the ethical requirements of consumers.

7. THE EU MEMBER STATES AS ECONOMIC ACTORS

Besides its activity as a direct regulator of the conduct of MNEs, the European Union could encourage positive developments in corporate conduct, by authorizing its Member States to reward the most deserving enterprises, thus providing companies with an incentive to comply with certain ethical standards.[239] The areas in which such incentives could be imagined are diverse. The Communication of the Commission on Corporate Social Responsibility mentions two examples: 'Making access to subsidies for international trade promotion, investment and export credit insurance, as well as access to public procurement, conditional on adherence to and compliance with the OECD guidelines for multinational enterprises, while respecting international commitments, could be considered by EU Member States and by other States adherent to the OECD Declaration on International Investment'.[240]

These tools can be described as levers by which, using its economic muscle as purchaser of public goods.[241] or as creditor or insurer, the State seeks to take into

---

[238] 'The European Social Agenda and the EU's International Partners', Brussels, 20–21 November 2001, at 11.

[239] States could also encourage private investors to invest selectively, by ensuring more transparency for the social, environmental, and ethical performance of companies (see, on Socially responsible investment and the contribution the Member States of the EU to its extension, the Green Paper of the Commission, Promoting a European framework for Corporate Social Responsibility (COM(2001) 366 final, 18.7.2001, para. 3.5; and the corresponding passage in the Communication of 2 July 2002 on Corporate Social Responsibility, COM(2002) 347 final, para. 5.5). This question is not developed in the present study. It would fit, rather, in the preceding Chapter: by facilitating transparency and thus informed choices being made by investors, States are still acting as regulators rather than as economic actors in the market.

[240] Communication of the Commission on Corporate Social Responsibility: A business contribution to Sustainable Development, COM(2002) 347 final, at 23.

[241] The potential of this tool should not be underestimated. The acquisition by the public authorities of goods, services, and works represents 14% of the GDP (Gross Domestic Product) in the EU: see *Single Market News*, March 2000, cited by P. Lefèvre, 'Les considérations sociales et environnementales dans les marchés publics européens', *Journal des tribunaux: Droit européen* (2000), at 245.

account certain not purely economic criteria in the decisions adopted by its public authorities on the market. The example of the debate on public procurement,[242] however, illustrates that, in comparison to social or environmental criteria, ethical criteria (the respect a corporation shows for human rights) remain susceptible to being more easily manipulated, and thus instrumentalized for less justifiable reasons, in particular for protectionist purposes. An index of this is that, whilst the Commission has presented interpretative communications on the Community law applicable to public procurement and the possibilities for integrating both social[243] and environmental[244] considerations into public procurement, it has not presented a similar communication on the integration of human rights concerns in such policies.

Directive 2004/18/EC of the European Parliament and of the Council of 31 March 2004, on the coordination of procedures for the award of public works contracts, public supply contracts, and public service contracts, provides that contract performance conditions may seek to favour the employment of people experiencing particular difficulty in achieving integration, the fight against unemployment, or the protection of the environment, or that they may include a requirement, for instance, that the contractors comply with the basic conventions concluded within the International Labour Organization (ILO), to the extent that these conventions are implemented in national legislation (Article 26). However, it does not provide for the possibility that a Member State may decide to award its public contracts only to economic operators which undertake to respect, ensure the respect of, and protect human rights in their spheres of activity and influence, and who effectively agree to submit to monitoring procedures which ensure that this undertaking is compiled with. There are no insuperable technical obstacles to providing for this possibility. In particular, authorizing States to rely on such an 'ethical clause' to select their contractors would not necessarily lack the required objectivity, and so would not create any risk of discrimination or nontransparent practices.

For instance, Member States could be authorized to require that economic operators wishing to compete for public contracts agree to abide by the Guidelines for Multinational Enterprises set up by the Organization for Economic Co-Operation and Development, and to comply with any procedures initiated within those Guidelines. Directive 2004/18/EC already provides that economic operators who have participated in a criminal organization, or who have been found guilty of

---

[242] The examples of the linkage of access to export credits to ethical criteria, and esp. to companies' compliance with the OECD Guidelines for Multinational Enterprises—as advocated by the European Parliament (Resolution on the Commission Green Paper on promoting a European framework for corporate social responsibility (COM(2001)366—C5-0161/2002—2002/2069(COS)), para. 27)—are not detailed here. See esp. the Dutch example, and a recent Belgian Bill proposed to that effect by Mr D. Van der Maelen (Wetsvoorstel ter bevordering van duurzaam en verantwoord ondernemen van Belgische bedrijven in het buitenland), on which the parliamentary discussion still has to be launched. A number of NGOs advocate the insertion of social, environmental, and ethical clauses in Council Directive 98/29/EC of 7 May 1998 on harmonization of the main provisions concerning export credit insurance for transactions with medium and long-term cover, OJ 1998 L 148/22.

[243] COM(2001) 566 final of 15.10.2001.   [244] COM(2001) 274 final of 4.7.2001.

corruption or of fraud to the detriment of the financial interests of the European Communities, or of money laundering, may be excluded from public contracts (Article 45). It would have been desirable, and an important contribution to enhancing the credibility of the discourse of the European Union institutions on corporate social responsibility, to go further. For instance, economic operators who have been found by a judgment having the force of *res judicata* to have committed, or aided and abetted to commit, or been complicit in, violations of the fundamental rights of workers as enumerated in the 1998 Declaration of the International Labour Conference on Fundamental Rights and Principles at Work, could be excluded from public contracts, just as under the current Directive they should be excluded if they have violated national legislation implementing Directives 2000/78/EC or 76/207/EEC, which relate to non-discrimination on the basis of race, ethnic origin, or sex. A similar exclusion could be imposed on those undertakings which have been found liable under the United States Alien Tort Claims Act 1789 (U.S.C. § 1350 (1994)), as such a finding would mean that the concerned undertaking has violated specific norms universally recognized as part of the 'law of nations'.

Indeed, the reasoning held by the European Court of Justice with respect to the integration of social or environmental criteria in public procurement policies of the Member States could be easily transposed to the insertion of ethical clauses in public contracts. Consider for instance the attitude of the Court when the Commission of the European Communities lodged an application against France, seeking a declaration that France had violated its obligations under European Community law by setting forth as an award criterion, in a number of contract notices for the construction and maintenance of school buildings by the Nord-Pas-de-Calais Region and the Département du Nord, a condition relating to employment linked to a local project to combat unemployment.[245] The Court considered that although, under Article 30(1) of Directive 93/37,[246] the criteria on which the contracting authorities are to base the award of contracts are either the lowest price only or, when the award is made to the most economically advantageous tender, various criteria according to the contract, such as price, period for completion, running costs, profitability, and technical merit, 'that provision does not preclude all possibility for the contracting authorities to use as a criterion a condition linked to the campaign against unemployment provided that that condition is consistent with all the fundamental principles of Community law, in particular the principle of non-discrimination flowing from the provisions of the Treaty on the right of establishment and the freedom to provide services', as long as the criterion is 'applied in conformity with all the procedural rules laid down in [Directive 93/37], in particular the rules on advertising'.[247] Although France was found to have violated its Community

---

[245] Case C-225/98, *Commission of the European Communities v. France* [2000] ECR I-7445 (judgment of 26 September 2000).

[246] Council Directive 93/37/EEC of 14 June 1993 concerning the coordination of procedures for the award of public works contracts, OJ 1993 L 199/54.

[247] Case C-225/98, *Commission of the European Communities v. France*, paras. 50–51.

obligations for a number of other reasons, the judgment of 26 September 2000 relies on a reading of previous case-law of the European Court of Justice[248] which implies that it may be extend, beyond social clauses, to environmental or ethical conditions.

With respect to environmental concerns, the extension was authorized by the Court before it was formally recognized by the European legislator in the public procurement Directive 2004/18/EC of 31 March 2004. In its judgment of 17 September 2002 in the case of *Concordia Bus Finland* a Finnish municipality took into account the environmental performance which could be satisfied in the execution of the contract to be awarded; the European Court of Justice considered that 'where the contracting authority decides to award a contract to the tenderer who submits the economically most advantageous tender, in accordance with Article 36(1)(a) of Directive 92/50,[249] it may take criteria relating to the preservation of the environment into consideration, provided that they are linked to the subject-matter of the contract, do not confer an unrestricted freedom of choice on the authority, are expressly mentioned in the contract documents or the tender notice, and comply with all the fundamental principles of Community law, in particular the principle of non-discrimination'.[250] Just as the requirements of environmental protection are to be integrated into the definition and implementation of Community policies and activities, this provision of Article 6 EC justifying, according to the Court, a reading of Article 36(1) of Directive 92/50 favourable to States wishing to take into account environmental criteria in the assessment of the economically most advantageous tender, the requirements of fundamental rights are ranked among the principles on which the Union is founded, and which are considered to be common to all its Member States.[251] Thus, nothing seemed to prevent an extension of the *Beentjes—Commission v. France—Concordia Bus Finland* line of cases to the integration of ethical criteria in the procurement policies of the Member States. In that context the absence of a formal recognition of that possibility in Directive 2004/18/EC of the European Parliament and of the Council of 31 March 2004 is clearly a source of disappointment.

Despite its limitations, the Interpretative Communication of the Commission on the Community law applicable to public procurement and the possibilities for integrating social considerations into public procurement, adopted on 15 October 2001, did not exclude such an extension. The third part of that Communication (Social Provisions applicable to Public Procurement) explicitly refers to a number of instruments, not

[248] Case 31/87 *Beentjes v. Netherlands State* [1988] ECR 4635, paras. 28 and 37.

[249] Article 36(1) of Council Directive 92/50/EEC of 18 June 1992 relating to the coordination of procedures for the award of public service contracts (OJ 1992 L 209/1) (defining the criteria on which the contracting authority may base the awarding of contracts where the award is made to the 'economically most advantageous tender', as 'various criteria relating to the contract: for example, quality, technical merit, aesthetic and functional characteristics, technical assistance and after-sales service, delivery date, delivery period or period of completion, price').

[250] Case C-513/99, *Concordia Bus Finland Oy Ab (previously Stagecoach Finland) v. Helsingin kaupunki et HKL-Bussiliikenne*, [2002] ECR 7213, para. 64 (judgment of 17 September 2002).

[251] Art. 6(1) TEU.

only from European Community law but also from the International Labour Organization, which protect fundamental social rights. There would in principle be no difficulty in extending such references to other instruments from international human rights law: respect for these instruments—as they are implemented in the national legislation of the Member States, which the European Court of Justice would recognize as embodying an imperative requirement of general interest which may justify national measures restricting the exercise of one of the fundamental freedoms of Community law—could then be defined as a condition for the awarding of public contracts, provided all the requirements of transparency and non-discrimination are respected.

8. CONCLUSION

This study has been about mechanisms, rather than substantive norms or criteria of liability. However, what was initially resented as a limitation turned out to be the approach best fitting to the subject matter. The mechanisms for imposing human rights obligations on MNEs fail us. The norms which MNEs should be obliged to respect, on the other hand, are available. Identifying them with the requisite precision should not prove to be an insuperable task. As all the other actors of society,[252] MNEs are firstly under a duty to respect the basic rights and freedoms of all who are affected by their activities and fall within their sphere of influence; and whenever their objective to make profit appears to conflict with the full preservation of the rights of others (employees, families of employees, neighbouring communities) the conditions under which States may restrict certain non-absolute rights or freedoms for public interest reasons should apply, *mutatis mutandis*, to the restrictions imposed by corporate actors of the rights and freedoms of those with whom they interact: these restrictions should be necessary for the fulfilment of the legitimate aims of the corporation, and they should remain within the limits required by the principle of proportionality.[253]

All other things being equal, the equation with the State authorities of the private party, with respect to the extent of the obligations imposed on the latter, will be all

---

[252] See Resolution 53/144 of the General Assembly of the United Nations, 'Declaration on the Right and Responsibility of Individuals, Groups and Organs of Society to Promote and Protect Universally Recognized Human Rights and Fundamental Freedoms', 8 March 1999 (A/RES/53/144). Although the Declaration, first approved by the Commission on Human Rights, recognizes that 'Each State has the prime responsibility and duty to protect, promote and implement all human rights and fundamental freedoms' (Art. 2(1)), it insists on the responsibility of each member of the society—individuals, groups, insititutions, and non-governmental organizations—in the promotion of human rights. According to Article 11 of the Declaration annexed to the Resolution, 'Everyone who, as a result of his or her profession, can affect the human dignity, human rights and fundamental freedoms of others should respect those rights and freedoms and comply with relevant national and international standards of occupational and professional conduct of ethics'.

[253] See Ratner, *supra* note 5, at 513–15. The voluminous case-law of the European Court of Human Rights concerning the application of the European Convention on Human Rights between private parties

the more justified if this private party is in a position of dominance which justifies this assimilation: where the corporation in fact exercises an element of governmental authority by delegation or is in a situation of monopoly and thus may coerce others (subcontractors, customers, employees) into interacting with it, where, therefore, it exerts the greatest power, the assimilation may be complete; where the corporation is one economic actor among others, in conditions of true competition, and is thus unable to impose itself on others with whom it deals, a less strict transposition of the duties of States to the corporation may be justified. Such an evaluation of the position of the corporation in comparison to that of the territorial State may especially be required where one wishes to go beyond the affirmation of an obligation to *respect*—i.e. not to violate the rights of others with whom the corporation interacts—to affirm an obligation of the corporation to *protect* or to *promote* the human rights of those persons under the sphere of influence of the corporation. Whether the corporation should, for instance, ensure that the children or its employees receive an adequate education and are not coerced into work, or whether it should use its leverage upon the local authorities to encourage democratization, may depend on whether or not the corporation is in fact in a sufficiently dominant position, either in a geographical area or in the host State in general, effectively to fulfil such obligations: responsibility should derive from control, and control is not an all-or-nothing concept, especially not with respect to private actors which, by definition, make no claim to being sovereign.

Not only must corporations, like other actors in society, respect the human rights of others; they must also not be complicit in the violations committed either by the States in which they invest or by the other private persons with whom they interact. The notion of complicity must of necessity supplement the imposition of the elementary obligation not to commit direct violations of human rights, or else it will be far too easy for corporations to escape any form of liability, civil or criminal, when participating in human rights violations—for example, by hiring a subcontractor to impose certain forms of forced labour or child labour, which the corporation itself would not be allowed to resort to directly; or by conducting operations in countries whose government bans unions or imposes racial discrimination, which the corporation will then present as not raising its own liability, as it simply 'benefits' from an environment created by the government. How far should the responsibility of the

illustrates how such a transposition, from obligations imposed on States in the field of human rights to obligations imposed on private actors, is relatively easy to perform. See e.g. the inadmissibility decision of 28 June 2001 in *Verlière v. Switzerland* (Appl. no. 41953/98) (complaint by the applicant that her activities has been spied upon by private detectives recruited by the insurance company from whom she had sought compensation for what she alleged to be consequences of a car accident); or the judgment by the Eur. Ct. H.R. of 29 February 2000, *Fuentes Bobo v. Spain* (Appl. no. 39293/98), § 50 (applicant discharged from the Spanish Television (TVE) after having made offensive public statements against the directors of his company, and having failed to obtain compensation from the Spanish courts for what he considered to be an unjustified dismissal, decided in violation of his freedom of expression: the Court simply applied to the relationship between two private parties the proportionality test developed in the context of the vertical relationships between individuals and public authorities).

corporation extend, if it is to go beyond the scope, strictly defined, of the violations it commits directly? The answer, it has been suggested above, may depend on the nature of the instruments which are used to assert this responsibility.

It therefore appears possible to derive from the standards existing in the international law of human rights certain duties imposed on legal persons, and in particular on multinational enterprises. Although the orthodox understanding of international law sees it as imposing enforceable obligations only *directly* on States or—exceptionally, and only with respect to certain international crimes—on natural persons, the norms codified in the international law of human rights lend themselves to such transposition. The problem of enforceability of these obligations remains, however, in situations where the MNE develops activities in States other than the State where it is incorporated. Neither the home State nor the host State of the investment has an incentive to take measures to ensure that the MNE will respect its obligations in international law. In the present stage of development of the international law of State responsibility, home States of MNEs are not under any obligation to act in that respect. And although host States may be under such an obligation because of their duty to protect the fundamental rights of all persons within their jurisdiction, they will, as a rule, be reluctant to invest in monitoring the activities of MNEs operating within their territory, because their primary objective is to make their territory attractive to foreign investment, rather than to adopt dissuasive measures.

It would be a mistake to think of the power thus exercised by MNEs, in the face of such unwillingness or incapacity of the States to impose on these actors a more stringent respect for social, environmental, or ethical standards, as a matter of fate. The power of MNEs should not be attributed to the sheer economic weight of these 'leviathans', as it may appear, for example, from the famous comparison between the GNP of certain countries and the total sales of the main multinationals.[254] It has its origin, rather, in the capacity of these enterprises to move their investments from one country to another, thus permanently holding both the countries in which they invest and those in which they are domiciled under the threat of a departure if the conditions offered by the host or the home country come to seem less attractive. However, what may appear in a static analysis as a disempowerment of the States confronted with a new form of sovereignty competing with theirs[255] is, it should be remembered, the result of the emergence of a global marketplace which is initially a creation of the States. Less than ever should we exculpate States from their alleged inability to tame the new leviathans.

---

[254] See Table 1.1 presented in the *1999 Human Development Report* published by the United Nations Development Programme, Oxford, Oxford University Press, 1999, at 32 (ranking countries and corporations according to these values and placing General Motors above Thailand or Norway, and Ford Motor Co. and Mitsui & Co. above Saudi Arabia).

[255] The authors of the study of the International Council on Human Rights Policy present their ambition thus: 'The concept of the sovereignty of states, which has been eroded by the development of human rights, should not be replaced by a new corporate sovereignty, which is unrestricted or unaccountable' (International Council on Human Rights Policy, *supra* note 2, at 10).

8

Human Rights Responsibilities of Businesses as Non-State Actors

DAVID WEISSBRODT AND MURIA KRUGER

In August 2003 the UN Sub-Commission on the Promotion and Protection of Human Rights approved the 'Norms on the Responsibilities of Transnational Corporations and Other Business Enterprises with regard to Human Rights' ('Norms')[1] in its resolution 2003/16.[2] The Norms represent a landmark step in holding businesses accountable for their human rights abuses and provide a succinct, but comprehensive restatement of the international legal principles applicable to businesses with regard to human rights, humanitarian law, international labour law, environmental law, consumer law, anti-corruption law, etc.

During the past half-century governments have codified international human rights law protecting the rights of individuals against governmental violations. With increasing attention to the emergence of international criminal law as a response to war crimes, genocide, and crimes against humanity, there has also been growing attention to individual responsibility for grave human rights abuses. In addition, international humanitarian law and international criminal law have placed obligations on armed opposition forces engaged in non-international armed conflicts. This web of human rights obligations, however, has not paid sufficient attention to some of the most powerful non-state actors in the world: transnational corporations and other business enterprises. With power should come responsibility,[3] and international human rights law needs to focus adequately on these extremely potent international non-state actors.

Having failed in the 1970s and 1980s to adopt a code of conduct for transnational corporations,[4] the United Nations has taken a new, human rights perspective not only on transnational corporations but on all business enterprises. The UN human

---

[1] UN Doc. E/CN.4/Sub.2/2003/12/Rev.2 (2003).

[2] Sub-Commission resolution 2003/16.

[3] M. Robinson, Address at the Second Global Ethic Lecture at the University of Tübingen, Germany (21 January 2002), reprinted in 'Globalization has to take human rights into account', *Irish Times*, 22 January 2002.   [4] *See infra* n 17 and corresponding text.

rights concerns arise from such fundamental developments as: the increasingly integrated global economy; the prominence of international trade and investment; the growth of information and communications technology facilitating rapid transmission of information; increasing privatization; concerns about the impact of globalization and trade on human rights;[5] an increase in consumer awareness about labour, environmental, and health conditions involved in the production of goods available for purchase;[6] shareholder and other stakeholder demands for greater openness and public accountability;[7] greater attention by more non-governmental organizations to the conduct of transnational corporations and other business enterprises;[8] and increased reliance upon voluntary compliance with international standards applicable to businesses.[9]

Transnational corporations are of particular concern in relation to recent global trends because they are active in some of the most dynamic sectors of national

---

[5] See C. Forcese, *Commerce with Conscience? Human Rights and Business Codes of Conduct* (1997); P. Utting, *Business Responsibility for Sustainable Development* (2000); Charnovitz, 'The Moral Exception in Trade Policy', 38 *Va. J. Int'l L.* (1998) 689.

[6] For example, consumer discontent that soccer/footballs were made by child labour led to a consumer boycott forcing the manufacturers to stop using child labour. See Robert J. Liubicic, 'Corporate Codes of Conduct and Product Labeling Schemes: The Limits and Possibilities of Promoting International Labor Rights Standards Through Private Initiatives', 30 *Law and Pol'y Int'l Bus* (1998) 111. Another example occurred in regard to the promotion of infant formula in developing countries. Certain companies were encouraging mothers in developing countries to use infant formula instead of breast-feeding. The use of infant formula led to increased infant mortality because of lack of clean water and because mothers were not properly instructed on how to use the formula. Once consumers learned about the increased infant mortality, they began boycotting Nestlé products. See Zelman, 'The Nestlé Infant Formula Controversy: Restricting the Marketing Practice of Multinational Corporations in the Third World', 3 *Transnat'l L.* (1990) 697. See also Weissbrodt, 'Strategies for the Selection and Pursuit of International Human Rights Objectives', 8 *Yale J. World Pub. Ord.* (1981) 62. Out of that controversy arose the World Health Assembly International Code of Marketing of Breast-Milk Substitutes (1981).

[7] The recent scandal with multinational giant, Enron, led to many changes in auditing and reporting guidelines so that consumers and investors will have a greater awareness of the actual financial conditions of the corporation. See Scherer and Francis, 'Lessons of Enron: How could no one have seen it? Bankruptcy forces a look at accounting, Wall Street practices, and pension plans', *Christian Science Monitor*, 16 January 2002.

[8] For example, Amnesty International and Human Rights Watch now specifically address human rights issues surrounding transnational corporations. Additionally, NGOs, such as CorpWatch, were created primarily to address the human rights issues that surround large multinational corporations. See Amnesty International and Prince of Wales International Business Leaders Forum, *Business and Human Rights: A geography of corporate risk* (2002); C. Avery, Amnesty International, *Business and Human Rights in a time of change* (February 2000), at <http://www.business-humanrights.org/Avery-Report.htm>; A. Ganesan/Human Rights Watch, *Business and Human Rights—The Bottom Line* (January 1999), at <http://www.hrw.org/advocacy/corporations/commentary.htm>. See also CorpWatch website, at <http://www.corpwatch.org> (visited 14 June 2002).

[9] See United Nations High Commissioner for Human Rights, Business and Human Rights, <http://www.unhchr.ch/global.htm> (visited 14 June 2002); United Nations Conference on Trade and Development, The Social Responsibility of Transnational Corporations, UN Doc. UNCTAD/ITE/IIT/Misc.21 at 6 (1999).

economies, such as the extractive industries,[10] telecommunications, information technology, electronic consumer goods, footwear and apparel, transport, banking and finance, insurance, and securities trading. They bring new jobs, capital, and technology. Some corporations make real efforts to achieve international standards by improving working conditions and raising local living conditions. They certainly have the capacity to assert a positive influence in fostering development. Some transnational corporations, however, do not respect international minimum human rights standards and can thus be implicated in abuses such as employing child labourers, discriminating against certain groups of employees, failing to provide safe and healthy working conditions as well as just and favourable conditions of work, attempting to repress independent trade unions and discouraging the right to bargain collectively, limiting the broad dissemination of appropriate technology and intellectual property, and dumping toxic wastes. Some of these abuses disproportionately affect developing countries, children, minorities, undocumented immigrants, and women who work in unsafe and poorly paid production jobs as well as indigenous communities and other vulnerable groups.

There is also increasing reason to believe that greater respect for human rights by companies leads to greater sustainability in emerging markets[11] and better business performance.[12] For example, observance of human rights aids businesses by protecting and maintaining their corporate reputation, and creating a stable and peaceful society in which businesses can prosper and attract the best and brightest employees.[13] Consumers have also demonstrated they are willing to pay attention to standards and practices used by a business regarding human rights and may even boycott products that are produced in violation of human rights standards.[14] There is also evidence that a growing proportion of investors seek to purchase shares in socially responsible companies.

---

[10] For an in-depth discussion of human rights in the oil industry, *see* A. Eide *et al.* (eds), *Human Rights and the Oil Industry* (2000). *See also* Human Rights Watch, *The Price of Oil, Corporate Responsibility and Human Rights Violations in Nigeria's Oil Producing Communities* (1999), *at* <http://www.hrw.org/reports/1999/nigeria/index.htm>; Human Rights Watch, *The Enron Corporation: Corporate Complicity in Human Rights Violations* (1999), *at* <http://www.hrw.org/reports/1999/enron/>. For case studies on human rights and the oil and high-tech industries, *see* Natural Heritage Institute *et al.*, *Beyond Good Deeds: Case Studies and a New Policy Agenda for Corporate Accountability* (2002).

[11] A large-scale study of evidence from developing countries found that emerging market companies gain financially from stability. *See* International Finance Corporation, Sustainability, Instituto Ethos, 'Groundbreaking Report Challenges Conventional Wisdom on Role of Business in Emerging Markets', Press Release No. 02/0098, 17 July 2002.

[12] *See* R. Cowe, *ABI Research Reports, Investing in Social Responsibility: Risks and Opportunities* (2001) (supporting the proposition that corporate social responsibility has a positive impact on businesses by increasing their potential for competitive advantage and increasing shareholder value through promotion of risk management).

[13] *See* Avery, *supra* n 8. *See also* United Nations High Commissioner for Human Rights, Business and Human Rights, <http://www.unhchr.ch/global.htm> (visited 14 June 2002). [14] *See supra* n 6.

All in all, business enterprises have increased their power in the world.[15] International, national, state, and local law-makers are beginning to realize that this power must be addressed, and there is a special need to address the human rights obligations of business enterprises.

The Norms are the first non-voluntary initiative accepted at the international level. Accordingly, the Norms have already attracted the attention of many scholars and others working in the field of corporate social responsibility. The Norms have also for this reason been welcomed by many non-governmental organizations (NGOs) and others who would like to use the Norms to begin holding large businesses accountable for their human rights violations.

This Chapter begins by briefly noting major developments in the creation of human rights standards for businesses and other methods to hold corporations accountable to human rights standards. Next, it provides a history of the drafting of the Norms by the Sub-Commission's Working Group on the Working Methods and Activities of Transnational Corporations. Then, it examines some of the major issues surrounding the creation of any international human rights standards for businesses, such as (1) to what extent human international obligations can be placed on non-state actors, and (2) whether it is appropriate to place human rights obligations on businesses. The Chapter concludes by discussing implementation procedures under the Norms.

1. DEVELOPMENTS IN CORPORATE CODES OF CONDUCT

One of the early efforts to hold corporations accountable to human rights standards occurred within the United Nations in the late 1970s and 1980s. The UN Commission on Transnational Corporations prepared the draft United Nations Code of Conduct for Transnational Corporations which was to be a statement from the international community regarding the international legal obligations of businesses.[16] Although the Commission spent approximately thirteen years drafting this document, the Code of Conduct was never fully adopted by the UN body.[17]

---

[15] A 2000 study found that 51 of the 100 largest economies in the world are corporations, while only 49 are countries; and the combined sales of the world's top 200 corporations are greater than the combined economies of all countries minus the biggest ten. Putting these findings in perspective, General Motors is bigger than Denmark; DaimlerChrysler is bigger than Poland; Royal Dutch/Shell is bigger than Venezuela; IBM is bigger than Singapore; and Sony is bigger than Pakistan. *See* S. Anderson and J. Cavanagh, *The Top 200: The Rise of Global Corporate Power* (2000), *at* <http://www.ips-dc.org/reports/top200text.htm>.

[16] Development and International Economic Cooperation: Transnational Corporations, UN Doc. E/1990/94 (1990); *see also* United Nations Draft International Code of Conduct on Transnational Corporations, 23 ILM 626 (1984).

[17] In 1972 the Economic and Social Council requested the Secretary-General to appoint a group of eminent persons to study the impact of multinational corporations on the world economy. In 1977 the United Nations Commission on Transnational Corporations began formulating a Code of Conduct

The Organization for Economic Co-operation and Development (OECD) undertook a similar effort in 1976 when it established its first Guidelines for Multinational Enterprises to promote responsible business conduct consistent with applicable laws.[18] In 2000 the OECD substantially updated and revised the Guidelines and added enhanced implementation procedures.[19] In 1977 the International Labour Organization (ILO) adopted its Tripartite Declaration of Principles concerning Multinational Enterprises[20] which incorporated relevant ILO conventions and recommendations.[21] For example, in March 2000 the ILO Governing Body incorporated into the Tripartite Declaration the 1998 Declaration on Fundamental Principles and Rights at Work and its Follow-Up, which had been adopted to modernize, strengthen, and ensure implementation of its system of labour standards.[22]

for Transnational Corporations; the most recent draft was completed in 1990, but the Code of Conduct was never concluded. *See* Lansing and Rosaria, 'An Analysis of the United Nations Proposed Code of Conduct for Transnational Corporations', 14 *World Competition* (1991) 35, at 37; Anderson, 'Respecting Human Rights: Multinational Corporations Strike Out', 2 *U. Pa. J. Lab. & Emp. L.* (2000) 463, at 474–75. Failure to agree on any one text for the Code of Conduct was due in large part to the differences between the desires of northern, developed countries and southern, developing countries, *see* S. C. van Fyk, *The OECD declaration and decisions concerning multinational enterprises: an attempt to tame the shrew* (1995), and the 'deep seated and persistent differences with respect to such issues as the applicability of principles of customary international law to investment relations, and the restraints to be placed on governments in such areas as nationalization of foreign property, treatment of foreign enterprises, jurisdiction and dispute settlement'. Asante, 'The Concept of the Good Corporate Citizen in International Businesses', in *Transnational Corporations: The International Legal Framework* (1994) 169, at 195. Many of the most controversial issues tackled by the first code, such as transfer pricing, transfer of technology, and taxation, are not included in the current Norms.

[18] Organization for Economic Cooperation and Development, Guidelines for Multinational Enterprises, 15 ILM 967 (1976). The OECD has established National Contact Points for handling inquiries and contributing to the solution of problems that may arise in connection with the OECD Guidelines. The OECD has also established the Committee on International Investment and Multinational Enterprises (CIME) that periodically or at the request of a Member country can hold an exchange of views on matters related to the Guidelines, *at* <http://www.oecd.org/daf/investment/guidelines/faq.htm> (14 June 2002). Over 30 cases have been submitted to the CIME, principally involving employment and industrial relations.

[19] OECD Guidelines for Multinational Enterprises, Revision 2000, *at* <http://www.oecd.org/daf/investment/guidelines/index.htm> (visited 14 June 2002).

[20] International Labour Organization, Tripartite Declaration of Principles concerning Multinational Enterprises and Social Policy (1977), 17 ILM 422, para. 6 (1978), *available at* <http://www.ilo.org/public/english/employment/multi/tridecl/index.htm>.

[21] See Ralph G Steinhardt, 'Corporate Responsibility and the International Law of Human Rights: The New *Lex Mercatoria*', Chapter 6 in this volume, at [203–05]. *See also* International Labour Organization, Updating of references annexed to the Tripartite Declaration of Principles concerning Multinational Enterprises and Social Policy, ILO Doc. GB.277/MNE/3 (2000).

[22] ILO Declaration on Fundamental Principles and Rights at Work and its Follow-Up, adopted by the International Labor Conference at its eighty-sixth session, Geneva, 18 June 1998. Follow-up and Promotion March 2000 by Subcommittee on Multinational Enterprises, ILO Doc. GB.277/MNE/1 (2000), *available at* <http://www.ilo.org/public/english/standards/relm/gb/docs/gb277/pdf/mne-3.pdf>. The ILO Declaration is monitored through a quadrennial survey and through interpretations rendered by the Subcommittee on Multinational Enterprises. *See also* International Labour Organization, Your Voice at

In addition, the ILO assists private voluntary initiatives to establish and implement their own codes of conduct.[23]

During the period when the United Nations, OECD, and ILO were preparing codes of conduct for businesses, other groups were also considering the obligations of businesses with regard to human rights conduct.[24] Throughout the 1980s and 1990s efforts grew as an increasing number of consumers, investors, local communities, NGOs, and others started to take note of and call for action regarding human rights violations by businesses. In January 1999 United Nations Secretary-General Kofi Annan proposed a Global Compact of shared values and principles at the Davos Conference.[25]

Governments have also begun to address issues with regard to the human rights conduct of businesses. In 1998 the European Parliament (EP) passed a resolution calling upon the European Union (EU) to draft a binding Code of Conduct for European Multinationals and to establish a monitoring mechanism,[26] leading to

---

Work, 'Global Report under the Follow-up to the ILO Declaration on Fundamental Principles and Rights at Work' (2000), *available at* <http://www.ilo.org/public/english/standards/decl/declaration/text/>.

[23] *See* International Labour Organization, The International Labor Organization and Private Voluntary Initiatives (2000).

[24] *See, eg,* The Sullivan Statement of Principles (4th Amplification), 8 November 1984, 24 ILM 1496 (1985). The Sullivan and similar codes are discussed in this volume in Steinhardt, *supra* n 21 at [183, 185–87] and in August Reinisch, 'The Changing International Legal Framework for Dealing with Non-State Actors', Chapter 2 in this volume, at [44].

[25] Secretary-General Kofi Annan, Address at the World Economic Forum in Davos, Switzerland (31 January 1999), in UN Doc. SG/SM/6448 (1999). *See* Steinhardt, *supra* n 21, at [206–07] for further discussion. Prior to adoption of the Norms, the staff of the Global Compact issued a statement of 24 July 2003, in support of the Norms, indicating 'From the perspective of the Global Compact, we always welcome efforts that help to clarify complex human rights questions and that foster practical changes that advance understanding and good practices. It is my understanding that the Draft Norms have already initiated significant educational efforts and we are looking forward to seeing how these efforts could contribute positively to the Global Compact.' E-mail message from Georg Kell (24 July 2003) (on file with the author). That statement responded to a letter from the four major NGO participants in the Global Compact who wrote to their partners in the Global Compact stating their concern that companies are being allowed to sign onto the Global Compact without having to follow through with reporting obligations. *See* Letter from Jeremy Hobbs, Oxfam International; Irene Kahn, Amnesty International; Michael Posner, Lawyers Committee for Human Rights; and Kenneth Roth, Human Rights Watch, to Louise Frechette, Deputy Secretary-General of the United Nations (7 April 2003) (on file with the author). *Ibid.; see also* GRI Chief Executive Responds to Release of the UN Sub-Commission on the Promotion and Protection of Human Rights Norms for Transnationals (13 August 2003) (on file with author) (stating that 'The Global Reporting Initiative (GRI) has welcomed the work of the [Sub-Commission], which it sees as a further step in catalyzing and focusing discussion on how human rights can be advanced around the world in measurable, concrete and practical ways').

[26] European Parliament (EP), *Resolution on EU standards for European Enterprises operating in developing countries: towards a European Code of Conduct*, EP Resolution of 15 January 1999 OJ 1999 C 104. In November 1999 a consultation campaign was launched with a two-day Conference of the Belgian Presidency in Brussels attended by more than 1,000 participants. The participants included representatives from many different groups, including businesses, trade unions, academics, and NGOs. *See* Reports of the Conference of the Belgian Presidency, *at* <http://www.socialresponsibility.be/> (last visited

the 'Green Paper on promoting a European Framework for corporate social responsibility'.[27]

In December 2000 the United Kingdom and United States governments, along with many of the leading extractive and energy companies, released the 'Voluntary Principles on Security and Human Rights in the Extractive Sector'.[28] The heightened awareness of human rights abuses by security forces hired by large corporations in the extractive and energy sectors led to the drafting of these Principles. The Principles attempt to address abuses by setting standards which extractive and energy companies should follow with regard to risk assessment, relations with public security, and relations with private security. Consumers are also responding to the call to hold businesses accountable for human rights, with the emergence of 'social responsible' investment and more conventional measures such as boycotts.[29]

Transnational corporations and other business enterprises themselves also have begun to consider the human rights implications of their activities, for example, by (1) carefully assessing the context in which they are investing or doing business; (2) planning and implementing internal business policies; and (3) establishing workplace codes of conduct as to overseas offices, subsidiaries, suppliers, and contractors. Not only have many businesses developed their own ethical codes, but trade groups, NGOs, and others also have written codes of conduct for businesses.

Despite all of the recent developments in the area of human rights and businesses, there remains a call for a comprehensive, non-voluntary set of international standards to hold all transnational corporations and other business enterprises accountable to the same level of international human rights standards.

2 October 2002). Transnational corporations, Member States, European institutions, NGOs, and other stakeholders made over 250 contributions to the Green Paper. *See* Europa, European Union On-Line, Responses to the Consultation to the Green Paper on CSR, *at* <http://europa.eu.int/comm/employment_social/soc-dial/csr/csr_index.htm> (visited 2 October 2002).

[27] *See* Reinisch, *supra* n 24, at [45] for discussion of the Green Paper. See also Olivier De Schutter, 'The Accountability of Multinationals for Human Rights Violations in European Law' Chapter 7 in this volume, at [228, 260–61]. Green Paper Promoting a European Framework for Corporate Social Responsibility, COM (2001) 366 final, July 2001. There has also been a follow-up communication, 'A Business Contribution to Sustainable Development' COM(2002) 347 final, July 2002. The purpose of the Green Paper was to begin a debate within the European Union on corporate social responsibility. *See* Green Paper, at 4. *See also* Castle, 'Firms may be forced to pay for pollution', *Independent*, 31 May 2002; Maitland and Mann, 'Inside Track: Challenge to voluntary preserve', *Financial Times*, 30 May 2002.

[28] United States/United Kingdom Voluntary Principles on Security and Human Rights in the Extractive Sector, *at* <http://www1.umn.edu/humanrts/links/volprinciples.html> (visited 2 October 2002). Six extractive industry companies signed on to the original agreement, including: British Petroleum, Chevron, Conoco, Freeport McMoran, Rio Tinto, Shell, and Texaco. The Netherlands, Norway, Exxon-Mobil, and Occidental Petroleum joined the agreement in 2002. Lorne Craner, U.S. Sees Corporations as Partners in Democracy, Address Before the National Policy Association (18 June 2002) *at* <usinfo.state.gov>.

[29] *See* Norms, *supra* n 1; Sub-Commission, Commentary on the Norms on the Responsibilities of Transnational Corporations and Other Business Enterprises with regard to Human Rights, UN Doc. E/CN.4/Sub.2/2003/38/Rev.2 (2003) [hereinafter Commentary].

2. DRAFTING HISTORY OF THE NORMS

The idea for a sessional Working Group on the Working Methods and Activities of Transnational Corporations arose from Sub-Commission resolution 1997/11,[30] which asked El-Hadji Guissé[31] (Sub-Commission member from Senegal) to present a working document to the Sub-Commission at its fiftieth session (in 1998) on the issue of human rights and transnational corporations. Mr. Guissé's document briefly addressed the impact of transnational economic actors on income inequality both nationally and internationally.[32] Mr. Guissé's document further raised concerns about the far-reaching impact of transnational corporation policies and practices: for example, the threat to environmental sustainability posed by transnational corporations.

In response to that paper, in its resolution 1998/8 of 20 August 1998 the Sub-Commission decided 'to establish for a three-year period a sessional working group of the Sub-Commission, composed of five of its members, taking into account the principle of equitable geographic distribution, to examine the working methods and activities of transnational corporations'.[33] The mandate of the sessional Working Group included tasks such as: identifying issues, and gathering and examining information regarding the effects of transnational corporations on human rights; examining investment agreements for their compatibility with human rights agreements; making recommendations regarding the methods of work and activities of transnational corporations in order to ensure the protection of human rights; and considering the scope of the state's obligation to regulate transnational corporations.

In 1999 the Working Group set its agenda for the next two years and ended by asking David Weissbrodt to prepare a draft code of conduct for transnational corporations.[34] At its second meeting in August 2000, the Working Group considered the first draft of the Norms.[35] During this discussion, two main issues

---

[30] *See* UN Doc. E/CN.4/Sub.2/1997/50 (1997).

[31] El Hadji Guissé has been a member of the Sub-Commission since 1990. Guissé is a lawyer and judge in Senegal, the current chairperson of the Working Group on the Working Methods and Activities of Transnational Corporations, and former Chairperson of the Sub-Commission on the Promotion and Protection of Human Rights.   [32] *See* UN Doc. E/CN.4/Sub.2/1998/6 (1998).

[33] UN Doc. E/CN.4/Sub.2/1998/45 (1998).   [34] *See* UN Doc. E/CN.4/Sub. 2/1999/12 (1999).

[35] *See* UN Doc. E/CN.4/Sub. 2/2000/12, paras. 26–58 (2000). For drafts of the documents considered by the working group in 2000, *see* UN Doc. E/CN.4/Sub.2/2000/WG.2/WP.1 (2000); E/CN.4/Sub.2/2000/WG.2/WP.1/Add.1 (2000) [hereinafter 2000 Code of Conduct]; and List of Principal Source Materials for the Draft Code of Conduct for Companies, UN Doc. E/CN.4/Sub.2/2000/WG.2/WP.1/Add.2 (2000). The document title has changed many times in the drafting process. The first draft to be considered by the Working Group was called the 'Draft Code of Conduct for Companies'. *See* 2000 Code of Conduct. Upon consideration of this name, those in attendance at the 2000 Sub-Commission meeting felt that the term 'code of conduct' was overused and might be misleading as many voluntary codes also referred to themselves as 'codes of conduct'. *See* UN Doc. E/CN.4/Sub.2/2000/WG.1/WP.1 at para. 27. The title of the second draft was the 'Draft Universal Human Rights Guidelines for Companies'. *See* Sub-Commission, Draft Universal Human Rights Guidelines for Companies, UN Doc. E/CN.4/Sub.2/2001/WG.1/WP.1/Add.1 (2001) [hereinafter 2001 Guidelines]. The term 'universal' was added pursuant to

arose: (1) whether the document should be non-voluntary or voluntary; and (2) whether the document should apply to all businesses or only transnational corporations. The Working Group further recognized the necessity of addressing issues such as implementation in conjunction with this drafting exercise. By the end of the 2000 session, David Weissbrodt was asked to continue to draft and update the standards for another year and Asbjørn Eide (Sub-Commission member from Norway)[36] was asked to prepare a paper on implementation of standards.

Pursuant to encouragement from the Working Group at its 2000 meeting to gather further comments on the 2000 Draft, a March 2001 seminar was held at the Office of the UN High Commissioner for Human Rights.[37] The participants included: members of the Working Group; representatives from non-governmental organizations interested in corporate responsibility, human rights, development, and the environment; representatives from companies; union representatives; and knowledgeable scholars. Individuals at the conference suggested many substantive formatting changes, such as adding a preamble, radically shortening the main text into broad provisions, and adding a commentary following each principle to address more specific issues.[38]

---

suggestions by those in attendance at a March 2001 seminar of experts in this field convened to gather input on the Guidelines. *See generally* UN Doc. E/CN.4/Sub.2/2001/WG.1/WP.1/Add.3 (2001), *available at* <http://www1.umn.edu/humanrts/links/draftguidelines-ad3.html>[hereinafter Seminar Report]. Upon consideration of this name at the 2001 Sub-Commission meeting, those in attendance felt that the term 'guidelines' was not indicative of the non-voluntary approach the document was meant to convey and that the word 'principles' may better indicate this approach. Further, it was mentioned that the word 'companies' was not inclusive of all business forms and the words 'business enterprises' may be more inclusive. Also, since the Working Group's mandate included a special focus on transnational corporations, the document title should also include the term 'transnational corporations' in the title. The name of the third draft was the 'Human Rights Principles and Responsibilities for Transnational Corporations and Other Business Enterprises'. UN Doc. E/CN.4/Sub.2/2002/WG.2/WP.1 (February 2002) [hereinafter 2002 Principles]. At its February 2002 meeting, the Working Group decided to include the word 'responsibilities' to reflect the nature of the obligations the document attempts to create. At the 2002 Sub-Commission meeting the name was once again changed, this time to the 'Norms of Responsibilities for Transnational Corporations and Other Business Enterprises with Regard to Human Rights'. *See* UN Doc. E/CN.4/Sub.2/2002/13 at 15–21 (2002) [hereinafter 2002 Responsibilities]. The name was changed due to bargaining between Working Group members and their desire to reflect the non-voluntary nature of the document. Since 2002, the name has remained relatively unchanged.

[36] Asbjørn Eide has been a member of the Sub-Commission since 1981 and is the chair of the United Nations Working Group on the Rights of Minorities. He is also the former director and present senior fellow of the Norwegian Institute of Human Rights and the former secretary-general of the International Peace Research Institute in Oslo.   [37] *See* Seminar Report, *supra* n 35.

[38] The suggestion to shorten the text into broad substantive provisions and then to follow each provision with a commentary was adopted and incorporated into subsequent drafts. The approach was based on the structure of several other UN human rights instruments, such as the United Nations Standard Minimum Rules for the Administration of Juvenile Justice ('The Beijing Rules'), GA Res. 40/33, 29 November 1985. Additionally, the order of the subjects in the Draft Guidelines was reformulated to follow the somewhat analogous provisions in Article 5 of the International Convention on the Elimination of All Forms of Racial Discrimination, GA Res. 2106 (XX), 21 December 1965.

At its third meeting in August 2001, Weissbrodt contributed a second draft of the document.[39] The Working Group also considered papers by Guissé on the impact of transnational corporation activities on the enjoyment of economic, social, and cultural rights,[40] and by Eide on responsibilities and procedures for implementation and compliance with regard to human rights guidelines for transnational corporations.[41]

At the Working Group's third session, there was recognition of a common desire to implement the Norms as a non-voluntary standard as opposed to a voluntary initiative. Despite this desire, the Working Group and others did not believe that the United Nations of the world at large was ready for a legally binding treaty; therefore the Norms would be more effectively implemented as 'soft' law.[42] Implemented as soft law, the Norms could be similar to many other UN declarations,[43] principles,[44] guidelines,[45] standards,[46] and resolutions[47] which interpret existing international law and summarize international practice without reaching the status of a treaty.

---

[39] UN Doc. E/CN.4/Sub.2/2001/WG.2/WP.1 and Add. 2 (2001); 2001 Guidelines, *supra* n 35; Seminar Report, *supra* n 35. [40] UN Doc. E/CN.4/Sub.2/WG.2/WP.3 (2001).

[41] Sub-Commission, Corporations, States and human rights: a note on responsibilities and procedures for implementation and compliance, UN Doc. E/CN.4/Sub.2/WG.2/WP.2 (2001) [hereinafter Eide Working Paper]. [42] See *infra* n 118.

[43] For examples of soft law 'declarations' *see* the Declaration on the Rights of Disabled Persons, GA Res. 3447 (XXX), 9 December 1975; Declaration on the Right to Development, GA Res. 41/128, 4 December 1986; Declaration on the Protection of All Persons from Enforced Disappearances, GA Res. 47/133, 18 December 1992; Declaration on the Protection of All Persons Belonging to National or Ethnic, Religious or Linguistic Minorities, GA Res. 47/135, 18 December 1992; Declaration on the Elimination of Violence Against Women, GA Res. 2263(XXII), 7 November 1967; Vienna Declaration and Platform of Action, A/CONF.177/20 (1995) and A/CONF.177/20/Add.1 (1995); and Fourth World Conference on Women, Beijing Declaration and Platform of Action, A/CONF.177/20 (1995) and A/CONF.177/20/Add.1 (1995).

[44] For examples of soft law 'principles' *see* Body of Principles for the Protection of All Persons under any Form of Detention or Imprisonment, GA Res. 43/173, 9 December 1988; Principles on the Effective Prevention and Investigation of Extra-Legal, Arbitrary and Summary Executions, ECOSOC Res. 1989/65, 24 May 1989; Guiding Principles on Internal Displacement; UN Doc. E/CN.4/1998/53/Add.2 (1998), noted in Comm. Hum. Rts. Res. 1998/50 (17 April 1998); Siracusa Principles on the Limitation and Derogation Provisions in the International Covenant on Civil and Political Rights, UN Doc. E/CN.4/1985/Annex 4 (1984); and the Johannesburg Principles on National Security, Freedom of Expression and Access to Information, UN Doc. E/CN.4/1996/39 (1995).

[45] For examples of soft law 'guidelines' *see* the Maastricht Guidelines on Violations of Economic, Social and Cultural Rights, Maastricht, 22–26 January 1997; Guidelines for the Regulation of Computerized Personal Data Files, GA Res. 45/95, 14 December 1990; Guidelines on the Role of Prosecutors, A/CONF.177/20 (1995) and A/CONF.177/20/Add.1 (1995); and UNHCR, UNHCR Revised Guidelines on Applicable Criteria and Standards relating to the Detention of Asylum-Seekers (1999).

[46] For examples of soft law 'standards' *see* the Paris Minimum Standards of Human Rights Norms in a State of Emergency, 79 *AJIL* (1985) 1072; Standard Rules on the Equalization of Opportunities for Persons with Disabilities, A/RES/48/96, 85th Plenary Meeting, 20 December 1993.

[47] For an example of an instrument using the word 'resolution' *see* Resolutions of the Geneva International Conference, Geneva, 26–29 October 1863, at <http://www1.umn.edu/humanrts/instree/1863b.htm>.

There was also continued debate as to whether the Norms should apply to all business entities or only to transnational corporations. The Working Group discussed this issue extensively in its 2000 and 2001 sessions and partially resolved the issue in the Sub-Commission's resolution of August 2001. Sub-Commission resolution 2001/3 asked the Working Group to 'contribute to the drafting of relevant norms concerning human rights and transnational corporations and other economic units whose activities have an impact on human rights'.[48] At its February 2002 session the Working Group decided that the Norms would apply to 'transnational corporations and other business enterprises'. It is worthy of note that the Norms prominently mention transnational corporations as a significant focus of concern, but still address the responsibilities of all businesses.[49]

Since the Working Group had not completed its tasks pursuant to its three-year mandate, the Sub-Commission decided in August 2001 to extend the Group's mandate for another three years.[50] The renewed mandate, while substantially similar to the old mandate, includes new or newly clarified activities such as: compiling a list of relevant instruments and norms concerning human rights with regard to transnational corporations; contributing to the drafting of relevant norms concerning human rights and transnational corporations and other economic units whose activities have an impact on human rights; and analysing and drafting norms for the establishment of a monitoring mechanism in order to apply sanctions to transnational corporations when appropriate.[51]

At an informal meeting in February 2002 the five members of the Working Group on the Working Methods and Activities of Transnational Corporations (Chairperson El-Hadji Guissé, Miguel Alfonso-Martínez,[52] Vladimir Khartashkin,[53] Soo-Gil Park,[54] and David Weissbrodt) created a revised draft for consideration at its session during the fifty-fourth session of the Sub-Commission in July/August 2002. The new draft of the Norms consisted of eighteen fundamental human rights norms with regard to business activities of transnational corporations and other business enterprises and included a section on definitions.[55] For the first time, the Norms and the Commentary were submitted as separate

---

[48] Sub-Commission Resolution 2001/3.   [49] *See* Norms, *supra* n 1, at para. 1.

[50] *See* Resolution 2001/3, *supra* n 48.   [51] *Ibid.*

[52] Miguel Alfonso-Martínez has been a member of the Sub-Commission since 1995. He is the Titular Professor in the Superior Institute for International Relations and has been a member of the Permanent Court of Arbitration since 1998.

[53] Vladimir Khartashkin has been a member of the Sub-Commission since 2002 and an alternate since 1998. He is a professor of international law at the People's Friendship University in Moscow, the Principal Research Officer at the Institute of State and Law of the Russian Academy of Sciences, and was the chairperson of Russian President Yeltsin's Commission on Human Rights.

[54] Soo-Gil Park has been a member of the Sub-Commission since 2000. He is a Distinguished Professor of the Graduate School of Advanced Studies (International Relations), Korea University, a former President of the United Nations Security Council, and a former Ambassador Extraordinary and Plenipotentiary and Permanent Representative to the United Nations in New York.

[55] *See* 2002 Principles, *supra* n 35.

documents at the fifty-fourth session of the Sub-Commission in July/August 2002.[56]

By the end of the Working Group's meetings at the fifty-fifth session of the Sub-Commission in 2002, a revised version of the Norms (taking into account comments made at the Working Group meetings) was attached to the 2002 Working Group Report with the aim of promoting even greater dissemination of the document.[57] Resolution 2002/8 of the Sub-Commission asked that the Norms and Commentary be disseminated as widely as possible, so as to encourage governments, intergovernmental organizations, non-governmental organizations, transnational corporations, other business enterprises, unions, and other interested parties to provide any suggestions, observations, or recommendations.[58] The Norms were also attached in the expectation that the Working Group would adopt the Norms in 2003 and send them to the Sub-Commission and eventually to the Commission for adoption.[59] As to the substance of the document, the Working Group believed that the Norms should focus attention on large transnational corporations, while still applying generally to all businesses. The Working Group compromised on language which states that a small, local business will not be held rigorously subject to the Norms if it can prove (1) it has no connection with a transnational corporation, (2) its impact is entirely local, and (3) there was no violation of the right to security as defined in the Norms.[60]

In March 2003 several NGOs organized a seminar in which they provided the Working Group members with detailed comments on the Norms. During that seminar, the Working Group received and responded to each issue raised by the NGOs in attendance. Immediately following the seminar, the Working Group considered in private session all comments received from the seminar and pursuant to the dissemination requested in resolution 2002/8. The Working Group then agreed upon a draft of the Norms to present at their meetings during the fifty-fifth session of the Sub-Commission in July/August 2003.[61]

During its meetings at the fifty-fifth session of the Sub-Commission, the Working Group resolved the key issue of the status of the Commentary to the Norms. It decided that the preamble to both the Norms and Commentary should refer to the Commentary as a 'useful interpretation and elaboration of the standards contained in the Norms'.[62] Then, after taking into consideration all suggestions received at its

---

[56] Three members of the Working Group submitted the Commentary: Vladimir Khartashkin, Soo-Gil Park, and David Weissbrodt. *See* UN Doc. E/CN.4/Sub.2/2002/WG.2/WP.1/Add.2 (February 2002) [hereinafter 2002 Principles with Commentary], *available at* <http://www1.umn.edu/humanrts/links/omig.html>. The Working Group lacked sufficient time to review comprehensively the Commentary to the Norms at its three full days of meeting in February 2002.

[57] *See* UN Doc. E/CN.4/Sub. 2/2002/13 at para. 15 (2002); Sub-Commission, The relationship between the enjoyment of economic, social and cultural rights and the right to development, and the working methods and activities of transnational corporations, Sub-Commission Resolution 2002/8.

[58] *See* Resolution 2002/8, *supra* n 57.   [59] *Ibid.*   [60] *See* Norms, *supra* n 1, at para. 21.

[61] *See* Norms, *supra* n 1, Commentary, *supra* n 29.

[62] *See* Norms, *supra* n 1, at pmbl; Commentary, *supra* n 29, at pmbl.

public meetings in 2003, the Working Group adopted a revised version of both the Norms and Commentary and forwarded the Norms to the Sub-Commission for approval.[63]

After consideration of the Norms, the Sub-Commission unanimously approved the Norms in its resolution 2003/16 of 14 August 2003.[64] Resolution 2003/16 also transmitted the Norms to the Commission on Human Rights for their eventual consideration, and asked the Commission to invite Governments, United Nations bodies, specialized agencies, NGOs, and other interested parties to provide comments on the Norms for the Commission's session in March–April 2005.[65] In addition to transmission to the Commission, resolution 2003/16 creates an initial procedure for implementation of the Norms. The resolution requests the Working Group to receive information from Governments, NGOs, business enterprises, individuals, groups of individuals, and other sources on the negative impacts of businesses and particularly information on the implementation of the Norms. The Working Group is then to invite the business concerned to provide responses to the information received, and to transmit its comments and recommendations to the relevant business, government, or non-governmental organization.[66] It also asks the Working Group to continue discussions exploring further possible procedures for implementation such as the other mechanisms identified in general terms in the Norms and Commentary.[67]

At both the Working Group and Sub-Commission meetings in 2003, many NGOs and others provided public statements in support of the Norms, including Amnesty International; Christian Aid; Human Rights Advocates; Human Rights Watch; Lawyers Committee for Human Rights; Federation Internationale des Ligues des Droits de l'Homme (FIDH); Forum Menschenrechte (Human Rights Forum); Oxfam; Prince of Wales International Business Leaders Forum; World Economy, Ecology and Development (WEED); and the World Organization Against Torture (OMCT). Additionally, Amnesty International provided a list of fifty-eight NGOs confirming their support for the Norms, and Forum Menschenrechte provided another list of twenty-six NGOs joining their statement in support of the Norms.

Immediately upon adoption, many of the NGOs listed above issued a press release welcoming the Sub-Commission's approval of these Norms.[68] Additionally, a few NGOs have already indicated their intent to begin using the Norms as standards for reporting on the human rights activities of businesses.[69] Further,

---

[63] *See* Sub-Commission, Report of the sessional Working Group on the Working Methods and Activities of Transnational Corporations, UN Doc. E/CN.4/Sub.2/2003/13 (2003) [hereinafter 2003 Working Group Report].   [64] *See* Resolution 2003/16, *supra* n 2, at para. 1.

[65] *Ibid.* at paras. 2 and 3.   [66] *Ibid.* at para. 5.   [67] *Ibid.* at para. 7.

[68] *See* Non-Governmental Organizations Welcome the New UN Norms on Transnational Businesses (13 August 2002) (on file with author).

[69] Amnesty International and Christian Aid began using a draft of the Norms as the basis for their assessment of business conduct and campaign efforts even before the Norms were adopted.

several transnational businesses have agreed to 'road-test' the Norms as part of their commitment to human rights.[70]

As for the future of the Norms and Commentary in the UN system, the Sub-Commission in adopting the Norms and transmitting the Norms to the Commission on Human Rights suggested that the Commission at its sixtieth session in March–April 2004 invite governments, United Nations bodies, specialized agencies, non-governmental organizations, and other interested parties to submit comments on the Norms to the Commission at its sixty-first session in 2005. Much education on the Norms and Commentary for businesses, unions, and governments remains to be done, however, before it is likely that the Commission will begin seriously considering or adopting the Norms and Commentary. Meanwhile, the Norms have already begun to enter into business practices and to be accepted as the most comprehensive definition of corporate social responsibilities.

3. GENERAL ISSUES RAISED IN DRAFTING THE NORMS

The drafting of any document which intends to place international human rights obligations upon business entities raises two principal questions: (1) to what extent can international obligations be placed on non-state actors; and (2) is it appropriate to place human rights obligations upon businesses? This section argues that international obligations already apply both directly and indirectly to non-state actors such as businesses, and further that it is appropriate to place human rights responsibilities upon businesses.

This foundation is key to the drafting exercise of the Norms. The Norms draw upon the existing web of international obligations which already apply, either directly or indirectly, to business entities and pull them together into one document which clearly and directly states the human rights standards applicable to businesses. The Norms make clear which human rights standards correctly and appropriately apply to businesses.

A. International Obligations of Non-State Actors

Article 2 of the OECD Convention on Combating Bribery of Foreign Public Officials in International Business Transactions states that '[e]ach Party shall take

---

[70] The aim of the 'Initiative for Respect in partnership with Mary Robinson and the Ethical Globalisation Initiative is to show leadership within the business sector on how human rights can be incorporated into the centre of the CSR [corporate social responsibility] and Governance debates'. (E-mail message of John Morrison, 26 August 2003, on file with author); *see also* John Morrison, *Business and Human Rights*, 2 NEW ACADEMY REVIEW 8 (2003). The seven founding companies of the Initiative are: ABB, Barclays Bank, National Grid Transco, Novartis, Novo Nordisk, MTV, and The Body Shop International. During their first meeting in Zurich during June 2003, the group agreed that one of the priorities should be to 'road-test' the Norms.

such measures as may be necessary, in accordance with its legal principles, to establish the liability of *legal persons* for the bribery of a foreign public official'.[71] This treaty makes clear that businesses are recognized and may be regulated by international law.[72] Similarly, the International Convention on Civil Liability for Oil Pollution Damage and the Convention on Civil Liability for Damage Resulting from Activities Dangerous to the Environment place responsibilities on businesses by extending their reach to 'legal persons'. Both define the persons liable to the convention as 'any individual or partnership or any public or private body, whether corporate or not, including a State or any of its constituent subdivisions'. One difficult question with regard to the Norms is whether human rights obligations may be imposed on non-state actors, such as transnational corporations and other business enterprises.[73] The Universal Declaration of Human Rights (Universal Declaration) announces the fundamental rights of individuals and places responsibility on both governments and other 'organs of society' for affording those rights. Particularly, it states:

The General Assembly, Proclaims this Universal Declaration of Human Rights as a common standard of achievement for all peoples and all nations, to the end that every individual and every *organ of society*, keeping this Declaration constantly in mind, shall strive by teaching and education to promote respect for these rights and freedoms and by progressive

---

[71] OECD Convention on Combating Bribery of Foreign Public Officials in International Business Transactions, 18 December 1997, S. Treaty Doc. 105-43 (1998), 37 ILM 1, *entered into force* 15 February 1999 (emphasis added). The OECD Convention makes it a crime to offer, promise, or give a bribe to a foreign public official in order to obtain or retain international business deals. The OECD Member countries and five non-member countries have ratified the treaty.

[72] *See* Ratner, *infra* n 73, at 482 (citing Art. 3 of the OECD Bribery treaty which states that 'The bribery of a foreign public official shall be punishable by effective, proportionate and dissuasive criminal penalties. The range of penalties shall be comparable to that applicable to the bribery of the Party's own public officials and shall, in the case of natural persons, include deprivation of liberty sufficient to enable effective mutual legal assistance and extradition.')

[73] *See* International Council on Human Rights, *Beyond Voluntarism: Human Rights and the developing international legal obligations of companies* (2002) [hereinafter Beyond Voluntarism]; Ratner, 'Corporations and Human Rights: A Theory of Legal Responsibility', 11 *Yale L.J.* (2001) 443 at 476 (arguing that the real question is what the rights and duties of non-state actors are, and not whether or not they exist); Paul, 'Holding Multinational Corporations Responsible Under International Law', 24 *Hastings Int'l & Comp. L. Rev.* (2001) 285; Blumber, 'Accountability to Multinational Corporations: The barriers presented by concepts of the corporate juridical entity', 24 *Hastings Int'l & Comp. L. Rev.* (2001) 297. *See also* Richard A. Higgott *et al.* (eds) *Non-State Actors and Authority in the Global System* (2000); Bas Arts *et al.* (eds), *Non-State Actors in International Relations* (2001); Panel, 'Human Rights and Non-State Actors', 11 *Pace Int'l L.* Rev. (1999) 205; Plenary Theme Panel, 'The Challenge of Non-State Actors', 92 *Am. Soc'y Int'l L. Proc.* (1998) 20; 'Non-State Actors and the Case Law of the Yugoslavia War Crimes Tribunal', 92 *Am. Soc'y Int'l L. Proc.* (1998) 48; Beard, 'International Security: Multiple Actors, Multiple Threats—Countering the Threat Posed by Non-State Actors in the Proliferation of Weapons of Mass Destruction', 92 *Am. Soc'y Int'l L. Proc.* (1998) 173; Farrior, 'State Responsibility in a Multiactor World: State Responsibility for Human Rights Abuses by Non-State Actors', 92 *Am. Soc'y Int'l L. Proc.* (1988) 299.

measures, national and international, to secure their universal and effective recognition and observance.[74]

'Organs of society' clearly includes actors beyond just the state, and very arguably includes non-state actors such as businesses.[75] Further, Article 29 of the Universal Declaration states that '*Everyone* has duties to the community in which alone the free and full development of his personality is possible',[76] and Article 30 states that no 'State, *group or person* [has] any right to engage in any activity or to perform any act aimed at the destruction of any of the rights or freedoms set forth therein'.[77]

Although the Universal Declaration is a declaration and not a treaty, several arguments can be made that the Universal Declaration does indeed create international binding obligations on States and which extend to non-state actors. One argument includes the fact that the UN Charter contains provisions that call upon States Members to participate in the promotion of human rights,[78] and the Universal Declaration is considered to be the authoritative and nearly contemporaneous interpretation of those human rights provisions.[79] Additionally, many of the

---

[74] Universal Declaration of Human Rights, GA Res. 217A (III), 26 June 1945, at preamble (emphasis added) [hereinafter Universal Declaration]. *See generally* International Council on Human Rights Policy, *Taking Duties Seriously: Individual Duties in International Human Rights Law, A Commentary* (1999).

[75] *See* Beyond Voluntarism, *supra* n 73, at 58–59 (stating that 'An "organ" in the sense used in the preamble suggests an institution or group which performs some function, in this case for "society".' It is not difficult to see that 'organs of society' encompass businesses, since they play a clear economic (and increasingly social) function in society.)

[76] Universal Declaration, *supra* n 74, at Art. 29(1) (emphasis added).

[77] *Ibid.* at Art. 30 (emphasis added). Additionally, Article 5(1) of both the International Covenant on Economic, Social, and Cultural Rights and the International Covenant on Civil and Political rights state that no 'State, group or person [has] any right to engage in any activity or to perform any act aimed at the destruction of any of the rights or freedoms recognized herein'. International Covenant on Civil and Political Rights, GA Res. 2200A (XXI), 16 January 1966, at Art. 5(1) [hereinafter Civil and Political Covenant]; International Covenant on Economic, Social, and Cultural Rights, GA Res. 2200A (XXI), 16 January 1966, at Art. 5(1) [hereinafter Economic and Social Covenant].

[78] *See* UNCIO XV, 335, Art. 1(3) (stating that one of the purposes of the United Nations is 'to achieve international cooperation in solving international problems of an economic, social cultural, or human-itarian character, and in promoting and encouraging respect for human rights and for fundamental freedoms for all without distinction as to race, sex, language, or religion'); Art. 55 (stating the United Nations shall promote 'universal respect for, and observance of, human rights and fundamental freedoms for all without distinction as to race, sex, language or religion'); and Art. 56 (stating that 'All Members pledge themselves to take joint and separate action in cooperation with the Organization for the achievement of the purposes set forth in Article 55').

[79] *See* Hannum, 'The Status of the Universal Declaration of Human Rights in National and International Law', 25 *Ga. J. Int'l & Comp. L.*(1995) 287, at 290; Sohn, 'The New International Law: Protection of the Rights of Individuals Rather than States', 32 *Am. U.L. Rev.*(1982) 1, at 16–17 (stating that The Universal Declaration has joined the UN Charter 'as a part of the constitutional structure of the world community'). *See also* Vienna Declaration and Programme of Action, UN GAOR, World Conference on Human Rights, 48th Sess., at 21–22, UN Doc. A/Conf.157/24 (Part I) (1993) (stating that the World Conference on Human Rights 'reaffirms the solemn commitment of all States to fulfill

individual articles of the Universal Declaration are considered to be customary international law.[80]

Several other instruments have followed the foundation laid by the Universal Declaration in extending human rights obligations to non-state actors either directly or indirectly. For example, Article 18 of the Declaration on Human Rights Defenders states that '[i]ndividuals, groups, institutions and non-governmental organizations have an important role to play...' in protecting and promoting human rights.[81] Article 2 of the International Convention on the Elimination of All Forms of Racial Discrimination (Race Convention) creates obligations for 'State[s], institution[s], group[s], [and] individual[s]'.[82] Similarly, Article 2(e) of the Convention on the Elimination of All Forms of Discrimination against Women requires states parties to 'take all appropriate measures to eliminate discrimination against women by any person, organization or enterprise' and Article 4(c) requires states parties to '[e]xercise due diligence to prevent, investigate, and in accordance with national legislation, punish acts of violence against women, whether those acts are perpetrated by the State or by private persons'.[83] Most recently, the Optional Protocol on the Convention on the Rights of the Child on the involvement of children in armed conflict specifically addresses 'armed groups distinct from the armed forces of a State'.[84] These examples show that there is no conceptual barrier to creating obligations for non-state actors and that the United Nations has viewed the conduct of non-state actors as conduct subject to international, universal standards.

Further extending responsibilities to non-state actors are several treaties which hold individuals accountable for their actions such as: (1) the Supplementary

---

their obligations to promote universal respect for, and observance and protection of, all human rights and fundamental freedoms for all in accordance with the Charter of the United Nations, other instruments relating to human rights, and international law. The universal nature of these rights is beyond question.')

[80] A state violates customary international law if it practises, encourages, or condones: genocide; slavery; murder or causing the disappearance of an individual; torture or other cruel, inhuman, or degrading treatment or punishment; prolonged arbitrary detention, systematic racial discrimination; and consistent patterns of gross violations of internationally recognized human rights. *See Restatement (Third) of Foreign Relations Law of the United States* §702 (1987). *See also* T. Meron, *Human Rights and Humanitarian Norms as Customary Law* (1989) (analysing the process for determining which rights have reached the level of international customary law).

[81] Declaration on the Right and Responsibility of Individuals, Groups and Organs of Society to Promote and Protect Universally Recognized Human Rights and Fundamental Freedoms, GA Res. 53/144, 8 March 1999, at Art. 18.

[82] International Convention on the Elimination of All Forms of Racial Discrimination, GA Res. 2106 (XX), 21 December 1965, at Arts. 2(1)(d).

[83] Convention on the Elimination of All Forms of Discrimination against Women, GA Res. 34/180, 18 December 1979, at Arts. 2(e) and 4(c).

[84] Optional Protocol to the Convention on the Rights of the Child on the involvement of children in armed conflict, GA Res. 54/263, 25 May 2000, at Art. 4(1).

Slavery Convention of 1957,[85] (2) the Genocide Convention,[86] (3) the Nuremberg Rules,[87] (4) the Rome Statute of the International Criminal Court,[88] (5) the Convention Against Torture,[89] and (6) Convention on Apartheid.[90]

In addition, while the Universal Declaration,[91] the International Covenant on Civil and Political Rights, and the International Covenant on Economic, Social, and Cultural Rights[92] focus principally on the duties of governments, they indicate that persons have both rights and responsibilities. The Committee on Economic, Social, and Cultural Rights Committee interpreted their respective Covenants to bind

[85] 'The act of enslaving another person or of inducing another person to give himself or a person dependent upon him into slavery, or of attempting these acts, or being accessory thereto, or being a party to a conspiracy to accomplish any such acts, shall be a criminal offence under the laws of the States Parties to this Convention and *persons* convicted thereof shall be liable to punishment'. Supplementary Convention on the Abolition of Slavery, the Slave Trade, and Institutions and Practices Similar to Slavery, 7 September 1956, 266 UNTS 3, at Art. 6 (emphasis added).

[86] '*Persons charged* with genocide or any of the other acts enumerated in article III shall be tried by a competent tribunal of the State in the territory of which the act was committed, or by such international penal tribunal as may have jurisdiction with respect to those Contracting Parties which shall have accepted its jurisdiction'. Convention on the Prevention and Punishment of the Crime of Genocide, 9 December 1948, 78 UNTS 277, at Art. 6 (emphasis added).

[87] 'The following acts, or any of them, are crimes coming within the jurisdiction of the Tribunal for which *there* shall be individual responsibility: (a) Crimes against Peace ... (b) War Crimes ... (c) Crimes against Humanity ...' Nuremberg Rules of the International Military Tribunal, *in* Agreement for the Prosecution and Punishment of the Major War Criminals of the European Axis, 8 August 1945, 82 UNTS 279 (emphasis added).

[88] 'The Court [created by the Statute] shall have jurisdiction over *natural persons* pursuant to this Statute. A person who commits a crime within the jurisdiction of the Court shall be individually responsible and liable for punishment in accordance with this Statute'. Rome Statute of the International Criminal Court, 17 July 1998, UN Doc. A/CONF.183/9 (1998), *reprinted in* 37 ILM 999 (1998), at Art. 25 (emphasis added). *See generally* Clapham, 'The Question of Jurisdiction under International Criminal Law over Legal Persons: Lessons from the Rome Conference on an International Criminal Court', in M.T. Kamminga and S. Zia-Zarifi (eds), *The Liability of Multinational Corporations under International Law* (2000) 139.

[89] 'Each State Party shall ensure that all acts of torture are offences under its criminal law. The same shall apply to an attempt to commit torture and to an act by any person which constitutes complicity or participation in torture'. Convention against Torture and Other Cruel, Inhuman or Degrading Treatment or Punishment, GA Res. 39/46, 10 December 1984.

[90] 'International criminal responsibility shall apply, irrespective of the motive involved, to *individuals*, members or organizations and institutions and representatives of the State, whether residing in the territory of the State in which the acts are perpetrated or in some other State'. International Convention on the Suppression and Punishment of the Crime of Apartheid, GA Res. 3068 (XXVIII) 30 November 1973, at Art. 3 (emphasis added).   [91] *See supra* nn 74 and 76.

[92] The preambles in both the Covenant on Civil and Political Rights and the Covenant on Economic, Social, and Cultural Rights have language stating that, 'The States Parties to the Present Covenant ... Realizing that *the individual, having duties to other individuals and to the community, is under a responsibility* to strive for the promotion and observance of the rights recognized in the present Covenant'. Civil and Political Covenant, *supra* n 77, at preamble; Economic and Social Covenant, *supra* n 77, at preamble (emphasis added). *See also supra* n 76.

businesses in regard to the rights to adequate food,[93] the highest attainable standard of health,[94] and privacy.[95]

Article 2 of the OECD Convention on Combating Bribery of Foreign Public Officials in International Business Transactions states that '[e]ach Party shall take such measures as may be necessary, in accordance with its legal principles, to establish the liability of *legal persons* for the bribery of a foreign public official.'[96] This treaty makes clear that businesses are recognized and may be regulated by international law.[97] Similarly, the International Convention on Civil Liability for

[93] General Comment 13 states, '[w]hile only States are parties to the Covenant and are thus ultimately accountable for compliance with it, all members of society—individuals, families, local communities, non-governmental organizations, civil society organizations, as well as the private business sector—have responsibilities in the realization of the right to adequate food. The State should provide an environment that facilitates implementation of these responsibilities. The private business sector—national and transnational—should pursue its activities within the framework of a code of conduct conducive to respect of the right to adequate food, agreed upon jointly with the Government and civil society'. Committee on Economic, Social, and Cultural Rights, General Comment 13, The right to adequate food (Art. 11) UN Doc. E/C.12/1999/5, para. 20 (1999).

[94] General Comment 13 extends the Covenant's reach to non-state actors with regard to the obligation to respect the right to health in Article 12 by stating, 'Violations of the obligation to respect are those State actions, policies or laws that contravene the standards set out in article 12 of the Covenant and are likely to result in bodily harm, unnecessary morbidity and preventable mortality. Examples include . . . the failure of the State to take into account its legal obligation regarding the right to health when entering into bilateral or multilateral agreements with other States, international organizations and other entities, such as *multinational corporations*.' Committee on Economic, Social, and Cultural Rights, General Comment 14, The right to the highest attainable standard of health, UN Doc. E/C.12/2000/4, para. 50 (2000) (emphasis added). Additionally, 'Violations of the obligation to protect follow from the failure of a State to take all necessary measures to safeguard persons within their jurisdiction from infringements of the right to health by third parties. This category includes such omissions as the failure to regulate the activities of *individuals, groups or corporations* so as to prevent them from violating the right to health of others; the failure to protect consumers and workers from practices detrimental to health, *e.g. by employers and manufacturers of medicines or food;* the failure to discourage production, marketing and consumption of tobacco, narcotics and other harmful substances; the failure to protect women against violence or to prosecute perpetrators; the failure to discourage the continued observance of harmful traditional medical or cultural practices; and the failure to enact or enforce laws to prevent the pollution of water, air and soil by extractive and manufacturing industries.' *Ibid.* at para. 51 (emphases added).

[95] General Comment 16 states that '[i]n the view of the Committee this right [to privacy, family, home, correspondence, honour, and reputation] is required to be guaranteed against all such interferences and attacks whether they emanate from State authorities or from natural *or legal persons*'. Human Rights Committee, General Comment 16 (Twenty-third session, 1988), Compilation of General Comments and General Recommendations Adopted by Human Rights Treaty Bodies, UN Doc. HRI/GEN/1/Rev.1 at 21, para.1 (1994) (emphasis added).

[96] *Supra* n 71.

[97] *See* Ratner, *supra* n 73, at 482 (citing Art. 3 of the OECD Bribery treaty which states that 'The bribery of a foreign public official shall be punishable by effective, proportionate and dissuasive criminal

Oil Pollution Damage and the Convention on Civil Liability for Damage Resulting from Activities Dangerous to the Environment place responsibilities on businesses by extending their reach to 'legal persons'. Both define the persons liable to the convention as 'any individual or partnership or any public or private body, whether corporate or not, including a State or any of its constituent subdivisions'.[98] Further, the Global Convention on the Control of Transboundary Movements of Hazardous Waste, which declares criminal any illegal movement of hazardous wastes, defines the 'persons' to be held responsible as any natural or legal person.[99]

The ILO Declaration on Fundamental Principles and Rights at Work[100] extends to both legal and non-legal persons. Members of the ILO include states, companies, and unions, thereby extending responsibilities to companies and unions as well as states. The OECD Guidelines for Multinational Enterprises set forth standards for multinational businesses, and explicitly mention the role of businesses to 'respect the human rights of those affected by their activities'.[101]

This body of law, varying in its applicability, demonstrates that (1) there is no conceptual barrier to applying international obligations to non-state actors such as businesses; (2) many international obligations already apply to businesses directly,[102] through the duties of states,[103] or through obligations of individuals who may be

---

penalties. The range of penalties shall be comparable to that applicable to the bribery of the Party's own public officials and shall, in the case of natural persons, include deprivation of liberty sufficient to enable effective mutual legal assistance and extradition').

[98] International Convention on Civil Liability for Oil Pollution Damage, *entered into force* 19 June 1975, Art. 1; Convention on Civil Liability for damage resulting from activities dangerous to the environment, 21 June 1993, 32 ILM 1228, at Art. 2(6). The Convention for Damage to the Environment is a regional instrument which is open to signature by the members of the Council of Europe and to nonmember states that have participated in its elaboration and the European Economic Community. *Ibid.* at Art. 32(1), *See* R. Picolotti and J.D. Taillant, *Human Rights Accountability of Private Business: A Question of Sustainable Development* (2000).

[99] United Nations Environment Programme Conference of Plenipotentiaries on the Global Convention on the Control of Transboundary Movements of Hazardous Wastes: Final Act and Text of Basel Convention, 22 March 1989, 28 ILM 649 (1989).

[100] ILO Declaration on Fundamental Principles, *supra* n 22.

[101] OECD Guidelines, *supra* n 19, §II.2.

[102] Direct application of law to legal entities such as businesses is a well accepted practice. Legal obligations already apply to businesses directly. Business entities, such as corporations, ordinarily have a legal identity distinct from their owners. *See* A. Conard, *Corporations in Perspective* (1976) 416; R.W. Hamilton, *Corporations Including Partnerships and Limited Liability Companies: Cases and Materials* (1998) 9. These business entities may be held responsible in tort for their corporate policies and decisions and may also be held vicariously responsible for the conduct of their employees within the scope of their employment. J.I. Diamond, *Understanding Torts* (1996) 221–23.

[103] Companies and similar entities are, from one perspective, legal constructs allowed to exist by virtue of state action. Accordingly in this view, a state should not create, nor allow to endure, a body that violates international human rights norms. At a minimum, states have the obligation not to allow violations by companies. For a discussion regarding the indirect obligations placed on companies via the direct obligation of states to regulate entities which the state creates, *see* Beyond Voluntarism, *supra* n 73, at 45–55.

company officers;[104] and (3) there may be rules which appropriately could be made to apply to businesses more explicitly. The Norms take these findings and use them as the foundation for the Working Group's drafting exercise. The Norms use the areas in which international human rights obligations have already been applied to non-state actors, and also take advantage of the areas in which a strong case can be made for applying such obligations to business enterprises,[105] and then take the next step: putting them all into one document to become the authoritative statement on the international human rights obligations of business enterprises.

B. The Role of Business Enterprises in Relation to Human Rights

Another issue in the creation of human rights standards for business is determining whether it is appropriate to place human rights obligations upon organizations whose primary purpose is to produce profit or effectively deliver goods and services.[106] Active concern for human rights helps: (1) ensure compliance with local and international laws; (2) satisfy consumer concerns; (3) promote stable legal environments; (4) build corporate community goodwill; (5) the selection of ethical, well managed, and reliable business partners; (6) produce a predictable, stable, and productive business enterprise; (7) keep markets open; and (8) increase worker productivity and retention.[107] Further, if human rights norms for business enterprises become widely accepted, businesses will enjoy greater predictability and consistency with regard to their responsibilities for protecting human rights. An authoritative set of human rights norms for businesses would thus ensure that these

---

[104] A 'firm' is a legal concept that usefully coordinates agreements among a variety of persons—some who give capital, some who manage, some who produce, etc. *See* R.H. Coase, *The Firm, The Market and the Law* (1988). The firm is actually a set of specialized agreements among persons in order to coordinate production or provide services in a more cost-effective manner. But the firm acts only by persons, whose fiduciary and other obligations constrain their acts. Hence, to the extent that firms are comprised of individuals and those individuals are bound by human rights treaties and other instruments, companies are effectively bound by the same provisions. *See* W. Holfield, *Fundamental Legal Conceptions* (1923) 197. Furthermore, in at least some countries corporations may be fined or subjected to relevant forms of criminal sanctions for employee conduct, if the criminal activity is not a personal aberration of an employee acting on his/her own, but reflects corporate policy. *See State v. Christy Pontiac-GMC, Inc.*, 354 N.W.2d 17 (Minn. 1984); *Commonwealth v. McIlwain School Bus Lines*, 423 A.2d 413 (Penn. 1980). In addition, there may be liability for the corporation if the crime has been committed by a 'directing mind' of the corporation. It has been argued that liability should also stem from the company's internal decision structures (its CIDs) and its ability to adjust its CIDs in the wake of harm caused. *See* C. Wells, *Corporations and Criminal Responsibility* (1983) 144.

[105] *See generally* Ratner *supra* n 73; Frey, 'The Legal and Ethical Responsibilities of Transnational Corporations in the Protection of International Human Rights', 6 *Minn. J. Global Trade* (1997) 153; Cassel, 'Corporate Initiatives: A Second Human Rights Revolution?', 19 *Fordham Int'l L. J.* (1996) 1963 (all three authors discuss methods for determining which human rights obligations are appropriate to place on business entities).

[106] For a discussion on the difficulty one industry has had trying to implement human rights standards and create better working conditions, *see* K. Schoenberger, *Levi's Children: Coming to Terms with Human Rights in the Global Marketplace* (2000). [107] Business and Human Rights, *supra* n 9, at 8–9.

responsibilities are clear, accessible, and unambiguous. A widely accepted set of human rights responsibilities articulated by the international community will help establish a level playing field for business competition. Such predictability is a basic foundation for commercial services, sustainable development, and prosperity.

Although it may be beneficial for transnational corporations and other business enterprises to embrace human rights standards, it may still be questioned if it is appropriate to impose human rights obligations on these business associations. Certainly, governments possess the principal responsibility of assuring the implementation of human rights and businesses should not be asked to take over the primary role of governments. The Norms have, since the beginning, noted the primary duty of governments to protect human rights and have evinced a strong commitment that nothing in the Norms shall diminish the human rights obligations of governments.[108] Hence, the most important paragraph of the Norms is the first, which provides:

States have the primary responsibility to promote, secure the fulfilment of, respect, ensure respect of and protect human rights recognized in international as well as national law, including ensuring that transnational corporations and other business enterprises respect human rights. Within their respective spheres of activity and influence, transnational corporations and other business enterprises have the obligation to promote, secure the fulfilment of, respect, ensure respect of and protect human rights recognized in international as well as national law, including the rights and interests of indigenous peoples and other vulnerable groups.[109]

This initial principle makes clear that it would be inappropriate to distract the United Nations and human rights advocates from their efforts to persuade governments to adopt and implement human rights law by focusing too much on the relatively new concerns of human rights abuses committed by corporations. One cannot, however, establish a requirement that governments must fulfil all of their human rights obligations before it would be appropriate to consider the responsibilities of businesses, individuals, and others. The human rights community should continue to press governments for improvement, but cannot meanwhile ignore abuses by individuals, business enterprises, and other organs of society. The growing power and transboundary reach of many large businesses have allowed at least some businesses to escape national legal responsibilities and thus require international attention.[110]

---

[108] The Savings Clause of the Norms states that '[n]othing in these Norms shall be construed as diminishing, restricting, or adversely affecting the human rights obligations of States under national and international law, nor shall they be construed as diminishing, restricting, or adversely affecting more protective human rights norms, nor shall they be construed as diminishing, restricting, or adversely affecting other obligations or responsibilities of transnational corporations and other business enterprises in fields other than human rights.' Norms, *supra* n 1, at para. 19.   [109] *Ibid.* at para. 1.

[110] *See* Grossman and Bradlow, 'Are We Being Propelled Towards a People-Centered Transnational Legal Order?', 9 *Am. U. J. Int'l L. & Pol'y* (1993) 1, at 8 (stating that 'The fact that they have multiple production facilities means that [transnational corporations] can evade state power and the constraints of national regulatory schemes by moving their operations between their different facilities around the world'). Stephens, 'Stefan A. Risenfeld Symposium 2001: The Amorality of Profit: Transnational Corporations and Human Rights', 20 *Berkeley J. Int'l L.* (2002) 45 (stating that 'international norms

Milton Friedman contended that 'there is one and only one social responsibility of business—to use its resources and engage in activities designed to increase its profits so long as it stays within the rules of the game, which is to say, engages in open and free competition, without deception or fraud'.[111] It is interesting to note that even Friedman's view that businesses should not pursue socially desirable objectives excluded two social policies: fraud and competition. These exceptions may be explained by the need to maintain the quality of the free market that he strenuously advocated. It is doubtful, however, that even Friedman would argue that corporations could pursue profit by committing genocide or using slave labour. Indeed, Friedman would likely have agreed that corporations can only pursue profits in ways that are consistent with legal limitations. That position is consistent with the views of many businesses and business managers who wish to be informed of the law and would be willing to comply with the law.

Ronald Coase developed an alternative paradigm to Friedman's understanding of how businesses should act, arguing that businesses are best understood by observing carefully their actual conduct rather than creating artificial models of how they ought to act.[112] The past ten years have demonstrated that major businesses are, in fact, becoming aware of the interplay between their businesses and their impact on individuals, communities, and the environment; realizing that respect for human rights leads to better business performance; and finding it beneficial to issue their own codes of conduct that go far beyond a narrow profit motive or legal mandates. Hence, the creation of human rights standards that help attract the best and brightest employees, solicit investments from investors who place at least some socially responsible screen on their stock holdings, and attract consumers who prefer to purchase goods made without child labour or unnecessarily soiling the environment are not contrary to the primary purpose of transnational corporations and other business enterprises. The creation of a uniform set of international human right standards would aid in this process by helping to make clear what human rights standards a company should follow and which business enterprises are meeting these standards.

If non-state actors, including businesses, can and should be subject to human rights responsibilities, some businesses have argued that they should only be subject to voluntary guidelines.[113] Many believe that business social responsibility is best achieved through the adoption and implementation of voluntary codes of conduct by transnational corporations and other business enterprises.[114] Because each business

enforced through international mechanisms or coordinated domestic approaches are essential to the effective regulation of corporate human rights abuses').

[111] M. Friedman, *Capitalism and Freedom* (1962) 133; *see also* Friedman, 'The Social Responsibility of a Business is to Increase Profits', *N.Y. Times*, 13 September 1970 (Magazine) at 32, 125.

[112] *See* Coase, *supra* n 104.

[113] *See* Joint views of ICC and the IOE on the Draft Human Rights Principles and Responsibilities for Transnational Corporations and Other Business Enterprises, 30 July 2002, on file with author.

[114] Prominent among such efforts is the UN Global Compact, which is a set of nine voluntary principles. *See supra* n 25.

is examining its own particular human rights situation, the resulting voluntary codes developed by each business enterprise may therefore more adequately reflect a particular set of business values adopted by the company or more adequately address the particular area of risk in greater depth. The involvement of a business in the drafting and implementation of its own code could lead to a greater level of internalization of corporate social responsibility and therefore also effectiveness.

The use of an entirely voluntary system of adoption and implementation of human rights codes of conduct, however, is not enough.[115] Voluntary principles have no enforcement mechanisms; they may be adopted by businesses for public relations purposes and have no real impact on business behaviour.[116] There is a need for outside verification that businesses are adequately incorporating and implementing the codes of conduct they adopt. In addition, there remains the issue of businesses which will not adopt a code of conduct on their own. Creating, adopting, and implementing a code of conduct takes time, money, and initiative on the part of the transnational corporation or other business enterprise, and many businesses may not be willing to put forward this type of effort without outside pressures.

After addressing issues regarding the applicability of international law to business entities, and the appropriate role of businesses in regard to human rights, it then becomes necessary to discuss the creation and implementation of such human rights standards.

4. IMPLEMENTATION

A. Methods of Creating Human Rights Norms for Transnational Corporations and Other Business Enterprises

The Norms as adopted are not a voluntary corporate social responsibility initiative. They include many implementation provisions, which indicates that they are not just aspirational statements of desired conduct. Further, Sub-Commission resolution 2003/16 included the creation of a mechanism for NGOs and others to submit information about businesses which are not meeting the minimum standards of the

---

[115] *See* Beyond Voluntarism, *supra* n 73, at 7 (stating that 'If self-regulation and market forces were the best means to ensure respect for human rights, one might expect, since this has been the dominant paradigm, the number of abuses attributable to companies to have diminished. In fact, in many parts of the world . . . [it] is precisely the opposite.')

[116] In January 2002 a group of individuals wrote a letter to the UN Secretary-General criticizing the Global Compact for further contributing to corporate misconduct by not requiring concrete conduct to improve human rights and for not containing any mechanism to hold companies responsible for violating the principles they voluntarily signed up to support. For a copy of the letter and a copy of the response from Kofi Annan, *see* The Global Compact Website, The UN Addresses Misunderstandings Surrounding Global Compact, *at* <http://www.unglobalcompact.org/irj/servlet/prt/portal/prtroot/com.sapportals.km. docs/uncontent/NewsEvents/SpeechesStatements/GC_misun.htm> (2 October 2002).

Norms.[117] The non-voluntary nature of the Norms therefore goes beyond the voluntary guidelines found in the UN Global Compact, the ILO Tripartite Declaration, and the OECD Guidelines for Multinational Enterprises.

The Norms, although not voluntary, are also not a treaty either. It would be unrealistic to suggest that human rights standards with regard to business enterprises should immediately become the subject of treaty obligations. The development of a treaty requires a high degree of consensus among nations. As discussed above, there have been some treaties and other international norms that apply to businesses and their officers, but there does not yet appear to be an international consensus on precisely what place businesses and other non-state actors have in the international legal order. Therefore, if the Norms are to become a treaty or customary norm, they would more than likely start with some form of 'soft' law drafting exercise.[118]

In preparation for drafting almost all human rights treaties, the United Nations begins with declarations, principles, or other soft law instruments, such as the Norms. Such steps are necessary to develop the consensus required for treaty drafting. The consensus surrounding some declarations has evolved quite quickly to prompt the development of a treaty. For example, the Declaration on the Protection of All Persons from Being Subjected to Torture and Other Cruel, Inhuman, or Degrading Treatment or Punishment of 1975[119] was followed quite rapidly by the Convention against Torture and Other Cruel, Inhuman, or Degrading Treatment or Punishment of 1984.[120] Some declarations, however, have not been codified in the form of treaties because of a lack of adequate consensus, for example, the Declaration on the Elimination of All Forms of Intolerance and of Discrimination Based on Religion or Belief.[121]

Any treaty takes years of preliminary work and consensus building before it has a chance of receiving the approval necessary to be adopted and enter into force. Even soft law instruments may take years to develop. For example, the UN Draft Declaration on the Rights of Indigenous Peoples[122] took twelve years of drafting in the Sub-Commission's Working Group on Indigenous Populations, has been the subject of deliberations in the Commission's Open-Ended Working Group for another eight years, and is likely to require some additional time.

---

[117] Resolution 2003/16 established the Working Group as a body to receive information from governments, NGOs, business enterprises, individuals, groups of individuals, and other sources on the negative impacts of businesses and particularly information on the implementation of the Norms. The Working Group is then to invite the business concerned to provide responses to the information received, and to transmit its comments and recommendations to the relevant business, government, or non-governmental organization. Resolution 2003/16, *supra* n 2, at para. 1.

[118] *See* Shelton, 'Compliance with International Human Rights Soft Law', in E.B. Weiss (ed), *International Compliance with Non-Binding Accords* (1998) 119.

[119] GA Res. 3452 (XXX), 9 December 1975.   [120] *See* Convention against Torture, *supra* n 89.

[121] GA Res. 36/55, 25 December 1981.

[122] Sub-Commission, Draft Declaration on the Rights of Indigenous Peoples, E/CN.4/Sub.2/1994/2/Add.1 (1994).

After drafting by lesser UN bodies, such as the Sub-Commission and the Commission, the General Assembly adopts and promulgates treaties. For example, after the General Assembly in 1948 adopted the Universal Declaration of Human Rights containing several provisions on economic and economic rights, it took eighteen years before the General Assembly in 1966 adopted and promulgated the International Covenant on Economic, Social, and Cultural Rights[123] as a multilateral treaty. Soft law standards, however, may be adopted at any one of the many different levels within the United Nations, although they are ordinarily considered more authoritative if they are adopted by higher organs such as the General Assembly. For example, the Norms could be adopted and promulgated: (1) at the Working Group level, such as the 'Body of Principles for the Protection of All Persons under Any Form of Detention or Imprisonment' adopted by the Working Group on Arbitrary Detention,[124] (2) at the Sub-Commission level, such as the resolution on 'Housing and property restitution in the context of the return of refugees and internally displaced persons',[125] (3) by the Commission on Human Rights, such as '[t]he protection of human rights in the context of human immunodeficiency virus (HIV) and acquired immunodeficiency syndrome (AIDS)',[126] (4) by the Economic and Social Council, such as the 'Principles on the Effective Prevention and Investigation of Extra-Legal, Arbitrary, and Summary Executions',[127] (5) and, of course, by the General Assembly, such as the 'Declaration on the Elimination of Violence against Women'.[128]

In addition to their status as soft law, the Norms also derive legal authority from their sources in treaties and customary international law. The Norms therefore act as a restatement of international legal principles applicable to companies.[129]

B. Avenues for Implementation

As the legal status of the Norms is developing, as it begins to be addressed by different international, intergovernmental, and non-governmental bodies, the methods of

---

[123] Economic and Social Covenant, *supra* n 77.

[124] UN Commission on Human Rights Working Group on Arbitrary Detention, Body of Principles for the Protection of All Persons under Any Form of Detention or Imprisonment regarding the situation of immigrants and asylum seekers, UN Doc. E/CN.4/2000/4/Annex 2 (1999).

[125] UN Sub-Commission on Prevention of Discrimination and Protection of Minorities, Housing, and property restitution in the context of the return of refugees and internally displaced persons, UN Doc. E/CN.4/SUB.2/RES/1998/26 (1998).

[126] UN Commission on Human Rights, Protection of human rights in the context of human immunodeficiency virus (HIV) and acquired immunodeficiency syndrome (AIDS), UN Doc. E/CN.4/RES/1997/33 (1997).

[127] Principles on the Effective Prevention and Investigation of Extra-Legal, Arbitrary, and Summary Executions, *supra* n 44.

[128] Declaration on the Elimination of Violence against Women, GA Res. 48/104, 1993.

[129] *Cf., e.g.*, International Law Commission, Draft Code of Offences against the Peace and Security of Mankind, Report of the International Law Commission on its 6th Session, UN Doc. A/2693 (1954); Draft Articles on Responsibility of States for Internationally Wrongful Acts, *in* Report of the International Law Commission on the Work of its Fifty-third Session, UN Doc. A/56/10 (2001).

implementation will continue to develop as different bodies consider the Norms. The Norms and Commentary do, however, contain some preliminary methods of implementation. Generally, the Norms start by discussing how businesses themselves can implement the Norms, and then move on to discuss how intergovernmental bodies (such as the United Nations), states, unions, and others can play a role in implementation. Resolution 2003/8 also set forth implementation methods and suggestions for further development of further mechanisms.[130]

1. Business Enterprises

Realizing that human rights obligations will be most effective if internalized as a matter of company policy and practice, the Norms on the Responsibilities of Transnational Corporations and Other Business Enterprises with Regard to Human Rights call upon businesses to adopt the substance of the Norms as the minimum standards for their own company codes of conduct or internal rules of operation and to adopt mechanisms for creating accountability within the company.[131]

The Norms then call upon companies to disseminate their adopted internal rules consistent with the Norms. Dissemination requires businesses to ensure that the Norms are communicated in a manner ensuring that all relevant stakeholders can understand their meaning.[132] Promulgation assures that those persons who are most affected by the company's actions know of the company's responsibility to promote and protect human rights.[133] It also ensures the company's responsibilities will be made known to the general public, further legitimating and institutionalizing the existence of its responsibilities.[134]

Business enterprises adopting and disseminating[135] their codes of conduct should then implement internal rules of operation in conformity with Norms. They should

---

[130] *See supra* n 117. Resolution 2003/16 also asks the Commission to consider establishing an open-ended working group to receive complaints on the Norms. *Ibid.* at para. 4.

[131] *See* Commentary, *supra* n 29.   [132] *See* Commentary, *supra* n 29, at para. 15(a).

[133] Adoption and dissemination by a company could create implicit contractual obligations, and thereby be used by stakeholders as a basis for advocacy or even litigation if the company fails to meet the standards stated in their promulgated human rights statements or assessments. *See* Ralph Steinhardt, Multinational Corporations and International Human Rights Law: The New Lex Mercatoria, Chapter 6 in this volume.

[134] In the United States, it may be in the corporation's interest to adopt and promulgate a corporate code of conduct. Corporations held criminally liable for the conduct of their agents can have their sentences reduced if the corporation has an 'effective compliance program' in place to detect and deter employee violations of the law while working for the corporation. U.S. Sentencing Comm'n, Guidelines Manual '8A1.2, application n 3(k) (1995). That sentencing guideline has been a great incentive for U.S. corporations to establish company codes of conduct.

[135] Another way of disseminating such assessments and making the assessments more comparable would be to establish a standardized numerical system for evaluating company performance under the Norms. One such standardized numerical system has been proposed by the Secretariat of the Caux Round Table. The Caux Round Table, Caux Round Table Self-Assessment and Improvement Program, <http://www.cauxroundtable.org/Implementation%20Tools.HTM> (visited 2 September 2003). Another means of verification would be through a corporate social audit similar to the current system used by public

provide training to managers and representatives in practices relevant to the Norms and inform all persons, enterprises, etc. who are potentially affected by dangerous conditions produced by the transnational corporation or business enterprise.[136] The Norms also address implementation issues with regard to each business's supply chain. They call upon businesses to apply and incorporate the Norms into their contracts with their business partners, and ensure that they only do business with others who follow standards similar to the Norms.[137] The Commentary also calls upon businesses to ensure that their supply chains are monitored as far as possible.[138]

A significant portion of implementation set forth in the Norms and Commentary involves monitoring. The Norms begin by calling on businesses to conduct internal monitoring. Businesses are to ensure that monitoring is transparent by disclosing the workplaces observed, remediation efforts undertaken, and other results of monitoring.[139] Businesses are also called upon to ensure that monitoring takes into account input from relevant stakeholders.[140] With regard to working conditions, unions are, of course, the principal stakeholders and in that context collective bargaining agreements cannot be replaced by the Norms or other mechanisms for corporate social responsibility.

Implementing the Norms also requires ensuring that businesses establish legitimate and confidential avenues for workers to file complaints regarding violations of the Norms, and to refrain from retaliatory actions against those workers that make complaints.[141] Once again, collective bargaining agreements and union procedures must be maintained. Businesses also must make a record of all complaints, take the proper steps to resolve the complaints, and take action to prevent reoccurrences.[142]

The Norms further call upon businesses periodically to report on and take other measures to fully implement the Norms.[143] The Commentary further calls on businesses to work in a transparent manner, by regularly disclosing information about their activities, structure, financial situation, and performance; as well as providing information regarding the location of their offices, subsidiaries, and factories.[144] Businesses must also inform individuals who may be harmed by conditions that the businesses have created.[145]

---

accountants for auditing company financial statements. The results of such an independent social audit could then be separately published or attached to the company annual report.

[136] *See* Commentary, *supra* n 29, at para. 15(b) and (e).

[137] The Norms call upon businesses to incorporate the Norms in all 'their contracts or other arrangements and dealings with contractors, subcontractors, suppliers, licensees, distributors, or natural or other legal persons that enter into any agreement with the transnational corporation or other business enterprise'. *See* Norms, *supra* n 1, at para. 15. The Norms do not call upon businesses immediately to stop doing business with others who do not comply with the Norms, but instead call upon businesses to 'initially work [with the partner] to reform or decrease violations, but if they will not change, . . . to cease doing business with them'. *See* Commentary, *supra* n 29, at para. 15(c).

[138] *See* Commentary, *supra* n 29, at para. 16(d).   [139] *Ibid.* at para. 16(c).

[140] *Ibid.* at para. 16(i).   [141] *Ibid.* at para. 16(d).   [142] *Ibid.* at para. 16(e).

[143] *See* Norms, *supra* n 1, at para. 15.   [144] *See* Commentary, *supra* n 29, at para. 15(d).

[145] *Ibid.* at para. 15(e).

Businesses must also engage in periodic assessment and the preparation of impact statements.[146] Assessments and impact statements should take into account comments made by stakeholders, and the results of any such assessments should be made available to all relevant stakeholders. Businesses are also called on to assess the human rights impact of major new projects.[147] Where an assessment shows inadequate compliance with the Norms, the Commentary calls upon the business to include a plan of action for reparation and redress.[148]

Business enterprises adopting and disseminating their codes of conduct should also work to improve their compliance with the Norms. One way of improving compliance would be periodic assessment and the preparation of impact statements. Any assessment of a company's performance under the Norms should be objective. For example, business management can conduct a self-assessment or they can retain outside consultants on a confidential basis with or without an assurance of confidentiality. Although self-assessment by a company's own management may be simpler and less expensive, such self-assessment may not yield results acceptable to outsiders. Confidential assessment by independent consultants may give company managers sufficient confidence to provide necessary information and would be more likely to be accepted by outsiders. Business enterprises with human rights concerns would be able to assess the situation and perhaps take steps to rectify any problems. Some outsiders may not, however, have confidence in the adequacy and certainly not in the transparency of confidential assessments. Both management self-assessments and assessments done by independent consultants could be made public. Such dissemination would increase the transparency and legitimacy of the evaluation process, but the expectation of publicity may discourage adequate disclosure of information. If an evaluation is expected to be made public, the standardized reporting system of the Global Reporting Initiative (GRI) could be used,[149] or a company could undergo evaluation by NGOs with expertise in the area, trade unions, labour associations, or governments.

In addition to assessment of past actions, businesses should prepare impact statements to describe and analyse any proposed actions that may have a significant impact on human rights as enumerated in the Norms. Impact statements can be used to examine ways to avoid or reduce adverse human rights consequences related to a proposed action. They include a description of the action, its need, anticipated benefits, an analysis of any human rights impact related to the action, an analysis of reasonable alternatives to the action, and identification of ways to reduce any

---

[146] *Ibid.* at para. 16(g) and (i). Impact statements can be used to examine ways to avoid or reduce adverse human rights consequences related to a proposed action. Impact statements include a description of the action, its need, anticipated benefits, an analysis of any human rights impact related to the action, an analysis of reasonable alternatives to the action, and identification of ways to reduce any negative human rights impacts.   [147] *Ibid.* at para. 15(g).

[148] *Ibid.* at para. 16(h).

[149] The GRI is an international, multi-stakeholder effort to create a common framework for voluntary reporting. *See* Global Reporting Initiative website, *at* <http://www.globalreporting.org> (visited 14 June 2002).

negative human rights impacts. All impact statements should be made available to stakeholders for comment before any action is taken with regard to the proposed action. Impact statements, similar to assessments, may be created by the company itself, through the use of independent consultants, or in cooperation with NGOs having expertise in the area, trade unions or labour associations, or governments.

2. United Nations

The Norms also provide several suggestions as to how the United Nations could aid in the implementation of the Norms. For example, the Norms suggest that human rights treaty bodies could use the Norms in the creation of additional reporting requirements for states.[150] The Norms could also be used by most of the human rights treaty bodies as the basis for their efforts to draft General Comments and Recommendations relevant to the activities of business enterprises.[151] The additional reporting requirements would request states to include reports about the compliance of business enterprises within their respective treaty regimes.[152] The treaty bodies could also use such a General Comment and thus the Norms in preparing their country conclusions and recommendations on states' compliance with existing treaty provisions. A further mechanism (not mentioned specifically in the Norms or Commentary) would be for the four treaty bodies with individual communications procedures to receive communications regarding governments that have failed to take effective action in response to business abuses under the respective treaties as elaborated by the Norms as well as by related General Comments and Recommendations.[153]

---

[150] *Ibid.* at para. 16(d). *See* Anne Bayefsky, *The UN Human Rights Treaty System in the 21st Century* (2000); Philip Alston and James Crawford eds, *The Future of Human Rights Treaty Monitoring* (2000).

[151] For example, the Committee on Economic, Social, and Cultural Rights might use the Norms in drafting, adopting, and applying a General Comment on the obligations of businesses to protect rights set forth in the International Covenant on Economic, Social, and Cultural Rights. *See e.g.* Committee on Economic, Social, and Cultural Rights, General Comment 7, The right to adequate housing (Art. 11(1)): forced evictions, UN Doc. E/C.12/1997/4 (1997); General Comment 13, The right to adequate food (Art. 11), UN Doc. E/C.12/1999/5, para. 20 (1999); General Comment 13, The right to the highest attainable standard of health, UN Doc. E/C.12/2000/4, para. 50 (1999); General Comment 15, The right to water, UN Doc. E/C.12/2002/11, para. 23 (2002); and Human Rights Committee, General Comment 16 (Twenty-third session, 1988), Compilation of General Comments and General Recommendations Adopted by Human Rights Treaty Bodies, UN Doc. HRI/GEN/1/Rev.1, para.1 (1994).

[152] Article 5 of the Convention on the Elimination of All Forms of Racial Discrimination requires states to regulate the activities of private parties extensively in order to prevent discrimination in areas such as the right to work, the right to form and join trade unions, and the right to housing. *See* International Convention on the Elimination of All Forms of Racial Discrimination, *supra* n 22, Art. 5. The Committee on the Elimination of All Forms of Racial Discrimination could increase its attention to a state's regulation of corporations and ask states particularly to report on corporate behaviour in light of the Norms. This same requirement could be used for reporting in connection with the Convention on the Elimination of Discrimination Against Women and the Convention on the Rights of the Child. *See also* UN Doc. E/CN.4/Sub.2/WG.2/WP.2 (2001).

[153] Mechanisms for individual complaints have been established under four principal human rights treaties. *See* Race Convention, *supra* n 82, at Art. 14; Convention Against Torture, *supra* n 89, at

The Commentary also mentions implementation by the special rapporteurs or other thematic procedures of the UN Commission on Human Rights. They could use the Norms, Commentary, and other relevant international standards for raising concerns about actions by business enterprises within their respective mandates. For example, the Commission's Special Rapporteur on adequate housing might express concerns about company actions that have resulted in forced evictions.[154] The Norms and Commentary could be used to create a new thematic procedure on transnational corporations and human rights within the context of the Commission or the General Assembly.

The Commentary further discusses its potential use by the UN and related institutions for determining which products and services to purchase and with which businesses to develop partnerships.[155] The Norms could also be used for the development of an interactive website to post international human rights standards in regard to businesses and to receive information from individuals and organizations about the conduct of businesses in compliance with the relevant standards and codes of conduct.[156]

3. Other intergovernmental organizations

The Norms further call upon other international and national mechanisms, already in existence or yet to be created, to implement the Norms through periodic monitoring and verification.[157] For example, a number of intergovernmental bodies may find the Norms useful in developing, amplifying, or interpreting their own standards. The ILO and OECD could take the Norms into account when making clarifications in their already existing standards for businesses. Similarly, the OECD could use the Norms in the context of their National Contact Points. The World Bank and its constituent institutions have adopted standards for loans relating to their impact on indigenous peoples, the environment, transfer of populations,

---

Art. 22(4) and (5); Optional Protocol to the International Covenant on Civil and Political Rights, G.A. res. 2200A (XXI). *See also* Eide Working Paper, *supra* n 41, at 12.

[154] The Norms may also be useful to the Special Rapporteurs on the right to food; on the highest attainable standard of health; on extra-judicial, summary, or arbitrary executions; and on the situation and fundamental freedoms of indigenous people. *See also* Eide Working Paper, *supra* n 41, at 12.

[155] *See* Commentary, *supra* n 29, at para. 16(b). For example, the UNHCR employs procurement standards that call for consideration of the vendor's environmental practices. UNHCR, UNHCR Guidelines for Environmentally Friendlier Procurement, OSCEA/STS (1996). UNICEF similarly uses procurement standards specifically regarding the suppliers' compliance with national child labour laws and involvement in the sale or manufacture of land mines. *See* UNICEF Procurement Information, *at* <http://www.supply.unicef.dk/business/procinfo.htm> (visited 2 September 2003). Sub-Commission Resolution 2002/8 explicitly recommended that the Norms be used for the development of procurement standards (*see* Resolution 2002/8, *supra* n 57, at para. 4(a)), but the Sub-Commission chose to focus on other implementation techniques in 2003.

[156] For an example of a website with an extensive amount of information on business and human rights, *see* Business & Human Rights: A Resource Website, *at* <http://www.business-humanrights.org> (visited 2 September 2003).   [157] *See* Norms, *supra* n 1, at para. 16.

sustainable development, and gender equality.[158] The Norms might be helpful in amplifying and interpreting those World Bank standards as well as encouraging further World Bank standards.

The World Trade Organization agreements, which generally prohibit states from creating trade limitations, contain several exceptions allowing states to restrict trade when certain conditions are met.[159] For example, in its Agreement on Sanitary and Phytosanitary Measures, the WTO prefers to follow international standards in determining if certain technical regulations that create trade limitations are necessary to protect human, animal, or plant life or health.[160] Similarly, the WTO's Agreement on Technical Barriers to Trade states that '[g]eneral terms for standardization and procedures for assessment of conformity shall normally have the meaning given to them by definitions adopted within the United Nations system and by international standardizing bodies'.[161] It is conceivable that the Norms could be considered one such international standard.

The Norms may also to be used for the creation of human rights standards on a region-by-region basis to address specific issues.[162] For example, after the passage of the North American Free Trade Agreement (NAFTA), two mechanisms were created to oversee the implementation of NAFTA with regard to environmental and labour standards. Those two mechanisms, the North American Agreement on Environmental Cooperation[163] and the Agreement on Labor Cooperation,[164] do not rely upon existing international standards for their decisions; however, the Norms could be used as a basis for fact-finding or interpreting the NAFTA standards. The European Parliament has adopted a resolution referring to basic

---

[158] See World Bank Operational Policy (OP) 4.0 et seq. (environmental protection and sustainable development guidelines); World Bank Operational Policies/Bank Procedures (OP/BP) 4.2 (protection of indigenous peoples and promotion); and Operational Policy (OP) 4.20 (promotion of gender equality).

[159] Article XX of the 1947 General Agreement on Tariffs and Trade states ten exceptions in which a State may use trade-restrictive measures, including justifications such as the protection of public morals; the protection of human, animal, or plant life or health; and the preservation of exhaustible natural resources. See Final Act Embodying the Results of the Uruguay Round of Multilateral Trade Negotiations, 15 April 1994, 33 ILM 1140, reprinted in The Results of the Uruguay Round of Multilateral Trade Negotiations: The Legal Texts (1994).

[160] Ibid. at Agreement on Sanitary and Phytosanitary Measures, Art. 2.1.

[161] Ibid. at Agreement on Technical Barriers to Trade, Art. 1.1. The International Standards Organization (ISO) has been recognized as one such standardizing body for establishing specifications for products. ISO has also prepared standards for management systems and has begun to consider developing corporate social responsibility standards from a consumer perspective. See International Standards Organization, Development of International Standards, <http://www.iso.org/iso/en/commcentre/pressreleases/2003/Ref846.html> (visited 2 September 2003).

[162] Examples of regional codes used to address specific issues include: The Sullivan Statement of Responsibilities, 4th Application, 8 Nov. 1984, 24 ILM 1464 (1985); Irish National Caucus; The MacBride Responsibilities (1984); Council of Economic Priorities Accreditation Authority; Maquiladora Standards of Conduct; Miller Responsibilities; Partner's Agreement to Eliminate Child Labor in the Soccer Ball Industry in Pakistan.

[163] See North American Agreement on Environmental Cooperation, 32 ILM 1480 (1993).

[164] See North American Agreement on Labor Cooperation, 32 ILM 1499 (1993).

international standards applicable to multinationals and calling upon the European Union to create a legally binding code of conduct for all multinationals headquartered in the European Union (EU).[165] In addition, the EU Commission requested a study of the possibility of creating a European Monitoring Platform (EMP) in connection with its code of conduct. Particularly, the Commission requested that creation of the EMP involve participation from northern and southern NGOs, as well as indigenous and local communities, to help ensure that the EMP protects individuals in host countries anywhere in the world. The EMP, once operating, would be open to receive complaints from community and/or workers' representatives, NGOs, individual victims, or other sources from all over the world with regard to actions taken by companies that violate the EU Code of Conduct. The Working Group may take lessons from the establishment of the EMP, or the EMP may ultimately decide to use the Norms to help draft or interpret the EU Code of Conduct. Certainly, the Norms would be more comprehensive and more effective in protecting human rights than the OECD Guidelines that contain only a single sentence on human rights.

Regional human rights commissions and courts should also use the Norms. For example, two European Court of Human Rights cases involving corporate environmental pollution negatively affecting private and family life under Article 8 of the European Convention on Human Rights have found states liable for not adopting regulations and pursuing inspections to prevent the corporate misconduct.[166] In such situations, regional courts could refer to the Norms in determining the obligation of states and thereby encourage states to monitor the conduct of businesses within their borders. Additionally, the African Commission on Human and Peoples' Rights could have used the Norms as an additional basis for its decision against the military government in Nigeria as to its involvement in and failure to limit the activities of oil companies in violating the economic and environmental rights of Ogoni residents.[167]

4. Unions

The Commentary encourages trade unions to use the Norms as a basis for negotiating agreements with businesses and monitoring compliance of businesses with the Norms.[168] The Norms guarantee freedom of association, including the right to establish and maintain trade unions, as well as effective recognition of the right to collective bargaining pursuant to the relevant conventions of the International

---

[165] European Parliament (EP), *Resolution on EU standards for European Enterprises operating in developing countries: towards a European Code of Conduct*, Resolution A4-0508/98 (1998).

[166] *Lopez Ostra v. Spain*, ECHR (1994), Series A, No. 303-C; *Guerra and Others v. Italy*, ECHR (1998) 1998-I, No. 64.

[167] *See Social and Economic Rights Action Center and the Center for Economic and Social Rights v. Nigeria*, African Comm. Hum. & Peoples' Rights, Comm. No. 155/96 (13–27 Oct. 2001).

[168] *See* Commentary, *supra* n 29, at para. 16(c).

Labour Organization. Unions and collective bargaining have a critical role to play in protecting the rights of workers, which should be reinforced by the Norms and other corporate social responsibility standards.

5. NGOs

The Commentary also encourages NGOs to use the Norms as the basis for their expectations of business conduct and for monitoring compliance of businesses with the Norms.[169]

6. Investors, lenders, and consumers

The Commentary mentions use of the Norms as the basis for ethical investment initiatives and other compliance benchmarks.[170] Self-assessments, assessments by consultants, independent social audits, etc. if done in accordance with the Norms could be used by individual investors and socially responsible mutual funds in making their investment decisions. Banks and other lending institutions may use this information in deciding whether to make loans. Consumers or consumer groups could use the Norms in formulating socially responsible purchasing decisions.

7. Business groups or trade associations

The Norms further call upon industry groups, for example a trade association, to use the Norms in their monitoring.[171] Industry groups might adopt or adapt the Norms as their own industry code of conduct for those businesses which are members. The Norms could be used by a consortium of business enterprises as a prerequisite of membership,[172] or could be used to support the creation of a labelling system to identify products and services created under the specific standards so as to promote ethical purchasing patterns.[173]

---

[169] *Ibid.* For an example of an NGO making a statement on human rights responsibilities it believes all companies should follow, *see* Mark Curtis, *Trade for Life: Making Trade Work for Poor People* (2001). As indicated above, some NGOs have already begun using the Norms as a basis for their assessment of company human rights behaviour. *See supra* n 69.

[170] *See* Commentary, *supra* n 29, at para. 16(c).   [171] *Ibid.* at para. 16(c).

[172] For example, Caux Round Table Responsibilities for Business (1986); Clean Clothes Campaign, Code of Labour Practices for the Apparel Industry Including Sportswear; and International Chamber of Commerce, Guidelines for International Investment and Business Charter for Sustainable Development.

[173] Although established by an NGO, the SA8000 is an example of a labelling system used to alert consumers to the conditions in which a product was produced. The SA8000, a human rights workplace standard development by Social Accountability International (SAI), allows retail and brand companies to join the SA8000 Signatory Program when they have demonstrated a commitment to achieving decent working conditions in their supply chains. To become a Signatory, each company defines the scope of its operations that it intends to bring into compliance with SA8000, develops a plan for achieving this goal, and issues annual progress reports to the public subject to verification by SAI before publication. Signatory

8. States

The Norms also call upon states to implement the Norms.[174] The Norms ask states to use the Norms to establish and reinforce the necessary legal or administrative framework with regard to the activities of each company having a statutory seat in that country, under whose law it was incorporated or formed, where it has its central administration, where it has its principal place of business, or where it is doing business.[175] The Norms also encourage use of the Norms by national courts in connection with determining damages, criminal sanctions, and in other respects, as established by national or international law.[176] In addition, in those countries where legislation already applies to the activities of business enterprises, courts could use the Norms to interpret legal standards.[177] For example, courts might refer to the Norms in assessing whether a company has provided consumers or investors with adequate information about their products and services.[178] In some countries compliance with the Norms might be relevant in determining liability for injuries caused by businesses and their officers.[179]

5. CONCLUSION

Globalization has been accompanied by an increase in the power of transnational corporations and other large businesses. With this increase in power comes an increase in responsibility. Many have called on international bodies to focus attention on the human rights conduct of large companies whose activities fall

benefits include the right to use the SA8000 Signatory logo. See SA8000 Signatory Benefits, at <http://www.cepaa.org> (visited 2 September 2003).

[174] *See* Norms, *supra* n 1, at para. 17.   [175] *Ibid.*   [176] *Ibid.* at para. 18.

[177] *See* Su-Ping Lu, 'Corporate Codes of Conduct and the FTC: Advancing Human Rights Through Deceptive Advertising Law', 38 COLUM. J. TRANSNAT'L L. 603 (2000) (discussing how company human rights codes of conduct may be used by courts to hold companies liable under deceptive advertising laws). Although not mentioned in the Norms or Commentary, states could further encourage or require businesses to file reports about their compliance with the Norms in a central office or could make the filing of such annual reports a requirement of business registration, licensing, securities law, tax law, consumer protection law, etc.

[178] The California Supreme Court upheld the right of consumers to sue a large corporation under the California state deceptive advertising laws for false statements regarding labour practices and working conditions in factories. *See Kasky v. Nike*, 27 Cal.4th 939, 45 P.3d 243 (2002), *cert. granted* 534 U.S. 3458 (2003), *cert. dismissed as improvidently granted.*

[179] For example, as a restatement of international legal principles applicable to companies, the Norms and particularly the underlying instruments could be used to identify the human rights violations that fall under the Alien Tort Claims Act (ATCA), 28 U.S.C. §1350 (1993). Actions under the ATCA have been brought against several large multinational corporations. *See Wiwa v. Royal Dutch Petroleum*, 2002 US Dist. LEXIS 3293 (S.D.N.Y. 2 Feb. 2002); *Abdullahi v. Pfizer*, 2002 US Dist. LEXIS 17436 (S.D.N.Y. 2002); *Doe/Roe v. Unocal*, Case Nos. 00-56603, 00-57197 (9th Cir. 2002); *Sarei v. Rio Tinto PLC*, 221 F. Supp. 2d 1116 (C.D. Cal. 2001); *Bano v. Union Carbide Corp.*, 273 F.3d 120 (2d Cir. 2001); *Bowoto v. Chevron*, Case No. C99-2506 CAL (N.D. Cal 1999); *Doe v. Gap*, Civ 99-329 (filed C.D. Cal., 13 Jan. 1999).

outside the ambit of any one country. The call is also to strengthen international authority and national will to deal with transnational corporations which are often so strong they may overpower the influence of any one country within its own borders.

In response to these demands, the UN Sub-Commission on the Promotion and Protection of Human Rights has adopted the Norms of Responsibilities of Transnational Corporations and Other Business Enterprises with Regard to Human Rights (the Norms). The Norms clarify the human rights obligations of businesses. Clarifying the duties of businesses may actually benefit businesses. There is a growing body of evidence that complying with human rights standards is beneficial to a company's bottom line. Consumers are more willing to take human rights conduct of a business into account. Businesses are also more likely to be exposed to liability for conduct that violates human rights standards. Clarification would provide greater guidance to businesses as to whether they should pursue a proposed course of conduct that might expose them to liability, consumer backlash, investor flight, and/or loss of the best and brightest employees.

The Norms represent a significant step towards establishing the international human rights obligations of transnational corporations and other business enterprises. The Norms help fill a major gap in the international human rights system. The Norms can also provide businesses with a level human rights playing field for global competition. Even with adoption of the Norms, implementation remains a key area for future development. While the Norms contain rudimentary mechanisms for implementation, the next step for the United Nations, states, businesses, unions, and others will be to continue to examine and develop effective methods of implementation.

Bibliography

MARY RUMSEY

NON-STATE ACTORS AND INTERNATIONAL LAW, GENERALLY

Anker D., 'Refugee Status and Violence Against Women in the "Domestic" Sphere: The Non-State Actor Question,' *Georgetown Immigration Law Journal*, Vol. 15 (2001), 391.

Armstrong P., 'Human Rights and Non-State Actors,' *Pace International Law Review*, Vol. 11 (1999), 239.

Arts B., 'Regimes, Non-State Actors and the State System: A "Structurational" Regime Model,' *European Journal of International Relations*, Vol. 6 (2000), 513.

——, Noortmann M., and Reinalda B. (eds.), *Non-State Actors in International Relations* (Aldershot: Ashgate, 2001).

Clapham A., *Human Rights in the Private Sphere* (Oxford: Oxford University Press, 1996).

Cook R., 'Accountability in International Law for Violations of Women's Rights by Non-State Actors,' in D. Dallmeyer (ed.), *Reconceiving Reality: Women and International Law* 93 (Washington, D.C.: American Society of International Law, 1993).

Dicker R., 'Human Rights and Non-State Actors,' *Pace International Law Review*, Vol. 11 (1999), 231.

Farrior S., 'State Responsibility in a Multiactor World: State Responsibility for Human Rights Abuses by Non-State Actors,' *Proceedings of the American Society of International Law*, Vol. 92 (1998), 299.

Haufler V., 'Crossing the Boundary Between Public and Private: International Regimes and Non-State Actors,' in V. Rittberger and P. Mayer (eds.), *Regime Theory and International Relations* (Oxford: Clarendon, 1993).

Higgott R., Underhill G. and Bieler A., *Non-State Actors and Authority in the Global System* (London: Routledge, 2000).

Hobe S., 'The Era of Globalisation as a Challenge to International Law,' *Duquesne Law Review*, Vol. 40 (2002), 655.

Hofmann R. (ed.), *Non-State Actors as New Subjects of International Law: International Law—From the Traditional State Order Towards the Law of the Global Community, Proceedings of an International Symposium of the Kiel Walther-Schücking-Institute of International Law, March 25 to 28, 1998* (Berlin: Duncker and Humblot, 1999).

Jochnick C., 'Confronting the Impunity of Non-State Actors: New Fields for the Promotion of Human Rights,' *Human Rights Quarterly*, Vol. 21 (1999), 56.

Josselin D. and Wallace W. (eds.), *Non-State Actors in World Politics* (Houndmills, Basingstoke, Hampshire, England: Palgrave, 2001).

Kälin W., 'Non-State Agents of Persecution and the Inability of the State to Protect,' *Georgetown Immigration Law Journal*, Vol. 15 (2001), 415.

Kiss A.-Ch. and Lammars J. G. (eds.) *Non-State Entities and International Law, Hague Yearbook of International Law*, Vol. 2 (Dordrecht: Martinus Nijhoff, 1989).

McCorquodale R., 'Overlegalizing Silences: Human Rights and Nonstate Actors,' *American Society of International Law Proceedings*, Vol. 96 (2002), 381.

Marx R., 'The Notion of Persecution by Non-State Agents in German Jurisprudence,' *Georgetown Immigration Law Journal*, Vol. 15 (2001), 447.

Moore J., 'From Nation State to Failed State: International Protection from Human Rights Abuses by Non-State Agents,' *Columbia Human Rights Law Review*, Vol. 31 (1999), 81.

Non-State Actors and International Law (2001–). (Dordrecht: Kluwer Academic Publishers).

Panel Discussion, 'Wrap-up: Non-State Actors and Their Influence on International Law,' 92 *Proceedings of the American Society of International Law*, Vol. 92 (1998), 380.

Plenary Theme Panel, 'The Challenge of Non-State Actors,' *American Society of International Law Proceedings*, Vol. 92 (1998), 20.

Risse T., 'International Institutions, Non-State Actors, and Domestic Change: The Case of Human Rights,' in *Protection of Human Rights in Europe, Collected courses of the Academy of European Law = Recueil des cours de l'Académie de droit européen* (The Hague: Kluwer Law International, 2000).

Risse-Kappen T. (ed.), *Bringing Transnational Relations Back In: Non-State Actors, Domestic Structures, and International Institutions* (Cambridge: Cambridge University Press, 1995).

Spiro P., Review Essay, 'Nonstate Actors in Global Politics,' *American Journal of International Law*, Vol. 92 (1998), 808.

Stubbs R. and Underhill G., *Political Economy and the Changing Global Order*, 2d ed. (New York: Oxford University Press, 2000).

NON-STATE ACTORS IN U.S. COURTS

Aceves W., 'Affirming the Law of Nations in U.S. Courts: The Karadzic Litigation and the Yugoslav Conflict,' *Berkeley Journal of International Law*, Vol. 14 (1996), 137.

Brandt M., Comment, 'Doe v. Karadzic: Redressing Non-State Acts of Gender-Specific Abuse under the Alien Tort Statute,' *Minnesota Law Review*, Vol. 79 (1995), 1413.

Kunstle D., Note, 'Kadic v. Karadzic: Do Private Individuals Have Enforceable Rights and Obligations under the Alien Tort Claims Act?,' *Duke Journal of Comparative and International Law*, Vol. 6 (1996), 319.

Lu J., Note, 'Jurisdiction over Non-State Activity under the Alien Tort Claims Act,' *Columbia Journal of Transnational Law*, Vol. 35 (1997), 531.

Walker J., 'Domestic Adjudication of International Human Rights Violations under the Alien Tort Statute,' *Saint Louis University Law Journal*, Vol. 41 (1997), 539.

REGULATION OF MULTINATIONAL ENTERPRISES, GENERALLY

Fatouros A., *Transnational Corporations: The International Legal Framework* (London: Routledge, 1994).

Hatem F., 'Quel cadre juridique pour l'activité des firmes multinationales?,' *Economie international*, Vol. 65 (1995), 71.

Merciai P., *Les enterprises multinationales en droit international* (Brussels: Bruylant, 1993).

Muchlinski P., 'Labour Relations,' in P. Muchlinski, *Multinational Enterprises and the Law* (Oxford: Blackwell, 1999) 457–490.

Seidl-Hohenveldern I., 'Corporations under International Law,' in I. Seidl-Hohenveldern, *Corporations in and under International Law* (Cambridge: Grotius Publications, 1987) 67–125.

Todarello V., Note and Comment, 'Corporations Don't Kill People—People Do: Exploring the Goals of the United Kingdom's Corporate Homicide Bill,' *New York Law School Journal of Human Rights*, Vol. 19 (2003), 481.

Wallace C., *Multinational Enterprise and Legal Control: Host State Sovereignty in an Era of Economic Globalization* (The Hague: Martinus Nijhoff, 2002)

——, 'The Scope for International Controls,' in C. Wallace, *Legal Control of the Multinational Enterprise* (The Hague: Martinus Nijhoff, 1983), 295–326.

MULTINATIONAL ENTERPRISES AND HUMAN RIGHTS IN INTERNATIONAL LAW

Addo M. (ed.), *Human Rights Standards and the Responsibility of Transnational Corporations* (The Hague: Kluwer Law International, 1999).

Amann D., 'Capital Punishment: Corporate Criminal Liability for Gross Violations of Human Rights,' *Hastings International and Comparative Law Review*, Vol. 24 (2001), 327.

Amnesty International, *Human Rights Principles for Companies: Report*, January 1998, ACT 70/01/98, http://web.amnesty.org/library/index/engact700011998.

Anderson J.C., 'Respecting Human Rights: Multinational Corporations Strike Out,' *University of Pennsylvania Journal of Labor & Employment Law*, Vol. 2 (2000), 463.

Archer W. and Ansell R., 'The Universal Declaration of Human Rights and Multinational Corporations in the Third World,' *University of New Brunswick Law Journal*, Vol. 47 (1998), 133.

Asante S., 'The Concept of the Good Corporate Citizen in International Business,' *ICSID Review/Foreign Investment Law Journal*, Vol. 4 (1989), 1.

Aubert M., Brama P., and Blum R., *Rapport d'information sur le rôle de compagnies pétrolières dans la politique internationale et son impact social et environnemental* (Paris: Assemblée National Française, 1999).

Avery C., *Business and Human Rights in a Time of Change* (London: Amnesty International, 2000), http://www.business-humanrights.org/Avery-Report.htm

Baade H., *Codes of Conduct for Multinational Enterprises: An Introductory Survey* (Deventer, The Netherlands: Kluwer, 1980.)

Baez C., Dearing M., Delatour M., and Dixon C., 'Multinational Enterprises and Human Rights,' *University of Miami International & Comparative Law Review*, Vol. 8 (1999–2000), 183.

Baker M., 'Private Codes of Conduct: Should the Fox Guard the Henhouse?,' *University of Miami Inter-American Law Review*, Vol. 24 (1993), 399.

——, 'Tightening the Toothless Vise: Codes of Conduct and the American Multinational Enterprise,' *Wisconsin International Law Journal*, Vol. 20 (2001), 89.

Barber J., *Minding Our Business: The Role of Corporate Accountability in Sustainable Development* (Washington: Integrated Strategies Forum, 1997).

Baxi U., 'Mass Torts, Multinational Enterprise Liability and Private International Law,' *Recueil des Cours*, Vol. 276 (The Hague: Martinus Nijhoff, 2000), 305–423.

Benson R., 'How Many Strikes Do Big Corporations Get? The Petition to Revoke Unocal's Corporate Charter,' *Guild Practitioner*, Vol. 55 (1998), 113.

Berg E., 'La négociation d'un code de conduite sur les sociétés transnationales au sein des Nations Unies,' in *Les Nations Unies et le droit international économique*, Colloque de Nice de la Société française pour le droit international (Paris: A. Pedone, 1986) 219–236.

Bergman M., 'The Norm-Creating Effect of a General Assembly Resolution on Transnational Corporations,' in F. Snyder and S. Sathirathai, *Third World Attitudes Toward International Law, an Introduction* (Dordrecht: Martinus Nijhoff, 1987) 231–256.

Billenness S., 'Beyond South Africa: New Frontiers in Corporate Responsibility,' *Business and Society Review*, Vol. 86 (1993), 28.

Blanpain R. (ed.), *Multinational Enterprises and the Social Challenges of the XXIst Century: The ILO Declaration on Fundamental Principles at Work, Public and Private Corporate Codes of Conduct* (The Hague: Kluwer Law International, 2000).

Bol J., 'Using the Inter-American System to Pursue International Labour Rights: A Case Study of the Guatemalan Maquiladoras,' *University of Toronto Faculty of Law Review*, Vol. 55 (1997), 351.

Bolivar M. de, 'A Comparison of Protecting the Environmental Interests of Latin-American Indigenous Communities from Transnational Corporations under International Human Rights and Environmental Law,' *Journal of Transnational Law & Policy*, Vol. 8 (1998), 105.

Branson D., 'The Social Responsibility of Large Multinational Corporations,' *Transnational Lawyer*, Vol. 16 (2002), 121.

Cahn D. and Holeman T., 'Business and Human Rights,' *Forum for Applied Research and Public Policy*, Vol. 14 (Spring 1999), 52.

Cao-Huy T. and Drai R. (eds.), *Multinationales et droits de l'homme* (Paris: Presses Universitaire de France, 1984).

Cassel D., 'Corporate Initiatives: A Second Human Rights Revolution?,' *Fordham International Law Journal*, Vol. 19 (1996), 1963.

Charney J., 'Transnational Corporations and Developing Public International Law,' *Duke Law Journal*, Vol. 1983, 748.

Charnovitz S., 'The Globalization of Economic Human Rights,' *Brooklyn Journal of International Law*, Vol. 25 (1999), 113.

Chopra S., 'Multinational Corporations in the Aftermath of Bhopal: The Need for a New Comprehensive Global Regime for Transnational Corporate Activity,' *Valparaiso University Law Review*, Vol. 29 (1994), 235.

Clapham A. and Jerbi S., 'Categories of Corporate Complicity in Human Rights Abuses,' *Hastings International and Comparative Law Review*, Vol. 24 (2001), 339.

Codes of Conduct: U.S. Corporate Compliance Programs and Working Conditions in Chinese Factories: Roundtable before the Congressional-Executive Commission on China, 108th Cong. (2003) (Washington: U.S. G.P.O.).

Commission of the European Communities, *Green Paper: Promoting a European Framework for Corporate Social Responsibility* (Brussels: Commission of the European Communities, 2001), http://europa.eu.int/comm/employment_social/soc-dial/csr/greenpaper.htm.

Compa L. and Diamond S. (eds.), *Human Rights, Labor Rights, and International Trade* (Philadelphia: University of Pennsylvania Press, 1996.)

——, and Hinchliffe-Darricarrere T., 'Enforcing International Labor Rights through Corporate Codes of Conduct,' *Columbia Journal of Transnational Law*, Vol. 33 (1995), 663.

Comprosky C., 'The Plight of the Street Children of Latin America Who Are Addicted to Sniffing Glue, and the Role and Responsibilities of Transnational Corporations,' *ILSA Journal of International and Comparative Law*, Vol. 8 (2002), 599.

Danailov S., 'The Accountability of Non-State Actors for Human Rights Violations: The Special Case of Transnational Corporations,' Geneva, October 1998, http://www.humanrights. ch/bildungarbeit/seminare/pdf/000303_danailov_studie.pdf.

The Danish Human Rights and Business Project, *Defining the Scope of Business Responsibility for Human Rights Abroad* (2001), http://www.humanrightsbusiness.org/resp_6.htm

Deak L., 'Customary International Labor Laws and Their Application in Hungary, Poland, and the Czech Republic,' *Tulsa Journal of Comparative and International Law*, Vol. 2 (1994), 1.

——, 'Customary International Labor Laws and Their Application in Russia,' *Tulsa Journal of Comparative and International Law*, Vol. 2 (1995), 319.

Deakin S. and Wilkinson F., 'Rights vs. Efficiency? The Economic Case for Transnational Labour Standards,' *Industrial Law Journal*, Vol. 23 (1994), 289.

Dell S., *The United Nations and International Business* (Durham N.C.: Duke University Press, 1990).

Desai M. and Redfern P. (eds.), *Global Governance: Ethics and Economics of the World Order* (London: Pinter, 1995).

Dickerson C., 'Culture and Trans-Border Effects: Northern Individualism Meets Third-Generation Human Rights,' *Rutgers Law Review*, Vol. 54 (2002), 865.

——, 'Human Rights: The Emerging Norm of Corporate Social Responsibility,' *Tulane Law Review*, Vol. 76 (2002), 1431.

Dieng A., 'Globalisation, Human Rights and the Rule of Law,' *International Commission of Jurists Review*, Vol. 61 (1999), 5.

Diller J., 'Responsabilité sociale et mondialisation: qu'attendre des codes de conduite, des labels sociaux et des pratiques d'investissement,' *Transnational Associations*, Vol. 51 (1999), 246.

——, and Levy D., Note and Comment, 'Child Labor, Trade and Investment: Toward the Harmonization of International Law,' *American Journal of International Law*, Vol. 91 (1997), 663.

Dine J., 'Multinational Enterprises: International Codes and the Challenge of Sustainable Development,' *Non-State Actors and International Law*, Vol. 1 (2001), 81.

Dodge W., 'Which Torts in Violation of the Law of Nations?,' *Hastings International and Comparative Law Review*, Vol. 24 (2001), 351.

Doelder H. de and Tiedemann K. (eds.), *La criminalisation du comportement collectif/Criminal Liability of Corporations: XIVth International Congress of Comparative Law* (The Hague: Kluwer Law International, 1996).

Dowling D., 'The Multinational's Manifesto on Sweatshops, Trade/Labor Linkage, and Codes of Conduct,' *Tulsa Journal of Comparative and International Law*, Vol. 8 (2000), 27.

Dubin L., 'The Direct Application of Human Rights Standards to, and by, Transnational Corporations,' *International Commission of Jurists Review*, Vol. 61 (1999), 35.

Duke J., 'Enforcement of Human Rights on Multi-National Corporations: Global Climate, Strategies and Trends for Compliance,' *Denver Journal of International Law and Policy*, Vol. 28 (2000), 339.

Dyson S., Comment, 'The Clash Between Corruption and Codes of Conduct: The Corporate Role in Forging a Human Rights Standard,' *Connecticut Journal of International Law*, Vol. 17 (2002), 335.

Eaton J., 'The Nigerian Tragedy, Environmental Regulation of Transnational Corporations, and the Human Right to a Healthy Environment,' *Boston University International Law Journal*, Vol. 15 (1997), 261.

Ebenroth C. and Karl J., *Code of conduct: Ansätze zur vertraglichen Gestaltung internationaler Investitionen* (Konstanz: Universitätsverlag, 1987).

Ehrenberg D., 'The Labor Link: Applying the International Trading System to Enforce Violations of Forced and Child Labor,' *Yale Journal of International Law*, Vol. 20 (1995), 361.

Elfstrom G., *Moral Issues and Multinational Corporations* (London: Macmillan, 1991).

Feld W., *Multinational Corporations and U.N. Politics: The Quest for Codes of Conduct* (New York: Pergamon Press, 1980).

Ferreira L., Note, 'Access to Affordable HIV/AIDS Drugs: The Human Rights Obligations of Multinational Pharmaceutical Corporations,' *Fordham Law Review*, Vol. 71 (2002), 1133.

Fisse B. and Braithewaite J., 'The Allocation of Responsibility for Corporate Crimes,' *Sydney Law Review*, Vol. 11 (1988), 468.

Forcese C., *Commerce with Conscience?: Human Rights and Business Codes of Conduct* (Montréal: International Center for Human Rights and Democratic Development, 1997).

———,'Deterring "Militarized Commerce": The Prospect of Liability for "Privatized" Human Rights Abuses,' *Ottawa Law Review*, Vol. 31 (1999/2000), 171.

Forsythe D., 'Human Rights and Multinational Corporations,' in D. Forsythe, *Human Rights and International Relations* (Cambridge: Cambridge University Press, 2000).

Frankental P., *Human Rights, Is It Any of Your Business?* (London: Prince of Wales Business Leaders Forum, c2000.)

———,'The UN Universal Declaration of Human Rights as a Corporate Code of Conduct,' *Business Ethics*, Vol. 11 (2002), 129.

Freeman B., Pica M., and Camponovo C., 'A New Approach to Corporate Responsibility: The Voluntary Principles on Security and Human Rights,' *Hastings International and Comparative Law Review*, Vol. 24 (2001), 423.

French P., *Collective and Corporate Responsibility* (New York: Columbia University Press, 1984).

Frey B., 'The Legal and Ethical Responsibilities of Transnational Corporations in the Protection of International Human Rights,' *Minnesota Journal of Global Trade*, Vol. 6 (1997), 153.

Frynas J. and Pegg, S. (eds.), *Transnational Corporations and Human Rights* (New York: Palgrave MacMillan, 2003).

Geer M., 'Foreigners in Their Own Land: Cultural Land and Transnational Corporations—Emergent International Rights and Wrongs,' *Virginia Journal of International Law*, Vol. 38 (1998), 331.

Gelatt T. and Orentlicher D., *Getting Down to Business: The Human Rights Responsibilities of China's Investors and Trade Partners* (New York: International League for Human Rights, 1992).

Genugten W.J.M. van, 'Multinationale ondernemingen en de rechten van de mens: van voorzichtige toenadering tot paradigmawisseling,' *Nederlands Juristenblad*, Vol. 75 (2000), 1231.

Gould E., 'Finding Common Ground: Improving Workers' Rights in Developing Countries,' *LBJ Journal of Public Affairs*, Vol. 10 (Spring 1998), 50.

Granatino K., Note, 'Corporate Responsibility Now: Profit at the Expense of Human Rights with Exemption from Liability?,' *Suffolk Transnational Law Review*, Vol. 23 (1999), 191.

Grosse R., 'Codes of Conduct for Multinational Enterprises', *Journal of World Trade Law*, Vol. 16 (1982), 414.

Guissé E.-H., *Working Document on the Question of the Relationship Between the Enjoyment of Human Rights and the Working Methods and Activities of Transnational Corporations*, E/CN.4/Sub.2/1998/6 (1998).

Gutto S., 'Responsibilities of States and International Corporations for Violation of Human Rights in the Third World within the Context of the New International Economic Order,' in K. Ginther and W. Benedek (eds.), *New Perspectives and Conceptions of International Law, An Afro-European Dialogue* (Vienna; New York: Springer, 1983), 32.

——, 'Violation of Human Rights in the Third World: Responsibility of States and TNCs,' in F. Snyder and S. Sathirathai (eds.), *Third World Attitudes Toward International Law: An Introduction* (Dordrecht: Martinus Nijhoff, 1987), 275.

Hamilton G., *Les entreprises multinationales: Effets et limites des codes de conduite internationaux* (Geneva: Presses Universitaires de France, 1984).

Hartman L. Arnold D.G., and Wokutch R.E. (eds.), *Rising above Sweatshops: Innovative Approaches to Global Labor Challenges* (Westport, Conn.: Praeger, 2003).

Hartmann T., *Unequal Protection: The Rise of Corporate Dominance and the Theft of Human Rights* (Emmaus, Penn.: St. Martin's Press, 2002).

Henderson C., 'Multinational Corporations and Human Rights in Developing States,' *World Affairs*, Vol. 142 (Summer 1979), 17.

Herrnstadt O., 'Voluntary Corporate Codes of Conduct: What's Missing?,' *Labor Lawyer*, Vol. 16 (2001), 349.

Ho L., Powell C., and Volpp L., '(Dis)assembling Rights of Women Workers along the Global Assembly Line: Human Rights and the Garment Industry,' *Harvard Civil Rights-Civil Liberties Law Review*, Vol. 31 (1996), 383.

Horn N. (ed.), *Legal Problems of Codes of Conduct for Multinational Enterprises* (Deventer: Kluwer Law International, 1980).

——, International Rules for Multinational Enterprises: The ICC, OECD, and ILO Initiatives, *American University Law Review*, Vol. 30 (1981), 923.

Human Rights Watch, *The Enron Corporation: Corporate Complicity in Human Rights Violations* (New York: Human Rights Watch, 1999), http://www.hrw.org/reports/1999/enron.

Huu Tru N., 'Les codes de conduite: un bilan,' *Revue generale de droit international public*, Vol. 96 (1992), 45.

Industrial Restructuring and Education Network Europe (IRENE), *Controlling Corporate Wrongs: Liability of Multinational Corporations—The Legal Possibilities, Initiatives and Strategies for Civil Society* (Tilburg: IRENE, 2000), http://www.indianet.nl/irene.html.

The International Council on Human Rights Policy, *Beyond Voluntarism: Human Rights and the Developing International Legal Obligations of Companies* (Versoix, Switzerland: The Council, 2002).

International Labour Organization, *Codes of Conduct and Multinational Enterprises* (Geneva: ILO, 2002) (CD-ROM).

——, *A Guide to the Tripartite Declaration of Principles Concerning Multinational Enterprises and Social Policy: Knowing and Using Universal Guidelines for Social Responsibility* (Geneva: ILO, 2002).

——, *Tripartite Forum on Promoting the Tripartite Declaration of Principles Concerning Multinational Enterprises and Social Policy: summary of proceedings*, Geneva 25–26 March. (Geneva: ILO, 2002).

——, 'Tripartite Declaration of Principles Concerning Multinational Enterprises and Social Policy,' *ILO Official Bulletin, Series A*, Vol. 83, No. 3 (2000).

——, 'Tripartite Declaration of Principles Concerning Multinational Enterprises and Social Policy,' *International Legal Materials*, Vol. 17 (1978), 422.

Jackson J., *Codes of Conduct for Multinational Corporations: An Overview* (Washington: Congressional Research Service, 2001).

Jägers N., 'Colloquium on the Liability of Multinational Corporations under International Law,' *International Law FORUM* (1999), 181.

——, *Corporate Human Rights Obligations: In Search of Accountability* (Antwerp: Intersentia, 2002).

Jenkins R., *Corporate Codes of Conduct: Self-Regulation in a Global Economy* (Geneva: UNRISD, 2001).

——, and Pearson R., *Corporate Responsibility and Labour Rights: Codes of Conduct in the Global Economy* (London: Earthscan, 2002).

Johnson J., Note, 'Public-Private-Public Convergence: How the Private Actor Can Shape Public International Labor Standards,' *Brooklyn Journal of International Law*, Vol. 24 (1998), 291.

Joseph S., 'An Overview of the Human Rights Accountability of Multinational Enterprises,' in M. Kamminga and S. Zia-Zarifi (eds.), *The Liability of Multinational Corporations under International Law* (The Hague: Kluwer Law International, 2000), 75–93.

——, 'Pharmaceutical Corporations and Access to Drugs: The "Fourth Wave" of Corporate Human Rights Scrutiny', *Human Rights Quarterly*, Vol. 25 (2003), 425.

——, 'Taming the Leviathans: Multinational Enterprises and Human Rights,' *Netherlands Journal of International Law*, Vol. 46 (1999), 171.

——, Kinley D., and McBeth A., 'The Human Rights Responsibilities of Corporations: A Legal Study,' *New Academy Review*, Vol. 2 (2003), 92.

Kamminga M., 'Holding Multinational Corporations Accountable for Human Rights Abuses: A Challenge for the EC,' in P. Alston (ed.), *The EU and Human Rights* (New York: Oxford University Press, 1999).

——and Zia-Zarifi S. (eds.), *Liability of Multinational Corporations under International Law* (The Hague: Kluwer Law International, 2000).

Kapstein E., 'The Corporate Ethics Crusade,' *Foreign Affairs*, Vol. 80 (Sept./Oct. 2001), 105.

Kapur R., 'From Human Tragedy to Human Rights: Multinational Corporate Accountability for Human Rights Violations,' *Boston College Third World Law Journal*, Vol. 10 (1990), 1.

Keay M., *Towards Global Corporate Social Responsibility*, Briefing Paper No. 3 (London: Royal Institute of International Affairs, 2002), http://www.riia.org/pdf/briefing_papers/ TGCSR%20BP.pdf.

King B., 'The UN Global Compact: Responsibility for Human Rights, Labor Relations, and the Environment in Developing Nations,' *Cornell International Law Journal*, Vol. 34 (2001), 481.

Kinley D., 'Human Rights, Globalization and the Rule of Law: Friends, Foes or Family?,' UCLA Journal of International Law and Foreign Affairs, Vol. 7 (Fall/Winter 2002–2003), 239.

——, 'International Human Rights as Legally Binding or Merely Relevant,' in S. Bottomley and D. Kinley (eds.), *Commercial Law and Human Rights* (Burlington, VT: Ashgate, 2001).

——, and Joseph S., 'Multinational Corporations and Human Rights: Questions about Their Relationship,' *Alternative Law Journal*, Vol. 27 (Feb. 2002), 7.

Kline J., *International Codes and Multinational Business: Setting Guidelines for International Business Operations* (Westport, Conn.: Quorum Books, 1985).

——, 'International Regulation of Transnational Business: Providing the Missing Leg of Global Investment Standards,' *Transnational Corporations*, Vol. 2 (1993), 153.

Kokkini-Iatridou D. and Waart P. de, 'Foreign Investments in Developing Countries: Legal Personality of Multinationals in International Law,' *Netherlands Yearbook of International Law*, Vol. 14 (1983), 87.

Kolk A., Tulder R., and Welters C., 'International Codes of Conduct and Corporate Social Responsibility: Can Transnational Corporations Regulate Themselves?,' *Transnational Corporations*, Vol. 8 (1999), 143.

Kothari M. and Krause T., 'Human Rights or Corporate Rights? The MAI Challenge,' *Tribune des droits humains*, Vol. 5 (1998), 16.

Kowalewski D., *Transnational Corporations and Caribbean Inequalities* (New York: Praeger, 1982).

Krug N., Note, 'Exploiting Child Labor: Corporate Responsibility and the Role of Corporate Codes of Conduct,' *New York Law School Journal of Human Rights*, Vol. 14 (1998), 651.

Lansing P. and Rosaria A., 'An Analysis of the United Nations Proposed Code of Conduct for Transnational Corporations,' *World Competition*, Vol. 14 (June 1991), 35.

Letelier I. and Moffitt M., 'Supporting Repression: Multinational Banks in Chile,' *Race and Class*, Vol. 20 (1978), 111.

Likosky M., 'Human Rights Risk, Infrastructure Projects and Developing Countries,' *Global Jurist*, Vol. 2 (2002), 1.

Lippman M., 'Transnational Corporations and Repressive Regimes: The Ethical Dilemma,' *California Western International Law Journal*, Vol. 15 (1985), 542.

——, 'Multinational Corporations and Human Rights,' in G. Shepherd and V. Nanda (eds.), *Human Rights and Third World Development* (Westport, Conn.: Greenwood, 1985), 249–272.

Little P., 'Human Rights and Multinational Corporations in the Modern Business Milieu,' *Law Institute Journal*, Vol. 75 (2001), 67.

Litvin D., *Empires of Profit: Commerce, Conquest and Corporate Responsibility* (New York: Texere, 2003).

Liubicic R., 'Corporate Codes of Conduct and Product Labelling Schemes: The Limits and Possibilities of Promoting International Labor Rights through Private Initiatives,' *Georgetown Journal of Law and Policy in International Business*, Vol. 30 (1998), 111.

Machan T. (ed.), *Business Ethics in the Global Market* (Stanford, CA: Hoover Institution Press, 1999).

Mahari J., *Codes of Conduct für multinationale Unternehmen: unter besonderer Berücksichtigung betriebswitschaftlicher und juristischer Gesichtspunkte* (Wilmington, DE: Morgan, 1985).

Manby B., *The Price of Oil: Corporate Responsibility and Human Rights Violations in Nigeria's Oil Producing Communities* (Human Rights Watch, 1999).

Manning C., 'Does Globalisation Undermine Labour Standards? Lessons from East Asia,' *Australian Journal of International Affairs*, Vol. 52 (July 1998), 133.

Marston G., 'The Individual (Including the Corporation) in International Law: Protection of Human Rights and Fundamental Freedoms,' *British Yearbook of International Law*, Vol. 55 (1984), 451.

McClintock B., 'The Multinational Corporation and Social Justice: Experiments in Supra-national Governance,' *Review of Social Economy*, Vol. 57 (Dec. 1999), 4.

McCrudden C., 'Human Rights Codes for Transnational Corporations: What Can the Sullivan and MacBride Principles Tell Us?,' *Oxford Journal of Legal Studies*, Vol. 19 (1999), 167.

Meeran R., 'Accountability of Transnationals for Human Rights Abuses—Part 1,' *The New Law Journal*, Vol. 148 (1998), 1686.

——, 'Accountability of Transnationals for Human Rights Abuses—Part 2,' *The New Law Journal*, Vol. 148 (1998), 1706.

Meyer W., *Human Rights and International Political Economy in Third World Nations: Multinational Corporations, Foreign Aid and Repression* (Westport, Conn.: Greenwood Publishing, 1998).

——, 'Human Rights and MNCs: Theory v. Quantitative Analysis,' *Human Rights Quarterly*, Vol. 18 (1996), 368.

——, and Stefanova B., 'Human Rights, the UN Global Compact, and Global Governance,' *Cornell International Law Journal*, Vol. 34 (2001), 501.

Model Code of Conduct for Transnational Corporations (Washington: World Peace Through Law Center, 1977).

Mokhiber R. and Weissman R., *Corporate Predators: The Hunt for Mega-Profits and the Attack on Democracy* (Monroe, Maine: Common Courage, 1999).

Moran T., *Beyond Sweatshops* (Washington: Brookings, 2002).

Mowery L., Note, 'Earth Rights, Human Rights: Can International Environmental Human Rights Affect Corporate Accountability?,' *Fordham Environmental Law Journal*, Vol. 13 (2002), 343.

Muchlinski P., Book Review, 'Human Rights Standards and the Responsibility of Transnational Corporations,' *Leiden Journal of International Law*, Vol. 13 (2000), 712.

——, 'Holding Multinationals to Account: Recent Developments in English Litigation and the Company Law Review, *The Company Lawyer*, Vol. 23 (2002), 168.

——, 'Human Rights and Multinationals: Is There a Problem?, *International Affairs*, Vol. 77 (Jan. 2001), 31.

——, 'Human Rights, Social Responsibility and the Regulation of International Business: The Development of International Standards by Intergovernmental Organizations,' *Non-State Actors and International Law*, Vol. 3 (2003), 123.

Multinational Monitor (Washington, D.C.: Corporate Accountability Research Group, c1980–).

Murray J., 'A New Phase in the Regulation of Multinational Enterprises: The Role of the OECD', *International Law Journal* (2001), vol. 20, no. 3, pp. 255–270.

New Academy Review (Manchester, UK: Respect Publications, 2002–).

Ochoa C., 'Advancing The Language of Human Rights in a Global Economic Order: An Analysis of a Discourse,' *Boston College Third World Law Journal*, Vol. 23 (2003), 57.

Oloka-Onyango J., 'Reinforcing Marginalized Rights in an Age of Globalization: International Mechanisms, Non-State Actors, and the Struggle for Peoples' Rights In Africa,' *American University International Law Review*, Vol. 18 (2003), 851.

O'Mahony P., *Multinationals and Human Rights* (Great Wakering, UK: Mayhew-McCrimmon, 1980).

Orentlicher D. and Gelatt T., 'Public Law, Private Actors: The Impact of Human Rights on Business Investors in China,' *Northwestern Journal of International Law and Business*, Vol. 14 (1993), 66.

Organisation for Economic Cooperation and Development (OECD), 'Guidelines for Multinational Enterprises,' *International Legal Materials*, Vol. 15 (1976), 967.

——, 'Guidelines For Multinational Enterprises [revised],' *International Legal Materials*, Vol. 40 (2001), 237.

——, *Multinational Enterprises in Situations of Violent Conflict and Widespread Human Rights Abuses*, Working Papers on International Investment, Number 2002/1 (Paris: OECD, 2002), http://www.oecd.org/dataoecd/46/31/2757771.pdf.

——, *OECD Principles of Corporate Governance*, OECD Doc. SG/CG(99) (Paris: OECD, 1999).

Oxman B. and Shelton D., International Decision, 'Decision Regarding Communication 155/96, Social And Economic Rights Action Center/Center For Economic And Social Rights v. Nigeria,' *American Journal of International Law*, Vol. 96 (2002), 937.

Panel Discussion, 'Corporate Codes of Conduct,' *American Society of International Law Proceedings*, Vol. 92 (1998), 265.

Panel Discussion, 'Human Rights, Multinational Business and International Financial Institutions,' *Proceedings of the American Society of International Law*, Vol. 88 (1994), 271.

Panel Discussion, 'The Multinational Enterprise as Global Corporate Citizen,' *New York Law Journal of International and Comparative Law*, Vol. 21 (2001), 1.

Paul J., 'Holding Multi-National Corporations Responsible under International Law,' *Hastings International and Comparative Law Review*, Vol. 24 (2001), 285.

——, 'The New Movements in International Economic Law,' *American University Journal of International Law and Policy*, Vol. 10 (1995), 607.

Paust J., 'Human Rights Responsibilities of Private Corporations,' *Vanderbilt Journal of Transnational Law*, Vol. 35 (2002), 801.

Perez-Lopez J., 'Promoting International Respect for Workers Rights through Business Codes of Conduct,' *Fordham International Law Journal*, Vol. 17 (1993), 1.

'Permanent Peoples' Tribunal on Global Corporations and Human Wrongs, University of Warwick, 22–25 March 2000, Findings and Recommended Action,' 2001 (1) *Law, Social Justice & Global Development Journal* (LGD), http://elj.warwick.ac.uk/global/issue/2001-1/ppt.html.

Perry A., 'Multinational Enterprises, International Economic Organisations and Convergence among Legal Systems,' *Non-State Actors and International Law*, Vol. 2 (2002), 23.

Piccioto S. and Mayne R., *Regulating International Business: Beyond Liberalisation* (London: Macmillan, 1999).

Ramasastry A., 'Corporate Complicity: From Nuremberg to Rangoon—An Examination of Forced Labor Cases and Their Impact on the Liability of Multinational Corporations,' *Berkeley Journal of International Law*, Vol. 20 (2002), 91.

——, 'Secrets and Lies? Swiss Banks and International Human Rights,' *Vanderbilt Journal of Transnational Law*, Vol. 31 (1998), 325.

Ratner S., 'Corporations and Human Rights: A Theory of Legal Responsibility,' *Yale Law Journal*, Vol. 111 (2001), 443.

Redmond P., 'Sanctioning Corporate Responsibility for Human Rights,' *Alternative Law Journal* Vol. 27 (Feb. 2002), 23.

——, 'Transnational Enterprise and Human Rights: Options for Standard Setting and Compliance,' *International Lawyer*, Vol. 37 (2003), 69.

Rees S. and Wright S. (eds.), *Human Rights, Corporate Responsibility: A Dialogue* (Sydney: Pluto Press, 2000).

Review of the U.N. Code of Conduct for Transnational Corporations: Hearing before the Subcomm. on Human Rights and International Organizations of the House Comm. on Foreign Affairs, 100th Cong. (1987) (Washington: U.S. G.P.O.).

Richter J., *Holding Corporations Accountable: Corporate Conduct, International Codes, and Citizen Action* (London: Zed Books, 2001).

Rix S., 'Globalisation and Corporate Responsibility,' *Alternative Law Journal*, Vol. 27 (Feb. 2002), 16.

Rodman K., ' "Think Globally, Punish Locally": Nonstate Actors, Multinational Corporations, and Human Rights Sanctions,' *Ethics and International Affairs*, Vol. 12 (1998), 19.

Rubin S., 'Transnational Corporations and International Codes of Conduct: A Study of the Relationship between International Legal Cooperation and Economic Development,' *American University Journal of International Law and Policy*, Vol. 10 (1995), 1275.

——, 'Transnational Corporations and International Codes of Conduct: A Study of the Relationship Between Legal Cooperation and Economic Development,' *American University Law Review*, Vol. 30 (1981), 903.

——, 'Transnational Corporations and International Law: An Uncertain Partnership,' *Chinese Yearbook of International Law and Affairs*, Vol. 4 (1984), 39.

Sajhau J.-P., *Ethique des affaires dans les industries THC (textile, habillement, chaussures): Les codes de conduite* (Geneva: International Labour Organization, 1997).

Santoro M., *Profits and Principles: Global Capitalism and Human Rights in China* (Ithaca, N.Y.: Cornell University Press, 2000).

Schabas W., 'Enforcing International Humanitarian Law: Catching the Accomplices,' *International Review of the Red Cross*, Vol. 83 (2001), 439.

Schierbeck J., *Industry and Human Rights: A Guide* (Copenhagen: Confederation of Danish Industries, 1998).

Schilling D. and Rosenbaum R., 'Principles for Global Corporate Responsibility,' *Business and Society Review*, Vol. 1995, 55.

Schmalenbach K., 'Multinationale Unternehmen und Menschenrechte,' *Archiv des Völkerrechts*, Vol. 39 (2001), 57.

Schoenberger K., *Levi's Children: Coming to Terms with Human Rights in the Global Marketplace* (New York: Atlantic Monthly Press, 2000).

Schwamm H., 'Pourquoi un code de conduite des Nations-Unies sur les sociétés transnationales,' *Revue du marché commun*, Vol. 1977, 523.

Schwartz P. and Gibb B., *When Good Companies Do Bad Things: Responsibility and Risk in an Age of Globalization* (New York: John Wiley, 1999).

Scott C., 'Multinational Enterprises and Emergent Jurisprudence on Violations of Economic, Social and Cultural Rights,' in A. Eide, C. Krause, and A. Rosas (eds.), *Economic, Social and Cultural Rights: A Textbook*, 2d ed. (The Hague: Kluwer Law International, 2001).

——, 'Translating Torture into Transnational Tort: Conceptual Divides in the Debate on Corporate Accountability for Human Rights Harms,' in C. Scott (ed.), *Torture as Tort: Comparative Perspectives on the Development of Transnational Human Rights Litigation* (Oxford: Hart Publishing, 2001), 45–64.

Sethi S., *Setting Global Standards: Guidelines for Creating Codes of Conduct in Multinational Corporations* (Hoboken, N.J.: Wiley, 2003).

Shelton D., Protecting Human Rights in a Globalized World, *Boston College International and Comparative Law Review*, Vol. 25 (2002), 273.

Siqueiros J., 'The Juridical Regulation of Transnational Enterprises,' in F. Snyder and S. Sathirathai (eds.), *Third World Attitudes Toward International Law, an Introduction* (Dordrecht: Martinus Nijhoff, 1987), 577–594.

Smith J., Bolyard W., and Ippolito A., 'Human Rights and the Global Economy: A Response to Meyer,' *Human Rights Quarterly*, Vol. 21 (1999), 207.

Sornarahaj M., 'Linking State Responsibility for Certain Harms Caused by Corporate Nationals Abroad to Civil Recourse in the Legal Systems of Home States,' in C. Scott (ed.), *Torture as Tort: Comparative Perspectives on the Development of Transnational Human Rights Litigation* (Oxford: Hart Publishing, 2001), 491–512.

Spar D., 'The Spotlight and the Bottom Line: How Multinationals Export Human Rights,' *Foreign Affairs*, Vol. 77 (Mar.-Apr. 1998), 7.

——, and Yoffie D., 'Multinational Enterprises and the Prospects for Justice,' *Journal of International Affairs*, Vol. 52 (1999), 557.

Status of U.N. Code of Conduct on Transnational Corporations: Hearing before the Subcomm. on Human Rights and International Organizations of the House Comm. on Foreign Affairs, 101st Cong. (1989) (Washington: U.S. G.P.O.).

Steinhardt R., 'Litigating Corporate Responsibility,' *Global Dimensions* (2001), http://www.globaldimensions.net/articles/cr/steinhardt.html

Stephens B., 'Corporate Liability: Enforcing Human Rights Through Domestic Litigation,' *Hastings International and Comparative Law Review*, Vol. 24 (2001), 401.

——, 'The Amorality of Profit: Transnational Corporations and Human Rights,' *Berkeley Journal of International Law*, Vol. 20 (2002), 45.

Sullivan R. and Frankental P., 'Can Companies Violate Human Rights?' *LawNow*, Vol. 26 (Oct-Nov 2001), 42.

Tiewul S., 'Transnational Corporations and Emerging Legal Standards,' in P. de Waart, P. Peters, and E. Denters (eds.), *International Law and Development* (Dordrecht: Martinus Nijhoff, 1988), 105–117.

Toftoy R., Note, 'Now Playing: Corporate Codes of Conduct in the Global Theater—Is Nike Just Doing It?,' *Arizona Journal of International and Comparative Law*, Vol. 15 (1998), 905.

U.N. Code of Conduct on Transnational Corporations: Hearing before the Subcomm. on International Economic Policy, Trade, Oceans and Environment of the Senate Comm. on Foreign Relations, 101st Cong. (1990) (Washington, D.C.: U.S. G.P.O.).

United Nations, *The Realization of Economic, Social and Cultural Rights—The Relationship Between the Enjoyment of Human Rights, in Particular, International Labour and Trade Union Rights, and the Working Methods and Activities of Transnational Corporations: Background Document Prepared by the Secretary-General*, UN Doc. E/CN.4/Sub.2/1995/11 (1995).

——, Centre on Transnational Corporations, *The United Nations Code of Conduct on Transnational Corporations* (London: Graham & Trotman, 1988).

——, *Commentary on the Norms on the Responsibilities of Transnational Corporations and Other Business Enterprises with Regard to Human Rights*, U.N. Doc. E/CN.4/Sub.2/2003/38/Rev.2 (2003).

——, Commission on Human Rights, *The Realization of Economic, Social and Cultural Rights: The Question of Transnational Corporations: Second Report of the Working Group*, U.N. Doc. E/CN.4/Sub.2/2000/12 (2000).

——, Commission on Human Rights, *Report of the Working Group on the Effects of the Working Methods and Activities of Transnational Corporations on Human Rights*, U.N. Doc. E/CN.4/Sub.2/2000/WG.2/WP.1 (2000).

——, Conference on Trade and Development (UNCTAD), *Social Responsibility*, U.N. Doc. UNCTAD/ITE/IIT/22 (2001).

——, 'Draft International Code of Conduct on Transnational Corporations,' *International Legal Materials*, Vol. 23 (1984), 626.

——, *The Impact of the Activities and Working Methods of Transnational Corporations on the Full Enjoyment of All Human Rights, in Particular Economic, Social and Cultural Rights and the Right to Development, Bearing in Mind Existing International Guidelines, Rules and Standards Relating to the Subject Matter: Report of the Secretary-General*, U.N. Doc. E/CN.4/Sub.2/1996/12 and Corr.1 (1996).

——, Non-Governmental Liaison Service, *Voluntary Approaches to Corporate Responsibility: Readings and a Resource Guide* (Geneva: UN Non-Governmental Liaison Service, 2002).

——, *Norms on the Responsibilities of Transnational Corporations and Other Business Enterprises with Regard to Human Rights*, U.N. Doc. E/CN.4/Sub.2/2003/12/Rev.2 (2003).

——, Sub-Commission on the Promotion and Protection of Human Rights, *Working Group on the Working Methods and Activities of Transnational Corporations*, U.N. Docs. E/CN.4/Sub.2/2003/13, E/CN.4/Sub.2/2002/13 at 15–21; E/CN.4/Sub.2/2002/XX; E/CN.4/Sub.2/2002/WG.2/WP.1; E/CN.4/Sub.2/2002/XX/Add.1; E/CN.4/Sub.2/2002/WG.2/WP.1/Add.1; E/CN.4/Sub.2/2002/XX/Add.2; E/CN.4/Sub.2/2002/WG.2/WP.1/Add.2; E/CN.4/Sub.2/2002/X/Add.1; E/CN.4/Sub.2/2002/WG.2/WP.1/Add.1; E/CN.4/Sub.2/2001/WG.2/WP.1; E/CN.4/Sub.2/2001/WG.2/WP.1/Add.1; E/CN.4/Sub.2/2001/WG.2/WP.1/Add.2; and E/CN.4/Sub.2/2001/WG.2/WP.1/Add.3.

——, *Transnational Corporations—Texts Relevant to an Annotated Outline Suggested by the Chairman of the Intergovernmental Working Group on a Code of Conduct: Report of the Secretariat*, U.N. Doc. E/C.10/AC.2/3 (1978).

——, *The Universe of Transnational Corporations: Report of the Secretary-General*, U.N. Doc. E/C.10/1993/11 (1993).

Urminsky M., *Self-Regulation in the Workplace: Codes of Conduct, Social Labelling and Socially Responsible Investment* (Geneva: ILO, 2001).

Wagner M., 'The International Legal Rights of Indigenous Peoples Affected by Natural Resource Exploitation: A Brief Case Study,' *Hastings International and Comparative Law Review*, Vol. 24 (2001), 491.

Waldmann R., *Regulating International Business through Codes of Conduct* (Washington: American Enterprise Institute for Public Policy Research, 1980).

Ward H., *Governing Multinationals: The Role of Foreign Direct Liability*, Briefing Paper: New Series No. 18 (London: Royal Institute of International Affairs, 2001), http://www.riia.org/riia

——, *Corporate Accountability in Search of a Treaty? Some Insights from Foreign Direct Liability*, Briefing Paper No. 4 (London: Royal Institute of International Affairs, 2002), http://www.riia.org/pdf/research/sdp/Corporate_Accountability_Insights.pdf

——, 'Securing Transnational Corporate Accountability Through National Courts: Implications and Policy Options,' *Hastings International and Comparative Law Review*, Vol. 24 (2001), 451.

Weiss T. and Lu D., *International Negotiations on the Code of Conduct for Transnational Corporations* (Washington, D.C.: Georgetown University, 1988).

Weissbrodt D., *Draft Human Rights Code of Conduct for Companies with Source Materials*, UN Doc. No. E/CN.4/Sub.2/2000/WG.2/WP.1/Add.1 (Geneva: United Nations, 2000).

——, 'Non-State Entities and Human Rights within the Context of the Nation-State in the 21st Century,' in M. Castermans-Holleman, F. van Hoof, and J. Smith (eds.), *The Role of the Nation-State in the 21st Century—Human Rights, International Organisations and Foreign Policy: Essays in Honour of Peter Baehr* (The Hague: Kluwer Law International, 1998), 175–195.

——, 'UN Guidelines for Companies,' *Amnesty International Human Rights and Business Matters* (2001), http://www.amnesty.org.uk/business/pubs/hrgc.shtml

——, *Principles Relating to the Human Rights Conduct of Companies: Working Paper*, U.N. Doc. No. E/CN.4/Sub.2/2000/WG.2/WP.1 (Geneva: United Nations, 2000).

Wells C., *Corporations and Criminal Responsibility*, 2nd ed. (Oxford: Oxford University Press, 2001).

——, 'Corporate Manslaughter: A Cultural and Legal Form,' *Criminal Law Forum*, Vol. 6 (1995), 45.

——, 'Corporations: Culture, Risk and Criminal Liability,' *Criminal Law Review* (1993), 551.

——, 'The Decline and Rise of English Murder: Corporate Crime and Individual Responsibility,' *Criminal Law Review* (1988), 788.

——, 'A Quiet Revolution in Corporate Liability for Crime,' *New Law Journal*, Vol. 145 (1995), 1326.

Westfield E., Note, 'Globalization, Governance, and Multinational Enterprise Responsibility: Corporate Codes of Conduct in the 21st Century,' *Virginia Journal of International Law*, Vol. 42 (2002), 1075.

Wheeler S., *Corporations and the Third Way* (Oxford: Hart Publishing, 2002).

Wiebalck A., *The European Economic Community Code of Conduct for Companies with Interests in South Africa: A Legal Appraisal* (Regensburg: S. Roderer Verlag, 1992).

Williams C., Remarks on Panel, 'Codes of Conduct and Transparency,' *Hastings International and Comparative Law Review*, Vol. 24 (2001), 415.

Williams O. (ed.), *Global Codes of Conduct: An Idea Whose Time Has Come?* (Notre Dame, Ind.: Notre Dame Press, 2000).

Wilson I., *The New Rules of Corporate Conduct: Rewriting the Social Charter* (Westport, Conn.: Quorum Books, 2000).

Wood S. and Scharffs B., 'Applicability of Human Rights Standards to Private Corporations: An American Perspective,' *American Journal of Comparative Law*, Vol. 50 (2002), 531.

Wouters J., Stuyk J., and Kruger T., *Principles of Proper Conduct for Supranational, State and Private Actors in the European Union: Towards a Ius Commune, Essays in Honour of Walter Van Gerven* (Antwerp: Intersentia, 2001).

Zarate J., 'The Emergence of a New Dog of War: Private International Security Companies, International Law, and the New World Disorder,' *Stanford Journal of International Law*, Vol. 34 (1998), 75.

Zuijdwijk T.J.M., 'Some Observations Concerning Codes of Conduct for International Business,' in Canadian Council on International Law/Conseil Canadien de Droit International, *Proceedings of the Annual Conference* (1986), 212–218.

MULTINATIONAL ENTERPRISES AND INTERNATIONAL HUMAN RIGHTS LAW IN U.S. COURTS

Abi-Saab G., 'The International Law of Multinational Corporations: A Critique of American Legal Doctrines,' in F. Snyder and S. Sathirathai (eds.), *Third World Attitudes Toward International Law: An Introduction* (Dordrecht: Martinus Nijhoff, 1987).

Adams Lien S., Comment, 'Employer Beware? Enforcing Transnational Labor Standards in the United States under the Alien Tort Claims Act,' *Journal of Small and Emerging Business*, Vol. 6 (2002), 311.

Ayoub L., 'Nike Just Does It—and Why the United States Shouldn't: The United States' International Obligation to Hold MNCs Accountable for Their Labor Rights Violations Abroad,' *DePaul Business Law Journal*, Vol. 11 (1999), 395.

Bade D., 'Corporate Responsibility and U.S. Import Regulations against Forced Labor,' *Tulsa Journal of Comparative and International Law*, Vol. 8 (2000), 5.

Becker D., Note, 'A Call for the Codification of the Unocal Doctrine,' *Cornell International Law Journal*, Vol. 32 (1998), 183.

Betz D., Note and Comment, 'Holding Multinational Corporations Responsible for Human Rights Abuses Committed by Security Forces in Conflict-Ridden Nations: An Argument Against Exporting Federal Jurisdiction for the Purpose of Regulating Corporate Behavior Abroad,' *DePaul Business Law Journal*, Vol. 14 (2001), 163.

Blumberg P., 'Asserting Human Rights Against Multinational Corporations under United States Law: Conceptual and Procedural Problems,' *American Journal of Comparative Law*, Vol. 50 (2002), 493.

Bowersett L., Casenote, 'Doe v. Unocal: Torturous Decision for Multinationals Doing Business in Politically Unstable Environments,' *Transnational Lawyer*, Vol. 11 (1998), 361.

Boyd K., 'Collective Rights Adjudication in U.S. Courts: Enforcing Human Rights at the Corporate Level,' *Brigham Young University Law Review*, Vol. 1999, 1139.

Breed L., Note, 'Regulating Our 21st-Century Ambassadors: A New Approach to Corporate Liability for Human Rights Violations Abroad,' *Virginia Journal of International Law*, Vol. 42 (2002), 1005.

Bridgeford T., Note and Comment, 'Imputing Human Rights Obligations on Multinational Corporations: The Ninth Circuit Strikes Again in Judicial Activism,' *American University International Law Review*, Vol. 18 (2003), 1009.

Cleveland S., Book Review, 'Global Labor Rights and the Alien Tort Claims Act,' *Texas Law Review*, Vol. 76 (1998), 1533.

Collingsworth T., 'Separating Fact from Fiction in the Debate over Application of the Alien Tort Claims Act to Violations of Fundamental Human Rights by Corporations,' *University of San Francisco Law Review*, Vol. 37 (2003), 563.

Developments in the Law, 'Corporate Liability for Violations of International Human Rights Law,' *Harvard Law Review*, Vol. 114 (2001), 2025.

Dhooge L., 'A Close Shave in Burma: Unocal Corporation and Private Enterprise Liability for International Human Rights Violations,' *North Carolina Journal of International Law & Commercial Regulation*, Vol. 24 (1998), 1.

Ellinikos M., 'American MNCs Continue to Profit from the Use of Forced and Slave Labor Begging the Question: Should America Take a Cue from Germany?,' *Columbia Journal of Law and Social Problems*, Vol. 35 (2001), 1.

Everett D., Comment, 'New Concern for Transnational Corporations: Potential Liability for Tortious Acts Committed by Foreign Partners,' *San Diego Law Review*, Vol. 35 (1998), 1123.

Foos D., 'Righting Past Wrongs or Interfering in International Relations? World War II-Era Slave Labor Victims Receive State Legal Standing After Fifty Years,' *McGeorge Law Review*, Vol. 31 (2000), 221.

Forcese C., Note, 'ATCA's Achilles Heel: Corporate Complicity, International Law and the Alien Tort Claims Act,' *Yale Journal of International Law*, Vol. 26 (2001), 487.

Gibney M. and Emerick R., 'The Extraterritorial Application of United States Law and the Protection of Human Rights: Holding Multinational Corporations to Domestic and International Standards,' *Temple International and Comparative Law Journal*, Vol. 10 (1996), 123.

Hall S., Note, 'Multinational Corporations' Post-Unocal Liabilities for Violations of International Law,' *George Washington International Law Review*, Vol. 34 (2002), 401.

Heil J., Comment, 'African Private Security Companies and the Alien Tort Claims Act: Could Multinational Oil and Mining Companies Be Liable?,' *Northwestern Journal of International Law and Business*, Vol. 22 (2002), 291.

Hong J., Note and Comment, 'Enforcement of Corporate Codes of Conduct: Finding a Private Right of Action for International Laborers Against MNCs for Labor Rights Violations,' *Wisconsin International Law Journal*, Vol. 19 (2000), 41.

Khalil S., Note, 'The Alien Tort Claims Act and Section 1983: The Improper Use of Domestic Laws to "Create" and "Define" International Liability for Multi-National Corporations,' *Hofstra Law Review*, Vol. 31 (2002), 207.

Kieserman B., Comment, 'Profits and Principles: Promoting Multinational Corporate Responsibility by Amending the Alien Tort Claims Act,' *Catholic University Law Review*, Vol. 48 (1999), 881.

Lambert L., Case Note, 'At the Crossroads of Environmental and Human Rights Standards: Aguinda v. Texaco, Inc.—Using the Alien Tort Claims Act to Hold Multinational Corporate Violators of International Laws Accountable in U.S. Courts,' *Journal of Transnational Law and Policy*, Vol. 10 (2000), 109.

Light S., Student Note, 'The Human Rights Injunction: Equitable Remedies under the Alien Tort Claims Act,' *Transnational Law and Contemporary Problems*, Vol. 9 (1999), 653.

McDonald K., 'Corporate Civil Liability under the U.S. Alien Tort Claims Act for Violations of Customary International Law During the Third Reich,' *St. Louis-Warsaw Transatlantic Law Journal*, Vol. 1997, 167.

Morrin D., Book Review, 'People Before Profits: Pursuing Corporate Accountability for Labor Rights Violations Abroad Through the Alien Tort Claims Act,' reviewing Corporate Predators: The Hunt for Mega-Profits and the Attack on Democracy, *Boston College Third World Law Journal*, Vol. 20 (2000), 427.

Osofsky H., 'Environmental Human Rights under the Alien Tort Statute: Redress for Indigenous Victims of Multinational Corporations,' *Suffolk Transnational Law Review*, Vol. 20 (1997), 335.

Peterson R., Comment, 'Political Realism and the Judicial Imposition of International Secondary Sanctions: Possibilities from John Doe v. Unocal and the Alien Tort Claims Act,' *University of Chicago Law School Roundtable*, Vol. 5 (1998), 277.

Rice E., Note, 'Doe v. Unocal Corporation: Corporate Liability for International Human Rights Violations,' *University of San Francisco Law Review*, Vol. 33 (1998), 153.

Ridenour A., Recent Development, 'Apples and Oranges: Why Courts Should Use International Standards to Determine Liability for Violation of the Law of Nations under the Alien Tort Claims Act,' *Tulane Journal of International and Comparative Law*, Vol. 9 (2001), 581.

Rosencranz A. and Campbell R., 'Foreign Environmental and Human Rights Suits Against U.S. Corporations in U.S. Courts,' *Stanford Environmental Law Journal*, Vol. 18 (1999), 145.

Ryf K., Note, 'Burger-Fischer v. Degussa AG: U.S. Courts Allow Siemens and Degussa to Profit from Holocaust Slave Labor,' *Case Western Reserve Journal of International Law*, Vol. 33 (2001), 155.

Sacharoff A., Note, 'Multinationals in Host Countries: Can They Be Held Liable under the Alien Tort Claims Act for Human Rights Violations?,' *Brooklyn Journal of International Law*, Vol. 23 (1998), 927.

Saunders L., Note, 'Rich and Rare Are the Gems They War: Holding De Beers Accountable for Trading Conflict Diamonds,' *Fordham International Law Journal*, Vol. 24 (2001), 1402.

Shaw C., Note, 'Uncertain Justice: Liability of Multinationals Under the Alien Tort Claims Act,' *Stanford Law Review*, Vol. 54 (2002), 1359.

Slaughter, A.-M. and Bosco D., 'Plaintiff's Diplomacy,' *Foreign Affairs*, Vol. 79 (Sept./Oct. 2000), 102.

Thadhani P., Note, 'Regulating Corporate Human Rights Abuses: Is Unocal the Answer?,' *William and Mary Law Review*, Vol. 42 (2000), 619.

Thames H., 'Forced Labor and Private Individual Liability in U.S. Courts,' *Michigan State University-DCL Journal of International Law*, Vol. 9 (2000), 153.

Tzeutschler G., 'Corporate Violator: The Alien Tort Liability of Transnational Corporations for Human Rights Abuses Abroad,' *Columbia Human Rights Law Review*, Vol. 30 (1999), 359.

Wells L., 'A Wolf in Sheep's Clothing: Why Unocal Should Be Liable under U.S. Law for Human Rights Abuses in Burma,' *Columbia Journal of Law and Social Problems*, Vol. 32 (1998), 35.

Zia-Zarifi S., 'Suing Multinational Corporations in the U.S. for Violating International Law,' *University of California Los Angeles Journal of International and Foreign Affairs*, Vol. 4 (1999), 81.

Index

Abu Ghraib prison (Iraq) 9
accomplice liability 65, *see also* complicity; corporate complicity
accountability, *see* human rights accountability
ACP States
  Cotonou Agreement 16, 255
Adidas 303
advocacy campaigns 48–9, 96–7
African Charter on Human and Peoples' Rights 101–2
African Commission on Human and Peoples' Rights 11
agency principle 33, 156
aggregation of knowledge 157–8
Akerlof, G.A. 304
Al-Qaida 16
Alcoa case 57
Alfonso-Martinez, Miguel 325
Alien Tort Claims Act (USA) 10, 26, 31–2, 55, 152, 153, 195, 197, 198–202, 218, 220, 265–7, 292, 293
  applicable law 272–4
  foreign sovereign immunity 201
  forum non conveniens 200, 201
  political question doctrine 200–1
Allende regime (Chile) 64, 144
American Convention on Human Rights 106
American exceptionalism 218
amicus curiae briefs 107
Amnesty International 102, 104, 107, 142, 151–2
  Human Rights Principles for Companies 173
Annan, Kofi 206, 320
Anti-Corruption Convention 1977 (OECD) 60
anti-personnel mines 103–4
Anti-Slavery International 97
Anti-Slavery Society 97, 101
apartheid 189, 220
  Sullivan Principles 180–1
apparel industry 182
applicable law 272–4
approximation of laws 55
armed conflict, *see* conflict situations
armed opposition groups 6, 15, 96

arms control 15
  EU code of conduct 297–300
Arthur Andersen (auditors) 141, 184
Article 19 107
Articles on the Responsibility of States for Internationally Wrongful Acts 23–4
Arts, B. 15
Asian Development Bank 212
Asian Human Rights Charter 72
attribution rules 155–7
Australia
  Criminal Code Act 1995 156, 158
  extraterritorial litigation 56
  organizational liability 158

Baku-Tblisi-Ceyahn oil pipeline 144, 162
Barcelona Traction case 122
Belgium 290
beneficiary complicity 162, 163
BHP Mining Company 56
bill of rights 113–14
Bin Laden, Osama 16
blame attribution theories 155–7
The Body Shop 11–12, 183
BP 144, 152
Braithwaite, J. 172, 173
branding 21, 181–2, 193
Bremer, Paul 10
Brent Spar 48
Bretton Woods institutions 207–9, *see also* International Monetary Fund; World Bank
bribery and corruption 60, 187–8
  Foreign Corrupt Practices Act (USA) 31, 60, 187–8, 194
  OECD convention 160, 328–9, 333
Brownlie, Ian 21–2, 94–5
Brussels Convention 263–4, 265, 266, 267, 281
  forum non conveniens doctrine and 268–72
Burma 152, 185, 189, 193, 195–6, 303, *see also* Myanmar
Bush administration (USA) 27
business associations 96, *see also* non-governmental organizations (NGOs)

business enterprises
human rights responsibilities 335–8, *see also*
    **multinational corporations; Norms on
    the Responsibilities of Transnational
    Corporations**
international obligations 328–35

CACI International 18
Cambior 56
Campaign for Labor Rights 204
Canada 56, 104
canon law 222
Cape Asbestos 56
Cape plc 152, 153, 154
capital mobilization 17
CARE 96
case studies 7–14
international organizations 8–9
private security contractors 9–11
private shopping centre 8
Shell Oil in Nigeria 11–14
UN-administered territories 8
Castro regime (Cuba) 60–1
Caux Roundtable 45, 186
Center for Constitutional Rights 10
**CESCR (Committee on Economic, Social and
    Cultural Rights)**, *see under* **United
    Nations**
Chafee Amendment 192
changing international legal framework
    37–8, 42–89
common features 62–74
direct accountability 82–9
extra-territorial regulation 53–61
indirect human rights enforcement 65–7
new positions and alliances 62–5
non-legal enforcement techniques 67–8, 69
privatization trends 75–6
State responsibility 78–82
underlying causes 74–8
voluntary codes of conduct 42–53, *see also*,
    codes of conduct
Cheng, B. 20
Chevron 152
child labour 185, 204–5, 255, 256
child rights
UN Convention on the Rights of the
    Child 102–3, 105, 234, 283–4, 285,
    286, 289, 331
child sexual exploitation
extra-territorial legislation 283–6, 289

child soldiers 18
Chile 64, 144, 152, 188
China 193
Chiquita 181
Christian Solidarity International (CSI) 108,
    109
civil liability 37, 69, 152–3, 228
corporations, *see* **corporate civil liability**
human rights litigation, *see* **Alien Tort Claims
    Act; human rights litigation**
civil society 3, 16, 27, 33, *see also*
    **non-governmental organizations
    (NGOs)**
definition 14
development of 18
globalization, opportunities of 18
international 22, 94
Clapham, Andrew 162, 233
Clean Clothes campaign 303
Climate Action Network 103
climate change 103
Climate Convention 28, 94, 103, 104
Climate Council 103
**Coalition for Environmentally Responsible
    Economies** 181
Coase, Ronald 219, 337
codes of conduct 26, 40, 42–53, 66, 67, 77, 89
common background 49
corporations, *see* **corporate codes of conduct**
European Union 45, 47, 53, 87, 295–308
good governance debate 49–52
government facilitation 45–6
ILA standards 47–8
increased use of 26, 42–3
international organizations 26, 45, 46–8, 52
motivation 49–52
NGOs 26, 48–9, 53
origin 26, 49–50
private initiative codes 44
privatization of human rights 42–3
supervision and enforcement deficit 26, 52–3
trade unions 44
UN forces 46–7
Cold War 7, 18, 20
Colombia 18, 152
commodification 220–1
Common Foreign and Security Policy 296
common law litigation, *see* **human rights
    litigation**
common purpose 165, 167
communis opinio scholarum 61

companies, *see* **multinational corporations
(MNCs)**
complicity 65, 161–2, *see also* **corporate
complicity; corporate criminal liability**
common purpose 165
criminal law, in 163–6, 167
English law 165–6, 167
groups 164
international law 164, 166–9, *see also* **state
responsibility**
joint enterprise 165, 167
Rome Statute, under 166–9, 174–5, 232
conflict diamonds 182, 224
conflict situations 6
changing nature of 18–19
private security contractors, use of 9–11, 18, 76
Congo-Brazzaville 64, 288
conscientious proxy statements 185
consumer boycotts 26, 37, 68, 69, 77, 321
consumer movements 7
Control Council Law 232
controlling mind approach
corporate criminal liability, to 33, 156
Copenhagen criteria 50
**Copenhagen Declaration on Social
Development** 254
**Copenhagen World Summit for Social
Development (1995)** 131, 254
core labour standards, promotion of 254–60,
see also **International Labour
Organization**
corporate accountability 13, 25, 30–5, 37, 40,
41, 52, 53, 63, 64, 65–7, 69, 73, 142–6,
152, 178–9, 212–13
civil liability, *see* **corporate civil liability**
codes of conduct, *see* **corporate codes of
conduct**
complicity 142–6, 152–4, 161–9
criminal law, use of 153–4
criminal liability 154–61, 231, 232, *see also*
corporate criminal liability
direct accountability 85–7, 88–9
European Convention on Human Rights 34,
229, 240–51
European Union law, in 34, 35, 227–9, 230,
252–312, *see also* **European
multinationals**
international law, under 230–40
legal framework 40–1, 42–61
national courts, before 88–9
non-legal enforcement mechanisms 68, 69

public procurement incentives 308–12
Shell Oil in Nigeria 11–14
social responsibility, *see* **corporate responsibility;
Corporate Social Responsibility**
state responsibility 82, 233–40
tort law, use of 152–3
UN Norms, *see* **Norms on Responsibilities of
Transnational Corporations**
corporate behaviour 25–6
corporate citizenship 186
corporate civil liability 35, 37, 66, 69, 178, 179,
194–202, 217, 218, 228, *see also* **human
rights litigation**
alien tort litigation 35, 198 202, 218
contextual wrongs 198–202
EU law, under 262–82
parent-subsidiary relationship 276–81
per se violations 196–8, 216
corporate codes of conduct 26, 31, 32, 35,
43–6, 51, 52, 53, 87, 172–3, 183,
224, 225
developments in 318–21
European multinationals 45, 53, 87, 295–308,
320, 321, 347, *see also* **European
multinationals**
Global Compact 206–7, 228, 320
human rights entrepreneurialism 183
ILO Tripartite Declaration 319
OECD guidelines 149, 172, 209–10, 304–7,
308, 309, 319, 334, 339
UN draft Code of Conduct 318
UN Norms, *see* **Norms on the Responsibilities
of Transnational Corporations**
corporate complicity 34, 65–7, 142–6, 152–4,
180, *see also* **corporate criminal liability**
beneficiary complicity 163
direct complicity 162–3
indirect complicity 162, 163
principles of 161–9
Shell Oil in Nigeria: case study 11–14
corporate crime 142, 154
human rights abuses 142–4, 150, 151–2, 162,
237
responsibility for, *see* **corporate complicity;
corporate criminal liability**
corporate criminal liability 33–4, 35, 87, 154,
228, 231, 232, 233
bribery and corruption conventions 159, 160
complicity principles 154–61, *see also*
corporate complicity
European law 35, 159, 160–1, 282–95

corporate criminal liability (*cont.*)
  international instruments 159–61
  militarized commerce 151–2, 162
  multinationals 153–4, 154–61, 231, 232
  regulatory regimes 169–74
  Rome Statute, applications from 168, 169
  State responsibility under international law,
    see **State responsibility**
  theories of 33, 154–61
    aggregation of knowledge 158
    blame attribution 155–7
    corporate culture 156, 158
    holistic theories 157–9
    identification theory 157, 158
    management failure 158
  vicarious liability 156–7
  war crimes 233
corporate culture 33, 156, 158
corporate disclosure 188–9
corporate fraud 141–2
corporate governance
  good governance debate 51–2
corporate international obligations
  328–35
corporate liability 72, *see also* **corporate
  civil liability; corporate complicity;
  corporate criminal liability**
  criminal law, use of 153–4
  tort law, use of 152–3
corporate personality
  international legal personality 71–2, 151,
    154, 155, 232
corporate regulation 169–74
  barriers to 170–1
  domestic regulation 31, 187–94
  globalization era, in 143–50
  international law regulation 30–5, 202–12
  self-regulation 31, 32, 43–6, 180–7, *see also*
    corporate codes of conduct
  social responsibility, *see* **corporate
    responsibility; Corporate Social
    Responsibility**
corporate responsibility 12–13, 30–5, 45, 51,
    177–212
  administrative law 191–2
  American exceptionalism 218
  aspirations *versus* obligations 218–19
  civil liability regime 194–202, 217
  codes of conduct, *see* **corporate codes of
    conduct**
  commodification, problem of 220–1

complicity, *see* **corporate complicity**
contextual wrongs 198–202, 216
criminal liability, *see* **corporate criminal
  liability**
domestic regulation 31, 187–94
ethical investment organizations 184–5
ethically responsible behaviour 51–2
EU framework 35, 45, 212
good governance 51–2
Holocaust restitution 192–3
human rights entrepreneurialism 180–7, 194,
    225
international regulation 30–5, 202–12
  Bretton Woods system 207–9
  Global Compact 206–7
  ILO Tripartite Declaration 203–5
  OECD 209–10
  UN Norms, *see* **Norms on the
    Responsibilities of Transnational
    Corporations**
  UN Sub-Commission on Human
    Rights 205–6
  Universal Human Rights Guidelines 32
  Voluntary Principles on Security and Human
    Rights 13, 212
  WTO 210–12
lex mercatoria, modern reconception of 31,
    221–6
market-based regimes 31, 32, 180–7
means, problem of 218–19
moral agency 217
normative problem 213–15
notice, problem of 215–17
objections to corporate human rights
    regime 213–21
per se violations 196–8, 216
remedies 219–20
securities regulation 188–9
Shell Oil in Nigeria 11–14
social accountability auditing and
    certification 184
social disclosure 188–9
social performance criteria 191–2
sustainable business 184–5
transactional controls 189–90
Corporate Social Responsibility (EU) 45,
    228, 229, 253, 259, 260–2, 282,
    302–3
  ambiguities 261
  definition 260
  Green Paper 35, 212, 281

indicators 261
positive impact 260–1
corporate veil, piercing of 276–81
corporations, *see* **multinational corporations
(MNCs)**
Corpus Iuris project 159, 168
Costello-Roberts **case** 80
Cotonou Agreement (EU-ACP) 16, 255
Council of Europe 159
**Country Assessment Guidelines (Levi
Strauss)** 183
criminal liability, *see also* **international criminal
liability**
complicity 34, 65, 163–9, *see also* **corporate
complicity**
corporations, *see* **corporate criminal liability**
English law 165–6, 167
groups 164
joint enterprise 165, 167
legal persons 231, 232–3
mens rea, 165
participatory liability 164, 165–9
Rome Statute, complicity under 166–9, 174–5
criminal organizations 96, 164, 231–2
CSR, *see* **Corporate Social Responsibility**
Cuba 60–1
customary international law 39
due diligence requirement 79
ICESCR and 120–3
MNCs, applicability to 151
Universal Declaration of Human Rights 39,
121
Cyprus 245

De Schutter, Olivier 34–5
debt relief 117, 136, 137
**Declaration on Fundamental Principles and
Rights at Work (ILO 1998)** 17, 52–3,
204, 254, 257–8, 319, 334
Denmark 160
developing countries
Community GSP scheme 255–7
economic protectionism 239, 253
EU trade and development co-operation
253–60
foreign direct investment 238
human rights in, EU promotion of 252–60
IMF assistance 116, 117, 131, 132–3, 135–6
multinationals, regulation of 23, 238–9, 253
preferential treatment 255–6
sustainable development 255–9

development, right to 114
development co-operation 253–60
diamond trade 182, 224
direct accountability 82–7
domestic regulation 53–4, 54–5
corporate responsibility 187 94
extra-territorial application 55–6
Drahos, P. 172, 173
Dreyfus Third Century Fund 185
Drittwirkung **debate** 38, 70
due diligence 79

Earth Summit (Rio de Janeiro 1992) 94
East Timor 7
ECJ, *see* **European Court of Justice**
Ecological Trust (Merrill Lynch) 185
economic, social and cultural rights 114
Covenant, *see* **International Covenant
on Economic, Social and Cultural
Rights**
IMF, application to 29–30, 113–38,
see further under **International
Monetary Fund**
economic globalization
state sovereignty, challenge to 145, 146–8
economic growth
foreign direct investment 238
IMF surveillance, objective of 131, 132–3
economic protectionism 239, 253
The Economist 10, 94
ECOSOC 39
national organizations, relations with 97
NGOS, relations with 97, 100, 108–9
effects doctrine 57
Eide, Asbjorn 323, 324
Elf Aquitaine 64
Elias, Juanita 33–4
emergency NGOs 49
Encyclopaedia of Public International Law 95
England, *see* **United Kingdom**
Enron 65, 141, 142, 152
Environmental Defence Fund 103
environmental NGOs 48, 96, 103
environmental responsibility 43, 181
standards 255–7
erga omnes **obligations** 122, 235
Eser 166
Ethical Banana 181–2
ethical investment 68, 69, 184–5, 261, 321, 348
ethical labelling 261
Ethical Trading Initiative (UK) 45–6

EU, *see* **European Union**
European Bank for Reconstruction and Development 212
European Commission of Human Rights 242
European Communities, *see* **European Union (EU)**
European Convention for the Prevention of Torture (1987) 102
European Convention on Human Rights 229, 240–51, 299
  corporate accountability, and 34, 229, 240
  individuals, protection of
    State Parties' obligations 244–7
  jurisdiction
    extra-territorial scope, restrictions on 240–4, 247
    national territory, and 240–4, 249–51
  NGO petitions 105–6
European Convention on the Recognition of the Legal
  Personality of International Non-Governmental Organizations 95–6, 97
European Court of Human Rights 27, 41, 80, 347
  amicus curiae briefs 107
  international organizations, complaints against 81, 83
  jurisdiction 83, 241, 243–7
  non-state actors, violations by 80–1
European Court of Justice 212
  annulment actions 84
  human rights protection 47, 62, 84–5
European Framework for Corporate Social Responsibility 212
European Monitoring Platform 35, 302, 347
European multinationals
  codes of conduct 45, 53, 87, 295–308, 347
    arms exports 297–300
    misleading advertising of practices 300–1
    model codes 281, 304–7
    monitoring compliance 301–3
    South Africa, enterprises operating in 295–7, 299
  human rights accountability 227–9, 230, 252–312, *see also* **Corporate Social Responsibility**
    civil liability 262–82
    codes of conduct, *see above*
    criminal legislation, harmonization of 286–91

criminal liability 33, 35, 159, 160–1, 282–95
European ATCA 262–7, 281
incentives 308
member states as economic actors 308–12
public procurement incentives 308–12
trade and development cooperation 34–5, 253–60
European Ombudsman 50
European Parliament 87
European Political Cooperation 296
European Social Agenda 307
European Social Charter 106
European Union (EU) 4, 34, 35, *see also* **European Union law**
  Copenhagen criteria 50
  core labour standards, promotion of 253–60
  corporate social responsibility, *see* **Corporate Social Responsibility**
  Cotonou Agreement 16, 255
  Generalised System of Preferences (GSP) 255–7
  human rights challenge to 84
  human rights obligations 46, 47, 62
  human rights promotion 47, 252, 253–60
  multinationals, accountability of, *see* **European multinationals**
  non-state actors, definition of 15
  public procurement contracts 308–12
  sustainable development, promotion of 255–9
  trade and development cooperation 34–5, 253–60
European Union law 73–4
  Convention on Corruption 159
  Convention on the Protection of the European Communities' Financial Interests 159
  corporate civil liability 262–82
  corporate codes of conduct 35, 295–308, *see also* **European multinationals**
  corporate criminal liability 33, 35, 159, 160–1, 282–95
  direct effect 252
  extra-territorial jurisdiction 26, 57
  functional treaty succession 83–4
  Fundamental Rights Charter 47, 252
  multinationals, human rights accountability of, *see* **European multinationals**
Eximbank statute 191–2
export controls and sanctions 31, 189–90, 193
Export-Import Bank (Eximbank) 191–2
extra-territorial regulation 26, 42, 56, 77, 88–9

effects doctrine 57
European Union 26, 57
Helms-Burton controversy 60–1
human rights enforcement 26, 55–61, 65
justifications for 58–61
litigation 55–6, 56–7, 88–9
revival 26, 53 61
sexual exploitation of children 283–6, 289
shared international interests 58–61
extractive industries 303
Shell Oil operations in Nigeria 11–14
voluntary principles on security and human
rights 13, 212, 220
Exxon-Mobil 183

Fair Labor Association (USA) 45
fair trade 181
Falk, Richard 22, 23
Federal Republic of Germany 66
financial institutions 64, 77, *see also*
International Monetary Fund;
World Bank
The Financial Times 13
Finland 160
forced labour 23, 66, 255, 256, 257
Forcese, C. 152, 162
Foreign Corrupt Practices Act (USA) 31, 60,
187–8, 194
foreign direct investment (FDI)
149–50, 238
foreign investment 17
foreign sovereign immunity 201
forum non conveniens 35, 56, 200, 201,
267–72
forum shopping 54–5, 267
Framework Convention on Climate Change,
see Climate Convention
France
corporate criminal liability 160
corporate disclosure 188–9
securities regulation 31
freedom of speech 8
Friedman, Milton 51, 180, 213, 223, 337
Frowein, Jochen 248, 249
Fruehauf affair 57
functional treaty succession 83

G7 Genoa summit 48
Garang, John 108
GATT 73, 83, 171, 210, 255
Gautier, Jean-Jacques 102

Generalised System of Preferences (GSP
scheme) 255–7
Geneva Conventions 70, 99, 289
Additional Protocol II (1977) 6
UN forces, applicability to 46–7
war crimes, prosecution of 59–60
Genocide Convention 196–7, 289, 332
Germany 66, 160
Gianviti, François 29–30
Gibraltar 81
global civil society 22
Global Climate Coalition 103
Global Compact 13–14, 45, 66, 206–7, 228,
339
global consumer boycotts 77
Global Convention on the Control of
Transboundary Movements of
Hazardous Waste 334
global governance 50–1
Global Reporting Initiative 342
Global Sourcing and Operating Guidelines
(Levi Strauss) 183
globalization 17, 72, 76–8, 349
civil society development, and 18
corporate regulation 143–50
growth of NGOs, and 97
human rights, of 77–8
meaning of 76
products of 77
state sovereignty, challenge to 145, 146–8
good governance debate 26, 38, 49–52
Greece 160
green portfolios 181
Greenpeace 48, 96, 103, 107
Gross Domestic Product
multinational revenues, comparisons with 17,
147, 148 (*table*)
Guantanamo 18
Guillaume, Gilbert 27, 93, 94
Guissé, El Hadji 322, 325

Handicap International 103
headquarters agreements 98–9
Heavily Indebted Poor Countries (HIPC)
Initiative 136, 137
Held 146, 150
Helms-Burton controversy 60–1
Henkin 151
Holocaust litigation 31, 66, 179, 192–3
Holy See 70
Howen, N. 305

Howitt Resolution (1999) 281, 283, 302, 303, 304
human rights 37–8
  privatization 42–3, 75–6
human rights abuses
  international organizations 82–4
  multinational corporations 9–11, 142–4, 150, 237, 317, *see also* **corporate accountability; corporate complicity; corporate criminal liability**
  impunity in international law 230–40
human rights accountability
  corporations, *see* **corporate accountability**
  direct accountability
    international law, under 82–7
    national courts, before 87–9
  EU annulment actions 84
  indirect enforcement 65–7
  international organizations 8–9, 26, 40, 46–8, 62–3
  mechanisms 78
  new positions and alliances 62–5
  NGOs, *see* **non-governmental organizations**
  State responsibility for non-state activities 79–82, 85, *see also* **State responsibility**
Human Rights Committee (UN) 41, 76, 79, 81–2, 86
human rights conditionality 178, 179, 190, 193
human rights courts 41–2, 106–7, 107
human rights entrepreneurialism 180–7, 194, 225
  codes of conduct 42–53, 183
  commercial advantages 186–7
  essential characteristic 186
  ethical investment organizations 184–5
  NGOs, rise of 185–7
  precursors 180–1
  rights-sensitive product lines and branding 31, 181–2
  social accountability auditing and certification 184
human rights forum shopping 54–5
human rights law 38–42, *see also* **international human rights law**
  extra-territorial regulation 53–61
  indirect enforcement 65–7, 79–82, 84
  international law, part of 38, 39, 73–4
  legal framework 38–42
  non-legal enforcement 67–8, 69
  non-state actors, applicability to 38
  unwritten law 39

human rights litigation 55–6, 60–1, 88–9
  alien tort litigation 31–2, 55, 152, 153, 195, 197, 198–202, 218, 220, 272
  applicable law 272–5
  Brussels Convention 263–7
  European multinationals, involving 262–82
  foreign sovereign immunity 201
  forum non conveniens, 267–72
  political question doctrine 200–1
human rights promotion 178
  EU trade and development co-operation 253–60
  multinational corporations 63–4, 71, 72
  new alliances 63–4
  NGOs 5, 13, 16, 96
human rights protection, *see* **human rights law; international human rights law**
Human Rights Watch 10, 96, 103, 104, 141, 142, 151–2
  corporate complicity, definition of 163
  Shell Oil in Nigeria, and 12, 13, 14

I G Farben 233
IBRD
  human rights accountability 63
ICC, *see* **International Criminal Court**
ICCPR, *see* **International Covenant on Civil and Political Rights**
ICRC, *see* **International Committee of the Red Cross**
ICSID Convention 85
identification liability 157, 158
ILO, *see* **International Labour Organization**
immunity dumping 54
import controls and sanctions 31, 189–90, 193
India 152
indirect complicity 162, 163
indirect human rights enforcement 65–7, 79–82, 84
individual responsibility 70, 71
  international law, under 230, 231–3
Indonesia 144, 185
information revolution 27, 77
inspection panel, *see* **World Bank**
Inter-American Court of Human Rights 41, 80, 107
inter-governmental organizations (IGOs) 93, 94, 96, 98
inter-State system
  NGO status under international law, and 93–111
INTERIGHTS 107

International Association of Lawyers against
    Nuclear Arms (IALANA) 93
International Bill of Rights 113–14
International Campaign to Ban Landmines 15,
    103–4
International Chamber of Commerce 45
international civil society 94
international claims
    NGO capacity to bring 105–7
International Commission of Jurists
    (ICJ) 101–2, 106, 109
International Committee of the Red Cross
    (ICRC) 28, 70, 105
    headquarters agreements 98–9
    international legal personality 28
International Confederation of Free Trade
    Unions
    Basic Code of Conduct covering Labour
        Practices 44
International Convention on Civil Liability
    for Damage Resulting from Activities
    Dangerous to the Environment 329,
    334
International Convention on Civil Liability for
    Oil Pollution Damage 329, 333–4
International Convention on the Elimination
    of All Forms of Discrimination against
    Women 234, 331
International Convention on the Elimination
    of All Forms of Racial
    Discrimination 234, 331
International Council on Human Rights
    Policy 172
International Court of Justice 19, 27, 39, 106,
    122, 241
International Covenant on Civil and Political
    Rights 29, 79, 113–14
International Covenant on Economic, Social
    and Cultural Rights 29, 113–14, 293,
    332, 340
    broader context 113–14, 131
    customary international law, whether part
        of 120–2, 137
    development, right to 114
    economic preconditions 131
    erga omnes obligations, whether part of 122
    IMF, and, *see also* International Monetary Fund
        applicability to 29, 118–30, 137
        direct effect 118–19
        economic growth as objective of IMF
            surveillance 132–3

indirect effect 123–4
international organizations, whether binding
    on 120–3
jus cogens, and 122
nature of 138
wider economic rights 131
workers' rights 131
International Criminal Court 7, 28, 87, 94,
    104, 105, 146, 155, 170, *see also* **Rome
    Statute**
    complicity under Rome Statute 164, 166–9,
        174–5
    jurisdiction
        juridical persons, over 232–3
        legal persons, over 154, 155, 232
        omissions from 27, 151, 154, 232
    NGOs, role of 94, 104, 105
international criminal liability 87
    complicity 143, 164, 166 9
    corporations 154–63, 164, 168–74, 230,
        232–3, *see also* **corporate criminal
        liability**
    individuals 231–3
    juridical persons 232–3
    Rome Statute, complicity under 166–9, 174–5
international criminal tribunals 7, 145–6, 155,
    197
International Development Association 136
International Emergency Economic Powers Act
    (USA) 191
International Federation of Red Cross
    Societies 99
international human rights law 37–8, *see also*
    **European Convention on Human
    Rights; Universal Declaration of Human
    Rights**
    changing framework 42–74
        underlying causes 74–8
    codes of conduct 42–53
    corporate responsibility and 177–226, *see also*
        corporate responsibility
    direct accountability 82–9
    domestic law, translation into 53–4
    extraterritoriality, revival of 53–61
    forum shopping 54–5
    general international law, and 38, 39, 72–4
    globalization effects 76–8
    indirect enforcement 65–7
    institutional framework 41–2
    international bill of rights 113–14
    international legal personality 69–72

international human rights law (*cont.*)
  legal framework 38–42
  new positions and new alliances 62–5
  non-legal means of enforcement 67–8, 69
  standard-setting 39, 75, 101–5
  state power, protection against 37–8
  state responsibility 78–82
  treaty obligations 39–41
international institutions 3, 64, 77
International Labour Organization (ILO) 28,
    32, 41, 100, 171, 345
  child labour, campaign against 204–5
  code of conduct 44
  Committee on Freedom of Association 106
  core labour standards 253–4
  corporate responsibility agenda 203–5
  Declaration on Fundamental Principles and
    Rights at Work (1998) 17, 52–3, 204,
    254, 257–8, 319, 334
  freedom of association procedure 106
  Subcommittee on Multinational Enterprises 52
  supervision mechanism 86
  Tripartite Declaration of Principles Concerning
    Multinational Enterprises 203–5, 319,
    339
  tripartite system 100–1
international law
  accountability of non-state actors 328–35
    direct accountability 82–7
    multinationals 151, 155, 169–74, 227–8,
      229, 230–40
  complicity, *see* **corporate criminal liability**;
    international criminal liability; state re-
    sponsibility
  cross-fertilization 73–4
  erga omnes obligations 122, 235
  extraterritoriality and 56–61
  fragmentation 72–3
  Helms-Burton controversy 60–1
  human rights law, and 38, 39, 72–4, *see also*
    international human rights law
  ICESCR, status of 120–2
  impunity of multinationals 230–40
  individual responsibility 230, 231–3
  jurisdictional conflicts 56–8
  jurisdictional principles 59
  jus cogens norms 122–3, 235
  NGOs, and 93–111, *see also*
    non-governmental organizations
  non-state actors, and 19–25, 69–72, 93–5
  objects of 19–20

  role and function, expansion of 145
  standard-setting 39, 75, 101–5
  State-centrism 17, 19, 21, 22, 36, 229, 231,
    235
  State responsibility, *see* **State responsibility**
  subjectivity/personality under, *see* international
    legal personality
  treaties, *see* **treaties**
  war crimes tribunals 145–6, 155, *see also*
    International Criminal Court
International Law Association (ILA)
  accountability standards 47–8
International Law Commission 197, 241
  international organizations, responsibility
    of 24–5
  State Responsibility, Articles on 23, 24, 236,
    246
International League for Human Rights 106
international legal personality 19–20, 24–5, 26,
    46, 69–72, 85
  corporations 71–2, 151, 154, 155, 232
  International Committee of the Red Cross 28
  international organizations 29, 46
  NGOs 95–6
  non-state actors 19, 20, 26, 69–72, 151, 154,
    155, 232
  United Nations 18, 29
**International Lesbian and Gay Association
    (ILGA)** 108
International Military Tribunal of Nuremberg,
    see **Nuremberg tribunal**
International Monetary Fund (IMF) 3, 6, 25,
    29, 144, 207
  adjustment programmes 129
  arrears of members 129
  decision-making organs 115
    State Parties' actions through 124–6
  developing countries, and 116, 117, 135–6
  economic, social and cultural human rights
    and 29–30, 113–38
    applicability of Covenant 118–30
    Articles of Agreement, considerations
      under 30, 130–6
    customary international law 120–3
    direct effect of Covenant 118–19
    economic growth, condition of 131, 132–3
    financial assistance 134–5
    indirect effect of Covenant 123–30
    indirect obligations of Fund 126–30
    State Parties' obligations 124–5, 126–30
  establishment 114

Extended Fund Facility (EFF) 117
financial assistance 133
   conditionality 125–6, 134
   developing countries 135–6
   General Resources 125–6, 134–5
financial role 115, 116, 117, 137
good governance, advocacy of 50
Heavily Indebted Poor Countries (HIPC)
   initiative 117, 136, 137
human rights concerns 8–9, 29–30, 63, 119,
   121, 207, 209, *see also* **economic, social**
   and cultural human rights (*above*)
intergovernmental agency 119
mandate and practice 116
   evolution of 116–18, 137
members' financial obligations to 129
members' international commitments, and 129
monetary agency 116, 117, 137
nature and role of 114–18, 119, 137
NGO links 64
Poverty Reduction and Growth Facility
   (PRGF) 117, 136
specialized agency 119, 130, 137–8
surveillance activities 129
UN, relationship with 29–30, 115–16, 118,
   119–20, 137–8
uniformity of treatment 116
International Olympics Committee (IOC) 99
international organizations 26, 28–30, 115, *see*
   also **International Monetary Fund**
   (IMF); United Nations; World Bank;
   World Trade Organization
codes of conduct 46–8, 52
definition 24, 40n
division of labour 115
good governance debate 50–1
human rights accountability 8–9, 26, 40, 46–8,
   62–3
   direct accountability 82–5
human rights advocacy and supervision 40–1
human rights obligations 46
human rights violations 82–4
international law, subjects of 29, 46
jurisdictional immunity 88
responsibility of 24–5
rule of law, subject to 138
International Programme on the Elimination of
   Child Labour (IPEC) 204–5
International Red Cross Conference 99
international standard-setting
NGOs, role of 101–5

international tribunals
direct accountability of non-state actors 82–7
International Union for the Conservation of
   Nature (IUCN) 99
internet 77, 97–8
investment
ethical 184–5, 348
Foreign Direct Investment (FDI) 149–50, 238
socially responsible 68, 69, 185, 261, 321
Investor Responsibility Research Center 225
Iraq 34
invasion of 21
private security contractors 9–11, 18
ISO 9000 184
ISO 14001 184
Italy 160, 161, 188
ITT 64, 143 4

Jackson-Vanik Amendment 190
Japan 188
joint enterprise 167
Josselin, D. 15
juridical persons
international criminal liability 232–3
jurisdiction, *see also* **Brussels Convention**
applicable law 272–5
conflicts 56–8, *see also* **extra-territorial**
   regulation
forum non conveniens 267–72
forum shopping 54–5, 267
immunity 88
principles 59
territorial jurisdiction, extension of 56–8
jus cogens norms 122–3, 235
Justice (NGO) 107

Kamminga, Menno T. 14, 27–8, 149
Khartashkin, Vladimir 325
Kimberley Process 182, 224
Kruger, Maria 32–3

labour rights 23, 131, *see also* **International**
   Labour Organization (ILO)
core labour standards, EU promotion of
   253–60
Declaration on Fundamental Principles and
   Rights at Work (1998) 17, 52–3, 204,
   254, 257–8
laissez-faire capitalism 223
Landmines Convention 28, 103–4, 105
Latin America 181

Lawyers Committee for Human Rights 104
legal framework
  changing nature of, *see* changing international
    legal framework
  development of procedures 41
  institutions 41–2
  meaning of 38–42
  traditional instruments 39, 40–1
legal personality, *see also* international legal
    personality
  NGOs 95–6, 97
legal persons
  international criminal liability 27, 232, 329–35
  international obligations 329–35
legislative harmonization 55
Levi Strauss 183
lex lata 78
lex loci delicti 274, 275
lex mercatoria 179, 221–4, 225
  modern reconception of 31, 32, 221, 24–6
liberation movements, *see* national liberation
    movements
Liberation Tigers of Tamil Eelam
    (Sri Lanka) 18
Liz Claiborne 183
Lome Agreements 255

Maastricht Guidelines on Violations of
    Economic, Social and Cultural Rights
    1997 82
MacBride Principles 44, 181
McCorquodale, R. 169
McLean, Andrew 298
Malaysia 185
Mandela, Nelson 220
manufacturing sector
  human rights abuses 144
Maquila Solidarity Network 204
Maquiladora Standards of Conduct 44
market-based self-regulation 31, 32, 180–7
Matthews case (ECHR) 81, 83
Mbaye, Keba 102
Medecins sans Frontières 96–7
Medico International 103
medieval law, *see lex mercatoria*
Meeran, Richard 154
mens rea 165
mercenaries 18
Merrill Lynch 185
Mexico 17
militarized commerce 151–2, 162

military commanders
  Rome Statute, liability under 166, 168
Miller Principles 44
Mines Advisory Group 103
misleading advertising of practices
  EU code of conduct 300–1
mobilization of shame 41
Model Code of Conduct for European
    businesses 304–7
Movement for the Survival of the Ogoni
    People 11
Muchlinski, P. 148–9, 153
Multilateral Agreement on Investment
    (MAI) 94, 98, 210
multilateral institutions 18
multinational corporations 3, 6, 7, 14, 23, 26,
    30–5, 98, 141–75, 149, *see also* European
    multinationals
  civil liability, *see* corporate civil liability
  codes of conduct, *see* corporate codes of
    conduct
  collusion 143–4
  complicity, *see* corporate complicity
  consumer boycotts 68, 69, 321
  criminal liability, *see* corporate criminal
    liability
  definitions 40, 142n, 148–50
  disclosure 188–9
  economic power 17, 147–8 (*table*) 318, 349
  foreign direct investment (FDI) 149–50,
    238
  human rights abuses 142–4, 150, 237, 317
    manufacturing sector 144
    militarized commerce 151–2, 162
  human rights accountability, *see* corporate
    accountability
  human rights forum shopping 54–5
  human rights obligations 22–3, 23, 32–3, 151,
    317, 318
  human rights promotion 63–4, 71, 72, 150–1,
    172–3
  international law, accountability under 85–6,
    151, 155, 170–2
  impunity 230–40
  international legal personality 72
  moral obligations 22, 36
  national courts, accountability before 88–9
  NGOs distinguished from 96
  OECD guidelines 149, 172, 209–10,
    304–7, 308, 309, 319, 334, 339
  outsourcing 150

regulation of, *see* **corporate regulation**
social accounting 64
social responsibility 35, 45, 212, 228, 229, *see
also* **corporate responsibility; corporate
social responsibility**
socially responsible investing 68, 69
states and, distinction between 170
terminology 30, 149
transformative capacity 170
UN Working Group 45, 322–7
Murray 172
Myanmar (Burma) 23, 65, 183, 288

Namibia 7
nation state 58, 59
demise of 74–5
National Contact Points (OECD) 52, 305–6,
345
national courts
direct accountability before 87–9
Norms, use of 349
national jurisdiction, extension of 56–8, *see also*
extra-territorial regulation
national legislation, *see* **domestic regulation**
national liberation movements 6, 7, 14, 96
Nazi Holocaust 192, 194
litigation arising from 31, 66, 179, 192–3
negative publicity 26
Netherlands 160, 188
New Economics Foundation (NEF) 48
New International Economic Order 7, 43
new International Economic Order 7
**NGO Coalition for an International Criminal
Court** 104
**NGO Group for the Convention on the Rights
of the Child** 103
NGOs, *see* **non-governmental organizations**
Nigeria, Shell Oil operations in 11–14, 144, 152
Nike 183
non-discrimination
employment, in respect of 255, 256, 257
non-governmental organizations (NGOs) 3,
14, 18, 27–8
advocacy/campaigning groups 48–9, 96–7
armed opposition groups, distinguished
from 96
coalitions 102–4, 111
codes of conduct 48–9, 53
companies, distinguished from 96
corporate social responsibility, and 185–7
criminal organizations, distinguished from 96

criticisms of influence of 93–5
cyclical role of 97
definition 28, 40n, 95–8
democratic nature of 111
ECOSOC, consultative status with 97, 100,
108–9
failings of 110–11
growth of 97–8
history of 97
human rights accountability 48–9, 63,
108–9
direct accountability 85–6
domestic law, under 88–9, 107
international law, under 85–6, 107–9,
109–10
human rights courts, claims before 106, 107
human rights entrepreneurialism, and
185–7
human rights obligations 108
human rights promotion 62, 64
independence of 110–11
influence of, growth in 27, 93–5
inter-governmental organizations, distinguished
from 96, 98
inter-State system, whether threat to 93–111
international character 97
international law, and
convention-drafting, role in 102–3
ECHR, right to petition 105–6
international claims, capacity to bring 28,
105–7
liability under 28, 107–9, 109–10
standard-setting role 101–5
status under 28, 93–111
treaty-concluding capacity 98–100
treaty-making capacity 100–5
internet mobilization 97–8
legal personality 95–6, 97, 98
liberation movements, distinguished from 96
Norms on Transnational Corporations,
and 348
political parties, distinguished from 96
range of groups 96
relief and assistance groups 96–7, 98
Seattle summit protests (1999) 94
States' international obligations towards
105–6
treaty-making, role in 28, 98–105
UN, consultative status with 97
violent protests 48
non-legal enforcement techniques 67–8, 69

non-state actors 3–6, *see also* **international organizations; multinational corporations (MNCs); non-governmental organizations (NGOs)**
accountability, *see* **human rights accountability**
armed opposition groups 15
definitions 14–19
EU concept of 15
evolution of 6–7, 17–18
expansion of role of 18–19
extra-territorial conduct, regulation of, *see* **extra-territorial regulation**
human rights obligations 22–3, 335–8
international legal framework 19, 20, 25–7, 37–89, 38–42, *see also* **changing international legal framework; international legal personality**
international obligations of 328–35
self-regulation, *see* **codes of conduct**
State responsibility 23–4, 78–82
terrorist groups 16–17
transnational dimension 15–16
UN concept 16–17
Norms on the Responsibilities of Transnational Corporations 32–3, 66–7, 71, 151, 173, 315–50
drafting history 322–8
implementation 338–49
assessment 342
business enterprises 341–4
business groups 348
complaints procedures 342
impact statements 342–3
improving compliance 342
intergovernmental organizations 345–7
internal monitoring 342
investors, lenders and consumers 348
NGOs 348
states 349
trade associations 348
trade unions 347–8
United Nations 343–5
issues raised in drafting 328–38
non-voluntary nature of 338–9
Norrie, A. 165
North American Agreement on Environmental Cooperation 346
North American Agreement on Labor Cooperation 346

North American Free Trade Agreement 346
Northern Ireland
MacBride Principles 181
Norway 160
not-a-cat syndrome 3–6
Nova Corporation 152
Nuremberg Rules 332
Nuremberg tribunal 87, 145, 231, 233
principles 197

Occidental Petroleum 152
OECD, *see* **Organization for Economic Cooperation and Development**
Offical Journal of the European Communities 256
Ogoniland (Nigeria)
Shell Oil operations 11, 144
oil companies, *see* **extractive industries; Shell Oil ombudsman offices** 50
Organization for Economic Cooperation and Development (OECD) 26, 30, 32, 254
Anti-Corruption Convention 1977 60
Bribery and Corruption Convention 160, 234, 328–9, 333
code of conduct 43–4
Committee on International Investment and Multinational Enterprises 306
Guidelines on Multinational Enterprises 149, 172, 209–10, 304–7, 308, 309, 319, 334, 339
human rights concerns 209–10
Multilateral Agreement on Investment (MAI) 94, 98, 210
National Contact Points 52, 305–6, 345
supervision mechanism 86
outsourcing 150, *see also* **privatization**
Oxfam 96
Ozone Action 103

Paris Club 136
Park, Soo-Gil 325
Pax Romana 109
Pentagon 10
Philippines 185
Physicians for Human Rights 103
Poland 160
political parties
NGOs distinguished from 96
Portugal 160–1

Poverty Reduction and Growth Facility
(PRGF) 117, 136
pressure groups 93, 94
Principles for Business 186
Princz case 66
private duties 70, 71
private law 70
private sector 8, 9–14, *see also* civil society;
non-governmental organizations
(NGOs)
citizens' groups 96
foreign investment 17
prisons 76
security contractors 9–11, 18, 76
shopping centres 8
State responsibility, and 79–82
privatization 17, 27
global trends 75–6
human rights protection 42–3, 75–6
security provision 9–11, 18, 76
Project on International Courts and
Tribunals 73
property rights 131
public procurement 228, 230
ethical clause 309
EU member states
social or environmental criteria, inclusion
of 308–12
public sector 14

Racketeer Influenced and Corrupt
Organizations Act (RICO) 10
Ramasastry, A. 151, 163
Rand, Ayn 223
Ratner, S. 169
Reagan, Ronald 181
Reagonomics 77
Red Crescent 98
Red Cross organizations 97, 98–9, *see also*
International Committee of the Red
Cross (ICRC)
Reebok 183
regional development banks
social concerns 212
regulation avoidance 54–5
extraterritorial litigation 55–61
Reinisch, August 25–6, 31
Reisman, Michael 21
relief and assistance groups 96–7, 98, *see also*
non-governmental organizations
(NGOs)

remedies 219–20
Report of the Panel of Eminent Persons on
United Nations–Civil Society Relations
(2004) 14
Resolution 1267 Committee (UN) 16
respondeat superior 156
Revolutionary Armed Forces of Colombia 18
Revolutionary United Front (Sierra
Leone) 18
rights-sensitive product lines and
branding 21, 181–2, 193
Rio Tinto 55
Rivers State Internal Security Task Force 12
Roman civil law 222
Rome Conference (1998) 94, 104
Rome Statute 34, 104, 151, 288–9, 332
commander/superior liability 166, 168
complicity under 164, 166–9, 174–5
corporate complicity 168–9
juridical persons, liability of 232–3
legal persons, liability of 154, 155, 232
Royal Dutch Shell, *see* Shell Oil
rule of law 138, 178, 179, 214
international organizations subject to 138
Russia 193
Rwanda 7, 145

SA 8000 178, 184, 224
Saro-Wiwa, Ken 11
Save the Children 96
Schabas, W. 166
Seattle summit (1999) 94
securities regulation 31, 188–9
security provision
privatization of 9–11, 18
self-determination, right to 7
self-regulation 42–5, 46, *see also* codes of
conduct
human rights entrepreneurialism 31, 32,
180–7
Sen, Amartya 239
service-providing NGOs
codes of conduct 49
sexual exploitation of children
extraterritorial criminal legislation 283–6,
289
shared international interests
extraterritoriality, justification for 58–61
shareholders 26, 41, 51–2
pressure by 184–5
primacy of 213

Shell Oil 48, 152, 183
  Nigerian operations 11–14, 144, 152, 267
  Plan for Ogoni (1996) 12
Siberian pipe-line disaster 57
Sierra Club 103
Sierra Leone 18
Singapore WTO Declaration (1996) 253–4
slave labour 23, 65, 66, 194, 257
slave trade 101
Slepak Principles 44
small and medium-sized enterprises 14
Smith, Adam, *Wealth of Nations* 223–4
social accountability 31, 177–8, 184
social accounting 64
social disclosure 188–9
social dumping 190
social labelling 228, 261
social performance criteria 191–2
social responsibility 179, 260, *see also* **Corporate Social Responsibility**
  investments 68, 69, 185, 261, 321
social standards, EU promotion of 255–60
South Africa 7, 31, 153, 154, 185, 189, 220
  EU enterprises operating in
    code of conduct for 295–7, 299
  Sullivan Principles 180–1
South African Truth and Reconciliation Commission 162
sovereign immunity
  corporations 201
Sovereign Order of Malta 70
Spain 160
special-interest groups 94, 96, *see also* **non-governmental organizations (NGOs)**
Special Representative of the UN Secretary-General for Children and Armed Conflict 18
specialized agencies 137–8, *see also* **International Monetary Fund**
specialized international courts 73
Srebenica 63
Sri Lanka 18
stakeholders 51–2
standard-setting 39, 75
  NGOs, role of 101–5
Starbucks 181
State
  declining role of 74–5
  extra-territorial jurisdiction 54, 55–61
  nation state 58, 59, 74–5

responsibility, *see* **State responsibility**
sovereignty, *see* **State sovereignty**
State-centrism 17, 19, 21, 22, 36, 229, 231, 235
State responsibility 23–4, 27, 168, 170, 230–1, 233–40, 241
  delegated activities, for 81–2
  European Convention on Human Rights 240–51
  host states 237–40
  individuals, obligation to protect 233–5, 244–7
  International Law Commission Articles 23, 24, 236, 246
  multinationals, for 170–1, 235, 237, 240
    foreign countries, operating in 235, 237, 247–9, 251
    national territory, operating within 237–40, 251
    nationals abroad, control over 235–7, 247–9, 251
  NGOs, obligations towards 105–6
  non-state actors, invoked by 23–4
  territorial notion of jurisdiction 240–4
  vicarious liability 78–82, 84
State sovereignty 4, 7, 21–2, 23
  challenges to
    economic globalization 145, 146–8
    international law 145–6
  demise of 74–5
Steinhardt, Ralph 31–2
stock markets
  ethical investment 185
Stubbs, R. 146
subjects of international law, *see* **international legal personality**
Sudan 108, 144, 189, 193
Sudan People's Liberation Movement 18
Sullivan Principles 44, 180–1
Supplementary Slavery Convention 332
Sur, Serge 94
sustainable business 184–5
sustainable development 255–60
Sweatshop Watch 204
Swiss Committee against Torture 102
Swiss Federal Council 99
Switzerland
  NGOs, agreements with 98–100

Taliban 16
Tamil Eelam 18

terminology 3–4, 14–19, 149
territorial jurisdiction, extension of 56–8, *see also* **extra-territorial regulation**
territorial nation state, *see* **nation state**
terrorist groups 3, 7, 16–17
Thailand 185
Thatcherism 77
Third Century Fund (Dreyfus) 185
third-party effects 38, 70
Third Reich 66
Thor Chemical Holdings 55–6, 152, 153
Titan International 18
Tomuschat, Christian 23
tort law, *see also* **corporate civil liability; human rights litigation**
    extraterritorial litigation 56
    MNC complicity, application to 152–3
Torture Convention (UN) 28, 102, 234, 289, 332, 339
    NGOs, role of 102
trade associations 348
trade liberalization 17
trade sanctions 31, 34, 189–90
trade statutes 193
trade unions 44, 96, *see also* **non-governmental organizations (NGOs)**
    UN Norms and 347–8
transnational civil society 22
transnational corporations (TNCs), *see* **multinational corporations**
treaties 28, 39, 98–105
    headquarters agreements 98–9
    human rights instruments 39–41
    NGOs, role of 28, 98–100, 100–5
    standard-setting 39, 75, 100–5
Turkey 144, 162, 245
Turkish Republic of Northern Cyprus 245
Tyumen Oil Company 192

UN, *see* **United Nations**
UNCTAD 255
Underhill, G.R.D. 146
UNESCO 20, 171
United Fruit (Guatemala) 143–4
United Kingdom
    complicity 165–6, 167
    corporate criminal liability 156, 157
    Ethical Trading Initiative 45–6
    extra-territorial litigation 55–6, 56–7
    identification theory 157
    multinationals, liability of 152–3, 156, 157

    private prisons 76
    securities regulation 31
    social disclosure 188–9
    Voluntary Principles on Security and Human Rights 212
United Nations 4, 6–7, 18, 26, 28, 93, *see also* **ECOSOC; Global Compact**
    administered territories, human rights accountability in 8–9
    Charter 21, 108
    Code of Conduct for Transnational Corporations 318
    Commission on Global Governance 50–1
    Commission on Human Rights 39, 108, 109, 114
    Commission on International Investment and Transnational Corporations 43
    Commission on Transnational Corporations 43
    Committee on Economic, Social and Cultural Rights (CESCR) 41, 71, 86, 332–3
    Committee on Economic, Social and Cultural Rights (CESR) 119, 123
    Committee on the Elimination of Discrimination against Women 79–80
    Committee on the Rights of the Child 103
    Convention against Torture 28, 102, 234, 289, 332, 339
    Convention on Apartheid 332
    Convention on Contracts for the International Sale of Goods 222
    Convention on the Rights of the Child 102–3, 105, 234, 283–4, 285, 286, 289
        Optional Protocol 331
    Declaration on the Elimination of All Forms of Intolerance and of Discrimination Based on Religion or Belief 339
    Declaration on the Protection of All Persons from Being Subjected to Torture 339
    Declaration on the Right and Responsibility of Individuals, Groups and Organs of Society to Promote ... Human Rights 107–9
    Draft Declaration on the Rights of Indigenous Peoples 339
    General Assembly 23, 99
    High Commissioner for Human Rights 186–7, 323
    human rights accountability 62–3
    Human Rights Committee 41, 76, 79, 81–2, 86

United Nations (*cont.*)
IMF, relationship with 29–30, 115–16, 118,
119–20, 137–8
International Law Commission 73
international legal personality 18, 29
military operations
human rights obligations 46–7
NGO consultative status 64, 97
non-state actors, definition of 16–17
Norms on Responsibilities of TNCs and
Business Enterprises, *see* **Norms on
Responsibilities of Transnational
Corporations**
State sovereignty 4
Sub-Commission for the Promotion and
Protection of Human Rights 25, 32, 315,
350
Working Group on the Activities of
Transnational Corporations 45, 322–7
United States of America 108
anti-trust law 56–7
Commission on International Religious
Freedom 189
corporate criminal liability 156, 158–9
Eximbank statute 191–2
extra-territorial litigation 55, 60–1, *see also*
Alien Tort Claims Act
Fair Labor Association 45
Foreign Corrupt Practices Act 31, 60, 187–8,
194
Helms-Burton controversy 60–1
Holocaust litigation 31, 66
human rights conditionality 179
International Emergency Economic Powers
Act 191
MNC liability 152–3
NGO influence, criticisms of 27
private security contractors in Iraq
9–11, 18
Securities and Exchange Commission 189
transactional controls 189–90
Voluntary Principles on Security and Human
Rights 212
United States Senate 10
Universal Declaration of Human Rights 71,
108, 113, 114, 138, 206–7, 209,
329–30, 332, 340
corporations, application to 150–1
customary international law, whether part
of 39, 121
property rights 131

**Universal Human Rights Guidelines for
Companies** 32
University of Paris II 94
Unocal 65, 152, 195–6, 225
Uruguay Round 171, 210
USA, *see* **United States of America**

Valdez Principles 181
vicarious liability
corporations 156–7
state responsibility 79–82, 84
Vietnam Veterans of America Foundation 103
violent street protests 48
voluntary agencies 14, 18, *see also*
non-governmental organizations
voluntary codes of conduct, *see* **codes of
conduct**
**Voluntary Principles on Security and Human
Rights in the Extractive Industries** 13,
212, 220, 321

Wal-Mart 17
Wallace, W. 15
war crimes 59–60
complicity principles 166–9
corporate liability 233
tribunals 145–6, 155, *see also* **International
Criminal Court**
Warri (Niger Delta) 13
Washington Consensus 77
Weiss, Edith Brown 24
Weissbrodt, David 32–3, 322, 323, 324
Wells, Celia 33–4
Westphalian system 58, 74
inter-state system, NGO threat to 94–5
white collar crime 142
Women's Caucus for Gender Justice 104
workers' rights, *see* **labour rights**
World Bank 3, 6, 144, 346
economic, social and cultural rights, and
114–16
good governance, advocacy of 50
human rights concerns 207–8
Inspection Panel 26, 42, 50, 208
NGO links 64
**World Business Council for Sustainable
Development** 103
**World Conference on Human Rights
(Vienna 1993)** 108, 114
World Diamond Council 182
World Health Organization 93, 171

World Order Models Project 22
World Summit for Social Development
    (Copenhagen 1995) 131, 254
World Tourism Organization 25
World Trade Organization (WTO) 6, 28, 32,
    193, 346
  Agreement on Sanitary and Phytosanitary
    Measures 346
  Agreement on Technical Barriers to Trade 346
  corporate social responsibility, and 210–12
  human rights, and 171, 190, 211–12
  NGO links 64, 109
  Seattle summit (1999) 94

Singapore Declaration 253–4
social clause 32, 61
social concerns, obstacles to introduction
  of 253–4
World War II 194
World Wildlife Fund (WWF) 103
WorldCom 141–2
WorldWatch Institute 103

Yugoslavia 7, 145, 197

Zia-Zarifi, S. 149
Zimbabwe 7